The HOLT HANDBOOK

THE HOLT HANDBOOK

THIRD EDITION

Laurie G. Kirszner
Philadelphia College of Pharmacy and Science

Stephen R. Mandell
Drexel University

Harcourt Brace College Publishers
Fort Worth   Philadelphia   San Diego
New York   Orlando   Austin   San Antonio
Toronto   Montreal   London   Sydney   Tokyo

Publisher	Ted Buchholz
Acquisitions Editor	Michael Rosenberg
Developmental Editor	Stacy Schoolfield
Senior Project Editor	Charlie Dierker
Manager of Production	Tad Gaither
Art & Design Supervisor	John Ritland
Text Design	Circa 86, Inc.

Library of Congress Cataloging-in-Publication Data

Kirszner, Laurie G.
   The Holt handbook / Laurie G. Kirszner, Stephen R. Mandell. — 3rd
ed.
       p.   cm.
   Includes index.
   ISBN 0-03-055543-4
   1. English language—Rhetoric—Handbooks, manuals, etc.
   2. English language—Grammar—1950- —Handbooks, manuals, etc.
   I. Mandell, Stephen R.   II. Title.
PE1408.K675   1992
808'.042—dc20   91-32652
                                                                        CIP

Address for Editorial Correspondence
Harcourt Brace College Publishers, 301 Commerce Street, Suite 3700, Fort
Worth, TX 76102

Address for Orders
Harcourt Brace & Company, 6277 Sea Harbor Drive,
Orlando, FL 32887
1-800-782-4479, or 1-800-433-0001 (in Florida)

Printed in the United States of America

3 4 5   071   9 8 7 6 5 4

Literary acknowledgments follow index.

Preface to the Instructor

When we planned *The Holt Handbook*, our aim was to create a true writer's handbook, one that would serve not only as a text and a reference guide but also as a companion. In preparing the first edition we concentrated on making the book inviting, accessible, useful, and interesting to both students and teachers. Although we relied extensively on new research in composition, we were careful to apply the results of this research in a practical and straightforward manner. Our hope was that its organization, its process approach, its emphasis on revision, and its focus on student writing would make *The Holt Handbook* truly a writing-centered text. In addition, we hoped that its descriptive approach to grammar and its nonthreatening tone would make it particularly appealing to students. Now six years after publication of the first edition, we are delighted to see that our book has been warmly and enthusiastically received.

The Third Edition at a Glance

- **A new section**—Part 2, "Thinking Critically"—devotes three chapters to reading critically, writing critical responses, reasoning logically, and writing argumentative essays.
- **A new section**—Part 9, "Writing in the Disciplines"—devotes four chapters to explaining and illustrating the conventions of writing in the humanities, social sciences, and natural and applied sciences.
- **Cross-References** in the margin clearly direct students to related discussions in other parts of the book.
- **Revision Close-up** boxes place special emphasis on revision throughout the book.
- **Writing Checklists, Revision Checklists, and Summary Boxes** enable students to find important information easily. These quick references are ideal for students who are searching for a particular piece of information or who want to refresh their memories about a specific subject.

continued

continued from previous page

- **Exercises and examples** have been carefully revised with special attention to gender-related, cross-cultural, and cross-curricular topics.
- **Expanded documentation chapter** clearly presents conventions and examples of MLA, APA, University of Chicago, and CBE documentation. MLA style is highlighted by color-bordered pages to differentiate it from other documentation styles.
- **Student Writer at Work** exercises enable students to practice revision strategies in the context of whole essays. These innovative and useful exercises appear throughout the text.
- **Guide to Writing with Computers** offers practical strategies and tips for writing, editing, and revising on a computer.
- **A new four-color design** uses color to highlight important information that appears in checklists, summary boxes, and cross-references.

As we began to revise *The Holt Handbook*, our goal was to retain the features that have made the book so successful while adding new material to make it an even more valuable resource. Thoughtful comments from users of the first two editions and our own careful reevaluation of each element of the book led us to make a number of changes in the third edition. In Part 1, we have retained the student essay, "The Kuomboka Ceremony," to illustrate the writing process. A more concise treatment, enhanced by a new design, makes the discussion sections and the Student Case Study segments genuinely complementary. In response to suggestions from readers, we have relocated the treatment of formal outlining to Chapter 40, "Writing a Research Paper" and have given additional coverage to using collaborative strategies and instructor's comments to revise. We have also streamlined and condensed Chapter 4's treatment of paragraphing and added new material on arranging details.

Because critical thinking is such an important part of the writing process, we now devote a separate part of the third edition to this subject. Chapter 5, "Reading Critically," includes a detailed treatment of critical reading, including distinguishing fact from opinion, evaluating support, recognizing bias, recording reactions, and formulating a critical response. Chapter 6, "Thinking Logically," explains the principles of inductive and deductive reasoning (including validity versus truth and the enthymeme); the chapter goes on to explain and illustrate many common logical fallacies. The section on induction now includes a discussion of making inferences. Chapter 7, "Writing an Argumentative Essay," traces a student's progress as she plans, shapes, writes, and revises an essay on the controversial topic of pit bull terriers. This essay now includes a library source.

We have carefully revised Parts 3–7. In Part 4 we place special emphasis on the treatment of comma splices and fused sentences and on shifts and mixed constructions. The most obvious changes in Part 5 are in Chapter 19, now called "Using the Dictionary and Building a Vocabulary," which combines two earlier chapters, and in the spelling chapter, which now includes a list of commonly confused words. In Part 6, the chapter on nouns and pronouns has been revised for clarity. Throughout Parts 3–7 we have edited and redesigned material on style, grammar, and punctuation and mechanics so that definitions, guidelines, notes, and key concepts are emphasized visually as well as stylistically. We have carefully scrutinized every example and exercise in these sections and have edited, revised, eliminated, or replaced material when necessary. In addition, headings have been reworded, redesigned, or relocated to make information easier to locate.

Part 8, "Writing with Sources," has also received considerable attention. In Chapter 37, "Research for Writing," we have significantly updated the section on library research to reflect changes arising from increased reliance on computer technology. In Chapter 38, "Working with Source Material," we have added material on distinguishing primary from secondary sources and expanded the discussion of note taking and the treatment of plagiarism. Chapter 39, "Documentation," has been thoroughly revised and redesigned. One major change is the addition of Chicago style, used in history and other disciplines. We have also added helpful reference indexes and moved some material to the newly created Part 9. The major changes in Chapter 40, "Writing a Research Paper," are the expansion of the section on preparing a formal outline and the inclusion of material on using photocopied sources.

Perhaps the most dramatic change in the content of *The Holt Handbook* is the addition to the third edition of Part 9, "Writing in the Disciplines." The section begins with Chapter 41, "Understanding the Disciplines," which explains the similarities and differences in research sources, writing assignments, and conventions of style and documentation among the disciplines. A comprehensive chart summarizes these differences. Chapters 42–44 ("Writing in the Humanities," "Writing in the Social Sciences," and "Writing in the Natural and Applied Sciences") explain and illustrate the sources, assignments, and conventions of style and documentation for the respective disciplines. These three chapters include a full-length research paper in APA style, as well as numerous excerpts from other assignments in various disciplines. Also in this section are three chapters formerly included in the "Writing Special Assignments" part of the second edition: "Writing Essay Examinations," "Writing About Literature," and "Practical Writing" (formerly "Writing Business Letters").

We have taken special care to make the third edition of *The Holt Handbook* even more teachable for the instructor—and more usable for the student—than the last edition. Throughout the text, we have almost doubled the number of boxed lists, charts, summaries, and other design elements that highlight the material that teachers and students consult most often. In addition, we have included two new features: marginal cross-references to identify related topics and "Revision Close-up" boxes to identify points students should keep in mind as they revise. We have taken special care to word headings so that they are clear and descriptive and to position them logically in the text. The result, we believe, is a superior reference work that not only guides writing and revision but enables writers to find and apply information quickly and easily.

In this edition *The Holt Handbook* continues to approach writing as a recursive process, giving students the opportunity to practice planning, shaping, and writing and revising. This approach, consistent with composition research, encourages students to become involved with every stage of the process and to view revision as a natural and ongoing part of their writing. The style, grammar, and mechanics and punctuation chapters present clear, concise definitions of key concepts followed by examples and exercises that gradually increase in difficulty and sophistication. Whenever possible, sentence-level skills are taught in groups of related sentences that focus on a single high-interest topic instead of in isolated sentences. This pedagogically sound methodology allows students to learn incrementally, practicing each skill as it is introduced. In this way students learn to recognize and revise sentence-level problems within longer units of discourse, duplicating the way that they must actually interact with their own writing. This approach has been useful to the thousands of students who have used the first two editions, and we continue to believe in its effectiveness.

The Holt Handbook is a classroom text, a reference book, a revision guide, and—above all—a writing companion that students can turn to for advice and guidance as they write in college and beyond. Our goal throughout remains the same: to translate the best of research in composition theory into practice. In addition, we still believe that we have an obligation to give not just the rule but the rationale behind it. Accordingly, we are careful to explain the principles that writers must understand to make informed choices about grammar, usage, rhetoric, and style. The result is a book that students and instructors can continue to use with ease, confidence, and, we hope, pleasure.

With this edition, an even more comprehensive ancillary package is available for instructors and students: an *Annotated Instructor's Edition* with helpful annotations and articles on teaching composition: *The Research Sourcebook: A Workbook for Research Papers; Supplementary Exercises; Diagnostic Tests;* The Writing Tutor, an interactive software program for Macintosh and IBM computers; PC-TYPE II, a full-function word processor for IBM computers; and Holt On-Line, an on-line version of the handbook for IBM computers. For complimentary copies of these teaching and learning aids, contact your local Harcourt Brace Jovanovich sales representative.

Acknowledgments

We wish to thank the following colleagues for their valuable comments and sound advice on the development of the first and second editions: Chris Abbott, University of Pittsburgh; Virginia Allen, Iowa State University; Stanley Archer, Texas A & M University; Lois Avery, Houston Community College; Rance G. Baker, Alamo Community College; Julia Bates, St. Mary's College of Maryland; John G. Bayer, St. Louis Community College/Meramec; Larry Beason, Texas A & M University; Al Bell, St. Louis Community College at Florissant Valley; Debra Boyd, Winthrop College; Margaret A. Bretschneider, Lakeland Community College; Pat

Bridges, Grand Valley State College; Alma Bryant, University of South Florida; Wayne Buchman, Rose State College; David Carlson, Springfield College; Patricia Carter, George Washington University; Faye Chandler, Pasadena City College; Peggy Cole, Arapahoe Community College; Sarah H. Collins, Rochester Institute of Technology; Charles Dodson, University of North Carolina/Wilmington; Margaret Gage, Northern Illinois University; Sharon Gibson, University of Louisville; Owen Gilman, St. Joseph's University; Margaret Goddin, Davis and Elkins College; Ruth Greenberg, University of Louisville; George Haich, Georgia State University; Robert E. Haines, Hillsborough Community College; Ruth Hamilton, Northern Illinois University; Iris Hart, Santa Fe Community College; John Harwood, Penn State University; Michael Herzog, Gonzaga University; Clela Hoggatt, Los Angeles Mission College; Keith N. Hull, University of Wyoming/Laramie; Anne Jackets, Everett Community College; Zena Jacobs, Polytechnic Institute of New York; LaVinia Jennings, University of North Carolina/Chapel Hill; D. G. Kehl, Arizona State University; Philip Keith, St. Cloud State University; George Kennedy, Washington State University; William King, Bethel College; Edward Kline, University of Notre Dame; Susan Landstrom, University of North Carolina/Chapel Hill; Marie Logye, Rutgers University; Helen Marlborough, DePaul University; Nancy Martinez, University of New Mexico/Valencia; Marsha McDonald, Belmont College; Vivien Minshull-Ford, Wichita State University; Robert Moore, SUNY/Oswego; George Murphy, Villanova University; Robert Noreen, California State University/Northridge; L. Sam Phillips, Gaston College; William Pierce, Prince George's Community College; Robbie Pinter, Belmont College; Nancy Posselt, Midlands Technical College; Robert Post, Kalamazoo Valley Community College; Richard N. Ramsey, Indiana University/Purdue University; Mike Riherd, Pasadena City College; Emily Seelbinder, Wake Forest University; Charles Staats, Broward Community College/North; Frank Steele, Western Kentucky University; Barbara Stevenson, Kennesaw College; Jim Stick, Des Moines Area Community College; James Sodon, St. Louis Community College at Florissant Valley; Josephine K. Tarvers, Rutgers University; Kathleen Tickner, Brevard Community College/Melbourne; George Trail, University of Houston; Daryl Troyer, El Paso Community College; Ben Vasta, Camden County

Community College; Connie White, Salisbury State College; Joyce Williams, Jefferson State Junior College; Branson Woodard, Liberty University; and Peter Zoller, Wichita State University.

We would like to express our appreciation to our colleagues who offered suggestions and advice for revisions to the third edition of *The Holt Handbook:* Lynne Diane Beene, University of New Mexico, Albuquerque; Elizabeth Bell, University of South Carolina; Jon Bentley, Albuquerque Technical-Vocational Institute; Debra Boyd, Winthrop College; Judith Burdan, University of North Carolina/Chapel Hill; Phyllis Burke, Hartnell College; Sandra Frisch, Mira Costa College; Gerald Gordon, Black Hills State University; Mamie Hixson, University of West Florida; Sue Ellen Holbrook, Southern Connecticut State University; Linda Hunt, Whitworth College; Rebecca Innocent, Southern Methodist University; Gloria John, Catonsville Community College; Gloria Johnson, Tennessee State University; Suzanne Liggett, Montgomery College; Richard Pepp, Massasoit Community College; Nancy Posselt, Midlands Technical College; Robert Peterson, Middle Tennessee State University; Randy Popkin, Tarleton State University; George Redmond, Benedict College; Linda Rollins, Motlow State Community College; Gary Sattelmeyer, Trident Technical College; Father Joseph Scallon, Creighton University; Emily Seelbinder, Queens College; Cynthia Smith, University of West Florida; Bill Stiffler, Harford Community College; Nancy Thompson, University of South Carolina, Columbia; Warren Westcott, Frances Marion College; Connie White, Salisbury State University; and Helen Yanko, California State University, Fullerton.

We extend special thanks to Sue Brizuela of the Philadelphia College of Pharmacy and Science for her careful attention to the material on library research and sources, and to Joel Nydahl of Babson College for sharing his knowledge of computers and composition. Thanks also go to Larry Bromley of the University of Texas at Arlington for his help.

Among the many people at HBJ who contributed to this project, we would like to single out Stacy Schoolfield, Michael Rosenberg, and Charlie Dierker, whose care and concern are reflected on every page; Laurie Runion, who skillfully coordinated the Annotated Instructor's Edition, and Tad Gaither and John Ritland, who contributed so much to the book's production and design.

Once again, we would like to thank our families—Mark, Adam, and Rebecca Kirszner and Demi, David, and Sarah Mandell—who gave us no editorial assistance, did not type the manuscript, and offered no helpful suggestions, but whose love and understanding helped make it all possible.

Finally, we would like to thank each other for making this book a collaboration in the truest sense.

Philadelphia   L.G.K.
January 1991   S.R.M.

Preface to the Student

The Holt Handbook is a comprehensive guide that you can consult whenever you have a question about grammar, usage, style, or rhetoric. We suggest that you read Part 1 of the book to become acquainted with the stages of the writing process and the techniques that good writers use when they write. Only after you are familiar with the choices that you have as a writer will you be able to place information about grammar, usage, sentence structure, and mechanics into perspective. As you use *The Holt Handbook,* you will notice that whenever possible we give advice, not rules. We believe that student writers do best when they have the freedom to make informed choices about their writing and are able to take into consideration the demands of varying audiences, purposes, and writing situations.

You can find material in *The Holt Handbook* in a number of ways. Individual chapters offer in-depth discussions of a wide variety of topics, and cross-references in the text point you to definitions and discussions of unfamiliar terms. Throughout the text, helpful **charts** and **summary boxes** highlight important material. As you write, they can help you locate information quickly and efficiently. We have also added **cross-reference symbols** (▶) to point you to particularly useful related material in other parts of the text. Finally, we have included **Revision Close-up boxes** to identify special issues that will concern you as you write and revise. These are shaded in red for easy reference.

The Holt Handbook has a number of other special features that will help you locate material.

The **"Guide to the Plan of the Book,"** at the front of the handbook, highlights key elements of the table of contents and gives an overview of the entire book. Use this guide when you are looking for a specific subject or a discussion that you know is part of a specific chapter.

The **left inside back cover** contains a list of **correction symbols** that your instructor may use to help you edit and revise your papers. These symbols consist of an abbreviation (*agree* for agreement, for example) and a combination of numbers and letters (such as *24a*) that refer you to a specific section of the text (chapter twenty-four, subsection a). You can locate the section of the book that you need by looking at the tabs on the top of each page.

A **Guide to Checklists** on the right inside back cover lists the Writing and Revision Checklists found throughout the book. Page references are included.

The **index** presents a detailed alphabetical listing of all subjects covered in the book. Because it lists all major topics, subtopics, and cross-references, the index is the most comprehensive guide to the text's contents.

The **glossary of usage** offers an alphabetical listing of commonly confused words (*continual/continuous*, for example) and other problems in usage (*data/datum*, for instance). Although this section does not eliminate the need to consult a dictionary, it enables you to solve many common problems.

The **glossary of grammatical terms** provides definitions of the grammatical and rhetorical terms that appear throughout *The Holt Handbook* as well as cross-references to the sections of the book that contain more detailed discussions of the terms.

When you use *The Holt Handbook*, keep in mind that at best it is a guide, not a final authority. To determine what is appropriate for a specific writing situation you must ultimately rely on your own sense of the language and your own assessment of your purpose and audience. Used with this principle in mind, *The Holt Handbook* should serve you well for the writing that you will do both in college and in your life beyond your years as a student.

L.G.K.
S.R.M.

Contents

Contents

6   Understanding Grammar 363

P A R T 1

Composing an Essay

Planning an Essay

Writing is a constant process of decision making, of selecting, deleting, and rearranging material.

The Writing Process

Planning: Consider audience, purpose, and assignment.
Shaping: Decide how to organize your essay.
Writing: Draft your essay.
Revising: ''Re-see'' what you have written; write additional drafts.
Editing: Check grammar, spelling, punctuation, and mechanics.
Proofreading: Check for typographical errors.

The neatly defined stages that make up the writing process communicate neither its complexity nor its flexibility. Although we will examine these stages separately, they actually overlap: as you seek

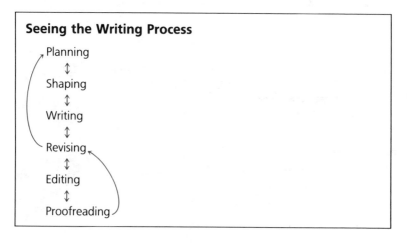

Seeing the Writing Process

Planning
⇕
Shaping
⇕
Writing
⇕
Revising
⇕
Editing
⇕
Proofreading

ideas you begin to shape your material; as you shape your material you begin to write; as you write a first draft you change your organization; as you revise you continue to discover more material. Moreover, the stages recur again and again throughout the writing process.

During your college years and in the years that follow, you will develop your own version of the writing process and use it whenever you write, adapting it to your audience, purpose, and writing situation.

1a   *Thinking About Writing*

Writing presents many situations in which you must think critically—make judgments, weigh alternatives, analyze, compare, question, evaluate, and engage in other decision-making activities. Virtually all writing demands that you make informed choices about your subject matter and about the manner in which you present your ideas.

Planning your essay—thinking about what you want to say and how you want to say it—begins well before you actually put your thoughts on paper in any organized way. This planning is as important a part of the writing process as the writing itself.

(1)   *Determining your purpose*

We write for a variety of purposes. One purpose might be simply to *express feelings or attitudes*, as in a diary, an autobiography, or a personal letter. Another might be to *persuade*. In this case you would try to convince your audience to agree with certain ideas and, often, to take some action, as in advertisements, proposals, and editorials. Another purpose might be to *convey information*, as in reports, news articles, textbooks, and encyclopedia entries. Still another could be to *give pleasure*, as in short stories, plays, novels, poems, and so on. You may also have additional, more specific aims or a combination of purposes.

The material you choose and the way you arrange and express it are determined by your purpose. For instance, a paper on summer camps could *inform*—explain how camping has changed in the past twenty years, for example. Such a paper would present pertinent facts and statistics straightforwardly. An advertisement designed to recruit potential campers would *persuade* by enumerating the benefits of the camping experience. Such an advertisement would stress positive details—the opportunity to meet new friends, for example—and deemphasize the possibilities of homesickness and rainy weather. A letter from a camper to a friend might try to *amuse*, describing all the things that would not appear in the promotional literature—mosquitoes, poison ivy, unheated cabins, institutional food, shaving cream fights, and so on. To *evaluate* the camping experience, a writer would aim for a balanced discussion of such things as recreational programs and sports facilities. In each case, your purpose determines which material you choose and how you present it.

College writing may call for any of a wide variety of approaches, but your general purpose is usually to convey information. As you do so, you try to demonstrate that you understand your subject and that you can make valid points about it.

Writing Checklist: Purpose

Is your purpose:

- to express feelings or attitudes?
- to persuade?
- to convey information?
- to give pleasure?
- to evaluate?
- to discover?
- to analyze?
- to debunk?
- to criticize?
- to satirize?

- to speculate?
- to warn?
- to reassure?
- to amuse?
- to take a stand?
- to identify problems?
- to suggest solutions?
- to define causes?
- to predict effects?

---

(2) *Identifying your audience*

Writing is often such a solitary activity that it is easy to forget about your audience. But except for personal diaries or journals, everything you write addresses an audience—a particular set of readers.

When you write, you may address many different kinds of audiences. As a citizen, consumer, or member of a community, civic, political, or religious group, you may respond to society's most pressing issues by writing letters to a newspaper editor; a public

4

official; a respresentative of a special interest group, business, or corporation; or another recipient you do not know well or at all. In your personal life, you may write notes and letters to friends and family and perhaps diary or journal entries to yourself. As an employee, you may write letters, memos, and reports to your superiors, to workers you supervise, or to workers on your level; you may also be called on to address customers or critics, board members or stockholders, funding agencies or the general public. As a student, you write essays, reports, and other papers addressed to one or more instructors and sometimes to other students or outside evaluators.

As you work through the writing process, you shape your paper increasingly in terms of what you believe your audience needs and expects. Your assessment of your readers' interests, educational level, biases, and expectations determines not only the information you include but also the emphasis, arrangement of material, and style or tone you choose.

The Academic Audience   A student very often writes for an audience of one: the instructor who assigns the paper. When addressing an instructor, you assume he or she represents a class of readers who apply accepted standards of academic writing.

What are these standards? Basically, instructors expect correct information, standard grammar and spelling, logical presentation of ideas, and some stylistic fluency. Instructors further ask that you define your terms and support your generalizations with specifics. They want to know what you know and whether you can express what you know clearly and accurately. Instructors assign written work to encourage you to use critical thinking skills, so the way you organize and express your ideas can be as important as the ideas themselves.

You can assume that all your instructors are specialists in their fields, so you can safely omit long overviews and basic definitions unless your instructor will need them to see how you have arrived at your ideas. But outside their areas of expertise, most instructors are simply general readers. If you think you may know more about a subject than your instructor does, be sure to provide ample background and definitions, examples, and analogies to make your ideas clear. Considering these factors helps you make the best possible writing choices.

Of course, each of your instructors is also a unique person with special knowledge and interests. Even though instructors generally

5

have similar overall requirements concerning the quality of your work, many will look for particular emphases or approaches. Your assessment of their special requirements also influences what and how you write.

The course for which you are writing will also influence your choices. If you decide to write about the underground mine fires that for years have been burning out of control near your hometown of Centralia, Pennsylvania, you would focus on different aspects of the topic for different courses.

Topic: Underground Fires	
Course	*Emphasis*
Chemistry	Origin of fire
Sociology	Relocation patterns of residents
Economics	Effects on local businesses and real estate
Psychology	Emotional impact of fires on children
Political Science	Role of federal or state government

Different academic disciplines also use their own formats, documentation styles, methods of collecting and reporting data, systems of formulas and symbols, technical vocabularies, and stylistic conventions. Instructors in different disciplines may therefore have different expectations.

See
Pt. 9 ◄

Writing Checklist: Audience

Is your audience

- an individual?
- a member of a group?
- specialized?
- general?

Can you identify your audience's

- needs?
- expectations?
- educational level?
- biases?
- interests?

Do you need to supply your audience with

- definitions?
- overviews?
- examples?
- analogies?

What special conventions does your audience expect concerning

- format?
- documentation style?
- methods of collecting and reporting
- data?
- systems of formulas and symbols?
- specialized vocabulary?
- writing style?

(3) Setting your tone

Your tone is the attitude you adopt as you write. This attitude, or mood, may be serious or frivolous, respectful or condescending, intimate or detached. It gives your readers clues about your feelings toward your material and helps them understand what you have to say. Therefore, your tone must remain consistent with your purpose and your audience as you shape, write, and revise your material.

How you feel about your readers—sympathetic or superior, concerned or indifferent, friendly or critical—is also revealed by your tone. For instance, if you identify with your readers or feel close to them, you use a personal and conversational tone. When you address a generalized, distant reader indirectly or anonymously, you use a more formal, impersonal tone.

When your audience is an instructor and your purpose is to inform, you should use an objective tone, neither too personal and informal nor too detached and formal (unless you are told otherwise). This paragraph from a student paper on the resistance to various drugs of a specific group of microorganisms achieves an appropriate tone for its audience (students in a medical technology lab) and purpose (to present information):

> One of the major characteristics of streptococci is that they are gram-positive. This means that after a series of dyes and rinses they take on a violet color. (Gram-negative organisms take on a red color.) Streptococci are also non-spore forming and non-motile. Most strains produce a protective shield called a capsule. They use organic substances instead of oxygen for their metabolism. This process is called fermentation.

An English composition assignment asking students to write a short, informal essay expressing their feelings about the worst job they ever had calls for an entirely different tone. The students's sarcastic tone effectively conveys his attitude toward his job, and his use of the first person encourages audience identification. Ironic comments ("good little laborer," "Now here comes the excitement") further establish his tone:

> Every day I followed the same boring, monotonous routine. After clocking in like a good little laborer, I proceeded over to a grey file cabinet, forced open the half-caved-in doors, and removed a staple gun, various packs of size cards, and a blue ball-point pen. Now here comes the excitement! Each farmer had a specific number assigned to his name. As his cucumbers were being sorted into their particular size, they were loaded into two-hundred-pound bins which I had to label with a stapled size card with the farmer's number on it. I had to complete a specific size card for every bin containing that size cucumber. Doesn't it sound wonderful? Any second grader could have handled it. And all the time I worked the machinery moaned and rattled and the odor of cucumbers filled the air.

In a letter applying for a job, however, the student would have different objectives. His distance from his audience and his purpose (to impress readers with his qualifications) would call for a much more objective and straightforward tone:

> My primary duty at Germaine Produce was to label cucumbers as they were sorted into bins. I was responsible for making sure each 200-pound bin bore the name of the farmer who had grown those cucumbers and also for keeping track of the cucumbers' sizes. Accuracy was extremely important in this task.

E X E R C I S E 1

Take as your general subject a book that you liked or disliked very much. How would each of the following writing situations affect the content, style, organization, tone, and emphasis of an essay on this book? Write an opening paragraph for each.

A journal entry recording your informal impressions of the book

An examination question that asks you to summarize the book's main idea

A book review for a composition class in which you evaluate both the book's strengths and its weaknesses

A letter to your local school board in which you try to convince your readers that, regardless of the book's style or content, it should not be banned from the local public library

An editorial for your school newspaper in which you try to persuade other students that the book is not worth reading

1b   *Getting Started*

Before you begin any writing task, be sure you understand the exact requirements of your assignment. It is very important that you keep these guidelines in mind as you write and revise. Do not make any guesses—and do not assume anything. Ask questions, and be sure you understand the answers.

Guidelines for Getting Started

What is the word, paragraph, or page limit?

How much time do you have to complete your assignment?

Is the assignment to be done in class or at home?

Can you take notes or do research?

If the assignment requires a specific format, do you know what its conventions are?

Sometimes an assignment allows you to choose your own topic. If so, choose a topic you know something about or want to learn about. Perhaps a class discussion or assigned reading suggests a topic; maybe you have seen a movie or television special or had a provocative conversation about an interesting subject. If so, you are off to a good start. If not, your instructor may be able to help you develop an unfocused idea into a workable topic.

(1)   *Exploring a topic*

Although you are sometimes able to choose your topic, your instructor's assignment generally limits your options. Sometimes it asks a specific question for you to answer: "How did the boundaries of Europe change following World War I?" "What are the advantages and disadvantages of the Federal Guaranteed Student Loan Program?" More often, it specifies a length, format, and particular subject area or gives a list of subjects from which to choose:

> Write a two-page critical analysis of a film. (Specifies length, format, and subject area)
>
> Write an essay explaining the significance of *one* of these court decisions: *Marbury* v. *Madison, Baker* v. *Carr, Brown* v. *Board of Education, Roe* v. *Wade.* (Gives list of specific subjects from which to choose)

Even in such cases, you cannot start to write immediately. You must narrow the assignment to a workable topic that suits your purpose and audience.

Narrowing an Assignment

Course	Assignment	Topic
Public Health	Analyze one effect of AIDS (Acquired Immune Deficiency Syndrome) on American society.	How has the spread of AIDS affected metropolitan-area blood banks?
Sociology	Identify and evaluate one resource available to the homeless population of one major American city.	The role of the Salvation Army in providing for Chicago's homeless
Freshman Composition	Describe a place that is very important to you.	Cape May: A town that never changes
Psychology	Write a three- to five-page paper assessing one method of treating depression.	How dogs interact with severely depressed patients

Begin exploring your topic by reviewing your options. Consider your assignment, your audience, and your purpose; also consider the things you know best and like best. If your assignment is to write about a place that is important to you, do not write about your dorm room because it is the first thing you think of or about the treasures of the Metropolitan Museum of Art because you think the topic sounds important. But if your dorm room represents your first taste of independence and your essay is about making a new start, it could be an ideal topic. If you know the collections at the Metropolitan well and plan to study art, you may legitimately use this knowledge in a paper about how your career goals developed. Still, do not automatically settle for a routine glance at the Mississippi River when you can describe Catfish Creek vividly.

Make certain that you understand the difference between what you *can* write about and what you *want* to write about. You may be very much interested in the Yukon but have nothing interesting to say about it; you may know more than you care to admit about McDonald's but not have the faintest desire to write about it. Your goal is to fill both requirements.

STUDENT CASE STUDY

GETTING STARTED

Throughout the first three chapters of this text, we will be following the writing process of George Panacheril, a freshman composition student who spent the first fourteen years of his life in Zambia. George's assignment was, "Write a short essay about a rite, ritual, or ceremony of a religion or an ethnic or community group with which you are familiar. Be sure your essay has a clearly stated thesis and helps readers to understand the ritual and its significance." The class had two weeks to complete the assignment, and library research was not permitted. The instructor explained that she would be requiring peer critiques, so students knew that their classmates would read and react to their papers.

George had no trouble thinking of several possible topics. He first considered rituals he had observed and participated in during his years as a secondary school student in the United States. These ceremonies— his first American Thanksgiving and Christmas, for instance—were freshest in his mind, so he thought he would best be able to write about them. But when he began to think more carefully about what to include in an essay on one of these topics, or on a community block party or a religious service, he realized that he was not very interested in such topics. Moreover, he thought his American audience would be most interested in something less familiar to them—for example, a ritual he had witnessed in Zambia. Once he narrowed his focus to Zambia, he was able to decide on a topic for his essay: the Kuomboka Ceremony, a yearly ritual during which the Lozi people, who live on a floodplain of the Zambezi River, move their village to higher ground for the duration of the rainy season.

EXERCISE 2

Read the following excerpt from Ron Kovic's autobiographical *Born on the Fourth of July*. Then list ten possible essay topics about your own childhood suggested by Kovic's memories of his. Each topic should be suitable for a short essay directed to your composition instructor. Your purpose is to give your audience a vivid sense of what some aspect of your childhood was like. Finally, choose the one topic you feel best qualified to write about, and explain the reasons for your choice.

When we weren't down at the field or watching the Yankees on TV, we were playing whiffle ball and climbing trees checking out birds' nests, going down to Fly Beach in Mrs. Zimmer's old car that honked the horn every time it turned the corner, diving underwater with our masks, kicking with our rubber frog's feet, then running in and out of our sprinklers when we got home, waiting for our turn in the shower. And during the summer nights we were all over the neighborhood, from Bobby's house to Kenny's, throwing gliders, doing handstands and backflips off fences, riding to the woods at the end of the block on our bikes, making rafts, building tree forts, jumping across the streams with tree branches, walking and balancing along the back fence like Houdini, hopping along the slate path all around the back yard seeing how far we could go on one foot.

And I ran wherever I went. Down to school, to the candy store, to the deli, buying baseball cards and Bazooka bubblegum that had the little fortunes at the bottom of the cartoons.

When the Fourth of July came, there were fireworks going off all over the neighborhood. It was the most exciting time of year for me next to Christmas. Being born on the exact same day as my country I thought was really great. I was so proud. And every Fourth of July, I had a birthday party and all my friends would come over with birthday presents and we'd put on silly hats and blow these horns my dad brought home from the A&P. We'd eat lots of ice cream and watermelon and I'd open up all the presents and blow out the candles on the big red, white, and blue birthday cake and then we'd all sing "Happy Birthday" and "I'm a Yankee Doodle Dandy." At night everyone would pile into Bobby's mother's old car and we'd go down to the drive-in, where we'd watch the fireworks display. Before the movie started, we'd all get out and sit up on the roof of the car with our blankets wrapped around us watching the rockets and Roman candles going up and exploding into fountains of rainbow colors, and later after Mrs. Zimmer dropped me off, I'd lie on my bed feeling a little sad that it all had to end so soon. As I closed my eyes I could still hear strings of firecrackers and cherry bombs going off all over the neighborhood. . . .

The whole block grew up watching television. There was Howdy Doody and Rootie Kazootie, Cisco Kid and Gabby Hayes, Roy Rogers and Dale Evans. The Lone Ranger was on Channel 7. We watched cartoons for hours on Saturdays—Beanie and Cecil, Crusader Rabbit, Woody Woodpecker—and a show with puppets called Kukla, Fran, and Ollie. I sat on the rug in the living room watching Captain Video take off in his spaceship and saw thousands of savages killed by Ramar of the Jungle.

I remember Elvis Presley on the Ed Sullivan Show and my sister Sue going crazy in the living room jumping up and down. He kept twanging this big guitar and wiggling his hips, but for some reason they were mostly showing just the top of him. My mother was sitting on the couch with her hands folded in her lap like she was praying, and my dad was in the other room talking about how the Church had advised us all that Sunday that watching Elvis Presley could lead to sin.

(2) Finding something to say

Once you have a topic, you can begin to discover ideas for your paper. One (or several) of the following strategies should prove helpful.

Strategies for Finding Something to Say

- Brainstorming
- Freewriting
- Keeping a journal
- Reading and observing
- Asking journalistic questions
- Asking in-depth questions

Brainstorming   One of the most useful ways to accumulate ideas is **brainstorming**. This strategy encourages you to recall pieces of information and to see connections among the pieces.

Begin by listing all the points you can think of that seem pertinent to your topic. Keeping your topic in mind, write down all the ideas that surface—comments, questions, single words, symbols, or diagrams—as quickly as you can. As the ideas begin to flow, write them down without pausing to consider their relevance or explain their significance. Your main goal is to let one idea suggest another, so do nothing to slow down your momentum. Only when you finish your brainstorming should you begin to group, sort, and classify the information on your list.

You can also brainstorm with your classmates in small groups that your instructor sets up, or you can enlist some friends to help you work through some ideas. Sometimes you can meet individually with your instructor and brainstorm about your paper. As others suggest ideas, write them down uncritically; you will sort through and evaluate them later. For now, unlock your mind and let your ideas flow freely, and do not be afraid to explore lines of thought that may at first seem unproductive. The unexpected perspectives or sudden shifts of thought that occur when you brainstorm can shed new light on your topic and suggest some interesting and original ideas.

Freewriting   Another strategy that can help you to discover ideas is **freewriting**. When you freewrite, you fix your mind on your topic and write *nonstop*, as quickly as you can, for a certain period of time—say, five minutes—without worrying about punctuation, spelling, or grammar, or about whether your mind is wandering. The momentum generated by this strategy encourages your mind to make connections and frees ideas that you may not be aware you have. If you run out of things to say about your topic, write about *anything*—the weather, a spot on the wall—until you pick up your subject again. When your time is up, look over what you have written and see if you have anything you can use. Occasionally you have nothing at all, but often you will see new details, a new approach to your topic, or even a new topic. Frequently you will find one good idea that you can use as the center of a new freewriting exercise.

Keeping a Journal   Professional writers sometimes keep **journals**, writing in them regularly whether or not they have a specific project in mind. Such a record of thoughts and ideas is a valuable resource when you run short of material. Journals, unlike diaries, do more than record personal experiences and reactions. In a journal you explore ideas as well as events and emotions, thinking on paper and drawing conclusions. You might, for example, explore the evolution of your position on a political issue or solve on paper a problem you find difficult to work through in your mind. A journal is an excellent place to record the evolution of your ideas about an assignment. You can also record quotations that mean something special to you or make notes about important news events, films, or conversations. A good journal is a scrapbook of ideas that you can leaf through in search of new material and new ways of looking at old material.

Reading and Observing   It is unlikely that all the ideas you need for your essay will already be in your mind, just waiting to be discovered. For this reason, it is important that you keep your eyes and ears open from the time you receive your assignment until you turn it in. As you read textbooks in various subjects or look through magazines and newspapers, be on the lookout for new ideas that pertain to your topic. Also, make a point of talking with friends or family about your topic.

If your instructor encourages you to do formal research, you can use material from nonprint sources such as films and television programs as well as material from books and articles. Interviews, telephone calls, letters, and questionnaires can be as fruitful as library research. But remember to document ideas that are not your own.

▶ See Pt. 8

Asking Journalistic Questions   Another way of finding something to say about your topic is to ask questions. Your answers to these questions will enable you to explore your topic in an orderly and systematic fashion. One strategy involves asking six simple questions: *Who? What? Why? Where? When? How?* Journalists often use these questions to assure themselves that they have touched on all angles of a story, and you can use them to see whether you have considered all sides of your topic.

Journalistic Questions

Who?	Where?
What?	When?
Why?	How?

Asking In-Depth Questions   If you have time, and if you want to generate ideas systematically, you can ask questions that suggest familiar ways of organizing material. These questions can not only give you a great deal of information about your topic but can also help you shape your ideas into paragraphs and whole essays. (As you review these questions, keep in mind that not every question will apply to every topic.)

In-Depth Questions

What happened? When did it happen? Where did it happen?	Suggests <u>narration</u> (account of your first day of school; a summary of Emily Dickinson's life)
What does it look like? What are its characteristics?	Suggests <u>description</u> (of the Louvre; of the electron microscope)

---

continued

continued from previous page

What are some typical cases or examples of it?	Suggests exemplification (three infant day-care settings; four popular fad diets)
How did it happen? What makes it work? How is it made?	Suggests process (how to apply for financial aid; how a bill becomes a law)
Why did it happen? What caused it? What does it cause? What are its effects?	Suggests cause and effect (events leading to the Korean War; the results of Prohibition; the impact of a new math curriculum on slow learners)
How is it like other things? How is it different from other things?	Suggests comparison and contrast (of the popular music of the 1950's and the 1960's; of two paintings)
What are its parts or types? Can they be separated or grouped? Do they fall into a logical order? Can they be categorized?	Suggests division and classification (components of the catalytic converter; kinds of occupational therapy; kinds of dietary supplements)
What is it? How does it resemble other members of its class? How does it differ from other members of its class?	Suggests definition (What is Marxism? What is photosynthesis? What is schizophrenia?)

If the questions that suggest *process* seem most productive, consider organizing your essay as a step-by-step explanation of a procedure; if the questions that suggest *cause and effect* yield the most material, perhaps you should devote part (or all) of your essay to **See 4f** ◀ tracing causes or predicting effects.

FINDING SOMETHING TO SAY

For his essay on the Kuomboka Ceremony, George Panacheril made the brainstorming list shown in Figure 1. Looking over his list, George saw some logical and sequential links among events, and he noticed that his brainstorming had uncovered a few interesting ideas—for in-

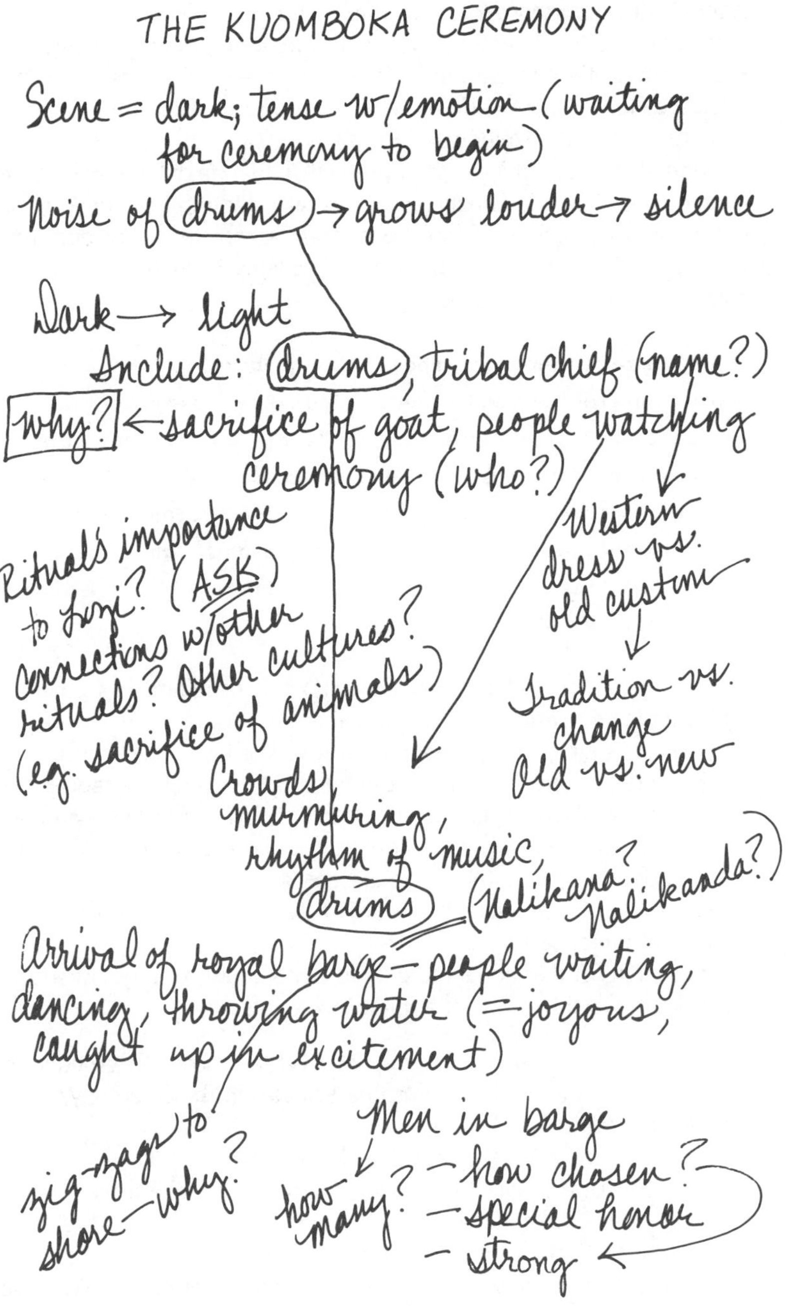

FIGURE 1 Brainstorming List

stance, the importance of the drums, and music in general, to the ceremony and the ceremony's blending of old and new elements. Not every item on the brainstorming list would appear in his essay, but the list did include some useful material and suggest some promising directions for further exploration.

George's brainstorming was so productive that he did not feel a need to freewrite. One additional step he did take, though, was to write an entry about his assignment in the journal he kept for his composition class. Here he began to explore the problems he might face as he continued the writing process:

```
     I know I can write about the Kuomboka. I have a good
topic, interesting and unusual, I think. I remember how
things looked, the first time at least, but I'm not sure I
can describe what I saw to this audience. It will be very
strange to them. I need to really create a scene, with a
lot of visual detail, and I need to describe what the
drums, the chief, and the barge look like. Also, how much
of my feelings should I include?
```

Meanwhile, George had to decide what kind of additional information on his topic he might need. He knew that his aunt, a journalist, would be a logical source of information because she had taken him to see the Kuomboka Ceremony. In a telephone conversation, he asked her to spell the words for tribal chief (Litunga) and royal barge (Nalikwanda). He also asked her to explain the significance of one element of the ritual that puzzled him: why the barge zigzags as it approaches the shore. When he had her answers, he recorded the information in his journal for future reference.

In a search for additional material to write about, George asked the journalistic questions, with the following results:

Who started the Kuomboka tradition? Who is most concerned with preserving the tradition? Who participates in the ceremony? Who witnesses it?
What is the ceremony? What does it mean?
Why does it take place? Why does it continue to take place?
Where does it take place?
When does it take place? When did it begin?
How is the chief chosen? How are the rowers chosen? How has the ceremony changed over the years?

These questions suggested both possible answers and additional questions. They encouraged George to begin thinking about including material about the ceremony's history and meaning and perhaps exploring the idea of how the ceremony had changed over the years.

George knew that his audience—his instructor and fellow students—would know nothing about the ceremony and that one of his most important goals was to help them visualize it; in addition, his assignment required him to communicate the significance of the ritual to his readers. Now he had to decide on the most effective way to do this.

After he had collected most of his ideas, George thought that a systematic review of the in-depth questions might help him to explore possibilities for shaping his essay. When George asked himself the questions relevant to description and process, he came up with a number of useful responses, which he added to his notes:

What does it look like? What are its characteristics?

suggests
description
Drums are wood covered with cowhide. Sky is black, then gray. Chief: white-haired, dressed in black. Barge: men with long wooden poles, thatched cabin for chief.

How did it happen?

suggests
process
It has happened the same way every time, for many years. The repeated process has become a ritual for the Lozi people. This predictable process and other familiar rituals may be what helps them keep their sense of identity.

With all this material, George felt ready to put his notes into a tentative order and start to shape his ideas into an essay.

EXERCISE 3

Make a brainstorming list on the topic you selected in Exercise 2. If you have trouble thinking of material to write about, try freewriting. Then write a journal entry assessing your progress.

EXERCISE 4

List all the sources you encounter in one day (people, books, magazines, observations, and so on) that could provide you with relevant information for the essay you are writing.

E X E R C I S E 5

Using the question strategies described earlier to supplement the work you did in Exercises 3 and 4, compile enough information for a short essay on your topic from Exercise 2.

Shaping Your Material

Grouping Ideas: Making a Topic Tree

When you begin to see the direction your ideas are taking, it is time to sort your notes, to sift through your ideas and choose those you can use to build the most effective essay. One way to do this is to make a **topic tree,** a diagram that enables you to group ideas logically, develop an overview of your topic, and see relationships among ideas.

Begin your topic tree by reviewing all your notes and writing down the three or four basic categories of information that seem most pertinent to your essay. Write these categories across the top of a piece of paper. Then go through your notes again, select points that are related to each category, and write each point under the relevant heading, drawing lines to connect each point to the more general heading above. Continue going through your notes and adding related points, skipping those that seem irrelevant. As you move down the page, you should move from general information to increasingly specific details.

Of course, you will add to, delete from, rearrange, and rewrite the points on your topic tree as you review your brainstorming list and other notes. When you finish, you can begin to see how your ideas are related and which are subordinate and which dominant. Seeing these relationships will help you to develop a tentative thesis.

Making a Topic Tree

- Review your notes carefully.
- Identify the three or four general categories of information most pertinent to your emerging essay.

continued

continued from previous page

- Copy these points across the top of a piece of paper.
- Review your notes again to select points related to each category.
- Copy points under relevant headings, moving from general information to increasingly specific details as you move down the page.
- Draw branches to connect points in each category.

STUDENT CASE STUDY

MAKING A TOPIC TREE

George Panacharil constructed the topic tree shown in figure 2.
Now George felt well on his way toward writing an effective essay. But before he could begin drafting his paper, he needed to bring his ideas into sharper focus: to find a thesis or central idea for his essay.

E X E R C I S E 1

Construct a topic tree from the work you did for Exercises 2, 3, and 4 in Chapter 1.

2b *Developing a Thesis*

Your **thesis** is the main idea of your essay, the central point your essay supports.

(1) *Defining an effective thesis*

An effective thesis clearly communicates your essay's main idea. It tells your readers not only what your essay's topic is but also how you will approach that topic and what you will say about it. Thus, the thesis reflects your essay's purpose. If your aim is to persuade, your thesis will take a strong stand (see **7a2**). If your purpose is to convey information, your thesis can present the specific points you will discuss or give an overview that suggests how the essay will be organized. A laboratory report, for instance, simply explains a process and does not take a position. To impose an argumentative thesis on such a report could be confusing or dis-

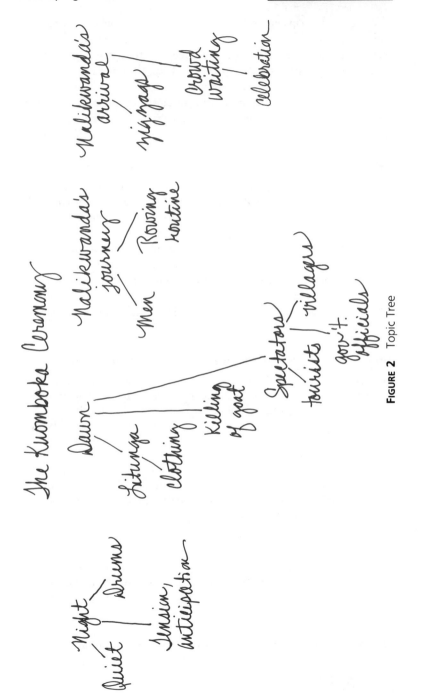

The Kuomboka Ceremony

Night
Quiet — Drums
tension,
anticipation

Dawn
Litunga
clothing
Killing
of goat
Spectators
tourists / villagers
gov't.
officials

Nalikwanda's
journey
Men
Rowing
routine

Nalikwanda's
arrival
zigzag
crowd
waiting
celebration

FIGURE 2 Topic Tree

23

tracting. A descriptive or narrative essay may be written to express feelings or convey impressions; its purpose may be simply to describe a scene or recount an experience, not to argue a point about that scene or experience. In such an essay, the thesis might reflect the organizing principle or dominant impression.

An effective thesis is more than a title, a statement of fact, or an announcement of your subject. Consider the differences among the following statements.

Title	Statement of Fact	Announcement
The Draft	The United States currently has no peacetime draft.	In this essay I will discuss our country's need for a draft.

Thesis   As our statesmen talk again of resisting aggression and demonstrating our will—as they talk, that is, of sending someone's sons (or daughters) to bear arms overseas—the only fair and decent answer to that question lies in a return to the draft. (James Fallows, "The Draft: Why Our Country Needs It")

Title	Statement of Fact	Announcement
Intelligence Tests	Intelligence tests are used extensively in some schools.	The paragraphs that follow will advance the idea that intelligence tests may be inaccurate.

Thesis   My intelligence, then, is not absolute but is a function of the society I live in and of the fact that a small subsection of that society has managed to foist itself on the rest as an arbiter of such matters. (Isaac Asimov, "Intelligence")

Title	Statement of Fact	Announcement
Music Videos	Music videos can enhance record sales.	As I will argue in this paper, music videos are an important part of our culture.

Thesis   The proliferation of music videos threatens to produce an entire generation of people who will all but miss out on the sublime, extremely personal element of music. (Eric Zorn, "Memories Aren't Made of This")

Title	Statement of Fact	Announcement
Math Anxiety	Math anxiety is a problem for many young girls.	My paper will attempt to show why young girls have problems with mathematics.

Thesis   Since ability in mathematics is considered by many to be unfeminine, perhaps fear of success, more than any bodily or mental dysfunction, may interfere with girls' ability to learn math. (Sheila Tobias, "Who's Afraid of Math, and Why?")

Title	Statement of Fact	Announcement
Prize Fighting and the Death of Benny Paret	Prize fighting is an inherently dangerous sport that resulted in the death of Benny Paret.	It is my opinion that prize fighting is a dangerous sport, and I intend to explain here how it caused Benny Paret's death.

Thesis   Put the blame [for Paret's death] where it belongs—on the prevailing mores that regard prize fighting as a perfectly proper enterprise and vehicle of entertainment. (Norman Cousins, "Who Killed Benny Paret?")

An effective thesis is carefully worded. In order to communicate your main idea, an effective thesis should be clearly and accurately worded, with careful phrasing that makes your meaning apparent to your readers. Often, it is expressed in a single, concise sentence. Your thesis should be direct and straightforward, avoiding vague, abstract language and overly complex terminology. It should include no unnecessary details that might confuse or mislead readers and make no promises that the essay will not fulfill. Although your thesis cannot enumerate every point your essay will develop, it may list your most important points; in any case, it should be specific enough to give readers a good idea of the essay's main points.

Finally, **an effective thesis accurately predicts your essay's direction, emphasis, and scope.** Your thesis should give an accurate overview of your essay, helping you to visualize the most effective way to arrange your material. Ideally, it suggests how your points are related, in what order your major points should be introduced, and where you should place your emphasis.

The following thesis statement conveys a good deal of information:

> Widely ridiculed as escape reading, romance novels are becoming increasingly important as a proving ground for many never-before-published writers and, most significantly, as a showcase for strong heroines.

First, this thesis tells you that this essay focuses primarily on what the writer considers to be the two major new roles of the romance novel: providing markets for new writers and (more importantly) presenting strong female characters. To a lesser extent, the role of the romance as escapist fiction may also be treated. The thesis statement even suggests a possible order for the various ideas discussed.

Introduction: Romance formulas; general settings; plots and characters; thesis

Body:

- Romance novels as escapist reading
- Romance novels as an outlet for unpublished writers
- Romance novels as a showcase for strong heroines

Conclusion: Review of major points; significance of recent developments; restatement of thesis

In an essay written according to this plan, the body paragraphs would provide the evidence necessary to support the thesis.

In the following example, the thesis suggests not only the order of the ideas but also a specific pattern of development:

> Romance novels may be extremely popular, but science fiction contributes more to the art of popular fiction.

The phrasing of the thesis clearly indicates that the essay *compares and contrasts* two kinds of popular fiction and concludes something about their relative merits.

See ◄ 4f

Writing Checklist: Identifying An Effective Thesis

- Does your thesis clearly communicate your essay's main idea? Does it suggest the approach you will take toward your material?

Does it reflect your essay's purpose?
- Is your thesis more than a title, a statement of fact, or an announcement of your subject?
- Is your thesis carefully worded?
- Does your thesis accurately predict your essay's direction, emphasis, and scope?

(2) Deciding on a thesis

Occasionally—especially if you know a lot about your topic—you may begin writing with a thesis in mind. Most often, however, your thesis evolves out of the reading, questioning, and grouping of ideas you do early in the writing process. If you have difficulty finding a thesis, try reviewing your notes or brainstorming list. Some writers find that doing focused freewriting at this stage helps. By concentrating on a key idea about your topic and then freewriting about it, you can frequently discover a possible thesis.

The thesis you develop as you plan your essay is only a tentative one. It gives you sufficient focus to guide you through your first draft, but you should expect to modify it in subsequent drafts. As you write and rewrite, you often see new connections and change your emphasis several times. It stands to reason, then, that you will constantly change and sharpen your thesis to keep it consistent with your paper's changing goals. Notice how the following pairs of thesis statements changed as the writers moved through successive drafts of their essays.

Developing a Thesis

Tentative Thesis	Revised Thesis
Professional sports can easily be corrupted by organized crime.	Although proponents of legalized gambling argue that organized crime cannot make inroads into professional sports, the way in which underworld figures compromised the 1919 World Series suggests the opposite.

continued

continued from previous page

Laboratory courses provide valuable educational experiences.	By providing students with the actual experience of doing scientific work, laboratory courses encourage precise thinking, careful observation, and creativity.
It is difficult to understand Henry Jame's short novel *The Turn of the Screw* without examining the personality of the governess.	A careful reading of Henry James's *The Turn of the Screw* suggests that the governess is an unreliable narrator, incapable of distinguishing appearance from reality.

(3) Stating your thesis

As a beginning writer, you may find it helpful to state your thesis early in your paper. Not only will this placement immediately signal the focus of your discussion to your readers, but it will also serve as a constant reminder to you of your essay's direction. Your thesis can appear anywhere in your essay, however, as long as it makes your essay's main idea clear to your readers. Where you state your thesis largely depends on the effect you wish your essay to have on a particular audience. In an argument, you may have to lead your readers gradually to your controversial thesis instead of stating it at once. To do otherwise could alienate a segment of your audience. In a research paper, you may have to present several paragraphs of background material before your audience is able to understand your thesis.

Although many of the essays you write in college will include a thesis, not all require it to be explicitly stated. Sometimes your thesis can be *implied* through the arrangement of the points in your essay. Like an explicit thesis, an implied thesis must clearly and specifically convey your essay's main idea to your readers. Professional writers often use this technique, preferring to make their points in a more subtle manner that allows readers to arrive at their own conclusions. For example, in "Letter from Birmingham Jail," Martin Luther King, Jr., prefers to let a chain of reasoning supported by many descriptive examples lead his readers to the implied thesis that people of good will should support his demonstrations in Birmingham, Alabama.

DEVELOPING A THESIS

As George reviewed his topic tree and notes and analyzed his thoughts, several possible thesis statements came to mind. At first he considered "The Kuomboka Ceremony is extremely important to many people," but he quickly realized that this statement was far too general and that it said nothing about why the ceremony was so important. Next he tried "The Kuomboka Ceremony is important both because it is fascinating to watch and because it represents a long-standing tradition to many people." This statement was closer to what he wanted to express, but it was still too vague. What he wanted to communicate, he knew, was the significance of the ritual, but he could not seem to identify what qualities made the ceremony so important. He had gathered plenty of useful information, but now he found himself wondering what the point of all the details was. He tried "If rituals like the Kuomboka Ceremony are allowed to die, the world will lose something vitally important," but he rejected this at once as inappropriately argumentative and impersonal. After considering and rejecting several additional statements, George finally decided on the following tentative thesis:

What is most amazing about the Kuomboka Ceremony is the way it has lasted through the years, maintaining tradition in the face of change.

This statement was specific enough to give George direction, and it was an idea he felt his description of the process could support.

EXERCISE   2

Analyze the following statements or topics, and explain why none of them qualifies as an efffective thesis. Be prepared to explain how each could be improved.

1. In the pages that follow, I will examine the use of pesticides in the Great Plains states.
2. The development of the nuclear freeze movement
3. How to apply for a civil service position
4. ROTC: Pro and Con
5. Medicare benefits many senior citizens, but it has some drawbacks.

6. The feminist position on pornography
7. Unemployment is rising steadily in the auto industry.
8. Welfare reform is sorely needed.
9. Benjamin Franklin was a statesman and scientist.
10. Most of my friends like running or skiing, but I prefer tennis.

EXERCISE 3

For three of the following topics, formulate a clearly worded thesis statement.

1. A literary work that has influenced your thinking
2. Cheating in college
3. The validity of SAT scores as the basis for college admissions
4. Should women in the military serve in combat?
5. Private vs. public education
6. Should college health clinics provide abortion services?
7. Is governmental censorship of art ever justified?
8. The role of the individual in saving the earth
9. The portrayal of minorities in film and television
10. Should smoking be banned from all public places?

EXERCISE 4

Read the following sentences excerpted from the essay "Territoriality and Dominance" by René Dubos. Then develop a thesis that will tie together the information in the sentences. Make sure that your thesis is well constructed and follows the requirements outlined in this chapter.

- Whenever the population density of a group increases beyond a safe limit, many of the low-ranking animals in the social hierarchy are removed from the reproductive pool.
- The remarkable outcome of these automatic mechanisms is that, in the case of many animal species, animal populations in the wild remain on the average much more stable than would be expected from the maximum reproductive potential.
- When males fight, the combat is rarely to the death.
- The losing animal is a struggle saves itself . . . by an act of submission, an act usually recognized and accepted by the winner.
- The view that destructive combat is rare among wild animals . . . is at variance with the "Nature, red in tooth and claw" legend. . . .
- Since ritualization of behavior is widespread among the higher apes, it is surprising that humans differ from them, as well as from most other animals, in practicing warfare extensively with the intent to kill.

E X E R C I S E 5

Review the topic tree you made in Exercise 1. Use it to help you to develop a thesis for an essay on the topic you chose in Exercise 2 in Chapter 1.

2c *Preparing an Informal Outline*

An **informal outline** is a blueprint for an essay, a plan that gives you more detailed, specific guidance than a thesis statement. You need not always prepare such an outline; a short essay on a topic with which you are familiar may require nothing beyond a thesis and a list of major divisions or main supporting points. More often, however, you need additional help. An informal outline arranges your main ideas and supporting points in an informal but orderly way to guide you as you write.

Preparing An Informal Outline

- Write down the categories and subcategories from your topic tree.
- Arrange the categories and subcategories in the order in which you will use them.
- Flesh out the plan with additional material from your brainstorming list, journal, or any other notes you may have.

For a short paper, an informal outline is usually sufficient. Sometimes, however—particularly when you are writing a long or complex essay—you will need to construct a formal outline. ► **See 40g**

PREPARING AN INFORMAL OUTLINE

Reviewing his notes and topic tree carefully, George selected material he could use and prepared the following informal outline.

INFORMAL OUTLINE: THE KUOMBOKA CEREMONY

Thesis: What is most amazing about the Kuomboka Ceremony is the way it has lasted through the years, maintaining tradition in the face of change.

Night (before ceremony)
  Quiet
    —insects
    —animals?
    —low rumble of drums
  Drums get louder
    —like kettle drum
    —wood and cowhide
  Fires start around the camp
Dawn (preparation for ceremony)
  People gather
    —tourists
    —villagers
    —goverment officials
  Litunga
    —black clothing
    —dignity
  Killing of goat
Nalikwanda's journey
  Men
    —strong warriors
    —honor
  Cabin for Litunga
  Rowing
    —men in unison, singing
    —boat speeds up
Nalikwanda's arrival
  Waiting crowd
    —dancing
    —drums
  Boat zigzags to shore
  Celebration

This informal outline guided George as he wrote his first draft.

EXERCISE 6

Review your notes and prepare an informal outline for a paper on the thesis you developed in Exercise 5.

Writing and Revising

3a Writing a Rough Draft

Because the purpose of a rough draft is to get your thoughts down on paper so that you can react to them, a rough draft is often messy and full of false starts. Experienced writers know that they will generally rewrite a paper several times. They expect to cross out words and sentences and to produce choppy, disconnected paragraphs. They realize that they will correct these problems when they revise.

As you write your draft, you may discover new questions and new perspectives. These represent departures from the paper you are planning, but they should not present a problem. If new ideas occur to you, follow them through. They may lead you to a better paper than the one you were planning.

In most cases, a rough draft focuses on the body paragraphs of your essay, with only a weak—or even nonexistent—introduction and conclusion. This is as it should be. In fact, students who struggle to write perfect opening and closing paragraphs are usually wasting their time: the effort slows them down, and these paragraphs are likely to change substantially in subsequent drafts. For these reasons, many experienced writers write their introductions and conclusions last.

Strategies for Writing a Rough Draft

- **Prepare your work area.** Once you begin to write, you should not have to stop because you need a sharp pencil, important notes, or anything else. Unscheduled breaks can ruin your concentration.
- **Fight writer's block. Writer's block**—an inability to start (or continue) writing—may be caused by fear that you will not write well

---

or that you have nothing to say. If you really do not feel ready to write, taking a short break may give your ideas time to incubate, which, in turn, may unlock new ideas. If you decide that you really do not have enough material to get you started, return to one of the strategies for finding something to say **(see 1b2)**. But remember, the least productive response to writer's block is procrastination.

- **Get your ideas down on paper as quickly as you can.** Do not worry about sentence structure, spelling, or finding exactly the right word. Concentrate on recording your points. Writing quickly helps you uncover new ideas or new connections between ideas.
- **Take regular breaks as you write.** Write one section of your essay at a time. When you have completed a section and have perhaps just begun or outlined the next section, take a break. Your unconscious mind may continue to focus on your assignment while you do other things. When you return to your essay, writing may be easier.
- **Leave yourself enough time to revise.** All writing benefits from revision, so be sure you have time to reconsider your work and to write as many drafts as necessary.

You will probably be revising much of what you write, and careful preparation of your first draft will make these revisions less painful.

Drafting with Revision in Mind

- **Write on every other line.** (If you type, triple space.) This makes errors more obvious and also gives you plenty of room to add new material or to try out new versions of sentences.
- **Develop a system of symbols**, each indicating a different type of revision. For instance, you can circle individual words or box longer groups of words (or even entire paragraphs) that you want to relocate. You can use an arrow to indicate the new location, or you can use asterisks or matching numbers or letters to indicate how you want to rearrange ideas. When you want to add words, use a caret like $\overset{\text{this}}{\wedge}$. You can also use proofreading symbols.
- **Write on only one side of a sheet of paper**. This technique enables you to reread your pages side by side. Writing on one side only also permits you to cut and paste without destroying material on the other side of the page. This strategy gives you the flexibility to keep reorganizing the sections or paragraphs of your paper until you find their most effective arrangement.

▶ See App.

If you are composing on a computer, revision is easier. You can delete words and sentences or relocate paragraphs simply by touching a few keys. But be careful not to discard information that you may need later.

STUDENT CASE STUDY

WRITING A ROUGH DRAFT

Notice that in this typed version of his first draft, George Panacheril's four body paragraphs correspond to the four major headings in his informal outline on page 31.

First Draft: The Kuomboka Ceremony

1   Of all the rituals I have observed or participated in, the one that I found the most interesting is the Kuomboka Ceremony. It is a truly important, even momentous event. What is most amazing abou the Kuomboka Ceremony is the way it has lasted through the years, maintaining tradition in the face of change.

2   All was still in the inky darkness of the African night, the silence punctuated by the sounds of various insects. Occasionally the inane laugh of the hyena or the screech of a baboon split the night. As I stood motionless, together with hundreds of others, a low throbbing sound filled the air. Soft, almost inaudible at first, the sound gradually increased in intensity as more and more drummers joined in. They were playing big drums which were essentially an African equivalent of the kettle drum. Made from wood, it was covered with stretched cowhide. The rhythms they placed were complex, highly intricate patterns which took years of practice to master. It was now midnight and the drums would not stop beating until the chief left the next morning, some seven hours later. This served as a signal and within minutes a number of fires had sprung up around the camp as the whole village came to life. The Kuomboka Ceremony had begun.

3   The sky was a dusky gray as the first rays of soft

sunlight heralded the dawn. Slowly people began to gather around the Litunga's hut. There were all kinds of people there, from foreign tourists with their cameras and tape recorders, to villagers dressed in animal skins and dilapidated, cast-off Western clothing. Looking through the crowd I was not surprised to see a few cabinet ministers and other top government officials present. Inside the thatched mud hut the Litunga was being prepared for the journey by the tribal elders. And then, for the first time since they had started, the big drums missed a beat; and then another. Then as they had started they gradually faded off until there was silence. In fact after the many hours of drumming you could almost hear the silence. All eyes turned expectantly toward the door of the chief's hut. As the Litunga stepped out into the light there was an explosion of smaller drums in a rapid, staccato beat that was very much like a high-speed pneumatic drill. Suddenly all around me people were clapping and dancing in time to the drums. The chief was an elderly man with white hair who walked with the help of a cane. In his left hand he carried a fly-whisk. He was dressed in black robes that hung down to his knees and black trousers and shoes, and carried himself with the dignity due his age and position. As the Litunga walked away from the hut a warrior standing a short distance away raised his knife to kill a goat.

4   As the crowd moved toward the river I caught my first glimpse of the royal barge, "the Nalikwanda." The two sides of the boat were lined with men who were all adjusting their costumes or fidgeting with the long wooden poles they each held. They were an elite group of men in the tribe, a select group of warriors with the power and stamina to row nonstop for ten hours. It was in fact a great privilege because in the many years to come they would be able to boast to their children and grand-children about how they had rowed on the Nalikwanda. In

the centre of the boat was a small thatched cabin which
was where the Litunga would sit during the journey.
Finally after much singing and dancing the chief stepped
into the boat and in a flurry of paddles the boat cast off
from the bank. Then on a given signal all the poles lifted
as one, and plunged into the water in perfect unison as
the boat began to move off. They sang as they rowed. One
man would sing a line of a song while they all lifted
their poles out of the water and then they would all sing
the second line as they completed the downward stroke. It
was an incredible sight—one hundred or so ten foot poles
rising and falling in perfect harmony as the spray flew.
The Nalikwanda slowly picked up speed until it was flying
along at an incredible pace. As far as we were concerned
this was the last we would see of the Nalikwand until it
reached the winter palace where we would be waiting for
it. Meanwhile a whole fleet of smaller boats set out as
the Lozi followed their chief to their new homes.

5   The waiting crowd rushed forward as the boat appeared
on the horizon. As the boat drew closer the drumming grew
more frenzied and people would spontaneously break into
dance. Women would dance down to the water's edge, scoop
up a handful of water and dance back, sprinkling the water
on those around them as a way of showing everyone how
happy they were. As the boat drew closer it suddenly
stopped and started to move backward. Then it moved
forward and again reversed direction. According to
tradition a direct approach to the shore would bring bad
luck, and so the boat zigzagged in this manner for about
half an hour before coming in to dock. In the winter
village the feast had been prepared and the potent local
beer had been brewed. That night the Lozi people
celebrated the successful completion of yet another
Kuomboka Ceremony.

6   This was one of several times I observed the Kuomboka

Ceremony. I still remember how moved I was and how much it meant to me to witness this age-old ritual.

EXERCISE 1

Write a rough draft of the essay you began planning in Chapter 1.

3b *Understanding Revision*

Revision does not simply follow planning, shaping, and writing as the next step in a sequence. Rather, it is a process you engage in from the moment you begin to discover ideas for your essay. As you work you are constantly rethinking your topic or thesis and reconsidering your ideas, their order, and the pattern in which you arrange them. Revision is a creative and individual aspect of the writing process, and everyone does it somewhat differently. You will have to do a lot of experimenting before you find the particular techniques that work best for you.

Inexperienced writers sometimes believe they have failed if their first drafts are not perfect, but more experienced writers expect to revise. They also differ from inexperienced writers in *how* they revise. Inexperienced writers tend to concentrate on words, spelling, and grammar. They might do little more than refine word choices, correct grammatical or mechanical errors, or recopy their papers to make them neater. Experienced writers, however, see revision as a series of internal upheavals. They are willing to rethink a thesis and to disassemble and reassemble an entire essay. Only by doing so can they find a voice and a shape for their writing.

In your rough draft, you tend to write without thinking much about your audience. In your next draft, you begin to shape your writing for others. Now you "re-see" what you have written and make the changes necessary to enable your readers to understand and appreciate your ideas. Thus, revision reflects not only your private criticism of your first draft but also your anticipation of your readers' reactions.

Writing with Your Reader in Mind

- **Present one idea at a time and summarize when necessary.**
  When you overload your paper with more information than readers
  can take in, you lose them. Readers should not have to backtrack
  constantly to understand your message.
- **Fulfill your reader's expectations.** Readers expect your paper to
  do what your thesis says it will do, with major points introduced in
  an understandable order and appropriate support developed in
  your body paragraphs. They also expect style, grammar, punctuation, and mechanics to be correct.
- **Provide clear signals to establish your essay's direction.**
  Repeating key points, constructing clear topic sentences, using
  transitional words and phrases to link ideas logically, and accurately
  identifying dominant and subordinate ideas all help provide conti-
  nuity.

3c Applying Strategies for Revision

Everyone revises differently, and every writing task demands a
slightly different kind of revision. Four strategies in particular can
help you revise.

(1) Using a formal outline

Making a formal outline of a draft helps you to check the structure of your paper. A formal outline reveals at once whether points
are irrelevant or poorly placed—or, worse, missing. It also reveals
the hierarchy of your ideas—which points are dominant and which
are subordinate. This strategy is especially helpful early in revision,
when you are reworking the larger structural elements of your essay.

See
40g

(2) Collaborating with peers

Instead of trying to imagine your audience, you can address a
real audience by asking a friend, classmate, or family member to
read your draft and comment on it (with your instructor's permission, of course). The response should tell you whether or not your
essay has the effect you intended and perhaps why it succeeds or
fails. Peer criticism can also be more formal. Your instructor may
conduct the class as a workshop, assigning the class to comment

on different students' essays. Or, he or she may ask you to exchange essays with other students and write evaluations of their work.

In either case, approach a fellow student's essay responsibly, and take the analysis of your own essay seriously.

Writing Checklist: Questions for Peer Criticism

- What is the main point of the essay? Is the thesis stated? If so, is it clearly worded? If not, how can the wording be improved? Is the thesis stated in an appropriate place?
- Is the essay arranged logically? Do the body paragraphs appear in an appropriate order?
- What ideas support the thesis? Does each body paragraph develop one of these ideas?
- Does each body paragraph have a unifying idea? Do you need topic sentences to summarize the information in the paragraphs? Are the topic sentences clearly related to the thesis?
- Is any additional supporting information needed? List any missing points. Is any information irrelevant? If so, indicate possible deletions.
- Are all the necessary transitions provided? Or would additional links between sentences or paragraphs help? If so, where are such links needed?
- Does the introductory paragraph attract your attention? Would another kind of introduction work better?
- Does the conclusion add interest to the essay and reinforce the thesis? Would another kind of conclusion be more appropriate?
- Is anything unclear or confusing?
- What is the essay's greatest strength?
- What is the essay's greatest weakness?

(3)   Using instructor's comments

Instructors' comments can also help you revise. In general, these comments fall into three categories.

Correction Symbols   Frequently an instructor will indicate an area of concern with one of the correction symbols listed on the inside front cover of this book. Instead of correcting a problem, the instructor will simply identify it and supply the number of the section in the handbook that deals with the error. After reading the appropriate section in the handbook, the student is able to make the necessary changes. The symbol and number beside the following sentence referred a student to 18g2, the section in the handbook that discusses sexist usage.

Equal access to jobs is a desirable goal for all (mankind.) 18g

Sexist Usage

After reading section 18g2, the student made this change.

Equal access to jobs is a desirable goal for everyone.

Marginal Comments   Instructors frequently make marginal comments when they read a paper. These comments may suggest rhetorical options, such as a new slant for an introduction or a more explicit thesis, or they may recommend stylistic changes such as more varied sentences. Instructors also use marginal comments to question a line of thought or to propose new directions for a discussion. In most cases, you should consider these comments to be suggestions rather than corrections. You may decide to incorporate these ideas into a revised draft of your essay, and then again, you may not. (For examples of instructors's marginal comments, **see 3d2.**)

Conferences   If your instructor's suggestions raise questions about the direction of your revision, arrange a conference. During a conference, you are able to respond to the instructor's questions and comments. If you do not think the instructor understands your point, say so. Sometimes you can clarify a line of thought simply by sharpening a sentence or choosing another word. Your instructor will help you explore choices by explaining some of the many options you have. Quite often, the give and take of a conference can help you bring into focus ideas that were only implied in a draft.

Getting the Most out of a Conference

- **Make an appointment.** Make an appointment with your instructor before coming to his or her office, and arrive on time. Do not barge in and expect him or her to drop everything to help you. (If you find you are unable to keep your appointment, be sure to call your instructor to reschedule it.)
- **Read your paper carefully.** Before coming to the conference, go over all the instructor's comments and suggestions. Look up all the correction symbols, and read the appropriate sections of the handbook. Make all the changes you can on your draft. If you are coming to a conference to discuss ideas for a paper in progress, be sure your instructor is aware of this fact.

- **Have a list of questions.** Do not expect the instructor to anticipate your questions. Preparing a list in advance will enable you to
  get the most out of the conference in the allotted time.
- **Bring your draft.** Come to the conference with a draft of your
  paper. Without it, both you and the instructor can talk only in gen-
  eralities about your writing. If you have several drafts, you may
  want to bring them all, but be sure you bring the draft that has
  the instructor's comments on it.
- **Take notes.** As you discuss your paper, write down any suggestions that you think are helpful. Chances are that if you do not
  write down important suggestions at the time you hear them, you
  will forget them when you revise.
- **Participate actively.** Be prepared to discuss your draft. Your
  instructor is there to help you clarify your thoughts and to answer
  your questions, but he or she does not expect to deliver a monologue. A successful conference is not one-sided; it should be an
  open exchange of ideas between you and your instructor.

(4) Using checklists

Using a **revision checklist**—either one your instructor prepares
or one you devise yourself—is a systematic way of examining your
writing. A checklist helps you focus on revising one element at a
time. Depending upon the problems you have and the time you
have to deal with them, you can survey your paper using all the
questions on the checklist or only some of them.

On pages 44–45 are five checklists keyed to sections of this text.
They parallel the normal revision process, moving in four stages
from largest to smallest elements and then considering the issues
of tone and style. These checklists may be more helpful when you
have become familiar with concepts discussed later in the book.
For now, you can certainly use the questions listed under "The
Whole Essay." You may also know from experience which questions apply to your current writing problems. As your understanding of the writing process increases and you are better able to
identify the strengths and weaknesses of your writing, you can
narrow the focus of your revision. Perhaps you will even add points
to the checklist. You can also use your teachers' comments to tailor
these checklists to your own needs.

Revision Checklist: The Whole Essay

- Did you present your ideas in a logical sequence? Can you think of a different arrangement that might be more appropriate for your purpose? **(See 2a)**
- Is your thesis clearly and specifically worded? **(See 2b)**
- Does each body paragraph support your thesis? **(See 2b)**
- Have you drawn explicit connections between your thesis and your supporting information? **(See 2b)**
- Have you discussed everything promised in your thesis? **(See 2b)**
- Have you included any irrelevant points? **(See 2b)**
- Did you summarize your progress as you went along? **(See 3b)**
- Do clear transitions between paragraphs allow your readers to follow your essay's structure? **(See 4d6)**

Revision Checklist: Paragraphs

- Does each body paragraph have one unifying idea? **(See 4c)**
- Are topic sentences clearly recognizable and linked to the thesis? **(See 4c1)**
- Do your body paragraphs contain enough detail to support your ideas? **(See 4e)**
- Do your introductory paragraphs arouse reader interest and prepare them for what is to come? **(See 4g2)**
- Are the relationships of sentences within paragraphs clear? **(See 4d)**
- Are your paragraphs constructed according to familiar patterns? **(See 4f)**
- Do your concluding paragraphs sum up your main points? **(See 4g3)**

Revision Checklist: Sentence Structure

- Have you strengthened sentences with repetition, balance, and parallelism? **(See 10c–d, 16a)**
- Are sentences overloaded with too many clauses? **(See 11c)**
- Have you used correct sentence structure? **(See Chs. 13 and 14)**
- Have you placed modifiers clearly and logically? **(See Ch. 15)**
- Have you avoided potentially confusing shifts in tense, voice, mood, person, or number? **(See 17a–d)**
- Are your sentences constructed logically? **(See 17f–g)**

- Have you used emphatic word order? **(See 10a)**
- Have you used sentence structure to signal the relative importance of clauses in a sentence and their logical relationship to one another? **(See 10b)**
- Have you eliminated nonessential words and needless repetition? **(See 11a–b)**
- Have you varied your sentence structure? **(See Ch. 12)**
- Have you combined sentences where ideas are closely related? **(See 12b)**

Revision Checklist: Word Choice

- Is your level of diction appropriate for your audience and your purpose? **(See 18a–b)**
- Have you selected words that accurately reflect your intentions? **(See 18c1)**
- Have you chosen words that are specific, concrete, and unambiguous? **(See 18c3–4)**
- Have you enriched your writing with figurative language? **(See 18e)**
- Have you eliminated jargon, neologisms, pretentious diction, cliches, ineffective figures of speech, and offensive language from your writing? **(See 18d,f,g)**

Revision Checklist: Tone and Style

- Is your tone consistent with your purpose? **(See 1a3)**
- Have you maintained the proper distance from your readers? **(See 1a3)**
- Is your style appropriate for your subject, purpose, and audience? **(See 18a–b)**

3d *Revising Your Drafts*

(1) *Revising the first draft*

After you finish your rough draft, set it aside for a day if possible. When you look it over, you will probably notice problems that need attention. You cannot solve every problem at once, however. It makes more sense to focus on only a few areas at a time and to rework your essay in several drafts. As you review your first draft, focus on your essay's *content, organization,* and *thesis.* Once you have given attention to these areas, you can attend to other problems more easily.

As you reread your draft, consider carefully the items in the Revision Checklist: The Whole Essay on page 44. As you review your first draft, you may also have the benefit of peer criticism or a conference with your instructor. If you do, consider these readers' comments carefully, focusing for now on their suggestions about content, organization, and thesis.

REVISING THE FIRST DRAFT

George Panacheril began his revision by reviewing the revision checklist The Whole Essay on page 44. He was confident that his essay included all the information that he felt was important and treated no irrelevant points. He also saw his organization as logical; it made sense to discuss the ceremony in chronological order, and the process pattern and transitions between stages were so clear that he could tell no stages had been omitted or presented out of order.

George felt satisfied that his thesis was consistent with his purpose and assignment and that it was worded clearly. He also believed that the body paragraphs of his essay, which emphasized the ceremony's tradition, supported his thesis quite well. All in all, he was satisfied with his draft.

However, when George discussed his essay with three fellow students, he discovered that he had a lot of work left to do. The students who read George's paper agreed with his own assessment of the essay's organization and thesis. Because the students knew little about his subject, however, they had many questions and comments:

Where is all this taking place?
Paragraphs are too long, and this makes the story hard to follow.
What is a Litunga?
You didn't tell the meaning of the ceremony. We need more background.
Why is the goat killed?
Why is the chief carrying a fly-whisk?
You need more on how things looked to you—the chief, the warriors, the barge, etc.
I think you should focus more on how you felt at the time—maybe add a paragraph about how this is an emotional event for you as a resident of that country. You seem to be just giving a description of the event

instead of expressing your feelings about what you've learned from it. I think you expected us to know too much.

After reading his classmates' comments on his draft and discussing their concerns with them, George decided not to add a separate paragraph about his feelings but rather to inject brief comments about his reactions wherever they seemed to be appropriate. His assignment did not ask him to tell what he had learned from the ritual or how he felt about it, so he thought a full paragraph on either of these subjects would be inconsistent with his purpose. He did decide to add a background paragraph explaining the ritual's significance (he planned to ask his aunt for help here) and to add more description of the scene and its participants. Now George went on to edit his first draft to reflect these decisions.

```
          First Draft: The Kuomboka Ceremony

1     Of all the rituals I have observed
or participated in, the one that I
found the most interesting is the Kuom-
boka Ceremony. It is a truly important,
even momentous event. What is most
amazing about the Kuomboka Ceremony is
the way it has lasted through the
years, maintaining tradition in the
face of change.
2     All was still in the inky darkness
of the African night, the silence punc-
tuated by the sounds of various
insects. Occasionally the inane laugh
of the hyena or the screech of a baboon
split the night. As I stood motionless,
together with hundreds of others, a low
throbbing sound filled the air. Soft,
almost inaudible at first, the sound
gradually increased in intensity as
more and more drummers joined in. They
were playing big drums which were
essentially an African equivilant of
```

the kettle drum. Made from wood, it was covered with stretched cowhide. The rhythms they played were complex, highly intricate patterns which took years of practice to master. It was now midnight and the drums would not stop beating until the chief left the next morning, some seven hours later. This served as a signal and within minutes a number of fires had sprung up around the camp as the whole village came to life. The Kuomboka Ceremony had begun.

3   The sky was a dusky gray as the first rays of soft sunlight heralded the dawn. Slowly people began to gather around the Litunga's hut. There were all kinds of people there, from foreign tourists with their cameras and tape recorders, to villagers dressed in animal skins and dilapidated, cast-off Western clothing. Looking through the crowd I was not surprised to see a few cabinet ministers and other top government officials present. Inside the thatched mud hut the Litunga was being prepared for the journey by the tribal elders. And then, for the first time since they had started, the big drums missed a beat; and then another. Then as they had started they gradually faded off until there was silence. In fact after the many hours of drumming you could almost hear the silence. All eyes turned expectantly toward the door of the chief's hut. As the Litunga stepped out into the light there was an

explosion of smaller drums in a rapid, staccato beat that was very much like a high-speed pneumatic drill. Suddenly all around me people were clapping and dancing in time to the drums. The chief was an elderly man with white hair who walked with the help of a cane. In his left hand he carried a fly-whisk. He was dressed in black robes that hung down to his knees and black trousers and shoes, and carried himself with the dignity due his age and position. As the Litunga walked away from the hut a warrior standing a short distance away raised his knife to kill a goat.

The emotionally charged atmosphere affected all of us and I could feel my feet twitching to the rhythm.

the

that is to a Lozichief what the sceptre in the crown jewels is to a British monarch.

As the blade of the panga swept up and down I shivered as I thought about the stories of how in days gone by a man had stood where the goat now lay.

I remember thinking how odd his clothing was in a ceremony of such symbolic importance. It was a measure of how the influence of western culture had started eroding the age-old customs of these people.

4   As the crowd moved toward the river I caught my first glimpse of the royal barge, "the Nalikwanda." The two sides of the boat were lined with men who were all adjusting their costumes or fidgeting with the long wooden poles they each held. *They were all clad in different arrangements of animal skins, their meticulously oiled bodies bare from the waist upward, glistening in the sunlight. Each rower wore a head dress made from the feathers of jacanas, maribou storks, herons, king-fisher, fish-eagles and other birds of the plains.*

It was a long, relatively narrow boat that sat low in the water. It was painted in a zebra-like pattern of vertical black and white stripes.

They were an elite group of men in the tribe, a select group of warriors with the power and stamina to row nonstop for ten hours. It was in fact a great privilege because in the many years to come they would be able to boast to their children and grand-children about how they had rowed on the Nalikwanda. In the centre of the boat was a small thatched cabin which was where the Litunga would sit during the journey. ⋀Finally after much singing and dancing *¶ new par* the chief stepped into the boat and in a flurry of paddles the boat cast off from the bank. Then on a given signal all the poles lifted as one, and plunged into the water in perfect unison as the boat began to move off. They sang as they rowed. One man would sing a line of a song while they all lifted their poles out of the water and then they would all sing the second line as they completed the downward stroke. It was an incredible sight—one hundred or so ten foot poles rising and falling in perfect harmony as the spray flew. The Nalikwanda slowly picked up speed until it was flying along at an incredible pace. As far as we were concerned this was the last we would see of the Nalikwanda until it reached the winter palace where would be waiting for it. Meanwhile a whole fleet of smaller boats set out as the Lozi followed their chief to their new homes.

5   The waiting crowd rushed forward

as the boat appeared on the horizon. As
the boat drew closer the drumming grew
more frenzied and people would sponta-
neously break into dance, ^which is the Zambian's way of expressing joy. Women would
dance down to the water's edge, scoop
up a handful of water and dance back,
sprinkling the water on those around
them as a way of showing everyone how
happy they were. As the boat drew
closer it suddenly stopped and started
to move backward. Then it moved forward
and again reversed direction. According
to tradition a direct approach to the
shore would bring bad luck, and so the
boat zigzagged in this manner for about
half an hour before coming in to dock.
In the winter village the feast had
been prepared and the potent local beer
had been brewed. That night the Lozi
people celebrated the successful completion of yet another Kuomboka Ceremony.

6   This was one of the several times
I observed the Kuomboka Ceremony. I
still remember how moved I was and how
much it meant to me to witness this
age-old ritual.

* add after ¶2

The Lozi people live on the Basuto Plains in the Western Province of the Republic of Zambia. This region which constitutes a section of the floodplain of the Zambezi River is subject to seasonal flooding and as a result every year these people have to move their village to higher ground in the rainy season. The annual trek from low to high ground is a ritual that goes *as far back as the beginning of the Lozi. The mass population movement is ceremonially initiated when the tribal chief, the Litunga, travels from his summer palace to his winter palace in a grand ceremony called the "Kuomboka."*

EXERCISE 2

Revise the large structure—content, organization, and thesis—of your essay, following the guidelines listed in the revision checklist The Whole Essay on page 44. Write a second draft reflecting your changes.

(2) Revising the second draft

REVISING THE SECOND DRAFT

Following is George's second draft, recopied from the edited first draft on pages 47–51. He submitted it to his instructor, whose correction symbols and comments appear on the manuscript.

Second Draft: The Kuomboka Ceremony

1   Of all the rituals I have observed   *What others*
or participated in, the one that I   *have you*
found the most interesting is the Kuom-   *observed?*
boka Ceremony. It is a truly important,   *Mention them*
even momentous event. What is most   *briefly here, or*
amazing about the Kuomboka Ceremony is   *try another*
the way it has lasted through the   *opening strategy.*
years, maintaining tradition in the   *See 4g1.*
face of change.

2   All was still in the inky darkness
of the African night, the silence punctuated by the sounds of various
insects. Occasionally the inane laugh

of the hyena or the screech of a baboon split the night. As I stood motionless, together with hundreds of others, a low throbbing sound filled the air. Soft, almost inaudible at first, the sound gradually increased in intensity as more and more drummers joined in. They were playing big drums which were essentially an African (equivilant) of

sp

the kettle drum. Made from wood, it was shaped like a giant gourd and was covered with stretched cowhide. The rhythms they played were complex, highly intricate patterns which took years of practice to master. It was now midnight and the drums would not stop beating until the chief left the next morning, some seven hours later. (This)

*ref. ?
see 22d1*

served as a signal and within minutes a number of fires had sprung up around the camp as the whole village came to life. The Kuomboka Ceremony had begun.

3   The Lozi people live on the Basuto Plains in the Western Province of the Republic of Zambia. This region which constitutes a section of the floodplain of the Zambezi River is subject to seasonal flooding and as a result every year these people have to move their village to higher ground in the rainy season. The annual trek from low to high ground is a ritual that goes as far back as the beginning of the Lozi. The mass population movement is ceremonially initiated when the tribal chief, the Litunga, travels from his

Good – this background really helps me understand the ritual's purpose

summer palace to his winter palace in a
grand ceremony called the "Kuomboka."

4   The sky was a dusky gray as the
first rays of soft sunlight heralded
the dawn. Slowly people began to gather
around the Litunga's hut. There were
all kinds of people there, from foreign
tourists with their cameras and tape
recorders, to villagers dressed in animal skins and dilapidated, cast-off
Western clothing. Looking through the
crowd I was not surprised to see a few
cabinet ministers and other top government officials present. Inside the
thatched mud hut the Litunga was being
prepared for the journey by the tribal
elders. And then, for the first time
since they had started, the big drums
missed a beat; and then another. Then
as they had started they gradually
faded off until there was silence. In
fact after the many hours of drumming
you could almost hear the silence. All
eyes turned expectantly toward the door
of the chief's hut.

cliché
see 18d

5   As the Litunga stepped out into
the light there was an explosion of
smaller drums in a rapid, staccato beat
that was very much like a high-speed
pneumatic drill. Suddenly all around me
people were clapping and dancing in
time to the drums. The emotionally
charged atmosphere affected all of us
and I could feel my feet twitching to
the rhythm. The chief was an elderly
man with white hair who walked with the

Nice – this is very dramatic

help of a cane. In his left hand he carried the fly—whisk that is to a Lozi chief what the ~~sceptre~~ in the crown jewels is to a British monarch. He was dressed in black robes that hung down to his knees and black trousers and shoes, and carried himself with the dignity due his age and position. I remember thinking how odd his clothing was in a ceremony of such symbolic importance. It was a measure of how the influence of Western culture had started eroding the age—old customs of these people. As the Litunga walked away from the hut a warrior standing a short distance away raised his knife to kill a goat. As the blade of the panga swept up and down I shivered as I thought about the stories of how in days gone by a man had stood where the goat now lay.

use American spelling (scepter) see 20a4

This helps support your thesis

6   As the crowd moved toward the river I caught my first glimpse of the royal barge, "the Nalikwanda." It was a long, relatively narrow boat that sat low in the water. It was painted in a zebra—like pattern of vertical black and white stripes. The two sides of the boat were lined with men who were all adjusting their costumes or fidgeting with the long wooden poles they each held. They were all clad in different arrangements of animal skins, their meticulously oiled bodies, bare from the waist upward, glistening in the sunlight. Each rower wore a head dress

good description— I can really see this scene.

made from the feathers of jacanas, maribou storks, herons, king-fishers,
fish-eagles and other birds of the
Plains. They were an elite group of men
in the tribe, a select group of warriors with the power and stamina to row
nonstop for ten hours. It was in fact a
great privilege because in the many
years to come they would be able to
boast to their children and grand-children about how they had rowed on the
Nalikwanda. In the centre of the boat
was a small thatched cabin which was
where the Litunga would sit during the
journey.

Great detail!
Readers won't
be familiar
with this
material and
your description
enables them to
picture what
you saw.

use American
spelling (center)
see 20 a4

7   Finally after much singing and
dancing the chief stepped into the boat
and in a flurry of paddles the boat
cast off from the bank. Then on a given
signal all the poles lifted as one, and
plunged into the water in perfect unison as the boat began to move off. They
sang as they rowed. One man would sing
a line of a song while they all lifted
their poles out of the water and then
they would all sing the second line as
they completed the downward stroke. It
was an incredible sight—one hundred or
so ten foot poles rising and falling in
perfect harmony as the spray flew. The
Nalikwanda slowly picked up speed until
it was flying along at an incredible
pace. As far as we were concerned this
was the last we would see of the Nalikwanda until it reached the winter palace where we would be waiting for it.

use two
unspaced
hyphens
see A-3

Meanwhile a whole fleet of smaller boats set out as the Lozi followed their chief to their new homes.

8   The waiting crowd rushed forward as the boat appeared on the horizon. As the boat drew closer the drumming grew more frenzied and people would spontaneously break into dance, which is the Zambian's way of expressing joy. Women would dance down to the water's edge, scoop up a handful of water and dance back, sprinkling the water on those around them as a way of showing everyone how happy they were. As the boat drew closer it suddenly stopped and started to move backward. Then it moved forward and again reversed direction. According to tradition a direct approach to the shore would bring bad luck, and so the boat zigzagged in this manner for about half an hour before coming in to dock. In the winter village the feast had been prepared and the potent local beer had been brewed. That night the Lozi people celebrated the successful completion of yet another Kuomboka Ceremony.

9   This was one of several times I observed the Kuomboka Ceremony. I still remember how moved I was and how much it meant to me to witness this age-old ritual.

Some things to think about before conference:
— Choice of tense (past, as though relating
the experience of your eyewitness rather
than present to describe a habitual action)
is problematic. Using present throughout
might make the essay more immediate.
— Introduction and conclusion seem
somehow tacked on. You might consider
whether they're even necessary. (Both ¶ 2
and your next to last ¶ are very strong.)

In this draft George had corrected many of his first draft's most obvious shortcomings in content and organization. Now he could consider elements like sentence structure and word choice, tone and style. To guide his revision he would have the benefit of his instructor's written comments in a conference. He would also review the rest of the revision checklists.

George had already added new material, occasionally changing words or phrasing. Now, following the advice of his instructor, George decided to edit or even perhaps delete his introduction and conclusion and to rewrite his essay in the present tense. He also decided to aim for a less wordy style and to carefully review his punctuation.

E X E R C I S E   3

Review the second draft of your paper, paying particular attention to paragraphing, topic sentences, and transitions and to the way you structure your sentences and select your words. If possible, ask a friend to read your draft and respond to the peer criticism questions in 3c2. Then revise your draft, incorporating any suggestions you find helpful.

(3) Preparing the final draft: editing and proofreading

After you have revised your drafts to your satisfaction, two final steps remain: editing and proofreading your paper.

Editing   When you edit, you concentrate on grammar and spelling, punctuation and mechanics. You will have done some of this work as you revised previous drafts of your paper, but now your *focus* is on editing. Approach your work as a critical reader would, reading each sentence carefully. As you proceed, you may find it helpful to review the items on the editing checklist that follows. Keep your preliminary notes, any sources you have used, and reference books (such as this handbook and an up-to-date college dictionary) nearby as you edit. If you are typing your paper on a computer, now is the time to run spelling and (with your instructor's permission) grammar and usage checks.

Revision Checklist: Editing for Grammar, Punctuation, Mechanics, and Spelling

Grammar

- Have you used the appropriate case for pronouns? **(See 22a–b)**
- Are pronoun references clear and unambiguous? **(See 22c–d)**
- Are verb forms correct? **(See 23a)**
- Are tense, mood, and voice of verbs logical and appropriate? **(See 23b–k)**
- Do subjects and verbs agree? **(See 24a)**
- Do pronouns and antecedents agree? **(See 24b)**
- Are adjectives and adverbs used correctly? **(See 25a–d)**

Punctuation

- Is end punctuation used correctly? **(See 26a–c)**
- Are commas used correctly? **(See Ch. 27)**
- Are semicolons used correctly? **(See Ch. 28)**
- Are apostrophes used correctly? **(See Ch. 29)**
- Are quotation marks used where they are required? **(See 30a–e)**
- Are quotation marks used correctly with other punctuation marks? **(See 30f)**
- Are other punctuation marks—colons, dashes, parentheses, brackets, slashes, and ellipsis marks—used correctly? **(See Ch. 31)**

Mechanics

- Is capitalization consistent with standard English usage? **(See Ch. 32)**
- Are italics used correctly? **(See Ch. 33)**
- Are hyphens used where required and place correctly within and between words? **(See Ch. 34)**
- Are abbreviations used where convention calls for their use? **(See Ch. 35)**

continued

continued from previous page

- Are numerals and spelled-out numbers used appropriately? **(See Ch. 36)**

Spelling

- Are all words spelled correctly? (Check a dictionary if necessary)

Proofreading   After you have completed your editing, type a final draft. Even when it is complete, however, you are still not finished. Now you must proofread, rereading every word carefully to make sure you did not make any errors as you typed. You must also make sure that the final typed copy of your paper conforms to your instructor's format requirements.

See ◄
App.

PREPARING THE FINAL DRAFT

After revising his second draft, George Panacheril edited, retyped, and proofread his essay. His final draft appears below.

Final Draft: The Kuomboka Ceremony

1   All is still in the inky darkness of the African night, the silence punctuated by the sounds of various insects. Occasionally, the inane laugh of the hyena or the screech of a baboon splits the night. As I stand motionless, huddled together with hundreds of others, a low throbbing sound fills the air. The people who have been talking stop to listen. Almost inaudible at first, the sound gradually increases in intensity as more and more drummers join in. As time goes on and I listen to more and more of the hypnotic throbbing, it begins to feel as though the drumming is within my own body. They are playing big drums, the African equivalent of kettle drums. Made from wood, they are shaped like giant gourds and covered with stretched cowhide. The rhythms the drummers play are complex, highly intricate patterns which take years of practice to master. It is now midnight and the drums will not stop beating until the chief leaves the

60

next morning, about seven hours from now. The drums serve
as a signal, and within minutes fires spring up around the
camp as the whole village comes to life. The Kuomboka
Ceremony has begun.

2   The Lozi people live on the Basuto Plains in the
Western Province of the Republic of Zambia. This region,
which constitutes a section of the flood plain of the
Zambezi River, is subject to seasonal flooding and, as a
result, every year these people have to move their village
to higher ground in the rainy season. The annual trek from
low to high ground is a ritual that goes as far back as
the beginning of the Lozi. The mass population movement is
ceremonially initiated when the tribal chief, the Litunga,
travels from his summer palace to this winter palace in a
grand ceremony called the "Kuomboka." Knowing that this
ceremony has continued for so many years, maintaining
tradition in the face of change, gives me confidence that
the rituals of the Lozi people will endure.

3   The sky is a dusky gray as the first rays of soft
sunlight appear. Slowly, people begin to gather around the
Litunga's hut. All kinds of people are there, from foreign
tourists with their cameras and tape recorders to
villagers dressed in animal skins and dilapidated cast-off
Western clothing. Looking through the crowd I am not
particularly surprised to see a few cabinet ministers and
other top government officials present, for at the
Kuomboka there are no racial, tribal, or social
distinctions.

4   Inside the thatched mud hut the Litunga is being
prepared by the tribal elders for the journey. Suddenly,
for the first time since they started, the big drums miss
a beat, and then another. Then they gradually fade off
until there is silence. After the many hours of drumming,
you can almost hear the silence. All eyes turn expectantly
toward the door of the chief's hut.

5   As the Litunga steps out into the light, there is an

explosion of smaller drums in a rapid, staccato beat that is very much like a high-speed pneumatic drill. Now all around me people are clapping and dancing in time to the drums. The emotionally charged atmosphere affects all of us, and I can feel my feet inadvertently moving to the rhythm. The chief, an elderly man with white hair, has to walk with the help of a cane. In his left hand he carries the fly-whisk that is to a Lozi chief what the scepter in the Crown Jewels is to a British monarch. He is dressed in black robes that hang down to his knees, and black trousers and shoes. He stands tall and proud and carries himself with the dignity due his age and position. It seems odd that he should wear Western clothes in a ceremony of such symbolic importance; it is a measure of how the influence of Western culture has started eroding the age-old customs of these people. As the Litunga walks away from the hut, a warrior standing a short distance away raises his knife to kill a goat. As the blade of the panga swishes through the air, my body twitches involuntarily. Originally, by tradition, a man would have knelt where the butchered goat now lies.

6   As the crowd moves toward the river, I catch my first glimpse of the royal barge, the Nalikwanda. A long, relatively narrow boat that sits low in the water, it is painted in a zebra-like pattern of vertical black and white stripes. The two sides of the boat are lined with men who are all adjusting their costumes or fidgeting with the long wooden poles each one holds. They are all clad in different arrangements of animal skins, and their meticulously oiled bodies, bare from the waist up, glisten in the sunlight. Each rower wears a headdress made from the feathers of jacanas, maribou storks, herons, kingfishers, fisheagles, and other birds of the plains. They are an elite group of tribesmen, a select group of warriors with the power and stamina to row nonstop for ten hours. There are smiles on their faces as they dream of

the day when they will be able to boast to their children
and grandchildren about how they rowed on the Nalikwanda.
In the center of the boat is a small thatched cabin, which
is where the Litunga will sit during the journey.

7   Finally, after much singing and dancing, the chief
steps into the boat, and in a flurry of paddles the boat
casts off the bank. Then, on a given signal, all the poles
lift as one and plunge into the water in perfect unison as
the boat begins to move off. The men sing as they row. One
man sings a line of the song while they all lift their
poles out of the water, and then they all sing the second
line as they complete the downward stroke. It is an awe-
inspiring sight—one hundred or so ten-foot poles rising
and falling in perfect harmony. The Nalikwanda slowly
picks up speed until it is flying along at an incredible
pace. The water around the boat turns white as it smashes
its way through the powerful mid-river currents. This is
the last we will see of the Nalikwanda until it reaches
the winter palace where we will be waiting for it.
Meanwhile, a whole fleet of smaller boats sets out as the
Lozi follow their chief to their new homes.

8   The waiting crowd at the winter palace rushes forward
as the boat appears on the horizon. As the boat draws
closer, the drumming grows more frenzied and people
spontaneously break into dance, which is the Zambian's way
of expressing joy. Women dance down to the water's edge,
scoop up handfuls of water, and dance back, sprinkling the
water on those around them as a way of showing everyone
how happy they are. Their joy is such that at this time
there is no distinction between those of the tribe and the
spectators. As people we all celebrate the success of a
great event and the continuation of a great tradition.

9   As the boat approaches the shore, it suddenly stops
and starts to move backward. Then it moves forward and
again reverse direction. According to tradition a direct
approach to the shore will bring bad luck, and so the boat

zigzags in this manner for about half an hour before
coming in to dock. In the winter village the feast has
been prepared, and the potent local beer has been brewed.
Tonight the Lozi people will celebrate the successful
completion of yet another Kuomboka Ceremony.

EXERCISE 4

What exactly has George changed between his second and third drafts?
List each of these changes and evaluate them as any careful reader would.
Are all his changes for the better? Are any other changes called for?

EXERCISE 5

Using the revision checklists in 3d4 as a guide, create a checklist that reflects
the specific concerns you need to consider to revise your essay. Then revise
your essay according to this checklist.

EXERCISE 6

Edit your essay, and then prepare a final draft, being sure to proofread it
carefully.

Writing Paragraphs

A **paragraph** is a group of related sentences, complete in itself, which forms a distinct unit of a longer piece of writing. Paragraphs serve three important functions in an essay:

1. They group sentences into units of thought that work as a whole to support an essay's main idea.
2. They provide visual breaks in the text that give readers a chance to pause and assimilate ideas.
3. They signal the movement of ideas in the essay. In most short essays, each paragraph presents a specific point contributing to a more general thesis. In longer essays, groups of related paragraphs, called **paragraph clusters,** may present the points.

4a   Determining When to Paragraph

By reinforcing your overall purpose, paragraphs help you control the organization of your paper and convey your ideas clearly to your readers.

When to Paragraph

- **To signal a shift in focus.** Whenever you move from one major idea to another in your essay, you begin a new paragraph.
- **To signal a shift in time or place.** In narrative or descriptive passages of an essay you may want to begin a new paragraph whenever you move your readers from one time or place to another.
- **To clarify sequence.** In enumerating points or tasks, you may begin a new paragraph every time you begin discussing a new

---

continued

continued from previous page

point in a sequence or a new stage in a process. These shifts are typically signaled by transitional words and phrases such as *first, second,* or *in the first case, in the second case.*

- **To make ideas more emphatic.** Writers underscore important ideas by isolating them in separate paragraphs.
- **To set off dialogue.** When recording dialogue, convention requires that you begin a new paragraph every time a new person speaks.
- **To set off introductions and conclusions.** Begin a new paragraph to signal the end of your introduction, and begin your conclusion with a new paragraph.

4b *Charting Paragraph Structure*

Charting the ideas in a paragraph helps you to recognize its underlying structure. You begin by assigning the sentence that expresses the main or **unifying idea** of the paragraph to level 1. If no sentence in the paragraph expresses the unifying idea, compose a sentence that does. Then, read each sentence of the paragraph. Assign to level 1 sentences as important as the one containing the unifying idea. Indent and assign to level 2 more specific sentences that qualify or limit the unifying idea. Indent again and assign to level 3 any sentences that support level-2 sentences. Do this for every sentence in the paragraph, assigning increasingly higher numbers to more specific sentences. Notice how charting reveals the structure of the following paragraph.

1 My grandmother told me that fifty years ago life was not easy for a girl in rural Italy.
  2 At the age of six a girl was expected to help her mother with household chores.
    3 Girls of this age were no longer permitted to play games or to indulge in childish activities.
  2 At the age of twelve, a girl assumed most of the responsibilities of an adult.
    3 She worked in the fields, prepared meals, carried water, and took care of the younger children.
    3 Education was usually out of the question; it was an unusual family that allowed a girl to enroll in one of the few convent schools that took peasant children.

The first sentence (level 1) of this paragraph introduces the unifying idea, and each level-2 sentence gives an illustration of that idea. The level-3 sentences support these examples with specifics.

Revision Close-up

Note that a properly constructed paragraph has only one level-1 sentence. If charting reveals more than one level-1 sentence, you will need to revise your paragraph, perhaps dividing it into two paragraphs **(see 4c2).**

By charting the sentences as you revise your paragraphs, you can make certain your paragraphs are *unified, coherent,* and *well developed.*

4c *Writing Unified Paragraphs*

A paragraph is **unified** when it focuses on a single idea and develops it. A paragraph without such a unifying idea is confusing and hard to follow.

You can create a unified paragraph by using a topic sentence and by ensuring that all the sentences in your paragraph support the unifying idea this topic sentence expresses.

(1) *Using topic sentences*

Although many experienced writers do not use topic sentences in all their paragraphs, they do organize each of their paragraphs around a single unifying idea. In some paragraphs, the topic sentence is **implied.** However, if you are a beginning writer, it makes good sense for you to use topic sentences to make your unifying idea clear both to you and to your readers.

Topic Sentence at the Beginning   When you use this option, you begin with a topic sentence and follow with support.

Using a topic sentence at the beginning of each paragraph is effective when you want your readers to see your paragraph's subject and main point immediately. Beginning with the topic sentence also helps you stay focused on your subject.

A Hindoo temple is a conglomeration of adornment. The lines of the building are completely hidden by the decorations. Sculptured figures and ornaments crowd its surface, stand out from it in thick masses, break it up into a bewildering series of irregular tiers. It is not a unity but a collection, rich, confused. It looks like something not planned but built this way and that as the ornament required. The conviction underlying it can be perceived: each bit of the exquisitely wrought detail had a mystical meaning and the temple's exterior was important only as a means for the artist to inscribe thereon the symbols of the truth. It is decoration, not architecture. (Edith Hamilton, *The Greek Way*)

Topic Sentence in the Middle   Placing a topic sentence in the middle of a paragraph enables you to build up to a point gradually or give background information before you state and develop your position. This strategy is especially effective if you are refuting opposing points of view or presenting unfamiliar or unexpected information.

African-American servicemen have played a role in the United States military since Revolutionary times. In the years before World War II, however, they were employed chiefly as truck drivers, quartermasters, bakers, and cooks. Then, in July 1941, a program was set up at Alabama's Tuskegee Institute to train black fighter pilots. Eventually, nearly one thousand flyers—about half of whom fought overseas— were trained there; sixty-six of these men were killed in action. Ironically, even as African-American servicemen were fighting valiantly against fascism in Europe, they continued to experience discrimination in the United States military. Black officers encountered hostility and even violence at officers' clubs. Enlisted men and women were frequently the target of bigoted remarks. Throughout the war, in fact, African-American servicemen were placed in separate, all-black units. This segregation was official army policy until 1948, when President Harry S. Truman signed an executive order to desegregate the military. (Student)

Topic Sentence at the End   Using a topic sentence at the end of a paragraph enables you to present controversial issues effectively. Leading off with a controversial statement can alienate an audience. However, if you lead your readers through a logical and carefully thought out argument and *then* present your conclusion, you are more likely to convince them that your conclusion is reasonable.

These sprays, dusts and aerosols are now applied almost universally to farms, gardens, forests, and homes—nonselective chemicals that have the power to kill every insect, the "good" and the "bad," to still the song of birds and the leaping of fish in the streams, to coat the leaves with a deadly film, and to linger on in soil—all this though the intended target may be only a few weeds or insects. Can anyone believe it is possible to lay down such a barrage of poisons on the surface without making it unfit for life? They should not be called "insecticides," but "biocides." (Rachel Carson, "The Obligation to Endure," *Silent Spring*)

Topic Sentence Implied At times you will want to avoid a direct statement of your unifying idea. In some situations—especially in narrative or descriptive paragraphs—a topic sentence can seem forced or artificial. In the following paragraph, the author wants readers to share her experience. To accomplish this goal, she implies her paragraph's unifying idea: that because she was a girl, she was considered inferior.

I am eight years old and a tomboy. I have a cowboy hat, cowboy boots, checkered shirt and pants, all red. My playmates are my brothers, two and four years older than I. Their colors are black and green, the only difference in the way we are dressed. On Saturday nights we all go to the picture show, even my mother; Westerns are her favorite kind of movie. Back home, "on the ranch," we pretend we are Tom Mix, Hopalong Cassidy, Lash LaRue (we've even named one of our dogs Lash LaRue); we chase each other for hours rustling cattle, being outlaws, delivering damsels from distress. Then my parents decide to buy my brothers guns. These are not "real" guns. They shoot "BBs," copper pellets my brothers say will kill birds. Because I am a girl, I do not get a gun. Instantly I am relegated to the position of Indian. Now there appears a great distance between us. They shoot and shoot at everything with their new guns. I try to keep up with my bow and arrows. (Alice Walker, "Beauty: When the Other Dancer Is the Self," *In Search of Our Mothers' Gardens*)

(2) Testing for unity

Each sentence in a paragraph should support its unifying idea. When you revise your paragraphs, look carefully for sentences that do not do so. You can bring your paragraph into focus by rewriting these sentences or, in some cases, by deleting them. The following paragraph contains sentences that wander from its subject:

One of the first problems students have is learning to use a micro-computer. All students were required to buy a computer before school started. Throughout the first semester we took a special course to teach us to use a computer. The Macintosh Classic has a large memory and can do word processing and spreadsheets. It has an eighty-character screen and a built-in disk drive. My parents were happy that I had a computer, but they were concerned about the price. Tuition was high, and when they added in the price of the computer, it was almost out of reach. To offset expenses, I arranged for a part-time job in the school library. Now I am determined to overcome my "computer anxiety" and to master my Macintosh by the end of the semester. (Student)

The lack of unity in the paragraph above becomes obvious when you chart its sentences.

1 One of the first problems students have is learning to use a microcomputer.
  2 All students were required to buy a computer before school started.
    3 Throughout the first semester we took a special course to teach us to use a computer.
1 The Macintosh Classic has a large memory and can do word processing and spreadsheets.
  2 It has an eighty-character screen and a built-in disk drive.
1 My parents were happy that I had a computer, but they were concerned about the price.
  2 Tuition was high, and when they added in the price of the computer, it was almost out of reach.
    3 To offset expenses, I arranged for a part-time job in the school library.
1 Now I am determined to overcome my "computer anxiety" and to master my Macintosh by the end of the semester.

Since each level-1 sentence represents a topic that should be developed in its own paragraph, this paragraph has not one but four topics. Instead of writing one unified paragraph, the writer has made a series of false starts.

To unify this paragraph around the idea of learning to use his computer, the writer took out the sentences about his parents' financial situation and the computer's characteristics, keeping only those details related to the unifying idea.

One of the first problems I had as a college student was learning to use my computer. All first-year students were required to buy a Macintosh Classic computer before school started. Throughout the first semester, we took a special course to teach us to use the computer. In theory this system sounded fine, but in my case it was a disaster. In the first place, the closest I had ever come to a computer was the hand-held calculator I used in math class. In the second place,

I could not type. And to make matters worse, many of the people in my computer orientation course already knew how to operate a computer. By the end of the first week I was convinced that I would never be able to work with my Macintosh.

EXERCISE 1

Each of the following paragraphs is unified by a central idea, but that idea is not explicitly stated. Identify the unifying idea of each paragraph, write a topic sentence that expresses it, and decide where in the paragraph to place it.

A. The narrator in Ellison's novel leaves an all-black college in the South to seek his fortune—and his identity—in the North. Throughout the story he experiences bigotry in all forms. Blacks as well as whites, friends as well as enemies, treat him according to their preconceived notions of what he should be, or how he can help to advance their causes. Clearly this is a book about racial prejudice. However, on another level, *Invisible Man* is more than the account of a young African-American's initiation into the harsh realities of life in the United States before the civil rights movement. The narrator calls himself invisible because others refuse to see him. He becomes so alienated from society—black and white—that he chooses to live in isolation. But, when he has learned to see himself clearly, he will emerge demanding that others see him too.

B. "Lite" can mean a product has fewer calories, or less fat, or less sodium, or it can simply mean the product has a "light" color, texture, or taste. It may mean none of these. Food can be advertised as 86 percent fat free when it is actually 50 percent fat, because the term "fat free" is based on weight and fat is extremely light. Another misleading term is "no cholesterol," which is found on some products that never had any cholesterol in the first place. Peanut butter, for example, contains no cholesterol—a fact that manufacturers have recently made an issue—but it is very high in fat and so would not be a very good food for most dieters. Sodium labeling presents still another problem. The terms "sodium free," "very low sodium," "low sodium," "reduced sodium," and "no salt added" have very specific meanings, frequently not explained on the packages on which they appear.

4d   *Writing Coherent Paragraphs*

A paragraph is **coherent** if all its sentences are logically related to one another.

You can achieve coherence in your paragraphs by arranging details according to an organizing principle and by using transitional words and phrases, pronoun reference, parallelism, and repeated key words.

(1) Arranging details

The sentences in a paragraph are like the pieces of a puzzle. Until you determine the relationship that exists among them, you have no clear idea what the whole looks like. Even if a paragraph's sentences are all about the same subject, they lack coherence until they are arranged according to an organizing principle. By arranging your thoughts in a definite order—*spatial, temporal,* or *logical*—you go a long way toward creating coherent paragraphs.

Spatial Order   Paragraphs arranged in spatial order establish the perspective from which readers will view details. For example, an object or scene can be viewed from top to bottom or from near to far. Spatial order is central to **descriptive paragraphs,** which tell how a person, place, or thing looks. Notice how the following descriptive paragraph begins on top of a hill, moves down to a valley, follows a river through the valley into the distance, and then moves to a point behind the speaker, where Mt. Adams stands.

See ◄ 4f2

> East of us rose another hill like ours. Between the hills, far below, was the highway which threaded south into the valley. This was the Yakima valley; I had never seen it before. It is justly famous for its beauty, like every planted valley. It extended south into the horizon, a distant dream of a valley, a Shangri-la. All its hundreds of low, golden slopes bore orchards. Among the orchards were towns, and roads, and plowed and fallow fields. Through the valley wandered a thin, shining river; from the river extended fine, frozen irrigation ditches. Distance blurred and blued the sight, so that the whole valley looked like a thickness or sediment at the bottom of the sky. Directly behind us was more sky, and empty lowlands blued by distance, and Mount Adams. Mount Adams was an enormous, snow-covered volcanic cone rising flat, like so much scenery. (Annie Dillard, "Total Eclipse")

Chronological Order   Paragraphs arranged in chronological order present details in sequence, using transitional phrases that establish the sequence of events—*at first, yesterday, later,* and so on. This type of organization is central to **narrative paragraphs,** which tell a story, recall a historical event, or relate an experience. The following narrative paragraph by an eighteenth-century naturalist is unified by the orderly sequence of events:

See ◄ 4f1

About midnight, having fallen asleep, I was awakened and greatly surprised at finding the most of my companions up in arms, and furiously engaged with a large alligator but a few yards from me. One of our company, it seems, awoke in the night, and perceived the monster within a few paces of the camp; when giving the alarm to the rest, they readily came to his assistance, for it was a rare piece of sport. Some took fire-brands and cast them at his head, whilst others formed javelins of saplings, pointed and hardened with fire; these they thrust down his throat . . . which caused the monster to roar and bellow hideously; but his strength and fury were so great, that he easily wrenched or twisted them out of their hands, and wielding and brandishing them about, kept his enemies at a distance for a time. Some were for putting an end to his life and sufferings with a rifle ball, but the majority thought this would too soon deprive them of the diversion and pleasure of exercising their various inventions of torture: they at length grew tired, and agreed in one opinion, that he had suffered sufficiently; and put an end to his existence. (William Bartram, *Travels of William Bartram*)

Chronological order is also used to arrange details in **process** paragraphs, which explain how something works or how to carry out a procedure. ▶ See 4f4

Logical Order   Paragraphs arranged in logical order present details or ideas in terms of their relationships to one another. Cause and effect, definition, example, comparison and contrast, and classification and division all use this arrangement. In addition, paragraphs that have a problem-and-solution or question-and-answer structure rely on logical order. The following paragraph is organized in a **problem-and-solution** pattern, beginning with a statement of the problem and going on to propose several solutions:

The injury rate in boxing presents a problem. Certainly other sports—football and motorcycle racing—have more deaths, but no other sport has as its sole object the disabling of an individual. Several reforms would help solve this problem. First, all boxers should wear protective equipment—head gear and kidney protectors, for example. This equipment is required in amateur boxing and should be required in professional boxing. Second, the object of boxing should be to score points, not to knock out opponents. An increased glove weight would make knockouts almost impossible. And finally, all fights should be limited to ten rounds. Studies show that most serious injuries occur in boxing between the eleventh and fifteenth rounds—when the boxers are tired and vulnerable. By limiting the number of rounds a boxer could fight, officials could substantially reduce the number of serious injuries. These reforms would bother fans at first, but eventually they would get used to them. The result of this temporary inconvenience would be a safer sport and, certainly, a more humane one. (Student)

The paragraph that follows has a **question-and-answer** structure. Notice how the question draws readers into the discussion.

Who is the elusive creature the reader? He is a person with an attention span of about twenty seconds. He is assailed on every side by forces competing for his time: by newspapers and magazines, by television and radio, by his stereo and videocassettes, by his wife and children and pets, by his house and his yard and all the gadgets that he has bought to keep them spruce, and by that most potent of competitors, sleep. The man snoozing in his chair with the unfinished magazine open on his lap is a man who was being given too much unnecessary trouble by the writer. (William Zinsser, "Simplicity," *On Writing Well: An Informal Guide to Writing Fiction*)

(2) Using transitional words and phrases

Transitional words and phrases—*but, similarly, also, on the other hand, moreover, in contrast, the same as, therefore, however,* and so on—aid coherence by indicating the relationships among sentences. By establishing logical and sequential connections, transitional words and phrases tie together ideas in a paragraph. The following paragraph shows how the omission of transitional words and phrases can make a passage difficult to understand.

Without transitional words and phrases

Napoleon certainly made a change for the worse by leaving his small kingdom of Elba. He went back to Paris, and he abdicated for a second time. He fled to Rochfort in hope of escaping to America. He gave himself up to the English captain of the ship *Bellerophon*. He suggested that the Prince Regent should grant him asylum, and he was refused. All he saw of England was the Devon coast and Plymouth Sound as he passed on to the remote island of St. Helena. He died on May 5, 1821, at the age of fifty-two.

Although the unifying idea of this paragraph is clearly stated, the exact chronological relationships among events is not. With no transitional words or phrases, the paragraph reads like a list of unconnected events. In the following paragraph, words and phrases such as *after, finally, once again,* and *in the end* provide the links that clarify the chronological order of the events in the passage:

Napoleon certainly made a change for the worse by leaving his small kingdom of Elba. After Waterloo, he went back to Paris, and he abdicated for a second time. A hundred days after his return from Elba, he fled to Rochfort in hope of escaping to America. Finally, he gave himself up to the English captain of the ship *Bellerophon*. Once again, he suggested that the Prince Regent grant him asylum, and once again, he was refused. In the end, all he saw of England was the Devon coast and Plymouth Sound as he passed on to the remote island of St. Helena. After six years of exile, he died on May 5, 1821, at the age of fifty-two. (Norman Mackenzie, *The Escape from Elba*)

Using Transitional Expressions

To Signal Sequence or Addition

and	besides
again	finally
also	furthermore
too	in addition
moreover	one . . . another
next	first . . . second . . . third
last	still

To Signal Time

at first	afterward
soon	at length
earlier	at the same time
before	now
after	as soon as
finally	meanwhile
then	in the meantime
later	until
next	immediately
during	eventually
subsequently	

To Signal Comparison

similarly	in comparison
likewise	also
by the same token	

To Signal Contrast

however	instead
but	even though
yet	on the one hand . . . on the
still	other hand

continued

continued from previous page

nonetheless	in contrast
on the contrary	although
despite	meanwhile
nevertheless	whereas

To Signal Examples

for example	namely
for instance	specifically
thus	

To Signal Narrowing of Focus

after all	specifically
in fact	that is
indeed	in other words
in particular	

To Signal Conclusions or Summaries

in summary	consequently
in conclusion	in other words
to conclude	thus
therefore	as a result

To Signal Concession

although	admittedly
granted	certainly
naturally	
of course	

To Signal Causes or Effects

because	consequently
hence	then
since	as a result
therefore	accordingly
so	

(3) Using pronouns

Because **pronouns** refer to nouns or other pronouns, they establish connections among sentences. Clear, well-placed pronoun references can lead readers through a paragraph. Unclear pronoun references, like those in the paragraph that follows, can make a writer's ideas difficult to follow:

> Like Martin Luther, John Calvin wanted to return to ^1
> principles of early Christianity described in the New Tes-
> tament. Martin Luther founded the evangelical churches ^2
> in Germany and Scandinavia, and he founded a number
> of reformed churches in other countries. A third Protes- ^3
> tant branch, episcopacy, developed in England. They ^4
> rejected the word *Protestant* because they agreed with
> Roman Catholicism on most points. They rejected the ^5
> primacy of the Pope. They accepted the Bible as the only ^6
> source of revealed truth, and they held that faith, not
> good works, defined a person's relationship to God.
> (Student)

Inexact
pronoun
reference

Unclear pronoun references make the paragraph confusing. Does *he* in sentence 2 refer to Luther or Calvin? Does *they* in sentence 4 refer to Luther and Calvin or to the three Protestant branches?

In this revision, clear pronoun references draw ideas together and establish coherence:

> 1 Like Martin Luther, John Calvin wanted to return to the principles
> 2 of early Christianity described in the New Testament. Martin Luther
> founded the evangelical churches in Germany and Scandinavia, and
> John Calvin founded a number of reformed churches in other coun-
> 3 tries. A third Protestant branch, episcopacy, developed in England.
> 4 Its members rejected the word *Protestant* because they agreed with
> 5 Roman Catholicism on most points. All these sects rejected the pri-
> 6 macy of the Pope. They accepted the Bible as the only source of
> revealed truth, and they held that faith, not good works, defined a
> person's relationship to God.

The writer has replaced *he* in sentence 2 with *John Calvin* and changed *they* in sentence 4 to *its members,* to which the sentence's second *they* now clearly refers. By adding the phrase *all these sects,* the writer makes clear that the two uses of *they* in sentence 6 refer to sects, not the episcopacy.

(4) Using parallel structure

Parallelism—the repeated use of similar grammatical structures— can help to establish coherence. The following paragraph does not use parallel structure:

▶ See 16a

> Thomas Jefferson was born in 1743 and died at Monti-
> cello, Virginia, on July 4, 1826. During his eighty-four years
> he accomplished a number of things. Although best known
> for his draft of the Declaration of Independence, Jefferson

Without
parallel
structure

was a delegate to the Continental Congress. Not only was Jefferson a patriot, he was also a profound thinker. During the Revolution he drafted the Statute for Religious Freedom. He drafted an ordinance for governing the West, and he formulated the first decimal monetary system. After being elected president, he abolished internal taxes, reduced the national debt, and made the Louisiana Purchase. Jefferson also designed Monticello and the University of Virginia. (Student)

The following revision shows how parallelism can strengthen paragraph coherence:

Thomas Jefferson was born in 1743 and died at Monticello, Virginia, on July 4, 1826. During his eighty-four years he accomplished a number of things. Although best known for his draft of the Declaration of Independence, Jefferson was a man of many talents who had a wide intellectual range. He was a patriot who was one of the revolutionary founders of the United States. He was a reformer who, when he was governor of Virginia, drafted the Statute for Religious Freedom. He was an innovator who drafted an ordinance for governing the West and devised the first decimal monetary system. He was a president who abolished internal taxes, reduced the national debt, and made the Louisiana Purchase. And finally he was an architect who designed Monticello and the University of Virginia.

Now the same basic sentence structure introduces each of Jefferson's accomplishments: *He was a patriot who* . . . ; *He was an innovator who* . . . ; *He was a president who* . . . ; *And finally he was an architect who.* . . . This presentation in parallel form helps the reader comprehend the material and at the same time adds emphasis (see **10c**).

(5) Repeating key words

Repeating key words or phrases—those essential to meaning—throughout a paragraph aids coherence by reminding readers how the sentences relate to one another and to the paragraph's unifying idea.

You should not repeat words and phrases monotonously—a well-written paragraph must have variety. But you have to balance the need to vary your vocabulary against your audience's need to understand what you have written. In the following paragraph, the absence of repeated key words or phrases that point to the paragraph's subject makes the discussion difficult to follow:

Mercury poisoning is a problem that has long been ₁
recognized. "Mad as a hatter" refers to the condition ₂
prevalent among nineteenth-century workers who manufactured felt hats. Workers in many other industries, such ₃
as mining, chemicals, and dentistry, were also affected. In

Without repeated key words or phrases

the 1950's and 1960's there were cases of poisoning in ₄
Minamata, Japan. Research showed that there were high ₅
levels of pollution in streams and lakes surrounding the
village. In the United States in 1969 a New Mexico fam- ₆
ily got sick from eating tainted food. Since then certain
pesticides have been withdrawn from the market, and ₇
chemical wastes can no longer be dumped into the ocean.
(Student)

The paragraph above demands a lot from readers. Sentence 1 introduces mercury poisoning as the topic of the paragraph, but sentences 2 through 7 never mention it. Readers must decide for themselves how the examples relate to the topic sentence. The following
revision shows how repetition of key words can help readers focus
on the subject:

1   Mercury poisoning is a problem that has long been recognized.
2 "Mad as a hatter" refers to the condition prevalent among nine-
     teenth-century workers who were exposed to mercury during the
3 manufacturing of felt hats. Workers in many other industries, such as
4 mining, chemicals, and dentistry, were similarly affected. In the
     1950's and 1960's there were cases of mercury poisoning in Mina-
5 mata, Japan. Research showed that there were high levels of mercury
6 pollution in streams and lakes surrounding the village. In the United
     States this problem came to light in 1969 when a New Mexico family
     got sick from eating food tainted with mercury. Since then pesticides
7 containing mercury have been withdrawn from the market, and chem-
     ical wastes can no longer be dumped into the ocean.

The use of the words *mercury* and *mercury poisoning* throughout
the paragraph now remind readers of the subject. Notice that to
avoid monotony the writer sometimes refers indirectly to this subject with phrases such as *similarly affected* (sentence 3) and *this
problem came to light* (sentence 6).

(6)   Achieving coherence among paragraphs

Most of the same methods you use to establish coherence within
paragraphs may also be used to link paragraphs. For example, you
can use transitional words and phrases, pronouns, parallel struc-

79

ture, and repeated key words. The following paragraph cluster shows
how some of these strategies work.

> A language may borrow a word directly or indirectly. A direct bor-
> rowing means that the borrowed item is a native word in the language
> it is borrowed from. *Festa* was borrowed directly from French and
> can be traced back to Latin *festa*. On the other hand, the word *alge-
> bra* was borrowed from Spanish, which in turn borrowed it from Ara-
> bic. Thus *algebra* was indirectly borrowed from Arabic, with Spanish
> as an intermediary.
>
> Some languages are heavy borrowers. Albanian has borrowed so
> heavily that few native words are retained. On the other hand, most
> Native American languages have borrowed little from their neighbors.
>
> English has borrowed extensively. Of the 20,000 or so words in
> common use, about three-fifths are borrowed. Of the 500 most fre-
> quently used words, however, only two-sevenths are borrowed, and
> because these "common" words are used over and over again in sen-
> tences, the actual frequency of appearance of native words is about 80
> percent. Morphemes such as *and, be, have, it, of, the, to, will, you,
> on, that,* and *is* are all native to English. (Victoria Fromkin and Rob-
> ert Rodman, *An Introduction to Language,* 4th ed.)

These three paragraphs form a tightly knit unit, and the topic sentences reinforce the structure. Each establishes coherence by including a variation of *A language may borrow.* In addition, some
form of the key words *language* and *borrow* appears in almost
every sentence.

EXERCISE 2

A. Read the following paragraph and determine how the author
   achieves coherence. Identify parallel elements, pronouns, repeated
   words, and transitional words and phrases that link sentences.

> Some years ago the old elevated railway in Philadelphia was torn
> down and replaced by the subway system. This ancient El with its
> barnlike stations containing nut-vending machines and scattered food
> scraps had, for generations, been the favorite feeding ground of flocks
> of pigeons, generally one flock to a station along the route of the El.
> Hundreds of pigeons were dependent upon the system. They flapped
> in and out of its stanchions and steel work or gathered in watchful
> little audiences about the feet of anyone who rattled the peanut-vend-
> ing machines. They even watched people who jingled change in their
> hands, and prospected for food under the feet of the crowds who
> gathered between trains. Probably very few among the waiting people
> who tossed a crumb to an eager pigeon realized that this El was like a

food-bearing river, and that the life which haunted its banks was dependent upon the running of the trains with their human freight. (Loren Eiseley, *The Night Country*)

B. Supplying the missing transitional words and phrases, revise the following paragraph to make it coherent.

The theory of continental drift was first put forward by Alfred Wegener in 1912. The continents fit together like a gigantic jigsaw puzzle. The opposing Atlantic coasts, especially South America and Africa, seem to have been attached. He believed that at one time, probably 225 million years ago, there was one supercontinent. This continent broke into parts that drifted into their present positions. The theory stirred conrovesy during the 1920's and eventually was ridiculed by the scientific community. In 1954 the theory was revived. The theory of continental drift is accepted as a reasonable geologic explanation of the continental system. (Student)

4e *Writing Well-Developed Paragraphs*

A paragraph is **well developed** when it contains the support—examples, statistics, opinions, and so on—readers need to understand the unifying idea.

The amount of support you need in a paragraph depends on your purpose, your audience, and the scope of your unifying idea. Just as charting structure can help you see whether a paragraph is unified, it can also help you determine whether it is well developed.

The following paragraph is not adequately developed.

From Thanksgiving until Christmas, children are saturated with ads for violent toys. Advertisers persist in thinking that only toys that appeal to children's aggressiveness will sell. Far from improving the situation, video games have escalated the arms race. The real question is why toy manufacturers continue to pour millions of dollars into violent toys, especially in light of the success of toys that promote learning and cooperation. (Student)

Charting the underlying structure of the paragraph reveals the problem.

1 From Thanksgiving until Christmas, children are saturated with ads for violent toys.
  2 Advertisers persist in thinking that only toys that appeal to children's aggressiveness will sell.

2 Far from improving the situation, video games have escalated the arms race.

2 The real question is why toy manufacturers continue to pour millions of dollars into violent toys, especially in light of the success of toys that promote learning and cooperation.

The first sentence of this paragraph is a level-1 sentence. The level-2 sentences expand the discussion, but the paragraph offers no level-3 examples. What kinds of toys appeal to a child's aggressive tendencies? Exactly what video games does the writer object to? The following revision includes specific examples that convincingly support the topic sentence (sentence 1).

From Thanksgiving until Christmas, children are saturated with ads for violent toys. Advertisers persist in thinking that only toys that appeal to children's aggressiveness will sell. One television commercial praises the merits of a commando team that attacks and captures a miniature enemy base. Toy soldiers wear realistic uniforms and carry automatic rifles, pistols, knives, grenades, and ammunition. Another commercial shows laughing children shooting one another with plastic rocket fighters and tanklike vehicles. Far from improving the situation, video games have escalated the arms race. The most popular video games involve children in realistic combat situations. One game lets children search out and destroy enemey rocket fighters in outer space. Other best-selling games simulate attacks on enemy fortresses or raids by hostile creatures. The real question is why toy manufacturers continue to pour millions of dollars into violent toys, especially in light of the success of toys that promote learning and cooperation.

4f Options for Paragraph Development

The pattern of a paragraph, like the pattern of an entire essay, reflects the way the writer thinks. Most of the time writers do not consciously decide in advance on a particular pattern of development and then write their paragraphs accordingly. Only in revision do they see the patterns into which their thoughts fall. At this point, when they see the direction a paragraph is taking, they can revise the topic sentence and rearrange information to support the unifying idea more effectively.

Of course paragraphs, like essays, can have more than one pattern of development. As a beginning writer, however, you should practice each pattern separately. After you have developed your paragraph skills, you may want to try combining various strategies in a single paragraph.

(1) What happened? (Narration)

Narrative paragraphs tell a story, but they do not necessarily follow strict chronological order. Sometimes a narrative can begin in the middle of a story or even at the end and then move back to the beginning. Careful use of transitions that signal sequence and time (**see 4d2**) keep the chronology clear.

In the following paragraph the topic sentence introduces the narrative. The sequence of events is signaled by the expressions *by midterms, by the end of the semester,* and *at the beginning of my second semester.*

> My academic career almost ended as soon as it began. Three weeks after I arrived at college, I decided to pledge a fraternity. By midterms I was wearing a straw hat and saying "Yes sir" to every fraternity brother I met. I ate lunch at the fraternity house, and when classes were over I ran errands for the fraternity members. After dinner I socialized and worked on projects with the other people in my pledge class. In between these activities I tried to study. Somehow I managed to write papers, take tests, and attend lectures. By the end of the semester, though, my grades had slipped and I was exhausted. It was then that I began to ask myself some important questions. Why was I putting myself through this? Why did I want to join a fraternity? I realized that I wanted to be popular, but not at the expense of my grades and my future career. At the beginning of my second semester I dropped out of the fraternity and volunteered to work in the biology lab. Looking back, I realize that it was then that I actually began to grow up. (Student)

(2) What does it look like? (Description)

To describe something you must first see it, and to see it you must first look at it part by part. In **descriptive** paragraphs you present your perception of these separate parts in such a way that they form a pattern for your readers. The most natural arrangement of details reflects the way you actually look at a scene or object: near to far, top to bottom, side to side, or front to back. The arrangement of details is made clear by transitions that identify the spatial relationships. Although many descriptive paragraphs do not have topic sentences, they must be unified by a **dominant impression,** a perception to which all the details contribute.

The following descriptive paragraph begins with a distant view of the Great Beach on Cape Cod and then moves closer. This organization makes it easy for readers to see the details, and the paragraph is unified by the writer's sense of the sand bar's mystery.

> The sand bar of Eastham is the sea wall of the inlet. Its crest overhangs the beach, and from the high, wind-trampled rim, a long slope well overgrown with dune grass descends to the meadows on the west. Seen from the tower at Nauset, the land has an air of geological simplicity; as a matter of fact, it is full of hollows, blind passages and amphitheatres in which the roaring of the sea changes into the far roar of a cataract. I often wander into these curious pits. On their floors of sand, on their slopes, I find patterns made of the feet of visiting birds. Here, in a little disturbed and claw-marked space of sand, a flock of larks has alighted; here one of the birds has wandered off by himself; here are the deeper tracks of hungry crows; here the webbed impressions of a gull. There is always something poetic and mysterious to me about these tracks in the pits of the dunes; they begin at nowhere, sometimes with the faint impression of an alighting wing, and vanish as suddenly into the trackless nowhere of the sky. (Henry Breston, *The Outmost House*)

(3)   What are some typical cases or examples of it? (Exemplification)

Exemplification paragraphs use specific illustrations to clarify a general statement. In the following paragraph a series of well-chosen examples supports the topic sentence, with the movement from one example to the next clearly signaled by the transitions *in addition* and *finally*.

> From an engineering standpoint alcohol could supplement oil as a fuel source. Alcohol could easily be substituted for diesel fuel if engineers implemented simple engine modifications and made ignition timing and fuel tank capacity changes. In addition, alcohol could be diluted with as much as thirty percent water and still burn in a home furnace. Farmers could use animal and plant waste to make enough fuel for their own consumption or could use the dried distiller's grain as a feed supplement. Finally, studies have shown that industrial consumers of fuel oil could, with little or no trouble, adapt their furnaces to use alcohol. (Student).

In the paragraph that follows, a single extended example gives readers enough detail to help them accept the author's point about hormone secretion and aggressiveness:

The influence of aggressiveness and dominance on hormones and sex reaches its peak in the case of small tropical fish called "cleaners," which feed off parasites that they remove from the skin of other fish. One species, studied on the Australian Great Barrier Reef, lives in groups of one male with a harem of three to six females; the male dominates the females and the larger, older females dominate the smaller, younger ones. If the male dies or is removed from the group, the largest of the females almost immediately begins to act like a male, carrying out typical male aggressive displays toward the other females. And within a couple of weeks *she actually turns into a male,* producing sperm instead of eggs! I am not suggesting, of course, that anything of the sort could occur in primates or other mammals; for one thing, most or all cleaner-fish females possess rudimentary testes, as mammalian females do not. Nonetheless, I find rather mind-blowing the fact that a female can change into a male simply by acting like one. (Robert Claiborne, *God or Beast*)

(4)   How did—or does—it happen? (Process)

Process paragraphs describe how something works, presenting a series of steps in strict chronological order. The topic sentence (when there is one) identifies the process, and the rest of the paragraph presents the steps involved. Throughout the paragraph, transitional terms such as *first, next, then,* and *finally* signal the organizational pattern and hold the paragraph together. Here, for example, is an explanation of the process by which members of the Supreme Court decide whether or not to grant an appeal:

Members of the court have disclosed, however, the general way the conference is conducted. It begins at ten A.M. and usually runs on until late afternoon. At the start each justice, when he enters the room, shakes hands with all others there (thirty-six handshakes altogether). The custom, dating back generations, is evidently designed to begin the meeting at a friendly level, no matter how heated the intellectual differences may be. The conference takes up, first, the applications for review—a few appeals, many more petitions for certiorari. Those on the Appellate Docket, the regular paid cases, are considered first, then the pauper's applications on the Miscellaneous Docket. (If any of these are granted, they are then transferred to the Appellate Docket.) After this the justices consider, and vote on, all the cases argued during the preceding Monday through Thursday. These are tentative votes, which may be and quite often are changed as the opinion is written and the problem thought through more deeply. There may be further discussion at later conferences before the opinion is handed down. (Anthony Lewis, *Gideon's Trumpet*)

Sometimes a process paragraph presents instructions. In this case its purpose is to enable readers to actually perform the process. Instructions are written in the present tense and, like commands, in the imperative mood: "Remove the cover . . . and check the valve." This directness of both tense and mood helps readers follow the directions more easily. The following paragraph presents a set of instructions:

If you have a photograph that hasn't been framed or mounted, sooner or later it will ripple or curl up at the corners. But you *can* treat the malady. Put the picture in a pan of room-temperature water. Take the photograph out after a few minutes. Shake the water drop-lets off it, then gently insert it in a folded paper towel. Put this flat packet on your ironing board. Cover the picture-side with more clean, white paper toweling. *Note:* Do not use a decorated towel! If you do, you'll transfer the design to your photograph. Set your *dry* iron on a low temperature, then iron across the towel. Now take the towel off. Lo and behold! A flat, ready-to-frame photograph! (Marcia D. Liles and Robert M. Liles, *Good Housekeeping Guide to Fixing Things Around the House*)

(5) What caused it? What are its effects? (Cause and effect)

Like narrative and process, **cause and effect** is concerned with events in time. But instead of focusing on the order in which events occur, cause-and-effect paragraphs explore why they occur and what happens because of them.

Revision Close-up

Cause-and-effect relationships are often complicated, so you should use topic sentences and transitional words and phrases (*one cause, another cause, a more important result, because, as a result*) to help clarify causal connections.

In the following paragraph the writer suggests a *cause* of thumb-sucking and then summarizes a study to support his assertion.

The main reason that a young baby sucks his thumb seems to be that he hasn't had enough sucking at the breast or bottle to satisfy his sucking needs. Dr. David Levy pointed out that babies who are fed every 3 hours don't suck their thumbs as much as babies fed every 4 hours, and that babies who have cut down on nursing time from 20 minutes to 10 minutes . . . are more likely to suck their thumbs than babies who still have to work for 20 minutes. Dr. Levy fed a litter of puppies with a medicine dropper so that they had no chance to suck during their feedings. They acted just the same as babies who don't get enough chance to suck at feeding time. They sucked their own and each other's paws and skin so hard that the fur came off. (Benjamin Spock, *Baby and Child Care*)

In the next paragraph a student identifies the *effects* of Saturday cartoon-watching on her younger brother. She begins by identifying the effects she will examine and then gives her examples and draws her conclusions.

Although I have not carried out a scientific study, I have noticed the effects of television violence on my younger brother. Every Saturday he goes on a four-hour television cartoon binge. His diet includes *G.I. Joe, Thunder Cats, He-Man, Teenage Mutant Ninja Turtles,* and occasionally *The Smurfs.* (He sneaks this one because he thinks he is too old for it.) As my brother watches the cartoons, he gets more and more excited. He runs and jumps around the room and has mock battles with furniture and imaginary enemies. Later, after he has finished watching, he and his friends act out things they have seen in the cartoons. Their games always involve fighting, shooting, stabbing, and killing. Even though some people might say that this aggressive behavior is normal for a six-year-old boy, I feel that television cartoons cause his play to be excessively violent. (Student)

(6) How is it like other things? How is it different? (Comparison and contrast)

Comparison-and-contrast paragraphs examine the similarities and differences between two subjects. Comparison emphasizes similarities, while contrast stresses differences.

Revision Close-up

When using comparison and contrast, be sure that the subjects you compare have elements in common and that you compare the same or similar qualities of both. Also be sure that the likenesses or differences are of some significance, not so obvious that a discussion of them would be pointless. Do not forget to use transitional words and phrases (*similarly, likewise, however, but, on the contrary, nevertheless*) to signal comparison or contrast and to indicate movement from one subject to another.

Comparison and contrast can be organized in one of two ways. First, you can compare and contrast the subjects point by point. This organization is especially useful in a complex paragraph in which your readers may have trouble keeping track of your points. The following paragraph uses **point-by-point** comparison.

> There are two Americas. One is the America of Lincoln and Adlai Stevenson; the other is the America of Teddy Roosevelt and the modern superpatriots. One is generous and humane, the other narrowly egotistical; one is self-critical, the other self-righteous; one is sensible, the other romantic; one is good-humored, the other solemn; one is inquiring, the other pontificating; one is moderate, the other filled with passionate intensity; one is judicious and the other arrogant in the use of great power. (J. William Fulbright, *The Arrogance of Power*)

By repeating *one* and *the other* the writer sets up a parallel structure. Not only does this technique aid coherence, it also emphasizes the ideas the writer wants to convey.

A second way to organize a comparison-and-contrast paragraph is to treat one subject in its entirety at the beginning of your paragraph and the other subject in its entirety at the end. This organization works well when you feel certain that your readers can remember what you have said about the first subject while they read about the second.

In the following paragraph the writer uses a **subject-by-subject** comparison, signaling the shift from one subject to the other with the transitional word *now*:

> This seems to be an era of gratuitous inventions and negative improvements. Consider the beer can. It was beautiful—as beautiful as the clothespin, as inevitable as the wine bottle, as dignified and reassuring as the fire hydrant. A tranquil cylinder of delightfully resonant metal, it could be opened in an instant, requiring only the application of a handy gadget freely dispensed by every grocer. Who can forget the small, symmetrical thrill of those two triangular punctures, the dainty *pffff*, the little crest of suds that foamed eagerly in the exultation of release? Now we are given, instead, a top beetling with an ugly, shmoo-shaped "tab," which, after fiercely resisting the tugging, bleeding fingers of the thirsty man, threatens his lips with a dangerous and hideous hole. However, we have discovered a way to thwart Progress, usually so unthwartable. *Turn the beer can upside down and open the bottom.* The bottom is still the way the top used to be. True, this operation gives the beer an unsettling jolt, and the sight of a consistently inverted beer can might make people edgy, not to say queasy.

But the latter difficulty could be eliminated if manufacturers would design cans that looked the same whichever end was up, like playing cards. What we need is Progress with an escape hatch. (John Updike, *Assorted Prose*)

An **analogy** is a special kind of comparison that explains an unfamiliar concept or object by likening it to a familiar one. Extended analogies resemble comparison-and-contrast paragraphs— with one important difference: whereas comparisons give equal weight to both things being compared, extended analogies use one part of the comparison for the *sole* purpose of shedding light on the other. Here an author uses the behavior of people to explain the behavior of ants:

Ants are so much like human beings as to be an embarrassment. They farm fungi, raise aphids as livestock, launch armies into wars, use chemical sprays to alarm and confuse enemies, capture slaves. The families of weaver ants engage in child labor, holding their larvae like shuttles to spin out the thread that sews the leaves together for their fungus gardens. They exchange information ceaselessly. They do everything but watch television. (Lewis Thomas, "On Societies as Organisms")

(7) What are its parts? (Division) Into what categories can its parts be arranged? (Classification)

In **division,** you take a single item and break it into its components. You could, for instance, divide blood into its various parts: plasma, white cells, red cells, and so on. In **classification,** you take many separate items and group them into categories according to qualities or characteristics they have in common. You could, for instance, group books according to subject, author, or size.

In the following paragraph, a student *divides* blood into several components. The opening sentence identifies the subject the paragraph will analyze, and subsequent sentences identify the components of blood, moving from the most frequently to the least frequently found elements.

The blood can be divided into four distinct components: plasma, red cells, white cells, and platelets. Plasma is 90 percent water and holds a great number of substances in suspension. It contains proteins, sugars, fat, and inorganic salts. Plasma also contains urea and other by-products from the breaking down of proteins, hormones, enzymes, and dissolved gasses. In addition, plasma contains the red blood cells that give it color, the white cells, and the platelets. The red cells are most numerous; they get oxygen from the lungs and release it in the tissues. The less numerous white cells are part of the body's defense against invading organisms. The platelets, which occur in almost the same number as white cells, are responsible for clotting. (Student)

The paragraph below establishes its subject, scientific frauds, and then goes on to *classify* frauds into three categories.

Charles Babbage, an English mathematician, reflecting in 1830 on what he saw as the decline of science at the time, distinguished among three major kinds of scientific fraud. He called the first "forging," by which he meant complete fabrication—the recording of observations that were never made. The second category he called "trimming"; this consists of manipulating the data to make them look better, or, as Babbage wrote, "in clipping off little bits here and there from those observations which differ most in *excess* from the mean and in sticking them on to those which are too small." His third category was data selection, which he called "cooking"—the choosing of those data that fitted the researcher's hypothesis and the discarding of those that did not. To this day, the serious discussion of scientific fraud has not improved on Babbage's typology. (Morton Hunt, *New York Times Magazine*)

Revision Close-up

Whether you classify or divide, your groups should be mutually exclusive; that is, items in one category should not also fit in another category.

(8) What is it? (Definition)

A **formal definition** includes the term you are defining, the class to which it belongs, and its attributes—the details that distinguish it from other members of its class.

Carbon is a nonmetallic element
(term)   (class to which it belongs)

occurring as diamond, graphite, and charcoal.
                    (distinguishing details)

An **extended definition,** which builds on this format, can be one or more paragraphs long. Such discussions may develop the definition with other patterns, defining *happiness,* for instance, by telling a story (narration), or defining a diesel engine by telling how it works (process). Extended definitions may also include the background or origins of a term and can define terms by telling what they are like (using synonyms) or what they are not (using negation).

The following paragraph develops an extended definition with exemplification. It begins with a straightforward definition of *gadget* and then cites an example.

A gadget is nearly always novel in design or concept and it often has no proper name. For example, the semaphore which signals the arrival of the mail in our rural mailbox certainly has no proper name. It is a contrivance consisting of a piece of shingle. Call it what you like, it saves us frequent frustrating trips to the mailbox in winter when you have to dress up and wade through snow to get there. That's a gadget! *(Smithsonian)*

EXERCISE 3

Determine one possible method of development for a paragraph on each of these topics. Then write a paragraph on one of the topics.

1. What love is (or is not)
2. How to cope with stress
3. The kinds of people who attend rock concerts
4. My worst job
5. American vs. Japanese cars
6. The connection between sleep and memory
7. Budgeting time wisely
8. Success
9. Making the perfect meal
10. Drinking and driving

4g · *Writing Special Kinds of Paragraphs*

So far we have been talking only about the paragraphs that carry the weight of your discussion. Other paragraphs have different functions, however. Although they do not follow all the principles we have discussed, they have a significant impact on how readers respond to your ideas.

(1) Transitional paragraphs

Longer essays frequently include one or more **transitional paragraphs** whose function is to signal a change in subject and provide a bridge between one section of an essay and another.

At their simplest, transitional paragraphs can be single sentences that move readers from one point to the next.

Let us examine this point further.

This idea works better in theory than in practice.

Of course there are other avenues we can explore.

Let us begin with a few estimates.

Sometimes writers use a transitional paragraph to present a concise summary of what they have already said. This technique reinforces important concepts by allowing readers to pause to consider what they have read before moving on to a new point. The following transitional paragraph uses a series of questions to restate some frightening points about overpopulation. The writer goes on to answer these questions in the next part of his essay.

> Can we bleed off the mass of humanity to other worlds? Right now the number of human beings on Earth is increasing by 80 million per year, and each year that number goes up by 1 and a fraction percent. Can we really suppose that we can send 80 million people per year to the Moon, Mars, and elsewhere, and engineer those worlds to support those people? And even so, nearly remain in the same place ourselves? (Isaac Asimov, "The Case Against Man")

(2) Introductions

An **introduction** prepares an audience for your essay. The preparation needed will depend on your subject, your audience, and the effect you want your paper to have.

Writing Introductions   Some introductions are straightforward, concerned primarily with presenting information. They begin by announcing the subject, limiting it, and then stating the thesis.

However, not all subjects appeal to all readers, so at times you must find a way to capture your audience's attention. Several strategies for effective introductions are listed below.

Strategies for Effective Introductions

Direct Announcement

Although modern architecture is usually not intricate in design, it often involves remarkable engineering accomplishments. Most people do not realize the difficulties an architect encounters when designing a "great" modern structure. The new wing of the Smithsonian in Washington, in its simplicity, is such a masterpiece of engineering and design. (Student)

Quotation

"It's far easier to explain why the moon shouldn't be there," says M.I.T. geophysicist Nafi Toksoz, "than to explain its existence." That may sound strange when the data amassed by the manned Apollo lunar missions should have settled, it seems, the age-old question of the moon's origin once and for all. But that just did not happen. Even after a decade of intensive study, lunar scientists are still trying to recreate the story of how the moon came to be. (Ben Patrusky, "Where Did the Moon Come From?")

Question

What kind of person goes to the movies at least three times a week? A film buff, that's who. Film buffs will go anywhere, almost any time, to see a movie they have missed. They spend much of their lives sitting in uncomfortable seats in darkened movie theaters. Even so, their hobby can be interesting, exciting, and rewarding. (Student)

Definition

Moles are collections of cells that can appear on any part of the body. With occasional exceptions, moles are absent at birth. They first appear in the early years of life, between ages two and six. Frequently moles appear at puberty. New moles, however, can continue to appear throughout life. During pregnancy new moles may appear and old ones darken. There are three major designations of moles, each with its own characteristics. (Student)

Unusual Comparison

Once a long time ago, people had special little boxes called refrigerators in which milk, meat, and eggs could be kept cool. The grandchildren of these simple devices are large enough to store whole cows, and they reach temperatures comparable to those at the South Pole. Their operating costs increase each year, and they are so complicated that few home handymen attempt to repair them on their own. Why has this change in size and complexity occurred in America? It has not taken place in many areas of the technologically advanced world (the average West German refrigerator is about a yard high and less than a yard wide, yet refrigeration technology in Germany is quite advanced). Do we really need (or even want) all that space and cold? (Appletree Rodden, "Why Smaller Refrigerators Can Preserve the Human Race")

Controversial Position

Most men live in harness. Richard was one of them. Typically he had no awareness of how his male harness was choking him until his personal and professional life and his body had nearly fallen apart. (Herb Goldberg, *The Hazards of Being Male*)

Revising Introductions   When you revise, keep in mind that a strong introduction brings readers into your essay. A weak one leaves them outside. For this reason, many writers like to present their thesis statements in their introductions. Whether or not it includes a thesis, your introduction should lead naturally into the body of your paper. It should not be at odds with your subject or seem imposed on it. It must also be consistent with the purpose, tone, and style of the rest of your essay. A serious, formal discussion should have the same kind of introduction. If your discussion is relaxed and informal, your introduction should also be. Finally, you should avoid opening statements that do no more than announce your subject ("In my paper I will talk about Lady Macbeth") or that undercut your credibility ("I don't know much about alternative energy sources, but here is my opinion of the subject").

Revision Checklist: Introductions

- Does your introduction capture your reader's attention?
- Does it contain the thesis of your essay?
- Does it lead naturally into the body of your essay?
- Is it consistent with the purpose, tone, and style of the rest of your essay?
- Does it avoid statements that simply announce your subject or that undercut your credibility?

In the following draft of an introduction, the writer simply announces the subject of the paper and does little to create interest or to clarify the paper's focus.

Ineffective Introduction

Dimensioned drawings are a standard method of pictorially communicating any object. In this paper I will discuss dimensioned drawings and show how they are used.

The revised introduction begins with a statement that immediately draws readers into the essay. It also defines the term *dimensioned drawing* and presents an accurate and engaging picture of what the essay will be about.

Effective Introduction

Every manufactured object, from a paper clip to a skyscraper, begins as a dimensioned drawing. Dimensioning, the process of drawing an object so it appears to have depth, is involved in at least one step of the production process. Because dimensioned drawings are a standard method of pictorially representing objects, the American National Standard Institute (ANSI) has established rules for placing dimensions on drawings. Despite these rules, experienced draftspersons have adopted their own methods of dimensioning objects, and for this reason, the art of dimensioning can be creative as well as precise.

(3)   Conclusions

Most essays have a **conclusion,** a carefully constructed ending that reinforces major ideas and gives readers a sense of completion. In short essays, the conclusion is usually only one paragraph; in longer essays, however, it can be longer.

Writing Conclusions   By restating your thesis or reviewing your main points, the conclusion gives readers the chance to make sure they have understood your essay.

Several strategies for effective conclusions are presented below.

Strategies for Effective Conclusions

Review of Main Points

As you can see, my grandmother is an unusual person. She is a dedicated nurse and a loving parent and grandparent. She has fought for the rights of others all her life, and she has raised children—both male and female—who follow her example. I am glad that I have had the opportunity to know her and to use her as a model for my own life. (Student)

Prediction

Looking ahead, prospects may not be quite as dismal as they seem. As a matter of fact, we are not doing so badly. It is something of a miracle that creatures who evolved as nomads in an intimate, small-band, wide-open-spaces context manage to get along at all as villagers or surrounded by strangers in cubicle apartments. Considering that our genius as a species is adaptability, we may yet learn to live closer and closer to one another, if not in utter peace, then far more peacefully than we do today. (John Pheiffer, "Seeking Peace, Making War")

Opinion

A piece of writing is never finished. It is delivered to a deadline, torn out of the typewriter on demand, sent off with a sense of

---

continued

continued from previous page

accomplishment and shame and pride and frustration. If only there were a couple more days, time for just another run at it, perhaps then . . . (Donald Murray, "The Maker's Eye: Revising Your Own Manuscripts")

Quotation

"Curiouser and curiouser," says Alice as she journeys through Wonderland. The same can be said by anyone who wanders through the maze of regulations contained in the tax code. Possibly someday our lawmakers will remedy this situation, but until then we are all victims of a tax system that is too complex for most people to understand and too unwieldy for the government to control. (Student)

Revising Conclusions   Like your introduction, your conclusion should be a logical extension of your essay. A conclusion should give readers a sense of closure. It should also fulfill the promises you make in your introduction, not introduce new points or go off in new directions. Your conclusion is your last word, and readers base their impressions of your writing on it. A weak or uninteresting ending detracts from an otherwise strong essay. Therefore, do not simply restate your introduction in different words or apologize or in any way cast doubt on your concluding points ("I may not be an expert" or "At least this is my opinion"). If you can, try to end with a statement that readers will remember or one that reinforces your essay's major point.

Revision Checklist: Conclusions

- Does your conclusion provide closure?
- Does it remind readers of the primary focus of your essay?
- Does it avoid restating the introduction's points?
- Does it avoid apologies?
- Does it end memorably?

The following draft of a conclusion goes off in a different direction from the rest of the essay. Instead of emphasizing the creative aspects of dimensioned drawing, it focuses on its precision.

INEFFECTIVE CONCLUSION

A draftsperson must know how to apply the rules of dimensioning. The draftsperson must know how to use the two types of dimension.

In addition, he or she must avoid inconsistencies. When a draftsperson changes the codes of a drawing, workers will waste a lot of time trying to decipher the illustration.

The revised conclusion reinforces the focus of the essay and re-states its major points, and it ends by emphasizing the major point of the essay—that dimensioned drawing is a creative activity that requires much skill and concentration.

EFFECTIVE CONCLUSION

In spite of the rules that govern the placement of dimensions on drawings, draftspersons have a great deal of flexibility in interpreting information. For instance, they can use different methods of dimen-sioning and labeling. In addition, draftspersons can align objects dif-ferently and modify the way relationships are shown. As long as workers are able to interpret a drawing quickly and easily, many vari-ations are possible. Over time, a draftsperson comes to realize that dimensioned drawing not only requires precision and concentration, but also creativity, intelligence, and artistic talent.

STUDENT WRITER AT WORK

WRITING PARAGRAPHS

The following draft of a student essay has a weak introduction and conclusion. Rewrite them to increase their effectiveness.

There are a number of things the government and auto manufacturers can do to reduce traffic deaths.

A passive restraint system automatically protects both driver and passenger in the event of a collision. Almost twenty years ago the government funded air bag research that it hoped would fill the need for such a system. The air bag, which inflates upon impact, automatically shields collision victims from injury. Several years ago Chrysler introduced driver-side air bags as standard equipment on all its new cars. As a result of Chrysler's actions, as well as public pressure, General Motors, Ford, and some Japanese manufacturers now include

continued

continued from previous page

air bags as standard equipment. This is not to say,
however, that air bags do not have critics. Some people
feel that they are both costly and unreliable. There is no
way of knowing for certain that air bags will work until
an accident occurs. Even so, experts feel that air bags
can do much to reduce automobile-related deaths.

Combination seat belt and shoulder harnesses are the
simplest and least expensive way to protect passengers in
a crash. Volkswagen has perfected an interlock system that
automatically buckles people into place when the door of
the car closes. Most American and Japanese car
manufacturers have not adopted this system, preferring
instead the driver-fastened harness. Whatever system
manufacturers use, government studies show that seat belts
could reduce the annual auto death rate by ten to twelve
thousand people. The problem, however, is that many people
just will not use seat belts. Insurance statistics show
that in states where seat belt use is not mandatory only
eleven to seventeen percent of all drivers wear their seat
belts regularly.

What can be done? First, the federal government
should require all new automobiles to have both driver-
side and passenger-side air bag systems. The money saved
in medical costs alone would more than offset the cost to
the consumer. Second, more state governments should pass
laws requiring riders to use seat belts. People riding
without fastened seat belts would receive tickets, just as
they would if they were speeding. In the states where laws
like this are already in effect, automobile injuries and
deaths have decreased significantly.

Certainly all these things would help.

PART 2

Thinking Critically

5

Reading Critically and Writing Critical Responses

The fact that something is printed in a book does not automatically establish it as free of bias or contradictions, let alone establish it as meaningful, insightful, or even accurate. For this reason, you should approach any text you read with a healthy skepticism. Your goal should be not simply to understand the literal meaning of what you read, but also to consider its subtleties—and, eventually, to assess the credibility of the writer and the soundness of his or her ideas.

As you read, remember that questioning or even challenging a writer's ideas is not heresy; in fact, scholars realize that probing other writers' ideas helps to create new interpretations, new perspectives, and new theories. The questioning process contributes to an ongoing intellectual debate in a particular field, a dialogue that helps to keep ideas current and fresh.

Approaching a text with a critical eye is no easy task; it requires you to marshal all your analytical and evaluative skills. And, before you even begin to read, you must agree to certain conditions.

Approaching a Text

- Keep an open mind.
- Withhold judgment.
- Acknowledge your own limitations and biases as a reader.
- Consider the possible reactions and questions of other readers—both to the text and to your ideas.

In addition, you must begin to develop a set of standards by which you will judge the text. For instance, will you be judging it in terms of its usefulness for a particular writing assignment? In terms of its consistency with the theories of a particular academic discipline or a particular school of criticism? On the basis of its logic? Its historical accuracy? Its willingness to break new ground? Any of these criteria is perfectly legitimate; which you select depends on your own critical stance.

Finally, you must be willing to read the text several times—at first simply to identify its subject and emphasis, then to understand its ideas, and eventually to make judgments about those ideas and to formulate a critical response.

5a   *Thinking Critically about Reading*

Thinking critically about what you read means more than just forming an opinion. You must be prepared to allow what you read to call your own ideas into question, and you must be prepared to seriously consider opposing points of view. As you read and take notes, remain open minded; realize that a text may test your own accepted beliefs and expose your own biases. Be willing to accept (or at least listen to) a particularly strong argument even if it goes against your own views. As you examine the ideas a writer presents in the text and the support used to make those ideas convincing, you should continue to examine—and to question—your own re- actions to those ideas.

(1)   *Distinguishing fact from opinion*

As you read and react critically to a text, you should be evaluating how effectively the writer supports his or her points. This support may be in the form of *fact* or *opinion*. As you read, you should be very careful to distinguish between fact and opinion as well as between opinion that is supported by examples, statistics, or expert testimony and opinion that is unsupported.

A **fact** is a verifiable statement that something is true or that something happened. We accept many facts because our senses confirm them: the sky is blue, water is wet. However, an individual's experience is limited, and we have to accept facts we are not able to verify personally. We accept that the planet Jupiter is 483 million miles from the sun and that it has an atmosphere of helium, hy- drogen, methane, and ammonia because we trust the reference sources that give us this information. In other cases, we may accept facts because an experiment demonstrates their truth. Keep in mind, however, that facts change as new information is uncovered or as situations change. To most Europeans who lived during the late fifteenth century, it was a *fact* that there was no sea route to India. Twenty-five years ago it was a *fact* that a person could not be given an artificial heart.

An **opinion** is a conclusion or belief that is not substantiated by proof and is, therefore, debatable.

FACT

Measles is a potentially deadly disease.

OPINION

All children should be vaccinated against measles.

An opinion may be *supported* or *unsupported.*

UNSUPPORTED OPINION

All children should be vaccinated against potentially deadly diseases, even if their parents' religious beliefs oppose this practice.

SUPPORTED OPINION

In 1991 in Philadelphia, several children enrolled in a church-related school whose religious doctrines oppose vaccination died of measles, a preventable disease. Because of the dangers posed by this failure to vaccinate children, all children should be vaccinated against potentially deadly diseases, even if their parents' religious beliefs oppose this practice.

(2) Evaluating a writer's support

The amount of weight an opinion carries varies according to the extent to which it is supported and to the nature of the support. The more reliable the support, the more convincing an opinion will be—and the more willing readers will be to accept it. Remember, though, that regardless of how it is supported, an opinion is not a fact. It never proves anything; it simply increases a statement's credibility.

An opinion may be supported with *examples, statistics,* or *expert testimony.*

An **example** is a specific illustration of a more general statement.

OPINION SUPPORTED BY EXAMPLES

The American Civil Liberties Union is an organization that has been unfairly characterized as left-wing. It is true that it has opposed prayer in the public schools, defended conscientious objectors, and challenged police methods of conducting questioning and searches of suspects. However, it has also backed the anti-abortion group Operation Rescue in a police brutality suit and presented a brief in support of a Republican politician accused of violating an ethics law.

Examples constitute adequate support only when they are sufficient, representative, and relevant. For instance, a text may cite just one example in an attempt to demonstrate that impoverished women are receiving high quality prenatal care. Even though a single detailed case study might be quite convincing, this one example is not enough to support such a controversial position. Moreover, the example may be exceptional and, therefore, not representative of the majority of poor women. Or, the example may be irrelevant—it may, for instance, cite the case of a woman who is not poor.

A **statistic** summarizes in numerical form a large number of specific examples.

OPINION SUPPORTED BY STATISTICS

A recent National Institute of Mental Health study concludes that mentally ill people account for more than 30 percent of the homeless population. Because so many homeless people have psychiatric disabilities, the federal government should seriously consider expanding the state mental hospital system.

To be convincing, statistics must be drawn from a reliable source. For example, statistics published in a journal known for its balanced treatment of the issues should carry more weight than those published in a journal known for its support of a particular cause or political position. Similarly, a newspaper poll of voters is likely to be more accurate than one commissioned by a candidate, who may wish to use the results to enhance his or her image. In addition, the statistical sample must be large enough to be meaningful. An article in the *Journal of the American Medical Association* recently noted that some researchers were publishing studies that included as few as ten participants. In many cases, the article pointed out, the results of such studies are misleading because a change in response by as few as two people can alter the results by twenty percent.

Expert testimony represents the opinion of recognized authorities in a particular field.

OPINION SUPPORTED BY EXPERT TESTIMONY

Clearly no young soldier ever really escapes the emotional consequences of war. As William Manchester, noted historian and World War II combat veteran observes in his essay "Okinawa: The Bloodiest Battle of All," "the invisible wounds remain" (72).

Expert testimony is only as convincing as the expert. The authority a writer cites should be a recognized expert in his or her field of study. In addition, the expert should support his or her claims with facts. Finally, the authority should approach the subject fairly and not be vulnerable to charges of bias (see 5a3).

Writing Checklist: Evaluating a Writer's Support

- Are enough examples provided?
- Are the examples representative, not aberrant?
- Are the examples selected relevant to the issue?
- Are the statistics drawn from a reliable source?
- Was the statistical sample large enough?
- Is the authority a recognized expert in his or her field?
- Does the authority support his or her claims with facts?
- Is the authority unbiased?

---

(3) Recognizing bias

As you read a text and form critical judgments about it, you should be alert for signs of the writer's bias. A **bias** is a predisposition to think a certain way. A writer is biased when he or she bases conclusions on preconceived ideas rather than evidence. Bias can creep into an argument without the knowledge of the writer; once present, it can not only distort information, but also undermine the credibility of the writer.

Obvious Bias   Some bias that you will encounter in your reading will be obvious and easy to detect.

Detecting Bias

- **Sexist or racist statements.** A writer who assumes that all doctors are male and that all nurses are female reflects a clear bias. A researcher who states that certain racial groups are intellectually superior to others is also presenting a biased view. In both cases, bias can cause the researcher to see only what he or she wants to see and to select data that support one outcome over all others. Thus, bias can undercut the writer's methods and distort his or her results.

- **A writer's stated beliefs.** In a recent article about the Middle East, a writer declared herself a strong supporter of the Palestinian position. This statement should tell you it is unlikely she will present an unbiased view of Israel's policies in the West Bank. Such a bias does not automatically invalidate the writer's points. On the contrary, she may offer an interesting perspective. What she will *not* do, however, is present a balanced view of the subject. For this reason it is essential that you explore other points of view before drawing your own conclusions.

- **Slanted language.** Slanted language can indicate a writer's bias. Saying "the politician presented an *impassioned* speech," gives one impression. Saying "the politician delivered a *diatribe*" gives another. Similarly, describing a person as "a Wall-Street type" is quite different from saying that she is well dressed and successful. In either case, language used to describe something determines the way a reader will perceive it.

- **Tone.** The tone of a piece of writing indicates a writer's attitude toward readers or toward his or her subject. As you read, ask yourself if the writer is being matter-of-fact, ironic, bitter, sarcastic, playful, tentative, angry, apologetic, or self-confident. In many cases, the tone of an essay can alert you to the possibility that the writer is slanting his or her case. An angry writer, for example, might not be able or willing to present an accurate account of an opponent's position, and an apologetic writer might inadvertently slant his or her case in an attempt to avoid offending readers.

- **Choice of examples.** As you read, try to evaluate a writer's use of examples. Frequently, the examples selected reveal the writer's biases—that is, a writer may include only examples that support a point and leave out examples that might contradict it **(see 5a2).**

- **Choice of experts.** In order to support a point effectively, a writer must present experts who represent a fair range of opinion. If, for instance, a writer discussing the president's economic policies toward Japan includes only statements by Republican economists or economists who advocate protectionism, he or she is presenting a biased case. The absence of statements by Democratic economists or economists who advocate free trade should alert you to this fact.

Subtle Bias   Other kinds of bias are so subtle that they are extremely difficult to detect. Cultural biases creep into a text when a writer accepts certain ideas as universal, not realizing that they are limited to the culture in which he or she lives. Assumptions about concepts such as material success, technology, progress, personal freedom, marriage, love, and children, for instance, are often cultural. A farmer in one South American country was shocked to hear a worker from the World Health Organization suggest that he should limit the size of his family. To him, a large number of male children meant prosperity and assured care in his old age. Similarly, the American emphasis on individual achievement is not universally shared. A Japanese business executive was recently quoted as saying that the problem with American workers is that they are more interested in themselves than in the welfare of the companies for which they work. Other biases can also affect a writer's thinking. Gender or social class, for instance, can determine how a writer views the world. Thus, ideas about the status of women or about the poor and how they should behave may be reflected in a writer's work.

EXERCISE 1

Read the following excerpt from a statement on comparable worth, a method by which some people seek to balance inequities in jobs occupied primarily by women. First, identify the facts and opinions in the excerpt. Then evaluate the support, using the checklist on page 104 as a guide. Finally, determine what biases the speaker seems to have. Make sure you underline the sentences and words that reveal her bias.

> My name is Phyllis Schlafly, president of Eagle Forum, a national profamily organization. I am a lawyer, writer, and homemaker.
>
> We oppose the concept called *comparable worth* for two principal reasons: (*a*) it's unfair to men and (*b*) it's unfair to women.
>
> The comparable worth advocates are trying to freeze the wages of blue-collar men while forcing employers to raise the wages of *some* white- and pink-collar women above marketplace rates. According to the comparable worth rationale, blue-collar men are overpaid and their wages should be frozen until white- and pink-collar women have their wages artificially raised to the same level. The proof that this is really what the comparable worth debate is all about is in both their rhetoric and their statistics.
>
> I've been debating feminists and listening to their arguments for more than a decade. It is impossible to overlook their rhetoric of envy. I've heard feminist leaders say hundreds of times, "It isn't fair that the man with a high school education earns more money than the women who graduated from college or nursing or secretarial school." That complaint means that the feminists believe that truck drivers,

electricians, plumbers, mechanics, highway workers, maintenance men, policemen, and firemen earn more money than feminists think they are worth. And how do the feminists judge "worth"? By paper credentials instead of by apprenticeship and hard work and by ignoring physical risk and unpleasant working conditions.

So the feminists have devised the slogan *comparable worth* to make the blue-collar man feel guilty for earning more money than women with paper credentials and to trick him into accepting a government-enforced wage freeze while all available funds are used to raise the wages of *some* women.

Statistical proof that the aim of comparable worth is to reduce the relative earning power of blue-collar men is abundantly available in the job evaluations commissioned and approved by the comparable worth advocates. You can prove this to yourself by making a job-by-job examination of *any* study or evaluation made with the approval of comparable worth advocates; it is always an elaborate scheme to devalue the blue-collar man.

For example, look at the Willis evaluation used in the famous case called *AFSCME v. State of Washington.* Willis determined that the electricians and truck drivers were overvalued by the state and that their "worth" was really far less than the "worth" of a registered nurse. More precisely, Willis produced an evaluation chart on which the registered nurse was worth 573 points, whereas the electrician was worth only 193 points (one-third of the nurse), while the truck driver was only worth 97 points (one-sixth of the nurse).

The federal court accepted the Willis evaluation as though it were some kind of divine law (refusing to listen to the Richard Jeanneret "PAQ" evaluation which produced very different estimates of "worth"). The federal court decision (unless it is overturned on appeal) means that the electricians and the truck drivers will probably have their salaries frozen until the state finds a way to pay the registered nurse three times and six times as much, respectively. [In a September 4, 1985, decision, the Ninth U.S. Circuit Court of Appeals overturned the decision.] (Phyllis Schlafly, "Comparable Worth: Unfair to Men and Women," *The Humanist,* May/June 1986)

5b *Recording Your Reactions*

Once you have read a text, you can begin to think about formulating a critical response to it. Annotating a text—recording your reactions to what you read in the form of notes in the margins or between the lines—can help you to express your own evaluation of a text's ideas. At first you may write down some relatively uncritical responses—for example, you may define new words, identify unfamiliar references, or jot down brief summaries to clarify points. Eventually, however, you will respond critically to the text. For instance, you may identify points that confirm (or challenge) your own thinking, question the appropriateness or accuracy of the writer's support, uncover the writer's biases, identify slanted language or faulty reasoning, or even question the writer's conclusion. Even if you are not an expert in a particular field, you are often able to question a writer's ideas—perhaps because you have different kinds of knowledge, a different perspective on an issue, or the ability to remain emotionally detached.

Questions such as the following can help you move beyond a text's literal meaning to consider its subtleties. Using such questions as a guide, you can begin to analyze, interpret, and evaluate a text and to consider its implications. In short, such questions can help you to develop your critical responses.

Questions for Reading Critically

- Do you agree with the points the writer is making?
- How would you characterize the writer's tone? How does the tone affect your response to the text?
- Is the writer's support primarily fact or opinion? **(See 5a1)**
- Does the writer present opinion as fact?
- Does the writer offer support for his or her opinions? If so, how convincing is this support? **(See 5a2)**
- Does the writer use valid reasoning? **(See 6a, 6b)**
- Does the writer use logical fallacies? **(See 6c)**
- Does the writer use unfair persuasion tactics such as appeals to prejudice or fear? **(See 7a8)**
- Does the writer oversimplify complex ideas?
- Does the writer make unsupported generalizations?
- Does the writer make reasonable inferences? **(See 6a2)**
- Does the writer represent the ideas of others accurately? Fairly?
- Does the writer distort the ideas of others or present them out of context? **(See 7a8)**
- Does the writer present a balanced picture of the issue?
- Are any alternative perspectives omitted?
- Does the writer omit pertinent information?

- Does the writer's language, tone, or choice of examples reveal any biases? If so, do the writer's biases reduce his or her credibility?
- Do your reactions reveal biases in your own thinking?
- Does the text challenge your own values, beliefs, and assumptions?

The passage below illustrates a student's reactions to a section of an article. After making these notes, the student is ready to draw her ideas together and write a critical response to the text.

One of the most compelling arguments about the Vietnam War is that it lasted as long as it did because of its "classist" nature. The central thesis is that because neither the decision-makers in the government *nor anyone they knew* had children fighting and dying in Vietnam, they had no personal incentive to bring the war to a halt. The government's generous college-deferment system, steeped as it was in class distinctions, allowed the white middle class to avoid the tragic consequences of the war. And the people who did the fighting and dying in place of the college-deferred were those whose voices were least heard in Washington: the poor and the disenfranchised.

I bring this up because I believe that the decline of the public schools is rooted in the same cause. Just as with the Vietnam War, as soon as the white middle class no longer had a stake in the public schools, the surest pressure on school systems to provide a decent education instantly disappeared. Once the middle class was gone, no mayor was going to get booted out of office because the schools were bad. No incompetent teacher had to worry about angry parents calling for his or her head "downtown." No third-rate educationalist at the local teachers college had to fear having his or her methods criticized by anyone that mattered.

The analogy to the Vietnam War can be extended even to the extent of the denial. It amuses me sometimes to hear people like myself

Is this comparison valid? (seems forced)

bias

Who are these people? Does he really represent them?

109

decry the state of the public schools. We
bemoan the lack of money, the decaying
facilities, the absurd credentialism, the high
foolishness of the school boards. We applaud
the burgeoning reform movement. And
everything we say is deeply, undeniably true.
We can see every problem with the schools
clearly except one: the fact that our decision to
abandon the schools has helped create all the
other problems. One small example: In the early
1980s, Massachusetts passed one of those tax
cap measures, called Proposition 2 1/2, which
has turned out to be a force for genuine evil in
the public schools. Would Proposition 2 1/2
have passed had the middle class still had a
stake in the schools? I wonder. I also wonder
whether 20 years from now, in the next round
of breast-beating memoirs, the exodus of the
white middle class from the public schools will
finally be seen for what it was. Individually,
every parent's rationale made impeccable
sense—"I can't deprive my children of a decent
education"—but collectively, it was a deeply
destructive act.

The main reason the white middle class fled,
of course, is race, or more precisely, the
complicated admixture of race and class and
good intentions gone awry. The fundamental
good intention—which even today strikes one
as both moral and right—was to integrate the
public classroom, and in so doing, to equalize
the resources available to all school children. In
Boston, this was done through enforced busing.
In Washington, it was done through a series of
judicial edicts that attempted to spread the good
teachers and resources throughout the system.
In other big city districts, judges weren't
involved; school committees, seeing the
handwriting on the wall, tried to do it
themselves.

However moral the intent, the result almost
always was the same. The white middle class
left. The historic parental vigilance I mentioned
earlier had had a lot to do with creating the
two-tiered system—one in which schools

Handwritten margin notes:
- *Is this "one small example" enough to support his claim?*
- *Oversimplification — Do all parents have same motives?*
- *Is this a valid assumption?*
- *Why does he assume intent was "good" & "moral"? Is he correct?*
- *?*

attended by the kids of the white middle class
had better teachers, better equipment, better
everything than those attended by the kids of
the poor. This did not happen because the white
middle-class parents were racists, necessarily; it
happened because they knew how to manipulate
the system and were willing to do so on behalf
of their kids. Their neighborhood schools
became little havens of decent education, and
they didn't much care what happened in the
other public schools.

Interesting point — but is it true?

In retrospect, this behavior, though perfectly
understandable, was tragically short-sighted.
When the judicial fiats made those safe havens
untenable, the white middle class quickly
discovered what the poor had always known:
There weren't enough good teachers, decent
equipment, and so forth to go around. For that
matter, there weren't even enough good *students*
to go around; along with everything else,
middle-class parents had to start worrying about
whether their kids were going to be mugged in
school.

slanted language (over emotional)

generalization?

Faced with the grim fact that their children's
education was quickly deteriorating, middle-
class parents essentially had two choices: They
could stay and pour the energy that had once
gone into improving the neighborhood school
into improving the entire school system—a
frightening task, to be sure. Or they could leave.
Invariably, they chose the latter.

Either/or fallacy? Were there other choices?

And it wasn't just the white middle class that
fled. The black middle class, and even the black
poor who were especially ambitious for their
children, were getting out as fast as they could
too, though not to the suburbs. They headed
mainly for the parochial schools, which
subsequently became integration's great success
story, even as the public schools became
integration's great failure. (Joseph Nocera,
"How the Middle Class Has Helped Ruin the
Public Schools," *Washington Monthly*, February
1989 reprinted in the *Utne Reader*, September/
October 1990)

EXERCISE 2

Read the following short article and answer the questions that follow, which have been adapted from the Questions for Reading Critically on p. 108.

"Go to Wall Street," my classmates said.
"Go to Wall Street," my professor advised.
"Go to Wall Street," my father threatened.

Whenever I tell people about my career indecisiveness, their answer is always the same: Get a blueprint for life and get one fast. Perhaps I'm simply too immature, but I think 20 is far too young to set my life in stone.

Nobody mentioned any award for being the first to have a white picket fence, 2.4 screaming kids and a spanking new Ford station wagon.

What's wrong with uncertainty, with exploring multiple options in multiple fields? What's wrong with writing, "Heck, I don't know" under the "objective" section of my résumé?

Parents, professors, recruiters and even other students seem to think there's a lot wrong with it. And they are all pressuring me to launch a career prematurely.

My sociology professor warns that my generation will be the first in American history not to be more successful than our parents' generation. This depressing thought drives college students to think of success as something that must be achieved at all costs as soon as possible.

My father wants me to emulate his success: Every family wants its children to improve the family fortune. I feel that desire myself, but I realize I don't need to do it by age 25.

This pressure to do better, to compete with the achievements of our parents in a rapidly changing world, has forced my generation to pursue definitive, lifelong career paths at far too young an age. Many of my friends who have graduated in recent years are already miserably unhappy.

My professors encourage such pre-professionalism. In upper level finance classes, the discussion is extremely career-oriented. "Learn to do this and you'll be paid more" is the theme of many a lecture. Never is there any talk of actually enjoying the exercise.

Nationwide, universities are finally taking steps in the right direction by re-emphasizing the study of liberal arts and a return to the classics. If only job recruiters for Wall Street firms would do the same.

"Get your M.B.A. as soon as possible and you'll have a jump on the competition," said one overly zealous recruiter from Goldman Sachs. Learning for learning's sake was completely forgotten: Goldman Sachs refused to interview anybody without a high grade-point average, regardless of the courses composing that average.

In other interviews, it is expected that you know exactly what you want to do or you won't be hired. "Finance?" they say, "What kind of finance?"

A recruiter at Dean Witter Reynolds said investment banking demands 80 to 100 hours of work per week. I don't see how anyone will ever find time to enjoy the gobs of money they'll be making.

The worst news came from a partner at Salomon Brothers. He told me no one was happy there, and if they said they were, they're lying. He said you come in here, make a lot of money and leave as fast as you can.

Two recent Wharton alumni, scarcely two years older than I, spoke at Donaldson, Lufkin & Jenrette's presentation. Their jokes about not having a life outside the office were only partially in jest.

Yet, students can't wait to play this corporate charade. They don ties and jackets and tote briefcases to class.

It is not just business students who are obsessed with their careers. The five other people who live in my house are not undergraduate business majors, but all five plan to attend graduate school next year. How is it possible that, without one iota of real work experience, these people are willing to commit themselves to years of intensive study in one narrow field?

Mom, dad, grandpa, recruiters, professors, fellow students: I implore you to leave me alone.

Now is my chance to explore, to spend time pursuing interests simply because they make me happy and not because they fill my wallet. I don't want to waste my youth toiling at a miserable job. I want to make the right decisions about my future.

Who knows, I may even end up on Wall Street.

(Michael Finkel, "Undecided—and Proud of It," *New York Times*)

1. What is the writer's main point? Do you agree with him?
2. How does he support this point?
3. Is his supporting information primarily fact or opinion? Does he support his opinions? Is the support convincing?
4. Where does the writer use expert testimony? How convincing are the experts he cites?
5. Should the writer have used other kinds of support? For example, should he have used statistics? If so, where? What kind of statistical evidence might have made his case more convincing?
6. Does the writer's language, tone, or choice of examples reveal any biases? What leads you to your conclusion?
7. The writer is a student at an Ivy League university. Do you think this

status might give him a limited or unrealistic view of college students' professional options?

8. Do you have any biases against the writer based on your assessment of his economic status, social class, or educational level?

9. The writer is a college senior. Do his age and his lack of experience in the working world make his article less credible to you?

EXERCISE 3

Draw a vertical line down the middle of a piece of paper. In the left-hand column, list the main points of the following short essay. In the right-hand column, write down your reactions to the writer's ideas. You may explain or clarify, question or contradict, probe for further information, or relate the writer's ideas to ideas of your own or to ideas from other sources. Use the Questions for Reading Critically on page 108 as a guide.

Week after week, Henrietta comes to clean my house. Despite her good humor, I don't think she much likes this kind of work, but it is all she can get without a high school diploma. She is a soft-spoken woman of 33, the divorced mother of four children. She knows where their father is, but they never see him and he contributes nothing to their support. The five of them survive on payments from Aid to Families With Dependent Children of $4,236 a year plus what I give her each week.

I met Henrietta through my husband, who teaches in an adult-education program, helping people earn a general equivalency diploma. Without such certification, they are disqualified from all but the most menial and irregular work. His students are predominantly women—most of them mothers, many in middle age—who have been placed in the program by the Arizona Department of Economic Security as part of an effort to shift them from public assistance to full employment. For their attendance they receive $3 a day. Funds and staff keep dwindling as the Federal Administration, despite recent protestations of concern about adult illiteracy, continues to slash at the program's resources. But the women keep coming.

*   *   *

Not long ago illiteracy had its 15 minutes of fame, which gave an emotional (though not a financial) boost to programs like the one my husband teaches in. I was surprised that women's groups did not take up the issue eagerly, for certain basic facts about women's lives make the question of illiteracy a particularly lively one.

Take the results, now familiar, of a 1985 study of divorced families by Lenore J. Weitzman, a sociologist: In the year following a divorce, the husband's standard of living rises 42 percent while that of the wife and children falls 73 percent. Also, in the past decade, teen-age pregnancies among all ethnic groups have increased, and many of these young women are choosing to try to raise their babies on their own. Some researchers predict that by the year 2000, virtually all poor people in this country will be women and children.

The problems that underlie such statistics are extraordinarily complex, and I do not mean to imply that we can sweep them away simply by teaching women to read, write and handle fractions. But neither do I belittle such capabilities. The woman solely responsible for herself and her children occupies a marginal position, socially and economically, at best. If she's illiterate, she might be pushed outside society's margins altogether.

The illiterate woman is essentially helpless to shape her own life. Unable to find work at wages that will support her family, she must live on public assistance that is inadequate for her needs and that, more important, reinforces her passivity. In such a situation, earning a high school diploma can be of enormous practical significance. Not only can she qualify for numerous jobs previously closed to her, but she becomes eligible for further training that might prepare her to work outside occupations traditionally held by women, which traditionally offer both low pay and low status. Moreover, she can assume an active stance, earning rather than receiving the money with which she feeds and shelters herself and her family. Thus, her entire relationship to society is transformed.

If, as seems to be the case, the majority of our children are going to be raised by single mothers, then the impact of a woman's literacy extends beyond her own social position and self-esteem. The children of a literate mother benefit enormously from the bedtime storytelling, the little notes, the help with a subtraction problem, the trips to the library—all the small commonplaces of literate life. Even more important, they see their mother, perhaps their only role model in the home, as a competent, self-defined and active element in their lives. Literacy might not be genetically inheritable, but it is passed down from generation to generation nonetheless.

Women are succeeding in these ways. Take Rita, one of my husband's students. The child of migrant workers, she loved school but could never keep up, so at 14 she dropped out and married. She has had nine "blessings," as she calls them; when the youngest started school, she went back herself and earned her general equivalency diploma. In fact, she was the student speaker at her graduation. She now works in a program for needy elderly people and attends a community college. Given the chance for such accomplishment, most women will take it. And though they are often timid at first, with encouragement most of them thrive.

* * *

Writing about women's literacy seems futile on the face of it. After all, my audience can, by definition, read; its members do not need to be persuaded of the virtues of literacy. But they might not have reflected on the ways literate women can work to swell their own ranks. They can, for one thing, volunteer in programs like my husband's, enabling an overtaxed staff with limited resources to reach further and more deeply. They can also lobby for an increase in those resources. The women entering these programs need ample support in the form of stipends, book allowances, flexible class hours, social and vocational counseling and day-care services. Henrietta's further education, for example, is interrupted every time her children are out of school.

These things would cost significantly less than a fleet of B-1 bombers, maybe even less than one B-1 bomber, and they would provide a more solid line of defense. Because at bottom, the strongest country is not the one with the classiest weapons and the most complicated technology. The strongest country is the one whose citizens, certain of their skills and worth, believe that they can take care of themselves and one another. (Nancy Mairs, "Hers" column, *New York Times*)

5c   *Writing a Critical Response*

After you have read critically and evaluated the ideas in the text, you may want to draw together your reactions to the text. Writing a critical response will help you to do this.

In a critical response you express the result of the interaction between you and the text. As in any convincing article or essay, the judgments and conclusions included in your response must be supported with specific examples. In addition, you must supply the logical and sequential links (transitions, topic sentences, and so on) that will help your readers to follow the progression of your ideas.

Before you begin writing your critical response, review your annotations. Carefully reconsider your judgments and reactions to the text in light of any biases you may have uncovered in your own thinking. Then, formulate a statement that summarizes your critical reactions to the text. As you write, begin by identifying your text and summarizing its position. Next, state your own position about the writer's stance and present your support: Summarize and respond to the writer's key points one by one, supporting your judgments with the ideas you wrote down as you annotated. At every stage, continue to test and reexamine your ideas and to remain as open-minded as possible to the ideas in the text—no matter how they may challenge (or even contradict) your own values or beliefs. Conclude by restating your critical response to the text. When you have finished, reread what you have written, making sure that it is as accurate, clear, and fair-minded as possible.

Writing Checklist: Formulating a Critical Response

Before writing:

- Review your annotations.
- Reconsider your judgments, taking your own biases into account.
- Formulate a statement of your critical reactions.

In your critical response:

- Identify your text and summarize the writer's position.
- State your position about the writer's stance.
- Summarize and evaluate the writer's key points.
- Restate your critical reaction to the text.
- Reread your response, checking for accuracy, clarity, and fair mindedness.

Following is a student's critical response to Joseph Nocera's "How the Middle Class Has Helped Ruin the Public Schools," an annotated section of which is reproduced on pages 109–111. In her remarks, the student uses her own knowledge, observations, and experiences to question and challenge Nocera's points.

Critical Response

Identification of text

 In his article "How the Middle Class Has Helped Ruin the Public Schools," published in the February 1989 issue of *The Washington Monthly,*

Summary of writer's position

Joseph Nocera tries to have it both ways. He is confessing the guilt he feels for contributing to the decline of public education and attacking those middle-class parents who have made the same

Statement of position about writer's stance.

choices he has made. What he seems to be asking his audience to do is to feel both sympathy and outrage towards parents in this situation. This is asking a lot.

Summary and
evaluation
of writer's
key points
(¶s 2–4)

Early in his essay Nocera tells readers that he moved to a small town because of its good public schools—which he attributes to "a large group of white middle-class parents deeply involved in the public school system" (67). He cites the "outrages" of public schools in Boston, Washington, and New York and concludes that "The destruction of the large public school systems in America is one of the great tragedies of our time" (67). Then, he apologetically explains that he has chosen, for the sake of his children's education, "not to stand and fight" (68). After all, he argues, "Parents aren't willing to sacrifice their children on the altar of their social principles" (71). Throughout the essay, he seems to assume his readers will agree with him simply because he is an ordinary middle-class parent.

Admitting that, as this typical middle-class parent, he has options poor parents do not have, Nocera tries to justify his private decision despite the widespread public disaster he admits it has helped to create. In doing so, he reveals his biases. At various points in his discussion he attacks the courts, unions, bureaucrats, and school committees. He talks about the nation's problems, but all his examples are drawn from the urban northeast, particularly Boston. He also suggests that any middle-class parents who, unlike himself, keep their children in public schools are sacrificing their children's education for some abstract social principles. This conclusion ignores the fact that some parents may consider the understanding of such social principles to be a valuable part of their children's education. In addition, not all urban public schools provide an inferior education. Finally, he reveals a racial bias when he makes the assumption that white middle-class students (and parents) are the most valuable in a school system and that without these ingredients the system is doomed.

Nocera's reasoning is sometimes faulty. For instance, when he says "Since the white middle class left, the system [in Boston] has simply fallen apart. Can this be sheer coincidence? I think not" (71) he is making a sweeping (and unsupported) generalization. He is also assuming that either white flight or coincidence—and no other factor—must have caused the schools' decline. Similarly, when he says the middle class could either try to improve the whole system or abandon it, he ignores the possibility of other options—such as working to improve one particular school in a system. Generalizations and oversimplifications like these reduce a complex issue to a simplistic, either-or situation. Given this limited perspective, it is not surprising that Nocera can offer no solution. Predictably, he believes change should come not from people like him but from those outside the system. In his conclusion Nocera reveals that what he is really looking for is not a platform from which to effect change but an opportunity for confession and a plea for forgiveness.

Restatement
of critical
reaction to
the text

The student who wrote the preceding critical response evaluated her source using her own knowledge. Sometimes, however, you will have to do research to help you analyze and evaluate the ideas of others.

Revision Close-up

If you use the ideas or words of a source to help you formulate a critical response, remember to clearly identify ideas that are not your own **(see 39a).**

EXERCISE 4

The letter below (*Utne Reader,* November/December 1990) was written by a Denver parent in response to Nocera's essay. Putting yourself in Nocera's place, write a brief critical response to this parent's ideas.

Multicultural Education

I believe Joseph Nocera's article is entirely accurate except for one major flaw. That flaw is the belief that sending your children to urban public schools is "sacrificing them." I believe it is in their best interest to do so.

I am a parent of four children in the Denver public school system. I have observed all of the rationalizations described in Nocera's article as dozens of good white liberals in our integrated neighborhood have fled to the suburbs and private schools. For years I tried to appeal to their altruism to support the schools. Then I realized that the reason I was sending my kids to the public schools was not "a sacrifice for my social principles" as Nocera would have us believe, but was actually because I knew it was in their own best interest, to help them learn how to relate and function within a multicultural, multiracial environment. Let me illustrate this point with personal anecdotes.

My son, who is a good fourth-grade student, asked why our friend's son was leaving our public school. I told him it was because "his parents didn't want him to be the only white boy in his class." Then I asked him, "Has that ever happened to you?" He pondered a moment and then said, "I don't think so. I can't remember." Actually, only the year before, he was the only white boy in his third-grade class, but he obviously had overcome any anxiety or prejudice or even awareness of this recent experience.

My daughter, who is a straight-A seventh grader, asked me, "What is an ethnic minority?" I explained that it was a small minority group like blacks. She said with a totally straight face, "Come on, Dad, blacks aren't a minority." In her world they aren't.

Duane Gall
Denver, CO

E X E R C I S E   5

Read the newspaper column below and, after highlighting and annotating it carefully, write a brief critical response to the ideas it discusses. Use the questions on page 108 and the checklist on page 117 to guide you.

The thought police are busy this year. With all the best intentions in the world—because aren't their intentions always honorable, from preserving the sanctity of the family to promoting racial equality?— they have proferred petitions, organized boycotts, brought lawsuits. Last week they even had the capacity to surprise us. They came out of left field, and they were represented by those people who traditionally have been the quirky, the avant-garde, the antithesis of the thought police type.

That is, actors.

In Central Park this summer, Morgan Freeman, a gifted actor who is black, has played Petruchio in "The Taming of the Shrew," and Denzel Washington, a gifted actor who is black, is portraying Richard III.

This is the way I choose to describe them. I use sentence structure to make their race, in this context, descriptive, not definitive. The definitive reasons they were chosen are clear: craft, and celebrity.

Actors' Equity, the union that represents them and others far less successful, believes that this is insufficient.

Last week Equity torpedoed a musical called "Miss Saigon," which includes parts for dozens of Asian actors. The celebrated actor Jonathan Pryce plays the Engineer in the London production, and was to do so on Broadway. Equity said it could not approve of Mr. Pryce playing the role, which he apparently does brilliantly, because the Engineer is Eurasian and Mr. Pryce is Caucasian.

That is, race as definition, not as description.

Let's be clear: this wish for politically correct casting goes only one way, the way designed to redress the injuries of centuries. When Pat Carroll, who is a woman, plays Falstaff, who is not, the casting is considered a stroke of brilliance. When Josette Simon, who is black, plays Maggie in "After the Fall" a part Arthur Miller patterned after Marilyn Monroe and which has traditionally been played, not by white women, but by blonde white women, it is hailed as a breakthrough.

But when the pendulum moves the other way, the actors' union balks. It is noted, quite correctly, that it is insufferable that roadshow companies of "The King and I" habitually use Caucasian men wearing eyeliner to play the King, rather than searching for suitable Asian actors. But the conclusion drawn from this is that a white man should never be permitted inside the skin of an Asian one, although all of acting is about getting inside someone else's skin, someone different, someone somehow foreign.

Anyone who has ever faced discrimination knows that bigotry begins when race, when gender, when ethnicity are applied as sole definition. The black man doesn't get into the country club; the savvy banker who is black might. The woman may not be a prime candidate for chief financial officer; the terrific numbers-cruncher who is a woman may get the job.

Actors are accustomed to this, too. How many of them have slunk off to coffee shops after a casting call, defeated and despondent after hearing "We're looking for a tall redhead."

Definitive can be limiting, reductive, making of a diverse group a collection of sameness.

Descriptive tries to force people to see us as individuals, with certain attributes, chief among them the proud one of race, the cherished one of gender, and the ineffable, unmistakable one of talent.

We women are familiar with what has become a tradition in the corporate culture. A woman is given an executive job, say vice president for human resources, and we all cheer. Except that, as the years go by, a woman is always vice president for human resources, but never anything else. Never controller. Never president. Vice president for human resources has become The Woman's Job. There is no need to worry about gender equity anymore.

Perhaps "Miss Saigon," if it ever comes to this country, will become the Asian show. An Asian actor will play the Engineer, and if he is seen as an Asian actor, he may never be offered Othello, or the Stage Manager in "Our Town," or the lead in a new John Guare play.

If he is seen as a brilliant actor who is Asian, it may be a different story.

It is dangerous to form a thought police force. Other people have been at it much longer; they have had months and months of fighting the ghost of Robert Mapplethorpe and trashing the righteous rage of Karen Finley. Who knows? One day one of them might run Actors' Equity.

And then perhaps Denzel Washington will not be playing Richard III. Perhaps there will be an open call for white male actors. Once you open certain doors, they swing both ways. (Anna Quindlen, "Error, Stage Left," *New York Times* Op-Ed)

Thinking Logically

An argument proceeds logically from facts to conclusions in two basic ways: **inductively,** moving from specific observations or experiences to a general conclusion, or **deductively,** moving from general statements held to be true or self-evident to more specific conclusions. Whether you proceed inductively or deductively depends on your topic, purpose, and audience. Many—probably most—arguments involve a combination of deductive and inductive reasoning, relying both on well-established beliefs and on conclusions drawn from evidence. For now, however, we will consider induction and deduction separately.

6a   *Reasoning Inductively*

An inductive argument moves from specifics to a general conclusion.

(1) Moving from hypothesis to conclusion

An inductive argument usually begins with the **hypothesis,** the idea the writer wants to investigate. Next, it examines the hypothesis by presenting evidence. Finally, the writer draws a conclusion based on the evidence. Consider the following outline of an argument's components:

HYPOTHESIS

    SAT's may not be very important to a particular college's admissions procedures.

EVIDENCE

- At Princeton University 50 percent of the admission decision is based on academic credentials and 50 percent on nonacademic factors.
- Academic factors include grades and rank in high school, SAT scores, achievement-test scores, and recommendations from teachers and counselors.
- Nonacademic factors include demonstration of leadership, extracurricular activities, sports, and a personal interview.
- Special attention may be given to athletes, minorities, and alumni and faculty children.
- The SAT is used as an admission requirement that cuts across all applicants.
- Less than 52 percent of applicants for a recent class with SAT verbal scores between 750 and 800 were accepted.
- Less than 39 percent of those with similar SAT math scores were offered admission.
- Approximately 18 percent of those with SAT verbal scores between 550 and 599 and over 19 percent of those with similar SAT math scores were admitted.

CONCLUSION

While important, the SAT scores are not always determining factors in the admission process. (Adapted from Jay Amberg, "The SAT")

No matter how much evidence you present, inductive conclusions are never absolutely certain, only highly probable. They are arrived at by what is called an **inductive leap.** The more observations you make, the narrower the gap between your observations and your conclusion and the better your chances of drawing a convincing conclusion. When, for example, a small child looks out the window, sees dark clouds, and predicts it will rain, he or she is making an inductive leap. The conclusion is sound because the child has seen clouds precede rain in the past. As the following passage shows, induction is central to scientific inquiry. Notice how the writer presents his observations and then makes the inductive leap to his conclusion that the songs of swamp sparrows are an example of learned behavior.

Male swamp sparrows brought into the laboratory as nestlings learn readily from taped songs of their species when these are played from the third to the eighth week of life. Full song develops some 9 months later and often contains a certain proportion of "syllables" that match the components on the training tapes. The diverse morphology of swamp sparrow syllables permits choice of a great variety of training patterns. Exposure to different syllables in infancy results in different patterns of adult singing. The conclusion that songs are learned is based on this capacity to match acoustic models and on the abnormality of songs of birds reared without exposure to the species song. (Peter Marler and Susan Peters, "Sparrows Learn Adult Song and More from Memory")

(2) Making inferences

When you make an inductive leap, you are actually making an **inference,** an observation about the unknown that is based on the known. For example, we commonly infer the size of people's incomes from the kinds of cars they drive or the kinds of houses they occupy. Similarly, an engineer infers the cause of a bridge collapse after finding signs of metal fatigue on a supporting girder, and a physician infers a diagnosis on the basis of observations of a patient's symptoms and behavior.

Suppose you are considering writing a paper about keeping your state free of the many soda bottles and cans that litter its towns and cities. Your research indicates that a number of possible solutions exist for this problem. The state could hire unemployed teenagers to pick up the litter. Brightly colored refuse containers could be placed prominently around the state to encourage people to dispose of bottles and cans properly. Finally, the state could enact a law that required a deposit from all those who bought beverages in bottles or cans. Reviewing your research, you find that your first two solutions have had no long-term effect on litter in the states that tried them. However, mandatory deposit laws, along with a prohibition of plastic beverage containers, significantly decreased the number of discarded bottles and cans in two states that instituted such programs. Still, because the conditions in your state are different from those in the states that you studied, you must make a leap from a known situation—the states you studied—to an unknown situation—your state. As a result of your analysis, you infer that the mandatory deposit law could be a good solution to your problem.

EXERCISE 1

Read the paragraphs below carefully, and answer the questions that follow them.

A. The role—and reputation—of pawn shops seems to be changing. Once considered by many to be somewhat seedy, disreputable establishments with an equally suspect clientele, pawn shops are now becoming more socially acceptable. As many as one out of every ten adult Americans borrows money from a pawn shop each year. In the past five years, the number of pawn-shop licenses has increased by more than a third in some states. Many individuals who cannot get credit from banks or other lending institutions are able to do so at pawn shops. They can borrow modest amounts of cash at no interest simply by presenting identification, offering a piece of collateral, and signing an agreement. Although often criticized for being legalized usurers or receivers of stolen goods, pawn-shop owners insist that they legitimately fill a gap in the loan business. Pawn-shop owners are working diligently to improve their image and have begun to attract middle-class and even upper-middle-class borrowers.

Which of the following statements can be inferred from the paragraph above?

1. More and more Americans are borrowing money.
2. Pawn shops are trying to improve their image by refusing to buy stolen goods.
3. Pawn shops are still not socially acceptable to some people.
4. Some states are trying to ban pawn shops because they are legalized usurers and receivers of stolen goods.
5. Pawn shops offer loans at no interest to qualified borrowers for any amount of money.

   B. Americans are becoming more ecologically aware with each passing year, but their awareness may be limited. Most people know about the destruction of rain forests in South America, for example, or the vanishing African elephant, but few realize what is going on in their own backyards in the name of progress. Even people who are knowledgeable about such topics as the plight of the wild mustang, the dangers of toxic waste disposal, and acid rain frequently fail to realize either the existence or the importance of "smaller" ecological issues. The wetlands are a good case in point. In his first State of the Union address, George Bush pledged there would be "no net loss" of wetlands in the U.S. But in recent decades, more than 500,000 acres of wetlands a year have been filled, and it seems unlikely that the future will see any great change. What has happened in recent times is that U.S. wetlands are filled in in one area and "restored" in another location, a practice that is legal according to Section 404 of the Clean Water Act, and one that does in fact result in "no net loss" of wetlands. Few see the problem with this. To most, wetlands are mere swamps, and getting rid of swamps is viewed as something positive. In addition, the wetlands typically contain few spectacular species—the sort of glamour animals, such as condors and grizzlies, that easily attract publicity and sympathy. Instead, they contain boring specimens of flora and fauna unlikely to generate great concern among the masses. Yet the delicate balance of the ecosystem *is* upset by the elimination or "rearrangement" of such marshy areas. True, cosmically speaking, it matters little if one organism (or many) is wiped out. But even obscure subspecies might provide some much-needed product or information in the future. We should not forget that penicillin was made from a lowly mold.

Which of the following statements can be inferred from the paragraph above?

1. The loss of even a single species may be disastrous to the ecosystem of the wetlands.
2. Even though the wetlands are considered swamps, most people are very concerned about their fate.
3. Section 404 of the Clean Water Act is not sufficient to protect the wetlands.
4. Few Americans are concerned about environmental issues.
5. Most people would agree that the destruction of rain forests is worse than the destruction of the wetlands.

EXERCISE 2

Read this essay carefully.

As Deerfield Academy, following Lawrenceville, departs from its traditional mission of single-sex education for boys, I, like others involved in girls' schools, am saddened that few voices were apparently raised to defend a mission I cannot help comparing to our own.

Advocates of single-sex education for girls are enthusiastic defenders of the cause. We feel validated every day in our classrooms, dormitories, councils of student government, science and computer laboratories and yearbook editing offices. We see growth, developing self-esteem, individuality and leadership all around us.

It is not that good co-educational schools cannot offer girls these things; it is that girls' schools do so consistently. We are a fail-safe producer of first-class citizenship for girls in a world in which they are not guaranteed this opportunity elsewhere. We, like the women's colleges, provide not only "equal opportunity, but every opportunity," to quote Dr. Nannerl Keohane, the president of Wellesley College.

A colleague of mine described a vignette in her all-girls kindergarten class: A small girl surveyed the room, arms akimbo, and sized up the situation. "Thank heavens," she said. "No boys in the block corner." No, there aren't. She won't have to establish her right to build with blocks, just as later on she won't have to elbow her way to the computer terminals or perhaps feel out of place spending extra time in the physics lab.

Her voice will be heard in class, her opinion sought—on every topic—and taken seriously. Whatever the athletic facilities, they are for her alone. Moreover, leadership roles are more available: Girls get experience in managing radio stations, editing student newspapers and literary magazines, heading the debate and mathematics teams—all without having to fight for a place in the sun, because sex stereotyping does not complicate life in the school.

Since failure is less threatening, risk-taking becomes more bearable. For example, like many girls' schools we have a wonderful dance program, but our dancers don't have to care if they don't have figures like the models in Seventeen magazine—and few teen-agers do. Like most people, they come in various shapes and sizes, yet they know no one will laugh at them or make disparaging remarks. So they learn to carry themselves with poise and grace, to be proud of their bodies—and stand a chance of becoming good dancers besides.

Relationships can flourish, both among peers and between students and adults. Communication with teachers and other adults is open and warm. Friendships grow strong and last long into adult life, as I have observed time and again by watching the alumnae of women's schools and colleges network and support each other in myriad ways. All this creates a learning and teaching atmosphere that is almost tangible: Our classrooms are lively, exciting places.

A graduate, finishing her sophomore year at a major New England (formerly all-male) college, visited Miss Porter's School last summer. She and I had known each other somewhat, had talked during her years with us but had never discussed the roles and expectations of women as such.

She and her friends were fighting for better health services for women at her college and were frustrated with their lack of progress. They were not being heard, she said. People were not taking them seriously. She talked about the climate of the classrooms, which she found alienating, and the effort she felt she must continually make to claim her equal place. The intensity and warmth of the conversation surprised me. "I wanted to talk to you," she said. "I knew you'd understand." That solidarity and that strength is what a women's single-sex school or college can provide.

We are sorry that Lawrenceville, and now Deerfield, did not feel that they could raise their voices in support of their historic educational environments. This is not a judgment—it is a sentiment—because women's schools, like women's colleges, find their mission constantly validated.

Ours is a co-educational world—no doubt about it—and single-sex education needs its defenders, promoters, believers and proselytizers.

Yes, some people think girls' schools are anachronisms, but they succeed, better than most people realize, and remain necessary in a world where men and women still do not work equally together as professionals. (Rachel Phillips Belash, "Why Girls' Schools Remain Necessary," *New York Times*)

Answer the following questions about the essay above.

1. What is Belash's hypothesis?
2. What examples does Belash offer to support her hypothesis? What additional examples could be offered?
3. Where does Belash make an inductive leap? What does she infer?
4. What is Belash's conclusion? Is this conclusion warranted in light of the information she presents?

6b *Reasoning Deductively*

Unlike induction, deduction begins with a general statement or proposition and establishes a chain of reasoning that leads to a conclusion. In order to study the process of deduction, we rely on a formal schematic called a syllogism. Devised by Aristotle, a **syllogism** is a three-part set of statements or propositions that contains a *major premise,* a *minor premise,* and a *conclusion.*

MAJOR PREMISE: All books from that store are new.
MINOR PREMISE: These books are from that store.
CONCLUSION: Therefore, these books are new.

In deduction, the premises contain all the information expressed in the conclusion: no terms are introduced in the conclusion that have not already appeared in the major and minor premises.

In a deductive argument, then, your conclusion must follow from your premises. Suppose you wish to argue that the government should take steps to protect people who live near nuclear power plants. You begin with the general statement that the government is obliged to protect its citizens. You then say that people who live near nuclear power plants are citizens. Your conclusion—that the safety of these residents should therefore be ensured—follows from these assumptions. Stated as a syllogism, your argument looks like this:

MAJOR PREMISE: All citizens should be protected by the government.

MINOR PREMISE: People who live near nuclear power plants are citizens.

CONCLUSION: Therefore, people who live near nuclear power plants should be protected by the government.

The strength of a deductive argument is that if your readers accept your premises, they usually grant your conclusion. Because your major premise is so important, it is a good idea to choose an idea that your audience already accepts as self-evident. Once you have established your premises, the force of logic alone should lead readers to accept your conclusion.

When you construct a deductive argument, you may state your conclusion explicitly and then support it, or you may lead up to a conclusion that is implied throughout. If your audience is likely to agree with your conclusion, state it at the outset. If not, proceed gradually. In the following deductive argument, the conclusion appears at the end:

> The primary function of a university is to discover and disseminate knowledge by means of research and teaching. To fulfill this function a free interchange of ideas is necessary not only within its walls but with the world beyond as well. It follows that the university must do everything possible to ensure within it the fullest degree of intellectual freedom. The history of intellectual growth and discovery clearly demonstrates the need for unfettered freedom, the right to think the unthinkable, discuss the unmentionable, and challenge the unchallenged. To curtail free expression strikes twice at intellectual freedom, for whoever deprives another of the right to state unpopular views necessarily also deprives others of the right to listen to those views. (Yale Committee, "Freedom of Expression at Yale")

(1) Distinguishing validity from truth

Before continuing, we should distinguish between arguments that are valid and arguments that are true. A **valid** argument is one whose conclusion logically follows from its premises. In other words, *validity* depends on the form of a syllogism. A **true** argument is one that makes accurate claims—that is, one in which the information contained by the propositions is in agreement with the facts. A **sound** argument must be both valid and true. However, an argument may be valid without being true or true without being valid. In the following example, the syllogism's argument is valid but not true:

MAJOR PREMISE: All politicians are male.

MINOR PREMISE: Patricia Schroeder is a politician.

CONCLUSION: Therefore, Patricia Schroeder is male.

As odd as it may seem, this syllogism's argument is valid. In the major premise, the phrase *all politicians* establishes that the entire class *politicians* is male. Once Patricia Schroeder is identified as a politician, the conclusion that she is male automatically follows. Common sense tells us, however, that Patricia Schroeder is female. Because the major premise of this syllogism is not true, any argument based on this premise also cannot be true. For this reason, even though the logic of the syllogism is correct, its argument is not.

(2) Constructing valid arguments

Just as a syllogism can be valid but not true, it can also be true but not valid.

Undistributed Middle Term   A syllogism in which the middle term is not distributed cannot have a valid conclusion.

MAJOR PREMISE: All fathers are male.
MINOR PREMISE: John Updike is a male.
CONCLUSION: Therefore, John Updike is a father.

Even though the premises of this syllogism are true, the conclusion—John Updike is a father—does not follow logically because the construction of the syllogism is faulty. The rule of logic is that the middle term, the term used in both the major and minor premises, must be *distributed*—that is, it must refer to all members of the group. In the preceding syllogism, however, this is not the case. In the major premise, *all fathers* is distributed because it refers to *all* individuals in the class designated as fathers. The term *male*, however, is undistributed and for this reason cannot be used as the middle term. Therefore, you cannot conclude that because John Updike is male, he is a father.

Consider this version of the preceding syllogism:

MAJOR PREMISE: All fathers are male.
MINOR PREMISE: John Updike is a father.
CONCLUSION: Therefore, John Updike is a male.

Now the distributed term *fathers* appears in both the major and the minor premises. Since *John Updike* is equated with the distributed middle term *fathers*, the conclusion that he is a male logically follows.

Shifting Meaning   A syllogism in which the meaning of a key term shifts cannot have a valid conclusion.

MAJOR PREMISE: Only man contemplates the future.
MINOR PREMISE: No woman is a man.
CONCLUSION: Therefore, no woman contemplates the future.

In the major premise, *man* is used to denote all human beings. In the minor premise, however, *man* refers to gender. As a result of this shift, the conclusion cannot be valid. You can correct this problem by making certain that the meaning of each key term in the syllogism remains the same.

MAJOR PREMISE: Only human beings contemplate the future.
MINOR PREMISE: No dog is a human being.
CONCLUSION: Therefore, no dog contemplates the future.

See
18g2   ◄ (Note that *human beings* is also preferable to *men* because it conforms to nonsexist usage.)

Negative Premises   A syllogism in which one of the premises is negative cannot have a valid affirmative conclusion.

MAJOR PREMISE: No handicapped persons may be denied employment because of their handicap.
MINOR PREMISE: Deaf persons are handicapped.
CONCLUSION: Therefore, deaf persons may be denied employment because of their handicap.

In the preceding syllogism, you cannot infer from the premises an affirmative relationship between *employment* and *deaf persons*. The only conclusion possible is a negative one. ("Therefore, *no* deaf persons may be denied employment because of their handicap.")

A syllogism in which both premises are negative cannot have a valid conclusion.

MAJOR PREMISE: Injured workers may not be denied workers' compensation.
MINOR PREMISE: Frank is not an injured worker.
CONCLUSION: Therefore, Frank may not be denied workers' compensation.

The two negative premises of this syllogism provide no links in the chain of reasoning established by the syllogism. Only if one of the premises is positive can a valid conclusion be reached.

MAJOR PREMISE: Injured workers may not be denied workers' compensation.

MINOR PREMISE: Frank is an injured worker.

CONCLUSION: Therefore, Frank may not be denied workers' compensation.

(3)   Recognizing enthymemes

As intellectually challenging as syllogisms can be, they do not present a realistic picture of how people actually form arguments. Many deductive arguments occur as statements in which assumptions are implied rather than stated. An **enthymeme** is a syllogism in which one of the premises—often the major premise—is unstated. Consider these assertions:

Melissa is on the Dean's List.

She is a good student.

These statements contain the minor premise and the conclusion of a syllogism. The reader must fill in the missing premise in order to complete the syllogism.

MAJOR PREMISE: All those on the Dean's List are good students.

MINOR PREMISE: Melissa is on the Dean's List.

CONCLUSION: Therefore, Melissa is a good student.

Enthymemes often occur as compound sentences which contain words that signal conclusions—*therefore, consequently, for this reason, for, so, since,* or *because.* Notice how *so* in the following sentence indicates the presence of an enthymeme.

Deer are intelligent creatures, *so* they should not be hunted.

After the major premise is supplied, the structure of the argument becomes clear.

MAJOR PREMISE: Intelligent creatures should not be hunted.

MINOR PREMISE: Deer are intelligent creatures.

CONCLUSION: Therefore, deer should not be hunted.

Some writers deliberately use unstated assumptions in an attempt to unfairly influence an audience. By keeping their basic assumptions ambiguous or by pretending that assumptions are so self-evident that they need not be stated, these writers hope to influence an audience unfairly. All one need do to counter arguments like these is challenge the soundness of the unstated assumption. For example, the mayor of a large city recently said that the city would not provide aid to the homeless because doing so would require an increase in taxes. In this case, the underlying assumption is that a city should not be required to do anything that would cause it to raise taxes. Although some people would agree with the sentiment the mayor expressed, others would disagree. In the same respect, a recent advertisement encouraged readers to purchase a certain luxury automobile because it was the product of Japanese engineering. The unstated assumption is that Japanese engineering produces the best luxury cars. Although this proposition may have merit, it is not self-evident—as German, Italian, and American automobile manufacturers would attest.

Review: Inductive and Deductive Arguments

	Inductive	Deductive
The argument begins	with a hypothesis.	with a general statement or proposition.
The argument is supported	with specific observations or conclusions.	with a chain of reasoning.
The conclusion	can only be probable, never certain.	can be sound or unsound.
The reasoning	progresses by means of inference. The argument makes a statement about the unknown based on what is known.	progresses by means of the syllogism. The argument makes a statement about the known based on what is known.

EXERCISE 3

Read this essay carefully.

A nation succeeds only if the vast majority of its citizens succeed. It therefore stands to reason that with immigrants accounting for about

40 percent of our population growth, the future economic and social success of the United States is bound up with the success of these new Americans. Demography, in a word, is destiny.

This is an important principle to keep in mind as we try to come to grips with the problems and opportunities presented by the flood of legal and illegal immigrants from Mexico and other parts of South and Central America, who now constitute by far our largest immigrant group.

How are we doing in our efforts to assimilate these largely Hispanic newcomers and provide them with a bright future? Some signs are disturbing.

John Garcia, associate professor of political science at the University of Arizona, writing in International Migration Review, finds that the average rate of naturalization of Mexican immigrants is one-tenth that of other immigrant naturalization rates. The Select Commission on Immigration and Refugee Policy made a similar finding. Increasingly, immigrants are separated from everyone else by language, geography, ethnicity and class.

The future success of this country is closely linked to the ability of our immigrants to succeed. Yet 50 percent of our children of Hispanic background do not graduate from high school. Hispanic students score 100 points under the average student on Scholastic Aptitude Test scores. Hispanics have much higher rates of poverty, illiteracy and need for welfare than the national average. This engenders social crisis.

Not all the indicators of assimilation are pessimistic: the success of many Indochinese immigrants has been gratifying. But the warning signs of nonassimilation are increasing and ominous.

America must make sure the melting pot continues to melt: immigrants must become Americans. Seymour Martin Lipset, professor of political science and sociology at the Hoover Institution, Stanford University, observes: "The history of bilingual and bicultural societies that do not assimilate are histories of turmoil, tension and tragedy. Canada, Belgium, Malaysia, Lebanon—all face crises of national existence in which minorities press for autonomy, if not independence. Pakistan and Cyprus have divided. Nigeria suppressed an ethnic rebellion. France faces difficulties with its Basques, Bretons and Corsicans."

The United States is at a crossroads. If it does not consciously move toward greater integration, it will inevitably drift toward more fragmentation. It will either have to do better in assimilating all of the other peoples in its boundaries or it will witness increasing alienation and fragmentation. Cultural divisiveness is not a bedrock upon which a nation can be built. It is inherently unstable.

The nation faces a staggering social agenda. We have not adequately integrated blacks into our economy and society. Our education system is rightly described as "a rising tide of mediocrity." We have the most violent society in the industrial world; we have startlingly high rates of illiteracy, illegitimacy and welfare recipients.

It bespeaks a hubris to madly rush, with these unfinished social agendas, into accepting more immigrants and refugees than all of the rest of the world and then to still hope to keep a common agenda.

America can accept additional immigrants, but we must be sure that they become American. We can be a Joseph's coat of many nations, but we must be unified. One of the common glues that hold us together is language—the English language.

We should be color-blind but linguistically cohesive. We should be a rainbow but not a cacophony. We should welcome different peoples but not adopt different languages. We can teach English through bilingual education, but we should take great care not to become a bilingual society. (Richard D. Lamm, "English Comes First," *New York Times*)

A. Answer the following questions about the essay above.

1. In developing the preceding argument, Richard D. Lamm relies on a number of basic premises, assumptions about his subject which he expects his audience to share. What are some of these assumptions?
2. In paragraph 1 Lamm presents a deductive argument. Express this argument as a syllogism.
3. What kinds of information does Lamm use to support his position? What other kinds of evidence could he have used?
4. Where does Lamm state his conclusion? Restate the conclusion in your own words.

B. Evaluate the soundness of these arguments. (If the argument is in the form of an enthymeme, supply the missing term before evaluating the argument.)

1. All immigrants should speak English. If they do not, they are not real Americans.
2. Richard Lamm was born in the United States and grew up in an English-speaking household. Therefore, he has no credibility on the subject of bilingualism.
3. Spanish-speaking immigrants should be required by law to learn English. After all, most Eastern European immigrants who came to this country early in the twentieth century learned English.
4. If immigrants do not care enough about our country to learn English, we should not allow them to become citizens.
5. Some immigrants have become financially successful even though they did not learn English. Obviously, then, learning English does not increase an immigrant's chances for success.

6. All Cuban immigrants speak Spanish. Former San Antonio Mayor Henry Cisneros speaks Spanish, so he must be a Cuban immigrant.
7. As Seymour Martin Lipset points out, bilingual societies can be threatened by tension and political unrest. Therefore, it is important that immigrants not be bilingual.

6c *Recognizing Logical Fallacies*

Fallacies are indefensible flaws in arguments. Because they closely resemble sound arguments, fallacious arguments can seem convincing. Unscrupulous writers intentionally use such arguments, and even well-intentioned writers sometimes slip into them without realizing it. When readers detect these fallacies, they see the writer as illogical—or, worse, dishonest. Here are some common fallacies to watch for as you read and write.

(1) Hasty generalization

A **hasty generalization** occurs when you draw a conclusion on the basis of too little supporting information. A single bad experience with an elected official is not enough to warrant the statement that you will never vote again. In the same respect, one stimulating class taught by a certain instructor does not mean that all classes she teaches will be equally interesting. The number of examples you need to support a conclusion depends on the type of claim you are making. A few examples could be enough to make the point that you and your former boyfriend or girlfriend were incompatible. Many more would be needed to support the statement that Hispanic writers have a difficult time getting their work published by mainstream American publishers.

(2) Sweeping generalization

Sometimes confused with the hasty generalization, the **sweeping generalization** occurs when you apply a generalization that is usually justified to a situation where it is not warranted. In other words, you apply a fair generalization to an exceptional situation and ignore the peculiarities of the situation. Consider, for example, this statement:

Everyone should exercise. Therefore, Eric would feel a lot better if he exercised.

Certainly, many people would agree that exercise is a healthy activity. It does not, however, mean that a particular person should exercise. What if, for example, he or she has a heart condition?

(3)   Equivocation

You are guilty of **equivocation** when you shift the meaning of a key word during an argument so that your conclusion seems to follow logically from your premises.

Equivocation can be subtle. Consider this statement:

> It is in the public interest for the government to provide for the welfare of those who cannot help themselves. The public's interest becomes aroused, however, when it hears of welfare recipients getting thousands of dollars by cheating or by fraud.

In the first sentence, *public interest* refers to social good, and *welfare* to well-being. In the second sentence, *the public's interest* refers to self-interest and *welfare* to financial assistance provided by the government.

(4)   The either/or fallacy

The **either/or fallacy** occurs when you analyze a complex situation as if it has only two sides when actually it has more. If you ask whether American involvement in Central America is beneficial or harmful, you acknowledge only two possibilities, ruling out all others. In fact, American involvement in some Central American countries may be beneficial, but in others it may be harmful. Or in any given country it may be *both* beneficial and harmful. Avoid the either/or fallacy by acknowledging the complexity of an issue. Do not misrepresent issues by limiting them.

Of course, *some* either/or situations lead to valid conclusions. In biology lab, a test either will or will not indicate the presence of a certain enzyme. To be valid, an either/or statement must encompass *every* possible alternative. The premise "Either Kim took the test or she did not" is valid. There are no other possibilities. But the premise "Either Kim took the test or she went to the Student Health Center" is an example of the either/or fallacy. To disprove the statement, all someone has to do is point out that Kim went somewhere else.

(5)   Post hoc, ergo propter hoc

Post hoc, ergo propter hoc is Latin for "after this, therefore because of this." The **post hoc** fallacy occurs when you mistakenly infer that because one event follows another in time, the events are causally related. Many arguments depend on establishing cause-and-effect relationships, but the link between the causes and effects presented must actually exist. In some arguments this is not the case. For example, after the United States sold wheat to the U.S.S.R., the price of wheat and wheat products rose dramatically. Many people blamed the wheat sale for this rapid increase. One event followed another closely in time, so people falsely assumed that the first event caused the second. In fact, a complicated series of farm-price controls that had been in effect for years was the actual cause of increases in wheat prices.

Make certain that you identify the actual causes and effects of the events you discuss. Cause-and-effect relationships are difficult to prove, so you may have to rely on expert testimony to support your claim.

(6) Begging the question

You **beg the question** when you restate the conclusion you intend to prove as a premise. Often this fallacy occurs when a person incorrectly assumes that a proposition is so obvious that it needs no proof. Consider this exchange:

"I believe in Darwin's Theory of Evolution."

"Why?"

"Because Darwin says it is so."

"But why should we believe Darwin?"

"Because he formulated the Theory of Evolution."

As you can see, this argument ends where it begins. The initial premise assumes the truth of Darwin's Theory of Evolution, which is exactly what is at issue. In other words, the argument goes in a circle.

Begging the question is not always as obvious as it is in the example above. In some cases it can be subtle.

Sadistic experiments on animals should be stopped because they clearly constitute cruel and unusual punishment.

Certainly sadistic experimentation is cruel. What has to be proven, however, is that the experiments actually are sadistic. By simply saying the same thing twice, the person making this argument side-steps this issue entirely.

(7) False analogy

Analogies—extended comparisons—are useful in arguments. They enable you to explain something unfamiliar by comparing it to something familiar (**see 4f6**). Skillfully used, an analogy can be quite convincing, as when Henry David Thoreau illustrates the futility of warfare by comparing an ant battle to a human battle. By itself, however, an analogy establishes nothing; it is no substitute for supporting information. In a freshman essay you might compare students at registration to rats in a maze: both are rewarded if they succeed and punished if they do not. But people are not rats, and you would still have to provide support if your purpose would show the shortcomings of the registration process.

A **false analogy** (or faulty analogy) assumes that because issues or concepts are similar in some ways, they are similar in other ways. On a television talk show recently, a psychiatrist was asked to explain why people commit crimes. He replied:

> Some people commit crimes because they are selfish or psychotic. Others are like pregnant women who know they shouldn't smoke but do anyway. They have a craving that they have to give in to. The answer is not to punish criminals, but to understand their behavior and to try to change it.

Admittedly, the analogy between a certain group of criminals and pregnant women who smoke is convincing. However, it oversimplifies the issue. A pregnant woman does not intend to harm her unborn child by smoking; many criminals do intend to harm their victims. To undercut the doctor's argument, you need only point out the shortcomings of his analogy.

(8) Red herring

The **red herring** fallacy occurs when you change the subject to distract your audience from the actual issue. Consider, for example, the statement "This company may charge high prices, but they do give a great deal of money to charity each year." The latter observation has nothing to do with the former but somehow manages to obscure it.

Many people use this fallacy when backed into a corner. By switching the subject, they hope to change direction and begin their argument on safer ground. Here is an example from a student essay:

> The appeals court should overturn the lower court's decision to allow females to attend previously all-male Central High School. One

can only wonder if the school board members who support this decision should not have more pressing things on their minds. Perhaps they should spend more time wondering how they will finance public education in this city next year.

This argument avoids discussing what it sets out to prove. Instead of explaining why women should not be allowed to attend Central High, the writer introduces an irrelevant point about financing public education.

(9) Argument to ignorance (argumentum ad ignorantiam)

The **argument to ignorance** fallacy occurs when you say that something is true because you cannot prove it false or say that something is false because you cannot prove it true. This fallacy occurred recently during a debate about allowing children who have been infected with AIDS to attend public school. A parent asked an AIDS researcher, "How can you tell me to send my child to school where there are children with AIDS? After all, you doctors can't say for sure that my child won't catch AIDS from these children." In other words, the parent was saying, "My children are likely to contract AIDS from other children in school because it has never been proven that they cannot." As persuasive as this line of reasoning can sometimes be, it is logically flawed. The fact remains that no evidence has been presented to support the speaker's conclusion.

(10) Bandwagon

The **bandwagon** fallacy occurs when you try to establish that something is true or worthwhile because everyone believes that it is ("20 million Frenchmen can't be wrong!"). This appeal is the same as saying that a television program must be good because it has high ratings. A recent newspaper editorial makes the point that a state should raise the speed limit on its highways to sixty-five miles an hour because nearly everyone exceeds the present fifty-five mile an hour limit. Instead of focusing on the lack of merit of the present limit, the editorial relies on an appeal to numbers. Certainly, the fact that many people ignore the speed limit is important, but this fact does not in itself establish that the speed limit should be raised.

(11) Skewed sample

The **skewed sample** is a problem that can occur during the collection of statistical evidence. To present accurate results, a statistical sample should be *representative;* that is, it should be typical of the broader population it represents. When a statistical sample is collected so that it favors one segment of the population over others, it is said to be *skewed.* For example, a study of the spending habits of Americans would most likely be skewed in favor of relatively affluent individuals if it were based on respondents chosen from lists of luxury-car owners. Similarly, census questions asked only in English would disproportionately skew results in favor of English-speaking respondents.

(12) You also (tu quoque)

The **you also** fallacy occurs when you say that a point has no merit because the person making it does not follow his or her own advice. Such an argument is irrelevant because it focuses attention on the person rather than on the issue being debated.

If you think that exercise is beneficial, why don't you exercise?

You're telling me to invest wisely? Look at how much money you lost in the commodities market last year.

(13) Argument to the person (ad hominem)

Arguments *ad hominem* attack a person rather than an issue. By casting aspersions on an opponent, they turn attention away from the facts of the case. Here are two examples:

That woman has criticized the president's commitment to equal rights for women. But she believes in parapsychology. She thinks that she can communicate with the dead.

Congressman Rodriguez supports the deployment of the MX missile. What do you expect from a man who worked for a defense contractor before he ran for public office?

When a topic is controversial, this tactic can work. But although you may persuade some people, others will recognize the fallacy and question your credibility.

(14)   Argument to the people (ad populum)

Arguments *ad populum* appeal to people's prejudices. A presidential candidate seeking support in a state whose textile industry has been hurt by foreign competition may allude to "foreigners who are attempting to overrun our shores." By exploiting prejudices of the audience, the candidate is able to avoid the concrete issues of the campaign. Of course, many political speeches contain emotional appeals—to patriotism, for instance—and this is fine. These appeals should be taken for what they are—an effort to establish good will—and should not substitute for specific support.

Guide to Logical Fallacies

- **Hasty Generalization**   Drawing a conclusion on the basis of too little evidence
- **Sweeping Generalization**   Applying a generalization that is usually true to a situation that may be an exception
- **Equivocation**   Shifting the meaning of a key word during an argument
- **Either/Or Fallacy**   Treating a complex issue as if it has only two sides
- ***Post Hoc***   Establishing an unjustified link between cause and effect
- **Begging the Question**   Stating a debatable premise as if it were true
- **False Analogy**   Assuming that because things are similar in some ways they are similar in other ways
- **Red Herring**   Changing the subject to distract your audience from the issue
- **Argument to Ignorance**   Saying that something is true because it cannot be proven false, or vice versa
- **Bandwagon**   Trying to establish that something is true because everyone believes it is true
- **Skewed Sample**   Collecting a statistical sample so that it favors one population over another
- **You Also**   Accusing a person of not upholding the position that he or she advocates
- **Argument to the Person**   Attacking the person and not the issue
- **Argument to the People**   Appealing to the prejudices of the people

EXERCISE 4

Identify the fallacies in the following statements. In each case, name the fallacy and rewrite the statement to correct the problem.

1. Dr. Spock is a brilliant physician. He should use his education to help the sick instead of criticizing the nation's nuclear policy.

2. My opponent says that he wants to be mayor. He has been divorced twice. Obviously, he should get his own life in order before he thinks of running for public office.

3. How can we not support railroads? Railroads are the arteries of our nation, and the trains are the lifeblood that bring sustenance to all parts of the country.

4. The school's mail-in registration program will either make things easier for students or result in total chaos.

5. During the last flight of the space shuttle, there was heavy rainfall throughout the entire Northeast. Therefore, the launch must have disturbed the weather patterns for that region of the country.

6. I just received a pamphlet that urges people to buy savings bonds. How can the government talk about saving? Look at the size of the national debt.

7. What former President Nixon did was wrong, but many people in public office have done a lot worse.

8. No truly intelligent person would deny that the government's welfare programs are shamefully mismanaged.

9. Public utilities must accept responsibility for their actions. Therefore, the public should make certain that the indigent and elderly get heat this winter.

10. No responsible scientist has been able to establish that smoking will definitely cause lung cancer in a particular individual. Therefore, we can ignore the warnings of the surgeon general.

7

Writing an Argumentative Essay

The major purpose of many essays is to convey information. In these essays you expect readers to accept your points at face value. In argument, however, you assume that your audience needs to be convinced that your claims are valid. When you set out to convince an audience, you rely on various appeals—to the emotions, to reason, and to ethics. But although most effective arguments combine a number of different kinds of appeals, their primary appeal is to reason.

When you write an argumentative essay, you follow the same process you use to construct any essay, but your purpose makes necessary some special strategies. Over and above these strategies, though, argument requires you not only to evaluate your own ideas but also to evaluate the ideas of others. In this sense, argument asks you to think critically.

7a Planning an Argumentative Essay

When you plan an argumentative essay, you must choose a debatable topic, formulate an argumentative thesis, define your terms, accommodate your audience, deal with opposing arguments, gather evidence, establish your credibility, and present your points fairly.

(1) Choosing a topic

You should base your argumentative essay on a *debatable* topic, one about which people disagree. "Chromium is a metallic element" is not debatable; it is a fact. But "We should not do business with South Africa even though we need South African chromite" is debatable. Reasonable people could debate this statement by presenting evidence for or against it.

In addition to being debatable, your topic should be one about which you know something. The more evidence you can provide, the more likely you are to sway your audience. General knowledge is seldom convincing by itself, so you will probably have to do some reading and perhaps some research. But remember, you must do more than rehash tired arguments that everyone has already heard. Unless you have something new to say, stay away from topics such as abortion, nuclear war, legalization of marijuana, and the death penalty.

You should also understand what you want to accomplish in an argumentative essay. Your purpose is to change or clarify your reader's view of an issue. To accomplish this end, you must be able to define both sides of an issue, isolate crucial points, and state your own ideas. If you cannot do so, you will not be able to make a very effective argument.

Finally, it helps if you care about your topic, but that is not an absolute requirement. In fact, when you feel very strongly about an issue, you may not be able to view it clearly. If this is the case, consider another topic, or consider writing an argument for the other side. (Dr. Samuel Johnson, the eighteenth-century lexicographer and critic, said that he preferred to argue on the wrong side of an issue because all the interesting things were to be said there.)

(2) Formulating an argumentative thesis

Your next step is to state your position in an argumentative thesis that asserts or denies something about your topic. Properly cast, this thesis lays the foundation for the rest of your argument.

Because the purpose of an argumentative essay is to convince readers to accept your position, your thesis must take a stand. One way to make sure that your thesis actually does take a stand is to formulate an **antithesis,** a statement that takes an arguable position opposite from yours. If you can create an antithesis, your main idea takes a stand. If you cannot, your statement needs further revision to make it an argumentative thesis.

THESIS	ANTITHESIS
Put the blame [for prize-fighter Benny Paret's death] where it	Paret's death cannot be blamed on the prevailing mores that

belongs—on the prevailing mores that regard prize-fighting as a perfectly proper enterprise and vehicle of entertainment.

regard prize-fighting as a perfectly proper enterprise and vehicle of entertainment.

(3) Defining your terms

You and your readers must agree about the terms you use in your argument. An argument that one rock group is superior to another means nothing unless your audience knows how you define *superior rock group.* Never assume that everybody will know exactly what you mean.

As a rule, you should avoid imprecise language. When you decide on a thesis, revise to eliminate vague words such as *wrong, bad, good, right,* and *immoral,* which convey different meanings to different people.

ORIGINAL: Censorship of pay TV would be wrong.

REVISED: Censorship of pay TV would unfairly limit free trade.

In the first sentence above, the thesis is vague and nearly meaningless; the revised thesis uses terms that can be clearly defined.

(4) Accommodating your audience

Plan your strategy with a specific audience in mind. The ideal situation is to address an audience with which you are familiar, but ideal situations are rare. Who are your readers? Are they unbiased observers or people deeply concerned about the issue you plan to discuss? Can they be cast in a specific role—concerned parents, victims of discrimination, irate consumers—or are they so diverse that they cannot be categorized? If you cannot be certain who your readers are, you will have to direct your arguments to a general audience (see 1a2).

In an argument your aim is to bring your audience to a position closer to your own. You cannot do this effectively if you expect your readers to accept what you say without question. You must instead deal with their objections and use evidence to support your conclusion.

(5) Dealing with opposing arguments

To argue effectively, you must know how to refute opposing arguments. You can do this by showing that opposing views are untrue, unfair, illogical, unimportant, or irrelevant. In an essay criticizing the unfair practices associated with whaling, a student refutes an argument against her position.

> Of course there are some who say Sea World only wants to capture a few whales. George Will makes this point in his commentary in *Newsweek*, pointing out how valuable the research on whales would be. Unfortunately, Will downplays the fact that Sea World wants to capture a hundred whales, not just "a few." And after releasing ninety whales, Sea World intends to keep ten for "further work." At hearings in Seattle last week, several noted marine biologists went on record condemning Sea World's research program. We must wonder, as they do, why Sea World needs such a large number of whales to carry out its project.

After acknowledging her opponent's position, the student questions its accuracy and supports her point by summarizing the testimony of several marine biologists.

When an opponent's position is so strong that it cannot be dismissed, admit that the point is well taken, and then, if possible, discuss its limitations. Martin Luther King, Jr., uses this tactic in his "Letter from Birmingham Jail."

> You express a great deal of anxiety over our willingness to break laws. This is certainly a legitimate concern. Since we so diligently urge people to obey the Supreme Court's decision of 1954 outlawing segregation in the public schools, at first glance it may seem rather paradoxical for us consciously to break laws. One may well ask: "How can you advocate breaking some laws and obeying others?" The answer lies in the fact that there are two types of laws: just and unjust. I would be the first to advocate obeying just laws. One has not only a legal but a moral responsibility to obey just laws. Conversely, one has a moral responsibility to disobey unjust laws. I would agree with St. Augustine that "an unjust law is no law at all."

King first acknowledges his audience's legitimate concern about his willingness to break laws. He then counters their objections by distinguishing between just and unjust laws. With this tactic King hopes to overcome audience resistance and gain support for his views.

Revision Close-up

When you acknowledge an opposing view, do not distort it or present it as ridiculously weak. This tactic, called creating a **straw man**, could seriously undermine your credibility.

(6) Gathering evidence

Most arguments are built on assertions (claims you make about your topic) backed by **evidence**—the supporting information, in the form of examples, statistics, or expert opinion, which reinforces your argument. You could, for instance, assert that law-enforcement officials are losing the war against violent crime. You could then support this assertion by referring to a government report stating that violent crime in the ten largest U.S. cities has increased during the last five years. This report would be one piece of persuasive evidence.

Certain assertions need no proof: statements that are *self-evident* ("All human beings are mortal"), statements that are true by *definition* (2 + 2 = 4), and *statements of fact* that you can expect the average person to know ("The Atlantic Ocean separates England and the United States"). Other kinds of assertions need supporting evidence.

Remember that an argumentative essay never proves a thesis conclusively—if it did, there would be no argument. The best you can do is to establish a high probability that your thesis is correct or establish that it is reasonable. Choose your supporting information with this idea in mind.

(7) Establishing your credibility

Clear reasoning, compelling evidence, and intelligent refutations go a long way toward making an argument solid. But in themselves, these elements are not sufficient to create a compelling argument. In order to sway readers, you have to convince them that you are someone they should listen to—in other words, that you have credibility.

Certain individuals, of course, bring credibility with them every time they speak. When a Nobel Prize winner in physics makes a speech about the need to control nuclear waste, we automatically assume that he or she knows the subject. But most people do not have this kind of authority and so must work to establish it—by finding common ground, demonstrating knowledge, and maintaining a reasonable tone.

Finding Common Ground   When you write an argument, it is tempting to go on the attack, emphasizing the differences between your position and those of your opponents. However, this tactic can antagonize not only readers who do not agree with you, but also those who might be sympathetic. Just as in labor negotiations and foreign policy, lack of agreement can cause animosity, mistrust, and eventually a total breakdown of communications. Writers of effective arguments know that they must avoid this deterioration at all costs. One way to avoid a confrontational posture, and thereby increase your credibility, is to think of the members of your audience as colleagues with whom you must collaborate to find solutions. Instead of verbally assaulting them, try to establish points of agreement. In this way, you establish common ground and work toward a resolution of the issue you are discussing.

Thomas Jefferson establishes common ground, for example, at the beginning of the Declaration of Independence when he presents the self-evident truths that he feels all people will accept. In "Letter from Birmingham Jail," Martin Luther King, Jr. also employs this strategy when he takes great pains to demonstrate to his audience of white clergy that they share the same goal—to fight injustice—and differ only on the methods that should be used to eliminate the problems. Of course, Thomas Jefferson could have attacked England, and Martin Luther King, Jr. could have called the white clergy bigots, but they knew that these comments would have alienated their audiences and undermined their own credibility.

Demonstrating Knowledge   Although writers tend to avoid using their personal experiences when they write an argument, pertinent personal experiences can show readers that you know a lot about your subject and thus give you some authority. Your attendance at a National Rifle Association conference can give you authority when you write an essay arguing for (or against) gun control. Similarly, the fact that you worked for a landscaping company can give you credibility when you argue for (or against) banning certain lawn-care products.

You can also establish credibility by showing you have done research into a subject. By mentioning important research sources you have consulted and documenting the information you got from them, you show readers that you have done the necessary groundwork. Including references to several sources—not just one—suggests to readers that you have a balanced knowledge of your subject.

Revision Close-up

Make certain that you document source material very carefully. Questionable sources, inaccurate documentation, and factual errors can undermine an argument. To many readers, an undocumented quotation or even an incorrect date can call an entire paper into question.

Maintaining a Reasonable Tone   The tone you adopt is almost as important as the information you convey. A confident tone helps convince readers that you have a firm grasp of your subject. Consider the difference between these statements:

TENTATIVE

In my opinion the savings and loan failures of 1990 and 1991 were probably precipitated by the Tax Reform Law of 1986.

CONFIDENT

The savings and loan failures of 1990 and 1991 were precipitated by the Tax Reform Law of 1986.

Avoiding sounding high-handed or pedantic. Talk *to* your readers, not *at* them. If you lecture your readers or appear to talk down to them, you will only succeed in alienating them. Remember, readers are more likely to respond to a writer who is conciliatory than one who is insulting. At the end of "Letter from Birmingham Jail," for example, Martin Luther King, Jr. deliberately understates his position, saying that he hopes that he did not go so far that he insulted his readers. In this way, King not only reassures his readers but also reinforces his thesis.

In addition, use moderate language. Words and phrases like *never, all,* and *in every case* can make your claims seem exaggerated and unrealistic. Learn to qualify your statements so that they seem reasonable. The statement "Mercy killing is never acceptable," for example, leaves no room for debate or differing points of view. A more conciliatory statement would be "In cases of extreme suffering one can understand a patient's desire for death, but in most cases the moral and social implications of mercy killing make it unacceptable." By qualifying your position, you demonstrate that you are making every effort to adopt a reasonable point of view.

Guidelines for Establishing Your Credibility

Finding Common Ground

- Identify the various sides of the issue.

continued

continued from previous page

- Identify the points on which you and your readers are in agreement.
- Work the areas of agreement into your argument.

Demonstrating Knowledge

- Include relevant personal experiences.
- Include relevant special knowledge of your subject.
- Include the results of any relevant research you have done.

Maintaining a Reasonable Tone

- Use a confident tone.
- Avoid sounding high-handed or pedantic.
- Use moderate language and qualify your statements.

(8) Being fair

The line between being persuasive and being unfair is a fine one, and no clear-cut rules exist to help you make this distinction. Writers of effective and sometimes brilliant argumentative essays are often less than fair to their opponents. We could hardly call Jonathan Swift "fair" when, in "A Modest Proposal," he implies that the English are cannibals. A supporter of George III would argue that Thomas Jefferson and the other writers of the Declaration of Independence were less than fair when they criticized British policy in America.

Of course, "A Modest Proposal" is bitter satire, and Swift employs overstatement to express his rage at social conditions. In justifying their break with England, the writers of the Declaration of Independence did not intend to be fair to the king. Argument promotes one point of view, so it is seldom objective.

For better or for worse, however, college writing requires that you stay within the bounds of fairness. To be sure that your support is not misleading or distorted, you should learn to avoid the following.

Distorting Evidence   Distortion is misrepresentation. Writers sometimes intentionally misrepresent their opponents' views by exaggerating them and then attacking this extreme position. For example, an incumbent senator delivered a speech in which he said that unless something was done soon, the Social Security Trust Fund would run out of money in ten years. He added that a possible solution was to eliminate certain cost-of-living increases that were due to go into effect. His opponent attacked him by saying that clearly he was in favor of curtailing benefits to older Americans. Where would he stop? Would he eliminate benefits? Would he scrap the whole Social Security system? What about Medicare? Medicaid? Welfare? Anyone who could support such actions, his opponent said, did not deserve public office.

The senator said only that something had to be done to keep the Social Security system solvent. His opponent could have challenged his assertion and his proposed solution with facts and figures. Instead, by distorting his position, she attacked it unfairly.

Quoting Out of Context   A writer or speaker quotes out of context by taking someone's words from their original setting and using them in another. When you select certain words from a statement and ignore others, you can change the meaning of what someone has said or implied. Consider this example:

Mr. N, township resident

   I don't know why you are opposing the new highway. According to your own statements the highway will increase land value and bring more business into the area.

Ms. L, township supervisor

   I think you should look at my statements more carefully. I have a copy of the paper that printed my interview and what I said was [*reading*]: "The highway will increase land values a bit and bring some business to the area. But at what cost? One hundred and fifty families will be displaced, and the highway will divide our township in half." My comments were not meant to support the new highway but to underscore the problems that its construction will cause.

By repeating only some of Ms. L's remarks, Mr. N alters her meaning to suit his purpose. In context, Ms. L's words indicate that although she acknowledges the highway's few benefits, she believes that its drawbacks outweigh them.

Slanting Supporting Information   When you select information that supports your case and ignore information that does not, you are slanting. For example, if you support your position that smoking should not be prohibited in public places by choosing only evidence provided by the American Tobacco Institute, you are guilty of slanting supporting information. Inflammatory language also biases your writing. A national magazine slanted its information, to say the least, when it described a reputed criminal as "a hulk of a man who looks as if he could burn out somebody's eyes with a propane torch." Although one-sided presentations do appear in newspapers and magazines, you should avoid such distortions when you seek to present a rational argument.

7b   *Shaping an Argumentative Essay*

In its simplest form, an argument consists of a thesis and supporting evidence. However, argumentative essays contain additional elements calculated to win audience approval and to overcome potential opposition. Depending upon your purpose and audience; you may choose to arrange these elements in various ways; in some cases, you may decide to omit one or more elements entirely.

Elements of an Argumentative Essay

The Introduction

The introduction of your argumentative essay orients your audience to your subject and helps to convince them that your subject is something about which they should be concerned. Here you can show how your subject concerns the reader, note why it is interesting, or explain how it has been misunderstood.

See
4g2 ◄

The Background Statement

In this section you present the background of the subject you will discuss. By giving readers an overview, you enable them to understand the more detailed points and refutations that you will present later. This section may include a narrative of past events, a summary of others' opinions on your subject, or a statement of the basic facts of an issue. Keep your background statement short; long, drawn-out discussions at this point will distract your readers from the focus of your argument.

The Thesis Statement

Your thesis statement can appear anywhere in your argumentative essay. Frequently, you present your thesis after you have given your readers an overview of your subject. However, in highly controversial arguments—those to which your audience might react negatively—you may

---

postpone your thesis until the end of your essay. Whatever the case, your thesis should clearly convey your position to your readers.

The Arguments in Support of Your Thesis

This section is the center of your essay; it contains the deductive or inductive arguments, or a combination of the two, that you will use to support your thesis. Here you present your points and the evidence you have gathered to support them.

One problem you may have at this stage is deciding on the arrangement of your points. Most often, you begin with your weakest argument and work up to your strongest. If you move in the opposite direction, your essay will be anticlimactic. Not only would you emphasize your weakest arguments by putting them last, but you would also make it appear as if these arguments were afterthoughts. If all your arguments are equally strong, you can arrange them in any way; however, you might want to begin with points with which your readers are already familiar and which they are likely to accept and then move on to relatively unfamiliar points. In this way, the familiar paves the way for the unfamiliar.

The Refutation of Opposing Arguments

In a face-to-face debate, you are confronted by the arguments against your thesis, and you have the opportunity to refute them. In an argumentative essay, however, you must bring these points up yourself: you must anticipate these arguments and question their soundness. If you do not confront these opposing arguments, doubts about your case will remain in the minds of your readers. If strong opposing arguments exist, admit their strengths and then refute the arguments early in your paper, before you present your own points. (If the opposing arguments are relatively weak, refute them after you have made your case.)

The Conclusion

Your conclusion can summarize key points, restate your thesis, reinforce the weaknesses of opposing arguments, or underscore the logic of your position. Most often, the conclusion restates in general terms the major arguments that you have marshaled in support of your thesis. This tactic brings your argument into focus and, for this reason, can have a powerful effect on readers. Many writers like to end their arguments with a strong last line, one calculated to stay in the minds of their readers. An apt quotation or a statement that crystallizes the sentiments or captures the intensity of your argument works well.

7c *Writing and Revising an Argumentative Essay*

(1) *Writing an argumentative essay*

The following draft of an essay contains many of the elements listed in the box on pages 154–155. The student, Lauren Sklar, was asked by her instructor to write an argument. She was told to rely primarily on her own experience, but she was given permission to include expert opinion supplied by her father, an amateur dog breeder. Library research, although not required, was permitted.

In Defense of Pit Bulls

Introduction

1   Throughout this coming year, many state legislatures will consider laws that could result in the persecution of an entire group of individuals. These laws make possible the confiscation of private property, the imposition of fines, and the criminal prosecution of people who are guilty of nothing more than owning a dog. As difficult as it may be to believe, these things are already happening to the thousands of people all over the United States who own a breed of dog commonly referred to as pit bulls.

Background
statement

2   The term <u>pit bull</u> is applied to a number of mixed breeds related to the American bull terrier. This animal is sleek, agile, strong loyal--and yes, lovable. Lately, these animals have achieved notoriety--especially on the television evening news--because of their attacks against human beings. The reports are usually accompanied by lurid pictures of the mangled limbs of victims and by adjectives such as "vicious" and "bloodthirsty." As a result of this publicity, some states have proposed laws that would make it a crime to own a pit bull. The

penalty for violating these laws is often
severe—destruction of the animal, stiff fines,
and sometimes even imprisonment of the owner.

Thesis   Not only are these prohibitions unconstitutional,
but they also reflect ideas about pit bulls that
are not supported by the facts.

Refutation of   3   It cannot be denied that the pit bull is a
opposing
arguments   formidable fighter and can be frightening when
provoked. Both adults and children have been
mauled by these animals, most often when they
unknowingly encroached on a pit bull's territory.
All dogs have strong territorial instincts and
will fight to protect their property. The pit
bull is no different. It will lunge from behind
a fence or actually attack an individual whom it
thinks is threatening an area that it has marked.

Refutation of   4   Although it is true that pit bulls have been
opposing
arguments   bred to be fighters, they are not people-haters.
As most owners will testify, attacking humans is
against the nature of pit bulls, just as it is
against the nature of most dogs. Certainly, pit
bulls have been used as weapons by some
individuals—inner-city gang members and drug
dealers immediately come to mind. But the fact
that these misguided owners abuse their animals
does not mean that the whole breed is bad and
should be outlawed. Outlawing pit bulls would
make as much sense as outlawing all automobiles
because just a few are used to commit crimes.

Deductive   5   In America a person is considered innocent
argument
until proven guilty. This principle is one of
the cornerstones of our democratic system of
government. Most people would agree that any law
that violates this precept is unjust and,
therefore, unconstitutional. Much of the
legislation that is aimed at pit bull owners,

however, subjects them to penalties before any harm has been done. One ordinance in Massachusetts makes it a crime to own the "Staffordshire pit bull terrier or bull terrier or any mixture thereof." This law mandates that pit bulls be destroyed, even if they are gentle animals. By indiscriminately condemning all pit bulls, such statutes clearly violate the owners' rights.

Inductive argument supported by expert opinion and personal experience

6   What is most disturbing about the recent movement to legislate against pit bull owners is how misinformed lawmakers seem to be. Take, for example, the charge that pit bulls are more vicious than other breeds. My father, who is an amateur breeder and who has handled pit bulls, says that no scientific evidence exists to support this claim. I myself have handled pit bulls and find them to be no more likely to bite than other dogs. In fact, according to my father, German shepherds, Labrador retrievers, Rottweilers, and assorted mongrels bite more frequently than do pit bulls. In the world of professional dog handlers and trainers, essayist and pit bull owner Vicki Hearne points out, "pit bulls are generally recognized as an amiable, easygoing lot." In this world, she notes, "there are no horror stories about pit bulls" (243).

Inductive argument supported by examples

7   Another area of misinformation concerns the severity of the injuries caused by pit bulls. Many dogs have the ability to inflict damage with their teeth. Every year thousands of dog bites are reported; most are minor, but some are quite severe. Although pit bulls have very powerful jaws and bite using a ripping motion, their bites are no more severe than those of many other breeds. According to my father, collies and

cocker spaniels, for example, not only bite more frequently, but also are responsible for many more serious injuries each year than are pit bulls. These breeds are high-strung, nervous, and unpredictable. In contrast, pit bulls, despite their reputations, are generally even-tempered, calm, and loyal.

Conclusion   8   It is understandable that state legislators want to protect people from the attacks of vicious dogs. But unlike existing laws that hold owners responsible for the actions of their pets, laws that apply to a single breed will not help the public. This shortsighted approach ignores the fact it is the individual dog, not the entire breed, that is dangerous. Outlawing an entire breed not only violates the rights of owners, but also undermines the freedom of all individuals.

Strong closing statement   By so doing, these proposed laws would seem to be more dangerous to the public than a pit bull could ever be.

Work Cited

Hearne, Vicki. "Consider the Pit Bull." The Contemporary Essay. Ed. Donald Hall. 2nd ed. New York: St. Martin's, 1989. 239–52.

(2) Revising an argumentative essay

You revise your argumentative essay using the same strategies you use for any essay (**see 3c**). In addition, you concentrate on the specific concerns of argument that are listed in the following checklist.

Revision Checklist: Argumentative Essays

- Is your topic debatable?
- Does your essay include an argumentative thesis?

continued

159

continued from previous page

- Have you adequately defined the terms you use in your argument?
- Have your considered the opinions, attitudes, and values of your audience?
- Have you identified and refuted opposing arguments?
- Have you supported your assertions with evidence?
- Have you established your credibility?
- Have you been fair? Have you been accurate?
- Are your arguments logically constructed?
- Have you avoided logical fallacies?
- Does the structure of your essay suit your material and your audience?
- Have you provided your readers with enough background information?
- Do you present your points clearly and organize them logically?
- Do you have an interesting introduction and a strong conclusion?

EXERCISE 1

The following paragraph was deleted by Lauren Sklar from the essay "In Defense of Pit Bulls." Was Lauren right to delete it? If it belongs in the essay, where would it go? Is it relevant? Logical? Jot down your responses in the margins of the essay, and be prepared to discuss them in class.

Another problem with these ordinances is that they ignore the fact that every decade seems to have its canine villains. During the nineteen forties the German shepherd achieved notoriety because of its use in concentration camps by the Nazis. In the nineteen fifties the chow was reputed to be a vicious animal that would turn without provocation on its owner. The seventies saw the Doberman pinscher take its place in the public mind as a fierce killer. No doubt several years from today the public will fix its gaze on another breed, and the pit bull will regain the anonymity that it formerly enjoyed. Although the laws that focus on a specific breed like the pit bull may be politically expedient, they do little to protect the public or to identify unsafe animals.

WRITING AN ARGUMENTATIVE ESSAY

Revise the following draft of an argumentative essay, paying particular attention to the essay's logic and to the use of support. Be prepared to explain the changes you made and how they make the essay more convincing. If necessary, revise further to strengthen coherence, unity, and style.

The Gun Question

Years ago, guns were essential for obtaining food to feed many families. However, since we started domesticating animals, guns have become less important for obtaining food. Instead, they have been widely used for crimes and have caused many accidents. When respected and used properly, however, guns can improve, protect, and even save many people's lives.

Some people feel that if guns were outlawed, fewer murders, robberies, and gun-related accidents would occur. These people do not know what they are talking about. If guns were taken away, only the honest citizens would give up their guns. The criminals and the government would be the only people who had guns. We would be at the mercy of outlaws and the good will of the government. Perhaps the people who oppose guns should worry more about tyranny than about the violation of criminals' rights.

Opponents of guns often suggest that all firearms in this country should be registered. The registration of firearms, however, is the first step toward confiscation. If firearms were confiscated, the next step would be a totalitarian government. There would be no armed citizenry to ensure that the Bill of Rights is enforced. Would the people who favor the registration of guns like it if the government took away their houses, their cars, or even their money?

The Constitution guarantees all citizens the right to

bear arms. The Founding Fathers realized that an armed citizenry is the best defense against tyranny. Look at some of the countries that have forbidden private citizens from owning guns. In Nazi Germany only the army could have guns. If a citizen was caught with a gun, he or she was killed. In the Soviet Union only certain people can own weapons. Anyone else who has a gun is thought to be an enemy of the state. The same holds true for Chile, Iran, and China.

In addition to protecting our rights, guns enable citizens to protect their lives. Every issue of The American Rifleman presents at least a dozen or more examples of honest people using guns to protect their lives and their possessions. These articles show how different types of people have been able to stop criminals. Store owners, housewives, and even children have used guns for protection against criminals. Anyone who cannot accept this evidence obviously has trouble accepting the truth.

Although some people fear guns and their misuse, guns are an important and beneficial factor in our lives. If guns were outlawed, only the criminals and the government would have guns. This fact should be enough to convince anyone how necessary guns are.

P A R T 3

Composing Sentences

8

Building Simple Sentences

8a   *Identifying the Basic Sentence Elements*

A **sentence** is an independent grammatical unit that contains a subject and a predicate and expresses a complete thought.

It came from outer space.

Easter Island is a Chilean island in the South Pacific.

A **simple subject** is a noun or noun substitute (*it, Easter Island*) that tells who or what the sentence is about. A **simple predicate** is a verb or verb phrase (*came, is*) that tells or asks something about the subject. The **complete subject** of a sentence, however, includes all the words associated with the subject, and the **complete predicate** includes not only the verb or verb phrase but all the words associated with it.

8b   *Constructing Basic Sentence Patterns*

A **simple sentence** consists of at least one subject and one predicate. The most basic English sentences may be built from one of the following five patterns.

(1) *Subject + intransitive verb (s + v)*

The simplest sentence pattern consists of only a subject and a verb or verb phrase.

The price of gold rose.

Stock prices may fall.

In both sentences the verbs (*rose, may fall*) are **intransitive**—that is, they have no direct objects. (A dictionary can tell you which verbs are transitive, which are intransitive, and which may be either, depending on context.)

(2)   Subject + transitive verb + direct object
(s + v + do)

In another pattern, the sentence consists of the subject, a transitive verb, and a direct object. A **transitive** verb is one that requires an object to complete its meaning in the sentence. A **direct object** indicates where the verb's action is directed and who or what is affected by it.

s   v   do
Van Gogh created The Starry Night.

s   v   do
Caroline saved Jake.

In each sentence the direct object tells *who* or *what* received the verb's action.

(3)   Subject + transitive verb + direct object + object
complement (s + v + do + oc)

This pattern, similar to the one above, includes an **object complement** that renames or describes the direct object.

s   v   do   oc
The class elected Bridget treasurer.

s v   do   oc
I found the exam easy.

In the first sentence the object complement is a noun that renames the object; in the second it is an adjective that describes the object.

(4)   Subject + linking verb + subject complement
(s + v + sc)

This kind of sentence consists of a subject, a **linking verb** (a verb that connects a subject to its complement) and the **subject complement** (the word or phrase that describes or renames the subject).

s   v   sc
The injection was painless.

s   v   sc
John Major became prime minister.

165

In the first sentence the subject complement is an adjective, called a **predicate adjective,** that describes the subject; in the second sentence the subject complement is a noun, called a **predicate nominative,** that renames the subject. In each case the linking verb can be seen as an equal sign, equating the subject with its complement (*John Major = prime minister*).

(5) Subject + transitive verb + indirect object + direct object (s + v + io + do)

In this sentence pattern the **indirect object** tells to whom or for whom the verb's action was done.

> s   v   io   do
> Cyrano wrote Roxanne a poem. (Cyrano wrote a poem for Roxanne.)

> s   v   io   do
> The officer handed Frank a ticket. (The officer handed a ticket to Frank.)

Basic Sentence Patterns

Subject + intransitive verb	s v The bell rang.
Subject + transitive verb + direct object	s v Octavio Paz won the 1990 do Nobel Prize.
Subject + transitive verb + direct object + object complement	s v do Artists and writers found Paris oc exciting.
Subject + linking verb + subject complement	s v The cowardly lion looked sc frightened.
Subject + transitive verb + indirect object + direct object	s The 1882 Chinese Exclusion Act v io denied a specific ethnic group do naturalization. (The act denied naturalization to a specific ethnic group.)

EXERCISE 1

In each of the following sentences underline the subject once, and underline the verb twice. Then label direct objects, indirect objects, subject complements, and object complements.

                              do

EXAMPLE: Scarlett O'Hara wore a green velvet dress.

1. Metro-Goldwyn-Mayer released the film version of Margaret Mitchell's novel *Gone with the Wind* in 1939.
2. Vivien Leigh played the fiery Scarlett O'Hara, a beautiful Southern belle.
3. Clark Gable co-starred as Rhett Butler.
4. Scarlett loved her home, the plantation called Tara.
5. Yankee soldiers looted and vandalized Tara.
6. Scarlett was angry.
7. She was also desperate.
8. She paid Rhett Butler a visit.
9. Scarlett requested a $300 loan from Rhett to pay Tara's taxes.
10. She painted Rhett an optimistic picture.
11. Rhett called her a liar.
12. Moreover, he refused her the loan.

8c   *Forming Questions and Commands*

The five basic sentence patterns are alike in one respect: all are statements that present first the subject and then the predicate. This standard word order varies for questions and commands.

(1) Questions

Questions in English can be formed in several ways.

Forming Questions

- Invert subject and verb
  (This is Maggie's farm. → Is this Maggie's farm?)
- Invert and add a form of *do* before the subject
  (Maggie lives here. → Does Maggie live here?)

---

continued

continued from previous page

- Begin sentence with *who, what, why, where, when,* or *how.*
  (Wes was late again. → Why was Wes late again?)
- Add a question mark
  (This is Maggie's farm? Wes was late again?)
- Add a phrase with inverted subject and verb at the end of the sentence
  (This is Maggie's farm, isn't it? Wes was late again, wasn't he?)

(2) Commands

To form commands, either use the second person singular (You stop that!) or simply leave out the sentence's subject (you), which is understood.

Go to your room.

March.

Stop that!

8d *Identifying Phrases and Clauses*

Individual words may be joined to build *phrases* and *clauses.*

(1) *Identifying phrases*

A **phrase** is a grammatically ordered group of related words that lacks a subject or predicate or both and functions as a single part of speech.

A **verb phrase** consists of an auxiliary verb and a main verb. (Time *is flying.*)

A **noun phrase** includes a noun or pronoun plus all related modifiers. (I'll climb *the highest mountain.*)

A **prepositional phrase** consists of a preposition, its object, and any modifiers of that object (see 8f1).

They discussed the ethical implications of the operation.

He was last seen heading into the sunset.

A **verbal phrase** consists of a verbal and its related objects, modifiers, or complements (see 8f2). A verbal phrase may be a **participial phrase,** a **gerund phrase,** or an **infinitive phrase.**

Encouraged by the voter turnout, the candidate predicted a victory. (participial phrase)

Taking it easy always makes sense. (gerund phrase)

The jury recessed to evaluate the evidence. (infinitive phrase)

An **absolute phrase** usually consists of a noun or pronoun and a participle, accompanied by modifiers (**see 8f3**).

Their toes tapping, they watched the auditions.

(2) Identifying clauses

A **clause** is a group of related words that includes a subject and a predicate. An **independent** (main) **clause** may stand alone as a sentence, but a **dependent** (subordinate) **clause** must always be accompanied by an independent clause.

[Lucretia Mott was an abolitionist.] [She was also a pioneer for women's rights.] (two independent clauses)

[Lucretia Mott was an abolitionist] [who was also a pioneer for women's rights.] (independent clause, dependent clause)

[Although Lucretia Mott was most widely known for her support of women's rights,] [she was also a prominent abolitionist.] (dependent clause, independent clause)

Depending on how they function in a sentence, dependent clauses may be classified as adjective, adverb, or noun clauses.

Adjective clauses, sometimes called **relative clauses,** modify nouns or pronouns and always follow the nouns or pronouns they modify. They are introduced by relative pronouns (**see 9b**). The adverbs *where* and *when* can be used as relative pronouns when the adjective clause modifies a place or time.

The television series *M*A*S*H,* which depicted life in an army hospital in Korea during the Korean War, ran for eleven years. (Adjective clause modifies the noun *M*A*S*H.*)

Celeste's grandparents, who were born in Romania, speak little English. (Adjective clause modifies the noun *grandparents.*)

The Pulitzer Prizes for journalism are prestigious awards that are presented in areas such as editorial writing, photography, editorial cartooning, and national and international reporting. (Adjective clause modifies the noun *awards.*)

Sophie's Choice is set in Brooklyn, where the narrator lives in a house painted pink. (Adjective clause modifies the noun *Brooklyn.*)

Adverb clauses modify single words (verbs, adjectives, or adverbs) or entire phrases or clauses. They are always introduced by subordinating conjunctions (see **9b**). Adverb clauses provide information to answer the questions *how? where? when? why?* and *to what extent?*

Exhausted after the match was over, Kim decided to take a long nap. (Adverb clause modifies the participle *exhausted.*)

To get to the coach before it turned into a pumpkin, Cinderella had to hurry. (Adverb clause modifies the infinitive phrase *to get to the coach.*)

Because 75 percent of its exports are fish products, Iceland's economy is heavily dependent on the fishing industry. (Adverb clause modifies independent clause, telling *why* the fishing industry is so important.)

Her unemployment insurance benefits were reduced when she found a part-time job. (Adverb clause modifies independent clause, telling *when* benefits were reduced.)

Noun clauses act as nouns (as subjects, direct objects, indirect objects, or complements) in a sentence. A noun clause may be introduced by a relative pronoun or by *whether, when, where, why,* or *how.*

Whatever happens to us will be for the best. (Noun clause serves as subject of sentence.)

They finally decided which candidate was best. (Noun clause serves as direct object of verb *decided.*)

What you see is what you get. (Noun clause serves as subject complement.)

Elliptical clauses are grammatically incomplete—that is, a part of the subject or predicate or the entire subject or predicate is missing. If the missing part can be easily inferred from the context of the sentence, such constructions are acceptable.

Although [they were] full, they could not resist dessert.

He has never been able to read maps as well as his brother [can read maps].

E X E R C I S E   2

Which of the following groups of words are independent clauses? Which are dependent clauses? Which are phrases? Mark each word group IC, DC, or P.

EXAMPLE: Coming through the rye. (P)

1. Beauty is truth.
2. When knights were bold.
3. In a galaxy far away.
4. He saw stars.
5. I hear a symphony.

6. Whenever you are near.
7. The clock struck ten.
8. The red planet.
9. Slowly I turned.
10. For the longest time.

8e   *Building Simple Sentences with Individual Words*

A simple sentence can consist of just a subject and predicate:

<u>Jessica</u> <u>fell</u>.

Simple sentences can also be considerably more elaborate:

Jessica fell in love.

Jessica fell in love with Henry.

Jessica almost immediately fell in love with Henry.

Jessica and her sister almost immediately fell in love with Henry.

Jessica and her younger sister Victoria almost immediately fell in love with the dashing Henry Goodyear.

Jessica and her lively younger sister Victoria almost immediately fell hopelessly in love with the very dashing and mysterious Henry Goodyear.

The addition of modifying words (*older, dashing,* and so on) and phrases (*with the dashing Henry Goodyear*) and the creation of compounds (*Jessica and her sister, dashing and mysterious*) can change the substance and the meaning of *Jessica fell* quite substantially.

(1)   *Building simple sentences with adjectives and adverbs*

Descriptive adjectives and adverbs enrich the meaning of a sentence. Reread our sample sentence:

Jessica and her lively younger sister Victoria almost immediately fell hopelessly in love with the very dashing and mysterious Henry Goodyear.

In this sentence, four adjectives describe nouns:

Adjective	Noun
lively	sister
younger	sister
dashing	Henry Goodyear
mysterious	Henry Goodyear

Four adverbs describe the action of verbs or modify adjectives or other adverbs:

Adverb	
almost	immediately (adverb)
immediately	fell (verb)
hopelessly	fell (verb)
very	dashing and mysterious (adjectives)

See
◄
Ch. 25

EXERCISE 3

Label all descriptive adjectives and adverbs in the following sentences.

                adj   adv
EXAMPLE: The red house perched unsteadily on the edge of the hill.

1. The matchmaker appeared one night out of the dark fourth-floor hallway of the graystone rooming house where Finkle lived, grasping a black, strapped portfolio that had been worn thin with use. (Bernard Malamud, "The Magic Barrel")
2. During these last decades the interest in professional fasting has markedly diminished. It used to pay very well to stage such great performances under one's own management, but today that is quite impossible. We live in a different world now. (Franz Kafka, "A Hunger Artist")
3. A school of minnows swam by, each minnow with its small individual shadow, doubling the attendance, so clear and sharp in the sunlight. (E. B. White, "Once More to the Lake")
4. Poetry is as universal as language and almost as ancient. (Laurence Perrine, *Sound and Sense*)
5. Every town and village along that vast stretch of double river front-

age had a best dwelling, finest dwelling, mansion—the home of its wealthiest and most conspicuous citizen. (Mark Twain, *Life on the Mississippi*)

E X E R C I S E 4

Using these five sentences as models, write five original simple sentences. Use adverbs and adjectives where the model sentences use them, and then underline and label these modifiers.

EXAMPLE: Cathy carefully put the baby bird in the nest.

He angrily called the old man into the kitchen.

1. Nick turned his head carefully away smiling sweatily. (Ernest Hemingway, *In Our Time*)
2. Outside, the fire-red, gas-blue, ghost-green signs shone smokily through the tranquil rain. (F. Scott Fitzgerald, "Babylon Revisited")
3. The pavement was wet, glassy with water. (Willa Cather, "The Old Beauty")
4. The therapy used for treating burns has been improved considerably in recent years. (Lewis Thomas, "On Medicine and the Bomb")
5. There was a strange, inflamed, flurried, flighty recklessness of activity about him. (Herman Melville, *Bartleby the Scrivener*)

(2) Building simple sentences with nouns and verbals

Words other than adjectives and adverbs can help you build richer simple sentences. These include nouns and verbals.

Nouns   Nouns can sometimes act as adjectives modifying other nouns.

He needed two cake pans for the layer cake.

Verbals   Verbals include present and past participles, infinitives, and gerunds.

▸ **See 21c2**

Verbals may act as modifiers.

All three living former presidents attended the funeral. (Present participle serves as adjective.)

The Grand Canyon is the attraction to visit. (Infinitive serves as adjective.)

The puzzle was impossible to solve. (Infinitive serves as adverb.)

Or verbals may act as nouns.

When the <u>going</u> gets tough, the tough get going. (Gerund serves as noun.)

<u>To err</u> is human. (Infinitive serves as noun.)

It took me an entire three-hour lab period to identify my <u>unknown</u>. (Past participle serves as noun.)

EXERCISE 5

1. List ten nouns that can be used as modifiers.

   EXAMPLES: <u>word</u> processor, <u>truck</u> stop, <u>peanut</u> butter

2. List ten participles that can be used as modifiers.

   EXAMPLES: crushed, ringing

3. Choosing words from your lists, write five original sentences, each of which includes both a noun and a participle used as modifiers.

   EXAMPLE: The <u>word</u> processor was a <u>crushed</u> mass of metal and plastic.

4. Then add adjectives and adverbs to enrich the sentence further.

   EXAMPLE: The <u>new</u> word processor was a <u>gruesomely</u> crushed mass of metal and plastic.

EXERCISE 6

For additional practice in building simple sentences using individual words, combine each of the following groups of sentences into one simple sentence that contains several modifiers. You will have to add, delete, or reorder words.

   EXAMPLE: The night was cold. The night was wet.
   The night scared them. They were terribly scared.

   REVISED: The cold, wet night scared them terribly.

1. The ship landed. The ship was from space. The ship was tremendous. It landed silently.
2. It landed in a field. The field was grassy. The field was deserted.
3. A dog appeared. The dog was tiny. The dog was abandoned. The dog was a stray.

4. The dog was brave. The dog was curious. He approached the space-craft. The spacecraft was burning. He approached it carefully.
5. A creature emerged from the spaceship. The creature was smiling. He was purple. He emerged slowly.
6. The dog and the alien stared at each other. The dog was little. The alien was purple. They stared meaningfully.
7. The dog and the alien walked. They walked silently. They walked carefully. They walked toward each other.
8. The dog barked. He barked tentatively. He barked questioningly. The dog was uneasy.
9. The alien extended his hand. The alien was grinning. He extended it slowly. The hand was hairy.
10. In his hand was a bag. The bag was of canvas. The bag was green. The bag was for laundry.

8f *Building Simple Sentences with Phrases*

You can also enrich your sentences with phrases. Because a phrase lacks a subject or predicate (or both), it cannot stand alone as a sentence. Within a sentence, however, phrases add information and provide connections between ideas.

▶ **See 8d1**

(1) Building simple sentences with prepositional phrases

A **preposition** relates a noun or noun substitute to the rest of the sentence. A **prepositional phrase** consists of the preposition, its object (the noun or noun substitute), and any modifiers of that object.

▶ **See 21f**

prep obj   modifier
Cumulus clouds are towers on bases that extend thousands of feet.
(Phrase functions as adjective modifying the noun *towers*.)

In this example the preposition *precedes* its object. Occasionally in writing and often in speech, however, the preposition appears after the object.

obj   prep
I see the person you are looking for.

Prepositional phrases can function in a sentence as adjectives or as adverbs.

Carry Nation was a crusader for temperance. (Prepositional phrase functions as adjective modifying the noun *crusader*.)

The Madeira River flows into the Amazon. (Prepositional phrase functions as adverb modifying the verb *flows*.)

EXERCISE 7

Read the following sentences. Underline each prepositional phrase, and then connect it with an arrow to the word it modifies. Finally, tell whether each phrase functions as an adjective or an adverb.

> EXAMPLE: Herz looked harassed enough to be the father of three or four small, mean, colicky children. (Philip Roth, *Letting Go*) (Prepositional phrase functions as an adjective.)

1. He stumbled down the back steps, hugging the thick book under his arm.   (Richard Wright, "The Man Who Was Almost a Man")
2. She looked at me, sitting in the chair before the cold stove, the sailor hat on her head.   (William Faulkner, "That Evening Sun")
3. It was Paul's afternoon to appear before the faculty of the Pittsburgh High School to account for his various misdemeanors.   (Willa Cather, "Paul's Case")
4. It struck the trunk of the apple tree, bounced back at an angle, and rolled steadily and stupidly onto the cement apron in front of the firehouse, where one of the trucks was parked.   (Richard Wilbur, "A Game of Catch")
5. Outside the town, along the tracks, there were barren trees and bushes below the embankment, snow-gray in the dark. And down among the trees and bushes there were makeshift houses made out of boxes and tin and old pieces of wood and canvas. You couldn't see them in the dark, but you knew they were there if you'd ever been on the road, if you had ever lived with the homeless and hungry in a depression.   (Langston Hughes, "On the Road")

EXERCISE 8

For additional practice in using prepositional phrases, combine each pair of sentences to create one simple sentence that includes a prepositional phrase. You may add, delete, or reorder words. Some sentences may have more than one correct version.

> EXAMPLE: America's drinking water is being contaminated. Toxic substances are contaminating it.
>
> America's drinking water is being contaminated by toxic substances.

1. Toxic waste disposal presents a serious problem. Americans have this problem.
2. Hazardous chemicals pose a threat. People are threatened.
3. Some towns, like Times Beach, Missouri, have been completely abandoned. Their residents have abandoned them.
4. Dioxin is one chemical. It has serious toxic effects.
5. Dioxin is highly toxic. The toxicity affects animals and humans.
6. Toxic chemical wastes like dioxin may be found. Over fifty thousand dumps have them.
7. Industrial parks contain toxic wastes. Open pits, ponds, and lagoons are where the toxic substances are.
8. Toxic wastes pose dangers. The land, water, and air are endangered.
9. In addition, toxic substances are a threat. They threaten our public health and our economy.
10. Immediate toxic waste cleanup would be a tremendous benefit. Americans are the ones who would benefit.

(2) Building simple sentences with verbal phrases

A **verbal phrase** consists of a verbal (participle, gerund, or infinitive) and its related objects, modifiers, or complements.

Some verbal phrases act as nouns. **Gerund phrases,** for example, like gerunds themselves, are always used as nouns, and infinitive phrases may also be used as nouns.

Making a living isn't always easy. (Gerund phrase serves as sentence's subject.)

Wendy appreciated Tom's being honest. (Gerund phrase serves as object of verb *appreciated*.)

The entire town was shocked by their breaking up. (Gerund phrase is object of preposition *by*.)

To know him is to love him. (Infinitive phrase *to know him* serves as sentence's subject; infinitive phrase *to love him* is subject complement.)

Some verbal phrases are also used as modifiers. **Participial phrases** are always used to modify nouns or pronouns, and **infinitive phrases** may function as adjectives or as adverbs.

Fascinated by Scheherazade's story, they waited anxiously for the next installment. (Participial phrase modifies pronoun *they*.)

The next morning young Goodman Brown came slowly into the street of Salem Village, staring around him like a bewildered man.

(Nathaniel Hawthorne) (Participial phrase modifies noun *Goodman Brown.*)

Henry M. Stanley went to Africa <u>to find Dr. Livingstone</u>. (Infinitive phrase modifies verb *went.*)

It wasn't the ideal time <u>to do homework</u>. (Infinitive phrase modifies noun *time.*)

Revision Close-up

See
15a2
15b1
When you use verbal phrases as modifiers, be especially careful not to create misplaced or dangling modifiers.

E X E R C I S E   9

For practice in using verbal phrases, combine each of these sentence pairs to create one simple sentence that contains a participial phrase, a gerund phrase, or an infinitive phrase. Underline and label the verbal phrase in your sentence. You will have to add, delete, or reorder words, and you may find more than one way to combine each pair.

EXAMPLE: Judy decorated her new jeans.
            She painted them with pink and yellow flowers.

            Judy decorated her new jeans,

                    participial phrase
            painting them with pink and yellow flowers.

1. In 1912 the textile workers of Lawrence, Massachusetts, went on strike. They were demonstrating for "Bread and Roses, too."
2. The workers wanted higher wages and better working conditions. They felt trapped in their miserable jobs.
3. Mill workers toiled six days a week. They earned about $1.50 for this.
4. Most of the workers were women and children. They worked up to sixteen hours a day.
5. The mills were dangerous. They were filled with hazards.
6. Many mill workers joined unions. They did this to fight exploitation by their employers.
7. They wanted to improve their lives. This was their goal.
8. Finally, twenty-five thousand workers walked off their jobs. They knew they were risking everything.
9. The police and the state militia were called in. Attacking the strikers was their mission.

10. After 63 days, the American Woolen Company surrendered. This ended the strike with a victory for the workers.

(Adapted from William Cahn, *Lawrence 1912: The Bread and Roses Strike*)

(3) Building simple sentences with absolute phrases

An **absolute phrase** is usually composed of a noun or pronoun and a past or present participle, along with its modifiers. Sometimes, however, an infinitive phrase functions as an absolute phrase. Absolute phrases act as modifiers, but they are not connected grammatically to any particular word or phrase in a sentence. Instead, an absolute phrase modifies the whole independent clause to which it is linked.

All things considered, I prefer Maine's cold winters to California's smog.

To make a long story short, our team lost.

Revision Close-up

When the participle in an absolute phrase is a form of the verb *be*, it is usually omitted.

They worked frantically, their time [being] almost up.

E X E R C I S E   10

For practice in using absolute phrases, combine each group of sentences to create one simple sentence that includes an absolute phrase. You will have to change, add, delete, or reorder some words.

EXAMPLE: Paris was beautiful.
Its streets were exceptionally clean.
Paris was beautiful, its streets [being] exceptionally clean.

1. Notre Dame stood majestically.
Its Rose Window glowed in the darkness.
2. We took a boat ride down the Seine.
Our feet were tired.
3. The Louvre is open six days a week.
Its doors are closed on Tuesdays.

4. The Jeu de Paume displays Impressionist paintings. Its exhibits show-case Manet, Degas, Renoir, and van Gogh.
5. We were forced to cut our vacation short.
   Our francs were spent.

(4) Building simple sentences with appositives

An **appositive** is a noun or a noun phrase that identifies, in different words, the noun or pronoun it follows.

> Roy Rogers's horse Trigger was a golden palomino. (appositive *Trigger* identifies noun *horse*)

> Farrington hated his boss, a real tyrant. (appositive *real tyrant* identifies noun *boss*)

Appositives expand a sentence by defining the nouns or pronouns they modify, giving them new names or adding identifying details. Appositives can substitute for the nouns or pronouns to which they refer.

> Francie Nolan, the protagonist of Betty Smith's novel *A Tree Grows in Brooklyn*, is determined to finish high school and make a better life for herself. (Francie Nolan = the protagonist of the novel)

> Grant, the son of a tanner on the Western frontier, was everything Lee was not. (Bruce Catton) (Grant = the son of a tanner)

As in the examples above, appositives are frequently used without special introductory phrases. They may also be introduced by *such as, or, that is, for example,* or *in other words.*

> A regional airline, such as Southwest, frequently accounts for more than half the departures at so-called second-tier airports.

> Rabies, or hydrophobia, was nearly always fatal until Pasteur's work.

E X E R C I S E   11

For practice in using appositives when you write, build ten new simple sentences by combining each of the following pairs. Make one sentence in each pair an appositive. You may need to delete or reorder words in some cases.

EXAMPLE: René Descartes was a noted French philosopher.
            Descartes is best known for his famous declaration, "I think, therefore I am."

René Descartes, a noted French philosopher, is best known for his famous declaration, "I think, therefore I am."

1. *I Know Why the Caged Bird Sings* is the first book in Maya Angelou's autobiography.
   It deals primarily with her life as a young girl in Stamps, Arkansas.
2. Catgut is a tough cord generally made from the intestines of sheep.
   Catgut is used for tennis rackets, for violin strings, and for surgical stitching.
3. Hermes was the messenger of the Greek gods.
   He is usually portrayed as an athletic youth wearing a cap and winged sandals.
4. Emiliano Zapata was a hero of the Mexican Revolution.
   He is credited with effecting land reform in his home state of Morelos.
5. Pulsars are celestial objects that emit regular pulses of radiation.
   Pulsars were first discovered in 1967.

(5) Building simple sentences with compound constructions

Compound constructions consist of two or more grammatically equivalent items, parallel in importance. Within simple sentences, compound words or phrases—subjects, predicates, complements, or modifiers—may be joined in one of three ways.

With commas:

He took one long, loving look at his '57 Chevy.

With the coordinating conjunctions *and, but, nor, or,* or *yet*:

They reeled, whirled, flounced, capered, gamboled, and spun.
(Kurt Vonnegut, Jr., "Harrison Bergeson")

With a pair of correlative conjunctions (*both/and, not only/but also, either/or, neither/nor, whether/or*):

Neither the twentieth-century poet Sylvia Plath nor the nineteenth-century poet Emily Dickinson achieved recognition during her lifetime.

Both milk and carrots contain Vitamin A.

EXERCISE 12

A. Expand each of the following sentences by using compound subjects and/or predicates.

> EXAMPLE: Bill played guitar.
> Bill and Juan played guitar and sang.

B. Then expand your simple sentence with modifying words and phrases, using compound constructions whenever possible.

> EXAMPLE: Despite "butterflies" and a restless audience, Bill and Juan played guitar and sang.

1. Cortés explored the New World.
2. Virginia Woolf wrote novels.
3. Edison invented the phonograph.
4. PBS television airs educational programming.
5. Thomas Jefferson signed the Declaration of Independence.

EXERCISE 13

To practice building sentences with compound subjects, predicates, and modifiers, combine the following groups of sentences into one.

> EXAMPLE: Marion studied. Frank studied. They studied quietly. They studied diligently.
> Marion and Frank studied quietly and diligently.

1. Robert Ludlum writes best-selling spy thrillers. Tom Clancy writes best-selling spy thrillers. John le Carré writes best-selling spy thrillers.
2. Smoking can cause heart disease. A high-fat, high-cholesterol diet can cause heart disease. Stress can cause heart disease.
3. Sylvia Plath was an important twentieth-century poet. Adrienne Rich was an important twentieth-century poet. They both frequently wrote about depression and despair.
4. Successful rock bands give concerts. They record albums. They make videos. They license merchandise bearing their names and likenesses.
5. Sports superstars like David Robinson and Andre Agassi earn additional income by making personal appearances. They earn money by endorsing products.

9

Building Compound and Complex Sentences

9a Building Compound Sentences

The pairing of similar elements—words, phrases, or clauses—to give equal weight to each is called **coordination**. Coordination can be used in simple sentences to join similar elements into compound subjects, predicates, complements, or modifiers. It can also join two independent clauses to form a compound sentence.

▶ See 8f5

Use Compound Sentences

- to show addition (*and, in addition to, not only . . . but also,* semi-colon)
- to show contrast (*but, however*)
- to show cause and effect (*so, therefore, consequently*)
- to present a choice of alternatives (*or, either . . . or*)

A **compound sentence** is formed when two or more simple sentences (independent clauses) are connected with coordinating conjunctions, conjunctive adverbs, correlative conjunctions, semicolons, or colons.

(1) Using coordinating conjunctions

Two independent clauses may be joined with a coordinating conjunction.

[The cowboy is a workingman], yet [he has little in common with the urban blue-collar worker]. (John R. Erickson, *The Modern Cowboy*)

[In the fall the war was always there], but [we did not go to it anymore]. (Ernest Hemingway, "In Another Country")

[She carried a thin, small cane made from an umbrella], and [with this she kept tapping the frozen earth in front of her]. (Eudora Welty, "A Worn Path")

Revision Close-up

When two independent clauses are joined by a coordinating conjunction, the first is nearly always followed by a comma. The comma may be omitted in very short sentences. The seven coordinating conjunctions are *and, or, nor, but, for, so,* and *yet.*

See ◄ 27a1

(2)   Using conjunctive adverbs and other transitional expressions

Two independent clauses may be joined with a conjunctive adverb or other transitional expression.

[Peter dropped Modern History]; instead, [he decided to take Educational Methods].

[The saxophone does not belong to the brass family]; in fact, [it is a member of the woodwind family].

[Aerobic exercise can help lower blood pressure]; however, [those with high blood pressure should still limit salt intake].

See ◄ 21e

See ◄ 4d2

Commonly used conjunctive adverbs include *consequently, finally, still,* and *thus.* Other commonly used transitional expressions include *for example, in fact, on the other hand,* and *for instance.*

Revision Close-up

When two independent clauses are joined by a conjunctive adverb or by any other transitional expression to form a compound sentence, the transitional phrase is always preceded by a semicolon and usually followed by a comma.

(3)   Using correlative conjunctions

See ◄ 21g

Correlative conjunctions can connect two independent clauses to form a compound sentence.

Sharon not only passed the exam, but she also received the highest grade in the class.

Either he left his coat in his locker, or he left it on the bus.

(4) *Using semicolons*

A **semicolon** can link two closely related independent clauses.

▶ See 28a

[Alaska is the largest state]; [Rhode Island is the smallest].

[Theodore Roosevelt was president after the Spanish American War]; [Andrew Johnson was president after the Civil War].

(5) *Using colons*

A colon can sometimes link two independent clauses.

▶ See 31a

He got his orders: he was to leave for France on Sunday.

They thought they knew the outcome: Truman would lose to Dewey.

EXERCISE 1

Bracket the independent clauses in these compound sentences.

EXAMPLE: [He was a man of few words], but [those few words were judiciously selected, weighed for quality, and delivered with expertise]. (Anita Brookner, *Hotel du Lac*)

1. We stand on the threshold of a great age of science; we are already over the threshold; it is for us to make that future our own. (Jacob Bronowski, *Science and Human Values*)
2. The players were not two persons, but two illustrious families; the game had been going on for centuries. (Jorge Luis Borges, "The Secret Miracle")
3. He blew the candle out suddenly, and we went inside. (Joseph Conrad, *Heart of Darkness*)
4. They had not shown much interest in the elephant when he was merely ravaging their homes, but it was different now that he was going to be shot. (George Orwell, "Shooting an Elephant")
5. The contempt of joggers and runners for the rest of humanity is often quite sincere, but I am not sure that it is deserved. (Joseph Epstein, *Familiar Territory*)

EXERCISE 2

After reading the following paragraph, use coordination to build as many compound sentences as you think your readers need to understand the links between ideas. When you have finished, bracket the independent clauses and underline the coordinating conjunctions, correlative conjunctions, or punctuation marks that link clauses.

The case of Alan Bakke presents an interesting footnote to the history of affirmative action legislation. Bakke applied to medical school at the University of California at Davis. He was rejected in 1973 and 1974. Bakke's grades were good. He said he was the victim of reverse discrimination. The medical school had designated sixteen out of every hundred slots for minority students. Bakke is white. Bakke said some minority students, less qualified than he, had been admitted. Bakke sued the University of California. The case went to the Supreme Court. In 1978, Bakke won his suit. Today, Bakke is a doctor.

EXERCISE 3

Add appropriate coordinating conjunctions, conjunctive adverbs, or correlative conjunctions as indicated to combine each pair of sentences into one well-constructed compound sentence that retains the meaning of the original pair. Be sure to use correct punctuation.

EXAMPLE: *Mad* was first published in 1952. It did not become a true magazine until July 1955. (coordinating conjunction)

Mad was first published in 1952, but it did not become a true magazine until July 1955.

1. The average American consumes 128 pounds of sugar each year. Most of us eat much more sugar than any other food additive, including salt. (conjunctive adverb)
2. Many of us are determined to reduce our sugar intake. We have consciously eliminated sweets from our diets. (conjunctive adverb)
3. Unfortunately, sugar is not found only in sweets. It is also found in many processed foods. (correlative conjunction)
4. Processed foods like puddings and cake contain sugar. Foods like ketchup and spaghetti sauce do, too. (coordinating conjunction)
5. We are trying to cut down on sugar. We find limiting sugar intake extremely difficult. (coordinating conjunction)
6. Processors may use sugar in foods for taste. They may also use it to help prevent foods from spoiling and to improve their texture and appearance. (correlative conjunction)
7. Sugar comes in many different forms. It is easy to overlook it on a package label. (coordinating conjunction)
8. Sugar may be called sucrose or fructose. It may also be called corn syrup, corn sugar, brown sugar, honey, or molasses. (coordinating conjunction)

9. No sugar is more nourishing than the others. It really doesn't matter which is consumed. (conjunctive adverb)
10. Sugars contain empty calories. Whenever possible, they should be avoided. (conjunctive adverb)   (Adapted from *Jane Brody's Nutrition Book*)

Write two sentences that imitate the following. Use the same parts of speech in making substitutions, and retain the function words (articles, prepositions, and conjunctions) of the model.

His clothes were a trifle outgrown, and the tan velvet on the collar of his open overcoat was frayed and worn; but for all that there was something of the dandy about him, and he wore an opal pin in his neatly knotted black four-in-hand, and a red carnation in his buttonhole.   (Willa Cather, "Paul's Case")

9b   *Building Complex Sentences*

When you want to indicate that one idea is less important than another, you subordinate the secondary idea to the primary one. You might put the secondary idea in a modifying phrase or in another, less emphatic position in the sentence. Another way to subordinate one idea to another is to place the main idea in an independent clause and the less important idea in a dependent clause. The result is a complex sentence.

A **complex sentence** consists of one simple sentence, which functions as an independent or main clause in the complex sentence, and at least one dependent or subordinate clause. **Independent clauses** can stand alone as sentences.

The hurricane began.

The town was evacuated.

Dependent clauses, introduced by subordinating conjunctions or relative pronouns, cannot stand alone.

After the town was evacuated

Which threatened to destroy the town

Dependent clauses must be combined with independent clauses to form sentences. The subordinating conjunction or relative pronoun links the independent and dependent clauses and shows the relationship between them.

dependent clause   independent clause
[After the town was evacuated], [the hurricane began].

independent clause   dependent clause
[Officials watched the storm], [which threatened to destroy the town].

Sometimes a dependent clause may be placed within an independent clause.

dependent clause
Town officials, [who were very concerned], watched the storm.

Depending on their function in a sentence, dependent clauses may be adverb, adjective, or noun clauses. Adverb clauses function in a sentence as adverbs, adjective clauses as adjectives, and noun clauses as nouns (**see 8d2**).

When the school board voted to ban Judy Blume's books, parents protested. (adverb clause)

The Graduate was the film that launched Dustin Hoffman's career. (adjective clause)

How the fight started remained a mystery. (noun clause)

Subordinating conjunctions introduce adverb clauses.

Commonly Used Subordinating Conjunctions		
after	in order that	unless
although	now that	until
as	once	when
as if	rather than	whenever
as though	since	where
because	so that	whereas
before	that	wherever
even though	though	while
if		

Relative pronouns introduce adjective clauses.

Relative Pronouns		
that	whatever	who (whose, whom)
what	which	whoever (whomever)

Noun clauses may be introduced by relative pronouns or by *whether, when, where, why,* or *how.*

EXERCISE 5

Bracket and label the independent and dependent clauses in these sentences, and then underline and label the subordinating conjunctions or relative pronouns. Finally, indicate the function of each dependent clause.

		sub. conj.	dep. clause

EXAMPLE: ["Jet-stream art" is created] [<u>when</u> paint thrown into the exhaust of a jet engine is spattered onto a giant canvas]. (dependent clause serves as an adverb)

1. The people were clustered thickly about the old man, all of them intermittently flicking glances toward me as they talked animatedly in their Mandinka tongue.   (Alex Haley, *Roots*)
2. When professional writers complete a first draft, they usually feel that they are at the start of the writing process.   (Donald M. Murray, "The Maker's Eye")
3. We cannot help regarding a camel as aloof and unfriendly because it mimics, quite unwittingly and for other reasons, the "gesture of haughty rejection" common to so many human cultures.   (Stephen Jay Gould, *The Panda's Thumb*)
4. These are both hopeful and frustrating times for those who want to improve the nation's science and math education.   (Arlen J. Large, *Wall Street Journal*)
5. Although there was always generosity in the Negro neighborhood, it was indulged on pain of sacrifice.   (Maya Angelou, *I Know Why the Caged Bird Sings*)

EXERCISE 6

Bracket the independent and dependent clauses in the following complex sentences. Then, using these sentences as models, create two new complex sentences in imitation of each. For each set of new sentences, use the same subordinating conjunction or relative pronoun that appears in the original.

1. I said what I meant.
2. Isadora Duncan is the dancer who best exemplifies the phrase "poetry in motion."
3. Because she was considered a heretic, Joan of Arc was burned at the stake.

4. The oracle at Delphi predicted that Oedipus would murder his father and marry his mother.
5. The ghost vanished before Hamlet could question him further.

E X E R C I S E   7

Use a subordinating conjunction or relative pronoun to combine each of the following pairs of sentences into one well-constructed sentence. The conjunction or pronoun you select must clarify the relationship between the two sentences. You will have to change or reorder words, and in most cases you have a choice of connecting words.

EXAMPLE: Some colleges are tightening admissions requirements.

The pool of students is growing smaller.

Although the pool of students is growing smaller, some colleges are tightening admissions requirements.

1. Some twelve million people are currently out of work. They need new skills for new careers.
2. Talented high school students are usually encouraged to go to college. Some high school graduates are now starting to see that a college education may not guarantee them a job.
3. A college education can cost a student more than $80,000. Vocational education is becoming increasingly important.
4. Students complete their work in less than four years. They can enter the job market more quickly.
5. Nurses' aides, paralegals, travel agents, and computer technicians do not need college degrees. They have little trouble finding work.
6. Some four-year colleges are experiencing growth. Public community colleges and private trade schools are growing much more rapidly.
7. The best vocational schools are responsive to the needs of local businesses. They train students for jobs that actually exist.
8. For instance, a school in Detroit might offer advanced automotive design. A school in New York City might focus on fashion design.
9. Other schools offer courses in horticulture, respiratory therapy, and computer programming. They are able to place their graduates easily.
10. Laid-off workers, returning housewives, recent high-school graduates, and even college graduates are reexamining vocational education. They all hope to find rewarding careers.

9c *Building Compound-Complex Sentences*

A **compound-complex sentence** consists of two or more independent clauses and at least one dependent clause.

dependent clause
[When small foreign imports began dominating the U.S.
independent clause
automobile industry], [consumers were very responsive], but [Ameri-
independent clause
can auto workers were dismayed].

dependent clause　　　　　independent clause
[As the ferry entered the harbor], [she stood up and made her way
down the deck against the light salt wind], and
dependent clause within independent clause
[Baxter], [who had returned to the island indifferently], [felt
independent clause
that summer had begun]. (John Cheever, "The Chaste Clarissa")

E X E R C I S E 8

In each of these sentences, identify subjects and verbs; bracket and label dependent and independent clauses; and identify each sentence as simple, compound, complex, or compound-complex.

1. Use of the telephone involves personal risk because it involves exposure; for some, to be "hung up on" is among the worst fears; others dream of a ringing telephone and wake up with a pounding heart. (John Brooks, *Telephone: The First Hundred Years*)
2. Although Intourist, the government travel organization, has made great strides in improving tourist facilities and the variety of things to do, the Soviet state still regards the foreign tourist as a blend of spy and ideological alien—a person to be watched, carefully segregated from the citizenry and, to the extent possible, educated in the wonders of Socialist democracy and achievements. (*New York Times*)
3. Though she was stout in build and stood erect, her slow eyes and parted lips gave her the appearance of a woman who did not know where she was or where she was going. (James Joyce, "The Dead")
4. This nation is even more litigious than religious, and the school prayer issue has prompted more, and more sophisticated, arguments about constitutional law than about the nature of prayer. (George F. Will, *Newsweek*)

5. The first time I ever went naked in mixed company was at the house of a girl whose father had a bad back and had built himself a sauna in the corner of the basement. (Garrison Keillor, *New Yorker*)

6. I am the son of Mexican-American parents, who speak a blend of Spanish and English, but who read neither language easily. (Richard Rodriguez, *Aria: A Memoir of a Bilingual Childhood*)

7. Winter was always the effort to live; summer was tropical license. (Henry Adams, *The Education of Henry Adams*)

8. Of course, only in extreme cases do graduates become dull immediately. (Wilfred Sheed, *New York Times*)

9. The most alarming of all man's assaults upon the environment is the contamination of air, earth, rivers, and sea with dangerous and even lethal materials. (Rachel Carson, *Silent Spring*)

10. At the age of 80, my mother had her last bad fall, and after that her mind wandered free through time. (Russell Baker, *Growing Up*)

EXERCISE 9

Choose one simple, one compound, one complex, and one compound-complex sentence from Exercise 8. Write an original sentence in imitation of each.

STUDENT WRITER AT WORK

BUILDING SENTENCES

A student in a freshman composition class was assigned to interview a grandparent and write a short paper about his or her life. When she set out to turn her grandmother's words into a paper, the student faced a set of choppy notes—words, phrases, and simple sentences—that she had jotted down as her grandmother spoke. She needed to fill out and combine these fragments and short sentences to produce varied, interesting sentences that would establish the relationships among her ideas. Read the notes, turn them into complete sentences when necessary, and combine sentences wherever it seems appropriate. Your goal is to build simple, compound, and complex sentences enriched by modifiers—without adding any information. When you have finished, revise further to strengthen coherence, unity, and style.

Notes

67 years old. Born in Lykens, PA (old coal—mining town).
Got her first paying job at 13. Her parents lied about her
age. Working age was 14. Parents couldn't afford all the
mouths they had to feed. Before that, she helped with the
housework. At work, she was a maid. Got paid only about a
dollar a week. Most of that went to her parents. Ate her
meals on job. Worked in house where 3 generations of men
lived. They all worked in the mines. Had to get up at 4
A.M. First chore was to make lunch for the men. She'd
scrub the metal canteens. Then she'd fill them with water.
Then she'd make biscuits and broth. Then she'd start
breakfast. Mrs. Muller would help. Cooking for 6 hungry
men was a real job. Then she did the breakfast dishes.
Then she did the chores. The house had 3 stories. She had
to scrub floors, dust, and sweep. It wasn't easy. Then
Mrs. Muller would need help patching and darning. She had
just enough time to get dinner started. Grabbed her meals
after the family finished eating. Had no spare time. When
not working she had chores to do at home. In spring and
summer she would grow vegetables. Canned vegetables for
her family. What was left over, she sold. Got married
at 16.

10

Writing Emphatic Sentences

When speaking, you add emphasis to your ideas with facial expressions, with gestures, and by raising or lowering your voice. When writing, you use other techniques to highlight important points.

Strategies for Writing Emphatic Sentences

- Use emphatic word order.
- Use emphatic sentence structure.
- Use parallelism and balance.
- Use repetition.
- Use active voice.

10a *Achieving Emphasis through Word Order*

Where you place your words, phrases, and clauses within a sentence emphasizes or deemphasizes their importance.

(1) Beginning with important ideas

Readers focus on the *beginning* and the *end* of a sentence, expecting the most important information to appear in these places. To convey emphasis clearly and forcefully, place key ideas in these positions. Look at the following sentence:

> In a landmark study of alcoholism, Dr. George Vaillant of Harvard followed 200 Harvard graduates and 400 inner-city, working-class men from the Boston area.

This sentence carries its key idea at the beginning. Greatest emphasis is therefore placed on the study itself, not on those who conducted it or who participated in it. Rephrasing changes the emphasis by focusing attention on the researcher and relegating the information about his work to a parenthetical phrase.

> Dr. George Vaillant of Harvard, in a landmark study of alcoholism, followed 200 Harvard graduates and 400 inner-city, working-class men from the Boston area.

Situations that demand a straightforward presentation—laboratory reports, memos, technical papers, business correspondence, and the like—call for sentences that present vital information first and qualify ideas later.

> The possibility of treating cancer with interferon has been the subject of a good deal of research.

> Whether or not dividends will be paid depends on the vote of the stockholders.

The first sentence emphasizes the new treatment, not the research; the second sentence stresses the question of dividends, not the vote. For technical and business audiences, artificially created suspense is inappropriate—especially if it means readers must wade through a series of qualifiers to get the point.

Revision Close-up

Because sentence beginnings are so strategic, the use of unemphatic, empty phrases like *there is* or *there are* in this position is generally ineffective.

UNEMPHATIC: There is heavy emphasis placed on the development of computational skills at MIT.

EMPHATIC: Heavy emphasis is placed on the development of computational skills at MIT.

or

MIT places heavy emphasis on the development of computational skills.

(2) Ending with important ideas

The ending of a sentence can be a very dramatic position for important ideas. Key elements may be placed at the end of a sentence in a number of conventional ways.

With a Colon or Dash   A colon or a dash can add emphasis by isolating an important word or phrase at the end of a sentence.

> Beth had always dreamed of owning one special car: a 1953 Corvette.

> The elderly need a good deal of special attention—and they deserve that attention.

With Subordinate Elements at the Beginning   Putting modifiers or other subordinate elements at the beginning of a sentence allows you to place more important elements in the naturally emphatic position at its end.

UNEMPHATIC

> The Philadelphia Eagles and the Pittsburgh Steelers became one professional football team, nicknamed the Steagles, during World War II because of the manpower shortage. (modifying phrases at end detract from main idea and weaken sentence)

EMPHATIC

> Because of the manpower shortage during World War II, the Philadelphia Eagles and the Pittsburgh Steelers became one professional football team, nicknamed the Steagles. (correctly emphasizes the newly created team)

With Climactic Word Order   **Climactic word order**, the arrangement of items in a series from the least to the most important, stresses the key idea—the last point—while building suspense and heightening interest.

When the key idea is buried in the middle of a sentence, the sentence will lack emphasis.

> Duties of a member of Congress include serving as a district's representative in Washington, making speeches, and answering mail. (Which duty is most important?)

When you use climactic word order, placing the key idea at the end, the momentum of the sentence gives this idea added force.

> The nation's most prominent orchestras all boast large annual budgets, locations in important cities, and the most talented musicians and conductors. (Talent is the key idea.)

Revision Close-up

Unless you have a good reason to do so, do not waste the end of a sentence on qualifiers such as conjunctive adverbs. In that position, a

196

qualifier loses its power as a linking expression that indicates the relationship between ideas. Put transitional phrases earlier, where they can fulfill their functions and add emphasis.

LESS EMPHATIC: Smokers do have rights; they should not try to impose their habits on others, however. (conjunctive adverb at end of clause)

MORE EMPHATIC: Smokers do have rights; however, they should not try to impose their habits on others. (conjunctive adverb at beginning of clause)

LESS EMPHATIC: We wanted the shelves to be water-resistant; we applied three coats of polyurethane for this reason. (transitional expression at end of clause)

MORE EMPHATIC: We wanted the shelves to be water-resistant; for this reason, we applied three coats of polyurethane. (transitional expression at beginning of clause)

EXERCISE 1

Underline the most important word group in each sentence of the following paragraph. Then identify the device the writer used to emphasize those key words. Are the key ideas placed at the beginning or end of a sentence? Does the writer use climactic order?

Buried in the basement of the computer center, often for hours on end, the campus computer hackers work. Day after day they sit at their terminals, working on games, class assignments, research projects, or schemes to conquer the world. Some computer hackers are totally absorbed in their terminals, pausing only for occasional meals or classes. A few hackers become almost reclusive, spending little time on recreational activities or social relationships. Sacrificing grades, exercise, dating, and contact with the outdoors, hackers structure their lives around their computers. With their own slang, their own habits, and their own hangouts, computer hackers tend to set themselves apart from their fellow students. But these computer addicts feel that the computer experience is worth the sacrifices they must make: Computers have opened up a whole new world for them.

(3) Using inverted word order

The word order of most sentences is subject-verb-object (or complement). When you depart from expected word order, you call attention to the word, phrase, or clause that you have inverted. You may even call attention to the entire sentence.

More modest and less inventive than Turner's paintings are John Constable's landscapes.

Here the writer calls special attention to the modifying phrase *more modest and less inventive than Turner's paintings* by turning the sentence around. Now the sentence stresses the comparison with Turner's work.

Revision Close-up

See ◄
12f1

Inverted word order should be used appropriately and in moderation. Misuse of this stylistic technique can distort your meaning; overuse makes your writing stiff and unnatural.

EXERCISE 2

Revise the following sentences to make them more emphatic. For each, decide which ideas should be highlighted, and group key phrases at sentence beginnings or endings, using climactic order or inverted order where appropriate.

1. Police want to upgrade their firepower because criminals are better armed than ever before.
2. A few years ago felons used so-called Saturday night specials, small-caliber six-shot revolvers.
3. Now semiautomatic pistols capable of firing fifteen to twenty rounds, along with paramilitary weapons like the AK-47, have replaced these weapons.
4. Police are adopting such weapons as new fast-firing shotguns and 9mm automatic pistols in order to gain an equal footing with their adversaries.
5. Faster reloading and a hair trigger are among the numerous advantages that automatic pistols, the weapon of choice among law enforcement officers, have over the traditional .38-caliber police revolver.

10b *Achieving Emphasis through Sentence Structure*

Skillful use of subordination can clarify a sentence's emphasis by deemphasizing less important ideas and emphasizing more important ones (**see 9b**).

emph 10b

(1) Using cumulative sentences

Most English sentences are classified as cumulative. A **cumulative sentence** begins with an independent clause that is followed by additional words, phrases, or clauses that expand or develop it:

> She holds me in strong arms, arms that have chopped cotton, dismembered trees, scattered corn for chickens, cradled infants, shaken the daylights out of half-grown upstart teenagers. (Rebecca Hill, *Blue Rise*)

Revision Close-up

Because it presents its main idea first, a cumulative sentence tends to be clear and straightforward. When you want to communicate an idea in a direct manner, a cumulative sentence is the appropriate choice.

(2) Using periodic sentences

A **periodic sentence** moves from supporting details, expressed in modifying phrases and dependent clauses, to the main idea, usually placed in the independent clause:

> Unlike the Pet Rock, which insulted the intelligence, and Rubik's Cube, which defied it, a big new hit on the toy scene tickles the imagination and captivates the eye. (*Time*)

In the preceding sentence, the writer adds emphasis to his main idea not only by placing it in the independent clause but also by keeping readers waiting for it. As the independent clause at the end of the sentence ties the clauses together, the writer emphatically makes his point.

In some periodic sentences the modifying phrase or dependent clause comes between subject and predicate:

> Columbus, after several discouraging and unsuccessful voyages, finally reached America.

Longer, more complex periodic sentences can be even more forceful. Piling up phrases and clauses, such sentences can gradually build in intensity, and sometimes in suspense, until a climax is reached in the independent clause:

> The problems of soiled artificial flowers, soggy undercrust, leaky milk cartons, sour dishrags, girdle stays jabbing, meringue weeping, soda

straws sticking out of bag lunches, shower curtains flapping out of the tub, creases in the middle of the tablecloth sticking up, wet boxes in the laundry room, roach eggs in the refrigerator motor, shiny seam marks on the front of recently ironed ties, flyspecks on chandeliers, film on bathroom tiles, steam on bathroom mirrors, rust in Formica drain-boards, road film on windshields—all were acknowledged and certified, probably for the first time ever, in "Hints from Heloise." (Ian Frazier, *New Yorker*)

Revision Close-up

Periodic sentences are generally more emphatic than cumulative sentences, but the most emphatic sentence is not always the best choice. Because the periodic structure forces readers to wait—or even to search—for the delayed main idea, periodic sentences tend not to be as straightforward as cumulative ones. In addition, a periodic sentence that is part of an unrelieved string of periodic sentences will lose its impact. Therefore, when deciding whether or not to use a periodic sentence, consider not only the emphasis you wish to achieve but also how directly you wish to communicate your ideas and how all the sentences in a passage work together.

E X E R C I S E   3

A. Bracket the independent clause(s) in each sentence, and underline each modifying phrase and dependent clause.
B. Label each sentence cumulative or periodic. Then, relocate the supporting details to make cumulative sentences periodic and periodic sentences cumulative, adding words or rephrasing to make your meaning clear.
C. Be prepared to explain how your revision changes the emphasis of the original sentence.

> EXAMPLE: [Feeling isolated, sad, and frightened], the small child sat alone in the train depot. (cumulative)
>
> The small child sat alone in the train depot, feeling isolated, sad, and frightened. (periodic)

1. However different in their educational opportunities, both Jefferson and Lincoln as young men became known to their contemporaries as "hard students."   (Douglas L. Wilson, "What Jefferson and Lincoln Read," *Atlantic Monthly*)
2. The road came into being slowly, league by league, river crossing by river crossing.   (Stephen Harrigan, "Highway 1," *Texas Monthly*)

3. Without willing it, I had gone from being ignorant of being ignorant to being aware of being aware. (Maya Angelou, *I Know Why the Caged Bird Sings*)

4. Over the course of the last eighteen months, no politician worth his weight in patriotic sentiment has missed a chance to congratulate one of the lesser nations of the earth on its imitation of American democracy. (Lewis H. Lapham, "Democracy in America?" *Harper's*)

5. To those of us who remain committed mainly to the exploration of moral distinctions and ambiguities, the feminist analysis may have seemed a particularly narrow and cracked determinism. (Joan Didion, "The Women's Movement")

6. [Henry] Moore's personal history is as familiar in outline as are his sculptures: his birth in 1898 as the seventh child of a Yorkshire coal-mining family; his early skill at carving; a conservative artistic education at the Royal College of Art, in London. (Kay Larson, *New York Magazine*)

EXERCISE 4

A. Combine each of the following sentence groups into one cumulative sentence, subordinating supporting details to main ideas.

B. Then combine each group into one periodic sentence. Each group can be combined in a variety of ways, and you will have to add, delete, change, or reorder words.

C. Be prepared to explain how the two versions of the sentence differ in emphasis.

> EXAMPLE: More people of color than ever before are running for office. They are encouraged by the success of minority candidates.
>
> CUMULATIVE: More people of color than ever before are running for office, encouraged by the success of minority candidates.
>
> PERIODIC: Encouraged by the success of minority candidates, more people of color than ever before are running for office.

1. Many politicians opposed the MX missile. They believed it was too expensive. They felt that a smaller, single-warhead missile was preferable.

2. Smoking poses a real danger. It is associated with various cancers. It is linked to heart disease and stroke. It even threatens nonsmokers.

3. Infertile couples who want children sometimes go through a series of difficult processes. They may try adoption. They may also try artifi-

cial insemination or in vitro fertilization. They may even seek out surrogate mothers.

4. The Thames is a river that meanders through southern England. It has been the inspiration for literary works such as *Alice's Adventures in Wonderland* and *The Wind in the Willows*. It was also captured in paintings by Constable, Turner, and Whistler.

5. Black-footed ferrets are rare North American mammals. They prey on prairie dogs. They are primarily nocturnal. They have black feet and black-tipped tails. Their faces have racoonlike masks.

E X E R C I S E   5

Combine each of the following sentence groups into one sentence in which you subordinate supporting details to main ideas. In each case, create either a periodic or a cumulative sentence, depending on which structure you think will best convey the sentence's emphasis. Add, delete, change, or reorder words when necessary.

> EXAMPLE: The fears of today's college students are based on reality. They are afraid there are too many students and too few jobs.
>
> The fears of today's college students—that there are too many students and too few jobs—are based on reality. (periodic)

1. Today's college students are under a good deal of stress. Job prospects are not very good. Financial aid is not as easy to come by as it was in the past.

2. Education has grown very expensive. The job market has become tighter. Pressure to get into graduate and professional schools has increased.

3. Family ties seem to be weakening. Students aren't always able to count on family support.

4. Students have always had problems. Now college counseling centers report more—and more serious—problems among college students.

5. The term *student shock* has recently been coined. This term describes a syndrome that may include depression, anxiety, headaches, and eating and sleeping disorders.

6. Many students are overwhelmed by the vast array of courses and majors offered at their colleges. They tend to be less decisive. They take longer to choose a major and to complete school.

7. Many drop out of school for brief (or extended) periods or switch majors several times. Many take five years or longer to complete their college education.

8. Some colleges are responding to the pressures students feel. They

hold stress-management workshops and suicide-prevention courses. They advertise the services of their counseling centers. They train students as peer counselors. They improve their vocational counseling services.

10c *Achieving Emphasis through Parallelism and Balance*

A **parallel sequence** gives a sentence emphasis and clarity by highlighting corresponding grammatical elements. Parallelism is used in situations where information must be conveyed clearly, quickly, and emphatically:

► See 16a

> We seek an individual who is a self-starter, who owns a late-model automobile, and who is willing to work evenings. (classified advertisement)

> Do not pass go; do not collect $200. (instructions)

> Discuss the role of woman in the short stories of Ernest Hemingway and F. Scott Fitzgerald, paying special attention to their relationships with men, to their relationships with other women, and to their roles in their jobs and/or marriages. (examination question)

> The Faust legend is central in Benét's *The Devil and Daniel Webster*, in Goethe's *Faust*, and in Marlowe's *Dr. Faustus*, (examination answer)

A **balanced sentence** is neatly divided between two parallel structures. Although balanced sentences are typically compound sentences made up of two parallel clauses, they can also be complex sentences. The symmetrical structure of a balanced sentence highlights correspondences or contrasts between clauses:

> In the fifties, the electronic miracle was the television; in the eighties, the electronic miracle was the computer.

> Alive, the elephant was worth at least a hundred pounds; dead, he would only be worth the value of his tusks, five pounds, possibly. (George Orwell, "Shooting an Elephant")

> When guns are outlawed, only outlaws will have guns.

Beyond helping you achieve emphasis, parallelism and balance can help you combine ideas and thus write more economically (see **Ch. 11**). In addition, the judicious use of balanced sentences helps you achieve sentence variety (see **Ch. 12**).

203

10d *Achieving Emphasis through Repetition*

Ineffective repetition makes sentences dull and monotonous as well as wordy:

> He had a good arm and <u>also</u> could field well, and he was <u>also</u> a fast runner.

> We got three estimates, and <u>the one we got from</u> the Johnson Brothers seemed more reasonable than <u>the one we got from</u> County Carpenters.

Effective repetition, however, can place emphasis on key words or ideas. For example, repeating a word or word group in a parallel series can add emphasis:

> They decided to begin again: <u>to begin</u> hoping, <u>to begin</u> trying to change, <u>to begin</u> working toward a goal.

Repeating a key word or phrase just once can also add emphasis:

> During those years when I was just learning to speak, my mother and father addressed me only <u>in Spanish; in Spanish</u> I learned to reply. (Richard Rodriguez, *Aria: A Memoir of a Bilingual Childhood*)

> If ever <u>two groups</u> were opposed, surely those <u>two groups</u> are runners and smokers. (Joseph Epstein, *Familiar Territory*)

Repetition may be restricted to a sentence, or it may continue throughout a paragraph—or even a paragraph cluster. In the following group of sentences, the parallel structure and repetition of *still* add emphasis, stressing how hard the author's mother worked:

> <u>Still</u> she sewed—dresses and jackets for the children, housedresses and aprons for herself, weekly patching of jeans, overalls, and denim shirts. She <u>still</u> made pillows, using the feathers she had plucked, and quilts every year—intricate patterns as well as patchwork, stitched as well as tied—all necessary bedding for her family. Every scrap of cloth too small to be used in quilts was carefully saved and painstakingly sewed together in strips to make rugs. She <u>still</u> went out in the fields to help with the haying whenever there was a threat of rain. (Donna Smith-Yackel, "My Mother Never Worked")

EXERCISE 6

Revise the sentences in this paragraph, using parallelism and balance whenever possible to highlight corresponding elements and using repetition of key words and phrases to add emphasis. (To achieve repetition, you must change some synonyms.) You may combine sentences and add, delete, or reorder words.

> Many readers distrust newspapers. They also distrust what they read in magazines. They do not trust what they hear on the radio and what television shows them either. Of these media, newspapers have been the most responsive to audience criticism. Some newspapers even have ombudsmen. They are supposed to listen to reader complaints. They are also charged with acting on these grievances. One complaint many people have is that newspapers are inaccurate. Newspapers' disregard for people's privacy is another of many readers' criticisms. Reporters are seen as arrogant, and readers feel that journalists can be unfair. They feel reporters tend to glorify criminals, and they believe there is a tendency to place too much emphasis on bizarre or offbeat stories. Finally, readers complain about poor writing and editing. Polls show that despite its efforts to respond to reader criticism, the press continues to face hostility. (Adapted from *Newsweek*)

10e *Achieving Emphasis through Active Voice*

The active voice is generally more emphatic—and more concise— than the passive voice.

PASSIVE: The prediction that oil prices will rise significantly can now be made by economists.

ACTIVE: Economists can now predict that oil prices will rise significantly.

The passive voice tends to focus your readers' attention on the action or on its receiver rather than on who is performing it. The receiver of the action is the subject of a passive sentence, so the actor fades into the background (*by economists*) or is omitted (*the prediction can now be made*). This deemphasis of the actor can make a sentence seem off-balance and lacking in force.

Sometimes, of course, you want to present the recipient of the action prominently. If so, it makes sense to use the passive voice. To stress the opening of the Western frontier, you would write:

▶ See 231

PASSIVE: The West was opened by Lewis and Clark. (*or* The West was opened.)

To stress the contribution of Lewis and Clark, however, you would write:

ACTIVE: Lewis and Clark opened the West.

The passive is also used when the identity of the actor is irrelevant or unknown.

The course was canceled.

Littering is prohibited.

The beaker was filled with a saline solution.

The passive voice occurs frequently in scientific and technical writing.

EXERCISE 7

Revise this paragraph to eliminate awkward or excessive use of passive constructions.

Jack Dempsey, the heavyweight champion between 1919 and 1926, had an interesting but uneven career. He was considered one of the greatest boxers of all time. Dempsey began fighting as "Kid Blackie," but his career didn't take off until 1919, when Jack "Doc" Kearns became his manager. Dempsey won the championship when Jess Willard was defeated by him in Toledo, Ohio, in 1919. Dempsey immediately became a popular sports figure; Franklin Delano Roosevelt was one of his biggest fans. Influential friends were made by Jack Dempsey. Boxing lessons were given by him to the actor Rudolph Valentino. He made friends with Douglas Fairbanks, Sr., Damon Runyon, and J. Paul Getty. Hollywood serials were made by Dempsey, but the title was lost by him to Gene Tunney, and Dempsey failed to regain it the following year. Meanwhile, his life was marred by unpleasant developments such as a bitter legal battle with his manager and his 1920 indictment for draft evasion. In subsequent years, after his boxing career declined, a restaurant was opened by Dempsey, and many major sporting events were attended by him. This exposure kept him in the public eye until he lost his restaurant. Jack Dempsey died in 1983.

STUDENT WRITER AT WORK

WRITING EMPHATIC SENTENCES

Identify the strategies a freshman composition student has used in this draft to add emphasis. Revise the draft to make sentences more emphatic, and then revise again if necessary to strengthen coherence, unity, and style.

Nuclear Power Plants: Threat to the Public

Nuclear power is a relatively new source of energy. Our reliance upon nuclear power increases as conventional sources of energy, such as coal and petroleum, are depleted. There has been much controversy concerning the safety of the reactors currently in use, however. Nuclear power plants are a constant threat to the public and to the environment.

It has been claimed by the nuclear power industry that its plants are safe. The industry points out that safety devices and procedures are rigid and that nuclear plants hold a safety record equal to that of conventional plants using coal or petroleum. These nuclear plants do not use coal or petroleum, however. Instead, they use highly radioactive substances. Safety standards at nuclear power plants should be even more rigidly enforced for this reason.

Many nuclear power plants are poorly built and designed. Some unscrupulous construction firms have been caught altering specifications or using shoddy materials to increase their profit margins. One nuclear reactor in California was designed to withstand massive earthquakes. However, some of the specifications were altered so that the foundation may have to be replaced or modified if it is to withstand an earthquake. Many nuclear plants have been plagued with faulty valves installed by firms that allegedly were aware of the defects.

A large number of poorly trained or inexperienced workers are among those employed as plant operators. The extent of the damage at Three Mile Island would not have been so great if the operators had been more experienced or better trained. Many operators failed their licensing test at Three Mile Island several years ago. This situation left only the minimum number of personnel required to operate the reactor "safely."

Until more research is done with regard to safety
procedures, design, and personnel of nuclear power plants,
these plants should be considered a threat to our
environment and to our lives. No more plants should be
built, and existing ones should be modified or shut down.
Nuclear energy should not be used unless facilities are
redesigned and thoroughly tested, although it can be a
good source of energy. Tighter government controls should
be imposed to protect the people and their environment.

Writing Concise Sentences

A concise sentence contains only the number of words necessary to achieve its effect or to convey its message. But a sentence is not concise simply because it is short. Conciseness is always related to content, to how much you have to say. If you can eliminate words without reducing the amount of information you present, you should do so.

Every word serves a purpose in a concise sentence. Because they are free of unnecessary words and convoluted constructions that come between writer and reader, concise sentences are also clear and emphatic.

Strategies for Writing Concise Sentences

- Eliminate nonessential words.
- Eliminate needless repetition.
- Tighten rambling sentences.

11a *Eliminating Nonessential Words*

One way to find out which words are essential to the meaning of a sentence is to underline the key words. Then, looking carefully at the remaining ones, you can see which are unnecessary or meaningless and delete them.

It seems to me that it doesn't make sense to allow any bail to be granted to anyone who has ever been convicted of a violent crime.

The underlining shows you immediately that none of the words in the long introductory phrase are essential. In revising, you might write this sentence:

> Bail should not be granted to anyone who has ever been convicted of a violent crime.

The new sentence includes all the key words and the minimum number of other words needed to give the key ideas coherence.

Nonessential words fall into three loose classifications: *deadwood, utility words,* and *circumlocution.*

(1)   Delete deadwood

Deadwood denotes unnecessary phrases that take up space and add nothing to meaning.

To be can be eliminated in certain contexts.

WORDY	CONCISE
Kareem Abdul-Jabbar was considered to be a great center.	Kareem Abdul-Jabbar was considered a great center.

You can often delete *who are, which are, that is,* and similar phrases that introduce adjective clauses.

WORDY	CONCISE
Shoppers who are looking for bargains often patronize outlets.	Shoppers looking for bargains often patronize outlets.
They played a racquetball game which was exhausting.	They played an exhausting racquetball game.
The box that was in the middle contained a surprise.	The box in the middle contained a surprise.

Removing deadwood from these wordy sentences turns the adjective clauses into simple modifying words or phrases, which in turn helps prevent rambling sentences (see 11c).

Revision Close-up

There is, there are, there were, and *it is* at the beginning of a sentence are frequently unnecessary.

There were many factors that influenced his decision to become a priest.	Many factors influenced his decision to become a priest.

It was lucky that he was able to get his friends to help him move.	He was lucky to get his friends to help him move.

Certain empty self-justifications and pompous sentence extenders too often appear as introductory phrases.

WORDY	CONCISE
With reference to your memo, the points you make are worth considering.	The points in your memo are worth considering.
In my opinion, the characters seem undeveloped.	The characters seem undeveloped.
As far as this course is concerned, it looks interesting.	This course looks interesting.
For all intents and purposes, the two brands are alike.	The two brands are essentially alike.
It is important to note that the results were identical in both clinical trials.	The results were identical in both clinical trials.

These and other expressions—*obviously, as the case may be, I feel, it seems to me, all things considered, without a doubt, in conclusion,* and *by way of explanation*—are simply padding. You may think they balance or fill out a sentence or make your writing sound more authoritative, but the reverse is true.

(2) Delete or replace utility words

Utility words are vague, all-purpose words that act as fillers and contribute nothing to a sentence. They may be nouns, usually those with imprecise meanings (*factor, kind, type, quality, aspect, thing, sort, field, area, situation,* and so on); adjectives, usually those with broad meanings (*good, nice, bad, fine, important, significant);* or adverbs, usually common ones concerning degree (*basically, completely, actually, very, definitely, quite*).

WORDY	CONCISE
The registration situation was disorganized.	Registration was disorganized.
His offer to share his lunch was a nice gesture.	His offer to share his lunch was a generous gesture.

The scholarship offered Fran a good opportunity to study Spanish.	The scholarship offered Fran an opportunity to study Spanish.
It was actually a worthwhile book, but I didn't completely finish it.	It was a worthwhile book, but I didn't finish it.

When you find yourself using a utility word, delete it or replace it with a more specific word. The result will be a more economical sentence.

(3) Avoid circumlocution

Taking a roundabout way to say something (using ten words when five will do) is called **circumlocution.** When you use long words, complicated phrases, and rambling constructions instead of short, concrete, commonly used words and phrases, you cannot write concise sentences. Notice how the revised versions of these sentences use fewer words and simpler constructions to say the same thing.

WORDY	CONCISE
The curriculum was of a unique nature.	The curriculum was unique.
It is not unlikely that the trend toward smaller cars will continue.	The trend toward smaller cars will probably continue.
Joel was in the army during the same time that I was in college.	Joel was in the army while I was in college.
It is entirely possible that the lake is frozen.	The lake may be frozen.

Wordy phrases can almost always be controlled or avoided. Always choose simple, easily understood terms; when you revise, strike out wordy, convoluted constructions.

Commonly Used Wordy Phrases

Instead of	Use
at the present time	now
at this point in time	now

for the purpose of	for
due to the fact that	because
on account of the fact that	because
until such time as	until
in the event that	if
by means of	by
in the vicinity of	near
have the ability to	be able to

EXERCISE 1

Revise the following paragraph to eliminate deadwood, utility words, and circumlocution. When a word or phrase seems superfluous, delete it or replace it with a more concise expression.

Sally Ride is an astrophysicist who was selected to be the first American woman astronaut. It seems that there were many good reasons why she was chosen. She is a first-rate athlete, and she did graduate work in X-ray astronomy and free-electron lasers. As a result of these and other factors, NASA accepted Ride as a "mission specialist" astronaut in the year 1978. Prior to that time, Ride had been a graduate student at Stanford who knew she had the capability of becoming a specialist in the area of theoretical physics. At NASA she helped to design the remote manipulator arm of the space shuttle, and at a later point she relayed flight instructions to astronauts until such time as she was assigned to a flight crew. Now, Ride teaches at the University of California. Although she is no longer employed by NASA, at this point in time she remains something quite definitely special: America's very first woman in space.

11b *Eliminating Needless Repetition*

Repetition of words or concepts can add clarity and emphasis to your writing, but unnecessary repetition annoys readers and obscures your meaning. Repeated words and **redundant** word groups (words or phrases that say the same thing in different words) are the chief problems. Consider the following sentences:

WORDY	CONCISE
Ernest Hemingway, one of the most <u>famous</u> and <u>well-known</u> <u>authors</u> in American literary history, is the <u>author</u> of <u>novels</u> like *The Sun Also Rises* and other <u>novels</u>. (*Famous* and *well-known* are redundant, while *author* and *novels* are repeated needlessly.)	Ernest Hemingway, one of the most famous writers in American literary history, is the author of *The Sun Also Rises* and other novels.

You can correct needless repetition in a number of ways.

(1)   Delete unnecessary repetition

The easiest way to correct needless repetition is to delete it.

WORDY	CONCISE
The childhood disease chicken pox occasionally leads to dangerous complications such as the disease known as Reye's Syndrome.	The childhood disease chicken pox occasionally leads to dangerous complications such as Reye's Syndrome.

(2)   Substitute a pronoun

You can substitute a pronoun for a repeated noun.

WORDY	CONCISE
Agatha Christie's Hercule Poirot solves many difficult cases. *The Murder of Roger Ackroyd* was one of Hercule Poirot's most challenging cases.	Agatha Christie's Hercule Poirot solves many difficult cases. *The Murder of Roger Ackroyd* was one of his most challenging cases.

(3)   Use elliptical clauses

You can use elliptical clauses, substituting commas for omitted words (see **27f1**).

WORDY	CONCISE
The Quincy Market is a popular tourist attraction in Boston; the White House is a popular	The Quincy Market is a popular tourist attraction in Boston; the White House, in Washing-

tourist attraction in Washington, D.C.; and the Statue of Liberty is a popular tourist attraction in New York City.	ton, D.C.; and the Statue of Liberty, in New York City.

(4) Use appositives

You can use appositives to eliminate unnecessary repetition.

WORDY	CONCISE
Red Barber was a sportscaster. He was known for his colorful expressions.	Red Barber, a sportscaster, was known for his colorful expressions.

(5) Create compounds

You can combine sentences to create compound subjects, compound objects or complements, or compound predicates. In the following sentence pairs, the revised sentences are not only more concise but also less choppy.

WORDY	CONCISE
Wendy found the exam difficult, and Karen also found it hard. Ken thought it was tough, too.	Wendy, Karen, and Ken all found the exam difficult. (compound subject)
Huckleberry Finn is an adventure story. It is also a sad account of an abused, neglected child.	*Huckleberry Finn* is both an adventure story and a sad account of an abused, neglected child. (compound complement)
In 1964 Ted Briggs was discharged from the Air Force. He then got a job with Maxwell Data Processing. He married Susan Thompson that same year.	In 1964 Ted Briggs was discharged from the Air Force, got a job with Maxwell Data Processing, and married Susan Thompson. (compound predicate)

(6) Use subordination

Finally, you can combine sentences so that one clause is subordinate to the other.

WORDY	CONCISE
One issue in the campaign was police brutality. Police brutality was on many voters' minds.	One issue in the campaign was police brutality, which was on many voters' minds.

Eliminate any unnecessary repetition of words or ideas in this paragraph. Also revise to eliminate deadwood, utility words, or circumlocution.

For a wide variety of different reasons, more and more people today are choosing a vegetarian diet. There are three kinds of vegetarians: strict vegetarians eat no animal foods at all; lactovegetarians eat dairy products, but they do not eat meat, fish, poultry, or eggs; and ovolactovegetarians eat eggs and dairy products, but they do not eat meat, fish, or poultry. Famous vegetarians include such well-known people as George Bernard Shaw, Leonardo da Vinci, Ralph Waldo Emerson, Henry David Thoreau, and Mahatma Gandhi. Like these well-known vegetarians, the vegetarians of today have good reasons for becoming vegetarians. For instance, some religions recommend a vegetarian diet. Some of these religions are Buddhism, Brahmanism, ·and Hinduism. Other people turn to vegetarianism for reasons of health or for reasons of hygiene. These people feel that meat is a source of potentially harmful chemicals, and they believe meat contains infectious organisms. Other people feel meat may cause digestive problems and may lead to other difficulties as well. Other vegetarians adhere to a vegetarian diet because they feel it is ecologically wasteful to kill animals after we feed plants to them. These vegetarians believe *we* should eat the plants. Finally, there are facts and evidence to suggest that a vegetarian diet may possibly help people live longer lives. A vegetarian diet may do this by reducing the incidence of heart disease and lessening the incidence of some cancers. (Adapted from *Jane Brody's Nutrition Book*)

11c   *Tightening Rambling Sentences*

Rambling, out-of-control sentences are the inevitable result of using nonessential words, unnecessary repetition, and complicated syntax. Making such sentences concise involves more than simply deleting a word or two. In fact, revising rambling sentences can require ruthless deletion. As you write and revise, the following techniques can help you keep your sentences under control.

(1)   *Eliminate excessive coordination*

Stringing a series of clauses together with coordinating conjunctions often creates a rambling sentence. Such excessive coordination is not only wordy but also misleading: it presents all your ideas as if they have equal weight when they do not.

WORDY

> Puerto Rico is the fourth largest island in the Caribbean, and it is predominantly mountainous, and it has steep slopes, and they fall to gentle coastal plains.

To revise this sentence, first identify the main idea, and then subordinate the supporting details. The revised sentence emphasizes the mountainous nature of Puerto Rico and recasts the other details as modifiers.

CONCISE

> Fourth largest island in the Caribbean, Puerto Rico is predominantly mountainous, with steep slopes falling to gentle coastal plains. *(National Geographic)*

(2) Eliminate excessive subordination

A series of adjective clauses is likely to produce a rambling sentence. To correct this problem, substitute concise modifying words or phrases for the adjective clauses.

WORDY	CONCISE
Moby-Dick, which is a book about a whale, was written by Herman Melville, who was friendly with Nathaniel Hawthorne, who encouraged him to revise the first draft of his novel.	*Moby-Dick,* a book about a whale, was written by Herman Melville, who revised the first draft of his novel at the urging of his friend Nathaniel Hawthorne.

Notice how two of the three dependent clauses in the first sentence have been eliminated. The sentence is now more economical and easier to read.

(3) Eliminate passive constructions

Although some situations call for passive voice (**see 23l**), the active voice, which communicates the same information in fewer words, is usually more emphatic.

WORDY	CONCISE
"Buy American" rallies are being organized by concerned Americans who hope jobs can be saved by such gatherings.	Concerned Americans are organizing "Buy American" rallies, hoping such gatherings can save jobs.
Water rights are being fought for in court by Indian tribes like the Papago in Arizona and the Pyramid Lake Paiute in Nevada.	Indian tribes like the Papago in Arizona and the Pyramid Lake Paiute in Nevada are fighting in court for water rights.

(4) Eliminate wordy prepositional phrases

Often you can tighten a rambling sentence by substituting single adjectives or adverbs for wordy prepositional phrases used as modifiers.

WORDY	CONCISE
The trip was one of danger but also one of excitement.	The trip was dangerous but exciting. (adjectives replace prepositional phrases)
He spoke in a confident manner.	He spoke confidently. (adverb replaces prepositional phrase)

(5) Eliminate wordy noun constructions

You can also tighten a rambling sentence by substituting strong verbs for convoluted noun phrases.

WORDY	CONCISE
The normalization of commercial relations between the United States and China in 1979 led to an increase in trade between the two countries.	When the United States and China normalized commercial relations in 1979, trade between the two countries increased.
We have made the decision to postpone the meeting until after the appearance of all the board members.	We have decided to postpone the meeting until all the board members appear.

EXERCISE 3

Revise the rambling sentences in this paragraph by eliminating excessive coordination and subordination, unnecessary use of the passive voice, and overuse of wordy prepositional phrases and noun constructions. As you revise, make your sentences more concise by deleting nonessential words and superfluous repetition.

Some colleges that have been in support of fraternities for a number of years are at this time in the process of conducting a reevaluation of the position of those fraternities on campus. In opposition to the fraternities are a fair number of students, faculty members, and administrators, who claim fraternities are inherently sexist, which they say makes it impossible for the groups to exist in a coeducational institution, which is supposed to offer equal opportunities for members of both sexes. And, more and more members of the college community see fraternities as elitist as well as sexist and favor their abolition. The situation has already begun to be dealt with at some colleges. For instance, Williams College made a decision in favor of the abolition of fraternities. At Wesleyan University a decision was made by officials to sever formal ties to all-male fraternities. This was done because of the university's inability to persuade the fraternities to consider the acceptance of women. In some cases, however, students, faculty, and administration remain wholeheartedly in support of fraternities, which they believe are responsible for helping students make the acquaintance of people and learn the leadership skills which they believe will be of assistance to them in their future lives as adults. Supporters of fraternities believe students should retain the right to make their own social decisions and that joining a fraternity is one of those decisions, and they also believe fraternities are responsible for providing valuable services and some of these are tutoring, raising money for charity, and running campus escort services. Therefore, they are not of the opinion that the abolition of fraternities makes sense.

STUDENT WRITER AT WORK

WRITING CONCISE SENTENCES

Revise this excerpt from an essay examination in American literature to make it more concise. After you have done so, revise further if necessary to strengthen coherence, unity, and style.

```
Oftentimes in the course of a literary work,
characters may find themselves misfits in the sense that
they do not seem to be a real part of the society in which
they find themselves. This problem often leads to a series
of genuinely serious and severe problems, conflicts either
```

between the misfits and their own identities or possibly between them and that society into which they so poorly fit.

In "The Minister's Black Veil" Reverend Hooper all of a sudden gives to the townspeople and members of his parish a surprise: a piece of black material which he has wrapped over his face, which causes readers to be as completely and thoroughly confused as the townspeople about the possible reason for the minister's decision to hide his face, until readers learn, in his sermon, that he is covering his face (from God, his fellow man, and himself) to atone for the sins of mankind. As far as readers can tell, they are never quite sure exactly why he is in possession of the notion that this act must be carried out by him, and they are never completely sure whether Reverend Hooper feels this guilt for some sin that may exist in his own past or for those sins that may have been committed by mankind in general, but in any case it is clear that he feels it is his duty to place himself in isolation from the world at large around him. To the Reverend, there is no solution to his problem, and he lives his whole entire life wearing the veil. Even after his death he insists that the veil remain covering his features, for it is said by the Reverend that his face could not be revealed on earth.

For Reverend Hooper, a terrible conflict exists within himself, and so Reverend Hooper voluntarily makes himself a misfit even at the expense of losing everything, even his true love Elizabeth.

Writing Varied Sentences

Varying your sentences will help you convey emphasis accurately and hold reader interest.

Strategies for Writing Varied Sentences

- Vary sentence length.
- Combine choppy simple sentences.
- Break up strings of compounds.
- Vary sentence types.
- Vary sentence openings.
- Vary standard word order.

12a *Varying Sentence Length*

A mixture of long and short sentences not only gives a pleasing texture to your writing but also keeps readers interested.

(1) *Mix long and short sentences*

A paragraph consisting entirely of short sentences (or entirely of long ones) can be dull:

> Drag racing began in California in the 1940's. It was an alternative to street racing, which was illegal and dangerous. It flourished in the 50's and 60's. Eventually, it became almost a rite of passage. Then, during the 70's, almost one-third of America's racetracks closed. Today, however, drag racing is making a modest comeback.

The following revision combines sentences to create units of various lengths:

> Drag racing began in California in the 1940's as an alternative to street racing, which was illegal and dangerous. It flourished in the 50's and 60's, eventually becoming almost a rite of passage. Then, during the 70's, almost one-third of America's racetracks closed. Today, however, drag racing is making a modest comeback.

(2)   Follow a long sentence with a short one

Using a short sentence after one or more long ones immediately attracts reader attention. This gear shifting, illustrated in the following passages, emphasizes the short sentence and its content while adding variety.

> There are two social purposes for family dinners—the regular exchange of news and ideas and the opportunity to teach small children not to eat like pigs. These are by no means mutually exclusive. (Judith Martin, "Miss Manners")

> In arguing the need for [vitamin] supplements, doctors like to point out that the normal diet supplies the RDA (Recommended Dietary Allowance) minimums. Nutritionists counter that the RDA, as established by the National Academy of Sciences, is only the minimum daily dose necessary to prevent the diseases associated with particular vitamin deficiencies. Over the years, vitamin boosters say, a misconception has grown that as long as there are no signs or symptoms of say, scurvy, then we have all of the vitamin C we need. Although we know how much of a particular vitamin or mineral will prevent clinical disease, we have practically no information on how much is necessary for peak health. In short, we know how sick is sick, but we don't know how well is well. (*Philadelphia Magazine*)

EXERCISE 1

A. Combine each of the following sentence groups into one long sentence.
B. Then, compose a relatively short sentence to follow each long one.
C. Finally, combine all the sentences into a paragraph, adding a topic sentence and any transitions necessary for coherence. Proofread your paragraph to be sure the sentences are varied in length.

1. Chocolate is composed of over 300 compounds. Phenylethylamine is one such compound. Its presence in the brain may be linked to the emotion of falling in love.

2. Americans now consume a good deal of chocolate. They eat an average of over nine pounds of chocolate per person per year. Belgians, however, consume almost fifteen pounds per year.
3. In recent years, Americans have begun a serious love affair with chocolate. Elegant chocolate boutiques sell exquisite bonbons by the piece. At least one hotel offers a "chocolate binge" vacation. The bimonthly *Chocolate News* for connoisseurs is flourishing. (Adapted from *Newsweek*)

12b *Combining Choppy Simple Sentences*

Strings of disconnected simple sentences can be tedious—and sometimes hard to follow as well. Revise such sentences by combining them with adjacent sentences, using coordination, subordination, or embedding.

(1) Use coordination

Coordination is one way to revise choppy simple sentences, such as these notes for part of a short paper on freedom of the press in America:

> John Peter Zenger was a newspaper editor. He waged and won an important battle for freedom of the press in America. He criticized the policies of the British governor. He was charged with criminal libel as a result, Zenger's lawyers were disbarred by the governor. Andrew Hamilton defended him. Hamilton convinced the jury that Zenger's criticisms were true. Therefore, the statements were not libelous.

The information is here, but the presentation is flat and lacks some of the links necessary for coherence. Coordination can add interest and clarity:

> John Peter Zenger was a newspaper editor. He waged and won an important battle for freedom of the press in America. He criticized the policies of the British governor, and as a result, he was charged with criminal libel. Zenger's lawyers were disbarred by the governor. Andrew Hamilton defended him. Hamilton convinced the jury that Zenger's criticisms were true. Therefore, the statements were not libelous.

This revision links two of the choppy simple sentences with *and* to create a compound sentence. The result is a slightly smoother paragraph.

(2)   Use subordination

Subordination clarifies the relationships among ideas. The following revision does so by changing two simple sentences into dependent clauses to create two complex sentences:

> John Peter Zenger was a newspaper editor. He waged and won an important battle for freedom of the press in America. He criticized the policies of the British governor, and as a result, he was charged with criminal libel. When Zenger's lawyers were disbarred by the governor, Andrew Hamilton defended him. Hamilton convinced the jury that Zenger's criticisms were true. Therefore, the statements were not libelous.

The revised paragraph now includes two complex sentences: one links ideas with a relative pronoun *(who)* and one with a subordinating conjunction *(when)*.

(3)   Use embedding

Embedding—working phrases, clauses, and sentences into other sentences—is another strategy for varying sentence structure. It is used effectively in the following revision:

> John Peter Zenger was a newspaper editor who waged and won an important battle for freedom of the press in America. He criticized the policies of the British governor, and as a result, was charged with criminal libel. When Zenger's lawyers were disbarred by the governor, Andrew Hamilton defended him, convincing the jury that Zenger's criticisms were true. Therefore, the statements were not libelous.

In this revision the sentence *Hamilton convinced the jury...* has been reworded to create a phrase *(convincing the jury)* that modifies the independent clause *Andrew Hamilton defended him.* Now the sentence has been embedded within another sentence.

The final revision of the original string of choppy sentences is a varied, readable paragraph that uses coordination, subordination, and embedding to vary sentence length but retains the final short simple sentence for emphasis. This revision, of course, represents only one of the many possible ways to achieve sentence variety.

EXERCISE 2

Using coordination, subordination, and embedding, revise this string of choppy simple sentences into a more varied and interesting paragraph.

The first modern miniature golf course was built in New York in 1925. It was an indoor course with 18 holes. Entrepreneurs Drake Delanoy and John Ledbetter built 150 more indoor and outdoor courses. Garnet Carter made miniature golf a worldwide fad. Carter built an elaborate miniature golf course. He later joined with Delanoy and Ledbetter. Together they built more miniature golf courses. They abbreviated playing distances. They highlighted the game's hazards at the expense of skill. This made the game much more popular. By 1930 there were 25,000 miniature golf courses in the United States. Courses grew more elaborate. Hazards grew more bizarre. The craze spread to London and Hong Kong. The expansion of miniature golf grew out of control. Then interest in the game declined. By 1931 most miniature golf courses were out of business. The game was revived in the early fifties. Today there are between eight and ten thousand miniature golf courses. The architecture of miniature golf remains an enduring form of American folk art. (Adapted from *Games*)

12c · *Breaking Up Strings of Compounds*

An unbroken series of compound sentences can be dull—and unemphatic (see 11c1). When you connect clauses only with coordinating conjunctions, you may fail to indicate emphasis or relationships accurately.

UNEMPHATIC

A volcano that is erupting is considered *active,* but one that may erupt is designated *dormant,* and one that has not erupted for a long time is called *extinct.* Most active volcanoes are located in "The Ring of Fire," a belt that circles the Pacific Ocean, and they can be extremely destructive. Italy's Vesuvius erupted in A.D. 79, and it destroyed the town of Pompeii. In 1883 Krakatoa, located between the Indonesian islands of Java and Sumatra, erupted, and it caused a tidal wave, and more than 36,000 people were killed. Martinique's Mont Pelée erupted in 1902, and its lava and ash killed 30,000 people, and this completely wiped out the town of St. Pierre.

EMPHATIC

A volcano that is erupting is considered *active;* one that may erupt is designated *dormant;* and one that has not erupted for a long time is called *extinct.* [compound sentence] Most active volcanoes are located in "The Ring of Fire," a belt that circles the Pacific Ocean. [simple sentence with modifier] Active volcanoes can be extremely destructive.

[simple sentence] Erupting in A.D. 79, Italy's Vesuvius destroyed the town of Pompeii. [simple sentence with modifier] When Krakatoa, located between the Indonesian islands of Java and Sumatra, erupted in 1883, it caused a tidal wave that killed 36,000 people. [compound-complex sentence with modifier] The eruption of Martinique's Mont Pelée in 1902 produced lava and ash that killed 30,000 people, completely wiping out the town of St. Pierre. [complex sentence with modifier]

EXERCISE 3

Revise the compound sentences in this passage so that the sentence structure is varied and the writer's meaning and emphasis are clear.

Dr. Alice I. Baumgartner and her colleagues at the Institute for Equality in Education at the University of Colorado surveyed 2,000 Colorado schoolchildren, and they found some startling results. They asked, "If you woke up tomorrow and discovered that you were a (boy) (girl), how would your life be different?" and the answers were sad and shocking. The researchers assumed they would find that boys and girls think there are advantages to being either male or female, but instead they found that both boys and girls had a fundamental contempt for females. Many elementary schoolboys titled their answers "The Disaster" or "Doomsday," and they described the terrible lives they would lead as girls, but the girls seemed to feel they would be better off as boys, and they expressed feelings that they would be able to do more and have easier lives.

Boys and girls alike realized that girls are judged by their looks more than boys, and both felt girls had to pay more attention to their looks, so all children perceived boys as having an advantage. In addition, boys and girls both valued boys' activities more highly, and boys and girls agreed that "women's work" is less valuable and less valued than "men's work." Both boys and girls also felt that boys are expected to behave differently, and they felt that boys could get away with more and be more active, but girls did have one advantage and that was that they could express their feelings openly.

Finally, both boys and girls agreed that boys are treated better and respected more than girls, so in other words there is a prejudice against females among both boys and girls, and this sex stereotyping is a psychological handicap for both men and women. (Adapted from *Redbook*)

12d *Varying Sentence Types*

You can vary sentence types by mixing **declarative sentences** (statements) with occasional **imperative sentences** (commands or requests), **exclamations,** and **rhetorical questions** (questions that the reader is not expected to answer).

IMPERATIVE SENTENCE

Modern dude ranches mix activities found at conventional resorts—golf, swimming, tennis, dances—with elements of the Old West. But some rather elaborate ranches may be quite expensive. Before planning a dude ranch vacation, then, consider your needs and interests carefully. You may be happier in a more modest (and less costly) setting.

EXCLAMATIONS

Tracks! Tracks! It seemed to the visionaries who wrote for the popular magazines that the future lay at the end of parallel rails. (E. L. Doctorow, *Ragtime*)

RHETORICAL QUESTION

Was it any wonder that seven members of the Continental Congress who had seen the draft of the Declaration of Independence had fled to Philadelphia, threatening to defect to King George III? Still, John Hancock had stood firm. Faithful John Hancock. Even now Hancock was scouring Philadelphia chicken coops, searching for a newborn chick with a quill so small that no one would be able to decipher his signature without a microscope. (Russell Baker, *New York Times Magazine*)

Revision Close-up

Other options for varying sentence types include mixing simple, compound, and complex sentences **(see 12b and c);** mixing cumulative and periodic sentences **(10b);** and using balanced sentences where appropriate **(see 10c).**

E X E R C I S E   4

The following paragraph is composed entirely of declarative sentences. To make it more varied, add three sentences—one exclamation, one rhetorical question, and one command—anywhere in the paragraph. Be sure the sentences you create are consistent with the paragraph's purpose and tone.

When the Fourth of July comes around, the nation explodes with patriotism. Everywhere we look we see parades and picnics, firecrackers and fireworks. An outsider might wonder what all the fuss is about. We could explain that this is America's birthday party, and all the candles are being lit at once. There is no reason for us to hold back our enthusiasm—or to limit the noise that celebrates it. The Fourth of July is watermelon and corn on the cob, American flags and sparklers, brass bands and more. Everyone looks forward to this celebration, and everyone has a good time.

12e   *Varying Sentence Openings*

In addition to varying sentence length and type, you can create variety by choosing different openings for your sentences. Rather than resigning yourself to beginning every sentence with the subject, strengthen your emphasis and clarify the relationship of a sentence to those that surround it by opening some sentences with modifying words, phrases, or clauses.

(1)   Adjectives, adverbs, and adverb clauses

You can begin a sentence with one or more *adjectives* or *adverbs* or with an *adverb clause*.

Proud and relieved, they watched their daughter receive her diploma. (adjectives)

Hungrily, he devoured his lunch. (adverb)

While Woodrow Wilson was incapacitated by a stroke, his wife unofficially performed many presidential duties. (adverb clause)

(2)   Prepositional phrases, participial phrases

You can begin a sentence with a *prepositional phrase* or a *participial phrase*.

For better or worse, alcohol has been a part of human culture through the ages. *(Consumer Reports)* (prepositional phrase)

Located on the west coast of Great Britain, Wales is part of the United Kingdom. (participial phrase)

(3) Coordinating conjunctions, conjunctive adverbs

To clarify the connection between two sentences, you can begin the second sentence with a *coordinating conjunction* or a *conjunctive adverb.*

The Big Bang may be the beginning of the universe, or it may be a discontinuity in which information about the earlier history of the universe was destroyed. But it is certainly the earliest event about which we have any record. (Carl Sagan, *The Dragons of Eden*) (coordinating conjunction)

Pantomime was first performed in ancient Rome. However, it remains a popular dramatic form today. (conjunctive adverb)

(4) Inverted appositives, absolute phrases

You can begin a sentence with an *inverted appositive* or with an *absolute phrase.*

A British scientist, Alexander Fleming is famous for having discovered penicillin. (inverted appositive)

His interests widening, Picasso designed ballet sets and illustrated books. (absolute phrase)

EXERCISE 5

Each of these sentences begins with the subject. Rewrite each so that it has a different opening, and then identify the opening strategy you used.

> EXAMPLE: Florence King, an acerbic-witted contemporary essayist, is to some a curmudgeon who dislikes everything and everybody.
>
> An acerbic-witted contemporary essayist, Florence King is to some a curmudgeon who dislikes everything and everybody. (inverted appositive)

1. *Confessions of a Failed Southern Lady,* a chronicle of King's early life, describes her peculiarly Southern family.
2. Herb, King's British intellectual dance-band musician father, educated himself quietly in his spare time.
3. Louise, her mother, was an ardent baseball fan, chain smoker, and world-class curser who didn't suffer fools gladly.
4. Granny, setting a good example, debated questions such as whether it is more ladylike to have a nervous breakdown or "female problems."

5. These people, with all their quirks and flaws, were the major influences, King contends, on her character and sense of humor.

12f *Varying Standard Word Order*

You can vary standard subject-verb-object (or complement) word order in two ways: by intentionally inverting this usual order, or by placing words between subject and verb.

(1) Invert word order

You can invert conventional word order by placing the complement or direct object *before* the verb instead of in its conventional position. Or, you can place the verb *before* the subject instead of after it.

In each of the following sentences, the unusual word order draws attention to what has been inverted:

(subject)
Nature   I   loved and, next to Nature, Art. (Walter Savage Landor)
(object)   (verb)

(complement)
The book was extremely helpful; especially useful was its index.
(verb) (subject)

Revision Close-up

Keep in mind that when it is overused, inversion loses its force and sounds unnatural.

---

(2) Separate subject from verb

Placing words or phrases between subject and verb is another way to vary standard word order.

Many states require that infants and young children ride in government-approved car seats because they hope this will reduce needless fatalities. (subject and verb together)

Many states, hoping to reduce needless fatalities, require that infants and young children ride in government-approved car seats. (subject and verb separated)

E X E R C I S E   6

The following sentences use conventional word order. Revise each in two ways: First, invert the sentence; then, vary the word order by placing words between subject and verb. After you have completed your revisions, create a varied five-sentence paragraph, choosing one version of each sentence. Be prepared to explain your choices.

> EXAMPLE: Exam week is invariably hectic and not much fun.
>
> Invariably hectic and not much fun is exam week.
>
> Exam week, invariably hectic, is not much fun.

1. The Beach Boys formed a band in 1961, and the group consisted of Brian Wilson, his brothers Carl and Dennis, their cousin Mike Love, and Alan Jardine, a friend.
2. The group's first single was "Surfin'," which attracted national attention.
3. Capitol Records signed the band to record "Surfin' Safari" because the company felt the group had potential.
4. The Beach Boys had many other top-twenty singles during the next five years, and most of these hits were written, arranged, and produced by Brian Wilson.
5. Their songs focused on California sun and good times and included "I Get Around," "Be True to Your School," "Fun, Fun, Fun," and "Good Vibrations."

STUDENT WRITER AT WORK

WRITING VARIED SENTENCES

Read this draft of a student essay carefully. Then, revise it to achieve greater sentence variety by varying the length, type, openings, and word order of the sentences. After you have done so, revise further if necessary to strengthen coherence, unity, and style.

Advertising: Newspapers versus Television

Advertising persuades by provoking the senses. It is big business. It exploits every conceivable method of enticing consumers to buy. Ads can be straightforward and informational. Or, they can be filled with intrigue, hilarity, or sexuality. They can prod the minds of the hungry, the self-indulgent, the imaginative, and the gullible. Every conceivable medium is used to advertise. Each has the same objective: to sell. Television and newspapers are perhaps the two most influential means of advertising. They reach the greatest number and widest range of people.

Advertisements in local newspapers lace the pages like a net. They lure the prospective catch with bait. This bait appears in the form of bold lettering and small dollar signs. But newspapers are for the serious-minded. People tend to believe things they read in black and white. So newspapers tend to report the facts. They announce store hours and liquidation sales. They support everything with numerous figures. Newspaper ads are concise and informative. They are also unpretentious and sensible. They attract attention to everything from barbells to diamond rings, using (for the most part) only facts.

Television is a completely different medium. It plays with emotion, fantasy, and impulse. It seeks to invoke an immediate response. Every viewer must remember a time when he or she got up from the couch to race to the refrigerator, victim of a commercial that promised Heavenly Hash satisfaction. Television uses only two of the five senses, sound and sight, but with careful calculation touch, smell, and taste can also be triggered, and therein lies television's strength. Viewers feel the excitement of driving a Pontiac LeMans up a mountain. They grind their teeth as they prepare to sail in a hang glider over the craggy California coast (chewing Wrigley's Spearmint Gum, of course). Emotionally charged sensationalism gets the message across.

Television ads roll right into viewers' living rooms. These advertisements sneak up on viewers. They play on their emotions. The ads appeal to greed, to competitiveness, to a desire for comfort and luxury. Newspaper ads finish the job. They tell where and when to buy. Readers already know why.

PART 4

Solving Common Sentence Problems

13

Sentence Fragments

A **sentence fragment** is an incomplete sentence, a phrase or clause punctuated as if it were a complete sentence.

A sentence may be incomplete because it lacks a subject or a **finite verb,** a verb that changes form to indicate person, tense, and number.

> Many astrophysicists now believe that galaxies are distributed in clusters. And even form supercluster complexes. (subject missing)

> Researchers are engaged in a variety of studies. All suggesting that a predisposition to alcoholism may be inherited. (finite verb missing)

> The streets of many large cities are home to increasing numbers of homeless people. Mentally or physically ill and unable to find shelter. (both subject and finite verb missing)

Revision Close-up

Participles *(suggesting)* and infinitives *(to find)* are verbals. Because they are not finite verbs, they cannot serve as main verbs in a sentence.

See
21c2 ◄

A sentence may also be incomplete because it is actually a dependent clause, introduced by a subordinating conjunction or by a relative pronoun.

> Bishop Desmond Tutu was awarded the Nobel Peace Prize. Because he struggled to end apartheid. (introduced by subordinating conjunction)

> The pH meter and the spectrophotometer are two scientific instruments. That changed the chemistry laboratory dramatically. (introduced by relative pronoun)

When readers cannot see where sentences begin and end, they have difficulty understanding what you have written. For instance, it is impossible to tell to which independent clause the fragment in the following sequence belongs:

> The course requirements were changed last year. Because a new professor was hired at the very end of the spring semester. I was unable to find out about this change until after preregistration.

Tests for Sentence Completeness

- A sentence must have a subject.
- A sentence must have a finite verb.
- A sentence cannot consist of a dependent clause alone. (A sentence cannot consist of a single clause that begins with a subordinating conjunction; unless it is a question, it cannot consist of a single clause beginning with *how, who, which, where, when, or why*.)

If your sentence does not pass these three tests, it is a fragment and should be revised. Once you determine that a sentence is incomplete, you can use one or more of the following strategies to revise the fragment.

Strategies for Revising Sentence Fragments

- Attach the fragment to an adjacent clause.

FRAGMENT: According to German legend, Lohengrin is the son of Parzival. And a knight of the Holy Grail.

REVISED: According to German legend, Lohengrin is the son of Parzival and a knight of the Holy Grail.

- Supply the missing subject and/or finite verb.

FRAGMENT: Lancaster County, Pennsylvania, is home to many Pennsylvania Dutch. Descended from eighteenth-century settlers from southwest Germany.

REVISED: Lancaster County, Pennsylvania, is home to many Pennsylvania Dutch. They are descended from eighteenth-century settlers from southwest Germany.

---

continued

continued from previous page

- Delete the subordinating conjunction or relative pronoun.

FRAGMENT: Property taxes rose sharply. Although city services showed no improvement.

REVISED: Property taxes rose sharply. City services showed no improvement.

When you correct sentence fragments, keep in mind that different strategies have different effects. Do not hesitate to revise corrected fragments further to achieve smooth, logically connected sentences that convey your emphasis accurately.

Revision Close-up

Supplying the missing subject or verb or deleting a subordinating conjunction or relative pronoun will correct many fragments, but these revision strategies may create choppy, disconnected sentences. Sometimes, for example, simple deletion of a subordinating conjunction will leave a necessary causal connection between two sentences unclear. Similarly, although attaching a fragment to an adjacent clause will produce the most concise revision, this strategy does not enable you to emphasize information by placing it in a separate independent clause.

See
Ch.
10, 11

Sentence fragments can take many forms. The following sections identify the grammatical structures most likely to appear as fragments and illustrate the most effective ways of revising each.

13a *Revising Dependent Clauses*

A **dependent clause** contains a subject and a verb, but it cannot stand alone as a sentence. Because it needs an independent clause to complete it, a dependent clause (also called a subordinate clause) must always be attached to at least one independent clause. You can recognize a dependent clause because it is always introduced by a subordinating conjunction or a relative pronoun (see 9b).

To correct fragments created when you punctuate dependent clauses incorrectly, you can use one of the following strategies:

(1) Join the dependent clause to a neighboring independent clause.
(2) Delete the subordinating conjunction or relative pronoun, creating a complete sentence with a subject and a finite verb. (In many cases, you will have to replace the relative pronoun with another word that can serve as the clause's subject.)

FRAGMENT: The United States declared war. Because the Japanese bombed Pearl Harbor. (Dependent clause is punctuated as a sentence.)

REVISED: The United States declared war because the Japanese bombed Pearl Harbor. (Dependent clause has been attached to an independent clause to create a complete sentence.)

REVISED: The Japanese bombed Pearl Harbor. The United States declared war. (Subordinating conjunction has been deleted; the result is a complete sentence.)

FRAGMENT: The battery is dead. Which means the car won't start. (Dependent clause is punctuated as a sentence.)

REVISED: The battery is dead, which means the car won't start. (Dependent clause has been attached to an independent clause to create a complete sentence.)

REVISED: The battery is dead. This means the car won't start. (Relative pronoun has been deleted; the substitution of *this* creates a complete sentence.)

EXERCISE 1

Identify the sentence fragments in the following paragraph, and correct each, either by attaching the fragment to an independent clause or by deleting the subordinating conjunction or relative pronoun to create a sentence that can stand alone. In some cases you will have to replace a relative pronoun with another word that can serve as the subject of an independent clause.

The drive-in movie came into being just after World War II. When both movies and cars were central to the lives of many Americans. Drive-ins were especially popular with teenagers and young families during the 1950's. When cars and gas were relatively inexpensive. Theaters charged by the carload. Which meant that a group of teenagers or a family with several children could spend an evening at the movies for a few dollars. In 1958, when the fad peaked, there were over 4,000 drive-ins in the United States. While today there are fewer than 3,000. Many of these are in the sunbelt, with most in California. Although many sunbelt drive-ins continue to thrive because of the year-round warm weather. Many northern drive-ins are in financial trouble. Because land is so expensive. Some drive-in owners break even only by operating flea markets or swap meets in daylight hours. While others, unable to attract customers, are selling their theaters to land developers. Soon drive-ins may be a part of our nostalgic past. Which will be a great loss for many who enjoy them.

13b   *Revising Prepositional Phrases*

A **prepositional phrase** consists of a preposition, its object, and any modifiers of the object (**see 8f1**). It cannot stand alone as a sentence.

To correct this kind of fragment most concisely, attach it to the independent clause that contains the word or word group modified by the prepositional phrase.

FRAGMENT: President Lyndon Johnson decided not to seek reelection. For a number of reasons. (Prepositional phrase is punctuated as a sentence.)

REVISED: President Lyndon Johnson decided not to seek reelection for a number of reasons. (Prepositional phrase has been attached to an independent clause.)

FRAGMENT: He ran sixty yards for a touchdown. In the final minutes of the game. (Prepositional phrase is punctuated as a sentence.)

REVISED: He ran sixty yards for a touchdown in the final minutes of the game. (Prepositional phrase has been attached to an independent clause.)

EXERCISE 2

Read the following passage and identify the sentence fragments. Then correct each one by attaching it to the preceding independent clause to form a sentence.

Most college athletes are caught in a conflict. Between their athletic and academic careers. Sometimes college athletes' responsibilities on the playing field make it hard for them to be good students. Often athletes must make a choice. Between sports and a degree. Some athletes would not be able to afford college. Without athletic scholarships. But, ironically, their commitments to sports (training, exercise, practice, and travel to out-of-town games, for example) deprive athletes of valuable classroom time. The role of college athletes is constantly being questioned. Critics suggest athletes exist only to participate in and promote college athletics. Because of the importance of this role to academic institutions, scandals occasionally develop. With coaches and even faculty members arranging to inflate athletes' grades to help them remain eligible. For participation in sports. Some universities even lower admissions standards. To help remedy this and other inequities, the controversial Proposition 48, passed at the NCAA convention in 1982, established minimum College Board scores and grade standards for college students. But many people feel that the NCAA remains overly concerned. With profits rather than with education. As a result, college athletic competition is increasingly coming to resemble pro sports. From the coaches' pressure on the players to win to the network television exposure to the wagers on the games' outcomes.

13c *Revising Verbal Phrases*

A **verbal phrase** consists of a present participle *(walking),* past participle *(walked),* infinitive *(to walk),* or gerund plus related objects and modifiers *(walking along the lonely beach)* (see 8f2). Because a verbal phrase does not contain a finite verb, it is not a complete sentence and should not be punctuated as one.

The most effective ways to correct a fragment created when you punctuate a verbal phrase as a sentence are either to attach the verbal phrase to a related independent clause or to change the verbal to a finite verb and add a subject.

FRAGMENT: In 1948 India became independent. Divided into the nations of India and Pakistan. (Participial phrase is punctuated as a sentence.)

REVISED: Divided into the nations of India and Pakistan, India became independent in 1948. (Participial phrase has been attached to the related independent clause to create a complete sentence.)

REVISED: In 1948 India became independent. It was divided into the nations of India and Pakistan. (Finite verb *was* and subject *it* have been added; the result is a separate independent clause.)

241

FRAGMENT: The pilot changed course. <u>Realizing the weather was</u> <u>worsening</u>. (Participial phrase is punctuated as a sentence.)

REVISED: The pilot changed course, realizing the weather was worsening. (Participial phrase has been attached to the related independent clause to create a complete sentence.)

REVISED: The pilot changed course. She realized the weather was worsening. (Finite verb *realized* has been substituted for the verbal *realizing* and subject *she* has been added; the result is a separate independent clause.)

E X E R C I S E   3

Identify the sentence fragments in the following paragraph, and correct each. Either attach the fragment to a related independent clause, or add a subject and a finite verb to create a new independent clause.

Many food products have well-known trademarks. Identified by familiar faces on product labels. Some of these symbols have remained the same, while others have changed considerably. Products like Sun-Maid Raisins, Betty Crocker potato mixes, Quaker Oats, and Uncle Ben's Rice use faces. To create a sense of quality and tradition and to encourage shopper recognition of the products. Many of the portraits have been updated several times. To reflect changes in society. Betty Crocker's portrait, for instance, has changed five times since its creation in 1936. Symbolizing women's changing roles. The original Chef Boy-ar-dee has also changed. Turning from the young Italian chef Hector Boiardi into a white-haired senior citizen. Miss Sunbeam, trademark of Sunbeam Bread, has had her hairdo modified several times since her first appearance in 1942; the Blue Bonnet girl, also created in 1942, now has a more modern look, and Aunt Jemima has also been changed. Slimmed down a bit in 1965. Similarly, the Campbell's Soup kids are less chubby now than in the 1920's when they first appeared. But the Quaker on Quaker Oats remains as round as he was when he first adorned the product label in 1877. The Morton Salt girl has evolved gradually. Changing several times from blonde to brunette and from straight- to curly-haired. But manufacturers are very careful about selecting a trademark or modifying an existing one. Typically spending a good deal of time and money on research before a change is made. After all, a trademark of long standing can help a product's sales. Giving shoppers the sense that they are using products purchased and preferred by their parents and grandparents.

13d   *Revising Absolute Phrases*

An **absolute phrase**—a modifying phrase that is not connected grammatically to any one word in a sentence—usually consists of a noun or pronoun plus a participle and any related modifiers. (Infinitive phrases sometimes function as absolute phrases; see 8f3.) An absolute phrase always contains a subject, but it lacks a finite verb and therefore cannot stand alone as a sentence.

To correct this kind of fragment, attach the absolute phrase to the clause it modifies, or substitute a finite verb for the participle or infinitive in the absolute phrase.

FRAGMENT: India has over 16 million child laborers. Their education cut short by the need to earn money. (Absolute phrase is punctuated as a sentence.)

REVISED: India has over 16 million child laborers, their education cut short by the need to earn money. (Absolute phrase has been attached to the clause it modifies.)

FRAGMENT: The Vietnam War memorial is a striking landmark. Its design featuring two black marble slabs meeting in a V. (Absolute phrase is punctuated as a sentence.)

REVISED: The Vietnam War memorial is a striking landmark. Its design features two black marble slabs meeting in a V. (Finite verb has been substituted for participle)

EXERCISE 4

Identify the sentence fragments in the following passage and correct each by attaching the absolute phrase to the clause it modifies or by substituting a finite verb for the participle or infinitive in the absolute phrase.

The domestic responsibilities of colonial women were many. Their fate sealed by the absence of the mechanical devices that have eased the burdens in recent years. Washing clothes, for instance, was a complicated procedure. The primary problem being the moving of some 50 gallons of water from a pump or well to the stove (for heating) and washtub (for soaking and scrubbing). Home cooking also presented difficulties. The main challenges for the housewife being the danger of inadvertently poisoning her family and the rarity of ovens. Even much later, housework was extremely time-consuming, especially for rural and low-income families. Their access to labor-saving devices remaining relatively limited. (Just before World War II, for instance, only 35 percent of farm residences in the United States had electricity.) (Adapted from Susan Strasser, *Never Done: A History of American Housework*)

13e · *Revising Appositives*

An **appositive**—a noun or noun phrase that identifies or renames the person or thing it follows—cannot stand alone as a sentence (**see 8f4**). An appositive must directly follow the person or thing it renames, and it must do so within the same sentence.

To correct a fragment created when an appositive is incorrectly punctuated as a sentence, attach the appositive to the independent clause that contains the word or word group the appositive renames.

FRAGMENT: Piero della Francesca was a leader of the Umbrian school. A school that remained close to the traditions of Gothic art. (Appositive, a fragment that renames *the Umbrian school,* is punctuated as a complete sentence.)

REVISED: Piero della Francesca was a leader of the Umbrian school, a school that remained close to the traditions of Gothic art. (Appositive has been attached with a comma to the noun it renames.)

Appositives included for clarification are sometimes introduced by a word or phrase like *or, that is, for example, for instance, namely,* or *such as.* These additions do not change anything: appositives still cannot stand alone as sentences. Once again, the easiest way to correct such fragments is to attach the appositive to the preceding independent clause.

FRAGMENT: Fairy tales are full of damsels in distress. Such as Snow White, Cinderella, and Rapunzel. (Appositive, a phrase that identifies *damsels in distress,* is punctuated as a sentence.)

REVISED: Fairy tales are full of damsels in distress, such as Snow White, Cinderella, and Rapunzel. (Appositive has been attached with a comma to the noun it renames.)

You can also correct an appositive that is a fragment by embedding the appositive within the related independent clause.

FRAGMENT: Some popular novelists are highly respected by later generations. For example, Mark Twain and Charles

Dickens. (Appositive, a phrase that identifies *some popular novelists,* is punctuated as a sentence.)

REVISED: Some popular novelists—for example, Mark Twain and Charles Dickens—are highly respected by later generations. (Appositive has been embedded within the preceding independent clause, directly following the noun it renames.)

For information on correct punctuation with appositives see 27d2. ► See 27d2

EXERCISE 5

Identify the fragments in this paragraph and correct them by attaching each to the independent clause containing the word or word group the appositive modifies.

The Smithsonian Institution in Washington, D.C., includes fourteen different buildings. Museums and art galleries. These include well-known landmarks. Such as the National Air and Space Museum and the National Gallery of Art. The Smithsonian also includes the National Zoo. Home of the giant pandas Ling-Ling and Hsing-Hsing. The Smithsonian contains many entertaining and educational exhibits. For example, the Wright Brothers' plane, Lindbergh's *Spirit of St. Louis,* and a moon rock. The Smithsonian also includes eleven other museums. The National Museum of American History, the National Museum of Natural History, the Hirshhorn Museum, the Freer Gallery, the Arts and Industries Building, the National Museum of American Art and National Portrait Gallery, the Renwick Gallery, the National Museum of African Art, The Castle, the Arthur M. Sackler Gallery, and the Anacostia Neighborhood Museum. The National Museum of American History contains one especially historic item. Edison's first light bulb. The National Museum of Natural History also includes a spectacular exhibit. A giant squid that washed ashore in Massachusetts in 1980. These and other entertaining and educational exhibits make up the Smithsonian. An attraction that should not be missed.

13f *Revising Compounds*

When detached from its subject, the last part of a **compound predicate** cannot stand alone as a sentence.

To correct this kind of fragment, connect the detached part of the compound predicate to the rest of the sentence.

FRAGMENT: People with dyslexia have trouble reading. And may also find it difficult to write. (Fragment, part of the compound predicate *have . . . and may also find,* is punctuated as a sentence.)

REVISED: People with dyslexia have trouble reading and may also find it difficult to write. (Detached part of the compound predicate has been connected to the rest of the sentence.)

The last part of a **compound object** or **compound complement** cannot stand alone as a sentence either. Be sure to attach such compounds to the rest of the sentence.

FRAGMENT: They took only a compass and a canteen of water. And some trail mix. (Fragment, part of the compound object *compass . . . canteen . . . trail mix,* is punctuated as a sentence.)

REVISED: They took only a compass, a canteen of water, and some trail mix. (Detached part of the compound object has been connected to the rest of the sentence.)

FRAGMENT: When their supplies ran out, they were surprised. And hungry. (Fragment, part of the compound complement *surprised and hungry,* is punctuated as a sentence.)

REVISED: When their supplies ran out, they were surprised and hungry. (Detached part of the compound complement has been connected to the rest of the sentence.)

EXERCISE 6

Identify the sentence fragments in this passage, and correct them by attaching each detached compound to the rest of the sentence.

One of the phenomena of the '90s is the number of parents determined to raise "superbabies." Many affluent parents, professionals themselves, seem driven to raise children who are mentally superior. And physically fit as well. To this end they enroll babies as young as a few weeks old in baby gyms. And sign up slightly older preschool children for classes that teach computer skills or violin. Or swimming or Japanese. Such classes are important. But are not the only source of formal education for very young children. Parents themselves try to raise their babies' IQs. Or learn to teach toddlers to read or to do simple math. Some parents begin teaching with flash cards when their babies are only a few months—or days—old. Others wait until their children are a bit older. And enroll them in day-care programs designed to sharpen their skills. Or spend thousands of dollars on "educational toys." Some psychologists and child-care professionals are favorably impressed by this trend toward earlier and earlier education. But most have serious reservations, feeling the emphasis on academics and pressure to achieve may stunt children's social and emotional growth.

13g   *Revising Incomplete Clauses*

Not all sentence fragments are short. In a long sentence with several modifiers, you can easily lose track of the direction of a sentence and leave it unfinished.

To correct such a fragment, you must add, delete, or change words to create a complete independent clause.

FRAGMENT: *Ancient Evenings,* Norman Mailer's 1983 novel, more than ten years in the making and considered by critics to be a major work, which is set in Egypt before the birth of Christ. (Subject *Ancient Evenings* has no predicate.)

REVISED: *Ancient Evenings,* Norman Mailer's 1983 novel, more than ten years in the making and considered by critics to be a major work, is set in Egypt before the birth of Christ. (Relative pronoun *which* has been deleted; *is set* is now the predicate of a complete independent clause.)

FRAGMENT: Because of Wright Morris's ambition to become a writer, which led him to travel to Paris just as Ernest Hemingway, Gertrude Stein, Samuel Beckett, and Henry Miller had. (Fragment contains no independent clause.)

REVISED: Wright Morris's ambition to become a writer led him to travel to Paris just as Ernest Hemingway, Gertrude Stein, Samuel Beckett, and Henry Miller had. (Subordinating conjunction *because* and relative pronoun *which* have been deleted, leaving one complete independent clause.)

REVISED: Because of Wright Morris's ambition to become a writer, he traveled to Paris just as Ernest Hemingway, Gertrude Stein, Samuel Beckett, and Henry Miller had. (Relative pronoun *which* has been deleted and some words have been changed, leaving a complete independent clause preceded by a dependent clause.)

247

EXERCISE 7

Identify the fragments in the following paragraph and correct each by adding, deleting, or changing words to create a complete independent clause.

The Brooklyn Bridge, completed in 1883 and the subject of poems, paintings, and films for many years, which helped it to capture the imagination of the public as well as the artist as few other structures have. Because artists like George Bellows, Georgia O'Keeffe, Andy Warhol, and Joseph Stella have used the bridge as a subject, and because it has appeared in the novels of John Dos Passos and Thomas Wolfe and the poems of Hart Crane and Marianne Moore, who have all seen it as a major symbol of America. The Brooklyn Bridge, also making an appearance in essays by writers like Henry James and Lewis Mumford and seen in films from *Tarzan's New York Adventure* and Laurel and Hardy's *Way Out West* to *Annie Hall* and *Sophie's Choice,* which ensured its visibility to the public. Over the years, the bridge has also turned up in songs, in Bugs Bunny cartoons, and on product labels, record jackets, and T-shirts, making it one of the most recognizable structures in America.

13h *Using Fragments Effectively*

In certain limited contexts, sentence fragments may be acceptable. For example, we commonly use fragments in speech and in informal writing:

See you later.

Back soon.

No sweat.

Could be trouble.

Just a note to let you know I got the loan. Sure will make things a lot easier next semester.

Advertising copywriters also use fragments:

Be all curls. Not all nerves.

Finally. Vegetables with no salt added.

Great taste in every bite, and only half the sugar.

Finally, journalists and creative writers frequently use fragments to achieve special effects—for instance, to represent casual conversation or to convey disconnected thinking:

> They tell me that apathy is in this year. Very chic. (Ellen Goodman, *Close to Home*)

> Then the curtains breathing out of the dark upon my face, leaving the breathing upon my face. A quarter hour yet. And then I'll not be. The peacefullest words. (William Faulkner, *The Sound and the Fury*)

Revision Close-up

Keep in mind that in most college writing situations, sentence fragments are not acceptable. Do not use incomplete sentences without carefully considering their suitability for your audience and purpose.

STUDENT WRITER AT WORK

SENTENCE FRAGMENTS

Carefully read this excerpt from a draft of a student essay. Identify all the sentence fragments, and determine why each is a fragment. Correct each sentence fragment by adding, deleting, or modifying words to create a sentence or by attaching the fragment to a neighboring independent clause. Finally, go over the draft again and, if necessary, revise further to strengthen coherence, unity, and style.

```
             from Ab Snopes: A Trapped Man

    Abner (Ab) Snopes, the father in William Faulkner's
story "Barn Burning," is trapped in a hopeless situation.
Disgusted with his lack of status, yet unable to do much
to remedy his dissatisfaction. He has little control over
his life, but he still struggles. Fighting his useless
battle as best he can.
    Ab is a family man. Responsible for a wife, children,
and his wife's sister. Unfortunately, he is unable to meet
his responsibilities. Such as providing a stable home for
```

his family. Evicted because of Ab's "barn burnings," the family constantly moves from town to town. With all its belongings piled on a wagon. But Ab continues to burn barns. Because he hopes that these acts will give him power as well as revenge.

To the rich landowners he works for, Ab is of little significance. Poor, uneducated, uncultured. There are many men just like him. Who can work the land. Ab understands this situation. But is unwilling to accept his inferior status. Consequently, he approaches new employers with arrogance. His actions and manner soon causing trouble. This behavior, of course, ensures his eventual dismissal. Ab feels that since he can never gain their respect. He should not even bother behaving in a civilized manner. So he insists on playing the role. Of a belligerent, raging man.

Ab's behavior sets in motion a self-fulfilling prophecy. Each time Ab's actions cause an employer to ask him to leave, his prophecy that he will be mistreated is fulfilled. He pretends that the failure is his employer's, not his own. And vents his frustration. By destroying their property wth fire. He also feels that such actions will earn him respect. People will be frightened of him, and he will create a name for himself. Only Ab's son, Sarty, sees the truth. That Ab is to his employers "no more . . . than a buzzing wasp."

14

Comma Splices and Fused Sentences

Comma splices and fused sentences are created when the proper connective or punctuation does not appear between independent clauses. In a **comma splice,** two independent clauses are joined only by a comma; in a **fused sentence,** two independent clauses are joined with no punctuation.

COMMA SPLICE:	Charles Dickens created the character of Mr. Micawber, he also created Uriah Heep.
FUSED SENTENCE:	Charles Dickens created the character of Mr. Micawber he also created Uriah Heep.
REVISED:	Charles Dickens created the character of Mr. Micawber. He also created Uriah Heep.

You can revise comma splices and fused sentences in one of four ways.

Revising Comma Splices and Fused Sentences

Comma Splice	*Fused Sentence*
1. Substitute a period for the comma.	1. Add a period between clauses.
2. Substitute a semicolon for the comma.	2. Add a semicolon between clauses.
3. Add an appropriate coordinating conjunction.	3. Add a comma and an appropriate coordinating conjunction.
4. Subordinate one clause to the other.	4. Subordinate one clause to the other.

14a *Revising with Periods*

Using a period to separate independent clauses creates two separate sentences. A comma splice or fused sentence can be revised in this way when the clauses are of equal importance but are not related closely enough to be joined in one sentence.

COMMA SPLICE: In the late nineteenth century Alfred Dreyfus, a Jewish captain in the French army, was falsely convicted of treason, his struggle for justice pitted the army and the Catholic establishment against the civil libertarians.

FUSED SENTENCE: In the late nineteenth century Alfred Dreyfus, a Jewish captain in the French army, was falsely convicted of treason his struggle for justice pitted the army and the Catholic establishment against the civil libertarians.

REVISED: In the late nineteenth century Alfred Dreyfus, a Jewish captain in the French army, was falsely convicted of treason. His struggle for justice pitted the army and the Catholic establishment against the civil libertarians.

Substituting a period is the best way to revise a comma splice created by the incorrect punctuation of a broken quotation.

COMMA SPLICE: "This is a good course," Eric said, "in fact, I wish I'd taken it sooner."

REVISED: "This is a good course," Eric said. "In fact, I wish I'd taken it sooner."

Revision Close-up

When using periods to revise comma splices and fused sentences, be careful to avoid creating strings of short, choppy sentences.

See ◄ 12b

14b *Revising with Semicolons*

If the two clauses of equal importance are closely related, and if you want to underscore that relationship, use a semicolon.

COMMA SPLICE:	In pre-World War II Western Europe only a small elite had access to a university education, this situation changed dramatically after the war.
FUSED SENTENCE:	In pre-World War II Western Europe only a small elite had access to a university education this situation changed dramatically after the war.
REVISED:	In pre-World War II Western Europe only a small elite had access to a university education; this situation changed dramatically after the war.

You can also use a semicolon to revise a comma splice or fused sentence when the ideas in the joined clauses are presented in parallel terms. In such cases, the semicolon emphasizes the parallelism between the two clauses (see 16a).

COMMA SPLICE:	Chippendale chairs have straight legs, Queen Anne chairs have curved legs.
FUSED SENTENCE:	Chippendale chairs have straight legs Queen Anne chairs have curved legs.
REVISED:	Chippendale chairs have straight legs; Queen Anne chairs have curved legs.

14c   *Revising with Coordinating Conjunctions*

If two closely related clauses are of equal importance, you can use an appropriate coordinating conjunction to indicate whether the clauses are linked by addition *(and)*, contrast *(but, yet)*, causality *(for, so)*, or a choice of alternatives *(or, nor)*.

COMMA SPLICE:	Elias Howe invented the sewing machine, Julia Ward Howe was a poet and social reformer.
FUSED SENTENCE:	Elias Howe invented the sewing machine Julia Ward Howe was a poet and social reformer.
REVISED:	Elias Howe invented the sewing machine, but Julia Ward Howe was a poet and social reformer. (Coordinating conjunction *but* shows emphasis is on contrast.)

Revision Close-up

Remember that you cannot correct a comma splice or fused sentence simply by adding a conjunctive adverb (*however, nevertheless, there-*

continued

continued from previous page

fore, and so on) or any other transitional expression *(for example, in fact, on the other hand)* between the independent clauses. If you do, you will still have a comma splice or fused sentence.

COMMA SPLICE:	The International Date Line is drawn north and south through the Pacific Ocean, largely at the 180th meridian, thus, it separates Wake and Midway Islands.
FUSED SENTENCE:	The International Date Line is drawn north and south through the Pacific Ocean, largely at the 180th meridian thus, it separates Wake and Midway Islands.
REVISED:	The International Date Line is drawn north and south through the Pacific Ocean, largely at the 180th meridian; thus, it separates Wake and Midway Islands.
REVISED:	The International Date Line is drawn north and south through the Pacific Ocean, largely at the 180th meridian. Thus, it separates Wake and Midway Islands.

See ◄
28c

14d *Revising with Subordinating Conjunctions or Relative Pronouns*

When the ideas in two clauses are not of equal importance, correct the comma splice or fused sentence by subordinating the less important idea to the more important one, placing the less important idea in a dependent clause. The subordinating conjunction or relative pronoun establishes the nature of the relationship between the clauses.

COMMA SPLICE:	Stravinsky's ballet *The Rite of Spring* shocked Parisians in 1913, its rhythms and the dancers' movements seemed erotic.
FUSED SENTENCE:	Stravinsky's ballet *The Rite of Spring* shocked Parisians in 1913 its rhythms and the dancers' movements seemed erotic.
REVISED:	Because its rhythms and the dancers' movements seemed erotic, Stravinsky's ballet *The Rite of Spring* shocked Parisians in 1913. (Subordinating conjunction *because* has been added to make the

original sentence's second clause subordinate to its first; the result is one complex sentence.)

COMMA SPLICE: Lady Mary Wortley Montagu had suffered from smallpox herself, she helped spread the practice of inoculation against the disease in eighteenth-century England.

FUSED SENTENCE: Lady Mary Wortley Montagu had suffered from smallpox herself she helped spread the practice of inoculation against the disease in eighteenth-century England.

REVISED: Lady Mary Wortley Montagu, who had suffered from smallpox herself, helped spread the practice of inoculation against the disease in eighteenth-century England. (Relative pronoun *who* has been added to make the original sentence's first clause subordinate to its second; the result is one complex sentence.)

Revision Close-up

In rare cases comma splices are acceptable. For instance, a comma is correct in dialogue between a statement and a tag question, even though each is a separate independent clause.

This is Ron's house, isn't it?

I'm not late, am I?

In addition, commas may connect two short *balanced* independent clauses, or two or more short parallel independent clauses, especially when one clause contradicts the other.

Commencement isn't the end, it's the beginning.

EXERCISE 1

Find the comma splices and fused sentences in the following paragraphs. Correct each in *two* of the four possible ways listed on page 251. If a sentence is correct, leave it alone.

EXAMPLE: The fans rose in their seats, the game was almost over.

The fans rose in their seats; the game was almost over.

The fans rose in their seats, for the game was almost over.

255

Entrepreneurship is the study of small businesses, college students are embracing it enthusiastically. Many schools offer one or more courses in entrepreneurship these courses teach the theory and practice of starting a small business. Students are signing up for courses, moreover they are starting their own businesses. One student started with a car-waxing business, now he sells condominiums. Other students are setting up catering services they supply everything from waiters to bartenders. One student has a thriving cake-decorating business, in fact she employs fifteen students to deliver the cakes. All over the country, student businesses are selling everything from tennis balls to bagels, the student owners are making impressive profits. Formal courses at the graduate as well as undergraduate level are attracting more business students than ever, several business schools (such as Baylor University, the University of Southern California, and Babson College) even offer degree programs in entrepreneurship. Many business school students are no longer planning to be corporate executives instead they plan to become entrepreneurs.

Animals are disappearing from the earth about one species a year has become extinct since 1900. Enormous dinosaurs once roamed the earth they became extinct some 65 million years ago. Huge mammals later flourished they included mastodons and mammoths. Over one hundred different species of these large mammals lived on earth, some of them were alive only 11,000 years ago. But these animals all vanished, no one is quite sure exactly why this happened. Hundreds of other species had developed and eventually died out before humans existed however after man appeared in North America extinction increased dramatically. Hunters killed animals for food, therefore some scientists believe it is possible that hunters exterminated the large animals. Other scientists attribute the animals' disappearance to climatic changes during the Ice Age. For instance, marked drops in temperatures ruined grazing lands, many animals died from exposure and starvation. Droughts also killed many animals the competition for grasslands was too much for them. Finally, it has been suggested that man did eliminate the animals however many had already been weakened by natural forces like disease and climatic changes.

E X E R C I S E   2

Combine each of the following sentence pairs into one sentence without creating comma splices or fused sentences. In each case, either connect the clauses into a compound sentence with a semicolon or with a comma and a coordinating conjunction, or subordinate one clause to the other to create a complex sentence. You may have to add, delete, reorder, or change words or punctuation.

1. Several recent studies indicate that many American high-school students have a poor sense of history. This is affecting our future as a democratic nation and as individuals.

2. Surveys show that nearly one-third of American seventeen-year-olds cannot identify the countries the United States fought against in World War II. One-third think Columbus reached the New World after 1750.

3. Several reasons have been given for this decline in historical literacy. The main reason is the way history is taught.

4. This problem is bad news. The good news is that there is increasing agreement among educators about what is wrong with current methods of teaching history.

5. History can be exciting and engaging. Too often it is presented in a boring manner.

6. Students are typically expected to memorize dates, facts, and figures. History as adventure—as a "good story"—is frequently neglected.

7. One way to avoid this problem is to use good textbooks. Texts should be accurate, lively, and focused.

8. Another way to create student interest in historical events is to use primary sources instead of so-called "comprehensive" textbooks. Autobiographies, journals, and diaries can give students insight into larger issues.

9. Students could also be challenged to think about history by taking sides in a debate. They would learn more about connections among historical events by writing essays rather than taking multiple-choice tests.

10. Finally, history teachers should be less concerned about specific historical details. They should be more concerned about conveying the wonder of history.

STUDENT WRITER AT WORK

COMMA SPLICES AND FUSED SENTENCES

Read the following answer to an economics examination question that asked students to discuss the provisions of the 1935 Social Security Act; correct all comma splices and fused sentences. After you have corrected the errors, go over the answer again and, if necessary, revise further to strengthen coherence, unity, and style.

In June of 1934 Franklin D. Roosevelt selected
Frances Perkins to head the new Committee on Economic
Security, its report was the basis of our current Social

Security program. The committee formulated two policies, one dealt with the employable the other with the unemployable. Roosevelt insisted that these programs be self-financing, as a result both employer and employee social insurance were required. In 1935 the Social Security Act was passed it attempted to categorize the poor and provided for federal sharing of the cost, but under local control. (The Social Security Act did not include a public works program, this feature of the New Deal was eliminated.)

Unemployment insurance was one major part of the Act. Funds were to be payable through public employment offices, also the money was to be paid into a trust fund. It was to be used solely for benefits an individual could not be denied funds even if work were available. The program provided for payroll taxes, in addition separate records were to be kept by each state. Old Age Survivor Insurance, another major provision of the Act, was for individuals over sixty-five it was amended in 1939 to cover dependents. One quarter of the recipients were disabled. Public Assistance was the third major part of the Act this program was designed to help children left alone by the death or absence of the parents and children with mental or physical disabilities. General assistance covered everything not included under the Public Assistance Program this coverage varied from state to state.

The Social Security Act stressed public administration of federal emergency relief assistance thus it forced reorganization of public assistance. These efforts differed from previous efforts earlier there were no clear guidelines defining which individuals should get aid and why. The Social Security Act attempted to eliminate gaps and overlaps in services.

15

Faulty Modification

Modifiers add information and show connections between ideas. They also expand and enrich sentences, helping you to communicate meaning accurately and precisely to your readers. Normally, a modifier is placed close to its **headword,** the word or phrase it modifies, and readers expect to find it there. **Faulty modification** is the awkward or confusing placement of modifiers or the modification of nonexistent words.

Faulty modification takes two forms: *misplaced modifiers* and *dangling modifiers.*

15a *Revising Misplaced Modifiers*

A **misplaced modifier** is a word or word group whose placement suggests that it modifies one word or phrase when it is intended to modify another. A misplaced modifier has no clear relationship with its headword. Consider the following sentence:

Faster than a speeding bullet, the citizens of Metropolis saw Superman flying overhead.

The placement of the introductory phrase makes it appear to modify *citizens,* yet it should modify *Superman.* Here is a corrected version:

The citizens of Metropolis saw Superman flying overhead, faster than a speeding bullet.

When writing and revising, take care to put modifying words, phrases, and clauses in a position that clearly identifies the headword and that does not awkwardly interrupt a sentence.

(1) Revising misplaced words

Readers expect to find modifiers directly before or directly after their headwords.

Dark and threatening, Wendy watched the storm. (Incorrectly placed adjectives *dark* and *threatening* seem to describe Wendy instead of the storm.)

Wendy watched the storm, dark and threatening. (Correct placement of modifier clarifies meaning.)

Certain modifiers—such as *almost, only, even, hardly, merely, nearly, exactly, scarcely, just,* and *simply*—should always immediately precede the words they modify. Different placements of these modifiers change the meaning of your sentence.

Nick *just* set up camp at the edge of the burned-out town. (He set up camp just now.)

Just Nick set up camp at the edge of the burned-out town. (He set up camp alone.)

Nick set up camp *just* at the edge of the burned-out town. (His camp was precisely at the edge.)

The imprecise placement of modifiers like these sometimes produces a **squinting modifier,** one that seems to modify either a word before it or one after it and to convey different meanings in each case. To avoid ambiguity, place the modifier so that it clearly modifies its headword.

SQUINTING: The life that everyone thought would fulfill her [totally] bored her. (Was she supposed to be totally fulfilled, or is she totally bored?)

REVISED: The life that everyone thought would totally fulfill her bored her. (Everyone expected her to be totally fulfilled.)

REVISED: The life that everyone thought would fulfill her bored her totally. (She was totally bored.)

E X E R C I S E   1

In the following sentence pairs, the modifier in each sentence points to a different headword. Underline the modifier and draw an arrow to the word it limits. Then explain the meaning of each sentence.

EXAMPLE: She just came in wearing a hat.
[She just now entered.]
She came in wearing just a hat.
[She wore only a hat.]

1. He wore his almost new jeans.
   He almost wore his new jeans.
2. He only had three dollars in his pocket.
   Only he had three dollars in his pocket.
3. I don't even like freshwater fish.
   I don't like even freshwater fish.
4. I go only to the beach on Saturdays.
   I go to the beach only on Saturdays.
5. He simply hated living.
   He hated simply living.

(2)   Revising misplaced phrases

Placing a modifying verbal or prepositional phrase incorrectly can change the meaning of a sentence or create an unclear or confusing sentence.

Misplaced Verbal Phrases   Certain verbal phrases act as modifiers (see 8f2). As a rule, place them directly before or directly after the nouns or pronouns they modify.

Roller-skating along the shore, Jane watched the boats.

She watched the car [rolling down the hill].

The incorrect placement of a verbal phrase that acts as a modifier can make a sentence convey an entirely different meaning or make no sense at all.

[Rolling down the hill], she watched the car.

Jane watched the boats [roller skating along the shore].

Misplaced Prepositional Phrases   When a prepositional phrase is used as an adjective, it nearly always directly follows the word it modifies.

This is a Dresden figurine [from Germany].

Created by a famous artist, Venus de Milo is a statue [with no arms].

Incorrect placement can give rise to confusion or even unintended humor.

Venus de Milo is a statue created by a famous artist [with no arms].

When used as adverbs, prepositional phrases usually follow their headwords.

Cassandra looked [into the future].

As long as the meaning of the sentence is clear, however, and as long as the headword is clearly identified, you can place an adverbial modifier in any alternative position.

He had been waiting anxiously at the bus stop [for a long time].

Revision Close-up

Be careful to avoid ambiguous placement of prepositional phrases serving as adverbs.

MISPLACED: She saw the house she built in her mind.
REVISED: [In her mind], she saw the house she built.
REVISED: She saw [in her mind] the house she built.

E X E R C I S E   2

Underline the modifying verbal or prepositional phrases in each sentence, and draw arrows to their headwords.

EXAMPLE: Calvin is the democrat running for town council.

1. The bridge across the river swayed in the wind.
2. The spectators on the shore were involved in the action.
3. Mesmerized by the spectacle, they watched the drama unfold.
4. The spectators were afraid of a disaster.
5. Within the hour, the state police arrived to save the day.
6. They closed off the area with roadblocks.
7. Drivers approaching the bridge were asked to stop.
8. Meanwhile, on the bridge, the scene was chaos.
9. Motorists in their cars were paralyzed with fear.
10. Struggling against the weather, the police managed to rescue everyone.

E X E R C I S E   3

Use the word or phrase that follows each sentence as a modifier in that sentence. Then draw an arrow to indicate its headword.

EXAMPLE: He approached the lion. (timid)
          Timid, he approached the lion.

1. The lion paced up and down in his cage, ignoring the crowd. (watching Jack)
2. Jack stared back at the lion. (fascinated yet curious)
3. The crowd around them grew. (anxious to see what would happen)
4. Suddenly Jack heard a growl from deep in the lion's throat. (terrifying)
5. Jack ran from the zoo, leaving the lion behind. (scared to death)

(3)   Revising misplaced dependent clauses

Dependent clauses that serve as modifiers—adjective clauses and adverb clauses—must be clearly related to their headwords. Adjective clauses usually appear immediately after the words they modify.

During the Civil War, Lincoln was the president [who governed the United States].

An adverb clause can appear in any of several positions, as long as the relationship to the clause it modifies is clear and its position conveys the intended emphasis.

During the Civil War Lincoln was president.

Lincoln was president during the Civil War.

To correct misplaced dependent clauses, make the relationship between modifier and headword clear.

MISPLACED ADJECTIVE CLAUSE

This diet program will limit the consumption of possible carcinogens, [which will benefit everyone]. (Will carcinogens benefit everyone?)

REVISED

This diet program, [which will benefit everyone], will limit the consumption of possible carcinogens.

MISPLACED ADVERB CLAUSE

They decided the house was haunted, but they changed their minds [when purple grass started growing out of the fireplace]. (This bizarre phenomenon reassured them?)

REVISED

They decided the house was haunted when purple grass started growing out of the fireplace, but they changed their minds.

263

REVISED

When purple grass started growing out of the fireplace, they decided the house was haunted, but they changed their minds.

EXERCISE 4

Relocate the misplaced verbal or prepositional phrases or dependent clauses so that they clearly point to the words or word groups they modify.

EXAMPLE: *Silent Running* is a film about a scientist left alone in space with Bruce Dern.

          Silent Running is a film with Bruce Dern about a scientist left alone in space.

1. She realized she had married the wrong man after the wedding.
2. *The Prince and the Pauper* is about an exchange of identities by Mark Twain.
3. The energy was used up in the ten-kilometer race that he was saving for the marathon.
4. He loaded the bottles and cans into his new Porsche, which he planned to leave at the recycling center.
5. The manager explained the sales figures to the board members using a graph.

(4) Revising intrusive modifiers

An **intrusive modifier** interrupts a sentence, making it difficult for readers to see the connections between parts of verb phrases, between parts of infinitives, or between subjects and their verbs or between verbs and their objects or complements.

Interrupted Verb Phrases   Revise when modifiers come between an auxiliary and a main verb.

AWKWARD: She had, without giving it a second thought or considering the consequences, planned to reenlist.

REVISED: Without giving it a second thought or considering the consequences, she had planned to reenlist.

AWKWARD: He will, if he ever gets his act together, be ready to leave on Friday.

REVISED: If he ever gets his act together, he will be ready to leave on Friday.

If a modifier is brief, it can usually interrupt a verb phrase.

She <u>had</u> always <u>planned</u> to reenlist.

He <u>will</u>, however, <u>be</u> ready to leave on Friday.

Longer interruptions, however, may obscure your meaning.

Interrupted Infinitives   Revise when modifiers interrupt an infinitive. As a rule, the parts of an infinitive should be together. When a modifier splits an infinitive—that is, comes between the word *to* and the base form of the verb—the sentence often becomes awkward.

AWKWARD: He hoped <u>to</u> quickly and easily <u>defeat</u> his opponent.

REVISED: He hoped <u>to defeat</u> his opponent quickly and easily.

AWKWARD: He decided <u>to</u> after he considered the possible risks <u>invest</u> all his money in stocks.

REVISED: After he considered the possible risks, he decided <u>to invest</u> all his money in stocks.

Revision Close-up

Although the general rule in writing is never to split an infinitive, it is occasionally necessary to do so. When the intervening modifier is short, and when the alternative is awkward or ambiguous, a split infinitive is permissible. In the following sentence, for example, a reader would have no trouble connecting the parts of the infinitive.

She expected <u>to not quite beat</u> her previous record.

Moreover, any revision using the same words is awkward or incoherent.

She expected not quite to beat her previous record.

She expected to beat not quite her previous record.

The only way to avoid a split infinitive in this case is to reword the original sentence.

She expected her score to be close to her previous record.

Because a revision often does not have exactly the same meaning as the original, it is sometimes necessary to split an infinitive. Before you decide to do so, however, be sure there is no other reasonable place for the modifier.

Interrupted Subjects and Verbs or Verbs and Objects or Complements   Revise if you have any doubts about letting a modifier stand between subject and verb or verb and object or complement.

It is standard practice to place even a complex or lengthy adjective phrase or clause between a subject and a verb or between a verb and its object or complement. An adverb phrase or clause in this position, however, may not be natural sounding or clear.

ACCEPTABLE: Major films that were financially successful in the thirties include *Gone with the Wind* and *The Wizard of Oz*. (Adjective clause between subject and verb does not obscure sentence's meaning.)

CONFUSING: The election, because officials discovered that some people voted twice, was contested. (Adverb clause intrudes between subject and verb.)

REVISED: Because officials discovered that some people voted twice, the election was contested. (Subject and verb are no longer separated.)

CONFUSING: A. A. Milne wrote, when his son Christopher Robin was a child, *Winnie-the-Pooh*. (Adverb clause intrudes between verb and object.)

REVISED: When his son Christopher Robin was a child, A. A. Milne wrote *Winnie-the-Pooh*. (Verb and object are no longer separated.)

EXERCISE 5

Revise these sentences so that the modifying phrases or clauses do not interrupt the parts of a verb phrase or infinitive or separate a subject from a verb or a verb from its object or complement.

EXAMPLE: A play can sometimes be, despite the playwright's best efforts, mystifying to the audience.

Despite the playwright's best efforts, a play can sometimes be mystifying to the audience.

1. The people in the audience, when they saw that the play was about to begin and realized that the orchestra had finished tuning up and had begun the overture, finally quieted down.
2. They settled into their seats, expecting to very much enjoy the first act.
3. However, most people were, even after watching and listening for twenty minutes and paying close attention to the drama, completely baffled.
4. In fact, the play, because it had nameless characters, no scenery, and a rambling plot that didn't seem to be heading anywhere, puzzled even the drama critics.

5. Finally one of the three major characters explained, speaking directly to the audience, what the play was really about.

15b *Revising Dangling Modifiers*

A **dangling modifier** is a word or phrase that cannot logically describe, limit, or restrict any word or word group in the sentence. In fact, its true headword does not appear in the sentence. Consider the following example:

Many undesirable side effects are experienced using this drug.

Using this drug appears to modify *side effects,* but this interpretation makes no sense. Because its true headword does not appear in the sentence, the modifier dangles.

One way to correct the faulty sentence is to add a word or word group that the dangling modifier can logically modify. To do so, you usually must change the subject of the main clause.

Patients using this drug experience many undesirable side effects.

Another way to correct a dangling modifier is to change the modifier into a dependent clause.

Many undesirable side effects are experienced when this drug is used.

The original incorrect sentence, like many sentences that include dangling modifiers, is in the passive voice. The true headword is absent because the passive construction *many undesirable side effects are experienced* does not tell *who* experiences the side effects. Changing the passive construction to active voice corrects the dangling modifier by changing the subject of the sentence's main clause from *side effects* to *patients,* a word the dangling modifier can logically modify. Sometimes, however, passive voice is a desirable stylistic option (see 23l). In such cases you may correct the dangling modifier by supplying the subject while retaining the passive voice.

Many undesirable side effects are experienced by patients using this drug.

Or, you may change the dangling modifier into a dependent clause.

Many undesirable side effects are experienced when this drug is used.

Correcting Dangling Modifiers

- Supply a word or word group that the dangling modifier can logically modify.
- Change the dangling modifier into a dependent clause.

The three most common kinds of dangling modifiers are dangling verbal phrases, dangling prepositional phrases, and dangling elliptical clauses.

(1) Revising dangling verbal phrases

Verbal phrases used as modifiers sometimes dangle in a sentence.

DANGLING PARTICIPIAL PHRASE

Using a pair of forceps, the skin of the rat's abdomen was lifted, and a small cut was made into the body with scissors. (Sentence contains no word the participial phrase can logically modify.)

REVISED

Using a pair of forceps, the technician lifted the skin of the rat's abdomen and made a small cut into the body with scissors. (Subject of main clause has been changed from *the skin* to *the technician*, a headword the participial phrase can logically modify.)

DANGLING PARTICIPIAL PHRASE

Paid in three installments, Brad's financial situation seemed stable. (Sentence contains no word the participial phrase can logically modify.)

REVISED

Because the grant was paid in three installments, Brad's financial situation seemed stable. (Modifying phrase is now a dependent clause.)

DANGLING INFINITIVE PHRASE

To make his paper accurate, all references were checked twice. (Sentence contains no word the infinitive phrase can logically modify.)

REVISED

To make his paper accurate, Don checked all references twice. (Subject of main clause has been changed from *references* to *Don*, a headword the infinitive phrase can logically modify.)

Dangling Infinitive Phrase

Music seemed to carry the children's minds away from reality to dream about the future. (Sentence contains no word the infinitive phrase can logically modify.)

Revised

Music seemed to carry the children's minds away from reality so that they were able to dream about the future. (Infinitive phrase is now a dependent clause.)

Dangling Gerund Phrase

The exhibit was very efficiently presented by using diagrams and photographs. (Sentence contains no word the gerund phrase can logically modify.)

Revised

By using diagrams and photographs, they presented the exhibit very efficiently. (Subject of main clause has been changed from the *exhibit* to *they*, a word the gerund phrase can logically modify.)

Dangling Gerund Phrase

By moving the microscope's mirror, light can be reflected off its surface up into the viewing apparatus. Sentence contains no word the gerund phrase can logically modify.)

Revised

When the microscope's mirror is moved, light can be reflected off its surface up into the viewing apparatus. (Gerund is now a dependent clause.)

(2) Revising dangling prepositional phrases

Prepositional phrases can also dangle in a sentence.

Dangling: With fifty pages to read, *War and Peace* was absorbing. (Sentence contains no word the prepositional phrase can logically modify.)

Revised: With fifty pages to read, Meg found *War and Peace* absorbing. (Subject of main clause has been changed from *War and Peace* to *Meg*, a word the prepositional phrase can logically modify.)

Dangling: On the newsstands only an hour, its sales surprised everyone. (Sentence contains no word the prepositional phrase can logically modify.)

REVISED: Because the magazine had been on the newsstands only an hour, its sales surprised everyone. (Prepositional phrase is now a dependent clause.)

(3) Revising dangling elliptical clauses

Elliptical clauses are dependent clauses from which part of the subject or predicate or the entire subject or predicate is missing. The absent words, therefore, must be inferred from the context. When such a clause cannot logically modify the subject of the sentence's main clause, it too dangles.

DANGLING: While still in the Buchner funnel, you should press the crystals with a clear stopper to eliminate any residual solvent. (Elliptical clause cannot logically modify subject of main clause.)

REVISED: While still in the Buchner funnel, the crystals should be pressed with a clear stopper to eliminate any residual solvent. (Subject of main clause has been changed from *you* to *crystals*, a word the elliptical clause can logically modify.)

DANGLING: Though a high-pressure field, I find great personal satisfaction in nursing. (Elliptical clause cannot logically modify subject of main clause.)

REVISED: Though it is a high-pressure field, I find great personal satisfaction in nursing. (Elliptical clause has been expanded into a complete dependent clause.)

E X E R C I S E 6

Eliminate the dangling modifier from each of the following sentences. Either supply a word or word group the dangling modifier can logically modify, or change the dangling modifier into a dependent clause.

EXAMPLE: Flying over Colorado, the Rocky Mountains looked spectacular. (dangling modifier)

Flying over Colorado, I thought the Rocky Mountains looked spectacular. (logical headword added)

As I flew over Colorado, the Rocky Mountains looked spectacular. (dependent clause)

1. Although architecturally unusual, most people agree that Buckminster Fuller's geodesic dome is well designed.

270

2. As an out-of-state student without a car, it was difficult to get to off-campus cultural events.
3. To build a campfire, kindling is necessary.
4. With every step upward, the trees became sparser.
5. Being an amateur tennis player, my backhand is weaker than my forehand.
6. When exiting the train, the station will be on your right.
7. Driving through the Mojave, the bleak landscape was oppressive.
8. By requiring auto manufacturers to further improve emission-control devices, the air quality will get better.
9. Using a piece of filter paper, the ball of sodium is dried as much as possible and placed in a test tube.
10. Having missed work for seven days straight, my job was in jeopardy.

STUDENT WRITER AT WORK

FAULTY MODIFICATION

Read this draft of a student's technical writing exercise, a description of a 10-cc syringe. Correct misplaced and dangling modifiers, and revise again if necessary to strengthen coherence, unity, and style.

Designed to inject liquids into, or withdraw them from, any vessel or cavity, the function of a syringe is often to inject drugs into the body or withdraw blood from it. Syringes are also used to precisely measure amounts of drugs or electrolytes that must be added to intravenous solutions.

There are available on the market today many different types of syringes, but the one most commonly used in hospitals is the 10-cubic-centimeter disposable syringe. Approximately 5 inches long, the primary composition of this particular syringe is transparent polyethylene plastic. The 10-cc syringe and the majority of other syringes all share the design of a round plunger or piston within a barrel.

The barrel of a syringe is a round, hollow cylinder about 4 1/2" long with a diameter of 3/8". The bottom end of the barrel has two outward extensions on its opposite sides, which are perpendicular to the cylinder. With a width equal to the diameter of the barrel, the length of these extensions is about 1/2". The purpose of these extensions is to enable one to hold with the forefinger and middle finger the barrel of the syringe while withdrawing the plunger with the thumb and third finger.

The barrel of the syringe is calibrated on the side in black ink subdivided into gradations of .2cc. At the top of the syringe the barrel abruptly narrows to a very small cylinder, 1/8" in diameter and 1/4" in length. This small cylinder is surrounded by another hollow cylinder with a slightly larger diameter. The inside wall of the outer cylinder is threaded like a corkscrew. The purpose of this thread is to secure the needle in place.

The other major part of the syringe is the plunger. The plunger is a solid, round cylinder that fits snugly into the barrel made of plastic. At the bottom of the plunger is a plastic ring the size of a dime, which provides something to grasp while withdrawing the plunger. The body of the plunger connects the bottom rim with the tip of the plunger, which is made of black rubber.

16

Faulty Parallelism

Parallelism is the use of similar grammatical elements in sentences or parts of sentences. It ensures that elements sharing the same function also share the same grammatical form—for instance, that verbs match corresponding verbs in tense, mood, and number.

16a   Using Parallelism

Effective parallelism adds force, unity, balance, and symmetry to your writing. It makes sentences clear and easy to follow and emphasizes relationships among equivalent ideas. It helps your readers keep track of ideas, and it makes sentences more emphatic, more concise, and more varied.

(1)   With items in a series

Coordinate elements—words, phrases, or clauses—in a series should be in parallel form.

As a vegetarian, he avoided meat, fish, and eggs.

Marijuana use, baby food consumption, and toy production are likely to decline as the United States population grows older.

Eat, drink, and be merry.

I came; I saw; I conquered.

Three factors influenced him: his desire to relocate; his need for greater responsibility; and his dissatisfaction with his current job.

(2) With paired items

Paired points or ideas (words, phrases, or clauses) should be presented in parallel terms. Parallelism conveys their equivalence and relates points to each other.

> Her note was short but sweet.

> Roosevelt represented the United States, and Churchill represented Great Britain.

> The research focused on muscle tissue and nerve cells.

> The more you study, the more you learn.

> Ask not what your country can do for you; ask what you can do for your country. (John F. Kennedy, Inaugural Address)

Correlative conjunctions (such as *not only/but also*, *both/and*, *either/or*, *neither/nor*, and *whether/or*) are frequently used to link paired elements. These phrases convey balance, so the terms they introduce should be parallel.

> The design team paid close attention not only to color but also to texture.

> Either repeat physics or take calculus.

> Both cable television and videocassette recorders continue to threaten the dominance of the major television networks.

Parallelism can also be used to highlight opposition between paired elements linked by the word *than*.

> Richard Wright and James Baldwin chose to live in Paris rather than to remain in the United States.

(3) In lists and outlines

Elements in a list should be expressed in parallel terms.

> The Irish potato famine had four major causes:
> 1. The establishment of the landlord-tenant system
> 2. The failure of the potato crop
> 3. The reluctance of England to offer adequate financial assistance
> 4. The passage of the Corn Laws

See ◀ 40g Elements in an outline should also be parallel.

Identify the parallel elements in these sentences by underlining parallel words and bracketing parallel phrases and clauses.

EXAMPLE: He is 81 now, [a tall man in a dark blue suit], [a smiling man with a nimbus of snowy white hair], and much of the world knows him [as the proponent of vitamin C to cure colds], [as a quixotic, vaguely ridiculed figure on the fringes of medicine]. (Maralyn Lois Polak, *Philadelphia Inquirer*)

1. You have lived an American dream when you begin the year setting pressure gauges for the Caterpillar Tractor Company in Peoria and end it building rocking chairs for your grandchildren. *(Newsweek)*
2. The public image [of the American woman] in the magazine and television commercials is designed to sell washing machines, cake mixes, deodorants, detergents, rejuvenating face creams, hair tints. (Betty Friedan, *The Feminine Mystique*)
3. Surgery restores to function broken limbs and damaged hearts with amazing safety and little suffering; sanitation removes from our environment many of the germs of disease; new drugs are constantly being developed to relieve physical pain, to help us sleep if we are restless, to keep us awake if we feel sleepy, and to make us oblivious to worries. (René Dubos, *Medical Utopias*)
4. Theoretically—and secretely, of course—I was all for the Burmese and all against their oppressors, the British. (George Orwell, "Shooting an Elephant")
5. As nations, we can apply to affairs of state the realism of science: holding to what works and discarding what does not. (Jacob Bronowski, *A Sense of the Future*)

Combine each of the following sentence pairs or sentence groups into one sentence that uses parallel structure. Be sure all parallel words, phrases, and clauses are expressed in parallel terms.

1. Originally, there were five performing Marx Brothers. One was nicknamed Groucho. The others were called Chico, Harpo, Gummo, and Zeppo.
2. Groucho was very well known. So were Chico and Harpo. Gummo soon dropped out of the act. And later Zeppo did, too.
3. They began in vaudeville. That was before World War I. Their first show was called *I'll Say She Is*. It opened in New York in 1924.

4. The Marx Brothers' first movie was *The Coconuts*. The next was *Animal Crackers*. And this was followed by *Monkey Business*, *Horsefeathers*, and *Duck Soup*. Then came *A Night at the Opera*.

5. In each of these movies, the Marx Brothers make people laugh. More importantly, they establish a unique, zany comic style.

6. In their movies, each man has a set of familiar trademarks. Groucho has a mustache and a long coat. He wiggles his eyebrows and smokes a cigar. There is a funny hat that Chico always wears. And he affects a phony Italian accent. Harpo never speaks.

7. Groucho is always cast as a sly operator. He always tries to cheat people out of their money. He always tries to charm women.

8. In *The Coconuts* he plays Mr. Hammer, proprietor of the run-down Coconut Manor, a Florida hotel. In *Horsefeathers* his character is named Professor Quincy Adams Wagstaff. Wagstaff is president of Huxley College. Huxley also has financial problems.

9. In *Duck Soup* Groucho plays Rufus T. Firefly, president of the country of Fredonia. Fredonia was formerly ruled by the late husband of a Mrs. Teasdale. Fredonia is now at war with the country of Sylvania.

10. Margaret Dumont is often Groucho's leading lady. She plays Mrs. Teasdale in *Duck Soup*. In *A Night at the Opera* she plays Mrs. Claypool. Her character in *The Coconuts* is named Mrs. Potter.

16b *Revising Faulty Parallelism*

When elements that have the same function in a sentence are not presented in the same terms, the sentence is flawed by **faulty parallelism.** Consider the following sentence:

FAULTY PARALLELISM

Many people in third-world countries suffer because the countries lack sufficient housing to accommodate them, sufficient food to feed them, and their health-care facilities are inadequate.

Because all three reasons have the same weight and are presented in a series connected by the coordinating conjunction *and,* readers expect them to be expressed in parallel terms. The first two elements satisfy this expectation:

sufficient housing to accommodate them . . .

sufficient food to feed them . . .

The third item in the series, however, breaks this pattern:

their health-care facilities are inadequate.

To create a clear, emphatic sentence, all three elements should be presented in the same terms.

> Many people in third-world countries suffer because the countries lack sufficient housing to accommodate them, sufficient food to feed them, and sufficient health-care facilities to serve them.

(1) Repeating parallel elements

Faulty parallelism occurs when a writer does not use parallel elements in a series or in paired points. Nouns must be matched with nouns, verbs with verbs, phrases and clauses with similarly constructed phrases and clauses, and so on, in places where they are expected.

FAULTY PARALLELISM	REVISED
Popular exercises for men and women include aerobic dancing, weight lifters, and jogging. (*Dancing* and *jogging* are gerunds; *weight lifters* is a noun phrase.)	Popular exercises for men and women include aerobic dancing, weight lifting, and jogging. (three gerunds)
Some of the side effects are skin irritation and eye irritation, and mucous membrane irritation may also develop. (*Skin irritation* and *eye irritation* are noun phrases; *mucous membrane irritation may also develop* is an independent clause.)	Some of the side effects that may develop are skin, eye, and mucous membrane irritation. (three nouns used as modifiers of *irritation*)
I look forward to hearing from you and to have an opportunity to tell you more about myself. (*Hearing from you* is a gerund phrase; *to have an opportunity* is an infinitive phrase.)	I look forward to hearing from you and to having an opportunity to tell you more about myself. (two gerund phrases)

(2) Repeating signals of parallelism

Faulty parallelism also occurs when a writer does not repeat words that signal parallelism: prepositions, articles, the *to* that is part of the infinitive, or the word that introduces a phrase or clause.

277

Although similar grammatical structures (verbs that match verbs, nouns that match nouns, and so on) may sometimes be enough to convey parallelism, sentences are clearer and more emphatic if other key words in parallel constructions are also parallel. Repeating these signals makes the boundaries of each parallel element clear. But be sure to include the same signals with *all* the elements in a series.

FAULTY PARALLELISM	REVISED
Computerization helps industry by not allowing labor costs to skyrocket, increasing the speed of production, and improving efficiency. (Does *not* apply to all three phrases, or only the first?)	Computerization helps industry by not allowing labor costs to skyrocket, by increasing the speed of production, and by improving efficiency. (Preposition *by* is repeated to clarify the boundaries of the three parallel phrases.)
The United States suffered casualties in the Civil War, French and Indian War, Spanish-American War and Korean War. (Without the repeated definite article, it is hard for readers to distinguish the four different wars.)	The United States suffered casualties in the Civil War, the French and Indian War, the Spanish-American War, and the Korean War. (The article *the* is repeated for clarity and emphasis.)
It may be easier to try remodeling than abandon a house. (Although *try* and *abandon* correspond, the sentence does not highlight their parallel structure; in fact, *remodeling* and *abandon* seem to be the paired elements.)	It may be easier to try remodeling than to abandon a house. (The *to* of the infinitive is repeated for clarity and emphasis.)
Koala bears are not as appealing as they look because they have fleas, they have bad breath, and a tendency to scratch. (Are *bad breath* and *a tendency to scratch* reasons why Koalas are unappealing, or are they incidental points?)	Koala bears are not as appealing as they look because they have fleas, because they have bad breath, and because they have a tendency to scratch. (The introductory words *because they have* are repeated for clarity and emphasis.)

(3)   Repeating relative pronouns

Faulty parallelism occurs when a writer fails to use a clause beginning with the relative pronoun *who, whom,* or *which* before one beginning with *and who, and whom,* or *and which.*

Like correlative conjunctions, *who...and who* and similar expressions are always paired and always introduce parallel clauses. When you omit the first part of the expression, you throw readers off balance.

INCORRECT: *The Thing,* directed by Howard Hawks, and which was released in 1951, featured James Arness as the monster.

REVISED: *The Thing,* which was directed by Howard Hawks, and which was released in 1951, featured James Arness as the monster.

In many cases, however, eliminating the relative pronouns produces a more concise sentence.

REVISED: *The Thing,* directed by Howard Hawks and released in 1951, featured James Arness as the monster.

E X E R C I S E   3

Identify and correct faulty parallelism in these sentences. Then underline the parallel elements—words, phrases, and clauses—in your corrected sentences. If a sentence is already correct, mark it with a *C* and underline the parallel elements.

EXAMPLE: Alfred Hitchcock's films include *North by Northwest, Vertigo, Psycho,* and he also directed *Notorious* and *Saboteur.*

REVISED: Films directed by Alfred Hitchcock include *North by Northwest, Vertigo, Psycho, Notorious,* and *Saboteur.*

1. The world is divided between those with galoshes on and those who discover continents.
2. Soviet leaders, members of Congress, and the American Catholic bishops all pressed the president to limit the arms race.
3. A national task force on education recommended improving public education by making the school day longer, higher teachers' salaries, and integrating more technology into the curriculum.
4. The fast-food industry is expanding to include many kinds of restaurants: those that serve pizza, fried chicken chains, some offering Mexican-style menus, and hamburger franchises.

5. The consumption of Scotch in the United States is declining because of high prices, tastes are changing, and increased health awareness has led many whiskey drinkers to switch to wine or beer.

STUDENT WRITER AT WORK

FAULTY PARALLELISM

In the following section of a draft of a paper written for a class in public health, a student discusses factors that must be taken into account by medical practitioners at the Indian Health Service. Correct the faulty parallelism, and revise again if necessary to strengthen coherence, unity, and style.

The average life-span of Native Americans is considerably lower than that of the general population. Not only is their infant mortality rate four times higher than that of the general population, but they also have a suicide rate that is twice as high as that of other races. Moreover, Native Americans both die in homicides more often than people of other races do and there are more alcohol-related deaths among Native Americans than among people of other races. Medical care available for them does not meet their needs and is presenting a challenge for the health professionals who serve them.

The Indian Health Service (IHS), a branch of the U.S. Public Health Service, is responsible for providing medical care to Native Americans who live on reservations. The IHS has been criticized for its inability to deal with cultural differences between health professionals and Native Americans—cultural differences that interfere with adequate medical care. In order to diagnose disease states, for prescribing drug therapy, and to counsel patients, health professionals need to acquire an understanding of Native-American culture. They must gain a working knowledge of Native Americans' ideas and feelings toward health and also God, relationships, and death. Only then can health professionals communicate their goals, provide quality medical care, and in addition they will be able to achieve patient compliance.

There are many obstacles to effective communication: hostility to white authority and whites' structured, organized society; language is another obvious barrier to communication; Native Americans' view of sickness, which may be different from Anglos'; and some Indian cultures' concept of time is also different from that of the Anglo health workers. Other problems are more basic: a physician cannot expect a patient to refrigerate medication if no refrigerators are available or dilute dosage forms at home or be changing wet dressings several times a day if clean water is not readily available nor quart/pint measuring devices to dilute stock solutions.

The defects in Native—American health care cannot be completely solved by the improvement of communication channels or making these channels stronger. But the health professional's communication with the Native—American patient can be effective enough so that medical staff can acquire an adequate medical history, monitor drug use, be alert for possible drug interactions, and to provide useful discharge counseling. If health professionals can communicate understanding and respect for Native—American culture and concern for their welfare, they may be able to meet the needs of their Native—American patients more effectively.

17

Shifts and Mixed Sentences

A **shift** is a change of tense, voice, mood, person, number, or type of discourse within or between sentences. **Mixed sentences**—which include *mixed constructions* and *faulty predication*—occur when two or more parts of a sentence do not fit together.

17a Shifts in Tense

The verb tenses within a sentence or a related group of sentences should not shift without good reason—to indicate changes of time, for example.

> *The Wizard of Oz* is a film that has enchanted audiences since it was made in 1939. (shift from present to past)

Generally, the tense of a verb in one clause of a sentence should be consistent with the tense of the verbs in the other clauses.

(1) Within a sentence

FAULTY: The judge told the defendant that he would not release him unless he promises to undergo therapy. (unwarranted shift from past to present)

REVISED: The judge told the defendant that he would not release him unless he promised to undergo therapy. (both verbs in past tense)

The following sentence is about a work of literature, so its action should be described in the present. The shift to the past (*drove*) in the dependent clause is therefore incorrect.

See ◄ 46c

FAULTY: The novel is about two friends who drove across the United States.

282

REVISED: The novel is about two friends who drive across the
United States.

Like works of literature, general truths are discussed in the present
tense.

FAULTY: Medical researchers know that asbestos caused cancer.

REVISED: Medical researchers know that asbestos causes cancer.

(2) In groups of sentences

The verb tenses within a series of related sentences should not
differ unless there is a logical reason for a shift.

ORIGINAL: One night I was driving late at night. Suddenly I see a
dog right in the path of my car. I slam on my brakes and
barely avoid hitting it. (unwarranted shift from past to
present tense)

REVISED: One night I was driving late at night. Suddenly I saw a
dog right in the path of my car. I slammed on my brakes
and barely avoided hitting it. (all verbs in past tense)

The following passage describes an event that occurs regularly
(each summer), so the verbs should be in the present tense. The
shift to the past tense throws readers off balance.

ORIGINAL: Each summer I spend a month at the shore. I lie on the
beach and let the sun drive away my troubles. The breeze
blows over the beach and cools the sand. I listened to a
radio on a nearby blanket and watched children playing
by the water.

REVISED: Each summer I spend a month at the shore. I lie on the
beach and let the sun drive away my troubles. The breeze
blows over the beach and cools the sand. I listen to a
radio on a nearby blanket and watch children playing in
the water.

17b   *Shifts in Voice*

Shifts in voice from active to passive may be necessary to give a
sentence like the one that follows proper emphasis:

▶ **See
23k**

Even though consumers protested, controls on the price of natural gas
were lifted.

Here the shift from active (*protested*) to passive (*were lifted*) enables the writer to keep the focus on consumer groups and the issue that they protested. To say *Congress lifted the price controls* would change the emphasis of the sentence.

Unwarranted shifts from active to passive, however, can be confusing and misleading. In the following sentence, for instance, the shift from active (*wrote*) to passive (*was written*) creates ambiguity:

> F. Scott Fitzgerald wrote *This Side of Paradise*, and later *The Great Gatsby* was written.

Although readers are able to tell that Fitzgerald wrote *This Side of Paradise*, they cannot be certain who wrote *The Great Gatsby*. Consistent use of the active voice makes this sentence clear:

> F. Scott Fitzgerald wrote *This Side of Paradise* and later wrote *The Great Gatsby*.

17c   *Shifts in Mood*

See
23g–i

As with tense and voice, unnecessary shifts in mood can be confusing and annoying.

INCONSISTENT:	It is important that a student buy a dictionary and uses it. (shift from subjunctive to indicative)
REVISED:	It is important that a student buy a dictionary and use it. (both verbs in the subjunctive)
INCONSISTENT:	Next, heat the mixture in a test tube and you should make sure it does not boil. (shift from imperative to indicative)
REVISED:	Next, heat the mixture in a test tube and be sure it does not boil (both verbs in the imperative)
INCONSISTENT:	The football player demanded that he get a raise and that he wants to play more often. (shift from the subjunctive to the indicative)
REVISED:	The football player demanded that he get a raise and that he play more often. (both verbs in the subjunctive)

17d   *Shifts in Person and Number*

Person is the form of a pronoun or verb that indicates who is speaking (first person—*I am, we are*), who is spoken to (second person—*you are*), and who is spoken about (third person—*he, she, it is; they are*). **Number** indicates one (singular—*novel, it*) or many (plural—*novels, they, them*).

Faulty shifts between the second- and the third-person pronouns cause most errors.

INCONSISTENT: When one looks for a loan, you compare the interest rates from several banks. (shift from third to second person)

REVISED: When one looks for a loan, one compares the interest rates from several banks.

REVISED: When you look for a loan, you compare the interest rates from several banks.

REVISED: When a person looks for a loan, he or she compares the interest rates from several banks.

Unwarranted shifts in number also create confusion within sentences. Make sure that singular pronouns refer to singular antecedents and plural pronouns to plural antecedents.

▶ See 24b

INCONSISTENT: If a person does not study regularly, they will have a difficult time passing organic chemistry. (shift from singular to plural)

REVISED: If a person does not study regularly, he or she will have a difficult time passing organic chemistry.

REVISED: If students do not study regularly, they will have a difficult time passing organic chemistry.

Revision Close-up

Although college writing follows standard conventions of pronoun-antecedent agreement, use of a plural pronoun referring to a singular antecedent is increasingly common in speech and in informal writing when such use enables the speaker or writer to avoid sexist language.

Buddy Holly and Janis Joplin each made a significant contribution with their music.

▶ See 18g2

EXERCISE 1

Read the following sentences, and eliminate any shifts in tense, voice, mood, person, or number. Some sentences are correct, and some will have more than one possible answer.

285

1. Gettysburg is a borough of southwestern Pennsylvania where some of the bloodiest fighting of the Civil War occurs in July 1863.
2. Giotto was born near Florence in 1267 and is given credit for the revival of painting in the Renaissance.
3. The early Babylonians divided the circle into 360 parts, and the volume of a pyramid could also be calculated by them.
4. During World War II General Motors expanded its production facilities, and guns, tanks, and ammunition were made.
5. Diamonds, the only gems that are valuable when colorless, were worn to cure disease and to ward off evil spirits.
6. First, clear the area of weeds, and then you should spread the mulch in a six-inch layer.
7. When one visits the Grand Canyon, you should be sure to notice the fractures and faults on the north side of the Kaibab plateau.
8. For a wine grape, cool weather means a higher acid content and a sour taste; hot weather means they will have lower acid content and a sweet taste.
9. Mary Wollstonecraft wrote *Vindication of the Rights of Women,* and then she wrote *Vindication of the Rights of Men.*
10. When one looks at the Angora goat, you should notice it has an abundant undergrowth.

17e *Shifts from Direct to Indirect Discourse*

Direct discourse reports the exact words of a speaker or writer. It is always enclosed in quotation marks and is often accompanied by an identifying tag (*he says, she said*).

> Commenting on his play, Eugene O'Neill said, "The script is written in blood and tears."

When a question is reported directly, the identifying tag indicates asking, and the sentence ends with a question mark.

> Rousseau asked, "Is it not obvious that where we demand everything, we owe nothing?

Indirect discourse summarizes the words of a speaker or writer. No quotation marks are used, and the reported statement is often introduced with the word *that.* Often, both pronouns and verb tenses in a reported statement are different from those in a directly quoted statement.

DIRECT DISCOURSE

> My instructor said, "I want your paper by this Friday."

INDIRECT DISCOURSE

My instructor said that he wanted my paper by this Friday.

Indirect reporting of a question includes a word like *who, what, why, whether, how,* or *if.* In addition, the pronouns and verb tenses of the original question change, and no question mark is used.

DIRECT QUESTION

The mayor asked, "Do you want to work in my reelection campaign?"

INDIRECT QUESTION

The mayor asked whether I wanted to work in his reelection campaign.

Shifts from direct to indirect discourse can lead to error because they invite illogical tense shifts.

FAULTY: William Dean Howells said that he felt the equality of things and "I believe in the unity of men." (unwarranted shift from indirect to direct discourse)

REVISED: William Dean Howells said that he felt the equality of things and that he believed in the unity of men. (Past tense indicates indirect discourse.)

REVISED: William Dean Howells said, "I feel the equality of things and I believe in the unity of men." (Present tense indicates direct discourse.)

E X E R C I S E   2

Transform the direct discourse in the following sentences into indirect discourse. Keep in mind that general truths stay in the present.

EXAMPLE: John F. Kennedy said, "Ask not what your country can do for you—ask what you can do for your country."

John F. Kennedy said that you should not ask what your country can do for you, but what you can do for your country.

1. Thoreau said, "I went to the woods because I wished to live deliberately."
2. In "Letter from Birmingham Jail" Martin Luther King, Jr., wrote, "I would be the first to advocate obeying just laws."
3. Steven Muller remarked, "I see an American society sadly in need of social services."

4. Psychologist B. F. Skinner observed, "Cultures are often judged by the extent to which they encourage self-observation."
5. "Why," asked Freud, "does our memory lag behind all our other psychic activities?"

17f *Mixed Constructions*

A **mixed construction** is a type of mixed sentence that occurs when a sentence begins with one grammatical strategy and then shifts to another. You can correct this type of mixed sentence by determining the focus of the sentence and revising it to reflect the meaning you want to convey.

> MIXED: Because she studies every day explains why she gets good grades.

The writer begins with a dependent clause (*Because she studies every day*), which should logically be followed by an independent clause. Instead, the writer uses the dependent clause as the subject of *explains*. The two parts of the sentence are, therefore, at odds with each other, and readers have trouble determining the meaning. The writer can correct this sentence by deleting *explains why*.

> REVISED: Because she studies every day, she gets good grades.

Mixed constructions can take many forms. Each of the groups of sentences below illustrates a common kind of mixed construction and presents some options for revision.

> MIXED: By calling for information is the best way to learn more about the benefits of ROTC. (adverbial phrase used as subject)
>
> REVISED: By calling for information you can learn more about the benefits of ROTC.
>
> REVISED: Calling for information is the best way to learn more about the benefits of ROTC.

> MIXED: Even though he published a paper on the subject does not mean he should get credit for the discovery. (adverb clause used as subject)
>
> REVISED: Even though he published a paper on the subject, he should not get credit for the discovery.
>
> REVISED: Publishing a paper on the subject does not necessarily warrant his getting credit for the subject.

MIXED: The book we found in the antique store, we took it to the museum to be appraised. (object used as the apparent subject)

REVISED: We took the book we found in the antique store to the museum to be appraised.

EXERCISE 3

Revise the following mixed constructions so that their parts fit together both grammatically and logically.

EXAMPLE: The people who had tickets, the ushers told them to line up on the right.

The ushers told the people who had tickets to line up on the right.

1. Despite the fact that she wrote *The Bluest Eye* did not mean that Toni Morrison won the Pulitzer Prize.
2. By trying to find a short route to India was how Columbus discovered the New World.
3. Because of a defect in design made the roof of the Hartford Stadium collapse.
4. The troops that advanced on Carthage, Scippio Africanus urged them to fight for the glory of Rome.
5. Even though she works for a tobacco company does not mean that she should be against laws prohibiting smoking in restaurants.

17g *Faulty Predication*

Faulty predication is a type of mixed sentence that occurs when a sentence's subject and predicate do not fit together logically. Faulty predication is especially common in sentences that contain a *linking verb*—a form of the verb *be*, for example—and a subject complement.

FAULTY: Mounting costs and declining advertising revenue were the demise of *Look* magazine in 1971.

This sentence states incorrectly that mounting costs and declining advertising *were* the demise of *Look* magazine when, in fact, they were *the reasons* for its demise. You can correct this problem by revising the sentence so that it includes a complement that can logically be equated with the subject.

REVISED: Mounting costs and declining advertising revenue were the reasons for the demise of *Look* magazine in 1971.

Faulty predication can also occur when intervening words obscure the connection between the subject and the verb. When you revise, be sure the connection between subject and verb is logical.

FAULTY: The purpose of Napoleon's campaign failed because of the severity of the Russian winter. (Intervening words obscure the relationship between the subject, *purpose,* and the verb, *failed.*)

REVISED: Napoleon's campaign failed because of the severity of the Russian winter. (*Napoleon's campaign* is now the sentence's subject.)

REVISED: The purpose of Napoleon's campaign was thwarted by the severity of the Russian winter. (The verb is now consistent with the subject.)

Another kind of faulty predication occurs when a clause beginning with *where* or *when* follows *is* in a definition. When you revise a clause containing a definition, be sure to use a noun or a noun phrase as both the subject and the subject complement.

FAULTY: Taxidermy is where you construct a lifelike representation of an animal from its preserved skin. (In definitions, *be* must be preceded and followed by nouns or noun phrases.)

REVISED: Taxidermy is the construction of a lifelike representation of an animal from its preserved skin. (The subject complement is now a noun phrase.)

A similar type of faulty predication occurs when the phrase *the reason is* precedes *because.*

FAULTY: The reason many people get cancer is because of environmental factors.

REVISED: Many people get cancer because of environmental factors.

REVISED: Environmental factors cause many people to get cancer.

A **faulty appositive** is a type of faulty predication in which an appositive is equated with a noun or pronoun which it cannot logically modify.

FAULTY: The salaries are high in professional athletics, such as football players. (*Professional athletics* is not the same as *football players.*)

REVISED: The salaries are high for professional athletes, such as football players. (football players = professional athletes)

EXERCISE 4

Revise the following sentences to eliminate faulty predication. Keep in mind that each sentence may be revised in more than one way.

EXAMPLE: Radioastronomy is when you use radio wavelengths to study the universe.

Radioastronomy is a branch of astronomy that uses radio wavelengths to study the universe.

1. Depression is where a person has a mood of helplessness and a feeling of inadequacy.
2. Competition is fierce among athletes, such as fencing and water polo.
3. The development of telescopes was made in considerable numbers and was found throughout Europe soon after their invention.
4. The reason the moon does not fall into the earth is because of centrifugal force.
5. Poor planning, complacency, and corruption were the defeat of the Turks in Arabia during World War I.

STUDENT WRITER AT WORK

SHIFTS AND MIXED SENTENCES

Following is an excerpt from a draft of a student's research paper on immigrant factory workers in New York City in the early twentieth century. In this section of her paper, the student focuses on a fire that contributed to the creation of stricter fire safety codes. Read the paragraphs and correct any mixed constructions, faulty predication, or unwarranted grammatical shifts. If necessary, revise further to strengthen coherence, unity, and style.

In one particularly compelling section of World of Our Fathers, Irving Howe describes the devastating 1911 fire at the Triangle Shirtwaist Company (304–6). In quoting an eyewitness account and contemporary reactions and by reproducing graphic photographs is how he added drama to his account of an already dramatic event. For instance, Howe quotes labor activist Rose Schneiderman, who said this was not the first time girls had been burned alive in this city, and "The life of men and women is so cheap and property is so sacred" (305).

In his book The Triangle Fire Leon Stein suggests
that the fire, in the ten-story Asch Building near
Washington Square in New York City, probably began with a
cigarette or spark in a rag bin. Some people in the
building apparently tried dousing the flames, but because
of rotted hoses and rusted water valves made efforts
useless (15).

The announcement of the many causes of the fire was
obvious. According to the investigating committee, the one
fire escape visible from Green Street collapsed after
fewer than twenty people escaped. In addition, although
sprinkler systems had been invented in 1895 did not mean
any were present in the Asch Building. They were
considered too expensive. Records show that six months
before the fire, the building was cited as a firetrap by
the city. The owners failed to make alterations was what
the report identified as a cause of the fire. Failure to
have regular fire drills and a lack of clearly marked
exits also contributed to the high death toll (Stein
117-119).

Because it was 4:30 P.M. on a Saturday when the fire
broke out meant there were 650 workers in the building.
The majority of these were young Jewish and Italian women,
and there was no common language spoken by them. By not
sharing a common language was one reason for the chaos
among the workers (Stein 14-15). When those on the ninth
floor found the fire exit doors locked, their panic
peaked. With their exit blocked, everyone was forced to
jump from the windows to avoid the intense fire that swept
through the building. Although it took fire fighters only
18 minutes to bring the fire under control, 146 workers
died.

PART 5

Using Words Effectively

Choosing Words

Choosing the right word is a complex process. Unfortunately, no clear rule exists for distinguishing the right word from the wrong one. The same word may be appropriate in one situation and inappropriate in another.

This chapter will acquaint you with the subtleties of language and help you to express yourself precisely and orginally in your college writing.

18a *Choosing an Appropriate Level of Diction*

Diction denotes word choice, particularly how appropriately you express an idea. Different audiences and occasions call for different *levels* of diction. You would think it odd, for example, if your history textbook said that Julius Caesar was the *guy* who ruled Rome, even though *man* and *guy* essentially mean the same thing. When you know who your readers are and what they expect, you can determine whether your level of diction should be *formal, informal,* or *popular*.

(1) Formal diction

When decorum is in order—in eulogies and other addresses, scholarly articles, formal reports, and some essays—readers expect formal diction. **Formal diction** calls for words familiar to an educated audience: *impoverished* rather than *poor, wealthy* or *affluent* rather than rich, intelligent rather than *smart, automobile* rather than *car*. Contractions, shortened word forms, and utility words such as *nice* (**see 11a2**) generally do not appear in formal diction.

Formal English is grammatically accurate, and often uses the impersonal *one* or the collective *we* rather than the more personal *I* and *you*.

The following passage from John F. Kennedy's inaugural address illustrates these characteristics. Although formal, Kennedy's diction is not stiff or artificial; rather, it is eloquent, graceful, and clear, with parallelism heightening its impact.

> Let the word go forth from this time and place, to friend and foe alike, that the torch has been passed to a new generation of Americans—born in this century, tempered by war, disciplined by a hard and bitter peace, proud of our ancient heritage, and unwilling to witness or permit the slow undoing of those human rights to which this nation has always been committed, and to which we are committed today at home and around the world.

Academics frequently use formal diction aimed at a learned audience, as the psychologist B. F. Skinner does in the following paragraph. Note that he expects his readers to be familiar with the terminology of his field and that he uses the collective *we* and *our* instead of the more personal *I* and *you*.

> We learn to perceive in the sense that we learn to respond to things in particular ways because of the contingencies of which they are a part. We may perceive the sun, for example, simply because it is an extremely powerful stimulus, but it has been a permanent part of the environment of the species throughout its evolution, and more specific behavior with respect to it could have been selected by contingencies of survival (as it has been in many other species). The sun also figures in many current contingencies of reinforcement: we move into or out of sunlight depending on the temperature; we wait for the sun to rise or set to take practical action; we talk about the sun and its effects; and we eventually study the sun with the instruments and methods of science. Our perception of the sun depends on what we do with respect to it. Whatever we do, and hence however we perceive it, the fact remains that it is the environment which acts upon the perceiving person, not the perceiving person who acts upon the environment. (*Beyond Freedom and Dignity*)

(2) Informal diction

Whereas formal diction is primarily a language of writing and formal addresses, **informal diction** is the language people use daily in conversation. It includes *colloquialisms, slang, regionalisms,* and occasionally *nonstandard language.* Although you will encounter informal diction quite frequently in your reading, limit its use in your college writing to imitating speech or dialect or to giving an essay a conversational tone.

Colloquialisms   **Colloquial diction** occurs most often in everyday speech. We use it when we are not concentrating on being grammatically correct, and it is perfectly acceptable in informal situations, where formal diction would be out of place.

Contractions—*isn't, won't, I'm, he'd*—are typical colloquialisms, as are shortened word forms—*phone* for *telephone, TV* for *television, dorm* for *dormitory, exam* for *examination,* for instance. Other colloquialisms include the placeholders *you know, sort of, kind of,* and *I mean* and the utility words *nice* for *good* or *acceptable, funny* for *odd,* and *great* meaning almost anything. Colloquial English also includes verb forms like *get across* for *communicate, come up with* for *find,* and *check out* for *investigate.*

In the following passage from J. D. Salinger's novel *The Catcher in the Rye,* the narrator, Holden Caulfield, uses colloquial diction:

> The book I was reading was this book I took out of the library by mistake. They gave me the wrong book, and I didn't notice it till I got back to my room. They gave me *Out of Africa,* by Isak Dinesen. I thought it was going to stink, but it didn't. It was a very good book. I'm quite illiterate, but I read a lot. My favorite author is my brother D. B., and my next favorite is Ring Lardner.

Slang   **Slang** words are extremely informal. Whether they are inventions or existing words redefined, they emerge to meet a need. They add spice to spoken language by calling attention to themselves. Words like *high, spaced out, dove, hawk, hippie, uptight, groovy, heavy, be-in, happening,* and *rip off* emerged in the 1960's as part of the counterculture surrounding rock music, drugs, and the protest against the United States involvement in Vietnam. During the 1970's technology, music, politics, and feminism influenced slang, giving us words and phrases like *high tech, hacker, input, disco, stonewalling, Watergate, nuke, burnout, macho,* and *male chauvinism.* Other 1970's words that are still with us include *humongous* and *lifestyle.* The 1980's have contributed expressions like *rap music, yuppie, fax, chocoholic,* and *crack.*

Revision Close-up

Slang varies with time and place and can become dated quickly. In time, slang can either become part of the language or fade into disuse. (Consider *beatnik, daddy-o,* and *hepcat.*) In college writing, use words classified as slang only when imitating speech or dialect.

Regionalisms   **Regionalisms** are words and expressions, commonly used in certain geographical areas, that may not be understood by a general audience. Regionalisms include words like *overshoe, fried cake,* and *angledog* and expressions like *take sick* and *come down with a cold.* In eastern Tennessee, for example, a paper bag is a *poke,* and empty soda bottles are *dope bottles.* Regionalisms also include old forms that have lost their meanings outside a particular area. For example, in Lancaster, Pennsylvania, which has a large Amish population, it is not unusual to hear an elderly person saying *darest* for *dare not* or *daresome* for *adventurous.*

In the following passage from his novel *As I Lay Dying,* William Faulkner uses regionalisms of the American South to add authenticity to his writing:

> "It's fixing up to rain," Pa says. "I am a luckless man. I have ever been." He rubs his hands on his knees. "It's that durn doctor, liable to come at any time. I couldn't get word to him till so late. If he was to come tomorrow and tell her the time was nigh, she wouldn't wait."

Revision Close-up

Regionalisms can make your writing more vivid. However, because they are an informal use of language and often have little meaning to an audience not familiar with a particular region's dialect, you should use them with care.

Nonstandard Language   **Nonstandard** (or **substandard**) refers to words and expressions that are not generally considered a part of standard English, even though many individuals use them when speaking. Included are words like *ain't, nohow, anywheres, nowheres, hisself, theirselves,* and *wait on* (instead of *wait for*).

Keep in mind that no absolute rules distinguish standard and nonstandard usage. In fact, this issue is currently the subject of much debate. Many linguists reject the idea of substandard usage altogether, arguing that this designation serves only to relegate both the language and those who use it to second-class status. Dictionaries and handbooks can at best only attempt to define the norms

See
19b9

of language. In the end, you will have to supplement the guidelines that these books provide with your own assessment of your audience and purpose to determine what is appropriate usage in a particular writing situation.

(3) Popular diction

Popular diction is the language of mass-audience magazines, newspapers, best sellers, and editorials. Conversational in tone, popular diction falls somewhere between formal and informal English. It does not employ words as precisely as formal English does, and it often includes colloquialisms, contractions, and the first person. Even so, popular diction generally uses correct grammar, avoiding slang and nonstandard language.

The following passage from *Esquire* illustrates many of these characteristics:

> Decade after decade of mediocre Disney films triumphed and stoked our sensibilities because the art itself, animation, is such a delight. It has been right from the start. In 1928, when Mickey Mouse as Steamboat Willie joins prototype Minnie to crank up a goat's tail in order to see musical notes leave the beast's mouth and dance to the tune of "Turkey in the Straw," the magic is already in full bloom. When Dumbo's ears flap and the ungainly mass finally soars, nobody cares where he's going. We love this creature; indeed we fall for Disney the way we fall in love: what the eye sees is more important than what the eye judges. (Max Apple, "Uncle Walt")

The contraction *he's* and the colloquial expressions *in full bloom, crank up,* and *fall for* give this piece a relaxed, conversational tone. However, the author also uses relatively formal words like *decade, prototype,* and *indeed* and the collective *we* and *our* instead of the more informal *I* and *you.*

(4) College writing

The level of diction appropriate for college writing depends on your assignment and your audience. A personal experience essay calls for a natural, informal style, but a research paper, an examination, or a report calls for a more formal vocabulary and a detached tone.

The following passage, which occasionally uses formal diction and includes no nonstandard language, contractions, or shortened word forms, illustrates the level of diction typical of much college writing:

> Deaf students face many problems. Their needs are greater than those of other students. Often ignored by hearing students, deaf students may develop a severe inferiority complex. Their inability to mix in a large group is another cause of this problem. Because deaf students communicate by sign language or by lip reading, they usually interact on a one-to-one basis. It is not at all unusual for deaf students to be in a classroom and not even realize that someone in the class is speaking. Other problems occur when people in the class first find out that a person has a hearing problem. Often, in an effort to try to help, people begin exaggerating their lip movements. This exaggerated lip movement, called "mouthing," makes it impossible for many deaf students to read lips. For this reason, many deaf students find it better to conceal a hearing impairment than to disclose it.

E X E R C I S E 1

This paragraph, from Sherwood Anderson's short story "I'm a Fool," is characterized by informal diction. Representing the speech of a young boy, it is laced with slang and grammatical inaccuracies. Underline the words that identify the diction of this paragraph as informal. Then rewrite the paragraph, using popular diction.

> You know how it is. Gee, she was a peach! She had on a soft dress, kind of a blue stuff and it looked carelessly made, but was well sewed and made and everything. I knew that much. I blushed when she looked right at me and so did she. She was the nicest girl I have ever seen in my life. She wasn't stuck on herself and she could talk proper grammar without being a school teacher or something like that. What I mean is, she was O.K. I think maybe her father was well-to-do, but not rich to make her chesty because she was his daughter, as some are. Maybe he owned a drug store or a drygoods store in their hometown or something like that. She never told me and I never asked.

E X E R C I S E 2

After reading the following paragraphs, underline the words and phrases that identify each as formal diction. Then choose one paragraph and rewrite it using a level of diction that you would use in your college writing. Use a dictionary if necessary.

In looking at many small points of difference between species, which, as far as our ignorance permits us to judge, seem quite unimportant, we must not forget that climate, food, etc., have no doubt produced some direct effect. It is also necessary to bear in mind, that owing to the law of correlation, when one part varies and the variations are accumulated through natural selection, other modifications, often of the most unexpected nature, will ensue.   (Charles Darwin, *The Origin of Species*)

I hope you are able to see the distinction I am trying to point out. In no sense do I advocate evading or defying the law, as would the rabid segregationist. That would lead to anarchy. One who breaks an unjust law must do so openly, lovingly, and with a willingness to accept penalty. I submit that an individual who breaks a law that conscience tells him is unjust, and who willingly accepts the penalty of imprisonment in order to arouse the conscience of the community over its injustice, is in reality expressing the highest respect for law.   (Martin Luther King, Jr., "Letter from Birmingham Jail")

18b   *Using Diction Appropriate to Purpose*

A word is *appropriate* if it suits the purpose for which it is intended. In general terms, a writer's purpose may be to convey information, to express personal feelings, or to persuade (see **1a1**).

(1)   Informative writing

Informative writing—the kind that appears in journals, magazines, newspapers, textbooks, expository essays, and examinations—conveys information to its readers. For the most part, it is factual and avoids words with emotional associations. It often relies on third-person pronouns instead of using *I* or *we*. The following example is from a student paper:

One method of disposing of nuclear wastes is to store them in air-cooled vaults. Most vaults of this type are large reinforced concrete buildings that are cooled by natural convection. An air-cooled vault requires at least 10,000 square feet of space to hold nuclear waste discharged from an atomic power plant. Spent fuel is packaged in lead containers and stored in compartments within the vault. Air flows through vents that line the inside of the chamber, keeping the vault at a constant temperature. A single air-cooled vault can store approximately 28.2 million pounds of spent fuel. This method of storage has two major drawbacks. First, it requires a large amount of space, and second, it costs $103 for each kilogram of fuel stored.

(2) Expressive writing

Expressive writing—the kind found in diaries, journals, letters, and personal experience essays—expresses the feelings of the writer. It uses words and phrases that evoke emotional images; relies on the personal pronouns *I* and *we*; and usually contains informal language, although it can also be formal, as in some autobiographies. The following paragraph is an example of expressive writing:

> *March 4.* When will it all end? The idiocy and the tension, the dying of young men, the destruction of homes, of cities, starvation, exhaustion, disease, children parentless and lost, cages full of shivering, staring prisoners, long lines of hopeless civilians plodding through mud, the endless pounding of the battle line. I can scarcely remember what it is like to be where explosions are not going off around me, some hostile, some friendly, all horrible; an exploding shell is a terrible sound. What keeps this war going, now that its end is so clear? What do the Germans think of us, and we of them? I do not think we think of them at all, or much. Do they think of us? I can think of their weapons, their shells, their machine guns, but not of the men behind them. (Donald Pearce, *Journal of War*)

(3) Persuasive writing

The purpose of **persuasive writing**—the kind that appears in argumentative essays, political tracts, advertising copy, editorials, and legal briefs—is to convince someone to act or to accept an idea. Words and phrases that convey value judgments and that reinforce the progression of an argument—*furthermore, consequently, accordingly,* and *therefore*—often appear. Persuasive essays may use either the first person *I* or *we* or the more formal third person *he, she, they,* or *one.* Persuasive writing may employ technical or other specialized terms to convince an audience of the validity of an assertion. The following paragraph, from an editorial in a college newspaper, is an example of persuasive writing:

> Students at this college wonder just how long they will have to put up with the dreadful conditions that exist in the cafeteria. The food is often overcooked and tasteless, and the facilities are always cramped and dirty. Even more important, the cafeteria's hours do not correspond to the needs of the students. For the past year the cafeteria has served lunch from eleven to one-thirty. A recent study conducted by

301

this paper revealed that almost 37 percent of all students have classes straight through this time period. As a result, these students must miss lunch entirely or eat "on the run." Accordingly, most students interviewed said they would like the cafeteria to serve light snacks and sandwiches all afternoon. So far, neither the management of the cafeteria nor the administration has responded to these concerns.

EXERCISE 3

Identify the primary purpose of each of the following paragraphs. Underline the words and phrases that help you make your determination.

There also was more than a hint of unseen mass in the finding last year by the High Energy Astronomical Observatory that an invisible ring of superheated gas circled the constellation Northern Cross like a halo. The halo extends 72 quadrillion miles. Its temperature is 3.5 million degrees, hot enough to create out of the gas in the halo as many as 10,000 new stars. Carrying powerful X-ray telescopes, HEAO was able to map 90 percent of the halo, which is invisible in space to any but an X-ray telescope. The halo is so hot that its light is paler than the sun's corona; surrounding bright stars and the background light of the galaxy are sufficient to wash out its light by the time it reaches Earth. (Thomas O'Toole, "Will the Universe Die by Fire or Ice?")

Why did I write it down? In order to remember, of course, but exactly what was it I wanted to remember? How much of it actually happened? Did any of it? Why do I keep a notebook at all? It is easy to deceive oneself on all those scores. The impulse to write things down is a peculiarly compulsive one, inexplicable to those who do not share it, useful only accidentally, only secondarily, in the way that any compulsion tries to justify itself. I suppose that it begins or does not begin in the cradle. Although I have felt compelled to write things down since I was five years old, I doubt that my daughter ever will, for she is a singularly blessed and accepting child, delighted with life exactly as life presents itself to her, unafraid to go to sleep and unafraid to wake up.   (Joan Didion, *Slouching Toward Bethlehem*)

College, then, may be a good place for those few young people who are really drawn to academic work, who would rather read than eat, but it has become too expensive, in money, time, and intellectual effort, to serve as a holding pen for large numbers of our young. We ought to make it possible for those reluctant, unhappy students to find alternative ways of growing up, and more realistic preparation for the years ahead.   (Caroline Bird, *The Case Against College*)

18c *Choosing the Right Word*

According to Mark Twain, the difference between the right word and almost the right word is the difference between the lightning and the lightning bug. If you use the wrong words—or even *almost* the right ones—you run the risk of misrepresenting your feelings and ideas.

(1) *Denotation and connotation*

A word's **denotation** is its explicit meaning, what it stands for without any emotional associations. A word's **connotations** are the emotional, social, and political associations that it has in addition to its denotative meaning. Denotative language is informative language, devoid of judgments or opinions. Connotations suggest feelings, attitudes, opinions, and desires.

Denotation and Connotation		
Word	**Denotation**	**Connotation**
Politician	Someone who holds a political office	Opportunist; wheeler-dealer
Fallout	Radioactive byproduct of an atomic explosion	Any consequence of a negative event
Institution	An organization or foundation, or the building housing it	A place where ill or elderly people are shut away

You would think that determining the denotative meaning of a word would present few problems, but this is not always so. Words can have different denotations for different people. The linguist S. I. Hayakawa points out that in England and in the United States the word *robin* denotes entirely different species of birds and that what the English call a sparrow is what we call a weaver finch. In addition, words can have similar but not identical meanings, and this too can cause confusion. For example, you make an error in denotation when you say *molecule* when you mean *atom* or *compound* when you mean *mixture*.

Selecting a word with the appropriate connotation is not always easy. Slang and colloquialisms sometimes give ideas unintended connotations. For instance, the sentence "In school we *mess around* with computers" gives the impression that your involvement with computers is not serious or important. If indeed your involvement is serious, it would be far better to say that in school you *work* with computers. Words that contain built-in judgments are another possible source of unintended connotations. For example, *mentally ill, insane, neurotic, crazy, psychopathic,* and *disturbed* have different social and political connotations that color the way people will respond. If you use these terms without considering their connotations, you run the risk of undercutting your credibility, to say nothing of confusing and possibly angering your readers.

You rely on denotative language when you want to describe things as they are. In laboratory reports, technical writing, examinations, and case studies, you use language that reinforces your objectivity and detachment. Opinion papers, arguments, and critical responses, however, require words that reinforce your critical judgments and therefore call for connotative language as well.

Most of the writing that you do, however, uses a combination of connotative and denotative language. Technical reports will sometimes use an analogy to explain an unfamiliar concept or situation, and literary analyses routinely employ precise denotative language to describe a scene or character. Used appropriately, both connotative and denotative language enable you to express your ideas and emotions clearly and effectively.

Revision Close-up

When you write, take the time to think about a word's emotional associations. Revise carefully, and be sure the words you use convey the connotations you intend them to.

E X E R C I S E 4

The following words have negative connotations. For each, list one word with a similar meaning whose connotation is neutral and another whose connotation is favorable.

EXAMPLE:	*Negative*	skinny
	Neutral	thin
	Favorable	slender

1. deceive
2. antiquated
3. egghead
4. pathetic
5. cheap

6. blunder
7. argumentative
8. politician
9. shack
10. stench

EXERCISE 5

Think of a trip you took. First, write a one-paragraph description that would discourage anyone from taking the same trip. Next, rewrite this paragraph, describing your trip favorably. Finally, rewrite your paragraph again, using neutral words that convey no judgments. In all three versions of your paragraph, underline the words that helped you to convey your impressions to your readers.

(2) Euphemisms

A **euphemism** is a term used in place of a blunt term that describes a subject that society considers disagreeable, frightening, or offensive.

In the Victorian era, direct reference to the body and its functions was disdained. Consequently, table supports were delicately referred to as *limbs,* and (to avoid saying *leg* and *breast*) people referred to the meat of a turkey as *dark* or *light.*

People still avoid discussing certain subjects, such as bodily functions, death, and certain social problems. Therefore, toilets are *lounges, bathrooms,* or *powder rooms.* (The word *toilet* itself is a euphemism for *dressing* or *shaving.*) We say that the dead have *passed on, gone to their reward,* or *departed,* and we call graveyards *resting places* or *memorial parks.* We refer to divorce as *marital dissolution,* adultery as an *affair,* the poor as *deprived,* and retarded children as *developmentally delayed.*

Revision Close-up

College writing is no place for euphemisms. Say what you mean—*pregnant,* not *expecting; died,* not *passed away; strike,* not *work stoppage; drunk,* not *inebriated;* and *used car,* not *preowned automobile.*

(3) Specific and general words

Specific words refer to particular persons, items, or events, while **general** words signify an entire class or group. *Queen Elizabeth II,* for example, is more specific than *monarch; topcoat* is more specific than *clothing;* and *Corvette* is more specific than *automobile.* General words are, of course, useful. Statements that use general words to describe entire classes of items or events are often necessary to convey a point. But such statements must also include specific words for support and clarity. The more specific your choice of words, the more vivid your writing will be.

Whether a word is general or specific is relative, determined by its relationship to other words. The following word chains illustrate increasing specificity, with the word farthest to the left denoting a general category or class and the one farthest to the right naming a specific, tangible member of that class.

General ⟶ Specific

history—American history—Civil War history—History 263
apparel—accessory—tie—bow tie—my blue bow tie
human being—official—president—Thomas Jefferson
reading matter—book—novel—*Native Son*
machine—vehicle—train—*Orient Express*

Using general words when specific words are needed produces vagueness. If you want your readers to visualize a certain building— say, the new wing of the National Gallery in Washington, D.C.— it is not enough to say that it has an angular shape. If you want your audience to "see" Picasso's *Guernica,* you must do more than note its mythic imagery.

(4) Abstract and concrete words

Abstract words—*beauty, truth, justice,* and so on—refer to ideas, qualities, or conditions that cannot be perceived by the senses. **Concrete** words, on the other hand, convey a vivid picture by naming things that readers can *see, hear, taste, smell,* or *touch.* As with general and specific words, whether a word is abstract or concrete is relative. The more concrete your words and phrases, the more vivid the image you evoke in the reader.

Abstract and Concrete

ABSTRACT

The night I stayed too late I was spellbound by the beautiful sights.

CONCRETE

The night I stayed too late I was hunched on the log staring spell-bound at spreading, reflected stains of lilac on the water. A cloud in the sky suddenly lighted as if turned on by a switch; its reflection just as suddenly materialized on the water upstream, flat and float-ing, so that I couldn't see the creek bottom, or life in the water under the cloud. Downstream, away from the cloud on the water, water turtles smooth as beans were gliding down with the current in a series of easy, weightless pushoffs, as men bound on the moon. (Annie Dillard, *Pilgrim at Tinker Creek*)

Of course we need abstract words to discuss concepts. The works of many great writers examine abstractions such as *truth, faith,* and *beauty,* but these writers know that they must go on to describe abstractions with concrete details. However, abstract terms can create problems for beginning writers, who may use them—without concrete supporting detail—to conceal fuzzy, inexact thinking.

In the following paragraph the overuse of abstract words creates a general and not very vivid description:

TOO ABSTRACT

The Balzac Monument is Rodin's most daring creation. The figure is unusual. Balzac is wrapped in a cloak in an interesting way. He has an unusual expression on his face.

Why is the figure of Balzac unusual? What is interesting about the way the cloak wraps the figure? What is the unusual expression on Balzac's face? When concrete words replace abstract words, the passage is much more informative.

MORE CONCRETE

The Balzac Monument is Rodin's most daring creation. The figure resembles a ghost or specter. Balzac seems to tower above us so that from a distance we see only his great size. Upon closer inspection we see that Balzac is wrapped in a cloak. From the indistinct lines of the cloak, Balzac's head emerges godlike, with eyes that stare off into the distance.

Revision Close-up

Imprecise diction often occurs when you use abstract terms such as *nice, great,* and *terrific* that say nothing and could be used in almost any sentence **(see 11a2).** These **utility words** indicate only enthusiasm. Replace them with more specific words.

VAGUE: The movie was good.

BETTER: The movie was an exciting and suspenseful mystery.

E X E R C I S E 6

Effective writing usually mixes specific and general words and abstract and concrete words. Read the following passage and underline words that are relatively specific and concrete. How do they make the paragraph more effective? Are any very general or abstract words used? How do they function? What impression does the writer want to convey?

Near the end of March, 1845, I borrowed an axe and went down to the woods by Walden Pond, nearest to where I intended to build my house, and began to cut down some tall arrowy white pines, still in their youth, for timber. It is difficult to begin without borrowing, but perhaps it is the most generous course thus to permit your fellow-men to have an interest in your enterprise. The owner of the axe, as he released his hold on it, said that it was the apple of his eye; but I returned it sharper than I received it. It was a pleasant hillside where I worked, covered with pine woods, through which I looked out on the pond, and a small open field in the woods where pines and hickories were springing up. The ice in the pond was not yet dissolved, though there were some open spaces, and it was all dark colored and saturated with water. There were some slight flurries of snow during the days that I worked there; but for the most part when I came out on to the railroad, on my way home, its yellow sand heap stretched away gleaming in the hazy atmosphere, and the rails shone in the spring sun, and I heard the lark and pewee and other birds already come to commence another year with us. They were pleasant spring days, in which the winter of man's discontent was thawing as well as the earth, and the life that had lain torpid began to stretch itself. (Henry David Thoreau, *Walden*)

EXERCISE 7

Revise this paragraph from a job application letter by substituting specific, concrete language for general or abstract words and phrases.

> I have had several part-time jobs lately. Some of them would qualify me for the position you advertised. In my most recent job, I sold products in a store. My supervisor said I was a good worker who possessed a number of valuable qualities. I am used to dealing with different types of people in different types of settings. I feel that my qualifications would make me a good candidate for your job.

18d *Avoiding Unoriginal Language*

Whenever possible, choose words that are original, vivid, and interesting, and avoid *jargon, neologisms, clichés,* and *pretentious diction,* which deaden writing and leave your meaning unclear.

(1) Jargon

Jargon refers to the specialized or technical vocabulary of a trade, profession, or academic discipline. Jargon is useful in the field for which it was developed, but outside that field it is often imprecise and confusing. Medical doctors tell patients that a procedure is *contraindicated* or that they are going to carry out a *differential diagnosis* of the symptoms that patients *present with.* Business executives ask for *feedback* or *input* and want departments to *interface* effectively. On a recent television talk show, a sociologist spoke about the need for *perspectivistic thinking* to achieve organizational goals. Is it any wonder that the befuddled host asked his guest to explain this term to the audience?

Jargon is often accompanied by overly formal diction, the passive voice, and wordy constructions. The following sentences contrast a passage choked by jargon with a simplified version:

> ORIGINAL: Procedures were instituted to implement changes in the parameters used to evaluate all aspects of the process.
>
> TRANSLATION: We began using different criteria to judge the process.

309

Although many people deliberately use jargon to impress their audience, its effect is usually just the opposite. When writing, avoid jargon and concentrate on a vocabulary that is appropriate for your audience and purpose.

(2) Neologisms

Neologisms are newly coined words that are not part of standard English. New situations call for new words, and frequently such words become a part of the language. The rapid development of the media and growth of scientific knowledge, for example, have introduced thousands of new words that have become part of Standard English.

Neologisms

quark:	A hypothetical subatomic particle
televangelist:	A member of the clergy whose primary ministry is a television audience
microelectronics:	A branch of electronics that deals with the miniaturization of electronic circuits and components

---

Other coined words, however, have not yet crossed into standard English; some of these may never be accepted. Many of these questionable neologisms are created when the suffixes *-wise* and *-ize* are added to existing words. Police officers say that a criminal must be *Mirandized*. Businesspeople *prioritize* before they *finalize* things *investmentwise*. Popular journalists and news commentators seem to attach these suffixes to many words—creating new words like *weatherwise, sportswise, timewise,* and *productwise*.

If you are not sure whether to use a term, look it up in your college dictionary. If it is not there, it is probably not standard English.

(3) Pretentious diction

Pretentious diction is language that is inappropriately elevated and wordy. In an effort to impress readers, beginning writers sometimes use pretentious diction: they elevate their style, overusing adjectives and adverbs, learned words, and poetic devices. Good writing is clear writing, and pompous or flowery language is no substitute for thought.

PRETENTIOUS DICTION

The expectations of offspring may be appreciably different from their parents'.

REVISED

Children's goals may be different from their parents'.

PRETENTIOUS DICTION

As I fell into slumber, I cogitated about my day ambling through the splendor of the Appalachian Mountains.

REVISED

As I fell asleep, I thought about my day hiking through the Appalachian Mountains.

Pretentious diction is not formal diction used in an inappropriate situation; it is always out of place. By calling attention to itself, it draws readers away from the point you are making. Contrast the following paragraphs in terms of clarity and appropriateness of imagery:

PRETENTIOUS

The Tammany Society [a political association] was an all-engulfing weed that rapidly overran and choked New York City's political gardens. Times were filled with danger for those who dared protest this corruption. Even the champion of the people—*The Sun*—refused to encourage the few flowers that dared to rear their heads in that field of briars. Although the situation improved somewhat in the hands of skillful gardeners, much corruption existed for years to come.

REVISED

The Tammany Society was a weed that quickly overran New York City. Times were hard for those who dared to speak against its spread; even *The Sun* did not encourage reformers. Although the situation improved somewhat in the hands of reform-minded politicians, much corruption existed for years to come.

(4) Clichés

Clichés are expressions that through overuse have lost all meaning. Familiar sayings like "This isn't my cup of tea," "We're in the

► See
18f1

same boat," "That's the last straw," and "Let's get down to brass tacks," for example, have lost their concrete associations and are now virtually meaningless.

Similarly, in many pat phrases, words become bound to other words. The phrases that result become so familiar that they lose their original impact. For example, political, social, or economic situations are often described as *rapidly deteriorating. Root causes* need to be uncovered, so *options are explored, Herculean efforts* are made, and sometimes *mutually agreeable solutions* are found. If not, *viable alternatives* may allow the two sides to *peacefully coexist.*

The purpose of college writing is always to convey information clearly; clichés do just the opposite.

E X E R C I S E   8

Rewrite the following passage, eliminating jargon, neologisms, pretentious diction, and clichés. Feel free to add words and phrases and to reorganize sentences to make their meaning clear. If you are not certain about the meaning or status of a word, consult a dictionary.

At a given point in time there coexisted a hare and a tortoise. The aforementioned rabbit was overheard by the tortoise to be blowing his horn about the degree of speed he could attain. The latter quadruped thereupon put forth a challenge to the former by advancing the suggestion that they interact in a running competition. The hare acquiesced, laughing to himself. The animals concurred in the decision to acquire the services of a certain fox to act in the capacity of judicial referee. This particular fox was in agreement, and consequently implementation of the plan was facilitated. In a relatively small amount of time the hare had considerably outdistanced the tortoise and, after ascertaining that he himself was in a more optimized position distancewise than the tortoise, he arrived at the unilateral decision to avail himself of a respite. He made the implicit assumption in so doing that he would anticipate no difficulty in overtaking the tortoise when his suspension of activity ceased. An unfortunate development racewise occurred when the hare's somnolent state endured for a longer-than-anticipated time frame, facilitating the tortoise's victory in the contest and affirming the concept of unhurriedness and firmness triumphing in competitive situations. Thus the hare was unable to snatch victory out of the jaws of defeat. Years later he was still ruminating about the exigencies of the situation.

Go through a newspaper or magazine and list the jargon, neologisms, pretentious diction, or clichés that you find. Then substitute more original words for the ones you identified. Be prepared to discuss your interpretation of each word and the word you chose to put in its place.

18e   *Using Figurative Language*

Language that adheres to the standard meaning or order of speech is called **literal language.** But writers must often go beyond literal meanings to **figurative language**—language that uses imaginative comparisons called **figures of speech.** A writer could say, "The moon was big and beautiful," but figurative language is more expressive: "The moon hung in the sky like one of the white balloons that decorated the bandstand."

Figurative language is not only for literary writing; it has its place in journalism, in college writing, and even in scientific and technical writing. Although you should not overuse figurative language, do not be afraid to use it when you think it will help you to communicate with a reader.

The most commonly used figures of speech are *simile, metaphor, analogy, personification, allusion, hyperbole,* and *understatement.*

(1)   Similes

A **simile** is a comparison between two essentially unlike items on the basis of a shared quality. Similes are introduced by a term such as *like* or *as.*

SIMILE: Like travelers with exotic destinations on their minds, the graduates were remarkably forceful. (Maya Angelou, *I Know Why The Caged Bird Sings*)

SIMILE: A cloud in the sky suddenly lighted as if turned on by a switch. (Annie Dillard, *Pilgrim at Tinker Creek*)

Revision Close-up

A simile must compare two *dissimilar* things. The first sentence below is not a simile, but the second one is:

continued

continued from previous page

> My dog is like your dog.
>
> My dog is as sleek as a seal.

(2) Metaphors

A **metaphor** also compares two essentially dissimilar things, but instead of saying that one thing is *like* another, it *equates* them.

Metaphors are compressed similes. Because of their economy of expression, they can convey ideas with considerable power.

> In its first days of operation, a new telescope orbiting the earth has returned infrared images showing previously unobserved features of distant galaxies and revealing cosmic "maternity wards" where clouds of interstellar gas appear at various stages of giving birth to stars. (John Noble Wilford, *New York Times*)

> Perhaps it is easy for those who have never felt the stinging darts of segregation to say, "Wait." (Martin Luther King, Jr., "Letter from Birmingham Jail")

Revision Close-up

For a metaphor to work, it has to employ images with which readers are familiar. If the comparison is too remote, readers will miss the point entirely. If it is too common, it will become a cliché **(see 18d4).**

(3) Analogies

See
4f6
An **analogy** explains an unfamiliar object or idea by comparing it to a more familiar one.

> An atom is like a miniature solar system.

> Robert Frost said that writing free verse is like playing tennis without a net.

> The circulatory system runs through the body like a network of rivers and streams.

Analogies can extend over several sentences or even several paragraphs.

Analogies work only when the subjects you are comparing have something in common. For example, drawing an analogy between tables and ants would not be useful because the items compared are too dissimilar. But explaining ants by comparing them to people— other social animals—makes good sense.

(4) Personification

Personification gives an idea or inanimate object human attributes, feelings, or powers. We use personification every day in expressions such as *The engine coughed.*

Personification can make an entity that is abstract or hard to describe more concrete and familiar. By doing so, it also makes your writing more precise and more interesting.

Truth strikes us from behind, and in the dark, as well as from before in broad daylight. (Henry David Thoreau, *The Journals*)

Institutions, no longer able to grasp firmly what is expected of them and what they are, grow slovenly and misshapen and wander away from their appointed tasks in the Constitutional scheme. (Jonathan Schell, *The Time of Illusion*)

(5) Allusion

An **allusion** is a reference—which readers are expected to recognize—to a well-known historical, biblical or literary person or event. Allusion enriches your readers' understanding by suggesting a relationship between your writing and something outside it. For example, suppose that you title an essay you have written about your personal goals "Miles to Go Before I Sleep." By reminding your readers of the concluding lines of Robert Frost's poem "Stopping by Woods on a Snowy Evening," you suggest your determination and self-discipline.

Literary allusions such as the one above can help to convey your emotional attitudes. *Biblical* allusions can allow you to express a moral attitude ("Be a good Samaritan"). *Historical* allusions, such as "Watergate was Richard Nixon's Waterloo," can elucidate current events by drawing parallels between a recent event (the political scandal that brought down the Nixon presidency) and an event of historical importance (Napoleon's crushing defeat).

(6) Overstatement (hyperbole)

Overstatement or **hyperbole** is an intentional exaggeration for emphasis. Its effect can be serious or humorous. For example, Sylvia Plath uses hyperbole in her poem "Daddy" when she compares her father to a Nazi storm trooper, and Jonathan Swift does so in his essay "A Modest Proposal" when he suggests that eating Irish babies would help the English solve their food shortage.

(7) Understatement

Where overstatement exaggerates, **understatement** downplays a situation or sentiment by saying less than what is really meant. When Mao-Tse Tung, former chairman of the People's Republic of China, said that a revolution was not a tea party, he was using understatement. When, after a hurricane, a survivor interviewed by a reporter said, "Well, it certainly was windy," she too was using understatement.

18f Avoiding Ineffective Figures of Speech

Effective figures of speech enrich your diction; ineffective figures of speech weaken it.

(1) Dead metaphors and similes

Metaphors and similes stimulate thought by calling up vivid images in a reader's mind. A **dead metaphor** or **simile**, however, has been so overused that it has become a pat, meaningless expression that evokes no particular visual image. Here are some examples:

beyond a shadow of a doubt	off the beaten path
crying shame	a shot in the arm
sit on the fence	smooth sailing
green with envy	dead as a doornail

off the track

the last straw

up in arms

sink or swim

Avoid dead metaphors and similes; instead, take the time to think of images that make your writing fresher and more vivid.

(2) Mixed metaphors

A **mixed metaphor** results when you combine two or more incompatible images in a single figure of speech. Mixed images leave readers wondering what you are trying to say—or leave them laughing. When you revise mixed metaphors, make your imagery consistent.

MIXED: Management extended an olive branch in an attempt to break some of the ice between the company and the striking workers. (break the ice with an olive branch?)

REVISED: Management extended an olive branch with the hope that the striking workers would pick it up. (Images are now consistent.)

(3) Strained metaphors

A **strained metaphor** compares two things that do not have enough in common to justify the comparison.

STRAINED: The plane was a fragment of candy falling through the sky.

In what sense is a plane comparable to a piece of candy? By comparing items that have a strong basis of comparison, the following revision creates an effective metaphor:

REVISED: The plane was a wounded bird falling through the sky.

EXERCISE 10

Read the following paragraph from Mark Twain's *Life on the Mississippi*, and identify as many figures of speech as you can.

Now when I had mastered the language of this water, and had come to know every trifling feature that bordered the great river as familiarly as I knew the letters of the alphabet, I had made a valuable acquisition. But I had lost something, too. I had lost something which could never be restored to me while I lived. All the grace, the beauty, the poetry, had gone out of the majestic river! I still keep in mind a certain wonderful sunset which I witnessed when steamboating was new to me. A broad expanse of the river was turned to blood; in the middle distance the red hue brightened into gold, through which a solitary log came floating black and conspicuous; in one place a long, slanting mark lay sparkling upon the water; in another the surface was broken by boiling, tumbling rings, that were as many-tinted as an opal; where the ruddy flush was faintest, was a smooth spot that was covered with graceful circles and radiating lines, ever so delicately traced; the shore on our left was densely wooded, and the somber shadow that fell from this forest was broken in one place by a long, ruffled trail that shone like silver; and high above the forest wall a clean-stemmed dead tree waved a single leafy bough that glowed like a flame in the unobstructed splendor that was flowing from the sun. There were graceful curves, reflected images, woody heights, soft distances; and over the whole scene, far and near, the dissolving lights drifted steadily, enriching it every passing moment with new marvels of coloring.

E X E R C I S E   11

Rewrite the following sentences, adding one of the figures of speech discussed above to each sentence to make the ideas more vivid and exciting. Identify each figure of speech you use, and be sure to use each of the five figures of speech at least once.

EXAMPLE: The room was cool and still.

The room was cool and still like the inside of a cathedral. (simile)

1. The child was small and carelessly groomed.
2. I wanted to live life to its fullest.
3. The December morning was bright and cloudy.
4. As I walked I saw a cloud floating in the sky.
5. House cats can be very lazy.
6. The sunset turned the lake red.
7. The street was quiet except at the hour when the school at the corner let out.
8. A shopping mall is a place where teenagers like to gather.
9. The president faced an angry Senate.
10. Education is a long process that takes much hard work.

18g   *Avoiding Offensive Language*

Racial, ethnic, and religious slurs, obscenities, and sexist language are offensive. Avoid the use of such language in your writing.

(1) *Racial, ethnic, and religious slurs*

When referring to any racial, ethnic, or religious group, use words with neutral connotations or words that the groups use in *formal* speech or writing to refer to themselves. The derogatory terms with which we are all too familiar are unacceptable in your writing.

Racial, ethnic, and religious stereotypes are also offensive. Avoid biased generalizations that brand certain groups as stupid, pushy, or tight with money, for instance.

(2) *Sexist language*

Sexist language ignores—and thereby undercuts—the political, economic, and social changes made by women and men. Insulting to both men and women, sexist language entails much more than the use of derogatory words such as *broad, hunk,* and *chick.* Assuming that some professions are exclusive to one sex—that, for instance, *nurse* denotes only women and *doctor* denotes only men—is also sexist. So is the use of job titles such as *postman* for letter carrier, *fireman* for firefighter, and *policeman* for police officer. Habits of thought and language change slowly, but they do change.

Sexist language also occurs when a writer fails to use the same terminology when referring to men and women. For example, you should refer to two scientists with Ph.D's not as Dr. Sagan and Mrs. Yallow, but as Dr. Sagan and Dr. Yallow. You should refer to two writers as James and Wharton, not Henry James and Mrs. Wharton.

In your writing, always use *women*—not *girls*—when referring to adult females. Use *Ms.* as the form of address when a woman's marital status is unknown or irrelevant. If the woman you are addressing refers to herself as Mrs. or Miss, however, use the form of address she prefers. Finally, avoid using the generic *he* or *him* when your subject could be either male or female. Use the third-person plural or the phrase *he or she* (not *he/she*).

TRADITIONAL: Before boarding, each passenger should make certain
that <u>he</u> has <u>his</u> ticket.

REVISED: Before boarding, passengers should make certain that they have their tickets.

REVISED: Before boarding, each passenger should make certain that he or she has a ticket.

Remember, however, not to overuse *his or her* or *he or she* constructions, which can make your writing repetitious and wordy.

Revision Close-up

When trying to avoid sexist use of *he* and *him*, be careful not to create ungrammatical constructions such as the following:

UNGRAMMATICAL: Before the publication of Richard Wright's novel *Native Son,* any unknown African-American writer had trouble getting their work published.

Although many educated speakers do use *they* and *their* in cases such as the one above, when doing so avoids an awkward alternative (*his or her* work published) or a sexist construction (*his* work published), you should avoid using a singular noun along with a plural pronoun in your college writing. Instead, use a plural noun.

GRAMMATICAL: Before the publication of Richard Wright's novel *Native Son,* unknown African-American writers had trouble getting their work published.

Alternatives for many common usage problems involving sexist language appear in the following chart.

Revising Sexist Language

Sexist Usage	Possible Revisions
1. A student should choose his courses carefully.	Students should choose their courses carefully.
	A student should choose his or her courses carefully.
2. Equality is a desirable goal for all men.	Equality is a desirable goal for everyone.
3. Mankind	People, human beings
Man's accomplishments	Human accomplishments
Man-made	Synthetic

4. The manager . . . he	The manager . . . he or she; the managers . . . they
The nurse . . . she	The nurse . . . he or she; the nurses . . . they.
The librarian . . . she	The librarian . . . he or she; the librarians . . . they
The lawyer . . . he	The lawyer . . . he or she; the lawyers . . . they.
5. Female doctor (lawyer, painter, etc.)	Doctor, (lawyer, painter, etc.)
6. Mailman Fireman Policeman/woman Salesman/woman/girl Businessman/woman	Letter carrier Firefighter Police officer Salesperson Businessperson
7. The girl at the desk answered the phone.	The person, the receptionist, the secretary
8. Women's libber Women's lib	Feminist Women's movement
9. Spinster Old maid	Single woman; no mention of marital status
10. Stewardess/Steward	Flight attendant
11. Phyllis Knable, wife of Dr. Peter Knable, was given the Benjamin Rush Award for her outstanding work as a surgeon.	Dr. Phyllis Knable was given the Benjamin Rush award for her outstanding work as a surgeon.
12. Linda Richards, mother of three, was the first woman to be inducted into the Leola branch of the International Association of Lions Clubs.	Linda Richards was the first woman to be inducted into the Leola branch of the International Association of Lions Clubs.
13. A professor works hard to get tenure. As a result, his wife must be supportive.	A professor works hard to get tenure. As a result, his or her spouse must be supportive; Professors work hard to get teunure. As a result, their spouses must be supportive.

continued

321

continued from previous page

| 14. Everyone should complete his application by Tuesday. | Everyone should complete his or her application by Tuesday; All students should complete their applications by Tuesday. |

E X E R C I S E   12

Suggest possible alternative forms for any of the following constructions which you consider sexist. In each case, comment on the advantages and disadvantages of the alternative you recommend. If you feel that a particular term is not sexist, explain why.

forefathers	longshoreman
man-eating shark	committeeman
manpower	(to) man the battle stations
workman's compensation	Girl Friday
men at work	Board of Selectmen
copy boy	stock boy
bus boy	cowboy
first baseman	man overboard
corpsman	fisherman
congressman	foreman

E X E R C I S E   13

These terms denote professions which have traditionally been linked with a particular gender. Now that the professions are open to both sexes, are any new terms needed? If so, suggest possible terms. If not, explain why not.

miner	farmer
mechanic	barber
soldier	rabbi
sailor	minister
rancher	bartender

E X E R C I S E   14

The following terms have emerged in the last few years as possible alternatives for older gender-specific words. Which do you believe are likely to become part of the English language? Which do you expect to disappear? Explain.

Coinage	*Older Form*
a. waitperson server	waiter or waitress
b. househusband homemaker	housewife
c. weatherperson	weatherman, weathergirl
d. chair chairwoman chairperson	chairman
e. spokesperson	spokesman

EXERCISE 15

Each of the following pairs of terms includes a feminine form which was at one time in wide use; all are still used to some extent. Which do you think are likely to remain in our language for some time, and which do you think will disappear? Explain your reasoning.

heir/heiress
benefactor/benefactress
murderer/murderess
actor/actress
hero/heroine
host/hostess
aviator/aviatrix
executor/executrix

author/authoress
poet/poetess
tailor/seamstress
comedian/comedienne
villain/villainess
prince/princess
widow/widower

EXERCISE 16

In recent years the word *parenting* has been introduced as a gender-free equivalent of *mothering*. How do the connotations of *parenting* differ from those associated with *mothering*? with *fathering*? Given those differences, what is your prediction about the continued use of *parenting* in years to come?

STUDENT WRITER AT WORK

CHOOSING WORDS

The following draft was written for a freshman composition class. Revise it for appropriateness, accuracy, and freshness, changing words and rewriting sentences as you see fit. If necessary, revise further to strengthen coherence, unity, and style.

Computers and Society

Computers are presently addressing many thorny problems that are just begging to be solved. In fact, their widespread use is making advances possible in many fields. At the present time computers are a major part of our environment, cutting down time-consuming chores and making our lives easier.

A computer is a device engineered to make computation easier and faster. Today the computer has taken the image of a highly sophisticated electronic complex. By transforming Base 10 into Base 2, the computer's binary coded hexadecimal system allows it to distinguish numbers through the use of electronic switches. An open switch represents a 0 state, and a closed switch represents a 1 state. By the use of programming, you can accomplish a desired result in a matter of milliseconds.

The computer's applications have spread like wildfire to almost every field of endeavor. In the fields of mathematics and science, the computer has been used in activities as diverse as studying the structure of the atom and sending satellites into space. Another recent application is the use of computers in hospitals to detect drugs and toxins in human blood. Because a doctor will be cognizant of poisoning immediately, he can embark upon an appropriate course of action and resuscitate the victim. This technique is a vast improvement over conventional laboratory analysis methods.

Computers can also be used at a person's residence to

make his daily life easier. For example, a computer can turn on and off lights even though a person is not home. Thus a thief can be thwarted in his attempt to violate a home. Likewise, a computer can direct a remote—controlled vacuum cleaner to make a house super—clean, and it can do laundry and dishes through the use of more automatic devices. Taking care of everyday financial matters can also be as easy as pie. In addition, alarm clocks can be programmed so members of the household could be awakened at different times.

In conclusion, the computer is a useful tool for society. It can be used beneficially in business and industry as well as in the home. And just as the automatic dishwasher has replaced doing dishes by hand, the computer will alter the way we do many things. The computer is an idea whose time has come and an idea that will open the door to the future.

19

Using the Dictionary and Building a Vocabulary

Exploring the Contents of a Dictionary

Like tools, different dictionaries are designed for different tasks. The most widely used type of dictionary, the one-volume **abridged dictionary** (also called a **desk dictionary** or a **college dictionary**), is ideal for daily use. Other types of dictionaries—including multi-volume, **unabridged dictionaries,** which give a great deal of specialized data, and the many **special-purpose dictionaries**—have their own special uses.

A dictionary is usually divided into three parts: the *front matter,* the *alphabetical listing,* and the *back matter.*

The **front matter** differs in each dictionary but generally contains a preface explaining how the dictionary is set up and guides for pronunciation and abbreviations. Some dictionaries include special material in the front matter. *The American Heritage Dictionary,* a standard reference dictionary, has articles focusing on the history of the language, dialects, usage and acceptability, and computers and language analysis.

The **alphabetical listing** is the largest section of every dictionary. Entries tell how a word is spelled, pronounced, and used, and some dictionaries also include information on stress, grammatical function, and *etymology* (history and origin of the word). On the basis of hundreds of examples of usage, lexicographers also classify word usage into categories such as *regional, slang,* and *preferred.* Dictionaries may disagree regarding these designations, however.

Meanings under each entry may also be arranged differently from one dictionary to another. Some dictionaries list meanings in historical order, with the oldest usage coming first; others list meanings in order of most frequent usage. Therefore, you cannot assume that the first definition under an entry is the preferred usage. You must look in the front matter to find out which principle of arrangement the lexicographers used.

The **back matter** also differs in each dictionary. Some dictionaries contain a list of weights and measures; others, an essay on punctuation; and still others, a glossary of foreign words. To get the most out of your dictionary, acquaint yourself with its back matter so that you can refer to it when the need arises.

Revision Close-up

Because the contents of these three sections differ from dictionary to dictionary, you should acquaint yourself with your dictionary's special features. Knowing exactly what your dictionary has to offer can help you get the most out of it as you write and revise.

19b *Using a Dictionary*

To fit a lot of information into a small space, abridged dictionaries use a system of symbols, abbreviations, and different typefaces. Each dictionary uses a slightly different system, so you should consult the front matter of your dictionary to determine how its system operates.

A labeled entry from *The American Heritage Dictionary,* 2nd College Edition is shown in Figure 1.

(1)   Guide words

To help you locate words, all dictionaries include a pair of guide words at the top corner of each page.

Couperin/court-martial
shriek · shut

The guide words indicate the first and last entries appearing on that page. The word on the left shows the first entry on the page, and the word on the right shows the last. All entries on the page fall alphabetically between these words.

Entry Word   Pronunciation   Usage Labels

cou·ple (kŭp'əl), *n.* **1.** Two items of the same kind; pair. **2.** Something that joins or connects two things together; link. **3.** (used with *a sing.* or *pl.verb*). **a.** A man and woman united, as by marriage or betrothal. **b.** Two people together. **4.** A few; several: *a couple of days.* **5.** *Physics.* A pair of forces of equal magnitude acting in parallel but opposite directions, capable of causing rotation but not translation. —*v.* **-pled, -pling, -ples.** —*tr.* **1.** To link together; connect: *coupled her refusal with an explanation.* **2. a.** To join as man and wife; marry. **b.** To join in sexual union. **3.** *Elect.* To link (two circuits or currents) as by magnetic induction. —*intr.* **1.** To form pairs; join. **2.** To copulate. **3.** To join chemically. [ME < OFr. < Lat. *copula,* bond.]

Synonyms: *couple, pair, duo, brace, yoke.* These nouns denote two of something in association. *Couple* refers to two of the same kind or sort not necessarily closely associated, though often it does apply to close relationship. Less formally the term may mean "few." *Pair* stresses close association and often reciprocal dependence of things (as in the case of gloves or pajamas). Sometimes it denotes a single thing with interdependent parts (such as shears or spectacles). *Duo* refers to partners in a duet. *Brace* refers principally to certain game birds, and *yoke* to two joined draft animals.

Usage: *Couple,* when referring to a man and woman together, may be used with either a singular or a plural verb, but the plural is more common. Whatever the choice, usage should be consistent: *the couple are spending their honeymoon* (or *is spending its honeymoon*).

Grammatical Function

Meanings

Etymology

Synonyms

Usage Note

Quotation

FIGURE 1 Sample Dictionary Entry

(2)   *Entry words*

The **entry word,** which appears in boldface at the beginning of the entry, gives the spelling of a word and any variant forms.

col · or *n.* Also chiefly British col · our

Dictionaries differ in their treatment of word division and compound words. *The American Heritage Dictionary,* for example, has *crossfire, The Concise Oxford Dictionary* has *cross-fire,* and *Webster's Ninth New Collegiate Dictionary* has *cross fire.*

(3)   *The pronunciation guide*

The pronunciation of a word appears in parentheses after the main entry (or between slashes [/ /] in *Webster's Ninth New Collegiate Dictionary*). Dictionaries use symbols to represent sounds, and an explanation of these symbols usually appears at the bottom of each page or across the bottom of facing pages throughout the alphabetical listing. (A full guide to pronunciation appears as part of the front matter of the dictionary.) The stressed syllable of a word is indicated by an accent mark ('). A secondary stress is indicated with a similar but lighter mark (').

(4) Part of speech labels

Dictionaries use abbreviations to indicate parts of speech and grammatical functions.

If a verb is regular, the entry provides only the base form of the verb.

help ... vb

If a verb is irregular, the entry lists the principal parts of the verb.

with · draw ... vb -drew ...; -drawn...; -drawing....

In addition, the entry indicates whether a verb is transitive, intransitive, or both.

in · fect ... vt

va · ca · tion ... vi

pen · e · trate ... vb ... vt ... vi

Part-of-speech labels also indicate the plural form of irregular nouns.

fly ... n pl flies

to · ma · to ... n pl -toes

a · lum · nus ... n pl -ni

moth · er-in-law ... n pl moth · ers-in-law

When the plural form is regular, it is not shown.

Dictionaries usually show the comparative and superlative forms of both regular and irregular adjectives and adverbs.

red ... adj redder; reddest

bad ... adv worse; worst

Revision Close-up

Most entries for regular adjectives and adverbs show the comparative and superlative forms with -er and -est. The fact that the entry shows -er and -est, however, does not mean that you cannot use more and most as an alternative way to form the comparative and the superlative. An entry without -er and -est always uses more and most to form the comparative and the superlative.

EXERCISE 1

Use your college dictionary to answer the following questions about grammatical function.

1. What are the principal parts of the following verbs: *drink, deify, carol, draw,* and *ring?*
2. Which of the following nouns can be used as verbs: *canter, aesthetic, minister, council, command, magistrate, mother,* and *lord?*
3. What are the plural forms of these nouns: *silo, sheep, seed, scissors, genetics,* and *alchemy?*
4. What are the comparative and superlative forms of the following adverbs and adjectives: *fast, airy, good, mere, homey,* and *unlucky?*
5. Are the following verbs transitive, intransitive, or both: *bias, halt, dissatisfy, die,* and *turn?* Copy the phrase or sentence from the dictionary that illustrates the use of each verb.

(5)   *Etymology*

The **etymology** of a word is its history, its evolution over the years. This information appears in brackets—[   ]—either before or after the list of meanings. The etymology traces a word back to its roots and shows its form when it entered English. For instance, *The American Heritage Dictionary* shows that *couple* came into Middle English (ME) (1150–1475) from Old French (OF) and into Old French from Latin (L). *Webster's Ninth New Collegiate Dictionary* shows *cup* to have the same form, *cuppe,* in both Old English (OE) and Middle English and to have come into English from the Latin *cuppa.*

(6)   *Meanings*

Some dictionaries, such as *The American Heritage Dictionary,* give the most common meaning first and then list less common ones. Others, such as *Webster's Ninth New Collegiate Dictionary,* begin with the oldest meaning and move to the most current ones.

Remember that a dictionary records the meanings that appear most regularly in speech and in writing. If a word is in the process of acquiring new meanings, the dictionary may not yet include them. Also remember that a dictionary meaning is primarily a record of the **denotations,** or exact meanings, of a word. Its emotional associations, or **connotations,** are not usually among the meanings listed, although some dictionaries do attempt to suggest them.

(7) *Synonyms and antonyms*

A dictionary entry often lists synonyms and occasionally antonyms in addition to definitions. **Synonyms** are words that have similar meanings, such as *well* and *healthy*. **Antonyms** are words that have opposite meanings, such as *courage* and *cowardice*. Dictionaries present synonyms—and sometimes antonyms—because they clarify the meanings of a word and also because they are useful to writers who want to vary their choice of words. However, no two words are exactly equivalent, so you must use synonyms carefully, making certain that the connotation of the synonym is as close as possible to that of the original word.

EXERCISE   2

Using your dictionary as well as your own knowledge, write a paragraph explaining the differences in the connotations of the words in one of the groups below.

1. car, automobile, limousine
2. cabin, shack, hovel
3. cry, weep, sob

4. portly, heavy, fat
5. slumber, sleep, snooze

(8) *Idioms*

Dictionary entries often show how certain words are used with other words in set expressions called **idioms.** Such phrases present problems for some native speakers and especially for non-native speakers, as you may know from your own study of other languages. For example, what are we to make of the expression *from the shoulder?* That it means "in a direct or outspoken manner of telling" is not at all apparent from its words. Such idiomatic phrases do not follow any rules; they have become fixed through custom and must be memorized.

Dictionaries also indicate the idiomatic use of prepositions. Under a usage note for the word *acquiesce,* for instance, *The American Heritage Dictionary* says that *acquiesce* is used with *in* when it takes a preposition. Similarly, we do not say that we *abide with* a decision or that we *interfere on* a performance. We say *abide by* and *interfere with.* The idiomatic use of prepositions is a matter of custom.

331

(9) Usage labels

Dictionaries use special labels to indicate restrictions on word meanings. Where such labels involve value judgments, dictionaries differ.

Usage Labels

Label	Definition	Example
1. Nonstandard/ Substandard	A word that is in wide use but not considered part of standard usage	*ain't*
2. Informal/ Colloquial	A word that is part of the language of conversation and acceptable in informal writing.	*I've* for *I have* *sure* for *surely*
3. Slang	A word appropriate only in extremely informal situations but, unlike regionalisms, widely used	*rip off* *prof* for *professor*
4. Dialect/Regional	A word or meaning of a word limited to a certain geographical region	*arroyo,* a word used in the Southwest to mean "deep gully" *potlatch,* a word used in the Northwest to mean "celebration"
5. Vulgar	A word that is offensive. This category includes words labeled **obscene,** which are extremely offensive, and words labeled **profane,** which show disrespect for the deity.	*crap*

6. Obsolete	A word that is no longer in use; this label applies only to words that have disappeared from the language	*egal* meaning "equal"
7. Archaic/Rare	A word or meaning of a word that was once common but now is seldom used; **archaic** differs from **rare,** which means that a word was never in common usage	*affright* meaning "to arouse fear or terror" (archaic) *nocent* meaning "guilty" or "harmful" (rare)
8. Poetic	A word used commonly only in poetry	*eve* for *evening* *o'er* for *over*
9. Foreign Language Labels	These identify expressions or words from other languages that are commonly used in English but are not considered part of the language.	*Adios,* Spanish for "goodbye" *Sine qua non,* Latin for "something that is essential"
10. Field Labels	These indicate that a word or meaning of a word is limited to a certain field or discipline (mathematics, biology, military, etc.).	*couple* (physics and electrical engineering)

EXERCISE 3

Use your college dictionary to find the restrictions on the use of the following words.

1. irregardless
2. apse
3. flunk
4. lorry
5. kirk
6. ope
7. whilst
8. integer
9. bannock
10. blowhard

(10)   General information

In addition to containing information about words, your abridged dictionary is an excellent source of general information. If you wanted to find out the year in which John Glenn orbited the earth, you might look up the entry *Glenn, John*. If you needed to find out after whom the Davis Cup is named, you would look up *Davis Cup*. When no other references are handy, your abridged dictionary can be extremely useful.

EXERCISE   4

To test the research capability of your dictionary, use it to answer the following questions.

1. Where is Kitty Hawk, the site of Wilbur and Orville Wright's first heavier-than-air powered flight?
2. How many satellites does the planet Uranus have?
3. What is the population of Los Angeles?
4. In what year did Martin Luther King, Jr., win the Nobel Peace Prize?
5. In what year did Edward VII of England abdicate?
6. Who was Grandma Moses?
7. After whom was the Ferris wheel named?
8. What is the atomic weight of sulfur?
9. What was Joseph Conrad's original name?
10. What is surrealism?

19c   *Surveying Abridged Dictionaries*

An **abridged dictionary** is one that is condensed from a more complete collection of words and meanings. A good hardback abridged dictionary will contain about 1,500 pages and about 150,000 entries. Paperback dictionaries usually contain fewer entries, treated in less detail. A paperback dictionary is adequate as a spelling reference that you can easily carry to class, but for home reference, any of the following hardback abridged dictionaries does a better job.

The American Heritage Dictionary of the English Language, 2nd Coll. ed. Boston: Houghton Mifflin, 1982.

This extensively illustrated dictionary was first published in 1969. The front matter of the dictionary discusses etymology, the history of language, usage and acceptability, dialects, and computers and language analysis. Within the alphabetical listing the principal and most current meaning appears first, with other meanings branching out from it. Throughout the dictionary, the editors have provided *usage notes* based on the responses of a panel of 100 experts. Synonyms and sometimes antonyms are also listed.

In general, this dictionary gives more guidance than any of the other abridged dictionaries listed here.

The Concise Oxford Dictionary of Current English, 8th ed. New York: Oxford University Press, 1990.

This no-nonsense dictionary contains no illustrations and gives little guidance on usage. It lists meanings according to the most common usage, includes illustrative quotations, and gives British as well as American spellings. Front and back matter is sparse: there is a short preface, and the back matter includes a table of weights and measures, the Greek and Russian alphabets, and a compendium of the principal monetary units of the world.

The Random House College Dictionary, rev. ed. New York: Random House, 1989.

This is an abridged version of the larger unabridged *Random House Dictionary of the English Language.* It lists meanings according to frequency of use and indicates informal and slang usage. It also gives synonyms and antonyms as well as geographical and biographical names. Illustrations are helpful but less extensive than those in *The American Heritage Dictionary.* Back matter includes a manual of style.

Webster's Ninth New Collegiate Dictionary. Springfield, MA: Merriam, 1990.

Like *The Random House College Dictionary,* this dictionary is an abridged version of a larger unabridged dictionary. Meanings are listed chronologically rather than according to frequency of usage, and historical information precedes each definition. *Webster's Collegiate* contains fewer illustrations than *The American Heritage Dictionary.*

Two new features characterize the ninth edition. First, entries are accompanied by dates showing how old a word is and when a definition came into use. Second, many entries are now followed by usage notes that discuss problems of usage and diction.

The front matter of this dictionary contains a detailed essay on the English language commissioned for this edition. Foreign words and phrases as well as biographical and geographical names appear in separate sections in the back matter.

> *Webster's New World Dictionary*, 3rd Coll. ed. Englewood Cliffs, NJ: Prentice-Hall, 1988.

This good basic dictionary presents meanings in historical order and indicates frequent usage. Foreign terms and geographical and biographical names are included in the alphabetical listing. Back matter includes information on mechanics, manuscript form, and punctuation.

NOTE: The name *Webster*, referring to the great lexicographer Noah Webster, is in the public domain. Because it cannot be copyrighted, it appears in the titles of many dictionaries of varying quality.

19d   *Surveying Unabridged Dictionaries*

In some situations you may need more information than your college dictionary offers. When you are looking for a detailed history of a word or when you want to look up an especially rare usage, you need to consult an unabridged dictionary. An **unabridged dictionary** attempts to present a comprehensive survey of all words in a language. Consequently, it gives a wider and more detailed treatment of entries than an abridged dictionary, with listings that may extend over several volumes.

> *The Random House Dictionary of the English Language*, 2nd ed., unabridged. New York: Random House, 1987.

This short unabridged dictionary—the shortest listed here—contains about 315,000 entries. In the process of updating the first (1966) edition, the editors have added 50,000 new words and 75,000 new definitions of old words.

> *Webster's Third New International Dictionary of the English Language.* Springfield, MA: Merriam, 1986.

This unabridged dictionary contains over 450,000 entries along with illustrations, some in color. Meanings appear in chronological order and are extensively illustrated with quotations. This dictionary does not, however, give much guidance on usage.

The Oxford English Dictionary. New York: Oxford University Press, 1933; 1986.

Consisting of twelve volumes plus four supplements, *The Oxford English Dictionary* offers over 500,000 definitions, historically arranged, and 2 million supporting quotations. The quotations begin with the earliest recorded use of a word and progress through each century either until the word becomes obsolete or until its latest meaning is listed. For this reason, many scholars consider *The Oxford English Dictionary* the best place to find the history of a word or to locate illustrations of its usage. However, *The Oxford English Dictionary* emphasizes British usage and does not treat American usage fully.

Also available is the compact edition, a photographic reduction of the entire thirteen-volume edition into two volumes. The one drawback of the compact edition is that it must be read with a magnifying glass.

The entry from *The Oxford English Dictionary* shown in Figure 2 illustrates the in-depth coverage offered by an unabridged dictionary.

courage ('kʌrɪdʒ), sb. Forms: 4-7 corage, curage, (4-6 corrage, 5 curag, coreage, 6 currage, courra(d)ge, 7 corege), 5- courage. [ME. corage, a. OF. corage, curage, later courage = Pr. and Cat. coratge, Sp. corage, It. coraggio, a Common Romanic word, answering to a L. type *coráticum, f. cor heart. Cf. the parallel ætáticum from ætát-em (AGE); and see -AGE.]

†1. The heart as the seat of feeling, thought, etc.; spirit, mind, disposition, nature. Obs.

c1300 K. Alis. 3559 Archelaus, of proud corage. c1386 CHAUCER Prol. 11 Smale fowles maken melodie..So priketh hem nature in here corages. c1430 Pilgr. Lyf Manhode i. xxxiii. (1869) 20 What thinkest in thi corage? c1430 Stans Puer 5 To all norture thi corage to enclyne. c1500 Knt. Curtesy 407 in Ritson Met. Rom. III. 213 In his courage he was full sad. 1593 SHAKS. 3 Hen. VI, ii. ii. 57 This soft courage makes your Followers faint. 1638 DRUMM. of HAWTH. Irene Wks. (1711) 163 Men's courages were growing hot, their hatred kindled. 1659 B. HARRIS Parival's Iron Age 41 The Spaniards..attacked it with all the force and maistry the greatest courages were able to invent.

†b. transf. Of a plant. Obs. (Cf. 'To bring a thing into good heart.')

c1420 Palladius on Husb. XI. 90 In this courage Hem forto graffe is goode.

†c. Applied to a person: cf. spirit. Obs.

1561 T. HOBY tr. Castiglione's Courtyer (1577) Vjb, The prowes of those diuine courages [viz. Marquesse of Mantua, etc.]. 1647 W. BROWNE Polex. II. 197 These two great courages being met, and followed by a small companie of the most resolute pirates.

†2. What is in one's mind or thoughts, what one is thinking of or intending; intention, purpose; desire or inclination. Obs. (Cf. 'To speak one's mind', 'to tell all one's heart'.)

c1320 Seuyn Sag. (W.) 2446 Lo her, sire, a litel pagel That schal sai the thi corage. c1386 CHAUCER Merch. T. 10 Swich a greet corage Hadde this knyght to been a wedded man. 1484 CAXTON Chivalry 7 Fayr frend what is your corage or entent. c1530 LD. BERNERS Arth. Lyt. Bryt. (1814)

277 Ye mayster dyscouered to her all his courage, how that he loued her. 1557 NORTH tr. Gueuara's Diall Pr. 93 b/1 The romaines had a great corage to conquere straunge realmes. 1568 GRAFTON Chron. II. 289 Many were taken of their owne corage, which might have scaped if they had list. 1607 SHAKS. Timon III. iii. 24 I'de such a courage to do him good. a1626 BACON Max. & Uses Com. Law xxii. 81 The law..shall..make construction that my minde and courage is not to enter into the greater bond for any menace.

†3. Spirit, liveliness, lustiness, vigour, vital force or energy; also fig. Obs.

a1498 WARKW. Chron. (Camden) 2 Thei..were greved with colde and rayne, that thei hade no coreage to feght. 1565 JEWEL Def. Apol. (1611) 505 In the Cardinals of Rome, Pride, Auarice, and Lechery are in their greatest Courage. 1630 R. Johnson's Kingd. & Commw. 249 They have horses of excellent courage. 1705 Lond. Gaz. No. 4182/4 A Chesnut Mare..of great Courage.

†b. Anger, wrath; c. Haughtiness, pride; d. Confidence, boldness. Obs.

c1386 CHAUCER Knt.'s T. (Harl.) 1154 The hunt[e] strangled with wilde bores corage. 1483 CAXTON G. de la Tour F iij b, [She] became..so grete of courage that also to the kynge her lord she bare not so grete reuerence as she ought. 1568 GRAFTON Chron. II. 285 Every man cryed and besought the king to have mercy..for Gods sake refraine your courage, ye haue the name of sovereigne noblenesse. 1590 SPENSER F.Q. III. x. 30 Trompart..Besought him his great corage to appease, And pardon simple man. 1608 MIDDLETON Trick to catch i. i, I will..set so good a courage on my state, That I will be believed.

†e. Sexual vigour and inclination; lust. Obs.

1541 BARNES Wks. (1573) 329/1 By the reason that priestes are so hoate of courage, and can not keepe theyr chastitie. 1577 B. GOOGE Heresbach's Husb. III. (1586) 129 If the Bull be not lusty enough about his businesse..his courage is also stirred up by the Mare, therefore..make refraine 1606 G. W[OODCOCKE] tr. Justin 56 Darius horse..by reason of the courage had to the Mare, forthwith neighed alowde. 1615 CROOKE Body of Man 45 If they be taken away, the iollity and courage of the Creature is extinguished.

4. That quality of mind which shows itself in facing danger without fear or shrinking; bravery, boldness, valour.

FIGURE 2 Entry from *Oxford English Dictionary*

19e *Analyzing Your Vocabulary*

Looking up a word in the dictionary is the first step toward learning its meaning and making it part of your vocabulary. In a sense, your vocabulary is composed of all the words you know. But this definition oversimplifies the situation. Actually you have four overlapping vocabularies that you use in various situations.

Your Four Vocabularies

Speaking vocabulary: the words you use in general conversation. For most people, this vocabulary consists of a few hundred words.

Writing vocabulary: the words you use when writing. This vocabulary is considerably larger than your speaking vocabulary, consisting of about 10,000 to 45,000 words. Many of the words in your spoken vocabulary are also part of your written vocabulary. But certain words—such as *satire, analogy, positron,* and *logarithm*—belong almost exclusively to your writing vocabulary.

Reading vocabulary: the words whose meanings you know but which you do not necessarily use in writing or in conversation. Words such as *plutocrat, elucidate,* and *equivocate* might fall into this category.

Guess vocabulary: words whose meanings you do not know exactly but can infer because the words are similar to ones you already know or because their context gives clues to their meanings.

Beyond these four vocabularies are words that you do not know and that you cannot figure out. These words you must look up in a dictionary.

19f *Building a Better Vocabulary*

A good vocabulary not only strengthens your performance on written examinations, papers, and oral reports, but also increases your ability to comprehend reading material and your instructors' comments in class. Without an extensive vocabulary, your ability to learn is limited. Broadly speaking, then, education is the learning of a new vocabulary, the words with which you express new ideas.

Learning new words takes work and, at first, a good deal of time. But as you proceed, your vocabulary increases and your task becomes easier.

(1) Become a reader

Reading in itself will not increase your vocabulary. But focusing on words as you read is one of the best ways of learning new words. Seeing words in context, remembering the sentences in which they appear and the ideas with which they are associated, helps you recall them later. Get into the routine of looking up new words as you encounter them and then writing them down along with their meanings. As your vocabulary grows, you will have to do this less often.

(2) Learn the histories of words

Many of the words you encounter have interesting histories, or **etymologies.** Knowing the etymology of a word can help you remember its definition. For example, *cliché,* meaning a worn-out expression, is a French word that refers to a plate used for printing. This meaning suggests the idea of being cast in metal from a mold. Hence a *cliché* is a fixed form of expression.

You can find the history of a word in any good college dictionary, or you can consult a specialized dictionary of etymology. As you build your vocabulary, consider whether the history of a word provides associations that help you remember it.

EXERCISE 5

Using your college dictionary, look up the histories of the following words. How does the history of each word help you remember its definition?

1. mountebank
2. pyrrhic
3. pittance
4. protean
5. gargantuan
6. cicerone
7. fathom
8. gossamer
9. rigmarole
10. maudlin

(3) Become familiar with roots, prefixes, and suffixes

The words you encounter in your college studies are sometimes long and complex. Usually, however, these words can be broken down into smaller units that give you clues to their meanings.

Roots   A **root** is a word from which other words are formed. Both *hypodermic* and *dermatologist,* for example, come from the Greek root *derma,* meaning "skin." *Manual* means working by hand, *manuscript* refers to a handwritten draft of a book, and *manufacture* literally means making a product by hand. All these words derive from the Latin root *manus*, meaning "hand."

Many scientific words are based on Latin and Greek roots. *Biography* contains the Greek root *graph*, meaning "to write," and *vacuum* contains the Latin root *vac*, meaning "empty." *Biology* contains the Greek root *bios*, meaning "life," as do *biosphere, biophysics, bionics,* and *biopsy*. When you come across words that contain *bio*, you already know half their meaning.

NOTE: Be careful when making generalizations based on roots, prefixes, and suffixes. Some words appear to have the same root but do not—for instance, *homosexual* (from the Greek *homos*, meaning "same") and *homo sapiens* (from the Latin *homo*, meaning "man").

Here are some common Latin and Greek roots whose meanings can help you identify and remember new words.

COMMON LATIN ROOTS

Latin Roots	Meanings	Examples
1. æquus	equal	equivocal, equinox
2. amare, amatum	to love	amiable
3. annus	year	annual
4. audire	to hear	audible
5. capere, captum	to take	capture
6. caput	head	caption, capital
7. dicere, dictum	to say, to speak	edict, diction
8. duco, ductum	to lead	aqueduct
9. facere, factum	to make, to do	manufacture
10. loqui, locutum	to speak	eloquence
11. lucere	to light	elucidate, translucent
12. manus	hand	manual, manuscript
13. medius	middle	mediate
14. mittere, missum	to send	admit, permission
15. omnis	all	omnipotent
16. plicare, plicatum	to fold	implicate
17. ponere, positum	to place	post, depose
18. portare, portatum	to carry	porter
19. quarere, quaesitum	to ask, to question	inquire
20. rogare, ragatum	to ask	interrogate

21. scribere, scriptum	to write	scribble
22. sentire, sensum	to feel	sense
23. specere, spectrum	to look at	inspect
24. spirare, spiratum	to breathe	inspire, conspire
25. tendere, tentum	to stretch	extend, attend
26. verbum	word	verb, verbiage

COMMON GREEK ROOTS

Greek Roots	Meanings	Examples
1. bios (bio-)	life	biology, biography
2. chronos (chrono-)	time	chronology
3. derma (derma-, -dermic)	skin	dermatologist, hypodermic
4. ethos (ethno-)	race, tribe	ethnic
5. gamos (-gamy, -gamous)	marriage, union	bigamy, bigamous
6. genos (gene-)	race, kind, sex	genetics, genealogy
7. geo-	earth	geology, geography
8. graphein (-graph)	to write	paragraph
9. helios (helio-)	sun, light	heliotrope
10. krates (-crat)	member of a group	plutocrat, democrat
11. kryptos (crypto-)	hidden, secret	cryptic, cryptogram
12. metron (-meter, metro-)	to measure	barometer, metronome
13. morphe (morph)	form	morphology
14. osteon (osteo-)	bone	osteopath, osteomyelitis
15. pathos (patho-, -pathy)	suffering, feeling	sympathy
16. phagein (phag)	to feed, to consume	bacteriophage
17. philos (philo-, -phile)	loving	bibliophile, philosophy
18. phobos (-phobe, phobia)	fear	Anglophobe, claustrophobia
19. photos (photo-)	light	photograph

continued

continued from previous page

20. pneuma	wind, air	pneumatic
21. podos (-pod, -poda)	foot	tripod, podiatrist
22. pseudein (pseudo-)	to deceive	pseudonym
23. pyr (pyro-)	fire	pyrotechnical
24. soma	body	psychosomatic
25. tele-	distant	telephone
26. therme (thermo-, -therm)	heat	thermometer

E X E R C I S E   6

Using the above list of roots, speculate about the meanings of the following words. If you cannot determine the exact meaning of a word, make the best guess you can. Check your definition against one that you find in your college dictionary.

1. amateur
   amative
2. pathology
   pathetic
3. photosensitive
   photoengraver
   photoelectric

4. audio
   audiometer
5. verbalize
   verbose
   verbalist

Prefixes   A **prefix** is a letter or group of letters put before a root or word that adds to or modifies it. The prefix *anti,* for example, means "against." When combined with other words, it forms new words.

antiaircraft	A weapon used against aircraft
antibiotic	A substance used to combat microorganisms
anticoagulant	A substance that suppresses the clotting of the blood
antidote	A remedy that counteracts poison
antifreeze	A substance used to stop a liquid from freezing.

Knowing even a few prefixes can help you to deduce the meanings of a great many words. Here is a list of prefixes which, combined with different roots, form thousands of words.

PREFIXES INDICATING NUMBER

Prefix	Meaning	Example	Definition
uni-	one	unify	To make into a unit
bi-	two	bimonthly	Every two months
duo-	two	duotone	Printed in two tones of the same color
tri-	three	triad	A group of three
quadri-	four	quadruped	A four-footed animal
tetra-	four	tetrachloride	A chemical with four chlorine atoms
quint-	five	quintuplets	Five offspring born in a single birth
pent-	five	pentagon	A five-sided figure
multi-	many	multilateral	Having many sides
mono-	one	monogamy	Having one spouse
poly-	many	polygamy	Having many spouses
omni-	all	omnivore	Eating all kinds of food

PREFIXES INDICATING SMALLNESS

Prefix	Meaning	Example	Definition
micro-	small	microscope	An instrument for observing small things
mini-	small	minibus	A small bus

PREFIXES INDICATING SEQUENCE AND SPACE

Prefix	Meaning	Example	Definition
ante-	before	antebellum	Before the war
pre-	before	prehistory	Before history
intro-	within	introspective	Looking into oneself
post-	after	postscript	A message written after the body of the letter
re-	back, again	review	To look at again
sub-	under	submarine	An underwater ship

continued

continued from previous page

super-	above	supervise	To look over the performance of others
inter-	between	international	Between nations
intra-	within	intramural	Within the bounds of an institution
in-	in, into	incorporate	To form into a body
ex-	out, from	exhale	to breathe out
circum-	around	circumnavigate	To sail or fly around (the earth, an island, etc.)
con-	with, together	congregate	To come or bring together

PREFIXES INDICATING NEGATION

Prefix	Meaning	Example	Definition
non-	not	nonpartisan	Not affiliated
in-	not	inactive	Not active
un-	not, the opposite of, against	unequal	Not equal
anti-	against	antiseptic	Free from germs
counter-	opposing	countermand	To revoke an order with another order
contra-	against	contradict	To speak against
dis-	not, the opposite of	dislike	To not like
mis-	wrong, ill	mislead	To give bad advice
mal-	bad, wrong, ill	malformed	Incorrectly shaped
pseudo-	false	pseudonym	A false name

EXERCISE 7

Review the preceding list of prefixes and supply one additional word and definition for each prefix.

Suffixes   **Suffixes** are syllables added to the end of a word or root that change its part of speech. For example, suffixes added to the verb *believe* form two nouns, an adjective, and an adverb.

believe	(verb)
believer	(noun)
believability	(noun)
believable	(adjective)
believably	(adverb)

English has relatively few suffixes that form verbs and adverbs. A large number of suffixes, however, form nouns and adjectives. Knowing the most common ones can help you to identify several words from a single base word.

VERB SUFFIXES

Suffix	Meaning	Example
-en	to cause to or become	cheapen, redden
-ate	to cause to be	activate, animate
-ify, fy	to make or cause to be	fortify, magnify
-ize	to make, to give, to practice	memorize, modernize

ADVERB SUFFIXES

The only regular suffix for adverbs is -ly, as in *slowly, wisely,* and *casually.*

ADJECTIVE SUFFIXES

Suffix	Meaning	Example
-al	capable of, suitable for	comical
-ial	pertaining to	managerial
-ic	pertaining to	democratic
-ly	a resemblance	sisterly
-ly	at specific intervals	hourly
-ful	abounding in	colorful
-ous, -ose	full of	porous, verbose
-ive	quality of	creative, adaptive
-less	lack of, free of	toothless
-ish	having the qualities of, preoccupied with	childish, bookish

NOUN SUFFIXES

Suffix	Meaning	Example
-ance, -ence	quality or state of	insurance, competence
-acy	quality or state of	piracy, privacy
-or	one who performs an action	actor
-arium, orium	place for	aquarium, auditorium
-ary	place for, pertaining to	dictionary
-cide	kill	suicide, homicide
-icle, -cle	a diminutive ending	icicle, corpuscle
-hood	state or condition of	childhood
-ism	quality or doctrine of	Marxism, conservatism
-ity	quality or state of	acidity
-itis	inflammation of	appendicitis
-ics	the science or art of	economics
-ment	act or condition of	resentment
-mony	resulting condition	testimony
-ology	the study of	biology, psychology

(4)   Learn words according to a system

Learning related words according to a system is far more effective than memorizing words at random. Consider the following pair of words.

duct	a tubular passage
aqueduct	a conduit designed to transport water

Both words share the Latin root *ducere* (to lead). Because you are already familiar with the word *duct,* you have a clue to the meaning of *aqueduct.* If you know that *aqua* is a Latin word meaning "water," you can easily remember the definition of the word.

Other words also share the root *ducere.*

conduct	to direct the course of
induct	to install, to admit as a member
viaduct	a series of spans used to carry a railroad over a valley or other roads
abduct	to carry off
deduct	to take away
ductile	capable of being fashioned into a new form

Learning these related words together would clearly be easier than learning them at random.

▶ See 20c4

Other word groupings also facilitate learning. You can, for example, study together words that are confusing because they sound so much alike.

imminent	about to occur
eminent	prominent
ascent	a rise
assent	agreement
capital	a seat of government
capitol	the building where the legislative body meets
principal	the most important; the head of a school
principle	a basic law or truth

You can also study together words that are confusing because they look somewhat alike.

marital	referring to marriage
martial	referring to war
descent	a downward movement
decent	characterized by good taste or morality

Finally, you can study together words that are confusing because their meanings are so closely associated with each other.

imply	to suggest
infer	to conclude
explicit	stated outright
implicit	implied, unsaid

20

Improving Spelling

Spelling errors distract readers and make it difficult for them to understand what you are trying to say. In some cases, incorrectly spelled words actually misrepresent your meanings, as when you use *equivalents* for *equivalence,* for example, or *benzene* for *benzoin.*

If spelling has always given you trouble, you will probably not become a good speller overnight. But the situation is not hopeless. Most people can spell even difficult words "almost" correctly; usually only a letter or two is wrong. For this reason, memorizing a few simple rules and their exceptions and learning the correct spelling of the most commonly misspelled words can make a big difference.

20a *Understanding Spelling and Pronunciation*

Because many words in English are not spelled as they are pronounced, sound alone does not necessarily indicate a word's spelling. For instance, *gh* is silent in *light* but pronounced *f* in *cough;* the ō sound is spelled differently in *mow, toe, though, sew,* and *beau.* These and other inconsistencies between English spelling and pronunciation create a number of problem areas to watch for.

(1) Vowels in unstressed positions

Many unstressed vowels sound exactly alike when we say them. For instance, it is hard to tell from pronunciation alone that the *i* in *terrible* is not an *a.* In general, the vowels *a,e,* and *i* are impossible to distinguish in the suffixes *-able* and *-ible, -ance* and *-ence,* and *-ant* and *-ent.*

comfortable servant   excellence
brilliance   compatible independent

(2) Silent letters in words

Some English words contain silent letters. The *b* in *climb* and *dumb* is silent, as is the *t* in *mortgage*. Silent letters at the beginning of a word are especially bothersome: you cannot look up the spelling of *gnu* (pronounced *new*) in a dictionary if you do not already know that it begins with a *g*. The spelling of words with silent letters follows no rules, so you have to memorize the spelling of words like the following as you encounter them.

aisle	depot	silhouette
condemn	knight	sovereign
climb	pneumonia	

(3) Words that contain letters or syllables not pronounced in informal speech

Most people pronounce words rather carelessly in everyday speech. Consequently, if they use pronunciation as a guide to spelling, they leave out, add, or misplace letters. The following words are often misspelled because they are pronounced incorrectly:

literature	quantity	lightning
February	recognize	probably
candidate	nuclear	specific
library	environment	surprise
government	disastrous	
perform	hundred	

(4) Variant forms of the same word

Some spelling problems occur because different forms of a word have different spellings.

Spelling problems can occur when the spellings of the verb and noun forms of a word are different.

advise (v)	advice (n)
renounce (v)	renunciation (n)
announce (v)	annunciation (n)
describe (v)	description (n)
omit (v)	omission (n)

Spelling differences also occur among the principal parts of irregular verbs.

arise, arose, arisen	ride, rode, ridden
drive, drove, driven	spring, sprang, sprung
grow, grew, grown	throw, threw, thrown

Irregular nouns change spelling when the plural is formed.

man, men	goose, geese
calf, calves	wife, wives
child, children	woman, women

Some words (such as *rime/rhyme*) have more than one accepted spelling. In addition, some words are spelled one way in the United States and another way in Great Britain. You should always consult a dictionary to determine the preferred American spelling.

American	*British*
color	colour
defense	defence
judgment	judgement
theater	theatre
traveled	travelled

(5) Homophones

Homophones are words—such as *accept* and *except*—that are pronounced alike but spelled differently.

See
20c4

20b *Learning Spelling Rules*

The few reliable rules that govern English spelling can help you overcome the general inconsistency between pronunciation and spelling. These rules have exceptions, but they are still useful guides.

(1) The *ie/ei* combinations

The old rule still stands: use *i* before *e* except after *c* or when pronounced *ay* as in *neighbor*.

i before *e*	*ei* after *c*	*ei* pronounced *ay*
belief	ceiling	neighbor
chief	conceit	weigh
field	deceit	freight
niece	receive	eight
piece	perceive	
friend		

There are a few exceptions to this rule: *either, neither, foreign, leisure, weird,* and *seize.* In addition, if the *ie* combination is not pronounced as a unit, the rule does not apply: *atheist, science.*

EXERCISE 1

Fill in the blanks with the proper *ie* or *ei* combination. After completing the exercise, use your dictionary to check your answers.

EXAMPLE: conc __ei__ ve

1. rec _____ pt
2. var _____ ty
3. caff _____ ne
4. ach _____ ve
5. kal _____ doscope

6. misch _____ f
7. effic _____ nt
8. v _____ n
9. spec _____ s
10. suffic _____ nt

(2) Doubling consonants

Some words double their final consonants before a suffix that begins with a vowel (*-ed, -ing*); others do not. Fortunately, there is a rule to distinguish them. The only words that double their consonants in this situation are those that meet the following criteria:

1. They have one syllable or are stressed on the last syllable.
2. They contain only one vowel in the last syllable.
3. They end in a single consonant.

The word *tap* satisfies all three conditions: it has only one syllable, it contains only one vowel (*a*), and it ends in a single consonant (*p*). Therefore, the final consonant doubles before a suffix beginning with a vowel (*tapped, tapping*). The word *relent* meets two of the above criteria (it has one vowel in the last syllable and it is stressed on the last syllable), but it does not end in a single consonant. Therefore, its final consonant is not doubled (*relented, relenting*).

(3) Prefixes

The addition of a prefix never affects the spelling of the root.

un + acceptable = unacceptable
dis + agree = disagree
mis + spell = misspell
dis + joint = disjoint

(For a more complete list of prefixes, see **19f3**.)

Some prefixes can cause spelling problems because they are easily confused or because they are pronounced alike although they are not spelled alike. Be especially careful of the prefixes *ante-/anti, en-/in-, per-/pre-,* and *de-/di-.*

antebellum	antiaircraft
encircle	integrate
perceive	prescribe
deduct	direct

(4) Suffixes

Silent e   When a suffix that starts with a consonant is added to a word ending in silent *e*, the *e* is generally kept: *hope/hopeful; lame/lamely; bore/boredom.*

Familiar exceptions include *argument, truly, ninth, judgment,* and *abridgment.*

When a suffix that starts with a vowel is added to a word ending in silent *e*, the *e* is generally dropped: *hope/hoping; trace/traced; grieve/grievance; love/lovable.*

Familiar exceptions include *changeable, noticeable,* and *courageous.* In these cases the *e* is kept so that the *c* or *g* will be pronounced like the initial consonants in *cease* or *gem* and not like the initial consonants in *come* or *game.*

EXERCISE 2

Combine the following words with the suffixes in parentheses. Determine whether you keep or drop the silent *e*, and be prepared to explain your choice.

> EXAMPLE: fate (al)
>   fatal

1. surprise (ing)   6. outrage (ous)
2. sure (ly)   7. service (able)
3. force (ible)   8. awe (ful)
4. manage (able)   9. shame (ing)
5. due (ly)   10. shame (less)

Words Ending in y   When a word ends in a consonant plus *y*, the *y* generally changes to an *i* when a suffix is added (beauty + ful = beautiful). The *y* is retained, however, when the suffix *-ing* is added (tally + ing = tallying). It is also retained when the *y* ends a proper name (McCarthy + ite = McCarthyite) and in some one-syllable words (dry + ness = dryness). Exception: city + scape = cityscape.

When a word ends in a vowel plus *y*, the *y* is retained (joy + ful = joyful; employ + er = employer). Exception: day + ly = daily.

E X E R C I S E   3

Add the endings in parentheses to the following words. Change or keep the final *y* as you see fit, and be prepared to explain your choice.

EXAMPLE: party (ing)
           partying

1. journey (ing)   6. sturdy (ness)
2. study (ed)   7. merry (ment)
3. carry (ing)   8. likely (hood)
4. shy (ly)   9. plenty (ful)
5. study (ing)   10. supply (er)

Seed **Endings**   Endings with the sound *seed* are nearly always spelled *cede*, as in *precede, intercede, concede,* and so on. The only exceptions are *supersede, exceed, proceed,* and *succeed.*

-Able, -ible   These endings sound alike, and they often cause spelling problems. Fortunately, there is a rule that can help you distinguish them. If the stem of a word is itself an independent word, the suffix *-able* is most commonly used. If the stem of a word is not an independent word, the suffix *-ible* is most often used.

*comfor*table	*compa*tible
*agree*able	*incred*ible
*dry*able	*plausi*ble

(5) Plurals

Most nouns form plurals by adding -s. This applies to words ending with consonants or with the vowels *a, e, i,* and *u.*

savage/savages	tortilla/tortillas
girl/girls	gnu/gnus
boat/boats	taxi/taxis

There are, however, a number of exceptions.

Words Ending in f or fe   Words ending in *f* or *fe* can form plurals in several ways. Some words ending in *f* or *fe* form plurals by changing the *f* to *v* and adding -es or -s.

knife/knives	wife/wives
life/lives	self/selves

Some words ending in *f* or *fe* just add -s.

belief/beliefs   proof/proofs

A few such words can form plurals either by adding -s or by substituting -ves for *f.*

scarf/scarfs/scarves   hoof/hoofs/hooves

Words ending in double *f* take -s to form plurals (*tariff/tariffs*).

Words Ending in y   Most words that end in a consonant followed by *y* form plurals by changing the *y* to *i* and adding -es.

baby/babies	blueberry/blueberries
seventy/seventies	worry/worries

Proper nouns, however, are exceptions: the *Kennedys* (never the *Kennedies*).

Words that end in a vowel followed by a *y* form plurals by adding -s.

monkey/monkeys	key/keys
turkey/turkeys	day/days

Words Ending in o   Most words that end in a consonant followed by *o* add -es to form the plural.

tomato/tomatoes   hero/heroes

Some, however, add -s.

silo/silos   piano/pianos
memo/memos   soprano/sopranos

Still other words that end in *o* add either *-s* or *-es* to form plurals.

memento/mementos/mementoes
mosquito/mosquitos/mosquitoes

Words that end in a vowel followed by *o* form the plural by adding *-s*.

radio/radios   stereo/stereos   zoo/zoos

Words Ending in s, ss, sh, ch, x, and z   These words form plurals by adding *-es*.

Jones/Joneses	lunch/lunches	box/boxes
mass/masses	latch/latches	tax/taxes
rash/rashes	ax/axes	buzz/buzzes

NOTE: Some one-syllable words that end in *s* or *z* double their final consonants when forming plurals (*quiz/quizzes*).

Compound Nouns   Compound nouns—nouns formed from two or more words—usually conform to the rules governing the last word in the compound construction.

welfare state/welfare states   snowball/snowballs

However, in compound nouns where the first element of the construction is more important than the others, the plural is formed with the first element (*sister-in-law/sisters-in-law*).

Irregular Plurals   Some words in English have irregular plural endings. No rules govern these plurals, so you have to memorize them.

child/children	ox/oxen
woman/women	louse/lice
man/men	mouse/mice
goose/geese	.

Foreign Plurals   Some words, especially those borrowed from Latin or Greek, keep their foreign plurals. When you use these words, you must look up their plural forms in your college dictionary if you do not know them.

Singular	Plural
criterion	criteria
datum	data
larva	larvae
memorandum	memoranda
stimulus	stimuli

Some foreign words have a regular English plural as well as the one from their language of origin.

Singular	Plural
hippopotamus	hippopotami, hippopotamuses
antenna	antennae, antennas

No Plural Forms   A few words use the same form for both the singular and the plural.

Singular	Plural
apparatus	apparatus
deer	deer
fish	fish (*also* fishes)
sheep	sheep
species	species

20c   *Developing Spelling Skills*

To develop good spelling skills, you must invest time and effort. In addition to studying the rules outlined in 20b, you can do the following things to help yourself become a better speller.

(1)   *Make your own spelling list*

Compile a list of your own problem words. When you write a first draft, circle any words whose spelling you are unsure of. Then look them up in your dictionary as you revise, and add them all (even those you have spelled correctly) to your list. When your instructor returns a paper, record any words you have misspelled. In addition, record problem words that you encounter when reading, including those from class notes and textbooks. It is especially important that you master the spellings of words that are basic to a course or given field of study.

(2) Uncover patterns of misspelling

Review your spelling list to see whether any patterns of misspelling emerge. Do you consistently have a problem with plurals or with *-ible/-able* endings? If so, review the spelling rules that apply to these particular problems. By using this strategy to get at the source of your spelling difficulties, you can eliminate the need to memorize single words.

(3) Fix each word in your mind

Once you isolate the words that you consistently misspell, take the time to think of associations that will help fix the correct spellings in your mind. For example, you can arrive at the correct spelling of *definite* (often misspelled *definate*) by remembering that it contains the word *finite*, which suggests the concept of limit, as does *definite*. You can recall the *a* in *brilliance* (often misspelled *brillience*) by remembering that brilliant people often get *A*'s in their classes. You can master the spelling of *criticism* by remembering that it contains the word *critic*.

Another way of fixing words in your mind is to write them down. When you review your spelling list, do not just *read* the words on it; *write* them. This repeated copying will help you remember the correct spellings.

(4) Learn to distinguish commonly confused words

Following is a list of words that are commonly confused because they look or sound alike. It is a good idea to take a group of these pairs of words—say, ten each day—and learn them. Copy each pair on a 3 × 5 card, and review them whenever you can. After isolating the word pairs that give the most trouble, you can concentrate on learning to distinguish them.

Commonly Confused Words   Following is a list of commonly confused homophones (words that sound alike but have different spellings and meanings) and words that create problems because they sound similar (for example, *accept* and *except*).

accept	to receive
except	other than
advice	recommendation
advise	to recommend
affect	to have an influence on (*verb*); an emotional response (*noun*)
effect	result (*noun*); to cause (*verb*)
all ready	prepared
already	by or before this or that time
allude	to refer to indirectly
elude	to avoid
allusion	indirect reference
illusion	false belief or perception
ascent	movement upward
assent	agreement
bare	uncovered
bear	to carry (*verb*); an animal (*noun*)
board	a wooden plank (*noun*); to get on an airplane, etc. (*verb*)
bored	uninterested
born	brought to life
borne	carried
brake	device for stopping
break	destroy, smash
buy	purchase
by	next to; near
capital	the seat of government; monetary assets
capitol	government building
cite	to quote, refer to
sight	the ability to see
site	a place
coarse	rough
course	path; class at school
complement	to complete or add to (*verb*); something that completes (*noun*)
compliment	praise
conscience	sense of right and wrong
conscious	mentally awake
council	governing body

counsel	advice (*noun*); to give advice (*verb*)
descent	downward movement
dissent	disagreement
desert	to abandon
dessert	sweet course at the end of a meal
device	an implement; a plan
devise	to invent
die	to lose life
dye	to change the color of something
discreet	reserved
discrete	individual, distinct
elicit	to draw out, evoke
illicit	unlawful; forbidden
eminent	prominent
immanent	inherent
imminent	about to happen
fair	equitable; light-complected
fare	a fee for transportation
forth	forward
fourth	referring to the number 4
gorilla	the animal
guerilla	a type of soldier or warfare
hear	to perceive by ear
here	in this place
heard	past tense of *hear*
herd	group of animals
hole	an opening
whole	complete
its	possessive of *it*
it's	contraction of *it is*
later	after a time
latter	the last in a series
lead	to guide or direct (*verb*); the metal (*noun*)
led	past tense of *lead*
lessen	to reduce
lesson	something learned
loose	not tight; unbound
lose	to misplace

maybe	perhaps
may be	might be
meat	flesh
meet	encounter
no	negative
know	to be certain
passed	past tense of *pass*
past	a previous time; a time gone by
patience	forbearance
patients	persons receiving medical care
peace	the absence of war; quiet
piece	a portion of something
persecute	to harrass or worry
prosecute	to institute criminal proceedings against
personal	private; one's own
personnel	employees
plain	unadorned
plane	an aircraft; a carpenter's tool
precede	to come before
proceed	to continue
principal	most important (*adjective*); head of a school (*noun*)
principle	a basic truth; rule of conduct
quiet	silent
quite	very
rain	precipitation
reign	to rule
rein	a strap, e.g., for a horse's bridle
raise	to build up
raze	to tear down
right	correct
rite	a ritual
write	to put words on paper
road	street, highway
rode	past tense of *ride*
scene	place of action; section of a play
seen	viewed
sense	perception, understanding
since	from a time in the past up to the present

stationary	standing still
stationery	writing paper
straight	unbending
strait	a water passageway
than	as compared with
then	at that time; next
their	possessive of *they*
there	in that place
they're	contraction of *they are*
through	finished; into and out of
threw	past tense of *throw*
thorough	complete
to	toward
too	also; more than sufficient
two	the number
waist	the middle of the body
waste	discarded material (*noun*); to squander (*verb*)
weather	atmospheric conditions
whether	in either case
weak	not strong
week	seven days
which	one of a group
witch	female sorcerer
who's	contraction of *who is*
whose	possessive of *who*
your	possessive of *you*
you're	contraction of *you are*

PART 6

Understanding Grammar

Identifying the Parts of Speech

The eight basic parts of speech—the building blocks for all English sentences—are *nouns, pronouns, verbs, adjectives, adverbs, prepositions, conjunctions,* and *interjections.* The part of speech to which a word belongs depends on its function in a sentence.

21a *Nouns*

Nouns name people, places, things, ideas, actions, or qualities.

A **common noun** names any of a class of people, places, or things: *artist, judge, building, event, city.*

A **proper noun**, always capitalized, refers to a particular person, place, or thing: *Mary Cassatt, Learned Hand, World Trade Center, Crimean War, St. Louis.*

A **mass noun** names a quantity that is not countable: *time, dust, work, gold.* Mass nouns are generally treated as singular.

A **collective noun** designates a group of people, places, or things thought of as a unit: *committee, class, navy, band, family.* Collective nouns are generally treated as singular unless the sentence clearly refers to the members of the group as individuals.

An **abstract noun** refers to an intangible idea or quality: *love, hate, justice, anger, fear, prejudice.*

21b *Pronouns*

Pronouns are words that may be used in place of nouns in a sentence. The noun for which a pronoun stands is called its **ante-**

cedent. There are eight types of pronouns. Different types of pronouns may have exactly the same forms, but they are distinguished by their functions in the sentence.

A **personal pronoun** stands for a person or thing: *I, me, we, us, my, mine, our, ours, you, your, yours, he, she, it, its, one, one's, him, his, her, hers, they, them, their, theirs.*

They made her an offer she couldn't refuse.

An **indefinite pronoun** functions in a sentence as a noun but does not refer to any particular person or thing. For this reason, indefinite pronouns do not require antecedents. Indefinite pronouns include *another, any, each, few, many, some, nothing, anyone, everyone, everybody, everything, someone, something, either,* and *neither.*

Many are called, but few are chosen.

A **reflexive pronoun** is one that ends with *-self* and refers to a recipient of the action that is the same as the actor: *myself, yourself, himself, herself, itself, oneself, themselves, ourselves, yourselves.*

They found themselves in downtown Pittsburgh.

Intensive pronouns have the same form as reflexive pronouns; they emphasize a noun or pronoun in the sentence.

Darrow himself was sure his client was innocent.

A **relative pronoun** introduces an adjective or noun clause in a sentence: *which, who, whom, that, what, whose, whatever, whoever, whomever, whichever.*

Gandhi was the charismatic man who helped lead India to independence. (introduces adjective clause)

Whatever happens will be a surprise. (introduces noun clause)

An **interrogative pronoun** introduces a question: *who, which, what, whom, whose, whoever, whatever, whichever.*

Who was that masked man?

A **demonstrative pronoun** points to a particular thing or group of things: *this, that, these, those.*

This is one of Shakespeare's early plays.

A **reciprocal pronoun** denotes a mutual relationship: *each other, one another.*

Ah, love, let us be true / to one another! (Matthew Arnold, "Dover Beach")

21c *Verbs*

(1) Recognizing verbs

A verb may express either action or a state of being.

He <u>ran</u> for the train. (action)

Elizabeth II <u>became</u> queen after the death of her father, George VI. (state of being)

Verbs can be classified into two groups: main verbs and auxiliary verbs (sometimes called helping verbs).

Main Verbs   A main verb carries most of the meaning in the sentence or clause in which it appears.

Bulfinch's *Mythology* <u>contains</u> a discussion of Greek mythology.

Emily Dickinson <u>anticipated</u> much of twentieth-century poetry.

A main verb is a **linking verb** when it is followed by a **subject complement**, a word or phrase that defines or describes the subject.

Carbon disulfide <u>smells</u> bad.

Commonly Used Linking Verbs

be	appear	remain	taste
become	believe	prove	feel
seem	grow	smell	turn

Auxiliary Verbs   Auxiliary verbs, such as *be* and *have*, combine with main verbs to form **verb phrases**. The auxiliary verbs indicate tense, voice, or mood.

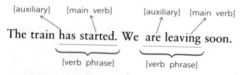

The train has started. We are leaving soon.

Certain auxiliary verbs, known as **modal auxiliaries,** indicate necessity, possibility, willingness, obligation, or ability.

In the near future farmers <u>might</u> cultivate seaweed as a food crop.

Coal mining <u>would</u> be safer if dust were controlled in the mines.

Modal Auxiliaries			
must	shall	might	need [to]
will	should	can	ought [to]
would	may	could	

(2) Recognizing verbals

Verbals, such as *known* or *running* or *to go,* are nonfinite verbs. That is, they do not change form to indicate person, tense, and number. They cannot serve as a sentence's main verb unless used with an auxiliary (*is going*). Verbals include *participles, infinitives,* and *gerunds.*

Participles   Virtually every verb has a **present participle,** which ends in *-ing (loving, learning, going, writing),* and a **past participle,** which usually ends in *-d* or *-ed (agreed, learned).* Some verbs have irregular past participles *(gone, begun, written).* Participles may function in a sentence as adjectives or as nouns.

Twenty brands of running shoes were displayed at the exhibition. (Present participle *running* serves as adjective modifying noun *shoes.*)

The crowded bus went right by those waiting at the corner. (Past participle *crowded* serves as adjective modifying noun *bus.*)

The wounded were given emergency first aid. (Past participle *wounded* serves as sentence's subject.)

Infinitives   An **infinitive**—the base form of the verb preceded by *to*—may serve as an adjective, an adverb, or a noun.

Ann Arbor was clearly the place to be. (Infinitive *to be* serves as adjective modifying noun *place.*)

They say that breaking up is hard to do. (Infinitive *to do* serves as adverb modifying adjective *hard.*)

Carla went outside to think. (Infinitive *to think* serves as adverb modifying verb *went.*)

To win was everything. (Infinitive *to win* serves as sentence's subject.)

Gerunds   **Gerunds,** special forms of verbs ending in *-ing,* are always used as nouns.

Seeing is believing. (Gerund *seeing* serves as sentence's subject; gerund *believing* serves as subject complement.)

He worried about interrupting. (Gerund *interrupting* is object of preposition *about*.)

Andrew loves skiing. (Gerund *skiing* is direct object of verb *loves*.)

NOTE: When the *-ing* form of a verb is used as a noun, as it is here, it is considered a *gerund;* when it is used as a modifier, it is a *present participle*.

21d *Adjectives*

Adjectives are words that describe, limit, qualify, or in any other way modify nouns or pronouns.

Descriptive adjectives, the largest class of adjectives, name a quality of the noun or pronoun they modify.

Strike while the iron is hot.

They ordered a chocolate soda and a butterscotch sundae.

The little one is the runt of the litter.

Some descriptive adjectives are formed from common nouns or from verbs *(friend/friendly, agree/agreeable)*. Others, called **proper adjectives,** are formed from proper nouns.

Eubie Blake was a talented American musician who died in 1983.

The Shakespearean or English sonnet consists of an octave and a sestet.

Two or more words may be joined, with or without a hyphen, to form a **compound adjective** *(foreign born, well-read)*. (See 34b1).

Another class of adjectives is composed of words like articles, pronouns, and numbers. When these words are used to limit or qualify nouns they are considered adjectives.

Articles *(a, an, the)*

The boy found a four-leaf clover.

Possessive adjectives (the personal pronouns *my, your, his, her, its, our, their, one's*)

Their lives depended on my skill.

Demonstrative adjectives *(this, these, that, those)*

This song reminds me of that song we heard yesterday.

Interrogative adjectives *(what, which, whose)*

Whose book is this?

Indefinite adjectives *(another, each, both, many, any, some,* and so on)

Both candidates agreed to return another day.

Relative adjectives *(what, whatever, which, whichever, whose, whosever)*

I forgot whatever reasons I had for leaving.

Numerical adjectives *(one, two, first, second,* and so on)

The first time I played I only got one hit.

21e *Adverbs*

Adverbs are words that describe the action of verbs or modify adjectives, other adverbs, or complete phrases, clauses, or sentences. They answer the questions "How?" "Why?" "Where?" "When?" "To what extent?" and "To what degree?"

He walked rather hesistantly toward the front of the room.

It seems so long since we met here yesterday.

Unfortunately, the program didn't run.

Cody's brother and sister were staggeringly unobservant. (Anne Tyler, *Dinner at the Homesick Restaurant*)

Interrogative adverbs—the words *how, when, why,* and *where*—introduce questions. (*Why* did the compound darken?)

Conjunctive adverbs join and relate independent clauses.

Commonly Used Conjunctive Adverbs

accordingly	furthermore	meanwhile	similarly
also	hence	moreover	still
anyway	however	nevertheless	then
besides	incidentally	next	thereafter
certainly	indeed	nonetheless	therefore
consequently	instead	now	thus
finally	likewise	otherwise	undoubtedly

Conjunctive adverbs may appear in any of several positions in a sentence.

> Jason forgot to register for chemistry. However, he managed to sign up during the drop/add period. (conjunctive adverb placed at beginning of sentence)

> Jason forgot to register for chemistry; however, he managed to sign up during the drop/add period. (conjunctive adverb placed at beginning of clause)

> Jason forgot to register for chemistry. He managed, however, to sign up during the drop/add period. (conjunctive adverb set within sentence)

> Jason forgot to register for chemistry. He managed to sign up during the drop/add period, however. (conjunctive adverb placed at end of sentence)

21f *Prepositions*

A **preposition** introduces a word or word group consisting of one or more nouns or pronouns or of a phrase or clause functioning in the sentence as a noun. The word or word group the preposition introduces is called its **object**.

prep obj   prep obj

They received a postcard from Bobby which told them about his trip

prep   obj

to the Soviet Union.

Frequently Used Prepositions

about	at	concerning	into
above	before	despite	like
across	behind	down	near
after	below	during	of
against	beneath	except	off
along	beside	for	on
among	between	from	onto
around	beyond	in	out
as	by	inside	outside

over	through	under	upon
past	throughout	underneath	with
regarding	to	until	within
since	toward	up	without

21g   *Conjunctions*

Conjunctions are words used to connect words, phrases, clauses, or sentences.

Coordinating conjunctions (*and, or, but, nor, for, so, yet*) connect words, phrases, or clauses of equal weight.

> He had to choose pheasant or venison. (Coordinating conjunction links two nouns.)

> ... of the people, by the people, and for the people (Coordinating conjunction links three prepositional phrases.)

> Thoreau wrote *Walden* in 1854, and he died in 1862. (Coordinating conjunction links two independent clauses.)

Correlative conjunctions, always used in pairs, also link items of equal weight.

▶ See 9a3

Frequently Used Correlative Conjunctions

both . . . and	not only . . . but also
either . . . or	whether . . . or
neither . . . nor	just as . . . so

> Both Hancock and Jefferson signed the Declaration of Independence. (Pair of correlative conjunctions links two nouns.)

> Either I will renew my lease, or I will move. (Pair of correlative conjunctions links two independent clauses.)

Subordinating conjunctions (*since, because, although, if, after, when, while, before, unless,* and so on) introduce adverb clauses. Thus, a subordinating conjunction connects the sentence's main (independent) clause with a subordinate (dependent) clause.

▶ See 9b

> Although drug use is a serious concern for parents, many parents are afraid to discuss it with their children.

> It is best to draw a diagram of your garden before you start to plant it.

Conjunctive adverbs, also known as adverbial conjunctions, are discussed in 21e.

21h *Interjections*

Interjections are words used as exclamations: *Oh! Ouch! Wow! Alas! Hey!* These words, which express emotion, are grammatically independent; that is, they do not have a grammatical function in a sentence. Interjections may be set off in a sentence by commas.

The message, alas, arrived too late.

Or, for greater emphasis, they can be punctuated as independent units, set off with an exclamation point.

Alas! The message arrived too late.

Other words besides interjections are sometimes used in isolation. These include words such as *yes, no, hello, good-bye, please,* and *thank you.* All such words, including interjections, may be collectively referred to as **isolates**.

Nouns and Pronouns

22a *Case*

Case is the form a noun or pronoun takes to indicate how it functions in a sentence. English has three cases: objective, subjective, and possessive.

As the English language developed, nouns generally lost their case distinctions and now change form only in the possessive case: the *cat's* eyes, *Bradley's* book. Therefore, discussions of case usually focus on the pronouns *I, we, he, she, they,* and *who,* which change forms in all cases.

Pronoun Case Forms

Subjective

| I | he, she | it | we | you | they | who | whoever |

Objective

| me | him, her | it | us | you | them | whom | whomever |

Possessive

| my | his, her | its | our | your | their | whose |
| (mine) | (hers) | | (ours) | (yours) | (theirs) | |

---

(1) Using the subjective case

SUBJECT OF A VERB

David and I bought the same kind of ten-speed bicycle. (*I* is the subject of a verb.)

SUBJECT COMPLEMENT

It was he the men were looking for. (*He* is the subject complement.)

SUBJECT OF A CLAUSE

The sergeant asked whoever wanted to volunteer to step forward. (*Whoever* is the subject of the noun clause *whoever wanted to step forward.*)

APPOSITIVE IDENTIFYING SUBJECT

Both scientists, Oppenheimer and he, worked on the atomic bomb. (*Oppenheimer and he* is an appositive identifying the subject *both scientists.*)

Revision Close-up

Using the proper case for subject complements sometimes creates forced-sounding constructions. Most people feel silly saying "It is I" or "It is he," and they use the more natural colloquial constructions "It's me" or "It's him" in speech or informal writing. In college writing, however, you should be careful to use proper pronoun case.

---

(2) Using the objective case

DIRECT OBJECT

Our sociology teacher likes Adam and me. (*Me* is a direct object of the verb *likes.*)

INDIRECT OBJECT

During the 1950's the *Kinsey Report* gave them quite a shock. (*Them* is the indirect object of the verb *gave.*)

OBJECT OF A PREPOSITION

In 1502 Leonardo da Vinci designed the fortifications of the city for him. (*Him* is the object of the preposition *for.*)

OBJECT OF AN INFINITIVE

Hoover did not want to anger Alfred E. Smith or him. (*Him* is the object of the infinitive *to anger.*)

OBJECT OF A GERUND

Finding her was not easy for Marlow. (*Her* is the object of the gerund *finding.*)

SUBJECT OF AN INFINITIVE

They told <u>him</u> to defend his flank against the French cavalry. (*Him* is the subject of the infinitive to *defend*.)

APPOSITIVE IDENTIFYING AN OBJECT

Rachel discussed both authors, <u>Hannah Arendt and her</u>. (*Hannah Arendt and her* is an appositive identifying the object *authors*.)

Revision Close-up

Discard the mistaken idea that *I* is always somehow more appropriate than *me*. In compound constructions like the following, *me* is correct.

He told Jason and <u>me</u> [not I] to run our computer program. (*Me* is the object of the verb *told*.)

Between you and <u>me</u> [not I] we own ten shares of stock. (*Me* is the object of the preposition *between*.)

Let's you and <u>me</u> [not I] go to the art museum. (*Me* is an appositive identifying *us*, direct object of the verb *let*.)

(3) Using the possessive case

A pronoun takes the **possessive case** when it indicates ownership (*our* car, *your* book). Some possessive forms—*his, hers, mine, ours, yours,* and *theirs*—may be used alone in a noun position.

The blue Volvo is <u>mine</u>.

Last year we all decided to plant gardens; <u>theirs</u> grew vegetables, and <u>ours</u> grew weeds.

Be sure to distinguish gerunds, which always function as nouns, from present participles functioning as adjectives (**see 21c2**). Use the possessive, not the objective, case before a gerund.

Napoleon approved of <u>their</u> [not *them*] ruling Naples. (*Ruling* is a gerund.)

Revision Close-up

Remember the distinction between the possessive pronoun *its* and the contraction *it's*. *Its* designates possession (*its* leg) while *it's* is the contraction of *it is* ("*It's* a nice day") or *it has* ("*It's* faded in the sunlight").

EXERCISE 1

Underline the correct form of the pronoun within the parentheses. Be prepared to explain why you chose each form.

> EXAMPLE: Alice Walker, Toni Morrison, and (she, her) are perhaps the most widely recognized African-American women writing today.

1. Both (he, him) and the homespun philosopher Will Rogers were born in Oklahoma.
2. Margaret Fuller, Susan B. Anthony, and (she, her) were early champions of women's rights in America.
3. Both Jimmy Carter and (he, him) wrote memoirs after leaving the presidency.
4. The librarian gave Sheila and (me, I) access to research materials about the Harlem Renaissance.
5. The traffic jam made (we, us) five minutes late.
6. The director objected to (me, my) being on the set.
7. (We, Us) Americans have a brief but rich history.
8. Marat, Robespierre, and (he, him) were the most radical members of the cabinet.
9. We appreciate (you, your) being here tonight.
10. The professor asked Doug and (me, I) to revise our essays.

22b Revising Common Errors: Case

(1) Implied comparisons with than or as

In constructions where words are left out but definitely understood, the case of a pronoun depends on the missing words. Implied comparisons using *than* or *as* are especially troublesome. When a sentence containing an implied comparison ends with a pronoun, your meaning dictates your choice of pronoun.

Darcy likes John more than I. *(more than I like John)*

Darcy likes John more than me. *(more than she likes me)*

Alex helps Dr. Elliott as much as I. *(as much as I help)*

Alex helps Dr. Elliott as much as me. *(as much as he helps me)*

(2) Who and whom

The case of the pronouns *who* and *whom* depends on their function *within their own clause*. When a pronoun serves as the subject, use *who* or *whoever;* when it functions as an object, use *whom* or *whomever.*

The Salvation Army gives food and shelter to whoever is in need. (*Whoever* is the subject of the verb *is* in the dependent clause *whoever is in need.*)

Shortly after leaving Oklahoma the Joads were reminded who they were and where they came from. (*Who* is the subject complement in the dependent clause *who they were and where they came from.*)

I wonder whom Rousseau influenced. (*Whom* is the object of *influenced* in the dependent clause *whom Rousseau influenced.*)

Whomever Stieglitz photographed, he revealed. (*Whomever* is the object of *photographed* in the dependent clause *Whomever Stieglitz photographed.*)

Revision Close-up

To determine the case of *who* at the beginning of a question, answer the question using a personal pronoun.

Who wrote *Gone with the Wind?* She wrote it. (Subject)

Whom do you want for mayor? I want her. (Object)

For whom is the letter? It is for him. (Object of a preposition)

Watch out for intervening phrases such as *I think, we know,* or *she* or *he says.* The choice of *who* or *whom* depends upon how the pronoun functions in its own clause. If intervening phrases cause problems, read the sentence without the intervening phrase.

Isaac Newton is the man who [we know] revolutionized the science of physics. (*Who* is the subject of the clause *who we know revolutionized the science of physics.*)

Revision Close-up

Although formal writing requires that *whom* be used for all objects, strict adherence to this rule can result in stilted constructions. In all but the most formal situations, current usage accepts *who* at the beginning of questions.

Who do you want for Mayor?

Who is the letter for?

EXERCISE 2

Using the word in parentheses, combine each pair of sentences into a single sentence. You may change word order and add or delete words.

EXAMPLE: Lee is a carpenter. Many people employ him. (whom)

Lee is a carpenter whom many people employ.

EXAMPLE: Ralph Waldo Emerson was a famous philosopher. He greatly influenced American transcendentalism. (who)

Ralph Waldo Emerson was a famous philosopher who greatly influenced American transcendentalism.

1. Ronald Reagan is a former president of the Screen Actors' Guild. He was president of the United States from 1980 to 1988. (who)
2. Charlie Parker was a jazz musician. They called him Bird. (whom)
3. Have you met the architect I. M. Pei? He designed the building. (who)
4. Octavio Paz is a poet, novelist, and essayist. He won the Nobel Prize for Literature in 1990. (who)
5. For three years she worked on a biography of Roosevelt. She once met him at a political dinner. (whom)

(3) Appositives

An **appositive** is a noun or noun phrase that renames the word it follows. The case of the pronoun in an appositive depends on the function of the word it describes. If the word functions as a subject or a subject complement, the pronoun takes the subjective case; if it functions as an object, the pronoun takes the objective case.

The Harlem Renaissance produced two particularly great writers, Langston Hughes and him. (*Writers* is the object of the verb *produced,* so the pronoun in the appositive phrase *Langston Hughes and him* takes the objective case.)

Two particularly great writers, Langston Hughes and he, were produced by the Harlem Renaissance. (*Writers* is the subject of the sentence, so the pronoun in the appositive phrase *Langston Hughes and he* takes the subjective case.)

(4) We *and* us *before a noun*

When a first-person plural pronoun precedes a noun, the case of the pronoun depends on the way the noun functions in the sentence.

Use *we* when the noun functions as the subject and *us* when it functions as an object.

> We women must stick together. (*Women* is the subject of the sentence; therefore, the pronoun *we* must be in the subjective case.)

> Teachers make learning easy for us students. (*Students* is the object of the preposition *for*; therefore, the pronoun *us* must be in the objective case.)

22c *Pronoun Reference*

An **antecedent** is the word or word group to which a pronoun refers. A pronoun reference is clear when readers can correctly identify the noun or pronoun to which it refers. In the following passage, notice how the underscored pronouns point clearly to the noun *warts*.

> Warts are wonderful structures. They can appear overnight on any part of the skin, like mushrooms on a damp lawn, full grown and splendid in the complexity of their architecture. Viewed in stained sections under a microscope, they are the most specialized of cellular arrangements, constructed as though for a purpose. They sit there like turreted mounds of dense impenetrable horn, impregnable, designed for defense against the world outside. (Lewis Thomas, *The Medusa and the Snail*)

22d *Revising Common Errors: Pronoun Reference*

(1) Ambiguous antecedents: this, that, which, *and* it

The meaning of a pronoun is **ambiguous** if the pronoun appears to refer to more than one antecedent. The pronouns *this, that, which,* and *it* are most likely to invite this kind of confusion. To ensure clarity make sure that each pronoun points to a specific antecedent.

AMBIGUOUS

> The accountant took out his calculator and completed the tax return. Then, he put it in his briefcase. (The pronoun *it* can refer either to *calculator* or to *tax return*.)

CLEAR

The accountant took out his calculator and completed the tax return. Then, he put the calculator in his briefcase.

AMBIGUOUS

Some one-celled organisms contain chlorophyll and are considered animals. This is one reason one-celled organisms are difficult to classify. (*This* can refer to the fact that some one-celled organisms are animals or to the fact that they contain chlorophyll. It could also refer to the implied idea that some one-celled organisms are not easily classified as plants or animals.)

CLEAR

Some one-celled organisms that contain chlorophyll are considered animals. This fact illustrates the difficulty of classifying single-celled organisms as either animals or plants.

Revision Close-up

If you are certain that no misunderstanding will occur, you can use *this, that, which,* or *it* to refer to a previous clause.

Visitors would constantly interrupt Edison. This made him angry.

Be careful, however. General references often invite confusion. For this reason, it is a good idea to avoid them in your college writing.

(2) Remote antecedents

The farther a pronoun is from its antecedent, the more difficult it is for readers to make a connection between them. As a result, readers lose track of meaning and must reread a passage to determine the connection.

AMBIGUOUS

Rumors of gold, letters from friends and relatives, and newspaper articles praising democracy persuaded many Czechs to come to America. By 1860 about 23,000 Czechs had left their country. Many immigrants were children under the age of twelve. By 1900, 13,000 Czech immigrants were coming to its shores each year.

The pronoun *its* in the last sentence is so far removed from its antecedent, *America,* that the reference cannot easily be understood. For clarity, the antecedent should be restated in the final sentence.)

CLEAR

> By 1900, 13,000 Czech immigrants were coming to America's shores each year.

(3) Unidentified antecedents

An unclear pronoun reference also occurs when a pronoun refers to a nonexistent antecedent.

> Our township has decided to build a computer lab in the elementary school. They feel that children should learn to use computers in fourth grade.

In the second sentence *they* seems to refer to *township* as a collective noun. Actually *they* refers to an antecedent that the writer has neglected to mention. Supplying the noun *teachers* eliminates the confusion.

> Our township has decided to build a computer lab in the elementary school. Teachers feel that children should learn to use computers in fourth grade.

Revision Close-up

References such as "*It* says in the paper" and "*They* said on the news" refer to unidentified antecedents and therefore are not acceptable in college writing. To correct this problem, substitute the appropriate noun for the unclear pronoun: "*The article* in the paper says...." and "In his commentary, *Ted Koppel* said...."

(4) Who, which and that

In general, *who* refers to people or to animals that have names. *Which* and *that* usually refer to objects, events, or animals and sometimes to groups of people.

> David Henry Hwang, who wrote the Tony Award-winning play *M. Butterfly*, also wrote *Family Devotions* and *FOB*.

> Bucephalus, who was Alexander the Great's horse, was famous for his bravery in battle.

> The spotted owl, which lives in old-growth forests, is in danger of extinction.

> Houses that are built today are usually more energy efficient than those built twenty years ago.

Revision Close-up

When you revise, make certain that you use *which* in nonrestrictive clauses, which are always set off with commas. In most cases, use *that* in restrictive clauses. *Who* may be used in both restrictive and nonrestrictive clauses.

See
27d1 ◄

E X E R C I S E   3

Analyze the pronoun errors in each of the following sentences about the Lewis and Clark expedition. After doing so, revise each sentence by substituting an appropriate noun or noun phrase for the underlined pronoun.

EXAMPLE: Jefferson asked Lewis to head the expedition, and Lewis selected him as his associate.

ANALYSIS: *Him* refers to a nonexistent antecedent.

REVISION: Jefferson asked Lewis to head the expedition, and Lewis selected Clark as his associate.

1. The purpose of the expedition was to search out a land route to the Pacific and to gather information about the West. The Louisiana Purchase increased the need for it.
2. The expedition was going to be difficult. They trained the men in Illinois, the starting point.
3. Clark and most of the men that descended the Yellowstone River camped on the bank. It was beautiful and wild.
4. Both Jefferson and Lewis had faith he would be successful in this transcontinental journey.
5. The expedition was efficient, and only one man was lost. This was extraordinary.

STUDENT WRITER AT WORK

NOUNS AND PRONOUNS

Following is part of a draft of an essay about John Updike. This section of the essay gives a plot summary of Updike's short story "A & P." Read the draft and revise it to correct errors in case and to eliminate inexact pronoun reference. After you have corrected the errors, go over the draft again and, if necessary, revise further to strengthen coherence, unity, and style.

John Updike's "A & P" is the fourteenth short story in the book <u>Pigeon Feathers</u>. It takes place in a small town similar to Updike's hometown. The character which has the significant role in "A & P" is Sammy, a cashier at the supermarket. Sammy is a nineteen-year-old boy that is just out of high school. He analyzes everyone who comes to the A & P to shop. It is him who is the narrator of the story.

The story takes place on a Thursday afternoon when three girls in bathing suits walk into the store. They are different from the other shoppers. Their manner and the way they walk make them different from them. Sammy notices that one of the girls, who he calls Queenie, leads the other girls. This appeals to him. He identifies with her because he feels that he too is a leader.

When the girls come to his check-out counter, he rings up their purchase. Suddenly the store manager, Lengel, begins scolding the girls for coming into the store in bathing suits. Sammy feels sorry for them, and in a gesture of defiance he quits. Sammy feels that him quitting is a rejection of him and all that he stands for. To Sammy, Lengel is a drab person that represents the narrow morality of the town.

Sammy quitting is the climax of the story. Sammy chooses to follow his conscience and in doing so pays the price. He feels that not following his ideals would be bad. Because he is young, however, he does not realize the significance of the act which he commits. For a moment Lengel and Sammy face each other, but he does not change his mind. Sammy feels that he has won his freedom. His confidence is short-lived, though. When he walks out into the parking lot, the girls are gone, and he is alone. It is then he realizes that the world is going to be hard for him from this point on.

Verbs

23a   Verb Forms

All verbs have four **principal parts** from which their tenses are derived: a **base form** (the form of the verb used with *I, we, you,* and *they* in the present tense),* a **present participle,** a **past tense form,** and a **past participle.** Most verbs in English are **regular** and form their principal parts with *-ing* and *-ed* or *-d* added to the base form. **Irregular** verbs, however, do not follow this pattern.

Principal Parts of Regular Verbs			
Base Form	**Present Participle**	**Past**	**Past Participle**
smile	smiling	smiled	smiled
talk	talking	talked	talked
jump	jumping	jumped	jumped

(1)   Standard verb forms

Consult a dictionary whenever you are uncertain about the form of a verb. If only the base form is listed, the verb is regular and forms both its past tense and past participle by adding *-d* or *-ed.* If the verb is irregular, the dictionary lists its forms, three if the past tense and past participle are different and two if the past tense and past participle are the same.

---

*NOTE: The verb *be* is so irregular that it is the one exception to this definition; its base form is *be.*

hide, v (past hid, pp hidden)
fall, v (past fell, pp fallen)
make, v (made)
spin, v (spun)

(2) Principal parts of irregular verbs

Many irregular verbs change an internal vowel in the past tense and past participle.

Base Form	Present Participle	Past	Past Participle
begin	beginning	began	begun
come	coming	came	come

Other irregular verbs not only change an internal vowel in the past tense but also add -n or -en to the past participle.

Base Form	Present Participle	Past	Past Participle
fall	falling	fell	fallen
rise	rising	rose	risen

Still other irregular verbs take the same form in both the past and the past participle forms.

Base Form	Present Participle	Past	Past Participle
bet	betting	bet (betted)	bet
have	having	had	had

Common Irregular Verbs

Base Form	Present Participle	Past	Past Participle
arise	arising	arose	arisen
awake	awaking	awoke, awaked	awoke, awaked
be	being	was/were	been
bear (carry)	bearing	bore	borne

continued

continued from previous page

Base Form	Present Participle	Past	Past Participle
beat	beating	beat	beaten
begin	beginning	began	begun
bend	bending	bent	bent
bet	betting	bet, betted	bet
bid	bidding	bid	bid
bind	binding	bound	bound
bite	biting	bit	bitten
bleed	bleeding	bled	bled
blow	blowing	blew	blown
break	breaking	broke	broken
bring	bringing	brought	brought
build	building	built	built
burn	burning	burned, burnt	burned, burnt
burst	bursting	burst	burst
buy	buying	bought	bought
catch	catching	caught	caught
choose	choosing	chose	chosen
cling	clinging	clung	clung
come	coming	came	come
creep	creeping	crept	crept
cut	cutting	cut	cut
deal	dealing	dealt	dealt
dig	digging	dug	dug
dive	diving	dived, dove	dived
do	doing	did	done
drag	dragging	dragged	dragged
draw	drawing	drew	drawn
drink	drinking	drank	drunk
drive	driving	drove	driven
eat	eating	ate	eaten
fall	falling	fell	fallen
feed	feeding	fed	fed
feel	feeling	felt	felt

Base Form	Present Participle	Past	Past Participle
fight	fighting	fought	fought
find	finding	found	found
fling	flinging	flung	flung
fly	flying	flew	flown
forbid	forbidding	forbade, forbad	forbidden, forbid
forget	forgetting	forgot	forgotten, forgot
forsake	forsaking	forsook	forsaken
freeze	freezing	froze	frozen
get	getting	got	gotten, got
give	giving	gave	given
go	going	went	gone
grind	grinding	ground	ground
grow	growing	grew	grown
hang (suspend)	hanging	hung	hung
hang (execute)	hanging	hanged	hanged
have	having	had	had
hear	hearing	heard	heard
hit	hitting	hit	hit
keep	keeping	kept	kept
know	knowing	knew	known
lay	laying	laid	laid
lead	leading	led	led
leap	leaping	leaped, leapt	leaped, leapt
learn	learning	learned, learnt	learned, learnt
lend	lending	lent	lent
let	letting	let	let
lie (recline)	lying	lay	lain
lie (tell an untruth)	lying	lied	lied
light	lighting	lighted, lit	lighted, lit
mow	mowing	mowed	mowed, mown
plead	pleading	pleaded, pled	pleaded, pled
prove	proving	proved	proved, proven

continued

continued from previous page

Base Form	Present Participle	Past	Past Participle
put	putting	put	put
read	reading	read	read
rid	ridding	rid, ridded	rid, ridded
ride	riding	rode	ridden
ring	ringing	rang	rung
rise	rising	rose	risen
run	running	ran	run
see	seeing	saw	seen
seek	seeking	sought	sought
set	setting	set	set
shake	shaking	shook	shaken
shed	shedding	shed	shed
shine	shining	shone	shone
shoe	shoeing	shod, shoed	shod, shoed
shrink	shrinking	shrank, shrunk	shrunk, shrunken
sing	singing	sang	sung
sink	sinking	sank	sunk
sit	sitting	sat	sat
slay	slaying	slew	slain
sneak	sneaking	sneaked	sneaked
sow	sowing	sowed	sowed, sown
speak	speaking	spoke	spoken
speed	speeding	sped, speeded	sped, speeded
spin	spinning	spun	spun
spring	springing	sprang	sprung
stand	standing	stood	stood
steal	stealing	stole	stolen
stick	sticking	stuck	stuck
strike	striking	struck	struck, stricken
strive	striving	strove	striven
swear	swearing	swore	sworn
swim	swimming	swam	swum
swing	swinging	swung	swung

Base Form	Present Participle	Past	Past Participle
take	taking	took	taken
teach	teaching	taught	taught
tear	tearing	tore	torn
think	thinking	thought	thought
throw	throwing	threw	thrown
tread	treading	trod	trodden, trod
wake	waking	woke	waked, woke, wakened
wear	wearing	wore	worn
weave	weaving	wove	woven
wed	wedding	wed, wedded	wed, wedded
weep	weeping	wept	wept
win	winning	won	won
wind	winding	wound	wound
wring	wringing	wrung	wrung
write	writing	wrote	written

E X E R C I S E   1

Complete the following sentences with an appropriate form of the verbs in parentheses.

> EXAMPLE: The inhabitants of Easter Island _____ Polynesian. (be)
>
> The inhabitants of Easter Island <u>are</u> Polynesian.

1. John Hancock _____ to write his name first on the Declaration of Independence. (choose)
2. In *The Scarlet Letter* Hester Prynne _____ the consequences of her guilt. (bear)
3. Before mechanization workers _____ the water out of the fabric by hand. (wring)
4. Daedalus warned his son what would happen if he _____ too close to the sun. (fly)
5. John Brown was _____ for his attack on Harpers Ferry, Virginia. (hang)

23b *Tense*

Tense is the form of a verb that indicates when an action occurred or when a condition existed. Tense, however, is not the same as time. The present tense, for example, indicates present time, but it can also indicate future time or a generally held belief.

English Verb Tenses

Simple Tenses

Present (I finish, she or he finishes)
Past (I finished)
Future (I will finish)

Perfect Tenses

Present perfect (I have finished, she or he has finished)
Past perfect (I had finished)
Future perfect (I will have finished)

Progressive Tenses

Present progressive (I am finishing, she or he is finishing)
Past progressive (I was finishing)
Future progressive (I will be finishing)
Present perfect progressive (I have been finishing)
Past perfect progressive (I had been finishing)
Future perfect progressive (I will have been finishing)

23c *Tense: Using the Simple Tenses*

(1) *Present tense*

The **present tense** usually indicates that an action is taking place when you are speaking or writing. With subjects other than singular nouns or third-person singular pronouns, the present tense uses only the base form of the verb.

I smile when I am nervous.

They wear wool in the winter.

With singular nouns or third-person singular pronouns, *-s* or *-es* is added to the base form.

She smiles when she is nervous.

He wears wool in the winter.

In addition to expressing action in the present, the present tense has some special uses.

Special Uses of the Present Tense

The rector opens the chapel every morning at six o'clock. (indicates that something occurs regularly)

The grades arrive next Thursday. (indicates future time)

Studying pays off. (states a generally held belief)

An object at rest tends to stay at rest. (states a scientific truth)

In *The Catcher in the Rye* Holden Caulfield spends a weekend wandering through New York City. (discusses the plot, characters, or meaning of literary works)

Notice that in some cases words like *every* and *next* help to indicate time.

---

(2) Past tense

The **past tense** is the form of the verb that indicates that an action has taken place. It is formed by adding *-d* or *-ed* to the base form or, for irregular verbs, by changing the form of the verb. The past tense has two uses.

Charles Lindbergh flew across the Atlantic Ocean on May 20, 1927. (indicates an action completed in the past)

When he was young, Mark Twain traveled across the mining towns of the Southwest. (indicates actions that recurred in the past but did not extend into the present)

(3) Future tense

The **future tense** indicates that an action will take place. A number of constructions can be used to indicate future action, including the present tense (**see 23c1**), but here we discuss future tense verb forms.

These verb forms consist of the auxiliaries *will* or *shall* plus the present tense. The future tense has the following uses:

> Halley's Comet will reappear in 2061. (indicates a future action that will definitely occur)

> The college has announced it will require all freshmen to buy microprocessors. (indicates intention)

> If you expose white phosphorous to oxygen, a violent reaction will occur. (indicates what will happen if certain conditions occur)

> The land boom in Florida will most likely continue. (indicates probability)

Revision Close-up

At one time *will* was used exclusively for the second- and third-person future of a verb, and *shall* was used for the first person. Except in formal usage, however, *shall* is now rare.

23d *Tense: Using the Perfect Tenses*

The perfect tenses designate actions that were or will be completed before other actions or conditions. The perfect tenses are formed with the appropriate tense form of the auxiliary verb *have* plus the past participle.

(1) Present perfect tense

The **present perfect** can indicate three types of continuing action that begin in the past.

> Dr. Kim has finished studying the effects of BHA on rats. (indicates an action that begins in the past and is finished when you are speaking or writing)

> My mother has invested her money wisely. (indicates an action that begins in the past and extends into the present)

> I have read all the books in the *Dune* series by Frank Herbert. (indicates an action that occurred at an unspecified past time)

(2) Past perfect tense

The **past perfect** has three uses.

By 1946 engineers had built the first electronic digital computer. (indicates an action occurring before a certain time in the past)

By the time Alfred Wallace wrote his paper, Darwin had already published *The Origin of Species*. (indicates that one action was finished before another one started)

We had hoped to visit the Kennedy Space Center on our trip to Florida. (indicates an unfulfilled desire in the past)

(3) Future perfect tense

The **future perfect** has two uses.

By Tuesday the transit authority will have run out of money. (indicates that an action will be finished by a certain future time)

By the time a commercial fusion reactor is developed, the government will have spent billions of dollars on research. (indicates that one action will be finished before another occurs in the future)

23e *Tense: Using the Progressive Tense Forms*

The tenses discussed so far, the simple tenses and the perfect tenses, are called **common forms.** They indicate a completed, momentary, or habitual action.

English also has **progressive forms** that express continuing action. The progressive forms consist of the appropriate tense of the verb *be* plus the present participle.

(1) Present progressive tense

The **present progressive** has two specific uses.

The volcano is erupting and lava is flowing toward the town. (indicates that something is happening when you are speaking or writing)

Law is becoming an overcrowded profession. (indicates that an action is happening even though it may not be taking place when you are speaking or writing)

(2) Past progressive tense

The **past progressive** has two uses.

Roderick Usher's actions were becoming increasingly bizarre. (indicates an action continuing in the past)

The French revolutionary Marat was stabbed to death while he was bathing. (indicates an action occurring at the same time in the past as another action)

(3) Future progressive tense

The **future progressive** has two uses.

The Secretary of the Treasury will be carefully monitoring the money supply. (indicates a continuing action in the future)

Next month NATO forces will be holding military exercises. (indicates a continuing action at a specific future time)

(4) Present perfect progressive tense

The **present perfect progressive** has only one use.

The number of women getting lung cancer has been increasing dramatically. (indicates action continuing from the past into the present and possibly into the future)

(5) Past perfect progressive tense

The **past perfect progressive** has only one use.

Before Julius Caesar was assassinated, he had been increasing his power. (indicates that one past action went on until a second occurred)

(6) Future perfect progressive tense

The **future perfect progressive** has only one use.

By eleven o'clock we will have been driving for seven hours. (indicates that an action will continue until a certain future time)

E X E R C I S E   2

A verb is missing from each of the following sentences. Fill in the form of the verb indicated in parentheses after each sentence.

EXAMPLE: The full moon _____ now. (rise: present progressive)
The full moon is rising now. (the action is happening when you are writing or speaking)

1. April showers _____ May flowers. (bring: present)
2. Before he sailed through the Straits of Magellan, Sir Francis Drake _____ Robert Dudley. (execute: past)

3. The movie *E.T.* _____ the contact between a traveler from outer space and an earth boy. (examine: present)
4. The Securities and Exchange Commission always _____ the interests of the public regarding the sale of securities. (protect: present perfect)
5. The Hindenburg _____ and people _____ to the ground. (burn, jump: present progressive)
6. Four engineers _____ on this system since March. (work: present perfect progressive)
7. The Environmental Protection Agency _____ cleaning up a chemical dump in North Jersey. (finish: present perfect)
8. Columbus _____ when the man on watch sighted land. (rest: past progressive)
9. By 1895 Sigmund Freud _____ the science of psychoanalysis. (develop: past perfect)
10. To Rutherford current models of the atom _____ questionable. (become: past progressive)

23f   *Using the Correct Sequence of Tenses*

The relationship among the verb tenses in a sentence is called the **sequence of tenses.** If the actions of all the verbs in a sentence occur at approximately the same time, the tenses should be the same.

When Katherine Hepburn <u>walked</u> on stage, the audience <u>rose</u> and <u>applauded</u>.

Often, however, a sentence contains several verbs describing actions that occur at different times. The tenses of the verbs must therefore shift. Which tense to use depends both on meaning and on the nature of the clauses in which the verbs occur.

(1)   *Verbs in independent clauses*

The tense of verbs that appear in adjacent independent clauses can shift as long as their relationships to their subjects and to each other are clear.

The debate <u>was</u> not impressive, but the election <u>will determine</u> the winner.

(2)   *Verbs in dependent clauses*

When a verb appears in a dependent clause, its tense depends on the tense of the main verb in the independent clause. When the main verb in the independent clause is in any tense except the past or past perfect, the verb in the dependent clause may be in any tense needed for meaning.

MAIN VERB	VERB IN DEPENDENT CLAUSE
Ryan knows	that Herman Melville wrote *The Confidence Man.*
The mayor will explain	why she changed her position.

When the main verb is in the past tense, the verb in the dependent clause is usually in the past or past perfect tense. When the main verb is in the past perfect, the verb in the dependent clause is usually in the past tense.

MAIN VERB	VERB IN DEPENDENT CLAUSE
George Hepplewhite was an English cabinetmaker	who designed distinctive chair backs.
The battle had ended	by the time reinforcements arrived.

(3) Infinitives in verbal phrases

When an infinitive appears in a verbal phrase, the tense it expresses depends on the tense of the main verb in the independent clause. The *present infinitive* (*to* plus the base form of the verb) indicates an action happening at the same time as or later than the main verb. The *perfect infinitive* (*to have* plus the past participle) indicates action happening earlier than the main verb.

MAIN VERB	INFINITIVE
I went	to hear Carlos Fuentes last week. (The going and hearing occurred at the same time.)
I want	to hear Carlos Fuentes tomorrow. (Wanting is in the present, and hearing is in the future.)
I would have liked	to hear Carlos Fuentes last week. (Both liking and hearing occur at the same time.)
I would like	to have heard Carlos Fuentes lecture. (Liking occurs in the present, and hearing would have occurred in the past.)

(4) Participles in verbal phrases

When a participle appears in a verbal phrase, its tense depends on the tense of the main verb in the independent clause. The *present participle* indicates action happening at the same time as the action of the main verb. The *past participle* or the *present perfect participle* indicates action occurring before the action of the main verb.

PARTICIPLE	MAIN VERB
Addressing the 1896 Democratic Convention,	William Jennings Bryan delivered his Cross of Gold speech. (The addressing and the delivery occurred at the same time.)
Having published his General Theory of Relativity,	Einstein worked on a Unified Field Theory. (The publishing occurred before the work on the Unified Field Theory.)

E X E R C I S E   3

From inside each pair of parentheses, choose the correct verb form. Make certain you check the sequence of the verb forms and are able to explain your choices.

EXAMPLE: Huckleberry Finn's friends and relatives mourned him, unaware that he _____ (staged, had staged) his death.

Huckleberry Finn's friends and relatives mourned him, unaware that he had staged his death. (The action occurred before the action of the main verb.)

1. Hamlet feigns madness after he _____ (discovers, discovered) his uncle's treachery.
2. I no longer eat red meat since I _____ (learned, have learned) that it is associated with some types of cancer.
3. In most of his novels, Nathaniel Hawthorne _____ (attempts, attempted) to show the effects of the past upon the present.
4. Because of the legal battles and bad press spawned by the lyrics of some rock bands, many music stores _____ (stopped, have stopped) carrying any material that could be deemed obscene.
5. When the president started to define his new economic policy, the press corps _____ (becomes, became) attentive.
6. Having directed conventional stage plays for years, Benita _____ (decided, had decided) to try something experimental.

397

7. When Zen masters present a koan, or riddle, to students, the students
_____ (solve, solved) them.

8. Henry David Thoreau was an American transcendentalist writer who
_____ (advocates, advocated) a life of simplicity.

23g *Mood*

Mood is the verb form that indicates a writer's basic attitude toward what he or she is saying.

MOOD

Type	Use	Example
Indicative mood	To express an opinion, state a fact, or ask a question	Margaret Sanger thought that family planning was necessary for social progress.
		Did the Phonecians develop a phonetic alphabet?
Imperative mood	To express commands and direct requests	[You] Read the next chapter.
		[You] Please finish today.
		Let us discuss the images of minorities created by television.
		Let's check our lab report.
Subjunctive mood	With *that* clauses, contrary-to-fact statements, and certain idiomatic expressions	The committee recommended that Houston be the site of next year's meeting.
		Hamlet acted as if he were mad.

23h   *Using the Indicative Mood*

The **indicative** is the mood used to express an opinion, state a fact, or ask a question. It may be used along with a form of *do* for emphasis.

Jackie Robinson had an impact on American professional baseball.

Did Margaret Mead say that behavioral differences are rooted in culture?

23i   *Using the Imperative Mood*

The **imperative** is the mood used in commands and direct requests. Usually the imperative includes only the base form of the verb without a subject.

(You) Use a dictionary.

(You) Please vote today.

When you include yourself in a command, use *let's* or *let us* before the base form of the verb.

Let us examine Machiavelli's view of human nature.

Let's go to the movies.

23j   *Using the Subjunctive Mood*

The *present subjunctive* uses the base form of the verb, regardless of the subject. The *past subjunctive* has the same form as the past tense of the verb. (The auxiliary verb *be*, however, takes the form *were* regardless of the number or person of the subject.) The *past perfect subjunctive* has the same form as the past perfect.

Dr. Gorman suggested that I study the Cambrian period. (present subjunctive)

I wish I were going to Europe. (past subjunctive)

I wish I had gone to the review session. (past perfect subjunctive)

The subjunctive is used in the following cases.

(1) That *clauses*

The subjunctive is used in *that* clauses after words such as *ask, suggest, require, recommend,* and *demand.*

> The report recommended that juveniles be given mandatory counseling.

> During the 1930's Louisiana politician Huey Long suggested that personal fortunes above a certain amount be liquidated.

> Captain Ahab insisted that his crew hunt the white whale.

(2) *Contrary-to-fact statements*

The subjunctive is used in conditional statements that are contrary to fact, including statements that express a wish. A **conditional statement** begins with a dependent *if* clause that presents a condition and concludes with an independent clause that presents the effect of that condition. If the effect is even slightly possible, use the indicative mood for the verb in the *if* clause.

> If a nuclear treaty is signed, the world will be safer. (A nuclear treaty is possible.)

If the condition is impossible or **contrary to fact,** use the subjunctive mood for the verb in the *if* clause.

> If Teller were there, he would have seen Oppenheimer. (Teller was not there.)

NOTE: A conditional clause beginning with *as if* is contrary to fact and should be in the subjunctive mood.

> The father acted as if he were having the baby. (The father couldn't be having the baby.)

A **wish** is a condition that does not exist; therefore, it should be expressed in the subjunctive mood.

> I wish I were more organized.

(3) *Idiomatic expressions*

The subjunctive is used in some special expressions.

> If need be, we will stay up all night to finish the report.

> Come what may, they will increase their steel production.

> Far be it for me to correct an expert.

> Special interest groups have, as it were, shifted the balance of power.

EXERCISE 4

Complete the sentences in the following paragraph by inserting the appropriate form (indicative, imperative, or subjunctive) of the verb in parentheses. Be prepared to explain your choices.

Harry Houdini was a famous escape artist. He _____ (perform) escapes from every type of bond imaginable: handcuffs, locks, straitjackets, ropes, sacks, and sealed chests underwater. In Germany workers _____ (challenge) Houdini to escape from a packing box. If he _____ (be) to escape, they would admit that he _____ (be) the best escape artist in the world. Houdini accepted. Before getting into the box he asked that the observers _____ (give) it a thorough examination. He then asked that a worker _____ (nail) him in the box. "_____ (place) a screen around the box," he ordered after he had been sealed inside. In a few minutes Houdini _____ (step) from behind the screen. When the workers demanded that they _____ (see) the box, Houdini pulled down the screen. To their surprise they saw the box with the lid still nailed tightly in place.

23k *Voice*

Voice indicates whether the subject of a verb acts or is acted upon. When the subject of a verb does something—that is, acts—the verb is in the **active voice.**

ACTIVE VOICE: Hart Crane wrote *The Bridge.*

When the subject of a verb receives the action—that is, is acted upon—the verb is in the **passive voice.**

PASSIVE VOICE: *The Bridge* was written by Hart Crane.

Revision Close-up

Because the active voice emphasizes the doer of an action, it is usually briefer, clearer, and more emphatic than the passive voice. For this reason, you should use active constructions in your college writing. Some situations, however, require use of the passive voice. Keep in mind that you should use passive constructions only when you have good reason to do so.

231 *Using the Passive Voice*

(1) When the doer is unknown or unimportant

The passive voice enables you to emphasize what happened when the person or thing acting is unknown or unimportant.

DDT <u>was found</u> in local soil samples. (Passive emphasizes finding of DDT, not who found it.)

We <u>were required</u> to embroider and I had trunkfuls of colorful dish towels, pillowcases, runners, and handkerchiefs to my credit. (Maya Angelou, *I Know Why the Caged Bird Sings*) (Passive emphasizes what they had to do, not who made them do it.)

(2) When the action should logically receive the emphasis

The passive voice also enables you to emphasize whatever logically receives, or is the logical object of, the action.

Darwin's faith in fixed species <u>was destroyed</u> on his five-year trip on the *Beagle*. (Emphasis is on fact that Darwin's faith was destroyed, not on who or what destroyed it.)

The art of the Greek sculptors of the great age <u>is known</u> to us by long familiarity. (Edith Hamilton, *The Greek Way*) (The passive emphasizes the art, not what we know about it.)

Numerical superiority <u>was achieved</u> by the Allies at the Battle of the Marne. (The passive enables the sentence to focus on numerical superiority.)

EXERCISE 5

Read the following paragraph, and determine which verbs are active and which are passive. Comment if you can on why the author used the passive voice in each case.

The human species is now undertaking a great venture that if successful will be as important as the colonization of the land or the descent from the trees. We are haltingly, tentatively breaking the shackles of Earth—metaphorically, in confronting and taming the admonitions of those more primitive brains within us; physically, in voyaging to the planets and listening for the messages from the stars. These two enterprises are linked indissolubly. Each, I believe, is a necessary condition for the other. But our energies are directed far more toward war. Hypnotized by mutual mistrust, almost never concerned for the species or the planet, the nations prepare for death. And because what we are doing is so horrifying, we tend not to think of it much. But what we do not consider we are unlikely to put right. (Carl Sagan, *Cosmos*)

23m *Changing from Passive to Active Voice*

You can change a verb from passive to active voice by making the subject of the passive verb the object of the active verb. The person or thing performing the action then becomes the subject of the new sentence.

PASSIVE: The novel *Frankenstein* was written by Mary Shelley.

ACTIVE: Mary Shelley wrote the novel *Frankenstein*.

You can easily change a verb from passive to active if the sentence contains an *agent* that performs the action. Often the word *by* follows the passive verb *(written by Mary Shelley)*, indicating the agent that can become the subject of an active verb.

If a passive verb has no agent, supply a subject for the active verb; if you cannot, keep the passive construction.

PASSIVE: Baby elephants are taught to avoid humans. (By whom are baby elephants taught?)

ACTIVE: Adult elephants teach baby elephants to avoid humans.

EXERCISE 6

Determine which verbs in the following paragraph should be changed from the passive to the active voice. Rewrite the sentences containing these verbs, and be prepared to explain your changes.

Rockets were invented by the Chinese about A.D. 1000. Gunpowder was packed into bamboo tubes and ignited by means of a fuse. These rockets were fired by soldiers at enemy armies and usually caused panic. In thirteenth-century England an improved form of gunpowder was introduced by Roger Bacon. As a result rockets were used in battles and were a common—although unreliable—weapon. In the early eighteenth century a twenty-pound rocket that traveled almost two miles was constructed by William Congreve, an English artillery expert. By the late nineteenth century thought was given to supersonic speeds by the physicist Ernst Mach. The sonic boom was predicted by him. The first liquid fuel rocket was launched by the American Robert

Goddard in 1926. A pamphlet written by him anticipated almost all future rocket developments. As a result of his pioneering work, he is called the father of modern rocketry.

23n *Changing from Active to Passive Voice*

You can change verbs from active to passive voice by making the object of the active verb the subject of the passive verb. The subject of the active verb then becomes the object of the passive verb.

ACTIVE: Sir James Murray compiled the *Oxford English Dictionary*.

PASSIVE: The *Oxford English Dictionary* was compiled by Sir James Murray.

Remember that an active verb must have an object or it cannot be put into the passive voice. If an active verb has no object, supply a subject or keep the active construction.

ACTIVE: Shakespeare wrote.

         _?_ was written by Shakespeare.

PASSIVE: *Twelfth Night* was written by Shakespeare.

E X E R C I S E   7

Determine which sentences in the following paragraph would be more effective in the passive voice. Rewrite those sentences, making sure that you can explain the reasons for your choices.

Thomas Eakins was a painter and sculptor who was born in Phila-delphia in 1844. Many people consider Eakins one of America's best nineteenth-century artists. Eakins, an innovative artist who knew anatomy and who insisted on working with nude models, led the move toward American realism. As a result, some people forced his resignation from the Pennsylvania Academy in 1886.

STUDENT WRITER AT WORK

VERBS

Revise this background section of a draft of a short paper on the writing of Samuel Pepys, the famous seventeenth-century English diarist. Look for inconsistencies in tense and mood and ineffective use of both passive and active voice. You may add words and phrases and rearrange sentences. After you have corrected the errors, go over the draft again and, if necessary, revise further to strengthen coherence, unity, and style.

Samuel Pepys was born on February 23, 1633, in a house in Shaftsbury Court, where the business of tailoring was carried out by his father. Samuel Pepys was the fifth child and second son of his family. A primary education was secured for Pepys with the aid of his father's cousin, Sir Edward Montagu. In 1650 Pepys enters Trinity College, Cambridge, and after transferring to Magdalene College a Bachelor of Arts Degree and a Master's Degree were eventually secured. In 1665 Pepys began a career in the navy. Between 1672 and 1679 various important offices were held by Pepys. He eventually rised to be secretary of the Admiralty, and many important duties were given to him. The revolution of 1688 terminated King James's reign, and also the career of Pepys was ended. On May 25, 1703, Pepys died and was buried beside his wife.

Throughout his life Pepys's true character was probably not known to those around him. Between 1660 and 1669, however, Pepys recorded his personal observations in his diary. This document was written in shorthand, French, Spanish, Latin, Greek, and invented ciphers. More than one hundred years after Pepys's death six volumes had been discovered by the Reverend John Smith, and in 1825 the first edition of The Diary was published. In the nine years he kept his diary, a brilliant and candid picture of Restoration life was given by Pepys. Today Pepys is regarded by most scholars as the most insightful of the English diarists.

Agreement

Agreement is the correspondence between words in number, gender, or person. Subjects and verbs agree in **number** (singular or plural) and **person** (first, second, or third); pronouns and their antecedents agree in number, person, and **gender** (masculine, feminine, or neuter).

24a *Subject-Verb Agreement*

Verbs should agree in number and person with their subjects: singular subjects have singular verbs, and plural subjects have plural verbs.

> SINGULAR: Hydrogen peroxide is an unstable compound.
>
> PLURAL: The characters are not well developed in most of O. Henry's short stories.

Present tense verbs, except *be* and *have,* add *-s* or *-es* when the subject is third-person singular. Third-person singular subjects include nouns; the personal pronouns *he, she, it,* and *one;* and many indefinite pronouns.

> The president has the power to veto congressional legislation.
>
> She frequently cites statistics to support her assertions.
>
> In every group somebody emerges as a natural leader.

Present tense verbs do not add *-s* or *-es* when the subject is first-person singular (*I*), first-person plural (*we*), second-person singular or plural (*you*), or third-person plural (*they*).

> I recommend that dieters avoid processed meat because of its high salt content.

In our Bill of Rights, we guarantee all defendants the right to a speedy trial.

At this stratum, you see rocks dating back fifteen million years.

They say that some wealthy people default on their student loans.

Subject-verb agreement is generally straightforward, but some situations can be troublesome. You can achieve proper agreement if you are familiar with the following conventions.

(1) Intervening phrases

Even if a modifying phrase comes between subject and verb, the verb should agree with the subject, not with a word in the intervening phrase.

The sound of the drumbeats builds in intensity in *The Emperor Jones*.

The games won by the intramural team are usually few and far between.

Revision Close-up

When phrases introduced by *along with, as well as, in addition to, including*, and *together with* come between subject and verb, the intervening phrases do not change the subject's number.

Heavy rain, together with high winds, causes hazardous driving conditions along the Santa Monica Freeway.

---

(2) Compound subjects joined by *and*

Compound subjects joined by *and* take plural verbs.

Air conditioning and power steering are two of the available options on most domestic automobiles.

There are, however, two exceptions to this rule.

- Some compound subjects joined by *and* stand for a single idea or person. These should be treated as a unit and given singular verbs.

Rhythm and blues is a forerunner of rock and roll.

- When *each* or *every* precedes a compound subject joined by *and*, the subject also takes a singular verb.

Every nook and cranny was searched before the purloined letter was found in plain sight on the mantel.

(3) Compound subjects joined by or

Compound subjects joined by *or* or by the correlative conjunctions *either . . . or* or *neither . . . nor* may take singular or plural verbs. If both subjects are singular, use a singular verb; if both subjects are plural, use a plural verb.

> Either radiation or chemotherapy is combined with surgery for the most effective results. (Both parts of the compound subject, *radiation* and *chemotherapy*, are singular, so the verb is singular.)

> Either radiation treatments or chemotherapy sessions are combined with surgery for the most effective results. (Both parts of the compound subject, *treatments* and *sessions*, are plural, so the verb is plural.)

When a singular and a plural subject are linked by *or*, or by the correlative conjunctions *either . . . or, neither . . . nor*, or *not only . . . but also*, the verb should agree with the subject that is nearer to it.

> Either radiation treatments or chemotherapy is combined with surgery for the most effective results. (Singular verb agrees with *chemotherapy*, the part of the compound subject closer to it.)

> Either chemotherapy or radiation treatments are combined with surgery for the most effective results. (Plural verb agrees with *treatments*, the part of the compound subject closer to it.)

Revision Close-up

When a compound subject is made up of nouns and pronouns that differ in person, the verb should agree in person as well as in number with the nearest element of the compound subject.

> Neither my running mate nor I wish to contest the election.

> Neither I nor my running mate wishes to contest the election.

(4) Indefinite pronouns

In most cases, you should use a singular verb when using an indefinite pronoun as a subject. Although some indefinite pronouns—*both, many, few, several, others*—are always plural, most— *another, anyone, everyone, one, each, either, neither, anything, everything, something,* and *somebody*—are singular.

Anyone is welcome to apply for a grant, providing certain financial qualifications are met.

Each of the chapters includes a review exercise.

Revision Close-up

Some indefinite pronouns—*some, all, any, more, most,* and *none*—can be singular or plural. In these cases the noun to which the pronoun refers determines whether the verb form should be singular or plural.

> Of course, some of this trouble is to be expected. (*Some* refers to *trouble;* therefore, the verb is singular.)

> Some of the spectators are getting restless. (*Some* refers to *spectators;* therefore, the verb is plural.)

---

(5) Collective nouns

A **collective noun** is singular in form but denotes a group of persons or things—for instance, *navy, union, association, group.* When a collective noun refers to a group as a unit, it takes a singular verb; when it refers to the individuals or items that make up the group, it takes a plural verb.

> To many people the royal family symbolizes Great Britain. (The family, as a unit, is the symbol.)

> After years of living together, the nuclear family begin to go their separate ways. (Each member leaves separately.)

Sometimes, however, even when usage is correct, a plural verb sounds awkward with a collective noun. If this is the case, rewrite the sentence to eliminate the awkwardness.

> After years of living together, the members of the nuclear family begin to go their separate ways.

Phrases that name a fixed amount—*three-quarters, twenty dollars, the majority*—are treated like collective nouns. When the amount is considered as a unit, it takes a singular verb; when it denotes part of the whole, it takes a plural verb.

> Three-quarters of those taking the math anxiety workshop improve dramatically. (All individuals in this group improve.)

> Three-quarters of his usual Social Security check is not enough. (Three-quarters denotes a unit.)

(6) *Singular subjects with plural forms*

Be sure to use a singular verb with a singular subject, even if the form of the subject is plural.

Statistics deals with the collection, classification, analysis, and interpretation of data.

Politics makes strange bedfellows.

In certain contexts, however, some of these words may actually have plural meanings. In these cases, a plural verb should be used.

Her politics are too radical for her parents. (*Politics* refers not to the science of political government but to political principles or opinions.)

The statistics prove him wrong. (*Statistics* denotes not a body of knowledge but the numerical facts or data themselves.)

Be sure that titles of individual works take singular verbs, even if their form is plural.

The Grapes of Wrath describes the journey of migrant workers and their families from the Dust Bowl to California.

This convention also applies to words referred to as words, even if they are plural.

Good vibes is a 1960's slang term meaning positive feelings.

See 20b5 ◄

(7) Inverted subject-verb order

Be sure a verb agrees with its subject, even when the verb precedes the subject.

Is either answer correct?

There but for fortune go you and I.

There are currently twelve circuit courts of appeals in the federal court system.

NOTE: The usual word order of a sentence is inverted with constructions involving *there is* or *there are*.

(8) Linking verbs

Be sure linking verbs agree with their subjects, not with the subject complement.

The problem was termites.

Here the verb *was* agrees with the subject *problem,* not with the subject complement *termites.* If *termites* were the subject, the verb would be plural.

Termites were the problem.

(9) Relative pronouns

When you use a relative pronoun (*who, which, that*) to begin a dependent clause, the verb in that clause should agree in number with the pronoun's antecedent. Because these pronouns have the same form for singular and plural, they provide no clues to subject-verb agreement.

The farmer is one of the ones who suffer during a grain embargo.

Here the verb *suffer* agrees with the antecedent *ones* of the relative pronoun *who.* Compare this sentence:

The farmer is the only one who suffers during the grain embargo.

Now the verb agrees with the antecedent *one,* which is singular.

EXERCISE 1

Each of these ten correct sentences illustrates one of the eight conventions just explained. Read the sentences carefully, and explain why each verb form is used in each case.

EXAMPLE: *Harold and Maude is* a popular cult film. (The verb is singular because the subject, *Harold and Maude* is the title of an individual work, even though it is plural in form.)

1. Jack Kerouac, along with Allen Ginsberg and William S. Burroughs, was a major figure in the "beat" movement.
2. Every American boy and girl needs to learn basic computational skills.
3. Aesthetics is not an exact science.
4. The audience was restless.
5. The Beatles' *Sergeant Pepper* album is one of those albums that remain popular long after the time they are issued.
6. All is quiet.
7. The subject was roses.
8. When he was young, Benjamin Franklin's primary concern was books.
9. Fifty dollars is too much to spend on one concert ticket.
10. "There are more things in heaven and earth, Horatio, than are dreamt of in your philosophy."

EXERCISE 2

Some of these sentences are correct, but others illustrate common errors in subject-verb agreement. If a sentence is correct, mark it with a C; if it has an error, correct it.

1. *I Love Lucy* is one of those television shows that almost all Americans have seen at least once.
2. The committee presented their findings to the president.
3. Neither Western novels nor science fiction appeal to me.
4. Stage presence and musical ability makes a rock performer successful today.
5. *It's a Wonderful Life,* like many old Christmas movies, seems to be shown on television almost daily from Thanksgiving to New Year's Day.
6. Hearts are my grandmother's favorite card game.
7. The best part of B. B. King's songs are the guitar solos.
8. Time and tide waits for no man.
9. Sports are my main pastime.
10. *Vincent and Theo* is Robert Altman's movie about the French Impressionist painter Van Gogh and his brother.

24b *Pronoun-Antecedent Agreement*

A pronoun must agree with its **antecedent**—the word or word group to which the pronoun refers—in number, person, and gender. Singular pronouns—such as *he, him, she, her, it, me, myself,* and *oneself*—should refer to singular antecedents. Plural pronouns— such as *we, us, they, them,* and *their*—should refer to plural antecedents. (See **21b** for a complete list of pronouns.) Pronouns must also agree with their antecedents in person (first, second, third) and gender (masculine, feminine, neuter). Several conventions govern pronoun-antecedent agreement.

(1) *More than one antecedent*

In most cases use a plural pronoun to refer to two or more antecedents connected by *and,* even if one or more of the antecedents is singular.

> Mormonism and Christian Science were influenced in their beginnings by Shaker doctrines.

However, if the compound antecedent denotes a single unit— one person or thing or idea—use a singular pronoun to refer to the compound antecedent.

> In 1904 the husband and father brought his family from Poland to America.

When the compound antecedent is preceded by *each* or *every,* use a singular pronoun.

> Every programming language and software package has its limitations.

Use a singular pronoun to refer to two or more singular antecedents linked by *or* or *nor.*

> Neither Thoreau nor Whitman lived to see his work read widely.

When one antecedent is singular and one is plural, however, you should be sure the pronoun agrees in person and number with the closer antecedent.

> Neither Great Britain nor the Benelux nations have experienced changes in their borders in recent years.

(2) Collective noun antecedents

Occasionally collective noun antecedents may require plural pronouns. If the meaning of the collective noun antecedent is singular, use a singular pronoun. If its meaning is plural, use a plural pronoun.

The teachers' union was ready to strike for the new contract its members had been promised. (All the members act as one.)

When the whistle blew, the team left their seats and moved toward the court. (Each member acts individually.)

Revision Close-up

Within any one sentence a collective noun should be treated consistently as either singular or plural. When one collective noun serves as both the subject of a verb and the antecedent of a pronoun, both verb and pronoun must agree with the noun. In this sentence, verb and pronoun are not consistent:

The teachers' union, ready to strike for the new contract its members had been promised, were still willing to negotiate.

Here the collective noun *union* is singular; the verb *were* is plural and, therefore, incorrect.

(3) Antecedent indefinite pronouns

Most indefinite pronouns—*each, either, neither, one, anyone,* and the like—are singular in meaning and should take singular pronouns. (Others may be plural—**see 24a4**—and require plural pronouns.)

Neither of these men is likely to have his proposal ready by the application deadline.

Each of these neighborhoods is like a separate nation, with its own traditions and values.

Everyone will get basic instruction in the modern foreign language of his choice.

Revision Close-up

Everyone presents some special problems for writers. Because *everyone* is singular in meaning and does not specify gender, convention says that it should be referred to by the singular pronoun *his*. But indefinite pronouns really denote members of both sexes, so many writers feel that using *his* is inaccurate. In speech, it is common to use the plural pronouns *they* or *their* to refer to *everyone*. In college writing, this is not acceptable.

Though it can be somewhat cumbersome if overused, one solution to this problem is to use *both* the masculine and feminine pronouns.

Everyone will get basic instruction in the modern foreign language of his or her choice.

Another solution is to change the subject and use a plural pronoun.

All students will get basic instruction in the modern foreign language of their choice.

▶ **See 18g2**

E X E R C I S E   3

Find and correct any errors in subject-verb and/or pronoun-antecedent agreement.

1. Either the Boy Scouts or the 4-H Program are offering special courses and publications to help latchkey children take care of themselves.
2. Gilbert and Sullivan's classic *The Pirates of Penzance* are revived frequently.
3. None of the lower forty-eight states is able to match Alaska's coal reserves.
4. A creole is a kind of language that comes into being when several different languages are spoken in an area. To make communication easier, speakers of each of these different languages tend to borrow from all the area's languages.
5. Although many students now enrolled in U.S. dental schools are female, as recently as 1979 there was only one oral pathologist, four endodontists, and six oral surgeons who were women.
6. A number of drugs currently banned in America is still routinely sold to "underdeveloped" countries by American manufacturers.
7. Alcohol use among college students, frequently associated with campus vandalism and traffic fatalities, are on the rise.
8. Since the 1960's, vegetarianism has moved apart from any particular religious, political, or ethical philosophy; now they have become a legitimate nutritional movement instead of a fad.
9. Neither paralegals, systems analysts, radiation therapy technologists, nor physician's assistants was in existence a generation ago.

10. Groups as diverse as Phyllis Schlafly's Eagle Forum, NOW, People for the American Way, and the DAR seeks to influence textbook selection committees.

EXERCISE 4

The ten sentences below illustrate correct subject-verb and pronoun-antecedent agreement. After following the instructions in parentheses after each sentence, revise each so that its verbs and pronouns agree with the newly created subject.

> EXAMPLE: One child in ten suffers from a learning disability.
> (Change *one child in ten* to *ten percent of all children.*)
> Ten percent of all children suffer from a learning disability.

1. The governess is seemingly pursued by evil as she tries to protect Miles and Flora from those she feels seek to possess the children's souls. (Change *The governess* to *The governess and the cook.*)
2. Insulin-dependent diabetics are now able to take advantage of new technology that can help alleviate their symptoms. (Change *diabetics* to *the diabetic.*)
3. All homeowners in shore regions worry about the possible effects of a hurricane on their property. (Change *All homeowners* to *Every homeowner.*)
4. Federally funded job-training programs offer unskilled workers an opportunity to acquire skills they can use to secure employment. (Change *workers* to *the worker.*)
5. Foreign imports pose a major challenge to the American automobile market. (Change *Foreign imports* to *The foreign import.*)
6. *Brideshead Revisited* tells how one family and its devotion to its Catholic faith affect Charles Ryder. (Delete *and its devotion to its Catholic faith.*)
7. *Writer's Digest* and *The Writer* are designed to aid novice and experienced writers as they seek markets for their work. (Change *writers* to *the writer.*)
8. Most American families have access to television; in fact, more have televisions than have indoor plumbing. (Change *Most American families* to *Almost every American family.*)
9. In Montana it seems as though every town's elevation is higher than its population. (Change *Every town's elevation* to *All the towns' elevations.*)
10. A woman without a man is like a fish without a bicycle. (Change *A woman/a man* to *Women/men.*)

AGREEMENT

Read the following draft of an English composition essay carefully, correcting all errors in subject-verb and pronoun-antecedent agreement. After you have corrected the errors, go over the draft again and, if necessary, revise further to strengthen coherence, unity, and style.

Marriage in the Ashanti Tribe

The Ashanti tribe is the largest in the small West African country of Ghana. The language of the Ashantis, Akan, is the most widely spoken in the country. The unity in the Ashanti tribe is derived from a golden stool which the Ashantis believe descended from the skies at the command of their chief priest. This unity has encouraged the Ashantis to create a system in which the family is so strong that the tribe has little need for formal support services. For instance, the tribe need few institutions to care for their orphans or homeless people. Among the Ashanti people, home and family means plenty of relatives, living and working and playing and worrying as well-knit units who live in single or neighboring households. Marriage among members of the Ashanti tribe is therefore a union of two families as well as two individuals.

In Ashanti, marriage is less an agreement entered into by two individuals before God or the justice of the peace than it is a social contract between two families, each of whom are represented by a partner to the marriage. Because a marriage binds two families together, it is not to be entered into hurriedly. In fact, everyone in the tribe fear the social consequences of an ill-conceived union. The families of both of the young people are active counselors during the courtship, and its wholehearted approval and endorsement is essential to the success of the marriage. The family seek the answers to many

questions. For instance, are the bride and bridegroom of
similar age? Have either been married before? If so, why
did the previous marriage fail? What is the history of the
family? Is the family in debt? Most important, of what
clan is the family?

When all the questions have been answered
satisfactorily, the man and the woman are married. The
respective troths—for bride and groom, for bride's family
and groom's family—are plighted in a quiet ceremony
without benefit of either clergy or justice of the peace.
The crucial part of the ceremony is the giving of a small
sum of money and various gifts and drinks by the family of
the groom to that of the bride. The actual value of such
payments are often small, amounting to about fifty dollars.
A royal family gives more and receives more. This money is
sometimes referred to as "bridewealth." It constitutes
only a token of the agreement reached between bride and
groom and between their families. In the giving and
receiving of the gifts the young people and their families
mutually pledge their faithfulness and support. When this
transaction has been witnessed by both families, the man
and woman are joined together as husband and wife. For
better or for worse, they are married.

25

Adjectives and Adverbs

Understanding Adjectives and Adverbs

Adjectives and adverbs are modifiers used alone or in combination to enrich sentences. **Adjectives** modify nouns and pronouns. **Adverbs** modify verbs; adjectives; other adverbs; or entire phrases, clauses, or sentences. Both adjectives and adverbs describe, limit, or qualify other words, phrases, or clauses.

The *function* of a word, not its *form*, determines whether it is classified as an adjective or an adverb. Although many adverbs (like *immediately* and *hopelessly*) end in *-ly*, others (like *almost* and *very*) do not. Moreover, some adjectives (like *lively*) end in *-ly*. Only by locating the modified word and determining its part of speech can you identify a modifier as an adjective or adverb.

Placement of Adjectives

Adjectives are commonly placed close to the nouns or pronouns they modify. They most often appear immediately *before* nouns and directly *after* linking verbs, direct objects, and indefinite pronouns.

They bought two shrubs for the yard. (before noun)

The name seemed familiar. (after linking verb)

The coach ran them ragged. (after direct object)

Anything sad makes me cry. (after indefinite pronoun)

Two or more adjectives can be placed *after* the noun or pronoun they modify.

The expedition, long and arduous, ended in triumph.

419

Placement of Adverbs

Adverbs are also usually located close to the words they modify. However, because they modify more kinds of words and word groups than adjectives do, they may occur in a greater variety of positions.

He walked slowly across the room.

Slowly he walked across the room.

He slowly walked across the room.

He walked across the room slowly.

25b *Using Adjectives*

Be sure to use an adjective—not an adverb—as a subject complement or an object complement (**see 21d**). A **subject complement** is a word that follows a linking verb and that modifies the sentence's subject, not its verb.

Linking Verbs

Linking verbs show no action; their function is to connect a sentence's subject and complement. Words that are or can be used as linking verbs include *seem, appear, believe, become, grow, turn, remain, prove, look, sound, smell, taste, feel,* and forms of the verb *be.*

Because a subject complement modifies the subject—a noun or pronoun—it must be an adjective.

Michelle seemed brave.

Here *seemed* shows no action and is therefore a linking verb. Because *brave* is a subject complement that modifies the noun *Michelle,* the adjective form is used. Compare the following sentence:

Michelle smiled bravely.

Here *smiled* shows action, so it is not a linking verb. *Bravely* modifies *smiled,* so it takes the adverb form.

Sometimes the same verb can either serve as a linking verb or convey action. Compare these two sentences:

He remained <u>stubborn</u>. (He was still stubborn.)

He remained <u>stubbornly</u>. (He remained, in a stubborn manner.)

When a word following a sentence's direct object modifies that object and not the verb, it is an **object complement**. Objects are nouns or pronouns, so their modifiers must be adjectives.

Most people called him <u>shy</u>. (Most people thought he was shy.)

Shy modifies the sentence's direct object (*him*), so the adjective form is correct. But in the following sentence *shyly* modifies the verb (*called*)—not the object—so the adverb form is used:

Most people called him <u>shyly</u>. (Most people were shy when they called him.)

25c *Using Adverbs*

Be sure to use an adverb—not an adjective—to modify verbs; adjectives; other adverbs; or entire phrases, clauses, or sentences (see 21e).

FAULTY: The majority of the class did <u>great</u> on the midterm. (adjective form used to modify verb)

My parents dress a lot more <u>conservative</u> than my friends do. (adjective form used to modify verb)

REVISED: The majority of the class did <u>well</u> (or <u>very well</u>) on the midterm.

My parents dress a lot more <u>conservatively</u> than my friends do.

Revision Close-up

In informal speech adjective forms such as *good, bad, sure, real, slow, quick,* and *loud* are often incorrectly used to modify verbs, adjectives, and adverbs. In college writing, however, be sure to avoid these informal modifiers and to use adverbs to modify verbs, adjectives, and other adverbs.

continued

continued from previous page

> **FAULTY:** The program ran <u>good</u> the first time we tried it.
>
> The new system performed <u>bad</u>.
>
> **REVISED:** The program ran <u>well</u> the first time we tried it.
>
> The new system performed <u>badly</u>.

EXERCISE 1

Revise each of the incorrect sentences in this paragraph so that only adjectives modify nouns and pronouns and only adverbs modify verbs, adjectives, or other adverbs. Be sure to eliminate informal forms. Place a check before any sentence that is correct.

The most popular self-help trend in the U.S. today is subliminal tapes. These tapes, with titles like "How to Attract Love," "Freedom from Acne," and "I Am a Genius," are intended to solve every problem known to modern society—quick and easy. The tapes are said to work because their "hidden messages" bypass conscious defense mechanisms. The listener hears only music or relaxing sounds, like waves rolling steady and slow. At decibel levels perceived only subconsciously, positive words and phrases are embedded, usually by someone who speaks deep and rhythmic. The top-selling cassettes are those to help you lose weight or quit smoking. The popularity of such tapes is not hard to understand. They promise easy solutions to complex problems. But the main benefit of these tapes appears to be for the sellers, who are accumulating profits real fast.

EXERCISE 2

Being careful to use adjectives—not adverbs—as subject complements and object complements, write five sentences in imitation of each of the following. Be sure to use five different linking verbs in your imitations of each sentence.

1. Julie looked worried.
2. Dan considers his collection valuable.

25d *Distinguishing Between Comparative and Superlative Forms*

Comparative and Superlative Forms

Form	Function	Example
Positive	Describes a quality; indicates no comparisons	big
Comparative	Indicates comparisons between two qualities (greater or lesser)	bigger
Superlative	Indicates comparisons among more than two qualities (greatest or least)	biggest

NOTE: Some adverbs, particularly those indicating time, place, and degree (*almost, very, here, yesterday,* and *immediately*), do not have comparative or superlative forms.

(1) The comparative degree

Adjectives   To indicate a *greater* degree, all one-syllable adjectives and many two-syllable adjectives (particularly those that end in *-y, -ly, -le, -er,* and *-ow*) add *-er* to form the comparative.

slow	slower
funny	funnier
lovely	lovelier

(Note that a final *y* becomes *i* before *-er* is added.)
   Other two-syllable adjectives and all long adjectives form the comparative with *more.*

famous	more famous
incredible	more incredible

NOTE: Many two-syllable adjectives can form the comparative with either *more* or *-er*—for example, *more lovely* or *lovelier.*
   All adjectives indicate a lesser degree with the word *less.*

lovely	less lovely
famous	less famous

423

Adverbs　Adverbs ending in *-ly* indicate a greater degree with *more*.

slowly　　　more slowly

Other adverbs use the *-er* ending to indicate a greater degree.

soon　　　sooner

Adverbs always indicate a lesser degree with the word *less*.

less slowly
less soon

Revision Close-up

Never use both *more* and *-er* to form the comparative degree.

FAULTY:　Nothing could have been more easier.
REVISED:　Nothing could have been easier.

(2)　The superlative degree

Adjectives　Adjectives that indicate the comparative with *-er* add *-est* to indicate the superlative (the *greatest* degree).

nicer　　　　　　nicest
funnier　　　　　funniest

Adjectives that indicate the comparative with *more* use *most* to indicate the superlative.

more famous　　　most famous
more challenging　most challenging

All adjectives indicate the least degree with the word *least*.

least interesting
least enjoyable

Adverbs　The majority of adverbs are preceded by *most* to indicate the greatest degree.

most quickly
most helpfully
most efficiently

Others use the *-est* ending to indicate the greatest degree.

soonest

All adverbs use *least* to indicate the least degree.

least willingly
least fashionably

Revision Close-up

Never use both *most* and *-est* to form the superlative degree.

FAULTY: Jack is the most meanest person in town.
REVISED: Jack is the meanest person in town.

(3) Irregular comparatives and superlatives

Some adjectives and adverbs do not conform to the rules presented above. Instead of adding a word or an ending to the positive form, they use different words to indicate each degree.

Irregular Comparatives and Superlatives

	Positive	Comparative	Superlative
ADJECTIVES:	good	better	best
	bad	worse	worst
	a little	less	least
	many, some, much	more	most
ADVERBS:	well	better	best
	badly	worse	worst

(4) Illogical comparisons

Many adjectives and adverbs have absolute meanings—that is, they can logically exist only in the positive degree. Good sense suggests that words like *perfect, unique, excellent, impossible,* and *dead* can never be used in the comparative or superlative degree.

FAULTY: The vase is the most unique piece in her collection.
REVISED: The vase in her collection is unique.

Although comparative and superlative forms of absolutes should be avoided in college writing, they may be used in informal contexts.

He revised eight times, always looking for the most perfect draft.

It was the most impossible course I ever took.

NOTE: Absolutes can be modified by words that suggest approaching the absolute state—*nearly* or *almost,* for example.

He revised until his draft was almost perfect.

EXERCISE 3

Supply the correct comparative and superlative forms for each of the adjectives or adverbs listed below. Then use each form in a sentence.

EXAMPLE: strange   stranger   strangest
The story had a *strange* ending. The explanation sounded *stranger* each time I heard it. This is the *strangest* gadget I have ever seen.

1. many
2. eccentric
3. confusing
4. bad
5. mysterious
6. softly
7. tremendous
8. well
9. often
10. tiny

25e *Using Nouns as Adjectives*

Many nouns can function as modifiers in a sentence.

He made a sandwich of turkey bologna, egg salad, and tomato slices on wheat bread.

Many familiar phrases, such as *space station, art history,* and *amusement park,* consist of a noun modifying another noun. In such cases using a noun as a modifier saves words. Overusing nouns as modifiers, however, can create clumsy—even incoherent—sentences.

CONFUSING: The Chestnut Hill Fathers' Club Pony League beginners spring baseball clinic will be held Saturday.

To revise cluttered sentences like the one above, restructure to break up long series of nouns. You can also substitute equivalent adjective forms, where such forms exist, or possessives for some of the nouns used as modifiers.

IMPROVED: The Chestnut Hill Fathers' Club's spring baseball clinic for beginning Pony League players will be held Saturday.

Of course, eliminating the passive voice would make this sentence even clearer.

On Saturday, the Chestnut Hill Fathers' Club will hold its spring baseball clinic for beginning Pony League players.

EXERCISE 4

Identify every noun used as a modifier in the following passage. Then revise where necessary to eliminate clumsy or unclear phrasing created by overuse of nouns as modifiers. Try substituting adjective or possessive forms, and rearrange word order where you feel it is indicated.

The student government business management trainee program is extremely popular on campus. The student government donated some of the seed money to begin this management trainee program, which is one of the most successful the university business school has ever offered to undergraduate students. Three core courses must be taken before the student intern can actually begin work. First, there is a management theory course given every spring semester in conjunction with the business school. Then, the following fall semester, students in the trainee program are required to take a course in personnel practices, including employee benefits. Finally, they take a business elective.

During the summer, the student interns are placed in junior management positions in large electronics, manufacturing, or public utility companies. This job experience is considered the most valuable part of the program because it gives students a taste of the work world.

STUDENT WRITER AT WORK

ADJECTIVES AND ADVERBS

Read carefully this draft of an essay, and correct errors in the use of adjectives and adverbs. Check to be sure adjectives modify nouns or pronouns and adverbs modify verbs, adjectives, or other adverbs; make sure the correct comparative and superlative forms are used; and eliminate any overuse of nouns as modifiers. After you have corrected the errors, go over the draft again and, if necessary, revise further to strengthen coherence, unity, and style.

Save the Harp Seals

What do rabbits, minks, foxes, and seals all have in common? Each is a victim of fashion. Many people want to own a fur coat real bad, and for those who can afford it, buying one seems to be a simple decision. This is all fine for the fur coat showroom salesperson who earns a commission on the sale, but what about the original owner of the fur? What about the animal who lost its life so its fur could sit on someone's shoulders? Too many animals have been slaughtered for just this reason, and in some cases the animals are skinned quick before they are even completely dead. Something sure must be done to stop the slaughter of these animals before they become extinct. The harp seal is an example of an animal in grave danger.

The harp seal has suffered a very large reduction in numbers during recent times because hunters have subjected these seals to mass slaughter. The issue is not only that the harp seals are butchered, but also that they are killed in the inhumanest manner possible.

The traditional method uses a gaff, which is a length of wood with a hook at one end and a spike at the other. Using this device, the hunter strikes the seal in the head with the hook. Some people consider this method painlessly; however, sometimes the spike misses the vital spot and the seal, still alive, is skinned by the hunter. Thus the gaff can prove painful indeed. The second method used is clubbing. Hunters who favor this technique use wooden clubs or great iron hooks. Seals often pull in their heads in alarm, covering their skulls with a thick layer of fat. It takes many powerful blows to penetrate the fat and kill the seal.

The seals are being killed in more greater numbers each year, and being killed savagely. Even the existing laws, which are supposed to help save the seals, have no effect. One such law limits the size and weight of the club, but if the clubs are made more lightly the only thing that will change is that more blows will be required to kill the seal. This law does not prevent the killings. Many other regulations are constantly being broken, and the problem of enforcement remains seriously. Meanwhile, the harp seals are the unwilling victims of brutal killings.

When will this mass slaughter end? If strong, immediate action is not taken, it will be too late for the animals. Something must be done quick before the harp seal becomes extinct.

PART 7

Understanding Punctuation and Mechanics

OVERVIEW OF SENTENCE PUNCTUATION

Commas, Semicolons, Colons, Dashes, Parentheses

(Further explanations and examples are located in the sections listed in parentheses after each example.)

SEPARATING INDEPENDENT CLAUSES

▶ *With a Comma and a Coordinating Conjunction*
The year was 2081, and everybody was finally equal. (Kurt Vonnegut, Jr., "Harrison Bergeron") (**27a1**)

▶ *With a Semicolon*
Paul Revere's *The Boston Massacre* is an early example of traditional American protest art; Edward Hicks's later "primitive" paintings are socially conscious art with a religious strain. (**28a**)

▶ *With a Semicolon and a Coordinating Conjunction*
If such a world government is not established by a process of agreement among nations, I believe it will come anyway, and in a much more dangerous form; for war or wars can only result in one power being supreme and dominating the rest of the world by its overwhelming military supremacy. (Albert Einstein, *Einstein on Peace*) (**28b**)

▶ *With a Semicolon and a Conjunctive Adverb*
Thomas Jefferson brought 200 vanilla beans and a recipe for vanilla ice cream back from France; thus, he gave America its all-time favorite ice-cream flavor. (**28c**)

SEPARATING ITEMS IN A SERIES

▶ *With Commas*
Chipmunk, racoon, and *Mugwump* are Native American words. (**27b**)

▶ *With Semicolons*
As ballooning became established, a series of firsts ensued: the first balloonist in the United States was 13-year-old Edward Warren, 1784; the first woman aeronaut was a Madame Thible who, depending on your source, either recited poetry or sang as she lifted

off; the first airmail letter, written by Ben Franklin's grandson, was carried by balloon; and the first bird's eye photograph of Paris was taken by a balloon. (Elaine B. Steiner, *Games*) (**28d**)

SETTING OFF ILLUSTRATIVE MATERIAL

▶ *With a Colon*
Each camper should bring the following: a sleeping bag, a mess kit, a flashlight, and plenty of insect repellent. (**31a1**)

▶ *With a Dash*
Walking to school by myself, losing my first tooth, getting my ears pierced, and starting to wear makeup—these were some of the milestones of my life. (**31b2**)

SETTING OFF NONESSENTIAL ELEMENTS

▶ *With a Single Comma*
His fear increasing, he waited to enter the haunted house. (**27d5**)
What do you think, Margie? (**27d6**)

▶ *With a Pair of Commas*
It was Roger Maris, not Mickey Mantle, who broke Babe Ruth's home run record. (**27d4**)

▶ *With a Pair of Dashes*
Although we are by all odds the most social of all social animals—more interdependent, more attached to each other, more inseparable in our behavior than bees—we do not often feel our conjoined intelligence. (Lewis Thomas, *Lives of a Cell*) (**31b1**)

▶ *With a Single Dash*
They could not afford to jump to conclusions—any conclusions. (Michael Crichton, *The Andromeda Strain*) (**31b1**)

▶ *With Parentheses*
It took Gilbert Fairchild two years at Harvard College (two academic years, from September, 1955, to June, 1957) to learn everything he needed to know. (Judith Martin, *Gilbert: A Comedy of Manners*) (**31c1**)

26

End Punctuation

26a *Using Periods*

Use **periods** to end declarative sentences (statements), mild commands, polite requests, and indirect questions. Also use periods in most familiar abbreviations and in dramatic and poetic references.

(1) *Ending a sentence*

Periods signal the end of a statement, a mild command or polite request, or an indirect question.

Something is rotten in the state of Denmark. (statement)

Be sure to have the oil checked before you start out. (mild command)

When the bell rings, please exit in an orderly fashion. (polite request)

They wondered whether it was safe to go back in the water. (indirect question)

(2)   *Marking an abbreviation*

Periods appear in most abbreviations.

Mrs. Robinson	Captain Newman, M.D.	25 B.C.
Mr. Spock	George McGovern, Ph.D.	N.Y., N.Y., U.S.A.
Ms. J. R. Jones	Sue Barton, R.N.	221b Baker St.
Dr. Kildare	9 P.M.	etc.

Punctuating with Abbreviations That Take Periods

At the End of a Sentence

If the abbreviation ends the sentence, do not add another period.

FAULTY: He promised to be there at 6 A.M..

REVISED: He promised to be there at 6 A.M.

However, do add a question mark after the abbreviation's final period if the sentence is a question.

Did he arrive at 6 P.M.?

Within a Sentence

If the abbreviation falls within a sentence, use normal punctuation after the abbreviation's final period.

FAULTY: He promised to be there at 6 P.M. but he forgot his promise.

REVISED: He promised to be there at 6 P.M., but he forgot his promise.

Acronyms   **Acronyms**—new words formed from the initial letters or first few letters of a series of words—do not include periods.

NATO	radar	OSHA	scuba
NOW	VISTA	SALT	CAT scan

Fannie Mae (Federal National Mortgage Association)
Gestapo (Geheime Staats Polizei)
Modem (modulator demodulator)

Frequently used capital-letter abbreviations   Familiar abbreviations of names of corporations, government agencies, and scientific and technical terms do not require periods.

CIA	NYU	IBM	FBI	WCAU-FM
EPA	CCC	DNA	IRA	AFT
MGM	RCA	HBO	UCLA	UFO

Shortened forms of words   Do not use a period after commonly accepted shortened forms of words (gym, dorm, math, and so on) or after abbreviations that do not require them. If you are unsure whether or not to use a period with a particular abbreviation, consult a good college dictionary.

(3)   Marking divisions in dramatic and poetic references

Periods separate act, scene, and line references in plays, and book and line references in long poems.

DRAMATIC REFERENCE   **POETIC REFERENCE**

Long Day's Journey into Night   *Paradise Lost* VII.163–67.
II.ii.1–5 (or 2.2.1–5.)

E X E R C I S E   1

Correct these sentences by adding missing periods and deleting superfluous ones. If a sentence is correct, mark it with a C.

EXAMPLE: Their mission changed the war

Their mission changed the war.

1. Julius Caesar was killed in 44 B.C.
2. Dr. McLaughlin worked hard to earn his Ph.D..
3. Carmen was supposed to be at A.F.L.-C.I.O. headquarters by 2 P.M.; however, she didn't get there until 10 P.M.
4. After she studied the fall lineup proposed by N.B.C., she decided to work for C.B.S.
5. Representatives from the U.M.W. began collective bargaining after an unsuccessful meeting with Mr. L Pritchard, the coal company's representative.

26b *Using Question Marks*

Use **question marks** at the end of direct questions to indicate questionable dates or numbers.

(1) Marking the end of a direct question

Use a question mark to signal the end of a direct question.

Who was that masked man? (direct question)

Who was it who asked, "Who was that masked man?" (question within a question)

Did he say where he came from, who his companion was, or where they were headed? (series of direct questions)

Did he say where he came from? Who his companion was? Where they were headed? (series of direct questions with each question asked separately)

Did he say where he came from? who his companion was? where they were headed? (series of direct questions; informal usage does not require capitalization of first word of each question)

"Is this a silver bullet?" they asked. (declarative sentence opening with a direct question)

They asked, "Could he have been the Lone Ranger?" (declarative sentence closing with a direct question)

NOTE: A pair of dashes or a pair of parentheses is used around a direct question within a declarative sentence.

Someone—a disgruntled office seeker?—is sabotaging the campaign.

Part of the shipment (three dozen cases?) was delayed.

(2) Marking questionable dates or numbers

Use a question mark in parentheses to indicate that a date or number is uncertain.

Aristophanes, the Greek author of satirical comic dramas, was born in 448 (?) B.C. and died in 380 (?) B.C.

The clock struck five (?) and stopped.

(3) Editing misused or overused question marks

Question marks are not used in the following situations:

After an Indirect Question   An indirect question calls for a period only.

> FAULTY: The personnel officer asked whether he knew how to type?
> REVISED: The personnel officer asked whether he knew how to type.

With Other Punctuation   A question mark is not used along with an exclamation point, comma, semicolon, or period.

> FAULTY: "Can it be true?," he asked.
> REVISED: "Can it be true?" he asked.
> FAULTY: Can you believe this run of good luck?!
> REVISED: Can you believe this run of good luck?

With Another Question Mark   It is incorrect to end a sentence with more than one question mark.

> FAULTY: You did what?? Are you crazy??
> REVISED: You did what? Are you crazy?

As an Indication of Attitude   Question marks are not used to convey sarcasm. Instead, suggest your attitude through word choice.

> FAULTY: I refused his generous (?) offer.
> REVISED: I refused his not-very-generous offer.

In an Exclamation   A question mark is not used after an exclamation phrased as a question.

> FAULTY: Will you please stop that at once?
> REVISED: Will you please stop that at once!

EXERCISE 2

Correct the use of question marks and other punctuation in the following sentences.

> EXAMPLE: She asked whether Freud's theories were accepted during his lifetime?
>
>   She asked whether Freud's theories were accepted during his lifetime.

1. He wondered whether he should take a nine o'clock class? Or would that be too early?
2. The instructor asked, "Was the Spanish-American War a victory for America?"?

3. Are they really going to China??!!
4. He took a modest (?) portion of dessert—half a pie.
5. "Is *data* the plural of *datum?*," he inquired.

26c *Using Exclamation Points*

Use an **exclamation point** is used to convey strong feeling—astonishment, drama, shock, and the like—at the end of an emphatic statement, interjection, or command.

(1) Marking emphasis

Use an exclamation point to signal the end of an emotional or emphatic statement, an emphatic interjection, or a forceful command.

Remember the Maine**!**

No**!** Don't leave**!**

Finish this job at once**!**

NOTE: An exclamation point can follow a complete sentence ("What big teeth you have!") or a phrase ("What big teeth!")

(2) Editing misused or overused exclamation points

Except for recording dialogue, exclamation points are almost never appropriate in college writing. Use exclamation points sparingly, even in informal writing. Too many exclamation points give readers the impression that you are overwrought, even hysterical. Exclamation points should not be used in the following situations:

With Mild Statements   Exclamation points are not used with mildly emphatic statements or with mild interjections or commands.

Please close the door behind you**.**

Stand by your man**.**

With Another Exclamation Point   It is incorrect to end a sentence with more than one exclamation point.

FAULTY: I could hardly believe my eyes!!!
REVISED: I could hardly believe my eyes**!**

With Other Punctuation   An exclamation point is not used along with a comma, period, semicolon, or question mark.

FAULTY: "Fire!," he shouted.
REVISED: "Fire!" he shouted.
FAULTY: You can't be serious?!
REVISED: You can't be serious!

As an Indication of Attitude   Do not use an exclamation point to suggest sarcasm or humor. Use word choice and sentence structure instead.

FAULTY: The team's record was a near-perfect (!) 0 and 12.
REVISED: The team's record was a far-from-perfect 0 and 12.

EXERCISE 3

Correct the use of exclamation points and other punctuation in these sentences.

EXAMPLE: "My God," she cried. "I've been shot!!!"

"My God," she cried. "I've been shot!"

1. Are you kidding?! I never said that.
2. When the cell divided, each of the daughter cells had an extra chromosome!
3. This is fantastic. I can't believe you bought this for me.
4. Wow. Just what I always wanted. A pink Cadillac.
5. "Eureka!," cried Archimedes as he sprang from his bathtub.

EXERCISE 4

Add appropriate punctuation to this passage.

Dr Craig and his group of divers paused at the shore, staring respectfully at the enormous lake Who could imagine what terrors lay beneath its surface Which of them might not emerge alive from this adventure Would it be Col Cathcart Capt Wilks, the MD from the naval base Her husband, P L Fox Or would they all survive the task ahead Dr Craig decided some encouraging remarks were in order

"Attention divers" he said in a loud, forceful voice "May I please have your attention The project which we are about to undertake—"

"Oh, no" screamed Mr Fox suddenly "Look out It's the Loch Ness Monster"

"Quick" shouted Dr Craig "Move away from the shore" But his warning came too late

The Comma

Use Commas ...

- To set off independent clauses **(27a)**
- To set off items in a series **(27b)**
- To set off introductory elements **(27c)**
- To set off nonessential elements **(27d)**
- In other conventional contexts **(27e)**
- To prevent misreading **(27f)**

27a *Setting Off Independent Clauses*

(1) *Comma plus coordinating conjunction*

Use a comma when you form a compound sentence by linking two independent clauses with a **coordinating conjunction** *(and, but, or, nor, for, yet, so)*.

> The year was 2081, and everybody was finally equal. (Kurt Vonnegut, Jr., "Harrison Bergeron")

> The bride was not young, nor was she very pretty. (Stephen Crane, "The Bride Comes to Yellow Sky")

No matter how many independent clauses a compound sentence has, use a comma before each coordinating conjunction.

> She had bonny children, yet she felt they had been thrust upon her, and she could not love them. (D. H. Lawrence, "The Rocking Horse Winner")

Use a comma after the first clause when correlative conjunctions link two independent clauses (**see 21g**).

Just as it's fascinating to find out where your barber gets his hair cut
or what the top chef eats, so it can be worthwhile to find out how top
brokers invest their own money. *(Money)*

NOTE: You may omit the comma if two clauses connected by a
coordinating conjunction are very short.

Seek and ye shall find.

Love it or leave it.

(2) Substituting a semicolon

You may use a semicolon—not a comma—to separate two clauses
linked by a coordinating conjunction when one or more of the
independent clauses already contains commas.

See
28b

> The tour visited Melbourne, the capital of Australia; and it continued
> on to Wellington, New Zealand.

You may also use a semicolon when one or more clauses are especially complex or when the second clause stands in sharp contrast
to the first.

> Helena wanted to marry her sister's brother-in-law in an elaborate
> outdoor wedding on June 24; but her parents thought she should wait
> until she turned 21 in September. (complex clauses)

> The advent of T.V. has increased the false values ascribed to reading,
> since T.V. provides a vulgar alternative. But this piety is silly; and
> most reading is no more cultural nor intellectual nor imaginative than
> shooting pool or watching *What's My Line?* (Donald Hall, "Four
> Kinds of Reading") (contrasting clauses)

In the sentences above, you could delete the coordinating conjunctions that follow the semicolons; however, using both makes the
separation between the clauses more emphatic.

EXERCISE 1

Combine each of the following sentence pairs into one compound sentence,
adding commas where necessary.

EXAMPLE: Emergency medicine became an approved medical specialty in 1979. Now pediatric emergency medicine is
become increasingly important. (and)

Emergency medicine became an approved medical specialty in 1979, and now pediatric emergency medicine is becoming increasingly important.

1. The Pope did not hesitate to vist his native Poland. He did not hesitate to meet with Solidarity leader Lech Walesa. (nor)
2. Agents place brand name products in prominent positions in films. The products will be seen and recognized by large audiences. (so)
3. Unisex insurance rates may have some drawbacks for women. They may be very beneficial. (or)
4. Cigarette advertising no longer appears on television. It does appear in print media. (but)
5. Dorothy Day founded the Catholic Worker movement over fifty years ago. Today her followers still dispense free food, medical care, and legal advice to the needy. (and)

27b *Setting Off Items in a Series*

(1) *Coordinate elements*

Use commas with three or more coordinate elements (words, phrases, or clauses in a series).

Chipmunk, raccoon, and *Mugwump* are Native American words. (series of words)

She is a child of her age, of depression, of war, of fear. (Tillie Olsen, "I Stand Here Ironing") (series of phrases)

Brazilians speak Portugese, Colombians speak Spanish, and Haitians speak French and Creole. (series of clauses)

Revision Close-up

In journalistic writing, the final comma is usually omitted. To avoid ambiguity, however, you should always use a comma between the last two items in a series—before the coordinating conjunction if the series includes one.

AMBIGUOUS

The party was made special by the company, the light from the hundreds of twinkling candles and the excellent hors d'oeuvres.

continued

continued from previous page

REVISED

The party was made special by the company, the light from the hundreds of twinkling candles, and the excellent hors d'oeuvres.

Do not use a comma to introduce or to close a series unless the context requires it.

FAULTY: The evaluators felt the most important criteria were, fat content, presence of artificial ingredients, and taste.

REVISED: The evaluators felt the most important criteria were fat content, presence of artificial ingredients, and taste.

FAULTY: Quebec, Ontario, and Saskatchewan, are three Canadian provinces.

REVISED: Quebec, Ontario, and Saskatchewan are three Canadian provinces.

See
28d NOTE: If phrases or clauses in a series already contain commas, separate the items with semicolons.

(2) Coordinate adjectives

Use a comma between two or more **coordinate adjectives**—adjectives that modify the same word or word group—unless they are joined by a conjunction.

She brushed her long, shining hair.

The fruit was crisp, tart, mellow—in short, good enough to eat.

The baby was tired and cranky and wet. (adjectives joined by conjunctions; no commas needed)

Sometimes several adjectives will all seem to modify the same noun, pronoun, or noun phrase when in fact one or more of them modifies another word or word group. In the sentence *Ten red balloons fell from the ceiling,* for instance, the adjective *red* modifies the noun *balloons,* but the adjective *ten* modifies the word group *red balloons.* In this case, only one adjective modifies the noun; the adjectives are not coordinate, so no comma is used.

NOTE: Numbers—such as *ten* in the example above—are not coordinate with other adjectives.

Tests for Comma Use with Series of Adjectives

1. If you can reverse the order of the adjectives, you need a comma.

She brushed her long, shining hair.

She brushed her shining, long hair.

> **If you cannot, the adjectives are not coordinate, and you should not use a comma.**

Ten red balloons fell from the ceiling.

Red ten balloons fell from the ceiling.

2. If you can insert *and* between the adjectives without changing the meaning of the sentence, use a comma.

She brushed her long, shining hair.

She brushed her long and shining hair.

> **If you cannot, the adjectives are not coordinate, and you should not use a comma.**

Ten red balloons fell from the ceiling.

Ten and red balloons fell from the ceiling.

E X E R C I S E   2

Correct the use of commas in the following sentences, adding or deleting commas where necessary. If a sentence is punctuated correctly, mark it with a C.

EXAMPLE: Neither dogs snakes bees nor dragons frighten her.

Neither dogs, snakes, bees, nor dragons frighten her.

1. Seals, whales, dogs, lions, and horses, are all mammals.
2. Mammals are warm-blooded vertebrates that bear live young, nurse them, and usually have fur.
3. Seals are mammals but lizards, and snakes, and iguanas are reptiles, and newts and salamanders are amphibians.
4. Amphibians also include frogs, and toads.
5. Eagles and geese and ostriches and turkeys chickens and ducks are classified as birds.

EXERCISE 3

Add two coordinate adjectives to modify each of the following combinations, inserting commas where required.

EXAMPLE: classical music

strong, beautiful classical music

1. distant thunder
2. silver spoon
3. New York Yankees
4. doll house
5. Rolling Stones

6. loving couple
7. computer science
8. wheat bread
9. art museum
10. new math

27c   *Setting Off Introductory Elements*

Use a comma to separate introductory elements from the rest of the sentence.

(1)   Introductory adverb clauses

Introductory adverb clauses, including elliptical adverb clauses (**see 8d2**), are generally set off from the rest of the sentence by commas.

Although the CIA used to call undercover agents *penetration agents,* they now routinely refer to them as *moles.*

When war came to Beirut and Londonderry and Saigon, the victims were the children.

While [he was] working in the mines, Paul longed for a better life.

If the adverb clause is short, you may omit the comma—*provided the sentence will be clear without it.*

When I exercise I drink plenty of water.

NOTE: When an adverb clause falls at the *end* of a sentence, no comma separates it from the independent clause (**see 27g7**).

(2)   Introductory phrases

Introductory phrases are usually set off from the rest of the sentence by commas.

Thinking that this might be his last chance, Scott struggled toward the Pole. (introductory participial phrase)

To succeed in a male-dominated field, women engineers must work extremely hard. (introductory infinitive phrase)

During the worst days of the Depression, movie attendance rose dramatically. (introductory prepositional phrase)

Revision Close-up

Commas do not follow gerunds and gerund phrases that serve as subjects rather than modifiers.

FAULTY: Laughing out loud, can release tension.

REVISED: Laughing out loud can release tension.

If the introductory phrase is short and no ambiguity is possible, you may omit the comma.

For the first time Clint felt truly happy.

After the exam I took a four-hour nap.

(3) *Introductory transitional expressions*

When they begin a sentence, conjunctive adverbs or other transitional expressions are usually set off from the rest of the sentence with commas.

Originally, the pleats in the cummerbunds worn with tuxedos were designed to conceal theater tickets.

Fortunately, Ralph got up the nerve to propose. Unfortunately, Alice turned him down.

E X E R C I S E   4

Add commas in this paragraph where they are needed to set off an introductory element from the rest of the sentence.

Once upon a time European "welfare states" supported ambitious social welfare programs. However these same governments today are having economic problems that are forcing them to seriously limit their social-welfare spending. In countries like Holland, Great Britain, and Germany unexpected economic and demographic conditions have forced governments to spend less. For instance longer life expectancies have made health care and old-age pensions more costly. In addition the declining birthrate has left fewer people to support the programs with tax revenues. Finally unemployed workers are placing a strain on unemployment insurance and disability insurance funds. Burdened by the increasing costs but unwilling to abandon social programs the nations of Western Europe are unable to invest in new businesses or industry. Because the governments cannot generate sufficient revenue to support them many programs are in serious trouble. (Adapted from "The Welfare Crisis," *Newsweek*)

27d Setting Off Nonessential Elements from the Rest of the Sentence

Certain elements at the beginning, middle, or end of a sentence are considered nonessential, or parenthetical. Although these words, phrases, or clauses do contribute to the meaning of the sentence, they are not essential to its meaning.

Designer jeans are a contradiction in terms, like educational television. (Fran Lebowitz)

There is no place I know of, other than the bathtub, where people should not have to worry about manners. (Judith Martin)

Commas should mark the boundaries of nonessential elements to keep them from blending into the rest of the sentence. (If the nonessential element falls at the beginning or end of a sentence, only one comma sets it off.)

(1) Nonrestrictive modifiers

Modifying phrases or clauses may be restrictive or nonrestrictive.

Restrictive modifiers limit the meaning of the word or word group they modify, and they should not be separated from it by commas. Consider the following sentence:

Men who were drafted when war was declared found themselves at a disadvantage.

Who were drafted when war was declared limits the noun *men* to only those who were drafted, and it is therefore *restrictive*. The modifying clause is essential to the meaning in this sentence of *men*, the noun it modifies. Without the modifying clause, the meaning of the sentence would change.

Nonrestrictive modifiers do not limit or particularize the words they modify; they merely supply additional information about them. Therefore, they are nonessential elements that should be set off by commas.

Men, who were drafted when war was declared, found themselves at a disadvantage.

In this sentence, the modifying clause *who were drafted when war was declared,* set off by commas, is nonrestrictive. The modifying clause in this case describes *all* the men, and therefore it is not essential to the meaning of the noun it modifies. Without the modifying clause, the sentence would still be about all the men.

Revision Close-up

Remember, when the modifier *is* essential to the meaning of the word it modifies, do *not* use a comma; when the modifier is *not* essential to the meaning of the word it modifies, *do* use a comma.

As the following examples illustrate, commas set off nonrestrictive modifiers *only*—never restrictive modifiers.

The counterculture hero who created Zap Comix during the 1960's has also had artwork displayed at the Whitney Museum of American Art. (restrictive clause)

Robert Crumb, who created Zap Comix during the 1960's, is credited with popularizing the slogan "Keep on Truckin'." (nonrestrictive clause)

Environmental groups have become much more militant in recent years; now the sincere and passionate demands that such groups make are inspiring recreational campers and the logging industry to mobilize against them. (restrictive clause)

Environmental groups have become much more militant in recent years; now their sincere and passionate demands, which groups like recreational campers and the logging industry oppose, are inspiring controversy. (nonrestrictive clause)

The president hoping to encourage Americans to become more physically fit was Dwight D. Eisenhower. (restrictive phrase)

President Eisenhower, hoping to encourage Americans to become more physically fit, created the President's Council on Youth Fitness. (nonrestrictive phrase)

or

Hoping to encourage Americans to become more physically fit, President Eisenhower created the President's Council on Youth Fitness. (nonrestrictive phrase)

Tests for Determining Whether a Modifier is Restrictive or Nonrestrictive

1. Is the modifier essential to the meaning of the noun it modifies (*The counterculture hero who created Zap Comix*—not just any counterculture hero)? If so, it is restrictive and does not take commas. If not, commas should set off the modifier.
2. Is the modifier introduced by *that (the sincere and passionate demands that such groups make)?* If so, it is restrictive. *That* cannot introduce a nonrestrictive clause.
3. Can you delete the relative pronoun without causing ambiguity or confusion *(the sincere and passionate demands [that] such groups make)?* If so, the clause is restrictive and requires no commas. (A relative pronoun that is not the subject of the relative clause can be deleted if the clause is restrictive. Relative pronouns that introduce nonrestrictive clauses, however, cannot be deleted.)
4. Can you rearrange the sentence so that the modifying phrase or clause precedes the word or word group it modifies *(Hoping to encourage Americans to become more physically fit, President Eisenhower . . .)?* If so, the modifier is nonrestrictive and requires a comma. Restrictive phrases and clauses, on the other hand, nearly always *follow* the words they modify.

Guidelines for Use of *That* and *Which*

That is used to introduce only restrictive clauses.

I bought a used car *that* cost $2000.

Which can be used to introduce both restrictive and nonrestrictive clauses.

RESTRICTIVE: I bought a used car *which* cost $2000.

NONRESTRICTIVE: The used car I bought, *which* cost $2000, broke down after a week.

Many writers, however, prefer to use *which* only to introduce nonrestrictive clauses.

EXERCISE 5

Insert commas where necessary to set off nonrestrictive phrases and clauses.

The Statue of Liberty which was dedicated in 1886 has undergone extensive renovation. Its supporting structure whose designer was the French engineer Alexandre Gustave Eiffel is made of iron. The Statue of Liberty created over a period of nine years by sculptor Frédéric-Auguste Bartholdi stands 151 feet tall. The people of France who were grateful for American help in the French revolution raised the money to pay the sculptor who created the statue. The people of the United States contributing over $100,000 raised the money for the pedestal on which the statue stands.

(2) Nonrestrictive appositives

An **appositive** is a noun or noun phrase that identifies or describes a noun, pronoun, or noun phrase (see 8f4). A **nonrestrictive appositive,** one that provides nonessential information about the word or words it modifies, is set off by commas.

> Steve Howe, relief pitcher for the Los Angeles Dodgers, struggled with a cocaine habit. (Appositive *relief pitcher for the Los Angeles Dodgers* further identifies Howe but is not essential to the meaning of *Steve Howe.*)

An appositive that is essential to the meaning of the word or word group it modifies is, however, **restrictive** and takes no commas.

> Orson Welles's film *Citizen Kane* has received great critical acclaim. (Without the appositive *Citizen Kane,* the sentence would imply that Welles directed only one film; therefore, the appositive is essential to the meaning of *Orson Welles's film* and to the sentence.)

Normally, an appositive is restrictive if it is more specific than the noun that precedes it.

(3) Conjunctive adverbs and other transitional expressions

Conjunctive adverbs—words like *however, therefore, thus,* and *nevertheless*—and **transitional expressions** like *for example* and *on the other hand* qualify, clarify, and make connections explicit, but they are not essential to meaning. ► **See 4d2**

When a conjunctive adverb or transitional expression interrupts a clause, it is set off by commas.

The House Ethics Committee recommended reprimanding two members of Congress. The House, <u>however,</u> overruled the recommendation and voted to censure them.

The Outward Bound program, <u>according to its staff,</u> is extremely safe.

A conjunctive adverb or similar expression at the end of a clause is still parenthetical, and it is separated from the rest of the sentence by a single comma.

Some things were easier after school started. Other things were a lot harder, <u>however.</u>

These transitional expressions are also usually set off by commas when they introduce a sentence (see **27c3**).

Revision Close-up

When a conjunctive adverb or transitional expression separates two independent clauses, it must be preceded by a semicolon or a period and followed by a comma **(see 28c).**

Laughter is the best medicine; of course, penicillin also comes in handy sometimes.

---

(4)   Contradictory phrases

A parenthetical phrase that expresses contrast is usually set off from the rest of the sentence by commas.

This medication should be taken after a meal, <u>never on an empty stomach.</u>

It was Roger Maris, <u>not Mickey Mantle,</u> who broke Babe Ruth's home run record.

(5)   Absolute phrases

An **absolute phrase** usually consists of a noun plus a participle. An absolute phrase is always set off by commas from the sentence it modifies.

<u>His fear increasing,</u> he waited to enter the haunted house.

A number of soldiers have vanished in Southeast Asia, <u>their bodies never recovered.</u>

If the participle is a form of *be,* however, it may be omitted (see **8f3**).

(6) Miscellaneous nonessential elements

Wherever they appear, certain nonessential elements are usually separated from the rest of the sentence by commas.

Tag Questions (Auxiliary Verb + Pronoun Added to a Statement)

This is your first day on the job, isn't it?

It seems possible, does it not, that carrots may provide some protection against cancer?

Names in Direct Address

I wonder, Mr. Honeywell, whether Mr. Albright deserves a raise.

Freddie, what's your opinion?

What do you think, Margie?

Mild Interjections

Well, it's about time.

NOTE: Stronger interjections may be set off by dashes or exclamation points (see 31b and 26c1).

Yes and No

Yes, we have no bananas.

No, we're all out of lemons.

EXERCISE 6

Set off the nonessential elements in these sentences with commas. If a sentence is correct, mark it with a C.

EXAMPLE: Piranhas like sharks will attack and eat almost anything if the opportunity arises.

Piranhas, like sharks, will attack and eat almost anything if the opportunity arises.

1. Kermit the frog is a muppet a cross between a marionette and a puppet.
2. The common cold a virus is frequently spread by hand contact not by mouth.
3. The account in the Bible of Noah's Ark and the forty-day flood may be based on an actual deluge.

453

4. More than two-thirds of U.S. welfare recipients, such as children, the aged, the severely disabled, and mothers of children under six, are people with legitimate reasons for not working.

5. The submarine *Nautilus* was the first to cross under the North Pole wasn't it?

6. The 1958 Ford Edsel was advertised with the slogan "Once you've seen it, you'll never forget it."

7. Superman was called Kal-El on the planet Krypton; on earth however he was known as Clark Kent not Kal-El.

8. Its sales topping any of his previous singles Elvis Presley's "Heart-break Hotel" was his first million seller.

9. Two companies Nash and Hudson joined in 1954 to form American Motors.

10. A firefly is a beetle not a fly and a prairie dog is a rodent not a dog.

27e *Using Commas in Other Conventional Contexts*

(1) *Around direct quotations*

In most cases, use commas to set off a direct quotation from the **identifying tag**—the phrase that identifies the speaker *(he said, she answered)*.

Emerson said to Thoreau, "I greet you at the beginning of a great career."

"I greet you at the beginning of a great career," Emerson said to Thoreau.

"I greet you," Emerson said to Thoreau, "at the beginning of a great career."

When the identifying tag comes between two complete sentences, however, the tag is introduced by a comma but followed by a period.

"Winning isn't everything," Vince Lombardi said. "It's the only thing."

If the first sentence of an interrupted quotation ends with a question mark or exclamation point, do not use commas.

"Should we hold the front page?" she asked. "After all, nothing much has happened this week."

See ◄
30f "Hold the front page!" he cried. "This is the biggest story of the decade."

(2) Between names and titles or degrees

Use a comma to set off a person's name from his or her title or degree.

Charles, Prince of Wales

Martin Luther King, Jr., Ph.D.

If the title or degree precedes the name, however, no comma is required.

Dr. Martin Luther King, Jr.

Prince Charles

No comma is used between a name and II, III, and so on.

Queen Elizabeth II

Andrew Bott III

(3) In dates and addresses

Use commas to separate items in dates and addresses.

August 9, 1975 (9 August 1975—no commas—also acceptable)

600 West End Avenue, New York, NY 10024

With hundreds watching, the space shuttle *Challenger* was launched on August 30, 1983, from Cape Canaveral, Florida.

NOTE: Commas are not used to separate the day from the month; when only the month and year are given, no commas are used (May 1968). No comma separates the street number from the street or the state name from the zip code. When a date or address punctuated with commas appears within a sentence, a comma follows its last element.

(4) In salutations and closings

Use commas in informal correspondence following salutations and closings and following the complimentary close in personal or business correspondence.

Dear John,

Dear Aunt Sophie,

Love,

Sincerely,

NOTE: Keep in mind that in business correspondence a colon, not a comma, always follows the salutation (**see 47a3**).

(5) In long numbers

Use commas with long numbers.

When writing a number of four digits or more, separate the numbers by placing a comma every three digits, counting from the right.

1,200   (comma optional with four digits)

12,000

120,000

1,200,000

Commas are not required in long numbers used in addresses, telephone numbers, zip codes, or years.

E X E R C I S E   7

Add commas where necessary to set off quotations, names, dates, addresses, and numbers in the following sentences.

1. India became independent on August 15 1947.
2. The UAW has over 1500000 dues-paying members.
3. Nikita Krushchev, former Soviet premier, said "We will bury you!"
4. Mount St. Helens, northeast of Portland Oregon, began erupting on March 27 1980 and eventually killed at least thirty people.
5. Located at 1600 Pennsylvania Avenue Washington D.C., the White House is a major tourist attraction.
6. In 1956, playing before a crowd of 64519 fans in Yankee Stadium in New York New York, Don Larsen pitched the first perfect game in World Series history.
7. Lewis Thomas M.D. was born in Flushing N.Y. and attended Harvard Medical School in Cambridge Massachusetts.
8. In 1967 2000000 people worldwide died of smallpox, but in 1977 only about twenty died.
9. "The reports of my death" Mark Twain remarked "have been greatly exaggerated."
10. The French explorer Jean Nicolet landed at Green Bay Wisconsin in 1634, and in 1848 Wisconsin became the thirtieth state; it has 10355 lakes and a population of over 4700000.

27f *Using Commas to Prevent Misreading*

Commas may be needed simply for clarity. Consider the following sentence:

Those who can, sprint the final lap.

Without the comma, *can* appears to be an auxiliary verb ("Those who can sprint....") and the sentence seems incomplete.

Commas that tell readers to pause prevent confusion and ambiguity. Use commas in two special situations.

(1) To indicate an omission

Use a comma to acknowledge the omission of a repeated word, usually a verb.

Pam carried the box; Tim, the suitcase.

Edwina went first; Marco, second.

(2) To separate repeated words

Use a comma to separate words repeated consecutively within a sentence.

Those of you who know me well, know well that I hate to get up in the morning.

Everything bad that could have happened, happened.

E X E R C I S E   8

Add commas where necessary to prevent misreading.

EXAMPLE: Whatever will be will be.

Whatever will be, will be.

1. According to Bob Frank's computer has three disk drives.
2. Da Gama explored Florida; Pizarro Peru.
3. By Monday evening students must begin preregistration for fall classes.
4. Whatever they built they built with care.
5. When batting practice carefully.
6. Brunch includes warm muffins topped with whipped butter and freshly brewed coffee.

EXERCISE 9

Commas have been intentionally deleted from some of the following sentences. Add commas where needed, and be prepared to explain why each is necessary. If a sentence is correct, mark it with a *C*.

1. The world is before you and you need not take it or leave it as it was when you came in.   (James Baldwin, *Nobody Knows My Name*)
2. The great secret known to internists but still hidden from the general public is that most things get better by themselves. Most things in fact are better by morning.   (Lewis Thomas, *Lives of a Cell*)
3. Her face was young and smooth and fresh-looking.   (Katherine Anne Porter, "Rope")
4. He was wearing his cape and had his cap on and he came directly toward my machine and put his arm on my shoulder.   (Ernest Hemingway, "In Another Country")
5. That she was in some way related to the girl though not of an age to be her mother was evident from their manner together.   (Shirley Hazzard, *The Transit of Venus*)
6. Every family is its own country and happy families are no more alike than peaceful nations.   (Frances Taliaferro, *Harper's*)
7. The downtown square is a brisk trading area its broad avenue resolving into a central square which framed by three-story buildings seems as though it is entirely walled.   (Joan Chase, *During the Reign of the Queen of Persia*)
8. It had rained long and hard during the night and an early morning mist drifted over Lake Placid. Tumbling low clouds covered the tops of the mountains that ringed the lake totally obscuring Whiteface highest of the peaks.   (Bernard F. Conners, *Dancehall*)
9. Dandelions crabgrass Queen Anne's lace lamb's quarters sheep sorrel and even bluegrass are but a small sample of a large constellation of alien plant species that have been assimilated into the ecology of North America.   (John C. Kricher, *Natural History*)
10. Oh I know intellectually that people have been circling the earth for centuries and there's nothing to it.   (Russell Baker, *New York Times Magazine*)

27g   *Editing Misused or Overused Commas*

Do not use commas ...

- Between two independent clauses **(27g1)**
- Around restrictive elements **(27g2)**

- Between inseparable grammatical constructions **(27g3)**
- Between a verb and a dependent clause to set off indirect quotations or indirect questions **(27g4)**
- Between coordinate phrases that contain correlative conjunctions **(27g5)**
- Between certain paired elements **(27g6)**
- Before an adverb clause at the end of a sentence **(27g7)**

(1) Between two independent clauses

Using a comma alone to connect two independent clauses creates a comma splice (see **Ch. 14**).

FAULTY: The season was unusually cool, nevertheless the orange crop was not seriously harmed.

REVISED: The season was unusually cool; nevertheless, the orange crop was not seriously harmed.

REVISED: The season was unusually cool. Nevertheless, the orange crop was not seriously harmed.

REVISED: The season was unusually cool, but the orange crop was not seriously harmed.

REVISED: Although the season was unusually cool, the orange crop was not seriously harmed.

(2) Around restrictive elements

Commas are not used to set off restrictive elements (see **27d1–2**).

FAULTY: Women, who seek to be equal to men, lack ambition.

REVISED: Women who seek to be equal to men lack ambition.

FAULTY: The film, *Wild at Heart,* was directed by David Lynch.

REVISED: The film *Wild at Heart* was directed by David Lynch.

FAULTY: They planned a picnic, in the park.

REVISED: They planned a picnic in the park.

FAULTY: The word, *snafu,* is an acronym for "situation normal—all fouled up."

REVISED: The word *snafu* is an acronym for "situation normal—all fouled up."

(3) Between inseparable grammatical constructions

A comma should not be placed between a subject and its predicate; a verb and its complement or direct object; a preposition and its object; or an adjective and the noun, pronoun, or noun phrase it modifies. Placing a comma between such constructions interrupts the logical flow of a sentence.

FAULTY: We think that anyone who can walk a straight line out of the office before lunch, ought to be able to travel the same route on the way back. (Advertisement, Spirits Council of the United States) (comma between subject and predicate)

REVISED: We think that anyone who can walk a straight line out of the office before lunch ought to be able to travel the same route on the way back.

FAULTY: Louis Braille developed, an alphabet of raised dots for the blind. (comma between verb and object)

REVISED: Louis Braille developed an alphabet of raised dots for the blind.

FAULTY: They relaxed somewhat during, the last part of the obstacle course. (comma between preposition and object)

REVISED: They relaxed somewhat during the last part of the obstacle course.

FAULTY: Wind-dispersed weeds include the well-known and plentiful, dandelions, milkweed, and thistle. (comma between adjective and words it modifies)

REVISED: Wind-dispersed weeds include the well-known and plentiful dandelions, milkweed, and thistle.

(4) Between a verb and a dependent clause to set off indirect quotations or indirect questions

Commas are not used between verb and dependent clause to set off indirect quotations or indirect questions.

FAULTY: Art Buchwald once said, that the problem with television news is that it has no second page.

REVISED: Art Buchwald once said that the problem with television news is that it has no second page.

FAULTY: The landlord asked, whether we would be willing to sign a two-year lease.

REVISED: The landlord asked whether we would be willing to sign a two-year lease.

(5) Between coordinate phrases that contain correlative conjunctions

Commas are not used between coordinate phrases that contain correlative conjunctions.

FAULTY: As a rule, college students thirty years ago had access to neither photocopiers, nor pocket calculators.

REVISED: As a rule, college students thirty years ago had access to neither photocopiers nor pocket calculators.

FAULTY: Both typewriters, and tape recorders were generally available, however.

REVISED: Both typewriters and tape recorders were generally available, however.

(6) Between certain paired elements

Commas are not used between two elements of a compound subject, predicate, object, complement, or auxiliary verb.

FAULTY: During the Middle Ages plagues, and pestilence were not uncommon. (Comma interrupts compound subject.)

REVISED: During the Middle Ages plagues and pestilence were not uncommon.

FAULTY: Women students age thirty-five and older are returning to college in large numbers, and tend to be very good students. (Comma interrupts compound predicate.)

REVISED: Women students age thirty-five and older are returning to college in large numbers and tend to be very good students.

FAULTY: Mattel has marketed a doctor's uniform, and an astronaut suit for its Barbie doll. (Comma interrupts compound object.)

REVISED: Mattel has marketed a doctor's uniform and an astronaut suit for its Barbie doll.

FAULTY: Bottled water appeals to many who believe it is pure, and fashionable. (Comma interrupts compound complement.)

REVISED: Bottled water appeals to many who believe it is pure and fashionable.

FAULTY: She can, and will be ready to run in the primary. (Comma interrupts compound auxiliary verb.)

REVISED: She can and will be ready to run in the primary.

REVISED: She can, and will, be ready to run in the primary.

461

(7) Before an adverb clause that falls at the end of a sentence

Commas are not used before an adverb clause that falls at the end of a sentence.

FAULTY: Jane Addams founded Hull House, because she wanted to help Chicago's poor.

REVISED: Jane Addams founded Hull House because she wanted to help Chicago's poor.

EXERCISE 10

Unneeded commas have been intentionally added to some of the sentences that follow. Delete any unnecessary commas. If a sentence is correct, mark it with a C.

EXAMPLE: Spring fever, is a common ailment.

Spring fever is a common ailment.

1. A book is like a garden, carried in the pocket. (Arab proverb)
2. Like the iodine content of kelp, air freight, is something most Americans have never pondered. *(Time)*
3. Charles Rolls, and Frederick Royce manufactured the first Rolls Royce Silver Ghost, in 1907.
4. The hills ahead of him were rounded domes of grey granite, smooth as a bald man's pate, and completely free of vegetation. (Wilbur Smith, *Flight of the Falcon*)
5. Food here is scarce, and cafeteria food is vile, but the great advantage to Russian raw materials, when one can get hold of them, is that they are always fresh and untampered with. (Andrea Lee, *Russian Journal*)

EXERCISE 11

In the following passage, punctuation errors have been deliberately made. Delete excess commas, and add any necessary ones. Be prepared to justify your revisions.

The most famous wild elephant in the world, lived in the mountain forest of Marsabit, in Kenya, and was called Ahmed. He was remarkable, for the beauty of his tusks. They descended, almost to the ground, in a graceful curve and their slender points were sharp, at the tip, and slightly raised. Ahmed was protected, from danger by special presidential decree. He was a symbol, of all the remaining animals running wild in Kenya and as such he was of some importance to both the science, and the business of supervising elephants. It would have been a very serious matter, if the president's wishes had been ignored, and Ahmed had been poached. Everywhere he went through the forest of Marsabit he was followed, by two armed forest rangers. When he left the safety of the mountain reserve, and wandered off into the surrounding desolation, his guards went, too. Because of this his position was always known, to the local authorities, and he became accustomed to people. He was very easy to photograph and every tourist, who came to Marsabit, wanted to see him. Thousands of visitors even made the uncomfortable trek, hundreds of miles away from their usual haunts, in order to view this singular beast.

But one night, in 1974, Ahmed died.   (Adapted from Patrick Marnham, *Harper's*)

The Semicolon

The **semicolon** is weaker than the period and stronger than the comma. It signals a shorter pause than the period but a longer pause than the comma. The semicolon is used only between items of equal grammatical rank: two independent clauses, two phrases, and so on.

Use Semicolons...

- To separate independent clauses **(28a)**
- To separate complex, internally punctuated clauses **(28b)**
- To separate clauses containing conjunctive adverbs **(28c)**
- To separate items in a series **(28d)**

28a   *Separating Independent Clauses*

Use a semicolon rather than a coordinating conjunction or a period between independent clauses that are closely related in meaning.

Paul Revere's *The Boston Massacre* is an early example of traditional American protest art; Edward Hicks's later "primitive" paintings are socially conscious art with a religious strain. (clauses related by contrast)

Separate sentences marked by periods would be correct but would fail to convey the close relationships between the clauses.

Revision Close-up

Using only a comma or no punctuation at all between independent clauses will produce a comma splice or a fused sentence **(see Chapter 14)**.

28b *Separating Complex, Internally Punctuated Clauses*

Use a semicolon instead of a comma between two clauses joined by a coordinating conjunction if one clause contains internal punctuation or is long or complex.

The semicolon in the following sentence not only distinguishes the two clauses but also emphasizes the warning at the end by isolating it:

> If such a world government is not established by a process of agreement among nations, I believe it will come anyway, and in a much more dangerous form; for war or wars can only result in one power being supreme and dominating the rest of the world by its overwhelming military supremacy. (Albert Einstein, *Einstein on Peace*)

EXERCISE 1

Add semicolons, periods, or commas plus coordinating conjunctions where necessary to separate independent clauses. Reread the paragraph when you have finished to make certain no comma splices or fused sentences remain.

EXAMPLE: *Birth of a Nation* was one of the earliest epic movies it was based on the book *The Klansman*.

Birth of a Nation was one of the earliest epic movies; it was based on the book *The Klansman*.

During the 1950's movie attendance declined because of the increasing popularity of television. As a result, numerous gimmicks were introduced to draw audiences into theaters. One of the first of these was Cinerama, in this technique three pictures were shot side by side and projected on a curved screen. Next came 3-D, complete with special glasses, *Bwana Devil* and *The Creature from the Black Lagoon* were two early 3-D ventures. *The Robe* was the first picture filmed in Cinemascope in this technique a shrunken image was projected on a screen twice as wide as it was tall. Smell-O-Vision (or Aroma-rama) was a short-lived gimmick that enabled audiences to smell what they were viewing problems developed when it became impossible to get one odor out of the theater in time for the next smell to be introduced. William Castle's *Thirteen Ghosts* introduced special glasses for cowardly viewers who wanted to be able to control what they saw, the red part of the glasses was the "ghost viewer" and the green part was the "ghost remover." Perhaps the ultimate in movie gimmicks accompanied the film *The Tingler* when this film was shown seats in the theater were wired to generate mild electric shocks. Unfortunately, the shocks set off a chain reaction that led to hysteria in the theater. During the 1960's such gimmicks all but disappeared, viewers were able once again to simply sit back and enjoy a movie.

E X E R C I S E   2

Combine each of the following sentence groups into one sentence that contains only two independent clauses. Use a semicolon to join the two clauses. You will need to add, delete, relocate, or change some words; keep experimenting until you find the arrangement that best conveys the sentence's meaning.

EXAMPLE: The Congo River Rapids is a ride at the Dark Continent in Tampa, Florida. Riders raft down the river. They glide alongside jungle plants and animals.

The Congo River Rapids is a ride at the Dark Continent in Tampa, Florida; riders raft down the river, gliding alongside jungle plants and animals.

1. Amusement parks offer exciting rides. They are thrill packed. They flirt with danger.
2. Free Fall is located in Atlanta's Six Flags over Georgia. In this ride, riders travel up a 128-foot-tall tower. They plunge down at 55 miles per hour.
3. In the Sky Whirl riders go 115 feet up in the air and circle about 75 times. This ride is located in Great America. Great America parks are in Gurnee, Illinois, and Santa Clara, California.
4. The Kamikaze Slide can be found at the Wet 'n Wild parks in Arlington, Texas, and Orlando, Florida. This ride is a slide 300 feet long. It extends 60 feet in the air.
5. Parachuter's Perch is another exciting ride. It is found at Great Adventure in Jackson, New Jersey. Its chutes fall at 25 feet per second.
6. Astroworld in Houston, Texas, boasts Greezed Lightnin'. This ride is an 80-foot-high loop. The ride goes from 0 to 60 miles per hour in four seconds and moves forward and backward.
7. The Beast is at Kings Island near Cincinnati, Ohio. The Beast is a wooden roller coaster. It has a 7400-foot track and goes 70 miles per hour. (Adapted from *Seventeen*)

28c *Separating Clauses Containing Conjunctive Adverbs*

Use a semicolon between two closely related independent clauses when the second clause is introduced by a conjunctive adverb or other transitional expression. (For a complete list of such expressions, **see 4d2.**)

> Thomas Jefferson brought 200 vanilla beans and a recipe for vanilla ice cream back from France; <u>thus,</u> he gave America its all-time favorite ice-cream flavor.

Within a clause, the position of a conjunctive adverb or other transitional expression may vary, and so will the punctuation (**see 21e**).

E X E R C I S E   3

Combine each of the following sentence groups into one sentence that contains only two independent clauses. Use a semicolon and the conjunctive adverb or transitional phrase in parentheses to join the two clauses, adding commas within clauses where necessary. You will need to add, delete, relocate, or change some words. There is no one correct version; keep experimenting until you find the arrangement you feel is most effective.

EXAMPLE: The Aleutian Islands are located off the west coast of Alaska. They are an extremely remote chain of islands. They are sometimes called America's Siberia. (in fact)

The Aleutian Islands, located off the west coast of Alaska, are an extremely remote chain of islands; in fact, they are sometimes called America's Siberia.

1. The Aleutians lie between the North Pacific Ocean and the Bering Sea. The weather there is harsh. Dense fog, 100-mile-per-hour winds, and even tidal waves and earthquakes are not uncommon. (for example)
2. These islands constitute North America's largest network of active volcanoes. The Aleutians boast some beautiful scenery. The islands are relatively unexplored. (still)
3. The Aleutians are home to a wide variety of birds. Numerous animals, such as fur seals and whales, are found there. These islands may house the largest concentration of marine animals in the world. (in fact)

467

4. During World War II, thousands of American soldiers were stationed on Attu Island. They were stationed on Adak Island. The Japanese eventually occupied both Attu and Kiska Islands. (however)
5. The islands' original population of native Aleuts was drastically reduced in the eighteenth century by Russian fur traders. Today the total population is only about 8500. The U.S. military and its employees comprise more than half of this. (consequently)   (Adapted from *National Geographic*)

28d   *Separating Items in a Series*

Use semicolons between items in a series when one or more of these items include commas. Without semicolons it may be difficult to distinguish the individual elements in the series.

Three papers are posted on the bulletin board outside the building: a description of the exams; a list of appeal procedures for students who fail; and an employment ad from an automobile factory, addressed specifically to candidates whose appeals are turned down. (Andrea Lee, *Russian Journal*)

As ballooning became established, a series of firsts ensued: the first balloonist in the United States was 13-year-old Edward Warren, 1784; the first woman aeronaut was a Madame Thible who, depending on your source, either recited poetry or sang as she lifted off; the first airmail letter, written by Ben Franklin's grandson, was carried by balloon; and the first bird's-eye photograph of Paris was taken by a balloon. (Elaine B. Steiner, *Games*)

Revision Close-up

Even when items in a series are brief, semicolons are required if any element in the series contains commas or other internal punctuation.

Laramie, Wyoming; Wyoming, Delaware; and Delaware, Ohio were the first three places they visited.

E X E R C I S E   4

Replace commas with semicolons where necessary to separate internally punctuated items in a series.

EXAMPLE: Luxury automobiles have some strong selling points: they are status symbols, some, such as the Corvette, appreciate in value, and they are usually comfortable and well appointed.

Luxury automobiles have some strong selling points: they are status symbols; some, such as the Corvette, appreciate in value; and they are usually comfortable and well appointed.

1. A quarter of a million Americans marched on Washington in 1983 to commemorate the twentieth anniversary of Dr. King's "I Have a Dream" speech, to remind the government that many Americans, even those who attended the 1963 march, are still without jobs and full equality, and to demonstrate for peace.

2. Steroids, used by some athletes, can be dangerous because they can affect the pituitary gland, causing a lowered sperm count, because they have been linked to the development of liver tumors, and because they can stimulate the growth of some cancers.

3. Tennessee Williams wrote *The Glass Menagerie,* which is about a handicapped young woman and her family, *A Streetcar Named Desire,* which starred Marlon Brando, and *Cat on a Hot Tin Roof,* which won a Pulitzer Prize.

4. New expressions like *outro,* used to designate the segment of a broadcast where the announcer signs off, *heavy breather,* used to describe a popular romance novel, *commuter marriage,* a union in which the partners live and work in different places, and *dentophobe,* a person who is afraid of dentists, are terms which have not yet appeared in most dictionaries.

5. Carl Yastrzemski is the former Red Sox star who replaced Ted Williams in 1961, joining Boston to play left field, who was chosen an all-star eighteen times, and who hit over 450 home runs in his career and was inducted into the Hall of Fame.

EXERCISE 5

Combine each of the following sentence groups into one sentence that includes a series of items separated by semicolons. You will need to add, delete, relocate, or change words. Try several versions of each sentence until you find the most effective arrangement.

EXAMPLE: Collecting baseball cards is a worthwhile hobby. It helps children learn how to bargain and trade. It also encourages them to assimilate, evaluate, and compare data about major league ball players. Perhaps most important, it encourages them to find role models in the athletes whose cards they collect.

Collecting baseball cards is a worthwhile hobby because it helps children learn how to bargain and trade; encourages them to assimilate, evaluate, and compare data about major league ball players; and, perhaps most important, encourages them to find role models in the athletes whose cards they collect.

1. A good dictionary offers definitions of words, including some obsolete and nonstandard words. It provides information about synonyms, usage, and word origins. It also offers information on pronunciation and syllabication.

2. The flags of the Scandinavian countries all depict a cross on a solid background. Denmark's flag is red with a white cross. Norway's flag is also red, but its cross is blue, outlined in white. Sweden's flag is blue with a yellow cross.

3. Over one hundred international collectors' clubs are thriving today. One of these associations is the Cola Clan, whose members buy, sell, and trade Coca-Cola memorabilia. Another is the Citrus Label Society. There is also a Cookie Cutter Collectors' Club.

4. Listening to the radio special, we heard "Shuffle Off to Buffalo" and "Moon Over Miami," both of which are about eastern cities. We heard "By the Time I Get to Phoenix" and "I Left My Heart in San Francisco," which mention western cities. Finally, we heard "The Star-Spangled Banner," which seemed to be an appropriate finale.

5. There are three principal types of contact lenses. Hard contact lenses, also called conventional lenses, are easy to clean and handle and quite sturdy. Soft lenses, which are easily contaminated and must be cleaned and disinfected daily, are less durable. Gas-permeable lenses, sometimes advertised as semihard or semisoft lenses, look and feel like hard lenses but are more easily contaminated and less durable.

28e *Editing Misused and Overused Semicolons*

Some writers use semicolons just because they feel that they are characteristic of a mature style. Others use them for variety. But semicolons are only called for in the contexts outlined in this chapter. In the following situations a semicolon is not used.

(1)   Between items of unequal grammatical rank

A semicolon is not used between a dependent and an independent clause or between a phrase and a clause.

FAULTY: Because new drugs can now suppress the body's immune reaction; fewer organ transplants are rejected by the body. (Semicolon incorrectly used between dependent and independent clause.)

REVISED: Because new drugs can now suppress the body's immune reaction, fewer organ transplants are rejected by the body.

FAULTY: Increasing rapidly; computer crime poses a challenge for government, financial, and military agencies. (Semicolon incorrectly used between phrase and clause.)

REVISED: Increasing rapidly, computer crime poses a challenge for government, financial, and military agencies.

(2)   To introduce a list

Use a colon, not a semicolon, to introduce a list.

FAULTY: The evening news is a battleground for the three major television networks; CBS, NBC, and ABC.

REVISED: The evening news is a battleground for the three major television networks: CBS, NBC, and ABC.

(3)   To introduce a direct quotation

A semicolon is not used to introduce a direct quotation (see 30a).

FAULTY: Marie Antoinette might not have said; "Let them eat cake."

REVISED: Marie Antoinette might not have said, "Let them eat cake."

(4)   To connect a string of clauses

Semicolons should be used selectively. Consider the following paragraph:

Art deco was a reflection of the jazz age of the roaring 1920's and more sober 1930's; at that time it was the dominant style, particularly in the United States. This was an art glorifying the machine; it was inspired by the speed of the automobile and airplane. It found expression in soaring skyscrapers and luxury ocean liners; streamlined statuettes, overstuffed furniture, and jukebox designs; and radio cabinets, toasters, and other kitchen gadgetry. Art deco was motivated by the vibrant energy released at the end of World War I; it was motivated by a faith in mechanized modernity; and it was also inspired by a joy in such new materials as glass, aluminum, polished steel, and shiny chrome.

Although semicolon use in the preceding paragraph is grammatically correct, the string of clauses connected by semicolons creates a monotonous passage. Compare the following paragraph.

Art deco was a reflection of the jazz age of the roaring 1920's and more sober 1930's when it was the dominant style, particularly in the United States. This was an art glorifying the machine and inspired by the speed of the automobile and airplane. It found expression in everything from soaring skyscrapers and luxury ocean liners to streamlined statuettes, overstuffed furniture, jukebox designs, radio cabinets, toasters, and other kitchen gadgetry. Art deco was motivated by the vibrant energy released at the end of World War I; a faith in mechanized modernity; and a joy in such new materials as glass, aluminum, polished steel, and shiny chrome. (William Fleming, *Arts & Ideas*)

EXERCISE 6

Read this paragraph carefully. Then add semicolons where necessary and delete excess or incorrectly used ones, substituting other punctuation where necessary.

Barnstormers were aviators; who toured the country after World War I, giving people short airplane rides and exhibitions of stunt flying, the name *barnstormer* was derived from the use of barns as airplane hangars. Americans' interest in airplanes had all but disappeared after the war; planes had served their function in battle, but when the war ended, most people saw no future in aviation. The barnstormers helped popularize flying; especially in rural areas. Some of them were pilots who had flown in the war; others were just young men with a thirst for adventure. They gave people rides in airplanes, sometimes they charged a dollar a minute. For most passengers, this was their first ride in an airplane, in fact, sometimes it was their first sight of one. In the early 1920's, people grew bored with what the barnstormers had to offer; so groups of pilots began to stage spectacular—but often dangerous—stunt shows. Then, after Lindbergh's 1927 flight across the Atlantic; Americans suddenly needed no encouragement to embrace aviation. The barnstormers had outlived their usefulness; and an era ended. (Adapted from William Goldman, *Adventures in the Screen Trade*)

The Apostrophe

Use an Apostrophe . . .

- To form the possessive case **(29a)**
- To indicate omissions in contractions **(29c)**
- To form plurals **(29d)**

29a *Forming the Possessive Case*

The possessive case indicates ownership, specifically or generally. In English the possessive case of nouns and indefinite pronouns is indicated in two ways: either with a phrase that includes the word *of* (the hands *of* the clock) or with an apostrophe and, in most cases, an -*s* (the clock's hands). Special forms are used to indicate the possessive case of personal pronouns.

▶ See 29b2

(1) Singular nouns and indefinite pronouns

To form the possessive case of singular nouns and indefinite pronouns, add -'*s*.

"The Monk's Tale" is one of Chaucer's *Canterbury Tales.*

When we would arrive at Dan's house was anyone's guess.

(2) Singular nouns ending in -s

To form the possessive case of singular nouns that end in -*s*, add -'*s* in most cases.

473

Reading Henry James's *The Ambassadors* was not Maris's idea of fun.

The class's time was changed to 8 A.M.

However, a few singular nouns that end with an *s* or *z* sound require only an apostrophe in the possessive case. This is because pronouncing the possessive ending as a separate syllable would create an awkward-sounding phrase.

For goodness' sake—are we really required to read both Aristophanes' *Lysistrata* and Thucydides' *History of the Peloponnesian War?*

An apostrophe is not used to form the possessive case of a title that already contains an -'*s* ending; use a phrase instead.

FAULTY: *A Midsummer Night's Dream's* staging
REVISED: the staging of *A Midsummer Night's Dream*

(3) Plural nouns ending in -s

To form the possessive case of regular plural nouns (those that end in -*s* or -*es*), add only an apostrophe.

The Readers' Guide to Periodical Literature is located in the reference section.

Two weeks' severance pay and three months' medical benefits were available to some workers.

The Lopezes' three children are identical triplets.

(4) Irregular plural nouns

To form the possessive case of nouns that have irregular plurals, add -'*s*.

Long after they were gone, the geese's honking could still be heard.

The Children's Hour is a play by Lillian Hellman; *The Women's Room* is a novel by Marilyn French.

The two oxen's yokes were securely attached to the cart.

NOTE: Noun plurals that are not possessive do not use apostrophes (see **29b1**).

(5) Compound nouns or groups of words

To form the possessive case of compound words or of word groups, add -'*s* to the last word.

The editor-in-chief's position is open.

He accepted the Secretary of State's resignation under protest.

This is someone else's responsibility.

(6) Two or more items

To indicate individual ownership of two or more items, add -'s to each item. To indicate joint ownership, add -'s only to the last item.

INDIVIDUAL OWNERSHIP

Ernest Hemingway's and Gertrude Stein's writing styles have some similarities. (Hemingway and Stein have two separate writing styles.)

JOINT OWNERSHIP

Gilbert and Sullivan's operettas include *The Pirates of Penzance* and *H.M.S. Pinafore*. (Gilbert and Sullivan collaborated on both operettas.)

EXERCISE 1

In these examples change the modifying phrases that follow the nouns to possessive forms that precede the nouns.

EXAMPLE: the pen belonging to my aunt
            my aunt's pen

 1. the songs recorded by Ray Charles
 2. the red glare of the rockets
 3. the idea Warren had
 4. the housekeeper Leslie and Rick hired
 5. the first choice of everyone
 6. the dinner given by Harris
 7. furniture designed by William Morris
 8. the climate of Bermuda
 9. the sport the Russells play
10. the role created by the French actress

EXERCISE 2

Wherever possible change each word or phrase in parentheses to its possessive form. In some cases you may have to use a phrase to indicate possession.

EXAMPLE: The (children) toys were scattered all over their (parents) bedroom.

The children's toys were scattered all over their parents' bedroom.

1. Jane (Addams) settlement house was called Hull House.
2. (*A Room of One's Own*) popularity increased with the rise of feminism.
3. The (chief petty officer) responsibilities are varied.
4. Vietnamese (restaurants) numbers have grown dramatically in ten (years) time.
5. (Harold Robbins) and (Jacqueline Susann) popular novels have sold millions of copies.

29b *Omitting the Apostrophe*

An apostrophe is not used with plural nouns that are not possessive or in the possessive case of personal pronouns.

(1) Plural nouns

Noun plurals that are not possessive never include apostrophes.

FAULTY	REVISED
The Thompson's aren't at home.	The Thompsons aren't at home.
The down vest's were very warm.	The down vests were very warm.
The Philadelphia Seventy Sixer's played well.	The Philadelphia Seventy Sixers played well.

(2) Personal pronouns

Personal pronouns never use apostrophes to form the possessive case. Rather, they have special possessive forms—*his, hers, its, ours, yours, theirs,* and *whose*—none of which include apostrophes.

FAULTY	REVISED
This ticket must be your's or her's.	This ticket must be yours or hers.
The next turn is their's.	The next turn is theirs.

The doll had lost it's right eye.

The next great moment in history is our's.

The doll had lost its right eye.

The next great moment in history is ours.

Revision Close-up

Be careful not to confuse the possessive form of the personal pronoun *it*(its) with the contraction *it's* (it is).

EXERCISE 3

In the following sentences, correct any errors in the use of apostrophes to form noun plurals or the possessive case of personal pronouns. If a sentence is correct, mark it with a C.

EXAMPLE: Dr. Sampson's lecture's were more interesting than her's.

Dr. Sampson's lectures were more interesting than hers.

1. The Schaefer's seats are right next to our's.
2. Most of the college's in the area offer computer courses open to outsider's as well as to their own students.
3. The network completely revamped its daytime programming.
4. Is the responsibility for the hot dog concession Cynthia's or your's?
5. Romantic poets are his favorite's.
6. Debbie returned the books to the library, forgetting they were her's.
7. Cultural revolution's do not occur very often, but when they do they bring sweeping change's.
8. Roll-top desk's are eagerly sought by antique dealer's.
9. A flexible schedule is one of their priorities, but it isn't one of our's.
10. Is yours the red house or the brown one?

29c Indicating Omissions in Contractions

Apostrophes are used to mark the omission of letters or numbers in contractions.

(1) Omitted letters

Apostrophes replace omitted letters in frequently used contractions that combine a pronoun and a verb (*he* + *will* = *he'll*) or the elements of a verb phrase (*do* + *not* = *don't*).

Commonly Used Contractions

it's (it is)	let's (let us)
he's (he is)	we've (we have)
who's (who is)	they're (they are)
isn't (is not)	we'll (we will)
wouldn't (would not)	I'm (I am)
couldn't (could not)	we're (we are)
don't (do not)	you'd (you would)
won't (will not)	

Although acceptable in speech and informal writing, contractions are not generally used in college writing except to reproduce dialogue or to create an informal tone deliberately.

Revision Close-up

Be especially careful not to confuse contractions with the possessive forms of personal pronouns **(see 22a3 and 29b2)**.

Contractions versus Possessive Forms

Contractions	*Possessive Forms*
Who's on first?	Whose book is this?
They're playing our song.	Their team is winning.
It's raining.	Its paws were muddy.
You're a real pal.	Your résumé is very impressive

(2) Omitted numbers

In informal writing an apostrophe may be used to represent the century in a year.

Crash of '29   Class of '94   '57 Chevy

In college writing, however, write out the year in full: *the Crash of 1929, the class of 1994, a 1957 Chevrolet.*

EXERCISE 4

In the following sentences correct any errors in the use of standard contractions or personal pronouns. If a sentence is correct, mark it with a C.

EXAMPLE: Who's troops were sent to Korea?

Whose troops were sent to Korea?

1. Its never easy to choose a major; whatever you decide, your bound to have second thoughts.
2. Olive Oyl asked, "Whose that knocking at my door?"
3. Their watching too much television; in fact, they're eyes are glazed.
4. Whose coming along on the backpacking trip?
5. The horse had been badly treated; it's spirit was broken.
6. Your correct in assuming its a challenging course.
7. Sometimes even you're best friends won't tell you your boring.
8. They're training had not prepared them for the hardships they faced.
9. It's too early to make a positive diagnosis.
10. Robert Frost wrote the poem that begins, "Who's woods these are I think I know."

29d *Forming Plurals*

The apostrophe plus -*s* is used to form plurals in some special cases. In these cases adding an -'*s* avoids a confusing combination that might obscure the fact that the word is plural.

Forming Plurals with Apostrophes

Plurals of Letters

The Italian language has no *j*'s or *k*'s.

Sesame Street helps children learn their ABC's.

Plurals of Numbers

Dick Button could make outstanding figure 8's.

Styles of the 1950's are back in fashion.

Many writers prefer to omit the apostrophe with plurals of numbers; either style is acceptable.

---

continued

continued from previous page

Plurals of Symbols

The +'s and -'s indicate positive and negative numbers, respectively.

The entire paper used &'s instead of *and*'s.

Plurals of Abbreviations Followed by Periods

Only two R.N.'s worked the 7-to-11 shift.

Four Ph.D.'s and seven M.D.'s attended the high school reunion.

Plurals of Words Referred to as Words

The supervisor would accept no *if*'s, *and*'s, or *but*'s.

His first sentence contained three *therefore*'s.

Revision Close-up

Letters, numerals, and words spoken of as themselves are always set in italic type **(see 33c)**; the plural ending is further distinguished by being set in Roman type. When you write or type, indicate italics by underlining. If no confusion is possible, you may omit the apostrophe, but you should still use italics where they are required.

The editor deleted all the *4*s in the report.

E X E R C I S E   5

In the following sentences, form correct plurals for the letters, numbers, and words in parentheses. Underline to indicate italics where necessary.

EXAMPLE: The word *bubbles* contains three (b).

The word *bubbles* contains three *b*'s.

1. She closed her letter with a row of (x) and (o) to indicate kisses and hugs.
2. The three (R) are reading, writing, and 'rithmetic.
3. The report included far too many (maybe) and too few (definitely).
4. His (4) and (9) were almost identical, and his (5) looked exactly like (s).
5. Her two (M.A.) were in sociology and history.

Quotation Marks

30a *Setting Off Direct Quotations*

Use quotation marks with **direct quotations** when you reproduce exactly a word, phrase, or brief passage from someone else's speech or writing. You must enclose the borrowed material in a pair of quotation marks.

> Gloria Steinem observed, "We are becoming the men we once hoped to marry."

Do not use quotation marks with **indirect quotations**—that is, when you report someone else's written or spoken words without quoting them exactly.

> Gloria Steinem observed that many women are now becoming the men they once hoped to marry.

Use single quotation marks to enclose a quotation within a quotation.

> Claire said, "It was Liberace who first said, 'I cried all the way to the bank.'"

Special punctuation problems occur when quoted material must be set off from phrases (such as *he said*) that identify its source. The following guidelines cover the most common problems.

(1) An identifying tag in the middle of a passage

Use a pair of commas to set off the identifying tag that interrupts a passage.

"In the future," pop artist Andy Warhol once said, "everyone will be world-famous for 15 minutes."

If the identifying tag follows a completed sentence but the quoted passage continues, use a period after the tag. Begin the new sentence with a capital letter, and place it within quotation marks.

"Be careful," Erin warned. "Reptiles can be tricky."

(2) An introductory identifying tag

Use a comma after the tag that introduces quoted speech or writing.

The Raven repeated, "Nevermore."

When you quote just a word or phrase, however, you may also introduce it without any punctuation.

The meteorologist said he expected March to be "unpredictable."

Use a colon instead of a comma before a long or formal quotation.

The Secretary of State announced: "All American citizens are asked to leave the area immediately. The instability of the military government and the acts of hostility toward Americans make this action necessary."

Use a colon before any quotation, even a brief one, if the introductory tag is an independent clause.

She gave her final answer: "No."

(3) An identifying tag at the end

Use a comma to set off the end of a quotation from the identifying tag that follows.

"Be careful out there," the sergeant warned.

If the quotation ends with a question mark or an exclamation point, however, that punctuation mark replaces the comma. The tag begins with a lower-case letter even though it follows end punctuation.

"Is Ankara the capital of Turkey?" she asked.

"Oh boy!" he cried.

If no identifying tag follows a quotation, use a period or other appropriate end punctuation after the quotation.

The principal said, "Education is serious business."

E X E R C I S E 1

Add single and double quotation marks to these sentences where necessary to set off direct quotations. Then add appropriate punctuation to set off direct quotations from identifying tags. If a sentence is correct, mark it with a C.

EXAMPLE: Wordsworth's phrase splendour in the grass was used as the title of a movie about young lovers.

Wordsworth's phrase "splendour in the grass" was used as the title of a movie about young lovers.

1. Mr. Fox noted Few people can explain what Descartes' words I think, therefore I am actually mean.
2. Gertrude Stein said You are all a lost generation.
3. Freedom of speech does not guarantee anyone the right to yell fire in a crowded theater she explained.
4. Dorothy kept insisting there was no place quite like home.
5. If everyone will sit down the teacher announced the exam will begin.

30b *Setting Off Titles*

Titles of short works and titles of parts of long works are enclosed in quotation marks (other titles are set in italics; **see 33a**).

Titles Requiring Quotation Marks

Articles in magazines, newspapers, and professional journals

"The Case for Syntactic Imagery" (*College English*)

---

continued

continued from previous page

Essays

"Fenimore Cooper's Literary Offenses"

Short stories

"Flying Home"

Short poems (those not divided into numbered sections)

"Daddy"

Songs

"The Star-Spangled Banner"

Chapters or sections of books

"Miss Sharp Begins to Make Friends" (Chapter 10 of *Vanity Fair*)

Speeches

"How to Tell a Story"

Descriptive titles of speeches, such as Kennedy's Inaugural Address, are not enclosed in quotation marks.

Episodes of radio or television series

"Lucy Goes to the Hospital" (*I Love Lucy*)

Single quotation marks indicate a title in a quotation already enclosed in double quotation marks.

I think what she said was, "Play it, Sam. Play 'As Time Goes By.'"

30c *Setting Off Words Used in a Special Sense*

Words used in a special sense are enclosed in quotation marks.

It was clear that adults approved of children who were "readers," but it was not at all clear why this was so. (Annie Dillard, *New York Times Magazine*)

It is often remarked that words are tricky—and that we are all prone to be deceived by "fast talkers," such as high-pressure salesmen, skillful propagandists, politicians or lawyers. (S. I. Hayakawa, "How Words Change Our Lives")

Coinages—invented words—also take quotation marks.

After the twins were born, the station wagon became a "babymobile."

When a word is referred to as a word, however, it is italicized (see 33c).

How do you pronounce *trough*?

Is their name spelled *Smith* or *Smythe*?

Revision Close-up

When you quote a dictionary definition, put the word you are defining in italics and the definition in quotation marks.

To *infer* means "to draw a conclusion"; to *imply* means "to suggest."

EXERCISE 2

Add quotation marks to the following sentences where necessary to set off titles and words. If italics are incorrectly used, substitute quotation marks.

> EXAMPLE: To Tim, social security means a date for Saturday night.
>
> To Tim, "social security" means a date for Saturday night.

1. *First Fig* and *Second Fig* are two of the poems in Edna St. Vincent Millay's *Collected Poems*.
2. In the article Feminism Takes a New Turn, Betty Friedan reconsiders some of the issues first raised in her 1964 book *The Feminine Mystique*.
3. Edwin Arlington Robinson's poem Richard Cory was the basis for the song Richard Cory written by Paul Simon.
4. *Beside* means next to, but *besides* means except.
5. In an essay on *An American Tragedy* published in *The Yale Review*, Robert Penn Warren noted, Theodore Dreiser once said that his philosophy of love might be called Varietism.

30d Editing Misused or Overused Quotation Marks

Although some writers use quotation marks to indicate special attention or emphasis quotation marks should not be used in the following situations.

(1) To convey special emphasis or sarcasm

FAULTY: William Randolph Hearst's "modest" home is a castle called San Simeon.

REVISED: William Randolph Hearst's far-from-modest home is a castle called San Simeon.

(2) To set off nicknames or slang

FAULTY: The former "Lady Di" became the Princess of Wales when she married Prince Charles.

REVISED: The former Lady Diana Spencer became the Princess of Wales when she married Prince Charles.

FAULTY: Dawn is "into" running.

REVISED: Dawn is very involved in running.

Revision Close-up

Do not make the mistake of thinking that quotation marks will make nonstandard or slang terms acceptable in college writing. Avoid substituting nicknames for full names or slang for standard diction.

---

(3) To enclose titles of long works

FAULTY: "War and Peace" is even longer than "Paradise Lost."

REVISED: *War and Peace* is even longer than *Paradise Lost.*

NOTE: Titles of long works are set in italics (see **33a**).

(4) To set off terms being defined

FAULTY: The word "tintinnabulation," meaning the ringing sound of bells, was used by Poe in his poem "The Bells."

REVISED: The word *tintinnabulation,* meaning the ringing sound of bells, was used by Poe in his poem "The Bells."

NOTE: Words that are defined should be italicized (see **33c**).

(5) To set off technical terms

FAULTY: "Biofeedback" is sometimes used to treat migraine headaches.

REVISED: Biofeedback is sometimes used to treat migraine headaches.

(6) To set off the title of a student essay

Do not use quotation marks around the title of your paper, whether it appears on a title page or at the top of the first page.

FAULTY: "Images of Light and Darkness in George Eliot's *Adam Bede*"

REVISED: Images of Light and Darkness in George Eliot's *Adam Bede*

(7) To set off indirect quotations

FAULTY: Freud wondered "what a woman wanted."

REVISED: Freud wondered what a woman wanted.

REVISED: Freud wondered, "What does a woman want?"

EXERCISE 3

In the following paragraph, correct the use of single and double quotation marks to set off direct quotations, titles, and words used in a special sense. Supply the appropriate quotation marks where required, and delete those not required. Be careful not to use quotation marks where they are not necessary.

In her essay 'The Obligation to Endure' from the book "Silent Spring," Rachel Carson writes: As Albert Schweitzer has said, 'Man can hardly even recognize the devils of his own creation.' Carson goes on to point out that many chemicals have been used to kill insects and other organisms which, she writes, are "described in the modern vernacular as pests." Carson believes such "advanced" chemicals, by contaminating our environment, do more harm than good. In addition to "Silent Spring," Carson is also the author of the book "The Sea Around Us." This work, divided into three sections (Mother Sea, The Restless Sea, and Man and the Sea About Him) was published in 1951.

30e Setting Off Dialogue, Long Prose Passages, and Poetry

(1) Dialogue

When you record dialogue, begin a new paragraph for each new speaker. Be sure to enclose the quoted words in quotation marks.

"Sharp on time as usual," Davis said with his habitual guilty grin.

"My watch is always a little fast," Castle said, apologizing for the criticism which he had not expressed. "An anxiety complex, I suppose." (Graham Greene, *The Human Factor*)

Notice that the phrases identifying the speaker (*Davis said, Castle said*) appear in the same paragraph as the speaker's words.

Revision Close-up

When you are quoting several paragraphs of dialogue by one speaker, begin each new paragraph with quotation marks. However, use closing quotation marks only at the end of the *entire quoted passage*, not at the end of each paragraph.

EXERCISE 4

Add appropriate quotation marks to the dialogue in this passage, beginning a new paragraph whenever a new speaker is introduced.

The next time, the priest steered me into the confession box himself and left the shutter back [so] I could see him get in and sit down at the further side of the grille from me. Well, now, he said, what do they call you? Jackie, father, said I. And what's a-trouble to you, Jackie? Father, I said, feeling I might as well get it over while I had him in good humor, I had it all arranged to kill my grandmother.

He seemed a bit shaken by that, all right, because he said nothing for quite a while. My goodness, he said at last, that'd be a shocking thing to do. What put that into your head? Father, I said, feeling very sorry for myself, she's an awful woman. Is she? he asked. What way is she awful? She takes porter, father, I said, knowing well from the way Mother talked of it that this was a mortal sin, and hoping it would make the priest take a more favorable view of my case. Oh, my! he said, and I could see that he was impressed. And snuff, father, said I. That's a bad case, sure enough, Jackie, he said. (Frank O'Connor, "First Confession")

(2) Long prose passages

A prose passage of more than four lines is set off from the body of a paper. Omit quotation marks and indent the text ten spaces from the left-hand margin. Double-space above and below the quotation, and double-space between lines within it. Introduce the passage with a colon.

The following portrait of Aunt Juley illustrates
several of the devices Galsworthy uses throughout The

Forsyte Saga, such as a journalistic detachment that is almost cruel in its scrutiny, a subtle sense of the grotesque, and an ironic stance:

> Aunt Juley stayed in her room, prostrated by the
> blow. Her face, discoloured by tears, was
> divided into compartments by the little ridges
> of pouting flesh which had swollen with
> emotion. . . . At fixed intervals she went to
> her drawer, and took from beneath the lavender
> bags a fresh pocket-handkerchief. Her warm heart
> could not bear the thought that Ann was lying
> there so cold. (329)

Similar characterizations appear throughout the book. . . .

Revision Close-up

When a long prose passage is a single paragraph or less, do not indent the first line. When quoting two or more paragraphs, indent each new paragraph three additional spaces.

If the long passage you are quoting already includes material quoted by the author, enclose those words in double quotation marks.

---

(3) *Poetry*

Three or fewer lines of poetry are treated like a short prose passage—enclosed in quotation marks and run into the text.

One of John Donne's best-known poems begins with the line, "Go and catch a falling star."

Two or more lines of poetry should be separated by a slash (/) (see **31e2**).

Alexander Pope writes, "True Ease in Writing comes from Art, not Chance, / As those move easiest who have learned to dance."

Four or more lines of poetry should be set off like a long prose passage (see **30e2**). For special emphasis, fewer lines may also be set off in this manner. Punctuation, spelling, capitalization, and indentation are reproduced *exactly*.

Wilfred Owen, a poet who was killed in action in
World War I, expressed the horrors of war with vivid
imagery:

> Bent double, like old beggars under sacks.
>
> Knock-kneed, coughing like hags, we cursed
>   through sludge.
>
> Till on the haunting flares we turned our backs
>
> And towards our distant rest began to trudge. (22)

30f Using Quotation Marks with Other Punctuation

Quotation marks frequently occur along with other punctuation marks. Sometimes the quotation marks are placed inside other punctuation, and sometimes they are placed outside.

(1) With final commas or periods

Quotation marks belong *outside* the comma or period at the end of a quotation.

Many, like Frost, think about "the road not taken," but not many really consider where it might have led them.

Janis Joplin sang, "Freedom's just another word for nothing left to lose."

(2) With final semicolons or colons

Quotation marks belong *inside* a semicolon or colon at the end of a quotation.

Students who do not pass the functional-literacy test receive "certificates of completion"; those who pass are awarded diplomas.

Taxpayers were pleased with the first of the candidate's promised "sweeping new reforms": a balanced budget.

(3) With question marks, exclamation points, and dashes

Quotation marks may be placed inside or outside a question mark, exclamation point, or dash at the end of a quotation, depending on the sentence's meaning.

If the question mark, exclamation point, or dash is part of the quotation, place the quotation marks *outside* the punctuation.

"Who's there?" she demanded.

"Stop!" he cried.

"Should we leave now, or—" Vicki paused, waiting for a sign from Joe.

If the question mark, exclamation point, or dash is not part of the quotation, place the quotation marks *inside* the punctuation.

Did you finish reading "The Black Cat"?

Whatever you do, don't yell "Uncle"!

The first essay—George Orwell's "Politics and the English Language"—made quite an impression on the class.

If both the quotation and the tag are questions or exclamations, place the quotation marks *inside* the punctuation.

Who asked, "Is Paris Burning"?

EXERCISE 5

Correct the use of quotation marks in the following sentences, making sure that the use and placement of any accompanying punctuation marks are consistent with accepted conventions. If a sentence is correct, mark it with a C.

EXAMPLE: The "Watergate" incident brought many new terms into the English language.

The Watergate incident brought many new terms into the English language.

1. Kilroy was here and Women and children first are two expressions *Bartlett's Familiar Quotations* attributes to "Anon."
2. Neil Armstrong said he was making a small step for man but a giant leap for mankind.
3. "The answer, my friend", Bob Dylan sang, "is blowin' in the wind".
4. The novel was a real "thriller," complete with spies and counterspies, mysterious women, and exotic international chases.
5. The sign said, Road liable to subsidence; it meant that we should look out for potholes.
6. One of William Blake's best-known lines—To see a world in a grain of sand—opens his poem Auguries of Innocence.

7. In James Thurber's short story The Catbird Seat, Mrs. Barrows annoys Mr. Martin by asking him silly questions like Are you tearing up the pea patch? Are you scraping around the bottom of the pickle barrel? and Are you lifting the oxcart out of the ditch?

8. I'll make him an offer he can't refuse, promised "the godfather" in Mario Puzo's novel.

9. What did Timothy Leary mean by "Turn on, tune in, drop out?"

10. George, the protagonist of Bernard Malamud's short story, A Summer's Reading, is something of an "underachiever."

Other Punctuation Marks

Using Other Punctuation

Use a colon . . .

- To introduce material **(31a)**
- Where convention requires it **(31a)**

Use dashes . . .

- To set off nonessential material **(31b)**
- To introduce a summary **(31b)**
- To indicate an interruption **(31b)**

Use parentheses . . .

- To set off nonessential material **(31c)**
- In other conventional situations **(31c)**

Use brackets . . .

- To set off comments within quotations **(31d)**
- In place of parentheses within parentheses **(31d)**

Use a slash . . .

- To separate one option from another **(31e)**
- To separate lines of poetry run into the text **(31e)**
- To separate the numerator from the denominator in fractions **(31e)**

Use an ellipsis mark . . .

- To indicate an omission in a quotation **(31f)**
- To indicate an omission within verse **(31f)**
- To indicate an unfinished statement **(31f)**

31a *Using Colons*

The **colon** is a strong punctuation mark that points ahead to the rest of the sentence, linking the words that follow it to the words that precede it.

(1) To introduce lists or series

Colons set off lists or series, including those introduced by phrases like *the following* or *as follows.*

> He looked like whatever his beholder imagined him to be: a bank clerk, a high school teacher, a public employee, a librarian, a fussy custodian, an office manager. (Norman Katkov, *Blood and Orchids*)

> Like croup and whooping cough, it was treated with remedies Ida Rebecca compounded from ancient folk-medicine recipes: reeking mustard plasters, herbal broths, dosings of onion syrup mixed with sugar. (Russell Baker, *Growing Up*)

Revision Close-up

A colon introduces a list or series *only* when an independent clause precedes the colon.

FAULTY: Each camper should be equipped with: a sleeping bag, a mess kit, a flashlight, and plenty of insect repellent. (*Each camper should be equipped with* is not a grammatically complete independent clause.)

REVISED: Each camper should bring the following: a sleeping bag, a mess kit, a flashlight, and plenty of insect repellent.

---

(2) To introduce explanatory material

Colons often precede the introduction of material that explains, details, exemplifies, clarifies, or summarizes. They frequently introduce **appositives,** constructions that identify or describe nouns, pronouns, or noun phrases. In such cases, the colon substitutes for a phrase like *for example, namely,* or *that is.*

> For dancers, the call to the dance begins with the body: an accident of birth which, nurtured and sculpted through years of rigorous training, culminates in the coveted invitation to join a professional ballet company. (*New York Times*)

Her hair was the longest and strangest Mrs. Miller had ever seen: absolutely silver-white, like an albino's. (Truman Capote, "Miriam")

Sometimes a colon separates two independent clauses: one general clause and a subsequent, more specific one that illustrates or clarifies the first.

A *U.S. News and World Report* survey has revealed a surprising fact: Americans spend more time at shopping malls than anywhere else except at home and at work.

Revision Close-up

When a complete sentence follows the colon, that sentence may or may not begin with a capital letter. However, if the sentence introduced by a colon is a quotation, its first word is always capitalized, unless it was not capitalized in the source.

---

(3) To introduce quotations

Colons are used to set off quotations that are introduced by a complete independent clause.

The French Declaration of the Rights of Man includes these words: "Liberty consists in being able to do anything that does not harm another person."

With great dignity, Bartleby repeated the words once again: "I prefer not to."

A long quotation is introduced by a colon whether or not the introductory tag is a complete clause (see **30e2**).

(4) In business letters

Use a colon after the salutation to introduce the body of a business letter (see **47a3**).

Dear Dr. Evans:

Thank you for your letter of April 12, in which you commented favorably on our plan to reclassify certain controlled substances.

(5) In special situations

Use colons in the following contexts where convention dictates their use.

Conventional Uses of Colons

To separate titles from subtitles

Family Installments: Memories of Growing Up Hispanic

Tennyson: The Unquiet Heart

To separate chapter from verse in Biblical citations

Judges 4:14

I Kings 11:8

To separate minutes from hours in numerical expressions of time

6:15 A.M.

3:03 P.M.

To separate place of publication from name of publisher in a list of works cited (see 39c2)

Fort Worth: Harcourt Brace Jovanovich, 1992.

---

(6) *Editing misused or overused colons*

After Such As, For Example, *and Similar Expressions*   Colons are not used after expressions like *such as, namely, for example,* or *that is.* These words serve the same purpose as the colon. Remember that a colon introduces a list or series only after an independent clause.

> FAULTY: The Eye Institute treats patients with a wide variety of conditions, such as: myopia, glaucoma, cataracts, and oculomotor dysfunction.

> REVISED: The Eye Institute treats patients with a wide variety of conditions, such as myopia, glaucoma, cataracts, and oculomotor dysfunction.

> REVISED: The Eye Institute treats patients with a wide variety of conditions: myopia, glaucoma, cataracts, and oculomotor dysfunction.

In Verb and Prepositional Constructions   Colons should not be placed between verbs and their objects or complements or between prepositions and their objects.

> FAULTY: James A. Michener wrote: *Hawaii, Centennial, Space,* and *Poland.*

496

REVISED: James A. Michener wrote *Hawaii, Centennial, Space,* and *Poland.*

FAULTY: Hitler's armies marched through: the Netherlands, Belgium, and France.

REVISED: Hitler's armies marched through the Netherlands, Belgium, and France.

EXERCISE 1

Add colons where required in the following sentences. If necessary, delete superfluous colons.

EXAMPLE: There was one thing he really hated getting up at 700 every morning.

There was one thing he really hated: getting up at 7:00 every morning.

1. Books about the late John F. Kennedy include the following *A Hero For Our Time; Johnny, We Hardly Knew Ye;* and *One Brief Shining Moment.*
2. Only one task remained to tell his boss he was quitting.
3. The story closed with a familiar phrase "And they all lived happily ever after."
4. The sergeant requested: reinforcements, medical supplies, and more ammunition.
5. She kept only four souvenirs a photograph, a matchbook, a theater program, and a daisy pressed between the pages of *William Shakespeare The Complete Works.*

31b *Using Dashes*

Commas are the mark of punctuation most often used to set off nonessential elements (**see 27d**), but dashes and parentheses also serve this function. While parentheses deemphasize the enclosed words, **dashes** tend to call attention to the material they set off.

Revision Close-up

When typing, indicate a dash with two unspaced hyphens; when writing, form a dash with an unbroken line about as long as two hyphens.

(1) To set off nonessential material

Explanations, qualifications, and appositives may be set off by dashes for emphasis or clarity.

Use a pair of dashes to set off parenthetical material within a sentence.

Although we are by all odds the most social of all social animals— more interdependent, more attached to each other, more inseparable in our behavior than bees—we do not often feel our conjoined intelligence. (Lewis Thomas, *Lives of a Cell*)

Use a single dash to set off material at the end of a sentence.

Most of the best-sellers are cookbooks and diet books—how not to eat it after you've cooked it. (Andy Rooney, *The New Yorker*)

(2) To introduce a summary

A dash is used to introduce a statement that summarizes a list or series before it.

Walking to school by myself, losing my first tooth, getting my ears pierced, and starting to wear makeup—these were some of the milestones of my childhood and adolescence.

"Study hard," "Respect your elders," "Don't talk with your mouth full"—Sharon had heard her parents say these things hundreds of times.

(3) To indicate an interruption

A dash is sometimes used in dialogue to mark a sudden interruption—for example, a correction, a hesitation, a sudden shift in tone, or an unfinished thought.

Groucho told the steward, "I'll have three hard-boiled eggs—make that four hard-boiled eggs."

"I think—no, I know—this is the worst day of my life," Julie sighed.

(4) Editing misused and overused dashes

Dashes give a loose, casual tone to a piece of writing; too many of them make a passage seem disorganized and out of control. Do not overuse dashes in academic writing, and do not use them carelessly in place of periods or commas or in any context that calls for other marks of punctuation. Compare these two paragraphs.

FAULTY (overuse of dashes)

> Registration was a nightmare—most of the courses I wanted to take—geology and conversational Spanish, for instance—met at inconvenient times—or were closed by the time I tried to sign up for them—it was really depressing—even for registration.

REVISED (moderate use of dashes)

> Registration was a nightmare. Most of the courses I wanted to take—geology and conversational Spanish, for instance—met at inconvenient times or were closed by the time I tried to sign up for them. It was really depressing—even for registration.

EXERCISE 2

Add dashes where needed in the following sentences. If a sentence is correct, mark it with a C.

> EXAMPLE: World War I called "the war to end all wars" was, unfortunately, no such thing.
>
> World War I—called "the war to end all wars"—was, unfortunately, no such thing.

1. Tulips, daffodils, hyacinths, lilies all of these flowers grow from bulbs.
2. St. Kitts and Nevis two tiny island nations are now independent after 360 years of British rule.
3. "But it's not" She paused and reconsidered her next words.
4. He considered several different majors history, English, political science, and business before deciding on journalism.
5. The two words added to the Pledge of Allegiance in the 1950's "under God" remain part of the Pledge today.

31c *Using Parentheses*

Like commas and dashes, **parentheses** may be used to set off interruptions within a sentence.

(1) To set off nonessential material

Parentheses may be used to set off nonessential material that expands, clarifies, defines, illustrates, or supplements an idea.

A compound may be used in any grammatical function: as noun (*wishbone*), adjective (*foolproof*), adverb (*overhead*), verb (*gainsay*), or preposition (*without*). (Thomas Pyles, *The Origin and Development of the English Language*)

It took Gilbert Fairchild two years at Harvard College (two academic years, from September, 1955, to June, 1957) to learn everything he needed to know. (Judith Martin, *Gilbert: A Comedy of Manners*)

When a complete sentence set off by parentheses falls within another sentence, it should not begin with a capital letter or end with a period.

Born in 1893, four years before Queen Victoria's Diamond Jubilee, at Cathedral Choir School, Oxford, where her father was headmaster, Sayers became a first-rate medievalist (she translated Dante) and a theologian (her miracle play, *The Man Born To Be King*, outsold her mystery novels in her lifetime); she died in 1957. (Barbara Grizzuti Harrison, *Off Center*)

If the parenthetical sentence does not interrupt another sentence, it must begin with a capital letter and end with a period, question mark, or exclamation point that falls within the closing parenthesis.

A few days later he called and asked me to come in and bring anything else I had written. (The only thing I had was a notebook full of isolated sentences like "She walked across the room wearing her wedding ring like a shield.") (Jeremy Bernstein, *New York Times Book Review*)

Revision Close-up

When a parenthetical element falls within a sentence, punctuation never precedes the opening parenthesis. Punctuation may follow the closing parenthesis, however.

(2) In special situations

Parentheses are used to set off letters and numbers that identify points on a list and around dates, cross-references, documentation, and the like.

All reports must include the following components: (1) an opening summary; (2) a background statement; and (3) a list of conclusions and recommendations.

Russia was finally victorious in the Great Northern War with Sweden (1700–1721).

Arvin believes that the novel has autobiographical elements (72).

The teachers' contract specifies that class size be limited to thirty-three (33) children.

NOTE: The last example illustrates a convention often used in legal and technical writing.

EXERCISE 3

Add parentheses where necessary in the following sentences. If a sentence is correct, mark it with a C.

> EXAMPLE: The greatest battle of the War of 1812 the Battle of New Orleans was fought after the war was declared over.
>
> The greatest battle of the War of 1812 (the Battle of New Orleans) was fought after the war was declared over.

1. George Orwell's *1984* 1949 focuses on the dangers of a totalitarian society.
2. The final score 45–0 was a devastating blow for the Eagles.
3. Belize formerly British Honduras is a country in Central America.
4. The first phonics book *Phonics is Fun* has a light blue cover.
5. Some high school students have so many extracurricular activities band, sports, drama club, and school newspaper, for instance that they have little time to study.

31d *Using Brackets*

Brackets are used in two special situations.

(1) *To set off comments within quotations*

Brackets are used within quotations to tell readers that the words enclosed are yours and not those of your source. Bracketed material may be a correction, an opinion, an explanation, or a clarification.

"Dues are being raised $1.00 per week [to $5.00]," the treasurer announced.

"The use of caricature by Dickens is reminiscent of the satiric sketches done by [Joseph] Addison and [Richard] Steele [in *The Spectator*]."

"Even as a student at Princeton he [F. Scott Fitzgerald] felt like an outsider."

"The miles of excellent trails are perfect for [cross-country] skiing."

If a quotation contains an error, indicate that the error is not yours by following the error with the italicized Latin word *sic* ("thus") in brackets.

"The octopuss [*sic*] is a cephalopod mollusk with eight arms."

Revision Close-up

Brackets are also used to indicate changes you make to tailor a quotation so that it fits the context of your sentence **(See 38d1)**.

(2) In place of parentheses within parentheses

When one set of parentheses falls within another, substitute brackets for the inner set.

In her narrative history of American education between 1945 and 1960 (*The Troubled Crusade* [New York: Basic Books, 1963], Diane Ravitch addresses issues like progressive education, race, educational reforms, and campus unrest.

31e Using Slashes

The **slash** is used in three situations.

(1) To separate one option from another

The either/or fallacy assumes that a given question has only two possible answers.

Will pass/fail courses be accepted for transfer credit?

The producer/director attracted more attention at the film festival than the actors.

When you use a slash to separate one option from another, do not leave a space before or after the slash.

Revision Close-up

Unless you are really presenting three alternatives (Bring a pencil or pen or both to the exam), the construction *and/or* (Bring a pencil and/or a pen to the exam) should be avoided. Instead use *and* or *or*.

> Bring a pencil and pen to the exam.
>
> Bring a pencil or pen to the exam.

(2) To separate lines of poetry run into the text

The poet James Schevill writes, "I study my defects / And learn how to perfect them."

When you use the slash to separate lines of poetry, leave a space both before and after the slash.

(3) To separate the numerator from the denominator in fractions

7/8

1 4/5

If your typewriter or computer has a special key for a particular fraction ($\frac{1}{2}$, $\frac{1}{4}$) use that instead of the slash.

31f *Using Ellipsis Marks*

(1) To indicate an omission in a quotation

The **ellipsis mark**—three spaced periods—is used to indicate words omitted from a quotation. When deleting material, be careful not to change the meaning of the original passage.

ORIGINAL

> When I was a young man, being anxious to distinguish myself, I was perpetually starting new propositions. But I soon gave this over; for I found that generally what was new was false. (Samuel Johnson)

WITH OMISSION

> When I was a young man, being anxious to distinguish myself, I was perpetually starting new propositions. But I soon ... found that generally what was new was false. (three spaced periods indicate omission)

If a punctuation mark occurs in the original text before the words that are deleted, include it in the quoted sentence ("If we give up now, ... we will answer to history.").

Deleting Words at the Beginning of a Quotation   When deleting *words at the beginning of a sentence* within a quoted passage, retain the period of the previous sentence before the ellipsis mark.

ORIGINAL

And Dickens tells of long mornings when he forced himself to stay at the desk making false starts, lest by giving up he should give up forever. For all his books already in print, he might just as well have been the common schoolboy who is told to write of his visit to Aunt Julia and who honestly finds nothing to say except that he arrived on Friday and left on Sunday. (Jacques Barzun, *Writing, Editing, and Publishing*)

WITH OMISSION

And Dickens tells of long mornings when he forced himself to stay at the desk making false starts, lest by giving up he should give up forever. . . . he might just as well have been the common schoolboy who is told to write of his visit to Aunt Julia and who honestly finds nothing to say except that he arrived on Friday and left on Sunday. (period retained; three equally spaced periods indicate omission)

Revision Close-up

Do not begin a quoted passage with an ellipsis mark.

FAULTY: Barzun notes that Dickens ". . . might just as well have been the common schoolboy. . . ."

REVISED: Barzun notes that Dickens "might just as well have been the common schoolboy. . ."

Deleting Words at the End of a Sentence   In deleting *words at the end of a sentence* within a quoted passage, retain the sentence period or other end punctuation, leaving a space between it and the ellipsis mark.

ORIGINAL

We hold these truths to be self-evident, that all men are created equal, that they are endowed by their Creator with certain unalienable rights, that among these are life, liberty and the pursuit of happiness. (The Declaration of Independence)

WITH OMISSION

> We hold these truths to be self-evident, that all men are created equal, that they are endowed by their Creator with certain unalienable rights. . . . (period retained; three equally spaced periods indicate omission)

Deleting One or More Complete Sentences   In omitting *one or more complete sentences from a quoted passage,* follow any end punctuation with a space and the ellipsis mark.

ORIGINAL

> Everywhere one meets the idea that reading is an activity desirable in itself. It is understandable that publishers and librarians—and even writers—should promote this assumption, but it is strange that the idea should have general currency. People surround the idea of reading with piety, and do not take into account the purpose of reading or the value of what is being read. (Donald Hall)

WITH OMISSION

> Everywhere one meets the idea that reading is an activity desirable in itself. . . . People surround the idea of reading with piety, and do not take into account the purpose of reading or the value of what is being read. (period retained; three equally spaced periods indicate omission)

Note that complete sentences must precede and follow the period plus ellipsis mark.

Guidelines for Punctuating and Placing Ellipsis Marks in Quotations

- "Countries were . . . not willing to compromise."
- "It was, . . . as if they wanted war."
- "Peace was to last only six months; . . . France would then attack."
- "During the summer ambassadors negotiated feverishly. . . ."
- "Self-interest would divert the German armies . . ." (147).
- "Who were the victors? . . ."

---

(2)   To indicate an omission within verse

When you omit one or more lines of poetry (or a paragraph or more of prose), use a complete line of spaced periods.

ORIGINAL: Stitch! Stitch! Stitch!
    In poverty, hunger, and dirt,
    And still with a voice of dolorous pitch,
    Would that its tone could reach the Rich,
     She sang this "Song of the Shirt!"
    (Thomas Hood)

WITH OMISSION: Stitch! Stitch! Stitch!
    In poverty, hunger, and dirt,
    . . . .
    She sang this "Song of the Shirt!"

(3) To indicate unfinished statements

An ellipsis mark can also be used to indicate an interrupted statement.

"If only . . ." He sighed and turned away.

This use is generally not appropriate in college writing unless you are reproducing dialogue.

EXERCISE 4

Read this paragraph and follow the instructions below it, taking care in each case not to delete essential information.

  The most important thing about research is to know when to stop. How does one recognize the moment? When I was eighteen or thereabouts, my mother told me that when out with a young man I should always leave a half-hour before I wanted to. Although I was not sure how this might be accomplished, I recognized the advice as sound, and exactly the same rule applies to research. One must stop *before* one has finished; otherwise, one will never stop and never finish. (Barbara Tuchman, *Practicing History*)

1. Delete a phrase from the middle of one sentence and mark the omission with ellipses.
2. Delete words at the begining of any sentence and mark the omission with ellipses.
3. Delete words at the end of any sentence and mark the omission with ellipses.
4. Delete one complete sentence from the middle of the passage and mark the omission with ellipses.

EXERCISE 5

Add appropriate punctuation—colons, dashes, parentheses, brackets, or slashes—to the following sentences. Be prepared to explain why you chose the punctuation marks you did. If a sentence is correct, mark it with a C.

EXAMPLE: There was one thing she was sure of if she did well at the interview, the job would be hers.

There was one thing she was sure of: if she did well at the interview, the job would be hers.

1. Mark Twain Samuel L. Clemens made the following statement "I can live for two months on a good compliment."
2. Liza Minnelli, the actress singer who starred in several films, is the daughter of Judy Garland.
3. Saudi Arabia, Oman, Yemen, Qatar, and the United Arab Emirates all these are located on the Arabian peninsula.
4. John Adams 1735–1826 was the second president of the United States; John Quincy Adams 1767–1848 was the sixth.
5. The sign said "No tresspassing *sic*."
6. *Checkmate* a term derived from the Persian phrase meaning "the King is dead" announces victory in chess.
7. The following people were present at the meeting the president of the board of trustees, three trustees, and twenty reporters.
8. Before the introduction of the potato in Europe, the parsnip was a major source of carbohydrates in fact, it was a dietary staple.
9. In this well-researched book (*Crime Movies* New York Norton, 1980), Carlos Clarens studies the gangster genre in film.
10. I remember reading though I can't remember where that Upton Sinclair sold plots to Jack London.

STUDENT WRITER AT WORK

Punctuation

Review Chapters 26–31; then read this student essay. Commas, semicolons, quotation marks, apostrophes, parentheses, and dashes have been intentionally deleted; only the end punctuation has been retained. When you have read the essay carefully, add all appropriate punctuation marks.

    The dry pine needles crunched like eggshells under
our thick boots.

Wont the noise scare them away Dad?

He smiled knowingly and said No deer rely mostly on smell and sight.

I thought That must be why were wearing fluorescent orange jumpsuits but I didn't feel like arguing the point.

It was a perfect day for my first hunting experience. The biting winds were caught by the thick bushy arms of the tall pines and I could feel a numbing redness in my face. Now I realized why Dad always grew that ugly gray beard which made him look ten years older. A few sunbeams managed to carve their way through the layers of branches and leaves creating pools of white light on the dark earth.

How far have we come? I asked. Oh only a couple of miles. We should be meeting Joe up ahead.

Joe was one of Dads hunting buddies. He always managed to go off on his own for a few hours and come back with at least a four-pointer. Dad was envious of Joe and liked to tell people what he called the real story.

You know Joe paid a fortune for that buck at the checking station hed tell his friends. Dad was sure that this would be his lucky year.

We trudged up a densely wooded hill for what seemed like hours. The sharp needled branches whipped my bare face as I followed close behind my father occasionally I wiped my cheeks to discover a new cut in my frozen flesh.

All this for a deer I thought.

The still pine air was suddenly shattered by four rapid gunshots echoing across the vast green valley below us.

Joes got another one. Come on! Dad yelled. It seemed as if I were following a young kid as I watched my father take leaping strides down the path we had just ascended. I had never seen him so enthusiastic before. I plodded breathlessly along trying to keep up with my father.

Suddenly out of the corner of my eye I caught sight of an object that didn't fit in with the monotony of trunks and branches and leaves and needles. I froze and observed the largest most majestic buck I had ever seen. It too stood motionless apparently grazing on some leaves or berries. Its coloring was beautiful with alternating patches of tan brown and snow white fur. The massive antlers towered proudly above its head as it looked up and took notice of me. What struck me most were the tearful brown eyes almost feminine in their gaze.

Once again the silence was smashed this time by my fathers thundering call and I watched as the huge deer scampered gracefully off through the trees. I turned and scurried down the path after my father. I decided not to mention a word of my encounter to him. I hoped the deer was far away by now.

Finally, I reached the clearing from where the shots had rung out. There stood Dad and Joe smiling over a fallen six-point buck. The purple-red blood dripped from the wounds to form a puddle in the dirt. The bucks sad brown eyes gleamed in the sun but no longer smiled and blinked.

Where have you been? asked Dad. Before I could answer he continued Do you believe this guy? Every year he bags the biggest deer in the whole state!

While they laughed and talked I sat on a tree stump to rest my aching legs. Maybe now we can go home I thought. But before long I heard Dad say Come on Bob I know theres one out there for us.

We headed right back up that same path and sure enough that same big beautiful buck was grazing in that same spot on the same berry bush. The only difference was that this time Dad saw him.

This is our lucky day he whispered.

I froze as Dad lifted the barrel of his rifle and

took careful aim at the silently grazing deer. I closed my eyes as he squeezed the trigger but instead of the deadly gun blast I heard only a harmless click. His rifle had jammed.

Use your rifle quick he whispered.

As I took aim through my scope the deer looked up at me. Its soulful brown eyes were magnified in my sight like two glassy bullseyes. My finger froze on the trigger.

Shoot him! Shoot him!

But instead I aimed for the clouds and fired. The deer vanished along with my fathers dreams. Dad never understood why it was the proudest moment of my life.

Capitalization

Familiarizing yourself with the conventions of capitalization is important. Conventions change, however, and if you are not certain whether a word should be capitalized, consult a recent dictionary.

32a Capitalize the First Word of a Sentence or of a Line of Poetry

The first word of a sentence, including a sentence of directly quoted speech or writing, should start with a capital letter.

> The square of the hypotenuse is equal to the sum of the squares of the other two sides.

> Shakespeare wrote, "Who steals my purse steals trash."

Do not capitalize a sentence set off within another sentence by dashes or parentheses.

FAULTY: Finding the store closed—It was a holiday—they went home.

REVISED: Finding the store closed—it was a holiday—they went home.

FAULTY: The candidates are Frank Lester and Jane Lester (They are not related).

REVISED: The candidates are Frank Lester and Jane Lester (they are not related).

When a complete sentence is introduced by a colon, capitalization is optional (**see 31a2**).

32b Capitalize Proper Nouns, Titles Accompanying Them, and Adjectives Formed from Them

Proper nouns—the names of specific persons, places, or things (Diana Ross, Madras, the Enoch Pratt Free Library)—are capitalized, and so are adjectives formed from proper nouns.

(1) Specific people's names

Clark Gable	Elvis Presley
Jackie Robinson	William the Conqueror

When a title precedes a person's name or is used instead of the name, it, too, is capitalized.

Dad	Pope John XXIII
Count Dracula	Justice Marshall

Titles that *follow* names or those that refer to the general position, not the particular person who holds it, are usually not capitalized. A title denoting a family relationship is never capitalized when it follows an article or a possessive pronoun.

CAPITALIZE	DO NOT CAPITALIZE
Grandma	my grandmother
Private Hargrove	Mr. Hargrove, a private in the army
Queen Mother Elizabeth	a popular queen mother
Senator John Glenn; the Senator (referring to a particular senator)	John Glenn, the senator from Ohio

Uncle Harry   my uncle

General Patton; the General   a four-star general
(referring to a particular general)

Titles or abbreviations of academic degrees are always capital-ized, even when they follow a name.

Perry Mason, Attorney at Law

Benjamin Spock, M.D.

Titles that indicate high-ranking positions may be capitalized even when they are used alone or when they follow a name.

the Secretary of Defense

the Speaker of the House

George Bush, President of the United States

(2) Names of particular structures, special events, monuments, vehicles, and so on

the *Titanic*   the Taj Mahal

the Brooklyn Bridge   Mount Rushmore

the World Series   the Eiffel Tower

NOTE: When a common noun such as *bridge, river,* or *lake* is part of a proper noun, it, too, is capitalized. Do not, however, capitalize such words when they complete the names of more than one thing (as in Kings and Queens counties).

(3) Places, geographical regions, and directions

Saturn   the Straits of Magellan

Budapest   the Western Hemisphere

Walden Pond   the Fiji Islands

The points of the compass are also capitalized when they denote particular geographical regions, but designations of directions are not.

The Middle West seemed like a wasteland to F. Scott Fitzgerald's Nick Carraway, so he decided to come East. (Capital letters necessary because *Middle West* and *East* refer to specific regions.)

Turn west at the corner of Broad Street and continue north until you reach Market. (No capitals used because *west* and *north* refer to directions, not specific regions.)

(4) Days of the week, months of the year, and holidays

Saturday	Ash Wednesday
January	Rosh Hashanah
Veterans Day	Labor Day

(5) Historical periods, events, and documents; names of legal cases and awards

the Battle of Gettysburg	the Treaty of Versailles
the Industrial Revolution	the Voting Rights Act
the Reformation	*Brown v. Board of Education*

(6) Philosophic, literary, and artistic movements

Naturalism	Dadaism
Romanticism	Fauvism
Neoclassicism	Expressionism

NOTE: Dictionaries vary in their advice on capitalizing these nouns, but current usage tends toward capitalization.

(7) Races, ethnic groups, nationalities, and languages

African-American	Korean
Hispanic	Dutch
Caucasian	Turkish

NOTE: When the words *black* and *white* refer to races, they have traditionally not been capitalized. Current usage is divided on whether or not to capitalize *black*.

(8) Religions and their followers; sacred books and figures

Muslims	the Talmud	Buddha
Jews	the Koran	the Virgin Mary
Islam	God	the Messiah
Judaism	the Lord	the Scriptures

NOTE: It is not necessary to capitalize pronouns referring to God unless the pronoun might also refer to another antecedent in the sentence.

CONFUSING: Alex's grandfather taught him to trust in God and to love all his creatures. (The word *his* could refer to either God or Alex's grandfather.)

REVISED: Alex's grandfather taught him to trust in God and to love all His creatures.

(9) *Political, social, athletic, civic, and other groups and their members*

New York Yankees

Democratic Party

International Brotherhood of Electrical Workers

National Organization for Women

National Council of Teachers of English

The Who

(10) *Businesses; government agencies; and medical, educational, and other institutions*

Congress	Lincoln High School
Environmental Protection Agency	University of Maryland

NOTE: When the name of a group or institution is abbreviated, the abbreviation uses capital letters in place of the capitalized words.

IBEW

NOW

NCTE

(11) *Trade names and words formed from them*

Pontiac	Coke
Sanka	Pampers
Kleenex	Xeroxing

NOTE: Trade names that have been used so often and for so long that they have become synonymous with the product—for example, frisbee, jello, victrola, and aspirin—are no longer capitalized. (Consult a dictionary to determine whether or not to capitalize a familiar trade name.)

(12) Specific academic courses

Sociology 201   English 101

NOTE: Do not capitalize a general subject area unless it is the name of a language.

Although his major was engineering, he registered for courses in sociology, English, and zoology.

(13) Adjectives formed from proper nouns

Keynesian economics	Elizabethan era
Freudian slip	Shakespearean sonnet
Platonic ideal	Marxist ideology
Aristotelian logic	Shavian wit

However, when words derived from proper nouns have lost their specialized meanings, do not capitalize them.

The china pattern was very elaborate.

We need a 40-watt bulb.

32c *Capitalize Important Words in Titles*

In general, all words in titles of books, articles, essays, films, and the like—including your own papers—are capitalized, with the exception of articles (*a, an,* and *the*), prepositions, conjunctions, and the *to* in infinitives. If an article, preposition, or conjunction is the *first* or *last* word in the title, however, it too is capitalized.

"Dover Beach"	*On the Waterfront*
The Declaration of Independence	*The Skin of Our Teeth*
	Of Human Bondage
Across the River and into the Trees	"Politics and the English Language"
Two Years before the Mast	

32d *Capitalize the Pronoun* I *and the Interjection* O

Even if the pronoun *I* is part of a contraction (*I'm, I'll, I've*), it is always capitalized.

Sam and I finally went to the Grand Canyon, and I'm glad we did.

The interjection *O* is also always capitalized.

Give us peace in our time, O Lord.

The interjection *oh*, however, is capitalized only when it begins a sentence.

NOTE: Many other single letters are also capitalized in certain usages. Check your dictionary if you are not certain whether to use a capital letter.

U-boat	Vitamin B
D-Day	an A in history
Model T	C major

32e Capitalize Salutations and Closings of Letters

In salutations of business or personal letters, always capitalize the first word. ▶ See 47a3

Dear Mr. Reynolds:

Dear Fred,

The first word of the complimentary close is also always capitalized.

Sincerely,   Very truly yours,

32f Editing Misused and Overused Capitals

Capital letters should not be used for emphasis or as an attention-getting device. If you are not certain whether a word should be capitalized, consult your dictionary.

(1) Seasons

Do not capitalize the names of the seasons—summer, fall, winter, spring—unless they are strongly personified, as in Old Man Winter.

(2) Centuries and loosely defined historical periods

Do not capitalize the names of centuries or general historical periods.

seventeenth-century poetry   the automobile age

But do capitalize names of specific historical, anthropological, and geological periods.

Iron Age   Paleozoic Era

(3) Diseases and other medical terms

Do not capitalize names of diseases or medical tests or conditions unless a proper noun is part of the name or unless the disease is an acronym.

polio   Apgar test   AIDS

Reye's syndrome   mumps   SIDS

EXERCISE

Capitalize words where necessary in these sentences.

EXAMPLE: John F. Kennedy won the pulitzer prize for his book *profiles in courage.*

John F. Kennedy won the Pulitzer Prize for his book *Profiles in Courage.*

1. The brontë sisters wrote *jane eyre* and *wuthering heights,* two nineteenth-century novels that are required reading in many english classes that study victorian literature.
2. It was a beautiful day in the spring—it was april 15, to be exact—but all Ted could think about was the check he had to write to the internal revenue service and the bills he had to pay by friday.
3. Traveling north, they hiked through british columbia, planning a leisurely return on the cruise ship *canadian princess.*
4. Alice liked her mom's apple pie better than aunt nellie's rhubarb pie; but she liked grandpa's punch best of all.
5. A new elective, political science 30, covers the vietnam war from the gulf of tonkin to the fall of saigon, including the roles of ho chi minh, the viet cong, and the buddhist monks; the position of presidents johnson and nixon; and the influence of groups like the student mobilization committee and vietnam veterans against the war.

6. When the central high school drama club put on a production of shaw's *pygmalion,* the director xeroxed extra copies of the parts for eliza doolittle and professor henry higgins so he could give them to the understudies.

7. Shaking all over, Bill admitted, "driving on the los angeles freeway is a frightening experience for a kid from the bronx, even in a bmw."

8. The new united federation of teachers contract guarantees teachers many paid holidays, including columbus day, veterans day, and washington's birthday; a week each at christmas and easter; and two full months (july and august) in the summer.

9. The sociology syllabus included the books *beyond the best interests of the child, regulating the poor,* and *a welfare mother;* in anthropology we were to begin by studying the stone age; and in geology we were to focus on the mesozoic era.

10. Winners of the nobel peace prize include lech walesa, former leader of the polish trade union solidarity; the reverend dr. martin luther king, jr., founder of the southern christian leadership conference; and bishop desmond tutu of south africa.

Italics

33a Setting Off Titles and Names

Italicize the titles of books, newspapers, magazines, and journals; pamphlets; films, television and radio programs; long poems; plays; long musical works; and paintings and sculpture. Also italicize names of ships, trains, aircraft, and spacecraft. All other titles are set off with quotation marks (**see 30b**).

Revision Close-up

Titles of your own essays, typed at the top of the first page or on a title page, are neither italicized nor placed within quotation marks. Names of sacred books, such as the Bible, and well-known documents, such as the Constitution and the Declaration of Independence, are also neither italicized nor placed within quotation marks.

Titles and Names Set in Italics

Books

David Copperfield   *A Connecticut Yankee in King Arthur's Court*

Newspapers

the *Washington Post*   *The Philadelphia Inquirer*

Articles and names of cities are italicized only when they are a part of a title.

Magazines

The Atlantic   *Scientific American*

Journals

New England Journal of Medicine

American Sociological Review

Pamphlets

Common Sense

Films

Casablanca   *Who's Afraid of Virginia Woolf?*

Punctuation is italicized when it is part of a title.

Television programs

Sesame Street   *Leave It to Beaver*

Radio programs

All Things Considered   *Prairie Home Companion*

Long poems

John Brown's Body   *The Faerie Queen*

Plays

Macbeth   *A Raisin in the Sun*

Long musical works

Rigoletto   *Eroica*

Paintings and sculpture

The Night Watch   *Guernica*

Ships

Lusitania   U.S.S. *Saratoga*

S.S. and U.S.S. are not italicized when they precede the name of a ship.

Trains

City of New Orleans   *The Orient Express*

Aircraft

the *Hindenburg*   *Enola Gay*

Only particular aircraft, not makes or types like Piper Cub or Boeing 707, are italicized.

Spacecraft

Sputnik   *Enterprise*

33b Setting Off Foreign Words and Phrases

Thousands of foreign words and phrases are now considered part of the English language. These words—*naive, lasso, chaperon,* and *catharsis,* for example—receive no special treatment. Foreign words and phrases not yet fully assimilated into the language, however, should be set in italics. (Foreign proper nouns are not italicized.)

The *carpe diem* theme is expressed in Andrew Marvell's poem "To His Coy Mistress."

Spirochaeta plicatilis, Treponema pallidum, and *Spirilbum minus* are all bacteria with corkscrew-like shapes.

If you are not sure whether a foreign word has been assimilated into English, consult a dictionary.

33c Setting Off Elements Spoken of as Themselves and Terms Being Defined

Italicize letters, numerals, words, and phrases when they refer to the letters, numerals, words, and phrases themselves.

Is that a *p* or a *g*?

I forget the exact address, but I know it has a *3* in it.

Does *through* rhyme with *cough?*

His pronunciation of the phrase *Mary was contrary* told us he was from the Midwest.

Italicize to set off words and phrases that you go on to define.

A *closet drama* is a play meant to be read, not performed.

33d Using Italics for Emphasis

Italics lend unusually strong weight to a word or phrase and should therefore be used in moderation. Overuse of italics interferes with the tone and even the meaning of what you write. Whenever possible, emphasis should be indicated by word choice and sentence structure. The following sentences illustrate acceptable use of italics for emphasis:

> As for protecting the children from exploitation, the chief and indeed only exploiters of children these days *are* schools. (John Holt, "School Is Bad for Children")

> Initially, poetry might be defined as a kind of language that says *more* and says it *more intensely* than does ordinary language. (Lawrence Perrine, *Sound and Sense*)

33e *Using Italics for Clarity*

Occasionally, it is necessary to italicize a word to avoid confusion or ambiguity when a sentence may have more than one meaning.

> This time Jill forgot the *key*. (Last time Jill forgot something else.)

> This time *Jill* forgot the key. (Last time someone else forgot the key.)

EXERCISE

Underline to indicate italics where necessary, and delete any italics that are incorrectly used. If a sentence is correct, mark it with a C.

> EXAMPLE: However is a conjunctive adverb, not a coordinating conjunction.
>
> However is a conjunctive adverb, not a coodinating conjunction.

1. I said Carol, not Darryl.
2. A *deus ex machina,* an improbable device used to resolve the plot of a fictional work, is used in Charles Dickens's novel Oliver Twist.
3. He dotted every i and crossed every t.
4. The Metropolitan Opera's production of Carmen was a real tour de force for the principal performers.
5. *Laissez-faire* is a doctrine that holds that government should not interfere with trade.
6. Antidote and anecdote are often confused because their pronunciations are similar.
7. Hawthorne's novels include Fanshawe, The House of the Seven Gables, The Blithedale Romance, and The Scarlet Letter.

8. Words like mailman, policeman, and fireman are rapidly being replaced by nonsexist terms like letter carrier, police officer, and firefighter.

9. A classic black tuxedo was considered de rigueur at the charity ball, but Jason preferred to wear his *dashiki.*

10. Thomas Mann's novel Buddenbrooks is a Bildungsroman.

Hyphens

Hyphens have two conventional uses: to break words at the end of a typed or handwritten line and to link words in certain compounds.

Breaking Words at the End of a Line

Whenever possible, avoid breaking a word at the end of a line; if you must do so, divide words only between syllables. Consult a dictionary to determine correct syllabication. Whenever you can, divide a word between prefix and root (sus · pending) or between root and suffix (develop · ment). Divide words that contain doubled consonants between the doubled letters (let · ter) unless the doubled letters are part of the root (cross · ing) or unless the doubled letters do not break into two syllables (ex · pelled). Do not end two consecutive lines with hyphens, and never divide a word at the end of a page.

Additional guidelines for determining how a word should be divided are listed below.

(1) One-syllable words

Never hyphenate one-syllable words. Keep a one-syllable word intact even if it is relatively long (*thought, blocked, French, laughed*). If you cannot fit the whole word at the end of the line, move it to the next line.

FAULTY: Mark Twain's novel *The Prin-*
           ce and the Pauper considers the
           effects of environment on personality.

525

REVISED: Mark Twain's novel *The Prince and the Pauper* considers
the effects of environment on personality.

(2) Short syllables

Never leave a single letter at the end of a line or carry one or
two letters to the beginning of a line. One-letter prefixes (like the
a- in *away*) or short suffixes (like *-y, -ly, -er,* and *-ed*) should not
be separated from the rest of the word. The suffixes *-able* and *-ible*
cannot be broken into two syllables.

FAULTY: Nadia walked very slowly a-
long the balance beam.

REVISED: Nadia walked very slowly along
the balance beam.

FAULTY: Amy's parents wondered whether the terrible twos would ever end.

REVISED: Amy's parents wondered whether the terrible twos would ever end.

(3) Compound words

If you must hyphenate a compound word, put the hyphen between
the elements of the compound. (For correct use of hyphens in compound words, see 34b.)

FAULTY: Environmentalists believe snowmo-
biles produce air and noise pollution.

REVISED: Environmentalists believe snow-
mobiles produce air and noise pollution.

If the compound already contains a hyphen, divide it at the existing
hyphen.

FAULTY: She met her ex-hus-
band on a blind date.

REVISED: She met her ex-
husband on a blind date.

(4) Illogical or confusing hyphenation

Some words contain letter combinations that look like other words.
To avoid confusing readers, do not isolate a fragment that can be
read as a separate word.

CONFUSING: The supervisor did not appreciate the facetious remark.

REVISED: The supervisor did not appreciate the
facetious remark.

(5) Numerals, contractions, and abbreviations

Contractions, numerals, acronyms, and abbreviations should not be divided. A hyphen is not used between a numeral and an abbreviation.

FAULTY: Whether or not the meeting began on time was-
n't important.

REVISED: Whether or not the meeting began on time
wasn't important.

FAULTY: The special program on child abuse was seen by over 23,-
000,000 Americans.

REVISED: The special program on child abuse was seen by over
23,000,000 Americans.

FAULTY: During the sixties, participation in RO-
TC declined on many college campuses.

REVISED: During the sixties, participation in ROTC
declined on many college campuses.

FAULTY: The balloon was launched at precisely 8-
P.M.

REVISED: The balloon was launched at precisely 8 P.M.

EXERCISE 1

Divide each of these words into syllables, consulting a dictionary if necessary; then, indicate with a hyphen where you would divide each word at the end of a line.

EXAMPLE: underground

un · der · ground

under-ground

1. transcendentalism
2. calliope
3. martyr
4. longitude
5. bookkeeper
6. side-splitting
7. markedly
8. amazing
9. unlikely
10. thorough

34b *Dividing Compound Words*

A **compound word** is composed of two or more words. Some familiar compound words are always hyphenated.

no-hitter   helter-skelter

Other compounds are always written as one word.

fireplace   peacetime   sunset

Finally, some compounds are always written as two separate words.

medical doctor   labor relations   bunk bed

Your dictionary can tell you whether a particular compound requires a hyphen: *snow job,* for instance, is two unhyphenated words; *snowsuit* is one word; and *snow-white* is hyphenated. Usage changes, however, so it is important to have a dictionary that is up to date.

Although hyphenization of compound words is not uniform, a few reliable rules do apply.

(1) In compound adjectives

A **compound adjective** is two or more words combined into a single grammatical unit that modifies a noun. When a compound adjective *precedes* the noun it modifies, its elements are joined by hyphens.

He stayed tuned to his favorite listener-supported radio station, waiting for a hard-hitting editorial.

The research team tried to use nineteenth-century technology to design a space-age project.

However, when a compound adjective *follows* the noun it modifies, it does not require a hyphen.

The three government-operated programs were run smoothly, but the one that was not government operated was short of funds.

Revision Close-Up

Compound adjectives that contain words ending in *-ly* are not hyphenated, even when they precede the noun.

> Many upwardly mobile families consider items like home computers, microwave ovens, and videocassette recorders to be necessities.

Use **suspended hyphens**—hyphens followed by space or by the appropriate punctuation and space—in a series of compounds that have the same principal elements.

The three-, four-, and five-year-old children were assigned to the same group.

(2) With certain prefixes or suffixes

Use a hyphen between a prefix and a proper noun or an adjective formed from a proper noun.

mid-July   pre-Columbian

Use a hyphen to connect the prefixes *all-, ex-, half-, quarter-, quasi-,* and *self-* and the suffixes *-elect* and *-odd* to a noun.

all-pro	quasi-serious
ex-senator	self-centered
half-pint	president-elect
quarter-moon	thirty-odd

NOTE: The words *selfhood, selfish,* and *selfless* do not include hyphens. In these cases *self* is the root, not a prefix.

(3) For clarity

Hyphenate to prevent misreading one word for another.

co-op	coop
re-form	reform
re-creation	recreation

Hyphenate to avoid hard-to-read combinations, like two *i*'s (*semi-illiterate*) or more than two of the same consonant (*shell-less*) in a row.

Hyphenate in most cases between a capital initial and a word when the two combine to form a compound.

A-frame   T-shirt

But check your dictionary; some letter- or numeral-plus-word compounds do not require hyphens.

B flat   F major

(4) In compound numerals and fractions

Hyphenate compounds that represent numbers below one hundred, even if they are part of a larger number.

the twenty-first century   three hundred sixty-five days

Compounds that represent numbers over ninety-nine (*two thousand, thirty million, two hundred fifty*) are not hyphenated. Therefore, in the expression *three hundred sixty-five days*, the compound *sixty-five* is hyphenated because it represents a number below one hundred, but no hyphens connect *three* to *hundred*.

Hyphenate fractions when they serve as compound modifiers.

a two-thirds share of the business

a three-fourths majority

Hyphens are not required in other cases, but most writers do use them.

PREFERRED: seven-eighths of the circle
ACCEPTABLE: seven eighths of the circle

(5) In newly created compounds

A coined compound, using a new combination of words as a unit, uses hyphens.

He looked up with a who-do-you-think-you-are expression on his face.

EXERCISE   2

Form compound adjectives from the following word groups, inserting hyphens where necessary.

EXAMPLE: a contract for three years

a three-year contract

1. a relative who has long been lost
2. someone who is addicted to video games

3. a salesperson who goes from door to door
4. a display calculated to catch the eye
5. friends who are dearly beloved
6. a household that is centered on a child
7. a line of reasoning that is hard to follow
8. the border between New York and New Jersey
9. a candidate who is thirty-two years old
10. a computer that is friendly to its users

EXERCISE 3

Add hyphens to the compounds in these sentences wherever they are required. Consult a dictionary if necessary.

EXAMPLE: Alaska was the forty ninth state to join the United States.

Alaska was the forty-ninth state to join the United States.

1. One of the restaurant's blue plate specials is chicken fried steak.
2. Virginia and Texas are both right to work states.
3. He stood on tiptoe to see the near perfect statue, which was well hidden by the security fence.
4. The five and ten cent store had a self service makeup counter and stocked many up to the minute gadgets.
5. The so called Saturday night special is opposed by pro gun control groups.
6. He ordered two all beef patties with special sauce, lettuce, onions, cheese, and pickle on a sesame seed bun.
7. The material was extremely thought provoking, but it hardly presented any earth shattering conclusions.
8. The Dodgers Phillies game was rained out, so the long suffering fans left for home.
9. Bone marrow transplants carry the risk of what is known as a graft versus host reaction.
10. The state funded child care program was considered a highly desirable alternative to family day care.

Abbreviations

Abbreviations save time and space. They also communicate meaning quickly and efficiently—but only when they are familiar to your readers.

Many abbreviations are acceptable only in informal writing and are not appropriate in college writing. Others are acceptable in scientific, technical, or business writing, or only in a particular discipline. If you are unsure whether to use a particular abbreviation, check a style manual in your field.

See ◄ 39f

35a Abbreviating Titles

Titles before and after proper names are usually abbreviated.

Mr. Walter Cronkite	Dr. Helen Zweizig
Henry Kissinger, Ph.D.	St. Jude

But military, religious, academic, and government titles are not abbreviated.

General George Patton	Professor Kenneth G. Schaefer
the Reverend William Gray	Senator Daniel Moynihan

Abbreviations like Gen., Rev., Sen., and the like are not acceptable before a surname alone or when they do not precede a proper name.

35b Abbreviating Technical Terms and Agency Names

Certain abbreviations are used in speech and in college writing to designate groups, institutions, people, substances, and so on. For example, businesses and government, social, and civic organizations are commonly referred to by initials. These abbreviations fall into two categories: abbreviations formed from capitalized initials (CIA) and those that are acronyms (CORE).

► See 26a2

Accepted abbreviations for terms that are not well known may also be used, but only if you have included the abbreviation in parentheses directly after your first mention of the full term.

Citrus farmers have been injecting ethylene dibromide (EDB), a chemical pesticide, into the soil for more than twenty years. Now, however, EDB has seeped into wells and contaminated water supplies, and it is a suspected carcinogen.

Revision Close-up

The extent to which abbreviations are used varies from discipline to discipline. Regardless of the discipline, however, excessive use of abbreviations can be confusing to your readers, so use them sparingly.

35c Abbreviating Designations of Specific Dates, Times of Day, Temperatures, and Numbers

50 B.C. (B.C. follows the date)   A.D. 432 (A.D. precedes the date)

6 A.M.   3:03 P.M.

20° C (Centigrade or Celsius)   180° F (Fahrenheit)

Always capitalize B.C. and A.D. You may, however, use either uppercase or lowercase letters for a.m. and p.m. (A.M., a.m., P.M., p.m.). Printers conventionally set A.M., P.M., B.C., and A.D. in small capital letters (A.M., P.M., B.C., A.D.). These abbreviations are used only when they are accompanied by numbers.

FAULTY: We will see you in the A.M.

REVISED: We will see you in the morning.

REVISED: We will see you at 8 A.M.

In technical writing you may use the abbreviation *no.* (number), but only before a specific number. This abbreviation may be written either *no.* or *No.*

FAULTY: The no. on the label of the unidentified substance was 52.

REVISED: The unidentified substance was labeled no. 52.

REVISED: The number on the label of the unidentified substance was 52.

In nontechnical writing *no.* is acceptable only in certain documentation formats.

CORRECT: *The Journal of the Institute for Socioeconomic Studies,* Vol. 11, No. 2, Spring 1977.

35d *Editing Misused and Overused Abbreviations*

Abbreviations are not used in the following cases.

(1) *Certain familiar Latin expressions*

Abbreviations of the common Latin phrases *i.e.* ("that is"), *e.g.* ("for example"), and *etc.* ("and so forth") are sometimes appropriate for informal writing, and they may occasionally be acceptable in a parenthetical note. In most college writing, however, an equivalent phrase should be written out in full.

INFORMAL: Poe wrote "The Gold Bug," "The Masque of the Red Death," etc.

PREFERABLE: Poe wrote "The Gold Bug," "The Masque of the Red Death," and other stories.

INFORMAL: Other musicians (e.g., Bruce Springsteen) have been influenced by Dylan.

PREFERABLE: Other musicians (for example, Bruce Springsteen) have been influenced by Dylan.

The Latin abbreviations *et al.* ("and others") and *cf.* ("compare") are used only in bibliographic entries.

Davidson, Harley, et al. *You and Your Motorcycle*. New York: Ten
    Speed, 1968.

(2) The names of days, months, or holidays

FAULTY: Sat., Aug. 9, was the hottest day of the year.

REVISED: Saturday, August 9, was the hottest day of the year.

FAULTY: Only twenty-three shopping days remain until Xmas.

REVISED: Only twenty-three shopping days remain until Christmas.

(3) Units of measurement

In informal and technical writing, some units of measurement
are abbreviated when preceded by a numeral.

The hurricane had winds of 35 m.p.h.

The new Honda gets over 50 m.p.g.

In general, however, write out such expressions, and spell out words
such as *inches, feet, years, miles, pints, quarts,* and *gallons.*

NOTE: Abbreviations for units of measurement are not used in the
absence of a numeral.

FAULTY: The laboratory equipment included pt. and qt. measures
          and a beaker that could hold a gal. of liquid.

REVISED: The laboratory equipment included pint and quart mea-
          sures and a beaker that could hold a gallon of liquid.

(4) Names of places, streets, and the like

Abbreviations of names of streets, cities, states, countries, and
geographical regions are common in informal writing and in correspondence. For college assignments these words should be spelled
out.

FAULTY	REVISED
B'way	Broadway
Riverside Dr.	Riverside Drive
Phila.	Philadelphia
Calif. or CA	California
Catskill Mts.	Catskill Mountains

EXCEPTIONS: The abbreviations *U.S.A.* (or *USA*) and *U.S.S.R.* (or
USSR) are often acceptable, as is *D.C.* (for District of Columbia)

in the phrase *Washington, D.C.* It is also permissible to use the abbreviation *Mt.* before the name of a mountain (*Mt. Etna*) and *St.* in a place name (*St. Albans*).

(5) Names of academic subjects

Names of academic subjects are not abbreviated.

FAULTY: Psych., soc., and English lit. are all required for graduation.

REVISED: Psychology, sociology, and English literature are all required for graduation.

(6) Parts of books

Abbreviations that designate parts of written works (*Pt. II, Ch. 3, Vol. IV*) should not be used within the text of a paper. Such abbreviations are acceptable only in documentation and bibliographic entries.

(7) People's names

FAULTY: Mr. Harris's five children were named Robt., Eliz., Jas., Chas., and Wm.

REVISED: Mr. Harris's five children were named Robert, Elizabeth, James, Charles, and William.

(8) Company names

The abbreviations *Inc., Bros., Co.,* or *Corp.* and the ampersand (&) are not used unless they are part of a firm's official name.

Company names are written exactly as the firms themselves write them.

Western Union Telegraph Company

Santini Bros.

Rohm & Haas

AT&T

Charles Schwab & Co., Inc.

Revision Close-up

Shortened forms of publishers' names—Harcourt, not Harcourt Brace Jovanovich—are preferred in MLA bibliographic citations **(see 39b2).**

Abbreviations for *company, corporation,* and the like are not used in the absence of a company name.

FAULTY: The corp. merged with a small co. in Pittsburgh.

REVISED: The corporation merged with a small company in Pittsburgh.

The ampersand (&) is used in college writing only in the name of a company that requires it or in citations that follow APA documentation style (**see 43c**).

(9) Symbols

The symbols %, =, +, #, and ¢ are acceptable in technical and scientific writing but not in nontechnical college writing.

FAULTY: The cost of admission represents a 50% increase over last year's price.

REVISED: The cost of admission represents a 50 percent increase over last year's price.

The symbol $ is acceptable in all types of writing, but only before specific numbers. It is not used as a substitute for the words *money* or *dollars.*

CORRECT: The first of her books of poetry cost $4.25 per copy.

FAULTY: The value of the $ has declined steadily in the last two decades.

REVISED: The value of the dollar has declined steadily in the last two decades.

EXERCISE 1

Correct any incorrectly used abbreviations in the following sentences, assuming that all are intended for an academic audience. If a sentence is correct, mark it with a *C*.

EXAMPLE: *Romeo & Juliet* is a play by Wm. Shakespeare.

Romeo and Juliet is a play by William Shakespeare.

1. The committee meeting, attended by representatives from Action for Children's Television (ACT) and NOW, Sen. Putnam, & the pres. of ABC, convened at 8 A.M. on Mon. Feb. 24 at the YWCA on Germantown Ave.

2. An econ. prof. was suspended after he encouraged his students to speculate on securities issued by corps. under investigation by the SEC.

3. Benjamin Spock, the M.D. who wrote *Baby and Child Care*, is a respected dr. known throughout the USA.

4. The FDA has banned the use of Red Dye no. 2 in food, but other food additives are still in use.

5. The Rev. Dr. Martin Luther King, Jr., leader of the S.C.L.C., led the famous Selma, Ala., march.

6. Wm. Golding, a novelist from the U.K., won the Nobel Prize for lit.

7. The adult education center, financed by a major computer corp., offers courses in basic subjects like introductory bio. and tech. writing as well as teaching programming languages like COBOL and FORTRAN.

8. All the bros. in the fraternity agreed to write to Pres. Dexter appealing their disciplinary probation under Ch. 4, Sec. 3, of the IFC constitution.

9. A 4 qt. (i.e., 1 gal.) container is needed to hold the salt solution.

10. According to Prof. Morrison, all those taking the MCAT's should bring two sharpened no. 2 pencils to the St. Joseph's University auditorium on Sat.

Numbers

Convention determines when to use a number (22) and when to spell out a number (twenty-two). Numerals are generally more common in scientific and technical writing, in journalism, and in informal writing, while numbers are more often spelled out in formal or literary writing. In certain contexts one option is preferred over the other.

Common sense and a knowledge of the conventions of a particular discipline should guide your final decision. If spelling out numbers is cumbersome, use figures. Whatever your choice, usage should be consistent, and numerals and spelled-out forms should generally not be mixed in the same passage.

36a Spelling Out Numbers That Begin Sentences

Never begin a sentence with a numeral. If a number begins a sentence, express the number in words.

FAULTY: 200 students are currently enrolled in freshman English.
REVISED: Two hundred students are currently enrolled in freshman English.

You may also reword the sentence, especially when the opening number is more than two words long.

CORRECT: Current enrollment in freshman English is 200 students.

36b Spelling Out Numbers That Can Be Expressed in One or Two Words

Unless a number falls into one of the categories listed in 36d, spell it out if you can do so in one or two words.

The Hawaiian alphabet has only twelve letters.

Class size stabilized at twenty-eight students.

Approximate numbers can often be expressed in one or two words.

Guards turned away more than ten thousand disappointed fans.

The subsidies are expected to total about two million dollars.

Revision Close-up

In some disciplines, such as the social sciences and engineering, the rule is to spell out all numbers less than ten and to use numerals for ten and above.

36c Using Numerals for Numbers That Cannot Be Expressed in One or Two Words

Numbers more than two words long are expressed in figures.

The pollster interviewed 3,250 voters before the election.

The dietitian prepared 125 sample menus.

When Levittown, Pennsylvania, was built in the early 1950's, the builder's purchases included 300,000 doorknobs, 153,000 faucets, 53,600 ice cube trays, and 4,000 manhole covers.

NOTE: To be consistent with the forms used in the last sentence above, the number 4,000 is expressed in figures even though it could be written in just two words.

36d *Using Numerals Where Convention Requires Their Use*

(1) Addresses

1600 Pennsylvania Avenue

10 Downing Street

111 Fifth Avenue, New York, New York 10003

(2) Dates

January 15, 1929   62 B.C.

November 22, 1963   1914–1919

(3) Exact times

9:16   10 A.M. (or 10:00 A.M.)   6:50

EXCEPTIONS: Spell out times of day when they are used with *o'clock: eleven o'clock,* not *11 o'clock.* Also spell out times expressed as round numbers: *They were in bed by ten.*

(4) Exact sums of money

$25.11

$6752.00 (or $6,752.00)

$25.5 million (or $25,500,000)

EXCEPTION: You may write out a round sum of money if the number can be expressed in fewer than three words.

five dollars   two thousand dollars

fifty-three cents   six hundred dollars

(5) Pages and divisions of written works

Numerals are used for chapter numbers; volume numbers; acts, scenes, and lines of plays; books of the Bible; and line numbers of long poems.

The "Out, out brief candle" speech appears in Act 5, scene 5, of *Macbeth* (lines 17–28); in Kittredge's *Complete Works of Shakespeare* it appears on page 1142.

(6) Measurements

When a measurement is expressed by a number accompanied by a symbol or an abbreviation, use figures.

55 mph	12″
32°	15 cc

(7) Numbers containing percentages, decimals, or fractions

80% (or 80 percent)	6 3/4
98.6	3.14

(8) Ratios, scores, and statistics

Children preferred Crispy Crunchies over Total Bran by a ratio of 20 to 1.

The Orioles defeated the Phillies 6 to 0.

The median age of the voters was 42; the mean age was 40.

(9) Identification numbers

Route 66	Track 8
Channel 12	Social Security number 146–07–3846

36e *Using Numerals with Spelled-out Numbers*

Even when all the numbers in a particular passage are short enough to be spelled out, figures are sometimes used along with spelled-out numbers to distinguish one number from another.

CONFUSING: The team was divided into twenty two-person squads.
CLEAR: The team was divided into twenty 2-person squads.
CONFUSING: They lived at 555 5th Avenue.
CLEAR: They lived at 555 Fifth Avenue.

E X E R C I S E   1

Revise the use of numbers in these sentences, being sure usage is correct and consistent. If a sentence uses numbers correctly, mark it with a C.

EXAMPLE: The Empire State Building is one hundred and two stories high.

The Empire State Building is 102 stories high.

1. *1984*, a novel by George Orwell, is set in a totalitarian society.
2. The English placement examination included a 30-minute personal-experience essay, a 45-minute expository essay, and a 100-item objective test of grammar and usage.
3. In a control group of two hundred forty-seven patients, almost three out of four suffered serious adverse reactions to the new drug.
4. Before the thirteenth amendment to the Constitution, slaves were counted as 3/5 of a person.
5. The intensive membership drive netted 2,608 new members and additional dues of over 5 thousand dollars.
6. They had only 2 choices: either they could take the yacht at Pier Fourteen, or they could return home to the penthouse at Twenty-seven Harbor View Drive.
7. The atomic number of lithium is three.
8. Approximately 3 hundred thousand school children in District 6 were given hearing and vision examinations between May third and June 26.
9. The United States was drawn into the war by the Japanese attack on Pearl Harbor on December seventh, 1941.
10. An upper-middle-class family can spend over two hundred fifty thousand dollars to raise each child up to age 18.

PART 8

Writing with Sources

Research for Writing

Research is the systematic study and investigation of a topic outside your own experience and knowledge. When you write a research paper, you may do **primary research**—conducting interviews and surveys, observing people and events—in addition to **secondary research**—reading other researcher's studies of your topic. Throughout this chapter, cross-references refer you to appropriate sections of the Student Case Study in Chapter 40, which illustrates and applies the research process.

37a *Mapping Out a Search Strategy*

A **search strategy** is a systematic process of collecting and evaluating source material, moving in a logical, orderly progression from general sources of information to more and more specific ones. A search strategy reflects the way research works: as your research becomes more focused, so do your ideas.

Search Strategy

- Set up conferences with instructor and librarian to plan search strategy and get names of helpful sources of information (books, organizations, experts, and so on).
- Visit reference area: survey encyclopedias, basic textbooks, and other general reference works to get an overview of your topic; pay particular attention to bibliographies.
- Plan and set up interviews; draft letters of inquiry; consider possibilities for field research.

- Consult catalog: locate articles recommended by experts or noted in basic reference works or their bibliographies.
- Search catalog for authors and titles: locate books recommended by experts or noted in basic reference works or their bibliographies.
- Search periodical indexes.
- Do database search if possible.
- Search catalog under subject.
- Use special library services if possible.
- Consult experts if necessary.
- Do field research if necessary.
- Return to reference area: consult specialized reference works as needed to fill in details.

The search strategy outlined above represents only one way to map out your progress, and many variations are possible. Remember, though, that although you map out your search strategy in advance, your plan should be flexible. You should be prepared to modify your search strategy as your objectives become more specific and your research becomes more focused (see **"Mapping Out a Search Strategy" in 40b Student Case Study.**)

37b *Doing Library Research*

Strategies For Doing Library Research

Before you start:

- Know the library's physical layout.
- Familiarize yourself with the library's holdings.
- Know the library's personnel.
- Be aware of the library's hours.

As you do research:

- Be sure to copy down or print out complete publication information—author, title, volume number, date of publication—that you will need to locate a particular source.
- Remember how to distinguish between a book and a periodical citation: a periodical citation includes an article title set in quotation marks.

(1) Reference sources for exploratory research

During **exploratory research** you get a preliminary sense of your topic and its possibilities. Your goal is to find a **research question** for your paper (see 40b). At this early stage you want to consult works that give useful overviews but that are not too technical. The exploration you do now can help you to familiarize yourself with key terms, people, and events relevant to your topic (see **40b and 40c Student Case Studies**). The following reference works are most useful for exploratory research.

General Encyclopedias   General multivolume encyclopedias such as *Encyclopedia Americana* and *Collier's Encyclopedia* contain information about many different subjects. Although general encyclopedias provide a good overview, they do not replace in-depth research.

Perhaps the most respected multivolume encyclopedia is *The New Encyclopaedia Britannica,* now in its fifteenth edition. The newest edition is divided into three sections: the *Propaedia,* a one-volume general subject index; the *Micropaedia,* a twelve-volume index containing brief articles; and the *Macropaedia,* a nineteen-volume detailed discussion of selected subjects listed in the *Micropaedia.* The information in the *Britannica* is invaluable, but this encyclopedia takes some getting used to. You can begin by searching the *Propaedia* for subject categories and then reading the brief articles in the *Micropaedia.* The longer discussions in the *Macropaedia* frequently contain brief bibliographies.

To get an overview of your topic in less time, use a one-volume general encyclopedia. Two of the best are *The New Columbia Encyclopedia* and *The Random House Encyclopedia.* Both contain many short entries listed in alphabetical order by subject. The cross-references and in-depth bibliographical information provided by the multivolume encyclopedias, however, do not appear in these short volumes. You may still have to consult a multivolume encyclopedia if you need more general information.

Encyclopedias, Dictionaries, and Bibliographies in Special Subjects These specialized reference works contain in-depth articles on single subjects in greater detail than do general encyclopedias, and articles sometimes include annotated bibliographies and cross-references. Specialized reference works are listed in Eugene P. Sheehy's *Guide to Reference Books,* available at the reference desk in most libraries. For information on specialized reference works used in specific disciplines, see the appropriate chapter in Part 9, Writing in the Disciplines. ▶ **See Part 9**

General Bibliographies   General bibliographies list books available in a wide variety of fields.

> *Books in Print.* A helpful index of authors and titles of every book in print in the United States. *The Subject Guide to Books in Print* indexes books according to subject area. *Paperbound Books in Print* is an index to all currently available paperbacks.
>
> *The Bibliographic Index.* A tool for locating bibliographies, this index is particularly useful for researching a subject that is not well covered in other indexes. Provides references to long bibliographies in books and brief ones in periodical articles.

Biographical References   Specialized biographical reference books provide valuable information about people's lives and times and bibliographic listings.

Living Persons

> *Who's Who in America.* Published every other year, this dictionary gives very brief biographical data and addresses of prominent living Americans.
>
> *Who's Who.* Concise biographical facts about notable living English men and women.
>
> *Current Biography.* Informal articles on living people of many nationalities.
>
> *American Men and Women of Science.* Information about prominent Americans in the physical, biological, social, and behavioral sciences.
>
> *Twentieth Century Authors.* Informal biographies of contemporary authors of many nationalities.

Deceased Persons

> *Dictionary of American Biography.* Considered the best of American biographical dictionaries. Offers articles on over thirteen thousand deceased Americans who have made contributions in all fields.
>
> *Dictionary of National Biography.* The most important reference work for English biography.
>
> *Webster's Biographical Dictionary.* Perhaps the most widely used biographical reference work. Includes people from all periods and places.
>
> *American Authors 1600–1900; European Authors 1000–1900; British Authors Before 1800; British Authors of the 19th Century.* These works provide biographical data on authors who wrote before the twentieth century.

549

Who Was When? A Dictionary of Contemporaries. A reference source for historical biography; covers 500 B.C. through the early 1970's.

Who Was Who in America. This series from 1607 to the present consists of nine volumes covering 1607–1985, the historical volume covering 1607 to 1896, and an index volume. These volumes, though useful, contain some inaccuracies.

(2) Reference sources for focused research

When you do **focused** research, you look for information with a specific research question in mind, returning to the library's reference area with more narrowly focused objectives. With your research question in mind, you use reference works to fill in specific details— facts, examples, statistics, definitions, quotations—to support your ideas (see **"Library Work"** in **40e Student Case Study**). The following reference works are most useful for focused research.

Unabridged Dictionaries   **Unabridged dictionaries,** such as the *Oxford English Dictionary,* are comprehensive works that give detailed information about words.

Special Dictionaries   These dictionaries focus on topics such as usage, synonyms, slang and idioms, etymologies, and foreign terms. For a list of special-purpose dictionaries see 19e.

Yearbooks and Almanacs   A **yearbook** is an annual publication that brings factual and statistical information on a subject up to date. An **almanac** provides lists, charts, and statistics about a wide variety of subjects.

World Almanac. Includes statistics about government, population, sports, and many other subjects. Includes a chronology of events of the previous year. Published annually since 1868.

Information Please Almanac. Could be used to supplement the *World Almanac* (each work includes information unavailable in the other) and is somewhat easier to read. Published annually since 1947.

Facts on File. A world news digest with index. Covering 1940 to the present, this work offers digests of important news stories from metropolitan dailies. Published weekly, *Facts on File* serves as a kind of current encyclopedia.

Editorials on File. Reprints important editorials from American and Canadian newspapers. Editorials represent both sides of controversial issues and are preceded by a summary of the principles involved.

Statistical Abstract of the United States. Summarizes the innumerable statistics gathered by the U.S. government.

Atlases   An **atlas** contains maps and charts and often a wealth of historical, cultural, political, and economic information.

> National Geographic Society. *National Geographic Atlas of the World,* 6th ed. 1990. This is the most up-to-date atlas available.

> *Rand McNally Cosmopolitan World Atlas.* A modern and extremely legible medium-sized atlas.

> *Times,* London. *The Times Atlas of the World,* five volumes, John Bartholomew, ed. Considered one of the best large world atlases. Includes inset maps for many cities. Very accurate and attractive maps throughout.

> Allen, James Paul and Eugene James Turner. *We The People: An Atlas of America's Ethnic Diversity.* Presents the ethnic diversity of the American people, including statistics on country of origin and maps of settlement in the U.S.

> Shepherd, William Robert. *Historical Atlas,* 9th ed. Covers period from 2000 B.C.. to 1955. Excellent maps showing war campaigns and development of commerce.

Quotation Books   A **quotation book** contains numerous quotations on a wide variety of subjects, often by well-known persons. Such quotations can be especially useful for your paper's introductory and concluding paragraphs.

> *Bartlett's Familiar Quotations.* Quotations are arranged chronologically by author. The volume also includes an index of authors and a key word index that can help you to find a quotation on a specific subject.

> *The Home Book of Quotations.* Quotations are arranged by subject. An author index and a key word index are also included.

(3)   Periodical indexes

In the early stages of your research, you may come across references to useful journal articles. After you copy down the necessary bibliographic information, you can proceed to the catalog that lists the journal, newspaper, and magazine holdings of your library. (In some libraries, periodicals may be listed in a separate catalog; in others, periodicals are listed in a single catalog along with books.) The catalog can tell you whether or not your library has the issues of the journals in which the articles you are looking for appear and where in the library those journals are housed. Libraries house periodicals in yearly bound volumes or in current issues located in the periodical section of your library. The words *microfiche, micro-*

print, or *microfilm* tell you that the periodicals have been stored photographically.

Later in your research, you consult specific periodical indexes as you search for additional articles to help you develop your research question. A **periodical index** lists articles from a selected group of magazines, newspapers, or scholarly journals. In some indexes entries are arranged according to subject; in others, entries are listed according to author. (Some periodicals have both kinds of listings.) The key to the abbreviations at the front of the volume enables you to use the index and gives all the information you need to compile your documentation and list of works cited. The entry in Figure 1 from the *Humanities Index* illustrates information contained in a citation from a periodical index. Once you locate potentially useful articles in the periodical index, you return to the catalog to locate the appropriate journals.

Many periodicals are indexed in computerized databases (**see 37b4**). Some specialized indexes are available only in computerized form and not in print. However, many articles in newspapers, magazines, and scholarly journals are indexed only in bound volumes or paperbound supplements kept in your library's reference section.

There are three levels of periodical indexes: general indexes, specialized indexes, and abstracting services.

General Indexes   General indexes lead you to articles in newspapers and popular magazines.

> *Readers' Guide to Periodical Literature.* This index lists articles that appear in more than 150 magazines for general readers. You have probably used this index before, and the fact that you are familiar with it may encourage you to consult it first. However, you should be aware of its limitations. First, the *Readers' Guide* indexes only

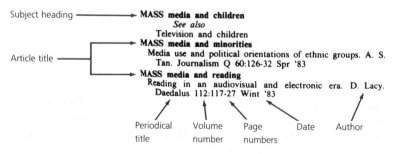

FIGURE 1   Entry from *Humanities Index*

552

popular periodicals, whose articles may oversimplify complex issues. Many of the periodicals indexed here are not suitable for college research. As a result, you must supplement information derived from such sources with material from more scholarly works. Second, even for popular periodicals, the *Readers' Guide* is neither as comprehensive nor as accessible as the *Magazine Index.*

Appearing in yearly volumes and paperbound supplements, articles in the *Readers' Guide* are listed and cross-referenced under subject headings.

Magazine Index. Now widely used in college libraries, this is an automated microfilm reader that indexes popular periodicals. It covers more periodicals (more than 400) than the *Readers' Guide* and is more up to date. In addition, it is easier to use. With the *Magazine Index* you can look at more than four years' worth of periodicals at a time; if you were using the *Readers' Guide,* you might have to look through many different volumes—bound volumes and supplements—to scan the same period.

New York Times Index. This is an excellent and reliable record of current events. In addition to news, it contains feature-length articles on issues of general interest. The *New York Times Index* lists major articles and features of the *Times* since 1851 by year or years. To find articles on a subject, locate the volume for the appropriate year. Articles are listed alphabetically by subject with short summaries. Supplements are published every two weeks. If your library subscribes to the *New York Times* microfilm service, you have access to every issue of the *Times* back to 1851. Articles give a contemporary view of a wide variety of subjects—everything from business and politics to literature and the arts.

Specialized Indexes   Specialized indexes lead you to articles in professional journals. The most commonly used of these volumes index scholarly periodicals that are largely American and fairly easy to obtain. Many of the articles listed in such indexes assume expert knowledge, but some are accessible to general readers. For information on specialized indexes used in specific disciplines, see the appropriate chapter in Part 9, Writing in the Disciplines.

► See
Part 9

Abstracting Services   Abstracting services have a wider scope than general or specialized indexes, with comprehensive, often international, listings of literature in a discipline. In addition to providing citations for journal articles, abstracting services also include **abstracts,** brief summaries of the articles' major points. As a beginning researcher you may find these indexes difficult to use. Still, abstracting services might be of some value to you now, enabling you to preview an article before you go to the trouble of searching for it, and they will be useful to you later in your academic career, as you do more serious research in your field of specialization. For information on abstracting services used in specific disciplines, see the appropriate chapter in *Writing in the Disciplines,* Part 9. Even if your library does not receive copies of these publications, you will be able to gain access to most of them if your library has online searching. For information about which abstracting services might be of value to you—and how to use them—consult a reference librarian.

See
◄ Part 9

(4) Database searches

Perhaps the fastest way to locate relevant information is to do a database search (**see "Library Work" in 40e Student Case Study**). Such a search enables you to use a computer to scan various **databases**—electronic indexes that list thousands of bibliographic sources. Most databases you will have occasion to use contain bibliographic citations; some contain abstracts that summarize entire books and articles. Not all databases are equally useful. Social science and natural science databases, for example, are currently more extensive than those in the humanities. Ask your librarian which databases would be appropriate for your subject matter and which journals and periodicals the relevant databases contain. If certain important journals are not included, you will have to supplement your search with bound periodical indexes (**see 37b3**).

One final word of caution: Database searching can be an expensive way to find information. Although most databases charge nominal fees, some charge more than a dollar per minute, while others charge by the entry. Be sure to ask your librarian to estimate the cost of your search before you begin.

In many college libraries the librarian carries out the search. However, many libraries have (or will soon have) equipment that enables students to do their own searches. Whatever system applies in your library, understanding the following general guidelines for carrying out a database search should make retrieving information easier.

Choosing Appropriate Databases   The first step in doing a computer search is determining which databases include the information you need. Many colleges subscribe to information services that provide access to hundreds of databases. By reviewing the databases available, you and your librarian can decide which ones are appropriate to your research. Among the useful databases most commonly available in college libraries are ERIC, PSYCINFO, and MLA Bibliography. In addition, most indexes (such as the *Humanities Index*, the *Social Sciences Index*, the *Business Index*, the *Education Index*, the *Art Index*, and many others) can be searched by computer in many libraries.

Narrowing Your Topic to Key Words   Before you begin a database search, you must define your topic in one or more **key words** (sometimes called *descriptors*). These words are your entry into the database, for they enable the computer to call up articles that contain your key words in their titles or abstracts. For this reason, the more precise your key words are, the more specific the information you get. For example, if your topic were "teaching science fiction," general key words like *science* or *teaching* would not be helpful to you, for they would yield literally thousands of references, most of them irrelevant. *Science fiction*, although narrower, would still yield several hundred—too many to be helpful. *Teaching and science fiction*, however, would yield about thirty references—a manageable number.

A list of key words and phrases accompanies each database. Some information services issue a printed book, called a **thesaurus,** that lists these words. Other databases contain a **dictionary** that can be called up on the video terminal. By consulting the thesaurus or the dictionary, you can determine which key words best describe your topic. If the first key word or words you have chosen do not yield enough information, you will have to try different ones or different combinations to search your topic.

Entering Key Words into the Computer   Once you have entered your key words, the computer will indicate the number of citations they will elicit. You can then decide whether you want a printout of these citations or whether you want to narrow your search. Keep in mind that you can search each key word individually, or you can examine key words in combination. By entering the combination *science fiction* AND *teaching,* for instance, you get only citations that contain *both* key words (e.g., "Using Science Fiction to Teach Children to Read"). By entering the combination *science fiction* OR *teaching,* you get citations that contain *either* key word.

Selecting the Format You Want for Each Citation   Before you print out the citations, you must select the format you prefer. You can command the computer to print only the bibliographic citation,

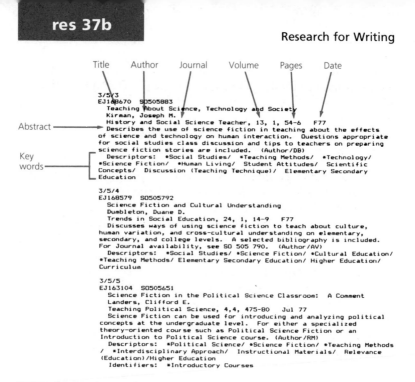

Title   Author   Journal   Volume   Pages   Date

```
3/5/3
EJ168670  SO505883
   Teaching About Science, Technology and Society
   Kirman, Joseph M.
   History and Social Science Teacher, 13, 1, 54-6   F77
```
Abstract ——
```
   Describes the use of science fiction in teaching about the effects
   of science and technology on human interaction.  Questions appropriate
   for social studies class discussion and tips to teachers on preparing
   science fiction stories are included.  (Author/DB)
```
Key
words ——
```
      Descriptors:  *Social Studies/  *Teaching Methods/  *Technology/
   *Science Fiction/  *Human Living/  Student Attitudes/  Scientific
   Concepts/  Discussion (Teaching Technique)/  Elementary Secondary
   Education
```

```
3/5/4
EJ168579  SO505792
   Science Fiction and Cultural Understanding
   Dumbleton, Duane D.
   Trends in Social Education, 24, 1, 14-9   F77
   Discusses ways of using science fiction to teach about culture,
human variation, and cross-cultural understanding on elementary,
secondary, and college levels.  A selected bibliography is included.
For Journal availability, see SO 505 790.  (Author/AV)
      Descriptors:  *Social Studies/ *Science Fiction/ *Cultural Education/
   *Teaching Methods/ Elementary Secondary Education/ Higher Education/
   Curriculum
```

```
3/5/5
EJ163104  SO505651
   Science Fiction in the Political Science Classroom:  A Comment
   Landers, Clifford E.
   Teaching Political Science, 4, 4, 475-80   Jul 77
   Science Fiction can be used for introducing and analyzing political
concepts at the undergraduate level.  For either a specialized
theory-oriented course such as Political Science Fiction or an
Introduction to Political Science course.  (Author/RM)
      Descriptors:  *Political Science/ *Science Fiction/ *Teaching Methods
   /  *Interdisciplinary Approach/  Instructional Materials/  Relevance
   (Education)/Higher Education
      Identifiers:  *Introductory Courses
```

FIGURE 2   Database printout

which gives the author, title, and journal reference, or you can command the fullest format, which gives you, in addition to the above, an abstract, publishing information, reprint costs, and additional key words. Between these two extremes a few other formats are usually available. Because computer time is costly, select the format that gives you only the information you need.

Making a Printout   You can print out all the citations, but if there are too many you may choose to print out only those published in certain years—all entries between 1988 and 1989, for example. For a paper on teaching science fiction, a student requested abstracts of all citations containing the key words *science fiction* AND *teaching*.

(5)   The catalog

All of the books in your college library are catalogued—that is, listed and described. Some libraries list their holdings in print form on cards which are arranged in drawers of **card catalogs.** These libraries have either a single catalog that interfiles author, title, and subject cards or two separate catalogs, one for author-title cards and another for subject cards. Books in the author-title file are alphabetized by author or by title; books in the subject catalog are alphabetized by subject. Other libraries have **online catalogs,** computerized systems that allow students to call up catalog entries by author, title, or subject on video terminals. (If the terminal is connected to a printer, students can get printouts of catalog entries.)

Early in your research, search books by author or title to see whether your library owns books mentioned in bibliographies or texts you have skimmed in the reference room, and to see where those books are located. Later, when you have narrowed the focus of your research and know more precisely the kind of information you are looking for, you search the catalog by subject for further information to support your tentative thesis.

If you have trouble finding your topic in the catalog, you can consult the index volume called *Library of Congress Subject Headings,* which is kept at the reference desk. Also keep in mind that the catalog itself contains cross-references that refer you to related subject headings. By using them, you can find more material related to your subject.

To locate a book on the library shelves, you need its **call number,** which appears with the entry in the catalog. The call number refers you to the general area of the library that houses books on your subject. The same call number that appears in the catalog is written on the spine of the book. When you find a book you need, look through the books shelved nearby. In itself, browsing is not an effective research technique, but as part of a focused search strategy, it can sometimes yield good results.

If you cannot find a book, go to the circulation desk for help. The book may be out, on reserve, or held in a different section of the library. If it has been checked out, the person at the desk will tell you when it is due back and, in many cases, will notify the borrower that someone else needs it.

(6) *Special library services*

Your most valuable resource is your librarian, a trained professional whose business it is to know how to locate information. Before you begin any complicated research project, you should ask your librarian about any of the following special services you may plan to use.

Interlibrary Loans   If you need a book or article that the library does not own, you can ask your librarian to arrange an interlibrary loan. Libraries can arrange to borrow books or acquire copies of articles from other college libraries or from the holdings of municipal and state libraries. However, because interlibrary loans may take several weeks, you may not be able to take advantage of this service unless you initiate the loan early in your research.

Special Collections   Your librarian can also help you locate special collections of books, manuscripts, or documents housed in your college library or nearby in the community. Churches, specialized libraries, government agencies, ethnic societies, historical trusts, and museums sometimes have books and articles that you cannot find anywhere else. Your librarian may be able to get you permission to use them.

Government Documents   Federal, state, and local governments publish a variety of print materials, ranging from consumer information to detailed technical reports. These documents vary widely in quality and complexity as well as in subject matter. Although some government documents may be overly technical—or overly simplistic—for your research needs, others can be valuable. Government documents are particularly useful sources of statistics.

Some government documents, such as *Statistical Abstract of the United States,* may be housed in your library's reference room. A large university library may have a separate government documents room or section with its own catalog or index; in smaller libraries, government documents may be shelved along with books and indexed in the main subject catalog. The *Monthly Catalog of U.S. Government Publications,* which may be located either among the indexes in the reference room or in a special government documents area, indexes many, but not all, publications of the federal government.

Vertical File   The **vertical file** is the place where libraries keep miscellaneous source materials that may or may not be suitable for research. This file includes pamphlets from a variety of organizations and interest groups, some requested by your library and others unsolicited. The file may also include newspaper clippings and other material collected by your librarians because of its relevance to the needs and interests of your college's population. Some sources, however, may not be acceptable or useful for research. Consult a reference librarian for help in evaluating the materials in your library's vertical file.

If Your Source Is Not Available

Problem	*Possible Solution*
Book checked out of library	Consult person at circulation desk.
Book not in library's collection	Call other nearby libraries. Ask instructor if he or she owns a copy. Arrange for interlibrary loan (if time permits).
Journal not in library's collection/article ripped out of journal	Arrange for interlibrary copy (if time permits). Check to see whether article is available on a database. Ask librarian whether article has been reprinted as part of a collection.

EXERCISE 1

What library research sources would you consult to find the following information?

1. A book review of Maxine Hong Kingston's *China Men* (1980)
2. Biographical information about the American anthropologist Margaret Mead
3. Books about Margaret Mead and her work
4. Information about the theories of Albert Einstein
5. Whether your college library has *The Human Use of Human Beings* by Norbert Wiener
6. How many pages there are in *On Death and Dying* by Elisabeth Kübler-Ross and how long the bibliography is
7. Where you could find other books on death and dying
8. Where you could find other books by Elisabeth Kübler-Ross
9. Articles about Walt Whitman's *Leaves of Grass*
10. Whether *Leaves of Grass* is presently available in a Norton Critical Edition

EXERCISE 2

Use the resources of your library to help you answer the following questions. Cite the source or sources of your answers.

559

1. What government publication could give you information about how to solar heat your home?
2. What government agency could you contact to find out what is being done to help the aging receive proper nutrition?
3. At what address could you contact Bruce Evans, an American artist?
4. At what university does the astronomer Carl Sagan teach?
5. What organizations could you contact to find out what is being done to prevent the killing of wolves in North America?
6. How could you get current information about the tobacco lobby?
7. What government agency could tell you what government services are available to resident aliens?
8. At what address could you contact Harold Bloom, a scholar who does work on nineteenth-century English literature?
9. Is there a government pamphlet that gives information about buying a new car?
10. How could you get current information about the Peace Corps?

37c *Gathering Information Outside the Library*

By relying exclusively on the library for research materials, you ignore important sources of more current information. Public service organizations, lobbies, and government agencies have available a wealth of current data. People who work in a field or who have a unique view of a situation are also excellent sources. Your problem as a researcher is finding these sources and obtaining information from them.

(1) Finding organizations

Numerous organizations offer literature, often free of charge, to interested parties. Your instructor or reference librarian may suggest appropriate organizations for you to contact, and local businesses, chambers of commerce, corporate public information departments, and government offices or publications may also direct you to potentially helpful groups. The most useful source of information, however, is the *Encyclopedia of Associations*. This valuable resource lists thousands of organizations by subject area. It also has a key word index, which enables you to discover whether or not an organization in a particular subject area exists. In addition to writing or calling for information, you can sometimes arrange to visit an organization, perhaps to observe a meeting or to interview a member (see "**Field Work: Observation**" in **40e Student Case Study**).

(2) Writing for information

Once you have identified people or organizations that may be able to supply useful information, your next step is to contact them directly and get their help (see "**Establishing Research Priorities**" in **40b Student Case Study**). If the organization is local or has a toll-free number, call to request information. If not, you may want to write a letter. Check with your instructor to be sure that writing for information is both necessary and appropriate and that you have enough time to wait for an answer. Whether you call or write, be sure you are prepared with the following information:

- The name of the person or department to contact
- The specific information you would like
- Why you want the information
- When you need it

For an explanation of how to write a letter requesting information, see **47d**.

(3) Finding people

An important step in your research is locating people who can suggest reliable and up-to-date sources of information. A meeting with your instructor may be all that you need to get started, or your instructor may refer you to someone else more familiar with your topic. Just one or two good contacts can help you to establish a research network: your first contact might suggest another, who in turn might suggest two more (see "**Consulting an Expert**" in **40b Student Case Study**).

Many excellent guides to people who are experts in various fields are available in the reference section of your library. Most of these guides focus on people in a particular area of endeavor.

Who's Who Among Black Americans
Who's Who and Where in Women's Studies
Who's Who in American Art
Who's Who in American Education
Who's Who in American Politics
American Men and Women of Science

Biographical Directory of the American Psychological Association
Contemporary Authors
Directory of The Modern Language Association

EXERCISE 3

You are beginning to gather information for the research projects outlined below. Whom in your college or your community might you approach to establish a research network? Write five exploratory questions that you would ask each person.

1. A paper for a biology course examining new developments in DNA recombinant research
2. A short paper for a history course in which you examine the validity of slave narratives for historical research
3. A research paper for a composition course in which you explore the possibility of scientists developing artificial intelligence
4. A paper for a political science course about the issues in a local election

(4) Observing people, places, objects, and events

Observation, so frequently used in scientific research, can be a useful source of information for papers in other disciplines (see **"Field Work: Walking Tour" in 40e Student Case Study**). For example, an art or music paper may be enriched by information gathered in a visit to a museum or concert; an education paper may include a report of a classroom observation; and a psychology or sociology paper may include observations of an individual's behavior or of group interaction.

Guidelines for Making Observations

- Determine in advance what information you hope to gain from your observations. This material should not be available from the library or other research sources.
- Decide exactly what you want to observe and where you are going to observe it.
- Make an appointment for your visit.
- Bring a small notepad or tape recorder so that you can keep a record of your observations.
- Bring any additional materials that you may need—a camera, videocassette recorder, or stop watch, for example.
- Afterwards, copy your observations onto notecards. Include the date, place, and time of your observations.

---

(5) Conducting an interview

Interviews often give you material that you cannot get by any other means—for instance, biographical information, a firsthand account of an event, or the views of an expert on a particular subject (see **"Field Work: Interviews" in 40e Student Case Study**). Interviews also allow you to prepare questions in advance and to follow up on the answers if necessary.

Your interview questions should elicit detailed, useful responses, and therefore, you should design them carefully. *Leading questions,* for instance, make some people defensive, and *vague questions* can confuse them. *Dead-end questions*—questions that call for yes/no answers, for example—yield limited information. As the following examples illustrate, the way you phrase a question determines the response to it:

The city intends to spend 2 billion dollars over the next ten years to rehabilitate the port area. Do you support this plan? Why or why not? (good question)

Are you against the city's innovative plans to rehabilitate the port area? (leading question)

What are your feelings about the port area? (vague question)

Do you think the port area should be developed? (dead-end question; likely to elicit a yes/no answer)

The success or failure of an interview often depends on how you prepare for it. First, learn something about your topic and about the person you are interviewing. Before interviewing the author of a new book, for example, you should have read it yourself.

Next, prepare a list of questions tailored to the subject matter and time limit of your interview. It is better to have a few questions that can be answered in depth than many that can be answered only superficially.

The kinds of questions you ask depend on the kind of information you are seeking. **Open-ended** questions elicit general information and allow a respondent great flexibility in answering:

How was this neighborhood's population different forty years ago?

Do you think students today are motivated? Why or why not?

If you could change something in your life, what would it be?

Closed-ended questions elicit specific information, enabling you to zero in on a subject:

Has your family become more or less religious over the past ten years? How do you account for this?

What is the most important health benefit of your findings concerning Vitamin C?

How much money did the government's cost-cutting programs actually save?

Guidelines for Conducting an Interview

- Always make an appointment.
- Prepare a list of specific questions, and phrase questions carefully.
- Do background reading about your topic. Be sure that you do not ask for information that you can easily find elsewhere.
- Have a pen and paper with you. If you want to tape the interview, get the respondent's permission in advance.
- Allow the person you are interviewing to complete an answer before you ask another question.
- Take notes, but continue to pay attention as you do so. Occasionally nod or make comments that show you are interested and that encourage the respondent to continue.
- Pay attention to the reactions of the respondent.
- Do not hesitate to deviate from your prepared list of questions if necessary to ask follow-up questions.
- At the end of the interview, thank the respondent for his or her time and cooperation.
- After the interview, send a brief note of appreciation.

---

(6) Conducting a survey

A survey enables you to gain new information by polling a variety of people. For some topics—a literary or historical analysis, for example—surveys have no usefulness. If, however, you are examining a contemporary social, psychological, or economic issue—the rise of racism on college campuses, for instance—a survey of attitudes or opinions could be extremely helpful. Before you start, keep in mind that conducting a survey requires a good deal of advance planning. If time is short, you should use another approach.

Begin by identifying the group of people you will poll. This group can be a **convenient sample**—for example, people in your chemistry lecture—or a **random sample**—names chosen from a telephone directory, for instance. When you choose a sample, your goal is to designate a population that is not only easily accessible to you, but also representative. You do not want, for example, a sample composed of all sophomores, all females, or all business majors—unless, of course, the goal of your survey is to poll only these groups.

Next, ask yourself what a survey might add to your paper. What gaps in your information do you expect to fill? What information can your survey provide that you could not get from reference books or individual interviews?

The number of people to poll is another consideration. To persuade readers that you are making a valid statement about an issue, you must have enough respondents to convince them that your sample is significant. If you poll ten people in your French class about an issue of college policy, and your university has ten thousand students, you cannot expect your readers to be convinced by your results. Scientific formulas exist to determine exactly what constitutes a significant sample, so if you plan to conduct a survey, you might want to consult a social science instructor for further information.

You must also be sure your questions are worded clearly and specifically designed to elicit the particular information you wish to get. Keep in mind that short-answer or multiple-choice questions, whose responses can be quantified, are much easier to handle than open-ended questions. Often open-ended questions yield so many kinds of responses that no valid conclusions can be drawn. Test the questions on a friend to be sure they are understandable and accurately phrased. Then, make any necessary modifications. Be sure you do not ask so many questions that respondents will lose interest and stop answering. Also, be sure that you do not ask biased or leading questions that oversimplify an issue by asking for an either/or response.

Although professional polling organizations distribute forms by mail, you have an advantage if you are surveying a population that you have access to—your classmates or neighbors, for example. If your population is your fellow students, you can slip questionnaires under their doors in the residence hall, or you can distribute them in the cafeteria during lunch, or (with the instructor's permission) you can give them out during a large lecture.

If your questionnaire is fairly brief—one that you think will take only a few minutes to fill out—the best way to ensure a high response rate is to allow respondents a specific amount of time and collect the forms yourself. If you believe they will need more time, or if you believe filling out forms on the spot will be disruptive or annoying, or if you think respondents may not want to be identified, you can request responses be returned to you—placed in a box set up in a central location, for instance. If you do not collect the forms yourself, be sure to set a deadline for their completion. Remember to set the deadline well in advance of when you need to begin analyzing responses.

If you have a manageable number of questions and respondents, you should be able to classify and categorize your responses fairly easily. If your questionnaire is complex, you may want to get a few friends to help you with this step. In any case, determining exactly what your results tell you is the most challenging (and the most unpredictable) part of the process. Counting is one thing, but determining what your various responses suggest is quite another. For example, even though only 20 percent of your respondents may be fraternity members, the fact that nearly all of them favor restrictions on hazing would be a fairly significant finding.

If your questions have addressed key concerns and generated a significant number of thoughtful responses, your results might suggest (or confirm) a tentative thesis for your paper—for example, that the current climate on your campus is (or is not) receptive to curriculum changes, restrictions on fraternity hazing, or seminars to decrease racism.

Guidelines for Conducting a Survey

- Determine what you want to know.
- Select your sample.
- Design your questions.
- Type and duplicate the questionnaire.
- Distribute the questionnaires.
- Collect the questionnaires.
- Analyze your responses.
- Decide how to use the results in your paper.

Working with Source Material

Once you have located sources of information for your paper, your next step is to read and evaluate them and to take notes. When you write your paper, you will use the information you have collected to support your points and to help you evaluate the work of others.

▶ See 40e

38a Reading Sources

Like writing, reading is an active process. When you read a text actively, you interact with it: You read and reread, identify and highlight key ideas and significant relationships, and begin to make marginal annotations.

The first steps in the process of active reading are *previewing* and *highlighting*.

(1) Previewing

The first time you encounter a text, you should skim it to gain a sense of the author's subject and emphasis. When previewing a book, begin by looking at its table of contents, especially at the sections that pertain to your topic. A quick glance at the index will reveal the kind and amount of coverage the book gives to subjects that may be important to you. As you leaf through the chapters, notice any pictures, graphs, or tables, reading the captions that appear under them. When previewing magazine articles, look at headlines or boxed excerpts that may appear throughout the text.

Also scan the introductory and concluding paragraphs for summaries of the author's main points. Journal articles in the sciences and social sciences often begin with summaries called **abstracts.** Read these as part of your previewing process.

In addition, look for the visual cues that writers of both books and articles use to stress ideas.

Visual Cues

Headings	Color
Capital letters	Italics
Underlining	Lists—with items numbered
Boxes	or set off with bullets (•)
Boldface	

Stylistic elements such as thesis statements, topic sentences, repeated key terms, transitional words and phrases, and transitional paragraphs can also help you gain an overview of a text and begin to react critically to its idea.

(2) Highlighting

When you preview a selection, you skim it to get a general idea of its subject and emphasis. When you **highlight,** you read a selection carefully, marking it to identify the key points and the relationship of one point to another. As you highlight, use a system of symbols and underlining to identify important ideas. (Never mark up books and articles that are not yours, however. If you are working with library material, photocopy the pages you need and then highlight them.) The symbols you use are up to you; the idea is to develop symbols that will clearly identify the visual and stylistic cues of a selection and that you will be able to understand when you reread them at a later time.

Highlighting Symbols

- Underline to indicate information you should read again.
- Box or circle key words or important phrases.

- Put a question mark (?) next to confusing passages, unclear points, or words you have to look up.
- Draw lines or arrows to show connections between ideas.
- Number points that appear in sequence.
- Draw a vertical line in the margin to set off an important section of text.
- Place an asterisk (*) next to an especially important idea.

The student who highlighted the following passage used a system of symbols to help her isolate the author's key ideas and to clarify the progression of ideas in the passage.

Public zoos came into existence at the ✱ beginning of the period which was to see the disappearance of animals from daily life. The zoo to which people go to meet animals, to observe them, to see them, is, in fact, a monument to the impossibility of such ✱ encounters. Modern zoos are an epitaph to a relationship which was as old as man. They are not seen as such because the wrong questions have been addressed to zoos.

When they were founded—the London Zoo in 1828, the Jardin des Plantes in 1793, the Berlin Zoo in 1844—they brought considerable ⟋① prestige to the national capitals. The prestige was not so different from that which had accrued to the private royal menageries. These menageries, along with gold plate, architecture, orchestras, players, furnishings, dwarfs, acrobats, uniforms, horses, art and food had been demonstrations of an emperor's or king's power and wealth. Likewise in the 19th century, public zoos were an endorsement of modern ⟋② colonial power. The capturing of the animals was a symbolic representation of the conquest of all distant and exotic lands. "Explorers" proved their patriotism by sending home a tiger or an elephant. The gift of an exotic animal to the metropolitan zoo became a token in subservient diplomatic relations.

Yet, like every other 19th century public institution, the zoo, however supportive of the ?⟨ideology of imperialism⟩ had to claim an

independent and civic function. The claim was
that it was another kind of museum, whose
purpose was to further knowledge and public
enlightenment. And so the first questions asked
of zoos belonged to natural history; it was then
thought possible to study the natural life of
animals even in such unnatural conditions. A
century later, more sophisticated zoologists such
as Konrad Lorenz asked behavioristic and
ethological questions, the claimed purpose of
which was to discover more about the springs
of human action through the study of animals
under experimental conditions. (John Berger,
About Looking)

Notice how symbols helped the student understand the passage.
For example, she underlined and starred the main idea of the passage and used arrows to show the relationship of one point to
another. In addition, she circled and put a question mark next to
unfamiliar words, phrases, and names—*ideology of imperialism,
ethological, behavioristic,* and *Konrad Lorenz*—that she will have
to look up. Finally, she numbered the two reasons why imperial
governments established public zoos. Once this student had highlighted the passage, she could go on to record her reactions to its
ideas—to ask questions, make connections, and draw tentative conclusions—in the form of marginal annotations.

See
5b ◀

EXERCISE 1

Preview the following passage, and then read it more carefully, highlighting
it to help you understand the writer's ideas. Then, answer the following
questions:

> What is the writer's subject?
> What is the writer's most important point?
> Which points are related?
> What is their relationship to one another?
> How does the writer make connections among related ideas clear?

A new attitude began to take effect in 1972 with the concept of
affirmative action and the enactment of the Equal Employment
Opportunity Act. Affirmative action is indispensable because it is
ethical in concept and practice.

Affirmative action is necessary because it opens doors to minorities
that never had been legally opened before in this country. Suddenly, it

was reasonable and appropriate to believe that a minority person could aspire to any profession or career he or she desired.

Thanks to affirmative action, young blacks in high school today are considered sane and reasonable to think of careers in medicine, law, business and so forth. At the same time, these young people are receiving legitimate support from family, friends, teachers and high school counselors.

Affirmative action provides a positive mind-set for minorities. The US government is saying it is legal and right for young blacks to believe in themselves. Strong affirmative action procedures truly are significant in raising the self-esteem and self-confidence of the previously dispossessed minorities.

For one to be told that he or she is less than equal when it comes to employment opportunities because of race, color or gender is devastating to the ego. This impact only can be felt clearly when an individual is the object of discrimination. An evil and ugly caste system arises when a person seeks a position and is told by those in authority that he or she is unfit or cannot pursue a certain course because of skin color.

Now, however, a job seeker can complete an application, go to an interview and have the chance to present him- or herself and his or her qualifications in areas previously closed to blacks. The program, supported by the federal government and court systems, was necessary to give everyone a chance.

Affirmative action encourages and gives hope to many formally disenfranchised blacks in this country. It is responsible for beginning to displace some of the anger in blacks, built up for decades by being told what they could not be and what they could not do.

This program builds hope and prohibits despair and violence. It has done more to diffuse and negate the attitude of blacks that they should burn it down, tear it up or start a race riot than any other major court or legal action in the past 20 years.

(Jerry B. Madkins, "Affirmative Action is Necessary and Ethical," *Personnel Journal*)

38b *Evaluating Sources*

Whenever you read, you should evaluate the potential usefulness of a source as soon as possible so that you will not waste time reading irrelevant material. Keep in mind that your reading should include a variety of sources that reflect a number of possible viewpoints.

(1) Distinguishing between primary and secondary sources

To evaluate a source, you should first be certain that you know whether you are reading a **primary** or a **secondary source**—that is, whether you are considering original documents and observations or interpretations of those documents and observations.

PRIMARY SOURCE

> [*United States Constitution: Amendment XIV (Ratified July 9, 1868). Section I.*]
> All persons born or naturalized in the United States, and subject to the jurisdiction thereof, are citizens of the United States and the state wherein they reside. No state shall make or enforce any law which shall abridge the privileges or immunities of citizens of the United States; nor shall any state deprive any person of life, liberty, or property, without the process of law; nor deny to any person within its jurisdiction the equal protection of the laws.

SECONDARY SOURCE

> [Paula S. Rothenberg, *Racism and Sexism: An Integrated Study*]
> Congress passed The Fourteenth Amendment . . . in July 1868. This amendment, which continues to play a major role in contemporary legal battles over discrimination, includes a number of important provisions. It explicitly extends citizenship to all those born or naturalized in the United States and guarantees all citizens due process and "equal protection" of the law.

For many research projects, primary sources such as letters, speeches, and data from questionnaires are essential. However, secondary sources supply the critical comments of scholars who know a good deal about the area you are studying. Still, keep in mind that the farther from an original source you get, the more chances exist for distortion and misinterpretation.

Primary and Secondary Sources

Primary Source	Secondary Source
Novel	Literary criticism
Diary, autobiography	Biography
Letters, historical documents, oral testimony	Historical commentary
Newspaper report	Editorial

Raw data from questionnaires	Social science paper
Observations/experiment	Scientific article
Television show/film	Critical analysis
Interview	Case study

(2) Evaluating print sources

One efficient way to evaluate a source and its author is to ask your librarian or your instructor for an opinion. But even if a source is highly recommended, it may not suit your needs.

To measure the usefulness of a print source, determine how *comprehensive* it is. How detailed is its treatment of your subject? Skim a book's table of contents and index for references to your topic. To be of any real help, a book should devote a section or chapter to your topic, not simply a footnote or a brief mention. For articles, read the abstract, or skim the entire article for key facts, looking closely at section headings, information set in boldface type, and topic sentences. An article should have your topic as its central subject, or at least as a major concern.

The date of publication tells you whether the information in a book or article is *current*. A discussion of computer languages written in 1966, for instance, is probably obsolete. Scientific and technological subjects usually demand state-of-the-art treatment. Even in the humanities, new discoveries and new ways of thinking lead scholars to reevaluate and modify their ideas over time.

Some classic works, however, never lose their usefulness. Although Edward Gibbon wrote *The History of the Decline and Fall of the Roman Empire* in the eighteenth century, the book still offers a valuable overview of the events it describes. Contemporary historians may interpret events differently, but Gibbon's information is sound, and the book is required reading for anyone studying Roman history. If a number of your sources cite certain earlier works, you should consult those works, regardless of their publication dates. Do, however, be alert for out-of-date information in such sources.

Another factor to consider is the *reliability* of your source. Is a piece of writing intended to inform or to persuade? Does the author have an ulterior motive? One way to judge the objectivity of a source is to find out something about its author. The source itself may contain biographical information, sometimes in a separate sec-

573

tion, or you can consult a biographical dictionary. Skim the preface to see what the author says about his or her purpose. What do other sources say about the author? Do they consider the author fair? Biased? Compare a few statements with another source—a textbook or an encyclopedia, for instance—to see whether an author seems to be slanting facts.

You should also determine how respected your source is. A contemporary review of a source can help you make this assessment. *Book Review Digest,* available in the reference section of your library, lists popular books that have been reviewed in at least three newspapers or magazines and includes excerpts from representative reviews. Scholarly books are indexed in *Book Review Index.* Although this book contains no excerpts, it does include citations that refer you to the periodicals in which books were reviewed.

You can also find out about the standing of a source in the scholarly community by consulting a special class of indexes called **citation indexes.** These books list all scholarly articles published in a given year that mention a particular source. Information is listed under the original article, the author of the article in which the original article is mentioned, or the subject. Seeing how often an article is mentioned and how it is regarded by others in the field can help you evaluate its reputation. Citation indexes are available for the humanities, the sciences, and the social sciences.

Revision Close-up

Be sure to examine carefully articles found in popular periodicals. You may consult popular sources for background or for leads, but remember that such sources are commercial. Because their aim is to sell copies to many people, their treatment may be superficial or sensational. For this reason, you should not rely on such material for your research.

(3) Evaluating nonprint sources

Nonprint sources—interviews, telephone calls, films, and so on—must also be evaluated. Here, too, you must consider the *scope* of the source—the extent to which it covers your topic. An interview with an expert on family planning who knows little about sex education may be an excellent source if your paper will focus on changing trends in birth control methods, but such an interview may not be worthwhile if your paper is about teenage pregnancy.

The *currency* of a nonprint source is also a factor. A 1970 television documentary on the topography of a Pacific island may still be accurate, but a documentary on the lives of its people may not reflect today's conditions at all.

Reliability is important, too. Is a radio feature on energy conservation part of a balanced news program or a thinly veiled commercial sponsored by a public utility? Is the material presented by experts in the field or by actors? Check the credits and acknowledgments, and read reviews to see which sources were consulted. Do the participants in a panel discussion on nuclear weapons all agree on how they should be deployed, or do they represent different points of view? Is a person you plan to interview fair and impartial or biased on some issues? Try to find out by consulting an instructor in a related field or by reading the person's work before the interview.

Guidelines for Evaluating Sources

- Is your source comprehensive?
- Is your source current?
- Is your source reliable?

EXERCISE 2

Read the following paragraphs carefully, paying close attention to the information provided about their sources and authors as well as to their content. Decide which sources would be most useful and reliable in supporting the thesis "Winning the right to vote has (or has not) significantly changed the role of women in national politics." Which sources, if any, should be disregarded? Which would you examine first? Be prepared to discuss your decisions.

1. Almost forty years after the adoption of the Nineteenth Amendment, a number of promised or threatened events have failed to materialize. The millennium has not arrived, but neither has the country's social fabric been destroyed. Nor have women organized a political party to elect only women candidates to public office. . . . Instead, women have shown the same tendency to divide along orthodox party lines as male voters. (Eleanor Flexner, *Century of Struggle*, Atheneum 1968. *A scholarly treatment of women's roles in America since the Mayflower, this book was well reviewed by historians.*)

2. In Kentucky a woman breezed to victory in the state's gubernatorial election. San Francisco's Mayor Dianne Feinstein won re-election

with an overwhelming 80 percent of the vote—then grew irritable at questions about whether she is available for the vice presidency. Houston's Mayor Kathy Whitmire fought off an oilman's spirited challenge and won re-election with more than 63 percent of the vote. ("Lessons from the Off-Off Year Vote," *Newsweek*, 1984)

3. Woman has been the great unpaid laborer of the world, and although within the last two decades a vast number of new employments have been opened to her, statistics prove that in the great majority of these, she is not paid according to the value of the work done, but according to sex. The opening of all industries to women, and the wage question as connected with her, are the most subtle and profound questions of political economy, closely interwoven with the rights of self-government. (Susan B. Anthony; first appeared in Vol. I of *The History of Woman Suffrage*; reprinted in *Voices from Women's Liberation*, ed. Leslie B. Tanner, NAL 1970. *An important figure in the battle for women's suffrage, Susan B. Anthony [1820–1906] also lectured and wrote on abolition and temperance.*)

4. Women . . . have never been prepared to assume responsibility; we have never been prepared to make demands upon ourselves; we have never been taught to expect the development of what is best in ourselves because no one has ever expected *anything* of us—or for us. Because no one has ever had any intention of turning over any serious work to us. (Vivian Gornick, "The Next Great Moment in History is Ours," *Village Voice* 1969. *The* Voice *is a liberal New York City weekly.*)

5. With women as half the country's elected representatives, and a woman President once in a while, the country's *machismo* problems would be greatly reduced. The old-fashioned idea that manhood depends on violence and victory is, after all, an important part of our troubles. . . . I'm not saying that women leaders would eliminate violence. We are not more moral than men; we are only uncorrupted by power so far. When we do acquire power, we might turn out to have an equal impulse toward aggression. (Gloria Steinem, "What It Would Be Like If Women Win," *Time* 1970. *Steinem, a well-known feminist and journalist, was one of the founders of* Ms. *magazine.*)

6. Nineteen eighty-two was the year that time ran out for the proposed equal rights amendment. Eleanor Smeal, president of the National Organization for Women, the group that headed the intense 10-year struggle for the ERA, conceded defeat on June 24. Only 24 words in all, the ERA read simply: "Equality of rights under the law shall not be denied or abridged by the United States or by any state on account of sex." Two major opinion polls had reported just weeks before the ERA's defeat that a majority of Americans continued to favor the amendment. (June Foley, "Women 1982: The Year that Time Ran Out," *The World Almanac & Book of Facts*, 1983)

7. The president of the National Women's Political Caucus, Sharon Rodine, grinned as she pronounced, "From Connecticut to Missouri to Oregon, women won great victories . . . 1990 is a clear rehearsal for the decade ahead." Ellen Malcolm, president of Emily's List, a fund-raising network for pro-choice Democratic women candidates, was almost effusive. "We have twenty Democratic women in the new Congress, an increase of two thirds since 1987," she said. Most significantly, Cardiss Collins, congresswoman from Chicago, will be joined by three more African Americans: Barbara-Rose Collins from Detroit; the eminent feminist civil rights activist Eleanor Holmes Norton from Washington D.C.; and the redoubtable Maxine Waters, who graduates to Congress after fourteen years as a state assemblywoman from Los Angeles. Returned to the House in this election were two other minority women: Ileana Ros-Lehtinen, a Florida Republican who is Cuban American, and Democrat Patsy T. Mink, an Asian American from Hawaii.

There may be twenty Democratic women in Congress this term, but the number of women remains the same. (Jane O'Reilly, "Running for Our Lives," *Glamour* Jan. 1991. *O'Reilly was a founding editor of* Ms. *as well as a newspaper columnist and a political correspondent for* Time. Glamour *is a fashion, beauty, and lifestyle magazine for young women.*)

38c   *Taking Notes*

Although it may seem like a sensible strategy, simply copying down the words of a source is the least efficient way to take notes. Experienced researchers know that it makes more sense to take notes that combine direct quotation with *paraphrase* and *summary*. By doing so, they ensure that they understand the material and see its relevance to their research. In fact, the very act of putting someone else's ideas into your own words helps you to gain a better understanding of what has been said. It is therefore a good idea to develop your skill in this area by paraphrasing or summarizing important material as soon as you finish reading it.

▶ See 40e2

(1)   *Writing a summary*

You summarize when you want to capture the general idea of a source. A **summary**, sometimes called a précis, is a brief restatement in your own words of the main idea of a passage, article, or entire book. When you write a summary, omit the examples, asides, and analogies that authors use to illustrate their points and to interest their readers. Be careful, however, not to leave out important points or to misrepresent an author's intention. In addition, do not include your own ideas or observations.

Before you write your summary, be sure that you thoroughly understand your source. After you have finished reading, restate the main idea in a sentence. Next, write your summary, using your one-sentence restatement as your guide. Your summary should present an overview of the original without using the exact language or phrasing.

Steps for Writing a Summary

1. Reread your source until you understand it.
2. Write a one-sentence restatement of the main idea.
3. Write the summary using the one-sentence restatement as your guide. Focus on what the text says, not on your own ideas or opinions.
4. Revise your summary, being sure that you have accurately condensed the original.
5. Add appropriate documentation.

Following is an original source and a summary of the source. Notice that the summary is much shorter than the original and that it gives only an overview of the passage.

ORIGINAL SOURCE

The religious and cosmic symbolism of the city reaches back to the early stages of human culture. It seems that in none of the great archaic cultures have cities been understood simply as settlements, arbitrarily established at a certain place and in a given form; both the placing and the shape of the cities were conceived as related, in a hidden or manifested form, to the structure of the universe. The most common form of this symbolism is the belief that the cities have astral or divine prototypes, or even descended from heaven; sometimes they were believed to have a relationship to the underworld. In both cases, however, they refer to an extraterrestrial reality. (Barasch, Moshe, "The City." *Dictionary of the History of Ideas*. Ed. Philip P. Wiener, 4 vols. New York: Scribner's, 1973. 1:427.)

SUMMARY

In ancient times cities had symbolic significance. They were seen, in part, as having a divine form—perhaps related to a heavenly or, less commonly, underworld counterpart (Barasch 1:427).

After you have written your summary, check to be sure that it conveys both the meaning and the spirit of the original. Make certain that you have not inadvertently used any of the author's exact words. (Of course, you can use *some* words from a source. As a rule, you can use the same proper nouns, simple words or technical terms as your source without documentation.) Reread your summary to see whether you can condense it further, and be sure that you have included documentation to identify the source you have summarized.

(2) Writing a paraphrase

A **paraphrase** is more specific than a summary; in fact, it is a detailed restatement in your own words of all your source's important ideas. It not only indicates the source's main points but also follows its order, tone, and emphasis. Often a paraphrase will quote key words or phrases from the original to convey the flavor of the source. Keep in mind, however, that when paraphrasing, you convey the *author's* ideas, not your own. Keep your own analyses, interpretations, and evaluations separate.

Begin your paraphrase by reading your source until you understand it. If the portion of your source to be paraphrased is long or complex, you might want to make an outline to clarify the progression of ideas. This approach may be time consuming, but in the long run it can help you write a clear and accurate paraphrase. Next, write your paraphrase, following the order, tone, and emphasis of the original source. Finally, add appropriate documentation.

Steps for Writing a Paraphrase

1. Reread your source until you understand it.
2. If necessary, make an outline.

---

continued

continued from previous page

3. Write your paraphrase, following the order, tone, and emphasis of the original.
4. Revise your paraphrase, being sure that it conveys the sense of the original and that you have not used the words or phrasing of the original without enclosing borrowed material in quotation marks.
5. Add appropriate documentation.

Below is a paraphrase of a passage that discusses a player's state of mind while playing a video game. Notice that although the paraphrase follows the order and emphasis of the original, and even quotes a key phrase, its wording and sentence structure are very different from those of the source.

ORIGINAL SOURCE

When you play a video game you enter into the world of the programmers who made it. You have to do more than identify with a character on the screen. You must act for it. Identification through action has a special kind of hold. Like playing a sport, it puts people into a highly focused, and highly charged, state of mind. For many people, what is being pursued in the video game is not just a score, but an altered state.

The pilot of a race car does not dare to take . . . attention off the road. The imperative of total concentration is part of the high. Video games demand this same level of attention. They can give people the feeling of being close to the edge because, as in a dangerous situation, there is no time for rest and the consequences of wandering attention feel dire. With pinball, a false move can be recuperated. The machine can be shaken, the ball repositioned. In a video game, the program has no tolerance for error, no margin of safety. Players experience their every movement as instantly translated into game action. The game is relentless in its demand that all other time stop and in its demand that the player take full responsibility for every act, a point that players often sum up by the phrase "One false move and you're dead." (Turkle, Sherry, *The Second Self: Computers and the Human Spirit.* New York: Simon & Schuster, 1984: 83–84.)

PARAPHRASE

The programmer controls the world of video games. Video games enable a player to merge with a character or object that is part of the game. This identification draws a player into the game. Like sports, video games put a player into an emotionally charged "altered state" (Turkle 83) that is a central part of the game.

Because video games demand a high degree of involvement, they can simulate the thrill of participating in a dangerous activity without the risks. Unlike pinball machines, video games provide no time to rest and no opportunity to correct errors in judgment. Every move a player makes appears at once on the screen. The game forces a player to adapt to its rules and to act carefully (83–84).

After you have written your paraphrase, reread it to make certain that you have not relied on the phrasing and syntax of the original and that you have put quotation marks around any words or phrases quoted directly from your source. Make sure that you have included all the important points of the original, and insert any transitional words or phrases that are needed to make your paraphrase flow smoothly. Finally, add separate documentation for each quotation you use—in addition to providing the source of the entire paraphrase.

(3) Recording quotations

You quote when you feel that an author's exact words will enhance your paper. When you **quote,** you copy an author's remarks just as they appear in a source, word for word and punctuation mark for punctuation mark. Pay particular attention to spelling and capitalization.

Revision Close-up

When recording quotations, be sure that you do not inadvertently leave out quotation marks. You may even want to circle them to be sure you notice them when you transfer them from your notes to your paper.

As a rule, avoid including numerous direct quotations in your papers. The use of one quotation after another interrupts the flow of your discussion and gives readers the impression that your paper is just a collection of other people's words. Quote only when something vital would be lost otherwise, and use only those quotations that support your points and provide a perspective that contributes to the effectiveness of your presentation. Before you include any quotation, ask yourself whether your purpose would be better served if you used your own words.

When to Quote

- Quote when a source's wording or phrasing is so distinctive that to summarize or paraphrase would diminish its impact. In such cases it is best to let the source speak for itself.
- Quote when a source's words lend authority to your presentation. If an author is a recognized expert on your subject, his or her words are as convincing as expert testimony at a trial.
- Quote when an author's words are so concise that paraphrase would create a long, clumsy, or incoherent phrase or would change the meaning of the original.
- Quote when you are going to disagree with a source. Using a source's exact words assures readers you are being fair to those on the other side of the issue and not setting up a straw man **(see 7a5).**

38d *Integrating Your Notes into Your Writing*

Once you have gathered material from your sources, you should not simply drop it into your paper. Instead, you should weave quotations, paraphrases, and summaries smoothly into the fabric of your discussion, adding analysis or explanation to increase coherence and to show why you are using each source's words or ideas. As you integrate borrowed material into your paper, you should be careful to differentiate your own ideas from those of your sources.

Revision Close-up

To avoid monotonous sentence structure, experiment with different methods of integrating source material into your paper.

1. Vary the verbs you use for attribution.

acknowledges	*discloses*	*implies*
suggests	*observes*	*notes*
concludes	*believes*	*comments*
insists	*explains*	*claims*
predicts	*summarizes*	*illustrates*

reports	finds	*proposes*
warns	*concurs*	*speculates*
admits	*affirms*	*indicates*

2. Vary the placement of the identifying phrase, putting it at the beginning or at the end of the quoted material, or even in the middle.

QUOTATION WITH ATTRIBUTION IN MIDDLE

"A serious problem confronting Amish society from the viewpoint of the Amish themselves," observes Hostetler, "is the threat of absorption into mass society through the values promoted in the public school system" (193).

PARAPHRASE WITH ATTRIBUTION AT END

The Amish are also concerned about their children's exposure to the public school system's values, notes Hostetler (193).

(1) Integrating quotations

Quotations should be smoothly embedded into sentences and introduced by identifying phrases when possible. In other words, they should be placed in context. Consider this passage:

> For the Amish, the public school system represents a problem. "A serious problem confronting Amish society from the viewpoint of the Amish themselves is the threat of absorption into mass society through the values promoted in the public school system" (Hostetler 193).

The direct quotation, awkwardly dropped into the passage above, could be worked into the sentence in this way:

> For the Amish, the public school system represents "the threat of absorption into mass society" (Hostetler 193).

Or you could use a **running acknowledgment,** in which you introduce the source of the quotation into the text.

> As John A. Hostetler points out, the Amish feel the public school system threatens them with "absorption into the mass society . . ." (193).

You could also combine quotation and paraphrase, quoting only a significant word or two and paraphrasing the rest.

According to John A. Hostetler, one of the most serious problems that the Amish face is a "threat of absorption" into the dominant culture posed by the public schools (193).

Changes Within Quotations   Sometimes you will have to alter a quotation to make it fit gramatically and logically into your paper. For example, you might have to supply the antecedent for a pronoun or change the verb tense of the original. If you alter words, *you must acknowledge your changes* by enclosing them in brackets (not parentheses).

AWKWARD: The Amish were traditionally opposed to the modern industrialized society around them. "They are a slow-changing, distinctive cultural group who place a premium on cultural stability rather than change" (Hostetler vii).

REVISED: The Amish were traditionally opposed to the modern industrialized society around them: "They [were] a slow-changing, distinctive cultural group who [placed] a premium on cultural stability rather than change" (Hostetler vii). (verb tense changed to match the paper's tense)

Omissions Within Quotations   You can reduce the length of quotations by substituting ellipsis points (three spaced periods) for the deleted words (see 31f1).

ORIGINAL: "Not only have the Amish built and staffed their own elementary and vocational schools, but they have gradually organized on local, state, and national levels to cope with the task of educating their children" (Hostetler 206).

REVISED: "Not only have the Amish built and staffed their own elementary and vocational schools, but they have gradually organized . . . to cope with the task of educating their children" (Hostetler 206).

When you omit a word or phrase at the beginning of a quoted passage, you do not use ellipsis points to indicate the omission.

FAULTY: For the Amish, the calendar year reflects agricultural activities and ". . . the kind of leisure and the customs that tend to become associated with seasons of the year" (Hostetler 94).

REVISED: For the Amish, the calendar year reflects agricultural activities and "the kind of leisure and the customs that tend to become associated with seasons of the year" (Hostetler 94).

Long Quotations   Occasionally, you may want to use a quotation consisting of more than four lines of text. Set off this quotation from the text by indenting it ten spaces from the margin. Double-space, do not use quotation marks, and introduce the long quotation with a colon. If you are quoting a single paragraph, do not indent the first line (see 30e2).

> According to Hostetler, the Amish were not always hostile to public education:
>
> > The one-room rural elementary school served the Amish community well in a number of ways. As long as it was a public school, it stood midway between the Amish community and the world. Its influence was tolerable, depending upon the degree of influence the Amish were able to bring to the situation. As long as it was small, rural, and near the community, a reasonable influence could be maintained over its worldly character. (196)

Revision Close-up

Use long quotations when you want to convey a sense of an author's style or thought process. Keep in mind, however, that long quotations can be distracting. They interrupt your discussion and, when used excessively, give the impression that you have relied too heavily on the words of others.

(2)   Integrating paraphrases and summaries

When you use paraphrases and summaries in your paper, you should make certain that your readers are able to differentiate your words from the words of your sources. If you do not, you risk misleading your readers and possibly being accused of plagiarism (see 38e4). The easiest way to avoid this problem is to surround your paraphrases and summaries with documentation—to introduce them with running acknowledgments and to end them with appropriate documentation.

MISLEADING

Art can be used to uncover many problems that children have at home, in school, or with their friends. For this reason, many therapists use art therapy extensively. Children's view of themselves in society is often reflected by their art style. A cramped, crowded art style using only a portion of the paper shows their limited role (Alschuler 260).

REVISED (WITH RUNNING ACKNOWLEDGMENT)

Art can be used to uncover many problems that children have at home, in school, or with their friends. For this reason, many therapists use art therapy extensively. According to William Alschuler in *Art and Self-Image,* children's view of themselves in society is often reflected by their art style. A cramped, crowded art style using only a portion of the paper shows their limited role (260).

In some cases running acknowledgments can be distracting—especially if you are weaving a number of examples from various sources into your discussion. In these situations, make certain that boundaries between your ideas and those of the sources are distinct and that you name each source in your documentation.

ORIGINAL (WITH RUNNING ACKNOWLEDGMENT)

The extent of colonial sympathy for the British cause has been widely debated, but even so certain conclusions can be drawn. According to William Appleton Williams, at least thirty-five and possibly sixty percent of the colonists initially sided with the British (235). Daniel Boorstin says after the war started, that number probably dropped to twenty percent (78). According to John Hope Franklin, however, at no time did the number of colonists loyal to England go below ten percent (45).

REVISED (WITHOUT RUNNING ACKNOWLEDGMENT)

The extent of colonial sympathy for the British cause has been widely debated, but even so certain conclusions can be drawn. At least thirty-five and possibly sixty percent of the colonists initially sided with the British (Williams 235). After the war started, that number probably dropped to twenty percent (Boorstin 78). At no time, however, did the number of colonists loyal to England go below ten percent (Franklin 45).

You should also be sure that a paraphrase or summary is consistent with your ideas. A clever idea or a particularly insightful observation is good only if it suits the purpose and tone of your paper. If it does not, it will mislead and possibly confuse your readers. You can make the relationship between your ideas and the ideas of your sources clear by using appropriate transitional words and phrases. Not only will such phrases ensure that your paraphrases and summaries are smoothly integrated into your discussion, they will also clarify your purpose. Notice that the sentence below gives no clue that the information provided by Woodward and Bernstein supports the paper's assertion. The transitional phrase in the revised version makes the causal connection clear.

CONFUSING: The chain of events that led to Richard Nixon's resignation is well known. According to Woodward and Bernstein, both Alexander Haig and Henry Kissinger urged Nixon to cut his ties with his aides (366).

REVISED: The chain of events that led to Richard Nixon's resignation is well known. According to Woodward and Bernstein, <u>for example,</u> both Alexander Haig and Henry Kissinger urged Nixon to cut his ties with his aids (366).

EXERCISE 3

Assume that in preparation for a paper on the topic "The effects of the rise of suburbia," you read the following passage from the book *Great Expectations: America and the Baby Boom Generation* by Landon Y. Jones. Reread the passage, and then write a one-paragraph summary. Next, paraphrase one paragraph. Finally, take notes that combine paraphrase with quotation, making certain to quote only when appropriate.

As an internal migration, the settling of the suburbs was phenomenal. In the twenty years from 1950 to 1970, the population of the suburbs doubled from 36 million to 72 million. No less than 83 percent of the total population growth in the United States during the 1950's was in the suburbs, which were growing fifteen times faster than any other segment of the country. As people packed and moved, the national mobility rate leaped by 50 percent. The only other comparable influx was the wave of European immigrants to the United States around the turn of the century. But as *Fortune* pointed out, more people moved to the suburbs every year than had ever arrived on Ellis Island.

By now, bulldozers were churning up dust storms as they cleared the land for housing developments. More than a million acres of farmland were plowed under every year during the 1950's. Millions of apartment-dwelling parents with two children were suddenly realizing that two children could be doubled up in a spare bedroom, but a third child cried loudly for something more. The proportion of new houses with three or more bedrooms, in fact, rose from one-third in 1947 to three-quarters in 1954. The necessary *Lebensraum* could only be found in the suburbs. There was a housing shortage, but young couples armed with VA and FHA loans built their dream homes with easy credit and free spending habits that were unthinkable to the baby-boom grandparents, who shook their heads with the Depression still fresh in their memories. Of the 13 million homes built in the decade before 1958, 11 million of them—or 85 percent—were built in the suburbs. Home ownership rose 50 percent between 1940 and 1950, and another 50 percent by 1960. By then, one-fourth of *all* housing in the United States had been built in the fifties. For the first time, more Americans owned homes than rented them.

We were becoming a land of gigantic nurseries. The biggest were built by Abraham Levitt, the son of poor Russian-Jewish immigrants, who had originally built houses for the Navy during the war. The first of three East Coast Levittowns went up on the potato fields of Long Island. Exactly $7900—or $60 a month and no money down— bought you a Monopoly-board bungalow with four rooms, attic, washing machine, outdoor barbecue, and a television set built into the wall. The 17,447 units eventually became home to 82,000 people, many of whom were pregnant or wanted to be. In a typical story on the suburban explosion, one magazine breathlessly described a volley-ball game of nine couples in which no less than five of the women were expecting.

38e *Avoiding Plagiarism*

Plagiarism is presenting another person's words or ideas as if they were your own. By not acknowledging a source, you mislead readers into thinking that the material you are presenting is yours when, in fact, it is the result of someone else's time and effort.

Some writers plagiarize deliberately, copying passages word for word or even presenting another person's entire work as their own. Students who do this are doing themselves and their classmates a great disservice. They are undercutting the learning process, thereby sacrificing the education that they are in college to obtain. If found out, they are usually punished severely. Some students have failed courses and even had degrees withheld because of plagiarism.

Most plagiarism, however, is accidental. It occurs when students are not aware of what constitutes plagiarism, or when they forget that a note they jotted down is really a direct quotation or that an idea they are using is really someone else's. Sometimes students simply forget to document a paraphrase or summary or forget to include quotation marks when they type their paper. Still, accidental plagiarism is often dealt with just as harshly as intentional plagiarism. Plagiarism is not taken lightly in education, business, or anyplace else. Plagiarism is theft.

In general, document all direct quotations, opinions, judgments, and insights of others that you summarize or paraphrase. You must also document information that is not well known, is open to dispute, or is not commonly accepted. Finally, document tables, graphs, charts, and statistics taken from a source (see 39a).

Common knowledge, information that you would expect most educated readers to know, need not be documented. You can safely use facts that are widely available in encyclopedias, textbooks, newspapers, and magazines without citing a source. Even if the information is new to you, if it is generally known, you need not indicate a source. You can usually assume that information that appears in several of your sources is generally known. Information that is in dispute, however, or that a particular person has discovered or theorized about, must be acknowledged. You need not, for example, document the fact that John F. Kennedy graduated from Harvard in 1940 or that he was elected president in 1960. You must, however, document a historian's analysis of Kennedy's performance as president or a researcher's recent discoveries about his private life.

You can avoid plagiarism by using documentation wherever it is required and by watching for the situations that cause the most common types of plagiarism.

Common Types of Unintentional Plagiarism

- Material from a source not acknowledged
- Paraphrase too close to its source
- Statistics not attributed to a source
- Writer's words and ideas not kept distinct from those of the source

---

(1) *Material from a source not acknowledged*

ORIGINAL

Historically, only a handful of families have dominated the fireworks industry in the West. Details such as chemical recipes and mixing procedures were cloaked in secrecy and passed down from one generation to the next. Families remain an important force in the industry. In the U.S., for instance, there are the Gruccis of Bellport, New York; the Zambellis of New Castle, Pennsylvania; the Rozzis of Loveland, Ohio; and the Souzas of Rialto, California. One effect of familial secretiveness is that, until recent decades, basic pyrotechnic research was rarely performed, and even when it was, the results were not generally reported in scientific journals. (Conkling, John A. "Pyrotechnics." *Scientific American* July 1990: 96.)

PLAGIARISM

John A. Conkling, the director of the American Pyrotechnics Association, points out that until recently, little scientific research was done on the chemical properties of fireworks, and when it was, <u>the results were not generally reported in scientific journals</u> (96).

The student who wrote this passage is guilty of plagiarism. Even though he documents the source of his information, he neglects to acknowledge that he borrows the source's exact wording. To correct this problem, the student should paraphrase the source's words or use quotation marks to acknowledge his borrowing.

CORRECT (PHRASE REWORDED)

John A. Conkling, the director of the American Pyrotechnics Association, points out that <u>research conducted on the chemical composition of fireworks was seldom reported in the scientific literature</u> (96).

CORRECT (PHRASE IN QUOTATION MARKS)

John A. Conkling, the director of the American Pyrotechnics Association, points out that until recently, little scientific research was done on the chemical properties of fireworks, and when it was, "<u>the results were generally not reported in scientific journals</u>" (96).

(2) Paraphrase too close to its source

ORIGINAL

Let's be clear: this wish for politically correct casting goes only one way, the way designed to redress the injuries of centuries. When Pat Carroll, who is a woman, plays Falstaff, who is not, casting is considered a stroke of brilliance. When Josette Simon, who is black, plays Maggie in *After the Fall,* a part Arthur Miller patterned after Marilyn Monroe and which has traditionally been played not by white women, but by blonde white women, it is hailed as a breakthrough.

But when the pendulum moves the other way, the actors' union balks. (Anna Quindlen, "Error, Stage Left." *New York Times* 12 Aug. 1990, sec. 1: 21.)

PLAGIARISM

Let us be honest. The desire for politically appropriate casting only goes in one direction, the direction intended to make up for the damage done over hundreds of years. When Pat Carroll, a female, is cast as Falstaff, a male, the decision is a brilliant one. When Josette Simon, a black woman, is cast as Maggie in *After the Fall*, a role Arthur Miller based on Marilyn Monroe and which has usually been played by a woman who is not only white but also blonde, it is considered a major advance.

But when the shoe is on the other foot, the actors' union resists (Quindlen 21).

Although this student documents the passage and does not use the exact words of her source, she closely imitates the syntax and phrasing of the source. In fact, all she has really done is substitute synonyms for the author's words; the distinctive style of the passage is still the author's. The student could have avoided plagiarism by substantially changing the syntax as well as the words of the original, using the ideas of the passage to support her own original conclusions about the subject.

CORRECT (PARAPHRASE; ONE DISTINCTIVE PHRASE PLACED IN QUOTATION MARKS)

Unfortunately, the actors' union supports "politically correct casting" only when it means casting a woman or minority group member in a role created for a male or a Caucasian. Thus, it is acceptable for actress Pat Carroll to play Falstaff or for black actress Josette Simon to play Marilyn Monroe; in fact, casting decisions such as these are praised. But when it comes to casting a Caucasian in a role intended for an African-American, Asian, or Hispanic, the union objects (Quindlen 21).

(3)   *Statistics not attributed to a source*

ORIGINAL

From the time they [male drivers between 16 and 24] started to drive, 187 of these drivers (almost two thirds) reported one or more accidents, with an average of 1.6 per involved driver. Features of 303 accidents are tabulated in Table 2. Almost half of all first accidents occurred before the legal driving age of 18, and the median age of all accidents was 19. One resulted in a fatality. Crashes involving death or injury were in the minority (14 percent); the large majority resulted in property damage only. The picture for this group of "normal" drivers was thus one of accidents of relatively mild character occurring well before adulthood. The emotional immaturity of this group is the most important factor related to the high frequency of accidents in this age group. (Schuman, Stanley, et al. "Young Male Drivers: Accidents and Violations." *JAMA* 50 (1983): 1027.)

PLAGIARISM

> By and large male drivers between the ages of 16 and 24 accounted for the majority of accidents. Of 303 accidents recorded in Michigan, almost one half took place before the drivers were legally allowed to drive at 18. Most of these accidents resulted in property damage and not in injury or loss of life. It seems likely that the immaturity of these drivers had a lot to do with their many accidents.

The student who used this information assumed that it was common knowledge—that it could be found in many sources and had been accepted as accurate by many experts in the field. These statistics, however, were the result of original research carried out by the authors of the journal article. Because both the statistics and the conclusion concerning the emotional immaturity of male drivers are the original contributions of the authors, they must be documented.

CORRECT

> According to one study, male drivers between the ages of 16 and 24 accounted for the majority of accidents. Of 303 accidents recorded almost one half took place before the drivers were legally allowed to drive at 18. Most of these accidents resulted in property damage and not in injury or loss of life. It seems likely that the immaturity of this group of drivers has a lot to do with their many accidents (Schuman et al., 1027).

(4) A writer's words and ideas not differentiated from those of the source

ORIGINAL

> [Emily Dickinson's] debt to Shakespeare was just as pervasive and even less visible. Poetic language in mid-nineteenth-century America had been reduced to a relatively flat and nerveless state, but he furnished her with clues for its resurrection. The major writers of the

preceding generation had not only finished their careers but had brought the older way to a dead end. For a poet to come of age at such a time, as she did, may have been a handicap in that it deprived her of a living tradition within which or against which to work. (Anderson, Charles R. *Emily Dickinson's Poetry: Stairway of Surprise*. New York: Holt, 1960: 145–46.)

Plagiarism

A careful reading of her poetry shows that Emily Dickinson was deeply concerned with language and the function of words. Although her style seems derivative, she actually creates a distinctive idiom all her own. Even so, many of her images show that she owed much to Shakespeare. Although she read many of the writers that had preceded her, they were of no use to her. She was in many respects "deprived...of a living tradition within which or against which to work" (Anderson 145–46).

Because the student who wrote this passage did not differentiate his ideas from those of his source, it appears that he borrowed only the quotation in the last sentence. Actually, the student used source material in the last three sentences of the passage. As a result, the student passes off some of his source's ideas as his own and unwittingly commits plagiarism. He could have clearly defined the boundaries of the borrowed material by placing a running acknowledgment *before* and documentation *after* the borrowed material. In the following example, notice that both the summary and the quotation are documented. (A quotation always requires separate documentation.)

Correct

A careful reading of her poetry shows that Emily Dickinson was deeply concerned with language and the function of words. Although her style seems derivative, she actually creates a distinctive idiom all her own. According to Charles R. Anderson, many of her images show that she owed much to Shakespeare. Although she read many of the writers that had preceded her, they were of no use to her (145). She was in many respects "deprived . . . of a living tradition within which or against which to work" (145–46).

Guidelines for Avoiding Plagiarism

- **Take careful notes.** Make certain that you have recorded information from your sources carefully and accurately.

continued

continued from previous page

- **Put all words taken from sources inside circled quotation marks,** and enclose your own comments within brackets.
- In your paper, **differentiate your ideas from those of your sources** by clearly introducing borrowed material with the author's name and by ending with documentation.
- **Enclose all direct quotations** used in your paper within quotation marks.
- **Review paraphrases and summaries in your paper** to make certain that they are in your own words and that any words and phrases from the original are quoted.
- **Document all direct quotations and all paraphrases and summaries** of your sources. (See Chapter 39 for a full discussion of documentation.)
- **Document all facts** that are open to dispute or that are not common knowledge.
- **Document all opinions, conclusions, figures, tables, graphs, and charts** taken from a source.

STUDENT WRITER AT WORK

WORKING WITH SOURCE MATERIAL

This student paragraph uses material from three sources, but its author has neglected to cite them. After reading the paragraph and the three sources that follow it, identify material that has been quoted directly from a source. Compare the wording against the original for accuracy, and insert quotation marks where necessary, being sure that the quoted passages fit smoothly into your text. Next, paraphrase passages that the student did not need to quote, and, after consulting Chapter 39, document each piece of information that requires it.

Student Paragraph: Oral History

Oral history became a legitimate field of study in 1948, when the Oral History Research Office was established by Allan Nevins. Like recordings of presidents' fireside chats and declarations of war, oral history is both oral and historical. But it is more: oral history is the creation of new historical documentation, not the recording or preserving of documentation that already exists. Oral history also tends to be more spontaneous and personal and less formal than ordinary tape recordings. Nevins's purpose was to collect and prepare materials to help future historians to better understand the past. Oral history has enormous potential to do just this, for it draws on people's memories of their own lives and deeds and of their associations with particular people, periods, or events. The result, when it is recorded and transcribed, is a valuable new source.

Source 1

When Allan Nevins set up the Oral History Research Office in 1948, he looked upon it as an organization that in a systematic way could obtain from the lips and papers of living Americans who had led significant lives a full record of their participation in the political, economic, and cultural affairs of the nation. His purpose was to prepare such material for the use of future historians. It was his conviction that the individual played an important role in history and that an individual's autobiography might in the future serve as a key to an understanding of contemporary historical movements. (Excerpted from Benison, Saul. "Reflections on Oral History." The American Archivist 28.1 [January 1965]:71.)

Source 2

Typically, an oral history project comprises an organized series of interviews with selected individuals or groups in order to create new source materials from the reminiscences of their own life and acts or from their association with a particular person, period, or event. These recollections are recorded on tape and transcribed on a typewriter into sheets of transcript. . . . Such oral

history may be distinguished from more conventional tape
recordings of speeches, lectures, symposia, etc., by the
fact that the former creates new sources through the more
spontaneous, personal, multitopical, extended narrative,
while the latter utilizes sources in a more formal mode
for a specific occasion. (Excerpted from Rumics,
Elizabeth. "Oral History: Defining the Term." Wilson
Library Bulletin 40 [1966]: 602.)

Source 3

Oral history, as the term came to be used, is the creation
of new historical documentation, not the recording or
preserving of documentation—even oral documentation—that
already exists. Its purpose is not, like that of the
National Voice Library at Michigan State University, to
preserve the recordings of fireside chats or presidential
declarations of war or James Whitcomb Riley reciting
"Little Orphan Annie." These are surely oral and just as
surely the stuff of history; but they are not oral
history. For this there must be the creation of a new
historical document by means of a personal interview.
(Excerpted from Hoyle, Norman. "Oral History." Library
Trends July 1972: 61.)

Documentation

Documentation is the formal acknowledgment of the sources you use in your paper. Your documentation enables your readers to judge the quality and originality of your work and to determine how authoritative and relevant each work you cite is. Different academic disciplines use different documentation styles. This chapter explains and illustrates the four most commonly used formats, the documentation styles recommended by the Modern Language Association (MLA), *The Chicago Manual of Style* (CMS), the American Psychological Association (APA), and the Council of Biology Editors (CBE).

39a *Knowing What to Document*

In general, you should document any information that is not yours, except information that is common knowledge. In addition to printed material, sources may include interviews, conversations, films, records, or radio or television programs. As a beginning researcher, you should document any material you think might need it. By doing so, you avoid any possibility of plagiarism.

► See 38e

What to Document

Do Document

- Direct quotations
- Opinions, judgments, and insights of others that you summarize or paraphrase

---

continued

continued from previous page

- Information that is not widely known
- Information that is open to dispute
- Information that is not commonly accepted
- Tables, charts, graphs, and statistics taken from a source

Do Not Document

- Your own ideas, observations, and conclusions
- Common knowledge: facts that are widely available in reference books, newspapers, and magazines
- Familiar quotations

Your documentation should clearly indicate the sources of all your information. Readers should not have to guess which passages you attribute to your sources and which statements you claim as your own. For this reason, you should avoid using single references to cover several unrelated borrowings throughout a passage. Instead, place documentation after each quotation and at the end of each paraphrase and summary passage. Be sure to place documentation so that it will not interrupt your ideas—ideally at the end of a sentence. Finally, be sure to differentiate your ideas from those of your sources by placing introductory phrases before, and documentation after, all borrowed material.

39b *Using MLA Format**

MLA format is recommended by the Modern Language Association of America, a professional organization of more than 25,000 teachers of English and other languages. It is also required by many teachers of other humanities disciplines at colleges throughout the United States and Canada. This method of documentation has three parts: parenthetical references in the text, a list of works cited, and content notes.

(1) *Parenthetical references in the text*

MLA documentation uses references inserted in parentheses within the text and keyed to a list of works cited at the end of the paper.

---

*MLA documentation format follows the guidelines set in the *MLA Handbook for Writers of Research Papers,* 3rd ed. New York: MLA, 1988.

A typical reference consists of the author's last name and a page number.

```
The colony's religious and political freedom appealed to
many idealists in Europe (Ripley 132).
```

If you use more than one source by the same author, shorten the title of each work to one or two key words, and include the appropriate shortened title in the parenthetical reference after the author's name.

```
Penn emphasized his religious motivation (Kelley, William
Penn 116).
```

If the author's name or the title of the work is stated in the text, do not include it in the parenthetical reference.

```
Penn's political motivation is discussed by Joseph P.
Kelley in Pennsylvania, The Colonial Years, 1681–1776
(44).
```

Punctuating Parenthetical References

Paraphrases and summaries [Parenthetical references appear *before* terminal punctuation marks.]

```
Penn's writings epitomize seventeenth–century
religious thought (Dengler and Curtis 72).
```

Quotations run in with the text [Parenthetical references appear *after* the quotation but *before* the terminal punctuation.]

```
As Ross says, "Penn followed his conscience in all
matters" (127).
```

```
We must now ask, as Ross does, "Did Penn follow Quaker
dictates in his dealings with Native Americans" (128)?
```

```
According to Williams, Penn's utopian vision was
informed by his Quaker beliefs . . ." (72).
```

Long quotations set off from the text [Parenthetical references appear two spaces *after* the final punctuation.]

continued

continued from previous page

> According to Arthur Smith, William Penn envisioned a
> state based on his religious principles:
>> Pennsylvania would be a commonwealth in
>> which all individuals would follow God's
>> truth and develop according to God's law.
>> For Penn this concept of government was
>> self-evident. It would be a mistake to see
>> Pennsylvania as anything but an expression
>> of Penn's religious beliefs. (314)

Sample MLA Parenthetical References

Directory of MLA Parenthetical References

1. Works by two or three authors
2. Works by more than three authors
3. Books with a volume and page number
4. Works without a listed author
5. Works that are one page in length
6. Indirect sources
7. More than one work
8. Literary works
9. An entire work
10. Tables and illustrations

1. Works by Two or Three Authors

One group of physicists questioned many of the
assumptions of relativity (Harbeck and Johnson 31).

For works with three authors, list the authors in the order in which
they appear on the title page, with *and* before the last name.

With the advent of behaviorism psychology began a new
phase of inquiry (Cowen, Barbo, and Crum 31–34).

2. Works by More Than Three Authors

For works with more than three authors, list only the first author,
followed by *et al.* ("and others") in place of the rest.

A number of important discoveries were made off the coast
of Crete in 1960 (Dugan et al. 63).

3. Books with a Volume and Page Number

A colon and a space separate volume and page numbers of books. The number before the colon is the volume number; the number after the colon is the page number. Do not use the words or abbreviations for *volume* and *page* in the entry.

```
In 1912 Virginia Stephen married Leonard Woolf, with whom
she founded the Hogarth Press (Woolf 1:17).
```

NOTE: To cite an entire volume, include the author's name followed by a comma and the abbreviation *vol.* (Woolf, vol. 1).

4. Works Without a Listed Author

For works without a listed author, use a shortened version of the title in the parenthetical reference. Begin the shortened title with the word by which it is alphabetized in the Works Cited list.

```
Television ratings wars have escalated during the past
ten years ("Leaving the Cellar" 102).
```

5. Works That Are One Page in Length

Omit the page reference if you are citing a one-page article.

```
It is a curious fact that the introduction of
Christianity at the end of the Roman Empire "had no
effect on the abolition of slavery" (Finley).
```

6. Indirect Sources

You should always try to get material from the original source, but sometimes you will have to use an indirect source. Indicate that the material is from an indirect source by using the abbreviation *qtd. in* ("quoted in") as part of the parenthetical reference.

```
Wagner stated that myth and history stood before him
"with opposing claims" (qtd. in Winkler 10).
```

7. More Than One Work

Cite each work as you normally would, separating one from another with semicolons.

```
The Brooklyn Bridge has been used as a subject by many
American artists (McCullough 144; Tashjian 58).
```

Keep these citations short, however, as long parenthetical references will distract readers. Whenever possible, present long references as content notes (see 39b3).

8. Literary Works

In citations to literary works it is often helpful to include more than only the author and page number. For example, the chapter number of a novel enables readers to locate your reference in any edition of the work to which you are referring. Similarly, Biblical citations include chapter and verse following an abbreviated title of the book (Gen. 5.12). In parenthetical references to prose works, begin with the page number, include a semicolon, and add any additional information that might be necessary.

```
In Moby-Dick Melville refers to a whaling expedition
funded by Louis XIV of France (151; ch. 24).
```

In parenthetical references to poems, separate the divisions and line numbers with periods.

```
In The Aeneid Virgil describes the ships as cleaving the
"green woods reflected in the calm water" (8.124). (In this
```
citation the reference is to book 8, page 124 of *The Aeneid*.)

In classic verse plays, the citation includes the act, scene, and line numbers (*Macbeth* 2.2.14–16 or II.ii.14–16).

9. An Entire Work

When citing an entire work rather than part of a work, all you need do is include the author's last name in your text.

```
Northrup Frye's Fearful Symmetry presents a complex
critical interpretation of Blake's poetry.
```

If you wish, you may mention the author's name in a parenthetical reference.

```
Fearful Symmetry presents a complex critical
interpretation of Blake's poetry (Frye).
```

10. Tables and Illustrations

When citing tables and illustrations, include the documentation below the illustrative material. (See the Appendix for the format for tables and illustrations.)

(2) Works Cited list

The *Works Cited* section appears at the end of your paper and lists all the research materials you have used. If your instructor tells you to list all the sources you read, whether you actually cited them or not, use the title *Works Consulted*.

Guidelines for Preparing the Works Cited Section

- If you have no explanatory notes, begin the list of works cited on a new page after the last page of text.
- Number the page on which the list of works cited begins as the next page of text—for example, if your paper ends on page 8, the *Works Cited* section begins on page 9.
- List the items in alphabetical order according to the authors' last names. If one of your sources is unsigned, as is the case with many magazine and newspaper articles, alphabetize by the first main word of the title (excluding *a, an,* or *the*).
- Type the first line of each entry flush with the left-hand margin, and indent subsequent lines of the entry five spaces from the left.
- Double-space the list of works cited within and between items.

An item in a list of works cited has three divisions, each separated by a period and two spaces.

Works Cited Format

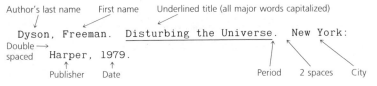

Author's last name   First name   Underlined title (all major words capitalized)

Dyson, Freeman. Disturbing the Universe. New York:
Double→
spaced Harper, 1979.
        ↑   ↑
     Publisher   Date   Period 2 spaces City

Sample MLA Works Cited Entries

Directory of MLA Works Cited Entries

Citations for Books

1. A book by one author
2. A book by two or three authors
3. A book by more than three authors
4. Two or more books by the same author

---

continued

continued from previous page

5. An edited book
6. An essay in an anthology
7. More than one essay from the same anthology
8. A multivolume work
9. The foreword, preface, or afterword of a book
10. A short story, play, or poem in an anthology
11. A short story, play, or poem in a collection of an author's work
12. A book-length poem
13. A book whose title contains a title that is normally enclosed within quotation marks
14. A book whose title contains a title that is normally underlined
15. A translation
16. A reprint of an older edition
17. A dissertation
18. An article in an encyclopedia
19. A pamphlet
20. A government publication

Citations for Articles

21. An article in a journal with continuous pagination through an annual volume
22. An article in a journal that has separate pagination in each issue
23. An article in a weekly magazine (signed/unsigned)
24. An article in a monthly magazine
25. An article that does not appear on consecutive pages
26. An article in a newspaper (signed/unsigned)
27. An editorial
28. A letter to the editor
29. A book review (titled/untitled)
30. An article whose title includes a title that is normally underlined
31. An article whose title includes a quotation or a title within quotation marks

Citations for Nonprint Sources

32. Computer software
33. Material from a computer information service
34. A lecture
35. A personal interview

36. A personal letter
37. A letter in a library's archives
38. A film
39. A videotape
40. A radio or television program
41. A recording

Citations for Books

1. A Book by One Author

Enter the full title of the book. To conserve space use a short form of the publisher's name; do not include *Incorporated, Publishers,* or *Company* after the name of the publisher. *Alfred A. Knopf, Inc.,* for example, is shortened to *Knopf,* and *Oxford University Press* becomes *Oxford UP.*

Bettelheim, Bruno. The Uses of Enchantment: The Meaning and Importance of Fairy Tales. New York: Knopf, 1976.

When citing an edition other than the first, indicate the edition number in the form used on the work's title page.

Gans, Herbert J. The Urban Villagers. 2nd ed. New York: Free, 1982.

2. A Book by Two or Three Authors

Only the first author's name is listed, with last name first. Subsequent authors' names should be listed first name first in the order in which they appear on the book's title page.

Davidson, James West, and Mark Hamilton Lytle. After the Fact: The Art of Historical Detection. New York: Knopf, 1982.

3. A Book by More Than Three Authors

For more than three authors, list only the first author followed by *et al.* ("and others").

Spiller, Robert E., et al., eds. Literary History of the United States. New York: Macmillan, 1974.

4. Two or More Books by the Same Author

Books by the same author are listed in alphabetical order by title. Three hyphens followed by a period take the place of the author's name after the first entry.

Thomas, Lewis. <u>The Lives of a Cell: Notes of a Biology Watcher</u>. New York: Viking, 1974.

———. <u>The Medusa and the Snail: More Notes of a Biology Watcher</u>. New York: Viking, 1979.

5. An Edited Book

An edited book is a work that has been prepared for publication by a person other than the author. If your emphasis is on the author's work, begin your citation with the author's name. If your emphasis is on the editor's work, begin your citation with the editor's name.

Bartram, William. <u>The Travels of William Bartram</u>. Ed. Mark Van Doren. New York: Dover, 1955.

Van Doren, Mark, ed. <u>The Travels of William Bartram</u>. By William Bartram. New York: Dover, 1955.

6. An Essay in an Anthology

When citing an essay appearing in an anthology, include the *full* span of pages on which the whole essay appears, even though you may cite only one page in your paper.

Lloyd, G. E. R. "Science and Mathematics." <u>The Legacy of Greece</u>. Ed. M. I. Finley. New York: Oxford UP, 1981, 256–300.

If the essay you cite has been published previously, include publishing data for the first publication followed by the current information along with the abbreviation *Rpt. in* ("Reprinted in").

Warren, Austin. "Emily Dickinson." <u>The Sewanee Review</u> 17 (1957): 132–77. Rpt. in <u>Emily Dickinson: A Collection of Critical Essays</u>. Ed. Richard B. Sewall. Englewood Cliffs: Prentice, 1963. 101–16.

NOTE: If you cite an essay that appears in a collection of the author's work, use the format illustrated in number 11.

7. More Than One Essay from the Same Anthology

If you cite more than one essay from the same anthology, list each essay separately, including a cross-reference to the entire anthology. List complete publication information for the anthology itself. In the cross-reference include only the author and title of the piece and the last name of the editor of the anthology, along with the appropriate page numbers.

Bolgar, R. R. "The Greek Legacy." Finley 429–72.

Davies, A. M. "Lyric and Other Poetry." Finley 93–119.

Finley, M. I., ed. The Legacy of Greece. New York:
    Oxford UP, 1981.

8. A Multivolume Work

If you are using only one volume of a multivolume work, refer to the volume you use.

Raine, Kathleen. Blake and Tradition. Vol. 1.
    Princeton: Princeton UP, 1968. 2 vols.

If you use two or more volumes of a multivolume work, cite the entire work.

Raine, Kathleen. Blake and Tradition. 2 vols.
    Princeton: Princeton UP, 1968.

If the volume you are using has an individual title, give the title after the author's name. Next, include the number of the volume that you are using followed by the title of the entire work.

Durant, Will, and Ariel Durant. The Age of Napoleon: A
    History of European Civilization from 1789 to 1815.
    New York: Simon, 1975. Vol. 11 of The Story of
    Civilization. 11 vols.

9. The Foreword, Preface, or Afterword of a Book

Taylor, Telford. Preface. Less Than Slaves. By
    Benjamin B. Ferencz. Cambridge: Harvard UP,
    1979. xiii–xxii.

10. A Short Story, Play, or Poem in an Anthology

Singer, Isaac Bashevis. "The Spinoza of Market Street."
    The Norton Anthology of Short Fiction. Ed. R. V.
    Cassill. 3rd ed. New York: Norton, 1986. 1210–24.

607

Shakespeare, William. Othello. The Moor of Venice.
Shakespeare: Six Plays and The Sonnets. Eds. Thomas
Marc Parrott and Edward Hubler. New York:
Scribner's, 1956.

11. A Short Story, Play, or Poem in a Collection of an Author's Work

Singer, Isaac Bashevis. "The Spinoza of Market Street."
The Collected Stories of Isaac Bashevis Singer. New
York: Farrar, 1983.

Pound, Ezra. "A Virginal." Selected Poems of Ezra
Pound. New York: New Directions, 1957. 23.

12. A Book-Length Poem

Eliot, T. S. The Waste Land. T. S. Eliot: Collected
Poems 1909—1962. New York: Harcourt, 1963. 51—70.
(The title of a book-length poem is underlined.)

13. A Book Whose Title Contains a Title That Is Normally Enclosed Within Quotation Marks

If the book you are citing contains a title enclosed in quotation marks, keep the quotation marks.

Herzog, Alan, ed. Twentieth Century Interpretations of
"To a Skylark." Englewood Cliffs: Prentice, 1975.

14. A Work Whose Title Contains a Title That Is Normally Underlined

If the work you are citing contains a title that you would normally underline (a novel, play, or long poem, for example), do not underline it.

Knoll, Robert E. ed. Storm Over The Waste Land.
Chicago: Scott, 1964.

15. A Translation

García Márquez, Gabriel. One Hundred Years of Solitude.
Trans. Gregory Rabassa. New York: Avon, 1971.

608

16. A Reprint of an Older Edition

Wharton, Edith. The House of Mirth. 1905. New York:
   Scribner's, 1975. (1905 is the original publication date.)

17. A Dissertation

Enter a published dissertation the way you would a book. Most American dissertations are published by University Microfilms International (UMI), so include the order number in your citation.

Spann, Marcella Joyce. An Analytical and Descriptive
   Catalogue of the Manuscripts and Letters in the
   Louis Zukofsky Collection at the University of Texas
   at Austin. Diss. U of Texas at Austin, 1969. Ann
   Arbor: UMI, 1970. 7010867.

Enclose the title of an unpublished dissertation within quotation marks.

Gainor, Charles Michael. "Cultural and Philosophical
   Determinants of Modern Economic Theory." Diss.
   Columbia U, 1984.

18. An Article in an Encyclopedia

Enter the title of an unsigned article just as it is listed in the encyclopedia. Because encyclopedia entries appear in alphabetical order, no volume number or page numbers are needed.

"Cubism." Encyclopaedia Britannica: Micropaedia. 1974.

For a signed article, enter the author's name, and then cite the article.

Monro, D. H. "Humor." The Encyclopedia of Philosophy.
   1974 ed.

19. A Pamphlet

Enter pamphlets as if they were books. If no author is listed, enter the underlined title first, and follow with publishing information.

Existing Light Photography. Rochester: Kodak, 1982.

20. A Government Publication

If the publication has no author, state the name of the government first, followed by the name of the agency and then the title of the pamphlet or bulletin.

> United States. President's Commission for the Study of
>   Ethical Problems in Medicine and Biomedical and
>   Behavioral Research. <u>Deciding to Forgo Life-</u>
>   <u>Sustaining Treatment: Ethical, Medical, and Legal</u>
>   <u>Issues in Treatment Decisions</u>. Washington: GPO,
>   1983.

Citations for Articles   Article citations contain the author's name; the title of the article, in quotation marks; and the underlined name of the journal. They also give the pages on which the full article appears. The abbreviations *p.* and *pp.* are not included.

21. An Article in a Scholarly Journal with Continuous Pagination through an Annual Volume

For an article in a journal with continuous pagination—for example, one in which an issue ends on page 172 and the next issue begins with page 173—include the volume number followed by the date of publication in parentheses. Follow the publication date with a colon, a space, and the page numbers.

> Huntington, John. "Science Fiction and the Future."
>   <u>College English</u> 37 (1975): 340–58.

22. An Article in a Scholarly Journal That Has Separate Pagination in Each Issue

For a journal with separate pagination in each issue—one in which each issue begins with page 1—add a period and the issue number after the volume number.

> Sipes, R. G. "War, Sports, and Aggression: An Empirical
>   Test of Two Rival Theories." <u>American</u>
>   <u>Anthropologist</u> 4.2 (1973): 65–84.

23. An Article in a Weekly Magazine (signed/unsigned)

Dates for articles follow military format, with the day preceding the month.

Bergley, Sharon. "Redefining Intelligence." <u>Newsweek</u> 14
    Nov. 1983: 123–24.

"Solzhenitsyn: A Candle in the Wind." <u>Time</u> 23 March
    1970: 70.

24. An Article in a Monthly Magazine

Roll, Lori. "Careers in Engineering." <u>Working Woman</u>
    Nov. 1982: 62.

25. An Article That Does Not Appear on Consecutive Pages

When an article does not appear on consecutive pages—that is,
when it begins on page 15, continues on page 16, and then skips
to page 86—include only the first page and a plus (+) sign.

Rodman, Selden. "Where Art Is Joy." <u>Caribbean Travel and
    Life</u> Oct. 1987: 58+.

26. An Article in a Newspaper (signed/unsigned)

Stipp, David. "Japanese Firms Find Little Success in the
    U.S. Small Computer Market." <u>Wall Street Journal</u> 11
    Sept. 1983, late ed.: 6.

"The Summit on Soviet Television." <u>Los Angeles Times</u> 13
    Dec. 1987, sec. 2: 3+.

27. An Editorial

"We Hear You, Mr. President." Editorial. <u>New York Times</u>
    11 Sept. 1983, late ed.: C11.

28. A Letter to the Editor

Bishop, Jennifer. Letter. <u>Philadelphia Inquirer</u> 10 Dec.
    1987: A26.

29. A Book Review (titled/untitled)

A citation for a review begins with the reviewer's name and is
followed by the title of the review (if any), the title and author of
the book reviewed, and the date on which the review appeared.

Prescott, Peter S. "A Movable Feast on Fiction." Rev.
    of The Assassination of Jesse James by the Coward,
    by Ron Hansen. Newsweek 14 Nov. 1983: 112.

Harris, Joseph. Rev. of Perspectives on Research and
    Scholarship in Composition, eds. Ben W. McLelland
    and Timothy R. Donovan. College Composition and
    Communication 38 (1987): 101–02.

NOTE: A citation for an unsigned review begins with the title of
the review, if any, or the title of the book reviewed.

30. An Article Whose Title Includes a Title That Is Normally Underlined

If an article title includes a title that you would normally underline
(to indicate italics), underline it in your Works Cited entry.

Leicester, H. Marshall, Jr. "The Art of Impersonation:
    A General Prologue to The Canterbury Tales." PMLA
    95 (1980): 213–24.

31. An Article Whose Title Includes a Quotation or a Title Within Quotation Marks

If a title contains material that is normally enclosed within quotation marks, use single quotation marks.

Nash, Robert. "About 'The Emperor of Ice-Cream.'"
    Perspectives 7 (1954): 122–24.

Citations for Nonprint Sources

32. Computer Software

Citations for computer software include the writer of the program, the title of the program, version (preceded by *vers*), the descriptive label *computer software*, the distributor, and the year of
publication. Follow with any pertinent information about the operating system.

Atkinson, Bill. MacPaint. Vers. 2.0b. Computer
    software. Apple, 1983. MacPlus, SE, System 6.0.

33. Material from a Computer Information Service

Enter material from a computer information service—BRS or DIALOG, for example—just as you would printed material. In addition, mention the information service and the identification numbers of the material at the end of the entry.

Baer, Walter S. "Telecommunications Technology in the
      1980's." Computer Science June 1984: 137+. DIALOG
      file 102, item 0346142.

34. A Lecture

Sandman, Peter. "Communicating Scientific Information."
      Communications Seminar, Dept. of Humanities and
      Communications. Drexel U, 26 Oct. 1990.

35. A Personal Interview

Cavett, Dick. Personal interview. 28 Dec. 1990.

   Sagan, Carl. Telephone interview. 8 June 1991.

36. A Personal Letter

Kingston, Maxine Hong. Letter to the author. 7 April
      1989.

A published letter is treated like a work in a collection.

37. A Letter in a Library's Archives

Stieglitz, Alfred. Letter to Paul Rosenberg. 5 Sept.
      1923. Steiglitz Archive. Yale, New Haven.

38. A Film

A citation for a film includes the title of the film (underlined), the distributor, and the date. You may also include other information such as the performers, the director, and the writer if this information would be of use to a reader.

Citizen Kane. Dir. Orson Welles. With Orson Welles,
      Joseph Cotton, Dorothy Comingore, and Agnes
      Moorehead. RKO, 1941.

If you are focusing on the contribution of a particular person, begin with that person's name (Welles, Orson, dir. *Citizen Kane.* . . .).

39. A Videotape

Arthur Miller: The Crucible. Videocassette. Dir.
   William Schiff. The Mosaic Group, 1987. 20 min.

Note that the title of the work being cited contains a title (*The Crucible*) that you would normally underline. This title is not underlined in the citation.

40. A Radio or Television Program

Kennedy. Writ. Reg Gadney. With Martin Sheen, John
   Shea, and Blair Brown. NBC. KNBC, Los Angeles. 20
   Nov. 1983.

41. A Recording

When citing a recording, list the composer, conductor, or performer (whichever you are emphasizing) followed by the artist, manufacturer, catalog number, and year of issue.

Boubill, Alain and Claude-Michel Schönberg. Miss Saigon.
   With Lea Salonga, Claire Moore, and Jonathan Pryce.
   Cond. Martin Koch. Geffen, DIDX006369, 1989.

In citing jacket notes or any material accompanying a recording, give the author's name, the title, and a description.

Marley, Bob. "Crisis." Lyrics. Bob Marley and the
   Wailers: Kava Island Records, 422-846 209-2, 1978.

(3) Content notes

Content notes—commentary on sources or additional information on content that does not fit smoothly into the text—may be used along with parenthetical documentation. Content notes are indicated by a raised number in the paper, which is keyed to the note. The full text of these notes appears on the first full numbered page, entitled *Notes*, following the last page of the paper and before the list of works cited. Content notes are double-spaced between and within entries.

For More Than One Source   Use content notes for references to numerous citations in a single reference. Many references within a single pair of parentheses will distract readers.

IN THE PAPER

Many researchers emphasize the necessity of having dying patients share their experiences.[1]

IN THE NOTE

[1]Kübler-Ross 27; Stinnette 43; Poston 70; Cohen and Cohen 31–34; Burke 1:91–95.

For Explanations   Use content notes to provide comments or explanations that are needed to clarify a point in the text.

IN THE PAPER

The massacre of the Armenians by the Turks during World War I is an event that the survivors cannot forget.[2]

IN THE NOTE

[2]For a firsthand account of these events, see Bedoukian 17–81.

39c *Using the Chicago Format*

The *Chicago Manual of Style** (CMS) is used in history as well as some other humanities disciplines. Chicago style has two parts: notes at the bottom of the page (footnotes) or at the end of the paper (endnotes) and bibliographic citations at the end of the paper.

(1) *Endnotes and footnotes*

The notes format uses a raised numeral in the text after source material you have either quoted or referred to. (If you are documenting a quotation, the note comes directly after it, not after the author's name or an identifying phrase.) This number corresponds

---

*The Chicago format follows the guidelines set in *The Chicago Manual of Style*. 13th ed. Chicago: University of Chicago Press, 1982.

to a number at the beginning of the note. Note numbers for foot-notes are typed slightly above the line (superscript). Note numbers for endnotes, however, may either be typed slightly above the line or on the line followed by a period and two spaces.

Type notes consecutively in the order in which they appear in the paper. Never put a period or any other mark of punctuation after a superscript number. Indent the first line of each note five spaces, and type subsequent lines flush with the lefthand margin. Use single-spacing within each entry and double-spacing between entries. If you are required to use footnotes, be sure the notes at the bottom of a particular page of your paper correspond to the note numbers in the text of the paper. List endnotes on a separate sheet entitled *Notes* at the end of your paper after the last page of text.

Endnote and Footnote Formats

IN THE TEXT

By November of 1942, the Allies had proof that the Nazis were engaged in the systematic killing of Jews.[1]

IN THE NOTE

[1]David S. Wyman, The Abandonment of the Jews: America and the Holocaust 1941–1945 (New York: Pantheon Books, 1984), 65.

Sample CMS Footnotes and Endnotes

Directory of CMS Footnotes and Endnotes

1. A book by one author
2. A book by two or three authors
3. A multivolume work
4. An edited book
5. An essay in an anthology
6. An article in an encyclopedia
7. An article in a scholarly journal with continuous pagination
8. An article in a scholarly journal with separate pagination in each issue
9. An article in a weekly magazine
10. An article in a monthly magazine
11. An article in a newspaper
12. Subsequent references

Citations for Books

1. A Book by One Author

¹Herbert J. Gans, <u>The Urban Villagers</u>, 2nd ed. (New York: Free Press, 1982), 100.

2. A Book by Two or Three Authors

²James West Davidson and Mark Hamilton Lytle, <u>After the Fact: The Art of Historical Detection</u> (New York: Alfred A. Knopf, 1982), 54.

3. A Multivolume Work

³Kathleen Raine, <u>Blake and Tradition</u> (Princeton: Princeton University Press, 1968), 1: 100.

⁴Will Durant and Ariel Durant, <u>The Age of Napoleon: A History of European Civilization from 1789 to 1815</u>, vol. 11, <u>The Story of Civilization</u> (New York: Simon and Schuster, 1975), 90.

4. An Edited Book

⁵William Bartram, <u>The Travels of William Bartram</u>, ed. Mark Van Doren (New York: Dover Press, 1955), 85.

5. An Essay in an Anthology

⁶G. E. R. Lloyd, "Science and Mathematics," in <u>The Legacy of Greece</u>, ed. M. I. Finley (New York: Oxford University Press, 1981), 256–300.

6. An Article in an Encyclopedia (Signed/Unsigned)

⁷<u>The Focal Encyclopedia of Photography</u>, 1965 ed., s. v. "Daguerreotype."

⁸<u>The Encyclopedia of Philosophy</u>, 1967 ed., s. v. "Hobbes, Thomas," by R. S. Peters.

NOTE: The abbreviation *s.v.* stands for *sub verbo*—under the word.

Citations for Articles

7. An Article in a Scholarly Journal with Continuous Pagination

¹John Huntington, "Science Fiction and the Future," <u>College English</u> 37 (Fall 1975): 340.

8. An Article in a Scholarly Journal with Separate Pagination in Each Issue

[2]R. G. Sipes, "War, Sports, and Aggression: An Empirical Test of Two Rival Theories," American Anthropologist 4, no. 2 (1973): 84.

9. An Article in a Weekly Magazine

[3]Sharon Bergley, "Redefining Intelligence," Newsweek, 14 November 1983, 123.

[4]"Solzhenitsyn: A Candle in the Wind," Time, 23 March 1970, 70.

10. An Article in a Monthly Magazine

[5]Lori Roll, "Careers in Engineering," Working Woman, November 1982, 62.

11. An Article in a Newspaper

[6]Raymond Bonner, "A Guatemalan General's Rise to Power," New York Times, 21 July 1982, sec. 1, p. 3.

12. Subsequent References

The first time you make reference to a work, use the full citation; subsequent references to the same work should list the author's last name, followed by a comma and a page number.

FIRST NOTE ON ESPINOZA

[1]J. M. Espinoza, The First Expedition of Vargas in New Mexico, 1692 (Albuquerque: University of New Mexico Press, 1940), 10–15.

SUBSEQUENT NOTE

[4]Espinoza, 69.

The Chicago Manual of Style allows the use of the abbreviation *ibid.* ("in the same place") for subsequent references to the same work as long as there are no intervening references. *Ibid.* takes the place of the author's name and the title.

FIRST NOTE ON ESPINOZA

[1]J. M. Espinoza, The First Expedition of Vargas in New Mexico, 1692 (Albuquerque: University of New Mexico Press, 1940), 10–15.

618

²Ibid., 69.

NOTE: Keep in mind that use of *Ibid.* is rapidly giving way to the style that uses the author's name in subsequent notes.

(2) Bibliography

List bibliographic entries in alphabetical order on a separate page after the last page of text or after the endnotes. In addition to the heading "Bibliography," Chicago style allows "Selected Bibliography," "Works Cited," and "Sources Consulted," depending on which more accurately reflects the works listed. Single-space within entries and double-space between them. The first line of each entry begins at the left-hand margin, and all subsequent lines are indented five spaces. Periods follow each of the main parts of the entry— author, title, and publication information spelled out in full.

Pages listing the notes and listing the bibliography should be numbered consecutively. In other words, if the last page of the paper is page 4, the endnotes page should be page 5, and the bibliography page should be page 6.

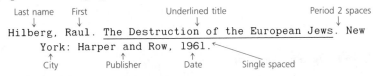

Last name   First   Underlined title   Period 2 spaces

Hilberg, Raul. The Destruction of the European Jews. New
        York: Harper and Row, 1961.
           City   Publisher   Date   Single spaced

Sample CMS Bibliographic Entries

Directory of CMS Bibliographic Entries

1. A book by one author
2. A book by two or more authors
3. A multivolume work
4. An edited book
5. An essay in an anthology
6. An article in an encyclopedia
7. An article in a scholarly journal with continuous pagination
8. An article in a scholarly journal with separate pagination in each issue
9. An article in a weekly magazine
10. An article in a monthly magazine
11. An article in a newspaper

Citations for Books

1. A Book by One Author

Gans, Herbert J. The Urban Villagers, 2nd ed. New York:
Free Press, 1982.

2. A Book by Two or More Authors

Davidson, James West and Mark Hamilton Lytle. After the
Fact: The Art of Historical Detection. New York:
Alfred A. Knopf, 1982.

3. A Multivolume Work

Raine, Kathleen. Vol. 1, Blake and Tradition. Princeton:
Princeton University Press, 1968.

Durant, Will and Ariel Durant. The Age of Napoleon: A
History of European Civilization from 1789 to 1815.
Vol. 11, The Story of Civilization. New York: Simon
and Schuster, 1975.

4. An Edited Book

Bartram, William. The Travels of William Bartram. Edited
by Mark Van Doren. New York: Dover Press, 1955.

5. An Essay in an Anthology

Lloyd, G. E. R. "Science and Mathematics." In The Legacy
of Greece, ed. M. I. Finley, 256–300. New York:
Oxford University Press, 1981.

6. An Article in an Encyclopedia (Unsigned/Signed)

The Focal Encyclopedia of Photography, 1965 ed., S. v.
"Daguerreotype."

The Encyclopedia of Philosophy. 1967 ed. S. v. "Hobbes,
Thomas," by R. S. Peters.

Citations for Articles

7. An Article in a Scholarly Journal with Continuous Pagination

Huntington, John. "Science Fiction and the Future."
College English 37 (Fall 1975): 340–58.

8. An Article in a Scholarly Journal with Separate Pagination in Each Issue

```
Sipes, R. G. "War, Sports, and Aggression: An Empirical
     Test of Two Rival Theories." American Anthropologist
     4, no. 2 (1973): 65–84.
```

9. An Article in a Weekly Magazine

```
Bergley, Sharon. "Redefining Intelligence." Newsweek, 14
     November 1983, 123.

"Solzhenitsyn: A Candle in the Wind." Time, 23 March
     1970, 70.
```

10. An Article in a Monthly Magazine

```
Roll, Lori. "Careers in Engineering." Working Woman,
     November 1982, 62.
```

11. An Article in a Newspaper

```
Bonner, Raymond. "A Guatemalan General's Rise to Power."
     New York Times, 21 July 1982, sec. 1, p. 3.
```

39d *Using APA Format**

APA format, which is used extensively in the social sciences, relies on short references—consisting of the last name of the author and the year of publication—inserted within the text. These references are keyed to an alphabetical list of references that follows the paper. APA format also permits content notes placed after the last page of the text.

(1) Parenthetical references in the text

APA style calls for a comma between the name and the date.

```
One study of stress in the workplace (Weisberg, 1983)
shows a correlation between. . . .
```

You should not include in the parenthetical reference information that appears in the text.

---

*APA documentation format follows the guidelines set in the *Publication Manual of the American Psychological Association.* 3rd ed. Washington, DC: APA, 1983.

```
In his study Weisberg (1983) shows a correlation. . . .
```
(author's name in text)

```
In Weisberg's 1983 study of stress in the
workplace. . . .
```
(author's name and date in text)

Sample APA Parenthetical References

Directory of APA Parenthetical References

1. Two publications by the same author(s), same year
2. A publication by two or more authors
3. An indirect source
4. Specific parts of a source
5. Two or more works within the same parenthetical reference
6. A long quotation

---

1. Two Publications by Same Author(s), Same Year

If you cite two or more publications by the same author that appeared the same year, the first is designated *a*, the second, *b* (e.g., Weisberg 1983a and Weisberg 1983b), and so on. These letter designations also appear in the reference list that follows the text of your paper.

```
He completed his next study of stress (Weisberg,
1983b). . . .
```

2. A Publication by Two or More Authors

When a work has two authors, both names are cited.

```
There is a current and growing concern over the use of
psychological testing in elementary schools (Albright &
Glennon, 1982).
```

If a work has more than two authors but fewer than six authors, mention all names in the first reference, and in subsequent references cite the first author followed by *et al.* and the year (Sparks et al., 1984). When a work has six or more authors, cite the name of the first author followed by *et al.* and the year.

When referring to multiple authors in your paper, join the last two names with *and*: According to Rosen, Wolfe, and Ziff (1988).

In parenthetical documentation, however, use an ampersand to join multiple authors (Rosen, Wolfe, & Ziff, 1988).

3. An Indirect Source

Indicate material from an indirect source by using the phrase *cited in* in the parenthetical reference.

```
Cogan and Howe offer very different interpretations of
the problem (cited in Swenson, 1990).
```

4. Specific Parts of a Source

When citing a specific part of a source, identify that part in your reference, using abbreviations for the words *page* ("p."), *chapter* ("ch."), and *section* ("sec.").

```
These theories have an interesting history (Lee, 1966,
p. 53).
```

5. Two or More Works Within the Same Parenthetical Reference

Identify works by different authors in alphabetical order.

```
. . . among several studies (Barson & Roth, 1985; Rose,
1987; Tedesco, 1982).
```

Identify works by the same author in order of date of publication.

```
. . . among several studies (Weiss & Elliot, 1982, 1984,
1985).
```

Identify works by the same author that appeared in the same year by designating the first *a*, the second *b*, and so on.

```
. . . among several studies (Hossack, 1985a, 1985b,
1985c, in press). (In press designates a work about to be
published.)
```

6. A Long Quotation

Parenthetical documentation for a long quotation (forty words or more) appears two spaces after the final punctuation.

```
Todd Gitlin sees a change in left-wing politics beginning
in 1969:
     Women had been the cement of the male-run movement;
     their 'desertion' into their own circles completed
```

the dissolution of the old boys' clan. While men
outside the hard—line factions were miserable with
the crumbling of their onetime movement, women were
riding high. (1987, p. 374)

NOTE: Long quotations are double-spaced and indented five spaces
from the left-hand margin.

(2) List of references

The list of all the sources cited in your paper falls at the end on
a new numbered page with the heading *References*. If you are listing
all works you consulted regardless of whether they are cited in your
paper, label your list *Bibliography*.

Items are arranged in alphabetical order, with the author's last
name spelled out in full and initials only for the author's first and
second names. Next comes the date of publication, title, and, for
journal entries, volume number and pages. For books, the city of
publication and publisher are also included.

Double-space all entries in your list of references. Type the first
line of each entry flush with the left-hand margin, and indent subsequent lines three spaces.

Guidelines for Arranging Works in the Reference List

- Single-author entries precede multiple-author entries that begin
  with the same name.

  Field, S. (1987). . . .

  Field, S., & Levitt, M. P. (1984). . . .

- Entries by the same author are arranged according to date of publication, starting with the earliest date.

  Ruthenberg, H., & Rubin, R. (1985). . . .

  Ruthenberg, H., & Rubin, R. (1987). . . .

- Entries by the same author and with the same date of publication
  are arranged alphabetically according to title. They include lowercase letters after the year.

  Wolk, E. M. (1986a). Analysis. . . .

  Wolk, E. M. (1986b). Hormonal. . . .

Reference List Format

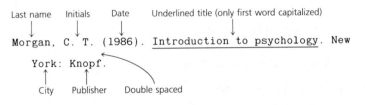

Last name   Initials   Date   Underlined title (only first word capitalized)

Morgan, C. T. (1986). Introduction to psychology. New

York: Knopf.

City   Publisher   Double spaced

Sample APA Reference List Entries

Directory of APA Reference List Entries

1. A book with one author
2. A book with more than one author
3. An edited book
4. A volume of a multivolume work
5. A book with a corporate author
6. An article in a scholarly journal with continuous pagination
7. An article in a scholarly journal with separate pagination
8. A magazine article
9. A newspaper article, unsigned
10. A newspaper article, signed
11. An article in an edited book
12. A government report

Citations for Books   Capitalize only the first word of the title and the first word of the subtitle. Underline the title and enclose the date, volume number, and edition number in parentheses.

1. A Book with One Author

Maslow, A. H. (1974). Toward a psychology of being.
    Princeton: Van Nostrand.

2. A Book with More Than One Author

Notice that both authors are cited with last names first.

Blood, R. O., & Wolf, D. M. (1960). Husbands and wives:
    The dynamics of married living. Glencoe: Free Press.

3. An Edited Book

Lewin, K., Lippitt, R., & White, R. K. (Eds.). (1985). Social learning and imitation. New York: Basic Books.

4. A Volume of a Multivolume Work

Gibb, C. A. (1969). Leadership. In G. Linzey and E. Aronson (Eds.), Handbook of social psychology (Vol. 4, pp. 205–282). Reading, MA: Addison–Wesley.

5. A Book with a Corporate Author

League of Women Voters of the United States. (1969). Local league handbook. Washington, DC: Author.

NOTE: When the author and publisher are the same, use the word *author* instead of repeating the publisher's name.

Citations for Articles　　Capitalize only the first word of the title and the first word of the subtitle. Do not underline the title of the article or enclose it in quotation marks. Give the journal title in full; underline the title and capitalize all major words. Underline the volume number and include the issue number in parentheses. Give inclusive page numbers.

6. An Article in a Scholarly Journal with Continuous Pagination through an Annual Volume

Miller, W. (1969). Violent crimes in city gangs. Journal of Social Issues, 27, 581–593.

7. An Article in a Scholarly Journal with Separate Pagination

Williams, S., & Cohen, L. R. (1984). Child stress in early learning situations. American Psychologist, 21 (10), 1–28.

8. A Magazine Article

Use *pp.* when referring to page numbers in magazines, but omit this abbreviation when referring to page numbers in journals.

McCurdy, H. G. (1983, June). Brain mechanisms and
intelligence. Psychology Today, pp. 61–63.

9. A Newspaper Article, Unsigned

Study finds many street people mentally ill. (1984, June
25). New York Times, p. 7.

10. A Newspaper Article, Signed

James, W. R. (1985, January 3). The unemployed and the
flat tax. The Wall Street Journal, pp. 1, 12. (article
appears on two separate pages)

11. An Article in an Edited Book

Tappan, P. W. (1980). Who is a criminal? In M. E.
Wolfgang, L. Savitz, & N. Johnston (Eds.), The
sociology of crime and delinquency (pp. 41–48). New
York:Wiley.

12. A Government Report

National Institute of Mental Health, (1987). Motion
pictures and violence: A summary report of research
(DHHS Publication No. ADM 91–22187). Washington, DC:
U.S. Government Printing Office.

(3) Content notes

APA format allows the use of content notes in your paper. These
notes are indicated by superscript numbers in the text. The notes
are listed on a separate page entitled *Footnotes* following the last
page of text. Double-space all notes, indenting the first line of each
note five spaces and beginning subsequent lines at the left-hand
margin.

IN THE TEXT

Skinner's behaviorist theories fell into disfavor and
were displaced by the ideas of cognitive psychologists.[1]

IN THE NOTE

> ¹Skinner himself remained largely unconvinced by the
> cognitive theorists. During a New York Times interview
> just two weeks before his death in 1990, he affirmed his
> belief in his model of human behavior.

39e *Using CBE Format**

Documentation formats recommended by the Council of Biology Editors (CBE) and distributed by the American Institute of Biological Sciences are used by authors, editors, and publishers in biology, botany, zoology, physiology, anatomy, and genetics. The *CBE Style Manual* recommends several documentation styles, including the number-reference format described below. Numbers inserted parenthetically in the text correspond to a list entitled "References" at the end of the paper. Works are arranged in the reference list in the order in which they are mentioned in the text and then numbered consecutively. When the list of references is typed, all lines begin at the left margin and are double-spaced.

Reference List Format

IN THE PAPER

> One study (1) has demonstrated the effect of low
> dissolved oxygen. Cell walls of. . . .

IN THE REFERENCE LIST

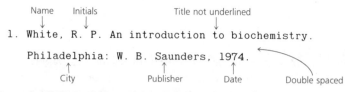

```
        Name    Initials              Title not underlined
          ↓        ↓                        ↓
  1. White, R. P. An introduction to biochemistry.

     Philadelphia: W. B. Saunders, 1974.
          ↑              ↑            ↑
         City         Publisher      Date         Double spaced
```

Sample CBE Reference List Entries

Directory of CBE Reference Entries

1. A book with one author
2. A book with more than one author

---

*CBE documentation format follows the guidelines set in the *CBE Style Manual.* 5th ed. Bethesda: Council of Biology Editors, 1983.

3. An edited book
4. A specific section of a book
5. An article in a scholarly journal with continuous pagination
6. An article in a scholarly journal that has separate pagination
7. An article with a subtitle
8. An article with no author
9. An article with discontinuous pagination

Citations for Books　For book entries, list the author(s), the title (with only the first word capitalized), the city of publication followed by a colon, the name of the publisher followed by a semicolon, and the year followed by a period. Do not underline book titles.

1. A Book with One Author

    1. Rathmil, P. D. The synthesis of milk and related
       products. Madison, WI: Hugo Summer; 1985.

2. A Book with More Than One Author

    2. Krause, K. F.; Paterson, M. K., Jr. Tissue culture:
       methods and application. New York: Academic Press,
       Inc.; 1973.

3. An Edited Book

    3. Marzacco, M. P., editor. A survey of biochemistry. New
       York: R. R. Bowker Co.; 1985.

4. A Specific Section of a Book

    4. Baldwin, L. D.; Rigby, C. V. A study of animal
       virology. 2nd ed. New York: John Wiley & Sons; 1984:
       121-133.

Citations for Articles　For journal articles list the author(s), the title of the article (with only the first word capitalized), the title of the journal (capitalized), the volume number followed by a colon, the inclusive page numbers of the article (followed by a semicolon), and the year (followed by a period).

5. An Article in a Scholarly Journal with Continuous Pagination

1. Bensley, K. Profiling women physicians. Medica 1: 140–145; 1985.

6. An Article in a Scholarly Journal That Has Separate Pagination

2. Wilen, W. W. The biological clock of insects. Sci. Amer. 234(2): 114–121; 1976.

7. An Article with a Subtitle

3. Schindler, A; Donner, K. B. On DNA: the evolution of an amino acid sequence. J. Mol. Evol. 8: 94–101; 1980.

8. An Article with No Author

4. Anonymous. Developments in microbiology. Int. J. Microbiol. 6: 234–248; 1987.

9. An Article with Discontinuous Pagination

5. Williams, S.; Heller, G. A. Special dietary foods and their importance for diabetics. Food Prod. Dev. 44: 54–62, 68–73; 1984.

39f   Using Other Documentation Styles

The following style manuals describe documentation formats different from the ones already discussed. When the need arises, consult them in your college library.

Chemistry

American Chemical Society. *Handbook for Authors of Papers in American Chemical Society Publications.* Washington: American Chemical Soc., 1978.

Geology

United States Geological Survey. *Suggestions to Authors of the Reports of the United States Geological Survey.* 6th ed. Washington DC: Dept. of the Interior, 1978.

Mathematics

American Mathematical Society. *A Manual for Authors of Mathematical Papers.* 7th ed. Providence: American Mathematical Soc., 1980.

Medical Sciences

American Medical Association. *Style Book: Editorial Manual.* 6th ed. Acton, MA: Publishing Sciences Group, 1976.

Physics

American Institute of Physics. Publications Board. *Style Manual for Guidance in the Preparation of Papers.* 3rd ed. New York: American Inst. of Physics, 1978.

See John Bruce Howell, *Style Manuals for the English-Speaking World* (Phoenix: Oryx, 1983) for other guides to style.

39g *Using Abbreviations*

Although many of the abbreviations that made documentation so tedious have been eliminated from the latest editions of style manuals, you should be familiar with certain abbreviations that you may encounter in your research.

Commonly Used Scholarly Abbreviations

anon.	anonymous
bk.	book
c., ca.	circa ("about"). Used with dates that are approximate, as in c. 1920 (approximately 1920).
cf.	confer ("compare")
ch.	chapter
col.	column
colloq.	colloquial
comp., comps.	compiled by, compiler(s)
diss.	dissertation
ed.	edition, editor, edited by
e.g.	*exempli gratia* ("for example")

continued

---

continued from previous page

et al.	*et alia* ("and others")
ff.	and the following pages, as in pp. 88 ff.
i.e.	*id est* ("that is")
illus.	illustrated by, illustration
l., ll.	line(s)
ms., mss.	manuscript(s)
n., nn.	note(s), as in p. 12, n. 1
NB	*nota bene* ("take notice")
n.d.	no date (of publication)
n.p.	no place (of publication), no publisher
n. pag.	no pagination
p., pp.	page(s)
rev.	revision, revised by; review, reviewed by
rpt.	reprint, reprinted by
sec.	section
supp.	supplement
trans.	translated by, translator, translation
vol.	volume

EXERCISE 1

The following are notes for a paper on approaches to teaching composition. Put them in the proper format for MLA parenthetical documentation, and then arrange them in the proper format for the list of works cited. (If your instructor requires a different method of documentation, use it instead.)

1. Page 2 in a book called Teaching Expository Writing by William F. Irmscher. The book has 188 pages and was published by Holt, Rinehart and Winston, which at that time was located in New York, in 1979. (author's name mentioned in the text of your paper)
2. Something Erika Lindemann said in a lecture on November 9, 1982. She called the talk Approaches to Teaching. (no name mentioned in text)
3. Irmscher's book again, this time pages 34, 35, and 36. (author's name mentioned in the text)
4. The Search for Intelligible Structure, an essay written by Frank J. D'Angelo in a book by Gary Tate and Edward P. J. Corbett that is

a collection of essays. Oxford University Press in New York published the book, and its copyright date is 1981. Your quotation is from the first page of the essay, which runs from page 80 to page 88. The book is called The Writing Teacher's Sourcebook. (no name mentioned in the text)

5. Page vii of the introduction to a book called Teaching Composition: 10 Bibliographical Essays, which Texas Christian University Press published in 1976 in Fort Worth. It was edited by Gary Tate. (no name mentioned in the text)

6. An article in *Time* on October 25, 1980, called Teaching Johnny to Write. You paraphrased a paragraph on page 73. The article ran from page 72 to page 79, and the last page was signed M. Hardy Jones. (no name mentioned in the text)

7. Page 61 in Teaching Expository Writing. (author's name mentioned in the text)

8. Using a Newspaper in the Classroom, which appeared in the Durham Morning Herald on page 1 of section D in the Sunday paper on November 14, 1982. It was written by Kim Best. (no name mentioned in the text)

9. Lee Odell's article in the February 1979 issue of College Composition and Communication. The article, called Teachers of Composition and Needed Research in Discourse Theory, ran from page 39 to page 45, and you got your information from page 41. That was volume 30 of the journal. (author's name mentioned in the text)

10. You found a book written by Erika Lindemann that you want to quote. You use material on pages 236 and 237 of the book, titled A Rhetoric for Writing Teachers, which was published in 1982 by the New York office of Oxford University Press. (no name mentioned in the text)

11. You decide you need to talk to someone with some experience at the University of North Carolina, so you interview English professor Robert Bain. You talked to him on November 5 and now you are quoting something he said. (no name mentioned in the text)

12. This material is from page 78 of that *Time* article. (no name mentioned in the text)

13. You summarize pages 179–185 of Irmscher. (author's name mentioned in the text)

14. You find the perfect conclusion on page 635 of volume 33 of College English in Richard Larson's article Problem-Solving, Composing and Liberal Education. This is the March 1972 issue and the article begins on page 635. (no name mentioned in the text)

Writing a Research Paper

THE RESEARCH PROCESS

Activity	Date Due	Date Completed
Moving from Assignment to Topic		
—understanding your assignment	_____	_____
—choosing a topic	_____	_____
—starting a research notebook	_____	_____
Focusing on a Research Question		
—mapping out a search strategy	_____	_____
—doing exploratory research	_____	_____
Assembling a Working Bibliography and Making Bibliography Cards		
—assembling a working bibliography	_____	_____
—making bibliography cards	_____	_____
Developing a Tentative Thesis		
Doing Focused Research and Taking Notes		
—reading sources	_____	_____
—taking notes	_____	_____

Planning Your Paper

	Activity	Date Due	Date Completed
Shaping Your Material	*Deciding on a Thesis*	_____	_____
	Preparing a Formal Outline	_____	_____
Writing and Revising	*Writing Your First Draft*	_____	_____
	Revising Your Drafts	_____	_____
	Preparing Your Final Draft	_____	_____

Doing research involves more than just absorbing the ideas of others; it requires you to think critically, evaluating and interpreting the ideas presented in your sources and developing ideas of your own. In addition, it requires strategic planning, careful time management, and the willingness to rethink, reformulate, and reshape ideas.

The sample schedule above will help you to manage your time as you write a research paper.

40a *Moving from Assignment to Topic*

(1) *Understanding your assignment*

Your research paper begins with an assignment. Before you can find a direction for your research within the guidelines of this assignment, you must be sure you understand it.

Writing Checklist: Understanding Your Assignment

- Are you to choose a topic from among a list of possible topics provided by your instructor?
- Have you been given a general subject area and asked to focus on one aspect of it?
- Are you being asked to select a topic on your own?

continued

635

continued from previous page

> - When is the completed research paper due?
> - About how long should it be?
> - Will you be given a specific research schedule to follow, or are you expected to set your own schedule?
> - Does your instructor expect you to take notes on note cards? To prepare a formal outline?
> - Will your instructor review note cards, outline, or drafts with you at regular intervals?
> - Are you to do research only in the library, or should you also use nonprint sources?
> - Does your instructor require you to keep a research notebook?
> - What paper format and documentation style are you to use?
> - What help is available to you—from your instructor, your fellow students, experts in the field your paper will explore, your library?

(2) Choosing a topic

Once you understand your assignment, you can look for a direction for your research. You begin this task by narrowing your focus to a topic you can explore within the limits of your assignment.

In most cases, your instructor will help you to choose a topic, either by providing a list of suitable topics or by assigning a general subject area—a famous trial, an event that happened on the day you were born, an ethnic group. Even in these instances, you will still need to choose one of the topics or narrow the subject area: decide on one trial, one event, one ethnic group. And even when you have made your choice, you will have to decide exactly how to approach that topic.

If your instructor prefers that you select a topic on your own, your task is somewhat more difficult: you must consider various topics and weigh both their suitability for research and your interest in researching them. You find a focus for your paper in much the same way you decide on a topic for a short essay: you brainstorm, ask questions, talk to people, and read widely. With a research paper, however, you know from the start that you will examine not only your own ideas on a topic, but also the ideas of others.

An effective research topic has four characteristics.

A Research Topic Should Be Neither Too Broad Nor Too Narrow
The subject areas on the list below are too general for research. The narrowed topics are more suitable starting points.

Subject Area	Topic
Computers	The possible negative effects of computer games on adolescents
Feminism	The relationship between the feminist movement and the use of sexist language
Mood-altering drugs	The use of mood-altering drugs in state mental hospitals

A topic must fit within the boundaries of your assignment. "Julius and Ethel Rosenberg: Atomic Spies or FBI Scapegoats?" is far too broad for a ten-page—or even a hundred-page—treatment. However, "One piece of evidence that played a decisive role in establishing the Rosenbergs' guilt" would probably be too narrow for a ten-page research paper—even if you could gain access to significant information. But how one newspaper reported the Rosenbergs' trial or how college students reacted at the time to the couple's 1953 execution for espionage might work.

A Research Topic Should Be Suitable for Research   Topics based exclusively on personal experience or on value judgments are not suitable for research. For example, "How attending an integrated high school has made me a more tolerant person" is a topic that can be supported only by self-analysis. Similarly, "The superiority of J. R. R. Tolkein's work to that of Frank Herbert" is an issue that might interest you, but neither research nor expert testimony can ever resolve it.

A Research Topic Should Be One That Can Be Researched in a Library to Which You Have Access   If your instructor gives you a specific topic or subject area to write about, he or she will probably have made sure that your library has the resources you need. If you choose your own topic, however, you will have to learn what your library has to offer and what its limitations are before you select a topic. For instance, the library of an engineering or business college may not have a large collection of journals about literature; the library of a small liberal arts college may not have extensive resources for technical or medical topics.

Finally, a Research Topic Should Be One in Which You Are Genuinely Interested   You will be deeply involved with this topic for many weeks—perhaps even for an entire semester—and your research will be most productive if you are able to see your paper as more than just an exercise. If you are interested in your topic, you

637

are more likely to see the research paper as an opportunity to discover new ideas and new connections among ideas.

(3)   Starting a research notebook

As soon as you have your assignment, you should start a **research notebook,** a combination journal of your reactions and log of your progress. A research notebook maps out your direction and keeps you on track; throughout the research process it defines and re-defines the boundaries of your assignment.

In this notebook you record lists of things to do, sources to check, leads to follow up on, appointments, possible community contacts, questions to which you would like to find answers, stray ideas, possible thesis statements or titles, and so on. Be sure to date your entries and to check off and date work completed; this will save you from repeating steps.

Some students use a spiral notebook that includes pockets to hold note and bibliography cards. Others use a small assignment book. Whatever kind of book you use, the research notebook can serve as a useful record of what has been done and what is left to do.

STUDENT CASE STUDY

MOVING FROM ASSIGNMENT TO TOPIC

Michael Schrader, a student in a freshman composition class, was given this assignment: "Write an eight- to ten-page research paper on some aspect of the immigrant experience in America, choosing *one* ethnic group and exploring *one* issue." This was to be a full-semester project, so Michael had fourteen weeks in which to research and write the paper. Throughout this chapter we will follow his progress.

Michael's instructor told the class that she would require regular conferences at which she would review each student's progress; a seg-ment of the assignment would be due at each meeting. She also would require each student to keep a research notebook, and she expected them to use nonprint as well as print sources. With these general guide-lines in mind, Michael began to think about his assignment.

Michael's mother's family was Italian, so he decided to do his paper on Italian Americans. His maternal grandparents lived in an Italian neigh-borhood and subscribed to ethnic newspapers and magazines. They had many friends among the political, religious, and social leaders of the community who could be of assistance to him. After discussing his topic with his mother, Michael decided to narrow his subject to the family life of Italian-American immigrants.

Assignment	Topic
Discuss one aspect of one ethnic group's immigrant experience	Family life of Italian-American immigrants

Michael began his research notebook by copying down his assignment and pasting the instructor's research schedule on the inside front cover, planning to check off each part of the project as he completed it. Next he jotted down the assignment's other requirements and the time of his first conference with his instructor. Then he recorded his topic and listed a few family members he thought might be able to help him. Now he was ready to move on to the next stage of his assignment: focusing on a research question.

E X E R C I S E   1

Using your own instructor's guidelines for selecting a research topic, choose a topic for your paper. Begin your research notebook by entering information about your assignment, schedule, and topic.

40b   *Focusing on a Research Question*

(1)   *Mapping out a search strategy*

The key to successful research lies in finding out what questions to ask. Your research should be guided by a **search strategy,** a plan for a systematic process of gathering and evaluating potential source material, moving from general to specific sources (**see 37a**). Your first meeting with your instructor can help you to map out a tentative search strategy for the project you have in mind. At this meeting your instructor can give you valuable suggestions and direct you to appropriate sources. As you continue your research, you will probably modify your search strategy, tailoring it to fit your changing priorities.

(2) Doing exploratory research

Exploratory research helps you to get an overview of your topic and an understanding of its possibilities. At this early stage, you want to explore the boundaries of your topic. One way to do this is to discuss your ideas with others. Teachers, librarians, family, and friends may all suggest possible sources—sometimes unexpected or unconventional ones—for your paper. Another way is to skim general reference works in your college library, noting bibliographical information. Your notes should identify potential sources and their locations, not the specific information each source contains.

As you do exploratory research, your goal is to formulate a **research question,** the question you want your research paper to answer. This question will help you to focus your exploratory research and guide your assembly of a working bibliography. By suggesting ideas to look for, it helps you to decide which sources to seek out, which to examine first, and which to skip. The answer to your research question will be expressed as your paper's **thesis,** the statement the body of your paper will support.

FOCUSING ON A RESEARCH QUESTION
Mapping out a Search Strategy

Michael Schrader approached his topic in an orderly, systematic way. He began his work on the topic "Family life of Italian immigrants" by conferring with his instructor, who helped him to outline a search strategy. She suggested that he start by consulting the *Harvard Encyclopedia of American Ethnic Groups,* which has listings for each ethnic group, and perhaps a general encyclopedia, which would provide an overview of his topic. Then she referred him to a colleague in the sociology department, Dr. Harold Kramer, who had recently done some research on Italians in the United States. To prepare for a meeting with Dr. Kramer, Michael visited the library's reference room. There he looked at the *Harvard Encyclopedia of American Ethnic Groups,* photocopying the helpful bibliography that followed the entry on Italians, and read the material about Italians under the entry "Migration" in the *Encyclopaedia Britannica.*

Consulting an Expert

Michael then met with Dr. Kramer and spent about twenty minutes with him reviewing potential sources. Dr. Kramer directed Michael to two classic works: Herbert Gans's *The Urban Villagers*, a 1962 study (revised in 1982) of Italian immigrants in Boston, and Nathan Glazer and Daniel F. Moynihan's *Beyond the Melting Pot*, a 1963 study of ethnic groups in New York City.

Next, Dr. Kramer thought Michael should look for journal articles on his topic, perhaps starting with the *Social Sciences Index*, which lists articles appearing in specialized journals such as the *American Sociological Review* and the *American Journal of Sociology*. He also suggested two specialized indexes, *Public Affairs Information Services* and *Sociological Abstracts*, pointing out that the library subscribes to information services whose databases include these two publications. Dr. Kramer also gave Michael a photocopy of a 1983 *New York Times* article about a major conference on Italian Americans that Dr. Kramer had attended.

In addition, Dr. Kramer strongly urged Michael to do some primary research. Specifically, he felt Michael should do field work, interviewing members of his own family, his grandparents' parish priest, and his grandfather's barber (the barber shop is the center of social life in Italian communities in Italy). He might observe his grandparents' neighborhood firsthand, and he might also ask the Sons of Italy, the largest Italian fraternal order, for material that could help him.

Dr. Kramer had many other suggestions. For instance, he thought Michael could try examining church records, census data, and other primary sources. Michael listened politely and took careful notes in his research notebook, but he knew that he did not have time to do everything Dr. Kramer suggested. As Michael took notes, he asked Dr. Kramer to spell unfamiliar names and to clarify his instructions. He listened especially carefully to Dr. Kramer's advice about what his priorities should be. After the interview, he sent a note to Dr. Kramer thanking him for his time.

Asking Questions

Michael's preliminary reading and his meeting with Dr. Kramer left him feeling somewhat overwhelmed, but it did suggest some questions he felt he could explore. He listed the most promising of those questions in his research notebook.

Why did Italian families come to the United States?
Where did they settle when they came here?
How are families in America different from those who remained in
    Italy?
How did World War II affect the Italian family in Italy?
What was the role of the church in maintaining stability in Italian immi-
    grant families?

What role does the church play in the family life of Italian Americans today?
What other institutions contribute to family stability?
What factors threaten family stability?

Establishing Research Priorities

During the next few days, Michael planned his research. He checked the latest editions of the Gans and the Glazer and Moynihan books out of the library, noting the titles of other books on his topic shelved nearby.

He also called his grandparents, asking them for their help in setting up interviews with the parish priest and the neighborhood barber. In a brief letter to the local Sons of Italy chapter, he explained the purpose of his paper and asked these questions: What activities does your group offer? What services do you provide, and how have they changed in the past fifty years? Do you collect statistics on family situations? Has your membership increased or decreased in the past fifty years? Finally, he asked for permission to attend an upcoming Sons of Italy meeting, which his grandfather had told him about, and he promised to send a copy of his finished paper to the organization for its files.

Next Michael went back to the library to get assistance with a database search of the indexes Dr. Kramer had suggested. However, the librarian he consulted told him that such a search would be more productive later in his research, after he had focused on a specific research question. This advice led Michael to postpone his search.

Michael had a few additional directions to pursue. He remembered seeing a film on educational television of director Martin Scorcese interviewing his Italian immigrant parents. He thought he might try to locate a copy of it, and perhaps look at some back issues of *Attenzione,* a popular magazine for Italian Americans to which his grandfather subscribed. Perhaps, too, informal telephone surveys of his Italian friends and relatives might yield information. He kept all these possibilities in mind as he continued his research, recording his ideas—and his progress—in his research notebook.

Focusing on a Research Question

When Michael reviewed his notes on his preliminary reading and discussion, he was able to decide on the research question he would pursue in his paper.

How did the Italian family change when Italians emigrated
to the United States?

This question guided the balance of his exploratory research and the assembly of his working bibliography.

40c *Assembling a Working Bibliography and Making Bibliography Cards*

(1) Assembling a working bibliography

Whenever you encounter a promising source, jot down its complete bibliographic information on a 3″ × 5″ card. You will use these cards to construct a **working bibliography,** which includes all the sources (print and nonprint) you will examine later when you do your concentrated research and take notes. This preliminary bibliography is neither permanent nor complete: you will probably discard some of the sources and add others. Even so, be careful to record full and accurate bibliographical data for each source so that you can find it if you do need it.

(2) Making bibliography cards

When you make a 3″ × 5″ bibliography card for a source that looks promising, include the following information.

Information on Bibliography Cards	
Book	*Article*
Author(s)	Author(s)
Title (underlined)	Title of article (in quotation marks)
Call number (for future reference)	Title of journal (underlined)
City of publication	Volume
Publisher	Date
Date of publication	Inclusive page numbers
Brief evaluation	Brief evaluation

You should also make cards for interviews (including telephone interviews), meetings, lectures, films, and other nonprint sources of information.

Your cards need not follow the format of your final bibliography, but bibliographic information must be *full* and *accurate*. If it is not, you may be unable to find sources later. Include a brief evaluation of each source, noting the kind of information the source contains, the amount of information offered, its relevance to your topic, and its limitations—whether it is biased or outdated, for instance.

As your research progresses, review your bibliography cards regularly. Once you have confirmed your research question, look over your cards again to reevaluate the usefulness of your sources. Select the cards that seem most useful, and make plans to reexamine the sources they describe. (Retain *all* the cards you have made, however, even those for sources that do not seem very promising. You may decide to use a rejected source later on when you have a definite thesis for your paper.) If you notice gaps, note where further research is needed.

ASSEMBLING A WORKING BIBLIOGRAPHY AND MAKING BIBLIOGRAPHY CARDS

During his exploratory research, Michael Schrader recorded evaluations of his sources as well as bibliographical data on 3″ × 5″ cards. Michael's first advisers had directed him to many of his most important sources and had given him good information about them. He knew, for instance, that the books by Gans and by Glazer and Moynihan, although not recent, were still considered important works. The participants in the conference on Italian Americans described in the *New York Times* article represented a variety of viewpoints that, if pursued, would give him a balanced picture.

After consulting with his grandparents, Michael was reassured that his personal interviews with the elderly barber and the parish priest would give him a view of changes in various aspects of Italian family life, at least in one community. He also decided that information from his grandparents, though limited to their own experience, could dramatize many points in his paper.

He was able to evaluate the usefulness of print sources he found on his own by reading abstracts of articles or skimming the prefaces or indexes of books. He decided, for example, that one 1948 article in the *American Journal of Sociology* would still be worth reading because, he noticed, it was included in bibliographies in Gans's book and in the *Harvard Encyclopedia of American Ethnic Groups.*

Two of Michael Schrader's bibliography cards are illustrated in Figures 1 and 2.

During his exploratory research, Michael noticed that many of his most promising sources suggested that Italian family life, while still

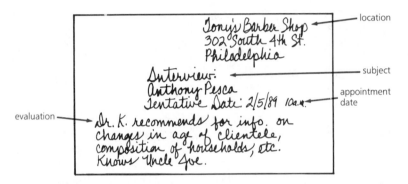

authors
title
publication data
evaluation

Glazer, Nathan
&
Moynihan, Daniel Patrick

325.7471
G46963

Beyond the Melting Pot
Cambridge, Mass.: MIT Press, 1970

Dr. K. says it's a classic. One chapter devoted to Italians. Also see Intro. and "The Catholics" (section of last chapter). Has bibliography and tables. Check Intro. to second edition for updated information.

FIGURE 1 Bibliography card—print source

Tony's Barber Shop
302 South 4th St.
Philadelphia

Interview:
Anthony Pesca
Tentative Date: 2/5/89 10a.m.

location

subject

appointment date

evaluation

Dr. K. recommends for info. on changes in age of clientele, composition of households, etc. Knows Uncle Joe.

FIGURE 2 Bibliography card—interview

strong, had deteriorated somewhat in this country. This information in turn suggested a possible answer to his research question about the changes in Italian-American family life.

EXERCISE 2

Do exploratory research to find a research question for your paper, carefully evaluating the relevance and usefulness of each source. Make a bibliography card for each source, and compile a working bibliography for your research paper in progress. When you have finished, reevaluate your sources and plan additional research if necessary.

40d *Developing a Tentative Thesis*

Your **tentative thesis** is a preliminary statement of what you think your research will demonstrate. This statement, which you will eventually refine into a thesis, will be the answer to your research question.

Your tentative thesis draws a preliminary conclusion about your topic; further research will lead you to accept, modify, or reject this assumption. At this point, the tentative thesis provides a direction for your focused research.

Developing a Tentative Thesis

Subject Area	Topic	Research Question	Tentative Thesis
Computers	The possible negative effects of computer games on adolescents	Do computer games have any negative effects on adolescents?	Computer games interfere with adolescents' ability to learn.
Feminism	The relationship between the feminist movement and the use of sexist language	What is the relationship between the feminist movement and the use of sexist language?	The feminist movement is largely responsible for the decline of sexist language.
Mood-altering drugs	The use of mood-altering drugs in state mental hospitals	How has the use of mood-altering drugs affected patients in state mental hospitals?	The use of mood-altering drugs has changed the population of state mental hospitals.

As you move through the research process, your tentative thesis and even your research question may change considerably. A line of inquiry may lead to a dead end, a key source may not be available, or a lead you uncover in your research may encourage you to branch out in a new direction. But whether or not you make major adjustments to your tentative thesis, it should grow increasingly more precise, eventually leading you to a thesis your research can support. ▶ **See 2b**

DEVELOPING A TENTATIVE THESIS

Michael Schrader's exploratory research led him not simply to a clearly focused research question ("How did the Italian family change when Italians emigrated to the United States?"), but also to a possible answer to that question: that, despite his initial assumptions, the family did not in fact change very much at all. The answer to his research question, which he recorded in his research notebook, became the tentative thesis which would guide his focused research.

```
In the United States, as in Italy, the family is the
Italian immigrant's most important resource.
```

EXERCISE 3

Following your own instructor's guidelines, develop a tentative thesis for your research paper.

40e *Doing Focused Research and Taking Notes*

Once you have decided on a tentative thesis, you are ready to begin your focused research and note taking.

(1) Reading sources

As you read, follow the reading strategies explained earlier: preview each source, skimming it quickly; read it carefully, highlighting ▶ **See 38c** potentially useful material; and annotate the source. Then, take notes in the form of summary, paraphrase, or direct quotation.

Your limited time makes it impossible for you to read all your print sources thoroughly, so read only those sections of a work that pertain to your topic. Before you begin, survey the work carefully, checking a book's index, and also the headings and subheadings in the table of contents, to determine which pages to read thoroughly and which to skim. Look carefully at abstracts and headings of articles.

(2) Taking notes

Take careful notes as you do library research, and be sure to take notes on nonprint sources—interviews, lectures, films, and so on—too. And remember, if you encounter a promising new source while you are taking notes, make a bibliography card for the new source immediately.

Note Cards   As they do library research, many people find it helpful to take notes on 4″ × 6″ index cards. (3″ × 5″ cards are too small to hold all the necessary information.) The advantages of index cards become obvious when you start arranging and rearranging your material. You seldom know where a particular piece of information belongs at first—or even whether you will use it. You will rearrange your ideas many times, and index cards make it easy for you to add and delete information and to experiment with different sequences. You cannot do that with notes on photocopies or on loose sheets of paper.

At the top of each note card, *include a short heading* that links the information on your card to some aspect of your topic. This heading will help you to make your outline and organize your notes.

Each card should accurately *identify the source* of the information you are recording. You need not include the complete citation, but you must include enough information to identify your source. "Gallo 53" would be enough to send you back to the bibliography card carrying the complete documentation for Patrick Gallo's *Old Bread, New Wine*. For one of two books by the same author, however, you need a more complete reference: "Gallo, *Old Bread* 53" would be necessary if you were using more than one book by Patrick Gallo. Be sure to identify each nonprint source with a brief descriptive heading. The rest of the card should carry the information you may decide to include in your paper.

Guidelines for Working with Note Cards

- **Put only one note on each 4″ × 6″ card.** If you do not do this, you lose the flexibility that is the whole point of this method of note taking.
- **Include everything now that you will need later** to understand your note. After a few weeks you will not remember the meaning of any but the most explicit notes.
- **Indicate the kind of information that appears on your note card.** If you copy a source's words, use quotation marks. If you use a source's ideas but not its words, do not use quotation marks. If you write down your own ideas, enclose them in brackets. This system will help you to avoid mixups—and plagiarism **(see 38e).**
- **Put an author's comments into your own words whenever possible.** Word-for-word copying is probably the most inefficient way to take notes. You may use quotations in your final paper, but for the most part you will summarize and paraphrase your source material **(see 38c),** adding your own observations and judgments. If you think you might like to quote an author's words, be sure to copy them accurately, transferring the author's exact words, spelling, punctuation marks, and capitalization to your note card.

Figure 3 illustrates two useful note-card formats, the first for a print source, the second for a nonprint source.

Photocopies   With the availability of photocopy machines in libraries, many researchers routinely copy useful portions of sources. As long as you record the bibliographic information for the source, this is a useful and time-saving strategy. As you prepare to photocopy material, however, keep the following guidelines in mind.

Guidelines for Working with Photocopies

- Bring exact change for the machine.
- Record full and accurate source information, including the page numbers, on the first page of each copy.
- Clip or staple together consecutive pages of a single source.
- Do not copy a source without reminding yourself—*in writing*—why you are doing so. In pencil or on removeable, self-stick notes, record your initial responses to the source's ideas, insert cross-references to other works or notes, and mark the boundaries of important sections.
- Photocopying can be expensive, so try to avoid copying material that is only marginally relevant to your paper.

Author, page

short heading ———————→ Emigration to Italy   Gans 205

note (summary, ———→ Italian immigrants brought their social structure
paraphrase, or
quotation)   to America. In the cities they usually "settled
in Italian neighborhoods, where relatives often
lived side by side, and in the midst of people
from the same Italian town. Under these
conditions the family circle was maintained

your comment   much as it had existed in Southern Italy."
(opinions, ———————→ [Gans bases his comments on immigrants in this
reactions, etc.)   section not on the Boston neighborhood he studied
but on a study of New York's East Harlem area by
Leonard Covello — see my bibliography card on
Covello.]

Family responsibilities   Sons of Italy meeting

One man responded angrily to Congressman
Flavio's suggestion that the 4th ward welcome
federal scatter-site housing, insisting the
family and the community -- not the federal
government -- should be responsible for its
poor. His statement was applauded.

FIGURE 3   Note card formats

Remember, however, that photocopied information is no substitute for the notes you must take for your paper. In certain limited
cases—for example, for short papers that require only a few notes—
the annotating and highlighting you do on copies may be all you
need. But for long, complex research assignments, using photocopies as a substitute for detailed notes has a number of drawbacks.
For one thing, the ease and efficiency of photocopying encourages
you to postpone decisions about the usefulness of your information.
You can easily accumulate so many photocopied pages that it will
be almost impossible to keep track of all your information. In
addition, photocopies are not flexible: a single page may include
notes that should be earmarked for several different sections of
your paper. This lack of flexibility makes it virtually impossible for
you to arrange your source material into any meaningful order.
Finally, your highlighting and annotations are usually not ready to

be incorporated into your paper. You will still have to paraphrase and summarize your source's ideas and make connections among them. Therefore, although preparing note cards is time consuming, it can actually save you a great deal of time in the long run.

DOING FOCUSED RESEARCH AND TAKING NOTES
Library Work

At the library, Michael now felt ready to do a database search. He had a specific research question in mind, and he thought he was close to deciding on a thesis. This time, the librarian agreed with him and recommended he search the *Social Sciences Index*. She consulted the **thesaurus,** a printed index listing key words **(see 37b4)** and advised him to begin by requesting all citations that included in their titles the phrases *Italian family* and *United States* or *Italian family* and *assimilation*. If these key words proved to be too specific to yield enough sources, he could widen his scope somewhat, requesting all citations that included the words *Italy, Italian,* or *Italians* and *family* or *families*.

When Michael received his printout, which included abstracts of articles, he read it carefully to identify the most promising articles. After locating them he took careful notes in the library (periodicals do not circulate), but he duplicated two especially useful pieces so that he would have them at home for reference.

In the catalog he found the call numbers of several books he had seen mentioned in other sources and then went to the shelves to find these and other books in his working bibliography. He skimmed each source and decided which to check out and what to photocopy. When he could not find a book, he tried to determine whether or not it had been checked out. If it had, he put a hold on it. When the librarian told him that one book on his list that the library did not have could be acquired through an interlibrary loan—but that this might take several weeks—Michael decided to look in another library, but he asked her to request the book anyway.

Field work

With his library research well underway, Michael set out for his grand-parents' neighborhood to begin his field work.

Walking Tour. He started by making observations and taking notes during a walk around the neighborhood. He noticed, for instance, an unusual number of elderly people in the community and a good many more children than in his own suburban neighborhood. He also saw four men in the barber shop, only one of whom was getting a haircut.

651

Interviews. Michael decided not to conduct a formal interview with his grandparents. He told them at the outset that he needed to find out the differences between family life in Italy and in America, but he did not ask prepared questions. Michael's primary role as interviewer was to guide them tactfully back to the topic whenever they digressed. As he expected, his grandparents were extremely generous with their reminiscences. In fact, his grandmother even showed him a letter his uncle had written to her in 1980 while he was in the army. Michael thought he might quote a section of it in his paper.

Before Michael interviewed the barber and the priest, he first learned something about them from his grandfather. He also prepared several questions that arose from his reading. Michael asked both men for permission to take notes and use a tape recorder. He asked Father D'Ancona about changes in the parish's marriage and divorce rates, in family size, in church attendance, and in sources of family tension. He also asked about general differences between family life in Italy and in the United States and about where the children of the parish settle when they marry, and why.

Michael's interview with Anthony Pesca, the barber, did not go as smoothly. People kept dropping into the barber shop to say hello and trade bits of news and gossip, so Michael finally arranged to continue the interview by telephone. When he reached Mr. Pesca, he had time to ask only a few general questions about the differences between Pesca's American-born and Italian-born customers and about the most obvious value conflicts between parents and children. Mr. Pesca did recommend, however, that Michael look at the community newspaper and the church bulletin board if he wanted to know what was going on in the neighborhood.

Follow-up. Michael felt he had accumulated some significant firsthand information to supplement his reading. He reviewed his notes, transferred portions of them onto 4" × 6" index cards, and recorded in his research notebook follow-up questions he wanted to ask and inconsistencies he needed to check. Finally, he wrote thank-you notes to Mr. Pesca and Father D'Ancona, taking the opportunity to ask Father D'Ancona another question: whether those who move out of the neighborhood bring their children back to be christened.

Observation. The Sons of Italy had answered Michael's letter and invited him to attend its next meeting. He noticed that the average age of the members at this meeting was about fifty and that the questions they asked the speaker revealed a conservative approach to social issues like welfare, taxes, and public housing. Toward the end of the meeting, Michael got some useful information: one particularly vocal person drew applause when he said that family and community—not public tax revenues—should be responsible for supporting and housing indigent persons. Michael jotted down these remarks and the audience reaction. When he got home, he put this note on an index card (see Figure 3) and also made a bibliography card for the meeting. Then he wrote a brief letter thanking the chapter president.

EXERCISE 4

Begin focused research for your paper, taking careful notes from your sources. Remember that your notes should include paraphrase, summary, and your own observations and reactions as well as direct quotations.

40f *Deciding on a Thesis*

Even after you have finished your focused research and note taking, your thesis remains tentative. Now you must refine this tentative thesis into a **thesis,** a carefully worded statement that draws a conclusion your research can support. This thesis will give your paper a clear focus and direction and will help you shape your material.

Your thesis should be consistent with the ideas you have formed and the source material you have explored. It should be considerably more focused and detailed than your tentative thesis, providing an overview of the main points your paper will make.

Deciding on a Thesis

Tentative Thesis	Thesis
Computer games interfere with adolescents' ability to learn.	Because they interfere with concentration and teach players to expect immediate gratification, computer games interfere with adolescents' ability to learn.

continued

continued from previous page

The feminist movement is responsible for the decline of sexist language.	By raising public awareness of careless language habits and changing the image of women, the feminist movement has helped to bring about a decline of sexist language.
The development of mood-altering drugs has changed the population of state mental hospitals.	It is the development of psychotropic (mood-altering) drugs, not advances in psychotherapy, that has made possible the release of large numbers of mental patients from state hospitals into the community.

If your thesis still does not convey a conclusion your research can support, you may need to reword it—or even revise it. Reviewing your notes carefully, perhaps grouping your note cards in different ways, may help you to decide on a suitable thesis. Or you may try other techniques—for instance, brainstorming or freewriting with your research question as a starting point, or asking questions about your topic. The thesis you finally decide on should be consistent with the kind and amount of source material you have collected and the ideas you have developed in response to that material.

DECIDING ON A THESIS

As Michael Schrader did his research, he revised his tentative thesis several times. He had begun with "In the United States, as in Italy, the family is the Italian immigrant's most important resource" because this was what he had expected his research to support. As he read, however, he found that after Italians emigrated from Italy, family ties seemed to have slightly eroded. He therefore modified his tentative thesis to reflect this realization: "Family life, while still the Italian immigrant's most important resource, is not as important in America as it was in Italy."

Throughout his research, Michael vacillated between these two statements. He had to decide which stand to take, but he had to take the stand his research would support, not the one he preferred. When he reread his note cards, he understood the reason for his indecision: to some extent his notes supported both thesis statements. His final thesis represented a compromise between the two.

```
Although emigration from Italy led to assimilation, which
weakened the family system to some extent, the Italian
family in the United States remains unusually close and
stable.
```

This thesis combines the idea of the erosion of family ties with the idea of continued strength in the family unit. It also indicates that Michael considers the latter more significant and that this is the point his paper will make.

EXERCISE 5

Read these three passages from various sources. Assume you are writing a research paper on the influences that shaped young writers in the 1920's. What possible thesis statements could be supported by the information in these passages?

1. Yet in spite of their opportunities and their achievements the generation deserved for a long time the adjective that Gertrude Stein had applied to it. The reasons aren't hard to find. It was lost, first of all, because it was uprooted, schooled away and almost wrenched away from its attachment to any region or tradition. It was lost because its training had prepared it for another world that existed after the war (and because the war prepared it only for travel and excitement). It was lost because it tried to live in exile. It was lost because it accepted no older guides to conduct and because it formed a false picture of society and the writer's place in it. The generation belonged to a period of transition from values already fixed to values that had to be created. (Malcolm Cowley, *Exile's Return*)
2. The 1920's were a time least likely to produce substantial support among intellectuals for any sound, rational, and logical program. Prewar stability and convention were condemned because all evidences of stability seemed illusory and artificial. The very lively and active interest in science was perhaps the decade's most substantial contribution to modern civilization. Yet in this case as well, achievement became a symbol of disorder and a source for disenchantment. (Frederick J. Hoffman, *The 20's*)

3. Societies do not give up old ideals and attitudes easily; the conflicts between the representatives of the older elements of traditional American culture and the prophets of the new day were at times as bitter as they were extensive. Such matters as religion, marriage, and moral standards, as well as the issues over race, prohibition, and immigration were at the heart of the conflict. (Introduction to *The Twenties*, ed. George E. Mowry)

EXERCISE 6

Carefully read over all the notes you have collected during your focused research, and develop a thesis for your paper.

40g Preparing a Formal Outline

Although many students will not prepare a formal outline for a short essay, a formal outline is almost essential for a longer or more complex writing project. A **formal outline** indicates the order in which you will present your ideas and the relationship of main ideas to supporting details. A formal outline is more polished than an informal one (**see 2c**). It is more strictly parallel and more precise, pays more attention to form, and presents points in the exact order in which you plan to present them in your draft.

A formal outline may be a topic outline or a sentence outline. In a **topic outline** each entry consists of a single word or a short phrase; in a **sentence outline** each entry is a complete sentence. Each of these outline forms has advantages and disadvantages. Because it uses complete sentences, a sentence outline is a more fully developed guide for your paper: you have a head start on your paper when you are able to use the sentences of your outline in your draft. This completeness, however, makes the sentence outline more difficult to construct, especially at an early stage of the writing process. A topic outline provides less precise guidance, but it is easier to prepare.

Formal outlines conform to specific conventions of structure, content, and style. If you follow the conventions of outlining carefully, your formal outline can help you to see that you have covered all relevant ideas in an effective order, with appropriate emphasis, within a logical system of subordination.

The Conventions of Outlining

Structure

- Outline format should be followed strictly:

I. First major division of your paper
  A. First secondary division
  B. Next secondary division
    1. First supporting example
    2. Next supporting example
      a. First specific detail
      b. Next specific detail
  II. Second major division

- Headings should not overlap.
- Each heading should have at least two subheadings.
- Each entry should be introduced by an appropriate letter or number, with the letter or number followed by a period.
- The first word of each entry should be capitalized.

Content

- Outline should include thesis statement.
- Outline should focus only on the body of the essay.
- Headings should be specific and concrete.
- Headings should be descriptive, clearly related to the topic to which they refer.

Style

- Headings of the same rank should be grammatically parallel.
- Sentence outlines should use complete sentences, with all sentences in the same tense.
- In a sentence outline, each entry should end with a period.
- Topic outlines should use words or short phrases, with all headings of the same rank using the same parts of speech.
- In a topic outline, entries should not be followed by end punctuation.

(1) Constructing a formal outline

Once you have a thesis, you should list the major points you tentatively plan to present in the order in which you think you will present them. This list serves as a general guide, and its divisions enable you to sort and categorize your note cards so that you can prepare a formal outline. To construct a formal outline for your paper, follow the steps below:

1. Check each card carefully to be sure it contains only one general idea or one brief related group of facts. If it does not, distribute the information among two or more cards. If the information on two cards overlaps, combine it on one card. Then be sure the headings on all your cards are accurate.

2. Lay out your note cards on a big table—or on the floor—and sort them into piles, one for each of your major points. (Keep a miscellaneous pile for notes that do not seem to fit anyplace. You may discard these notes later, or you may find—or make—a place for them in your paper when you construct your formal outline.)

3. Check your categories for balance. What if, for example, most of your notes support only three of your four major points? You have two options: (1) do more research to support the fourth point; or (2) drop it, narrow the scope of your paper, and revise your thesis. A review of your notes should tell you which course to take.

4. Guided by the headings in the upper left-hand corner of each card, sort and organize the cards *within* each group. Within each group, put related information together in an order that highlights the most important ideas and subordinates lesser ones. Once again, do some discarding, setting aside note cards that do not fit into your emerging scheme. (And remember to retain these cards. They may fit a new line of inquiry as you experiment with different arrangements.)

5. Review the order of your list of major points to be sure the sequence is right.

6. When you are satisfied with the arrangement, make a formal outline, with subdivisions corresponding to those of your note cards. This outline can be either a topic outline or a sentence outline.

7. Review your completed outline. This review can reveal potential problems—for instance, whether you lack supporting information in a particular area or have placed too much emphasis on a relatively unimportant idea, whether ideas are illogically or ineffectively placed, or whether similar concepts turn up in different parts of your plan.

Remember that this outline is only a guide for you to follow as you draft your paper and that it very likely will change as you write and revise. The final outline, written after your paper is complete, will serve as a guide for your readers.

PREPARING A FORMAL OUTLINE

Michael listed the four major divisions that emerged as he did his focused research.

Thesis: Although emigration from Italy led to

assimilation, which weakened the family system to some

extent, the Italian family in the United States remains unusually close and stable.

I. Family relationships in Italy

II. Changes resulting from emigration

III. Current status of Italian family

IV. Projections for future of Italian family

Following this list, Michael sorted his note cards into four groups. When he was satisfied with his arrangement, he went on to organize the cards *within* each group. This process forced him to consider the relevance of each piece of information and to discard material that seemed irrelevant to his paper. When Michael had finished sorting his note cards, he constructed the topic outline that follows. (A sentence outline appears with his paper on pp. 671–673.)

Thesis: Although emigration from Italy led to assimilation, which weakened the family system to some extent, the Italian family in the United States remains unusually close and stable.

I. Immigrants from southern Italian villages
   A. In Italy
      1. Separate customs maintained
      2. Identification with family and village
   B. In America
      1. Italian customs recreated
      2. Identification with Italy
II. Italian villagers' reliance on extended family
   A. Patriarchal structure
      1. Mother's responsibilities
      2. Father's responsibilities
   B. Children's roles
      1. Sons
      2. Daughters
III. Italians' insulation from outside world
   A. Family as refuge
   B. Distrust of outsiders
IV. Italian Americans' aloofness
   A. "Little Italys"
      1. Remain in northeastern United States
      2. Improve neighborhoods

   3. Often make two-generational moves

   4. Live near parents and siblings

  B. Family-oriented society

 V. Changes experienced in United States

  A. Employment for women

  B. Parent-child conflicts

  C. Changes in family system

   1. Family less patriarchal

   2. Sex roles less rigid

   3. Friends preferred over relatives

 VI. Family closeness and stability

  A. Family closeness

   1. Extended family more important

   2. Elderly relatives welcomed

   3. Emotional and social support provided

  B. Family stability

   1. Low divorce, separation, and desertion rates

   2. Low intermarriage rate

EXERCISE 7

Review your notes and your thesis carefully. If you have not already done so, make a list of the major points you plan to cover in your paper. Sort and group your note cards accordingly, and construct a formal topic outline for your paper.

40h   *Writing Your First Draft*

When you are ready to write your first draft, lay out your notes in the order in which you intend to use them. Follow your outline as you write, moving from one entry to the next and using your notes as you need them.

Your paragraphs will probably correspond to subdivisions of your outline, at least in this draft. As you write, make an effort to supply transitions between sentences and paragraphs. These transitions need not be polished; you will refine them in subsequent drafts. But if you leave them out entirely at this stage, you may forget what they are, which will make revising difficult.

You will not be able to write the whole draft in a single sitting, but do plan to write in segments that you can complete without interruption. One major heading from your outline, for instance, is a realistic goal for a morning or afternoon of writing. Once you get started, you will find that the time you spent taking careful, accurate notes and preparing a formal outline will pay off.

If words do not come easily, freewriting for a short period can get you started. Sometimes leaving your paper for only five or ten minutes gives you a fresh view of your material. Another good strategy for overcoming writer's block is beginning your drafting with the section for which you have the most material.

Remember, the purpose of the first draft is to get ideas down on paper so that you can react to them. You should *expect* to revise, ▶ See 3b so postpone precise word choices and refinements of style. As you write, jot down questions to yourself or points that need further checking; leave space for material you plan to add; and bracket phrases or whole sections that you may move or delete. In other words, lay the groundwork for a major revision. Remember that even though you are guided by an outline and notes, you are not bound to follow their content or sequence exactly. As you write, new ideas or new connections among ideas may occur to you. Jot them down as they come to mind, and plan to incorporate them in your next draft. If you find yourself deviating from your thesis or outline, reexamine them to see whether the departure is justified. (For information about drafting your essay on a computer, see the **Guide to Writing with Computers.**) ▶ See p. A9

(1)   The parts of the paper

Like most essays, the research paper has an introduction, a body, and a conclusion. In your first draft, however, you pay most attention to the body of your paper; in fact, you should not spend much time planning an introduction or conclusion for a rough draft. Your ideas will take shape as you write, and you will want to refine your opening and closing paragraphs later to reflect your revisions.

Introduction   You begin the introduction by identifying your topic and establishing those aspects you will discuss. You can, for example, survey previous research in a field or provide background for a problem. Next, state your thesis—the position you will support in the rest of the paper. You might then go on to summarize briefly your major supporting points (the major divisions of your outline) in the order in which you will present them. This overview of your thesis and support provides a smooth transition into the body of your paper.

Body   As you draft the body of your paper, indicate its direction with strong topic sentences that correspond to the divisions of your outline.

```
     The immigrants maintained their Old World family
system in the United States.
```

You can also use headings if they are a convention of the discipline in which you are writing.

```
Family Solidarity
     Family solidarity gave the southern Italian family
its essential unity and cohesiveness.
```

Even in your first draft, descriptive headings and topic sentences will help you to keep your discussion under control.

See
4f   Use different patterns of development to shape the individual sections of your paper, and be sure to connect ideas with transitional words and phrases. The same principles that apply to writing effective paragraphs and essays also apply to writing research papers.

Conclusion   Restate your thesis in your conclusion. This is especially important in a long paper because by the time your readers get to the end, they may have lost sight of your thesis. After this restatement, you can end your paper with a summary of your major points, a call for action, or perhaps an apt quotation. Just remember that your conclusion must be based on your supporting data and that it should help persuade your readers to accept your thesis.

(2)   *Working source material into your paper*

A good research paper evaluates and interprets its sources, comparing different ideas and synthesizing conflicting points of view. As a writer, your job is to draw your own conclusions, consolidating information from various sources into a paper that presents a coherent, original view of your topic to your readers.

Your source material must be smoothly integrated into your paper, with the opinions of one source blended in with those of another so that the relationship between them is apparent. This is easy to do when one source supports another. If, however, two sources present conflicting interpretations, be especially careful to use precise language and accurate transitions to make the contrast readily apparent (For instance, "Although Gans suggests the situation has changed, a later study reveals. . . ."). You will then have a context for making your own comments and drawing conclusions. If different sources present incomplete information about a subject, blend details from each source *carefully,* keeping track of which details come from which source, to reveal the complete picture.

Revision Close-up

As you write your rough draft, *be sure to record all source information fully and accurately. Include every source and page number,* as Michael Schrader does in the paragraphs from his draft on page 665.

EXERCISE 8

Write a draft of your paper, being careful to incorporate source material smoothly and to record source information accurately. Begin with the section for which you have the most material.

40i *Revising Your Drafts*

To make revising easier, follow the guidelines recommended in Chapter 3: double-space, write on only one side of your paper, and so on. Be careful to recopy your source information accurately on *each draft,* placing the documentation as close as possible to the material it identifies. (For information on revising with a computer, **see the Guide to Writing with Computers.**) A good way to start revising is to check to see that your thesis still suits your paper. Make an outline of your draft, and compare it with the outline you made before you began the draft. If you find significant differences, you will have to refine your thesis or rewrite sections of your paper.

► **See 3b**

When reconsidering your draft, follow the revision procedures that apply to any paper. In addition, ask yourself the following questions that apply specifically to research papers.

► **See 3c–d**

Revising a Research Paper

- Should you do more research to find support for certain points?
- Do you need to reorder the major divisions of your discussion?
- Should you rearrange the order in which you present your points within those divisions?
- Do you need to add section headings?
- Are sources smoothly integrated into your paper?
- Are direct quotations blended with paraphrase, summary, and your own observations and reactions?
- Are they woven smoothly into the text?
- Do you introduce source material with running acknowledgments?
- Have you analyzed and interpreted the ideas of others rather than simply stringing those ideas together?

If your instructor allows peer criticism, take advantage of it. The first draft is primarily for you. As you move toward a final draft, however, you should think more and more about your readers' reactions. Testing out your draft at this point can be extremely helpful.

You will probably take your paper through several drafts, changing different parts of it each time or working on one part over and over again. After editing your original draft thoroughly, you should write or type out a corrected version and make additional corrections on that draft before typing your final version.

WRITING AND REVISING

When Michael Schrader revised his first draft, he made changes in structure and style. Using his note cards as a guide, Michael had drafted the paragraphs illustrated in Figure 4, but when he reviewed this section he saw that he had simply copied material from his note cards without introducing it, adding proper transitions, or drawing his own conclusions. In his next draft (see Figure 5) he tried to incorporate his source material more smoothly, reworking three skimpy paragraphs into one unified whole that blended material from three sources with his own observations and conclusions.

Italian-Americans, even gangsters, typically maintain very close and highly stable family relationships (Glazer and Moynihan 196).
In addition, Italians are more likely to have relatives over 60 living with them

> (Goodman). In a walking tour of a typical
> Italian-American neighborhood, I noticed a
> large proportion of elderly residents often
> accompanied by children and grandchildren
> as they conducted routine errands and
> shopping. This convinced me that generations
> remain close.
>   Even though households may not include
> members of the extended family, the family
> relationships are close; the family provides
> close emotional support and serves as a
> social network (Gans 46).

FIGURE 4   First draft

Clear topic sentence
reflects main idea

> After they emigrated from Italy to America,
> the Italian-American family continued to be
> extremely close. Today Italians remain
> more likely than most other ethnic groups to
> have relatives over 60 living with them
> (Goodman). A walking tour of a typical
> urban Italian-American neighborhood
> confirmed this, revealing a large proportion
> of elderly residents, often accompanied by
> children and grandchildren as they
> conducted routine errands and shopping.

Support: examples from
reading and first-hand
observation

> Even when members of the extended family
> are not actually part of the household, the
> relationships among family members are
> close; the family provides close emotional
> support and also serves as a social network
> (Gans 46). In fact, even Italian-American
> gangsters typically maintain very close and
> highly stable family relationships
> (Glazer and Moynihan 196).

FIGURE 5   Revised draft

E X E R C I S E   9

Following the guidelines in 40i and in 3c and 3d, revise your research paper until you feel you are ready to prepare your final draft.

40j   *Preparing Your Final Draft*

When you complete your revision, prepare the final version of your formal outline (usually a sentence outline) to hand in with your paper, and prepare your documentation and your list of works cited. After you have finished these tasks, edit your draft and all related material—outline, documentation, works cited list, and so on.

Before you begin typing your final draft, stop for a moment to consider your title. It should be descriptive enough to tell your readers what your paper is about, and, ideally, it should create interest in your subject. The following titles are interesting as well as descriptive.

"Is the Welfare State Replacing the Family?" Mary Jo Bane, *The Public Interest*

"The Limited American, the Great Loneliness, and the Singing Fire: Carl Sandburg's 'Chicago Poems.' " William Alexander, *American Literature*

Your title should also be consistent with the purpose and tone of your paper. For example, you would hardly want a humorous title for a paper about the death penalty or world hunger. Still, your titles can be engaging and to the point and sometimes even provocative. Often a quotation from one of your sources suggests a likely title. Michael Schrader used "The Italian Family" as the working title for his paper, but his final title—"The Italian Family: 'Stronghold in a Hostile Land' "—which included a quotation from one of his sources, conveyed his paper's thesis more dramatically.

Now you can proceed to type your final draft. (See the Appendix for full information on manuscript preparation.) Before you hand in your manuscript, read it through one last time, proofreading for grammar, spelling, or typing errors you may have missed. Pay particular attention to notes and bibliographic references. Remember that every error takes away from the credibility of your whole paper. If your instructor gives you permission, you may make *minor* corrections on your final draft with correction fluid or by neatly crossing out a word or two and writing or typing the correct word or phrase above the line. If you find a mistake that you cannot correct neatly, however, retype or reprint the page. Once you are satisfied that your manuscript is as accurate as you can make it, you are ready to hand it in.

E X E R C I S E   10

Edit your research paper, including notes and list of works cited, and then type it according to the format your instructor requires. Proofread your typed copy carefully before you hand it in.

THE COMPLETED PAPER

Michael Schrader's completed research paper, "The Italian Family: 'Stronghold in a Hostile Land,' " appears on the pages that follow. The paper, which uses MLA documentation style, is accompanied by a sentence outline, explanatory notes, and a list of works cited. Annotations opposite each page of the manuscript comment on stylistic and structural aspects of the paper; explain the format for proper documentation; illustrate various methods of incorporating source material into the paper; and highlight some of the choices Michael made as he moved from note cards to first draft to completed paper.

If your instructor does not require a title page, include all identifying information—your name, the name of the course, your instructor's name, and the date—in the upper left-hand corner of your paper's first page, one inch from the top and flush with the left-hand margin. The title should be centered two spaces below the last line of this heading. Type your name and the number *1* in the upper right-hand corner, one-half inch from the top.

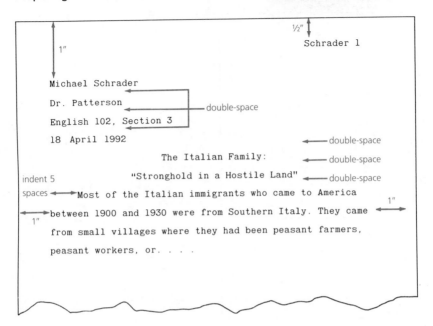

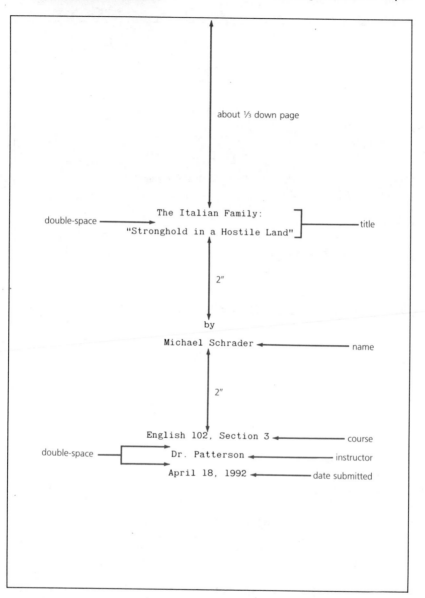

½"

Schrader i

name, page number
on every page

1"

center ──────────► Outline
double-space ──────────►

Thesis: Although emigration from Italy led to
        assimilation, which weakened the family system to
        some extent, the Italian family in the United
        States remains unusually close and stable.

I.   Most Italian immigrants came to America from the
     Mezzogiorno.

     A. In Italy, each village was separate and unique.

        1. Each village had its own customs.

        2. Villagers identified with family and village.

     B. In America, Italians recreated their Italian vil- ◄── 1"
        lages.

        1. Italians in America established customs and
           living conditions like those in Italy.

        2. In America, Italians began to identify with
           other Italians.

1" ◄──
II. Most Italians from the Mezzogiorno were of the <u>con-
     tadini</u> or <u>giornalieri</u> classes, which relied heavily
     on the extended family.

     A. The southern Italian family was usually
        patriarchal.

        1. The mother maintained the home and managed the
           finances.

        2. The father earned the money and made all major
           decisions.

     B. Children's roles mirrored adult roles.

Schrader ii

       1. Parents prepared their sons to be heads of households.

       2. Parents prepared their daughters to love and obey their husbands.

III. Family solidarity insulated the <u>contadino</u> family from the hostile outside world.

    A. Barzini sees the family as a "stronghold" and a "refuge."

    B. Italians did not trust outsiders.

IV. Italians in America have remained somewhat aloof.

    A. Immigrants often joined fellow villagers in urban "Little Italys."

       1. Most Italians remain in northeastern United States.

       2. Italians are more likely to improve old neighborhoods than to relocate.

       3. Two generations often move to suburbs together.

       4. Italians are more likely to live near parents and siblings than are other ethnic groups.

    B. Immigrants maintain a family-oriented society in America.

V. The Italian family in America has undergone many changes.

    A. Some women have sought employment.

    B. Conflicts have occurred between parents and children.

Schrader iii

    C. The family system has changed.

        1. The family has become less patriarchal and
more
democratic.

        2. Third—generation Italian Americans have
relaxed the rigid sex roles of Old World
society to some extent.

        3. Third—generation Italian Americans often
prefer to associate with friends rather than
relatives.

VI. Despite changes, the family remains close and
stable.

    A. The Italian family remains close.

        1. The extended family has become more important.

        2. Italians are more likely than other ethnic
groups to open their homes to elderly
relatives.

        3. The family provides emotional and social
support.

    B. The Italian family remains stable.

        1. Italians have low rates of divorce,
separation, and desertion.

        2. Italians have a low intermarriage rate.

Beginning with the first page of your paper, type your last name and the page number one-half inch from the top in the upper right-hand corner. Do not use punctuation before or after the page number. Leave one-inch margins.

Title typed 1" from top of page

Two spaces between title and first line of paper

¶1: Introduction, presenting background information

Information is available in several sources and is therefore considered general knowledge. For this reason, no documentation is required.

Thesis statement

¶2: Introduces discussion of outline point IA [Each village was self-contained and unique.]

First two sentences of ¶2 present information available in several sources; therefore, it does not require documentation.

"Francis Femminella and Jill Quadagno note. . . ." introduces material from source. Beginning the summary with the authors' names and closing it with parenthetical documentation clearly identifies the boundaries of the borrowed material.

½"

1"

Schrader 1

The Italian Family:

Double-space ⟶ "Stronghold in a Hostile Land"

¶1 Most of the Italian immigrants who came to America between 1900 and 1930 were from Southern Italy. They came from small villages where they had been peasant farmers, peasant workers, or artisans. When they emigrated to America, these southern Italians brought with them their close family system and their enormous respect for the family unit. Even with all of the demands and pressures of adjusting to life in a foreign country, the family remained the number-one priority for the Italians. Today, this is still true among Italian Americans. Some assimilation did occur after migration, but it did not take place to the same degree as it did with other ethnic groups. Although emigration from Italy led to assimilation, which weakened the family system to some extent, the Italian family in the United States remains unusually close and stable.

¶2 The southern peasant Italians came to America from a region known as the Mezzogiorno, which consisted of six provinces south and east of Rome. Each village in this region was self-contained, with its own local church and bell tower, and the language, manners, and mores differed from village to village. Francis Femminella and Jill Quadagno note that in Italy, the people did not see themselves as Italians; instead,

1"

<u>61–64</u> refers to four pages of source material, summarized here to convey general ideas rather than specific detail.

¶3: Transitional paragraph. Introduces outline point II [Most Italians from the Mezzogiorno were of the *contadini* or *giornalieri* classes, which relied heavily on the extended family.]

¶4: Outline point IIA [The southern Italian family was usually patriarchal.]

Schrader 2

they identified with their families, villages, and towns.
When the Italian villagers migrated to America, they
naturally sought out their paisani, their fellow
villagers, who had already come to the United States.
There they tried to establish customs and living
conditions similar to those they had left behind. In fact,
Italian immigrants did not really take on an Italian
ethnic identity until after they arrived in America
(61–64).

¶3   As Herbert Gans notes, most southern Italians
belonged to the peasant class of farmers called the
contadini or to the class of day laborers known as
giornalieri. Both these groups were very poor (199–200).
Femminella and Quadagno believe that it was because of
this poverty, and because they were exploited by
landowners, that these classes rejected the social
institutions of the rest of the country and came to rely
almost exclusively on the family (65). For the southern
Italian, however, family meant not only husband, wife, and
children, but also grandparents, uncles, aunts, and
cousins—in fact, all blood relatives—and even
godparents.

¶4   According to Femminella and Quadagno, the southern
Italian family is usually seen as patriarchal, but
although the father was the head of the family, the mother
had a great deal of power. For example, the mother was
responsible for maintaining the home, the true center of

<u>65–66</u> indicates that preceding material summarizes two pages in the source.

Quotation woven into last sentence of paragraph.

¶5: Outline point IIB [Children's roles mirrored adult roles.]

<u>Old Bread 152</u> indicates that information is a paraphrase of source material. A short title is included because two books by Gallo are used in this paper.

¶6: Outline point IIIA [Barzini sees the family as a "stronghold" and a "refuge."]

Both references in ¶6 cite the same source; two separate references are needed because a direct quotation requires its own reference.

Long quotation is introduced by a running acknowledgment.

Schrader 3

the family; for arranging her children's marriages; and for managing financial affairs. The father made all major decisions that involved the family's relationship with the world at large and, of course, was responsible for earning a living (65–66). In short, as Virginia Yans–McLaughlin points out, the Italian family was "father–dominated but mother–centered" (84).

¶5   Children were a very important part of the family, and the roles defined for them by their parents mirrored traditional adult roles. For instance, Patrick Gallo observes that although parents of the peasant class wanted their children to be well educated in proper behavior, their expectations were very different for their sons and their daughters. Male children were taught to be patient, to have inner control over their emotions, and to show respect for their elders and acknowledge their wisdom. The females were taught household skills and encouraged to develop qualities that would enable them to take their place as the center of the family (<u>Old Bread</u> 152).

¶6   Family solidarity gave the southern Italians a sense of unity and cohesiveness (Gallo, <u>Old Bread</u> 152). Within the family, a strong value system protected each individual from a hostile environment. Luigi Barzini describes the role of the family in Italian society in this way:

> The Italian family is a stronghold in a hostile
> land; within its walls and among its members, the

Over four lines long, this quotation is typed as a block, indented ten spaces from the left margin, double-spaced, with two spaces above and below. No quotation marks are used. Because the quotation is a single paragraph, no further paragraph indentation is needed. Note that in a long quotation, final punctuation is placed before the parenthetical reference.

The reference qtd. in Gallo, *Old Bread* 152 indicates that the Barzini quotation was cited in Gallo's *Old Bread, New Wine*.

¶7: Outline point IIIB [Italians did not trust outsiders.]

Quotation is blended into last sentence of paragraph. Direct quotation is used here because wording of original is distinctive and hard to paraphrase.

¶8: Transitional paragraph. Introduces outline point IV [Italians in America have remained somewhat aloof.]

Schrader 4

individual finds consolation, help, advice, provision, loans, weapons, allies, and accomplices to aid in his pursuits. No Italian who has a family is ever alone. He finds in it a refuge in which to lick his wounds after a defeat, or an arsenal and a staff for his victorious drives. (qtd. in Gallo, <u>Old Bread</u> 152)

The Italian family was so strongly bonded that it became the most powerful single unit to the individual. Since Southern Italy was perceived as threatening and lawless, the family was the only unit the individual could rely on.

¶7   The southern Italian family rarely became entangled in conflicts outside its own close—knit unit. If individuals placed any type of trust outside the family, they were considered by members of their own family to be taking risks that in the end could cause them to lose everything. To go outside the family for help was just not done since by so doing Italians would be placing themselves in a situation where "the form was alien, the access unequal, the rules unknown, and the justice pernicious" (Gallo, <u>Old Bread</u> 156).

¶8   As Yans—McLaughlin points out, the Italians came to America with a culture that was in many ways different from a rapidly developing industrial society, a society that needed their labor but rejected their "unusual" customs. The extent to which they were successful in staying apart from the larger society can be seen through

Two references indicate that the paragraph's information comes from two different sources.

¶9: Outline point IVA [Immigrants often joined fellow villagers in urban "Little Italys."]

Paragraph 9 uses paraphrase, summary, and direct quotation from four sources. See page 650 for Michael's note card for Gans 205 (his own comments appear in brackets).

Three references indicate paraphrase of source material.

Original source for Femminella and Quadagno 77: "According to the 1960 census, nearly 70 percent of Italian-Americans are concentrated in the northeastern portion of America."

Original source for Glazer and Moynihan 187: "Even the trek to the suburbs, when it does occur among Italians, is very often a trek of families of two generations, rather than simply of the young. And it is striking how the old neighborhoods have been artfully adapted to a higher standard of living rather than simply deserted, as they would have been by other groups, in more American style."

an examination of the characteristics of Italian—Americans today. Although assimilation has occurred, cultural traditions, maintained by strong family ties, have affected the relationship of the Italians to American society (79). In addition, Yancy, Ericksen, and Juliani believe that the Italians have become increasingly aware that their ethnic identity has been maintained by the stability and isolation of their communities and by their reliance on the services and institutions offered by their communities (399).

¶9 Many Italian families migrated to America to join relatives or friends from their villages. At the beginning of the immigration, many Italians settled into areas known as "Little Italys," urban neighborhoods "where relatives often lived side by side, and in the midst of people from the same Italian town. Under these conditions, the family circle was maintained much as it had existed in Southern Italy" (Gans 205). To a great extent, these "Little Italys" have been maintained, becoming extended families for their residents. The 1960 census showed that almost 70 percent of Italian Americans were still clustered in the northeastern region of the United States (Femminella and Quadagno 77). Glazer and Moynihan note that second— and third—generation Italian Americans are more likely to work to improve old neighborhoods than to move. When they do leave the old neighborhoods, children and parents often move together (187). National Opinion Research Center

Original source for Femminella and Quadagno 77: "of all the ethnic groups, Italians most often live in the same neighborhood as their parents and siblings and visit them every week."

See page 650 for Michael's note card for the Sons of Italy meeting.

The last sentence of paragraph 9 sums up main idea of paragraph and clarifies connections among sources' ideas.

¶10: Outline point IVB [Immigrants maintain a family-oriented society in America.]

61 indicates paraphrase of a source. The original reads: "The society which these peasants left behind is frequently termed 'familistic' because the nuclear and extended family, rather than the individual or the community, dominated social life to such an extent that an individual's primary social role was his or her role in the family."

¶11: Outline points VA and B [Some women have sought employment. Conflicts have occured between parents and children.]

Paragraph 11 opens with a transitional phrase ("Despite this cohesiveness. . . .") introducing a discussion of the changes the family experienced in America and relating them to the preceding discussion. The paragraph combines paraphrase, summary, and direct quotation from two print sources and two interviews.

surveys have found that Italians are more likely than other ethnic groups to live in the same neighborhood as their closest family members and to visit them regularly (Femminella and Quadagno 77). Italian Americans also exhibit a strong sense of loyalty to and responsibility for their paisani, insisting, for instance, that family and community should house and support their own indigents rather than relying on government agencies (Sons of Italy). It is clear that many Italian Americans value their ethnic solidarity and their independence from the larger society.

¶10 Italian immigrants have by and large maintained their Old World family system in the United States. As Yans-McLaughlin observes, the type of society they left behind is frequently referred to as "familistic" because the individual's social role was defined primarily by the family (61). In the United States as in Italy, the importance of the family over the community or the individual was maintained, and this too kept Italians somewhat aloof from outsiders.

¶11 Despite this cohesiveness, the first-generation Italian family in America was in transition. It was torn between the Italian culture transmitted by the family and the American culture transmitted by American institutions. As Femminella and Quadagno point out, many changes occurred when the family came to America. When the Italian immigrants arrived in America, many were faced with

<u>71</u> indicates paraphrase of a source.

Comments of interview subjects, summarized, are introduced by running acknowledgments. Interview subjects are listed in the Works Cited section at the end of the paper.

Note that even though the quotation begins in the middle of a sentence, an ellipsis mark (. . .) is not used.

Source for <u>Gallo, *Old Bread* 159</u> uses present tense. To tailor the quotation to the sentence, the verb *are* was dropped.

Notice the number at the end of paragraph 11, which refers readers to a content note. Michael includes material in this note that would distract readers if it were included in the text. The note itself does not present information that is necessary to the discussion, but it does shed light on Michael's research.

¶12: Outline point VC [The family system has changed.]

Paragraph 12 opens with a transitional phrase (''Although some patterns did remain the same. . . .'') to signal movement from discussion of adherence to Old World family system to focus on changes within the family. The topic sentence is supported by information from two sources.

Schrader 7

difficulties in finding work. It was often necessary for
the mother to go out and find a job. In Southern Italy,
the mother rarely left the house to go out and work, but
in America her employment was often necessary for the
family's survival. Some researchers view this as a
breakdown of the Italian—American family, but others
disagree, believing women took only those jobs that they
felt were in line with the family value system——for
instance, work in a factory that employed other Italian—
American women (71). Father Vincent P. D'Ancona, a
parish priest in the heavily Italian South Philadelphia
area, reports that even today a wife's or mother's need
to seek employment remains one of the primary sources
of family tension, whether the need is economic or
emotional. Conflicts also occurred among parents
and their children——even though many
children agreed that their parents were "too good to fight
with" (Gallo, Old Bread 159). Both Father D'Ancona and
barber Anthony Pesca, long—time residents of South
Philadelphia, observe that today parents and children
(despite their love and respect for each other) regularly
engage in heated quarrels over issues like dating and
curfews, use of drugs and alcohol, and church attendance.
The most sensitive issue, Father D'Ancona believes, is the
desire of a child to live outside the community or to
marry a non—Italian.[1]

¶12   Although some patterns did remain the same, the Old

Summary of main points of Campisi article is introduced by a running acknowledgment citing author, date, and title of this important study.

<u>443–49</u> cites the entire article, indicating that the material represents a summary of the article. Because the author's name appears in the text, only the page numbers are noted parenthetically.

Three references are made to Herbert Gans's book-length study, which is the source of the paraphrase and quotation in this paragraph. Running acknowledgments clearly distinguish information in Gans's original 1962 study from material added in the second edition (1982) and points made by Gans himself from conclusions drawn by Crispino and only cited by Gans.

Michael's discussion of the Crispino study cited by Gans blends a direct quotation smoothly into the sentence. Because it is clear that Crispino is quoted by Gans, there is no need to include the abbreviation *qtd. in* as part of the citation. Ellipses indicate the omission of an un-

Schrader 8

World family system changed as time went on. Paul J.
Campisi's often-cited 1948 study, "Ethnic Family Patterns:
The Italian Family in the United States," examines the
changes between the southern Italians and first- and
second-generation Italian Americans. One of the major
changes this study found was that although the peasant
family was primarily ruled by the father, by the second
generation the family had become democratic, with the
father's position more equal to that of the mother and
children. Campisi also found that the influence of Italian
culture was growing weaker, with more and more cultural
values shaped by the larger society rather than by the
family (443-49). As recently as 1962, however, Herbert
Gans noted that the husband was still the breadwinner and
the wife's primary responsibilities were still her home
and children. In fact, in Gans's working-class population,
the roles of husband and wife were clearly differentiated
(50-52). But in the 1982 update of his study, when he
considers the third generation of Italian Americans,
Gans finds that even in Italian urban neighborhoods, "the
traditional social segregation of husbands and wives has
been reduced considerably, although some men remain
reluctant to help with childrearing and housework" (231).
In his study, Gans cites an unpublished study of
Bridgeport, Connecticut, by James Crispino. As Gans notes,
Crispino reports that while his third-generation Italian
Americans felt very close to their relatives, more and

necessary word. The original source reads: "Increasingly, friends replaced family members as preferred associates, *however,* and many were
not Italian-American or peers they had known since childhood." The
last sentence sums up the paragraph's main point and ends with a
number that refers to a content note. Again, the information in this
note would have interrupted the flow of the discussion, so the decision
to put it in a note was a sensible one.

¶13: Outline point VIA [The Italian family remains close.]

Paragraph 13 begins with a transitional phrase ("Despite these
changes. . . ."), which introduces information directly supporting the
paper's thesis.

The paragraph includes summary, paraphrase, and direct quotation
from five different sources—four print sources and Michael's own observations. See page 665 for an earlier draft of part of this paragraph.

Palisi 49–50 indicates that the preceding sentences summarize information from two pages of a source.

Goodman's article is one page long; therefore, no page number is
included in the citation.

more often "friends replaced family members as preferred
associates . . . and many were not Italian American or
peers they had known since childhood" (230). It is clear,
then, that some aspects of the traditional family systems
are changing.[2]

¶13 Despite these changes, however, the Italian–American
family has remained close–knit and stable. After coming to
America, the Italian–American family continued to be
extremely close. In fact, in one study, which involved
fifty first–generation and ninety second–generation
Italian–American adults from an ethnic neighborhood in New
York City, researchers found that the extended family was
more important to second–generation than to first–
generation Italian Americans. Although the second–
generation family had generally become larger, relatives
tended to live in closer physical proximity and to have
closer and more extensive social ties with one another
(Palisi 49–50). Today, Italians remain more likely than
members of most other ethnic groups to have relatives over
sixty living with them (Goodman). A walking tour of a
typical urban Italian–American neighborhood seems to
support this conclusion, showing a large proportion of
elderly residents, often accompanied by children and
grandchildren as they go about routine errands and
shopping. Even when members of the extended family are not
actually part of the household, the relationships among
family members are close; the family provides emotional

¶14: Outline point VIB [The Italian family remains stable.]

Paragraph 14 combines paraphrase, summary, and direct quotation from three sources.

Ellipsis mark indicates that nonessential material has been deleted from the end of a sentence.

¶15: Conclusion

Topic sentence of paragraph 15 indicates paragraph will draw paper's ideas together.

Schrader 10

support and also serves as a social network (Gans 46). In fact, even Italian—American gangsters typically maintain very close and highly stable family relationships (Glazer and Moynihan 196).

¶14   The stability of the Italian family is reflected in the low rates of divorce and intermarriage. The 1970 census showed that only about 3 percent of all Italian Americans were divorced and that the divorce rate was not significantly higher for younger Italians. Alfred J. Tella, special adviser to the Director of the Census Bureau, notes that despite increasing affluence, Italian Americans retain closer family ties than other groups. Tella sees the fact that Italians as a group get fewer divorces as one indication of this continued closeness (Goodman). Glazer and Moynihan support this view. They say: "That the family is 'strong' is clear. Divorce, separation, and desertion are relatively rare. Family life is considered the norm for everyone . . ." (197). Moreover, two separate studies show Italians to have one of the lowest intermarriage rates; therefore, it can be concluded that they retain a high degree of ethnic identity (Femminella and Quadagno 74).

¶15 Several conclusions may be drawn about the Italian—American family today. Assimilation has occurred, but the notion of the importance of family has been passed down from generation to generation and has remained an important characteristic of

Direct quotations from a personal letter and a scholarly source both stress the continuing importance of family to Italian Americans, reinforcing the paper's thesis.

Schrader 11

the Italian—American family. As Frank Mucci, a third—generation Italian American says, "You can't do without your family, and they can't do without you. Your family has to stay your first responsibility, no matter what happens." So far, the stable Italian family system has survived through the years, and it seems likely to continue to do so. As Patrick Gallo notes, "The family for the southern Italian remains the supreme societal organization" (<u>Ethnic</u> 87).

This page is numbered.

Notes 1 and 2 are explanatory notes that provide supplementary information to the reader.

½″

Schrader 12

1″

center ⟶ Notes
double-space ⟶

[1]Because of the many interruptions in the interview with Mr. Pesca, I was unable to determine which issue he views as most likely to produce serious conflict between parents and children.

[2]The nomination of Congresswoman Geraldine Ferraro, an Italian–American wife and mother, as the Democratic vice-presidential candidate in 1984 seems to support the impression that the role of women in the Italian family is changing.

Every page of the works cited section is numbered.

The first entry illustrates the correct form for a signed journal article by a single author. Note that it provides inclusive pagination.

Use alphabetical order

Indent 5 spaces

Double-space between and within entries

Entry illustrates form for a book with more than one author.

Entry identifies the subject of a personal interview.

Entry refers to an article by Femminella and Quadagno in a book edited by Mindel and Habenstein.

The List of Works Cited contains two works by Patrick Gallo. Note that the author's name is not repeated; instead, three unspaced hyphens, followed by a period, are used.

Entry identifies a book with a single author.

Entry refers to a signed newspaper article, giving section and page number of the article.

Entry refers to a personal letter.

Entry identifies the subject of a telephone interview.

½"
1"
Schrader 13

center ⟶ Works Cited
double-space ⟶
Campisi, Paul J. "Ethnic Family Patterns: The Italian

indent ⟵⟶ Family in the United States." American Journal of
five
spaces   Sociology 53 (1948): 443–49.

    D'Ancona, Father Vincent P. Personal interview. 10 Feb.

       1992.

    Femminella, Francis X., and Jill S. Quadagno. "The Italian

       American Family." Ethnic Families in America. Ed.

       Charles H. Mindel and Robert W. Habenstein. New York:

Two   Elsevier, 1976. 61–88.
spaces
Gallo, Patrick, J. Ethnic Alienation. Cranbury, N.J.:

       Fairleigh Dickinson UP, 1974.

    ---. Old Bread, New Wine. Chicago: Nelson–Hall, 1981.

    Gans, Herbert J. The Urban Villagers. 2nd ed. New York:

       Free, 1982.

    Glazer, Nathan, and Daniel Patrick Moynihan. Beyond the

       Melting Pot. 2nd ed. Cambridge, Mass.: MIT P., 1970.

    Goodman, Walter. "Scholars Find Bad Image Still Plagues

       U.S. Italians." New York Times 15 Oct. 1983, late

       ed.: B25.

    Mucci, Frank. Letter to author's grandmother. 17 Nov.

       1980.

    Palisi, Bartolomeo S. "Ethnic Generation and Family

       Structure." Journal of Marriage and Family 28

       (1966): 49–50.

    Pesca, Anthony. Telephone interview. 10 Feb. 1992.

Entry refers to a meeting the author attended.

Entry refers to a neighborhood walking tour taken by the author.

Entry refers to a signed journal article with more than one author.

Schrader 14

Sons of Italy Meeting. Philadelphia, Pa. 30 March 1992.

Walking Tour. South Philadelphia. 10 Feb. 1992.

Yancy, William L., Eugene Ericksen, and Richard N.
    Juliani. "Emergent Ethnicity: A Review and
    Reformulation." <u>American Sociological Review</u> 41.3
    (1976): 391–403.

Yans-McLaughlin, Virginia. <u>Family and Community: Italian
    Immigrants in Buffalo</u>. Ithaca: Cornell UP, 1977.

PART 9

Writing in the Disciplines

41

Understanding the Disciplines

All instructors—regardless of academic discipline—have certain basic concerns when they read a paper. They expect to see standard English, correct grammar and spelling, logical thinking, and clear documentation of sources. In addition, they expect logical organization, convincing support, and careful editing. Despite these similarities, however, instructors in various disciplines have different ideas about what they expect in a paper.

One way of putting these differences into perspective is to think of the various disciplines as communities of individuals who gather together to discuss issues that concern them. Just as in any community, the community of scholars who write within a discipline have agreed upon certain conventions. Without these conventions it would be difficult or even impossible for them to communicate effectively with one another. What would happen, for example, if everyone writing about literature used a different documentation format or a different specialized vocabulary? The result would be chaos. To a large extent, then, learning to write in a particular discipline involves learning the conventions that govern its discourse.

41a *Research Sources*

Gathering information is basic to all disciplines, but not all of them rely on the same resources. In the humanities, for example, library research is an important part of most studies. Although some historians will carry out interviews and some literary scholars will collect quantifiable data, most people who work in the humanities spend a great amount of time reading primary and secondary sources.

Those who work in the social sciences will also spend a lot of time surveying the literature on a particular topic. But they will also rely heavily on nonprint sources of information: observation of behavior, interviews, and surveys, for example. Because of the kind of data they generate, social scientists must be able to use statistical methodology and to record their results in charts, graphs, and tables. Those who work in the natural sciences (such as biology, chemistry, and physics) and the applied sciences (engineering and computer science, for example) rely almost exclusively on **empirical data**—information gained through controlled laboratory experiments or from mathematical models. They use the data they collect to formulate theories that try to explain their observations.

The information you gather in the library, in the field, or in the laboratory will help you support the conclusions you formulate when you write. Whether you want to make a point about the color gray in a work by Herman Melville or about the effect of a particular amino acid on the respiratory system, your intent is the same: to explain something or to convince readers of something. In either case, solid evidence is a necessary part of any well-researched paper.

The kind of evidence that is acceptable and persuasive, however, varies from discipline to discipline. Students of literature often use quotations from fiction or poetry to support their assertions, while historians are likely to refer to documents, letters, and court or church records. Social scientists frequently rely on statistics to support their conclusions; those in the natural sciences use the results of controlled experiments. In addition, certain kinds of evidence may be more acceptable in one discipline than in another. For example, **anecdotal evidence**—evidence derived from the testimony of an individual—may be important to a social scientist studying the living conditions in urban public housing. However, anecdotal evidence will be of little or no use to a epidemiologist studying a measles outbreak in the South Bronx (unless, of course, it is supported by empirical evidence).

Scholars often use the opinions of recognized experts in a particular field to support their ideas. The weight that is given to these opinions can vary from discipline to discipline. A historian carrying out a Marxist analysis of Western industrialism, for example, will most likely use the ideas of Karl Marx to support his or her assertions. A feminist literary critic will probably cite the work of other well-respected feminist critics to reinforce his or her points. Although scientists frequently begin papers with a literature survey, however, they base their arguments not on interpretations of expert opinion, but on empirical evidence. Even so, this does not mean that scientific research somehow yields more objective conclusions than does research in other disciplines. The history of science is filled with examples of researchers seeing what they want to see, whether it be canals on Mars, a cure for cancer, or room-temperature fusion. In the same respect, expert opinion never proves anything conclusively. The best one can say is that expert opinion can help a writer construct a convincing (and sometimes even a compelling) case.

41b *Writing Assignments*

Because each discipline has a different set of concerns, the kind of writing assigned varies from course to course. A sociology course, for example, may require a statistical analysis, while a literature course will ask for a literary analysis. Therefore, it is not enough simply to know the material about which you are asked to write. You must also be aware of what the instructor in a particular discipline expects to receive. For example, when your art history instructor asks you to write a paper on the Brooklyn Bridge, she does not expect you to write an analysis of Hart Crane's poem "The Bridge"—a topic suitable for a literature class—nor does she want a detailed discussion of the chemical composition of the steel used in bridge building—a topic suitable for a materials engineering class. What she might expect is for you to discuss the use of the bridge as an artistic subject—as it is in the paintings of Joseph Stella and the photographs of Alfred Steiglitz, for example.

When you get any assignment, make certain you understand exactly what you are being asked to do. If you have any doubt, ask your instructor for guidance. You should begin by trying to acquaint yourself with issues that are of continuing interest to those who publish in areas related to your topic. Take the time to look through your text and class notes or browse through relevant periodical indexes in the library to get a sense of the theories, concerns, and controversies that pertain to your topic. Keep in mind, however, that this advice does not mean you should write only about areas that researchers have already explored. On the contrary, papers that take chances, that make links between disciplines—using some lines from "The Bridge" as part of your art history paper to shed some light on the power of the bridge as a literary and artistic symbol, for example—may be the most valuable and enlightening.

41c *Conventions of Style and Documentation*

(1) *Style*

Specialized Vocabulary   Learning a discipline is analogous to moving to a foreign country and not knowing the language. At first, you observe people from a distance. Eventually, as you learn a few words, you begin to communicate—if only slightly—with the natives. Finally, after you can speak the language well, you become actively involved with those around you and, if you are lucky, participate in the life of the community. Only by learning the specialized vocabulary of a field can you communicate with those who work in it. Once you know this vocabulary, you can begin to participate in the conversations and debates that define the discipline.

When you write a paper for a course, you should try to use the specialized vocabulary of people who work in the discipline. When you write a paper for a literature course, for example, use the terms you have heard in class and read in your textbook—*point of view, persona,* and *imagery,* for example. Do the same for your other classes. It makes no sense to use inexact words or colloquial phrases when the discipline offers a vocabulary that will enable you to express concepts accurately and concisely. What other words, for example, would you use to denote mitosis, ecosystem, or osmosis without using these specific terms? Keep in mind, however, that you must be careful to use specialized words correctly and accurately.

Revision Close-up

Although technical terms facilitate communication inside a discipline, they can do exactly the opposite when used outside the discipline **(see 18d1).**

Level of Diction   Within any field, particular assignments have different degrees of formality and different stylistic characteristics.

Regardless of discipline, research papers are usually formal: they contain learned words, are grammatically correct, avoid contractions and colloquialisms, and use third person pronouns. Proposals—whether they are in the humanities, social sciences, or natural sciences—also are relatively formal.

Other assignments, by their very nature, are less formal than proposals and research papers. Because its purpose is to present an individual's personal reactions, a response statement uses subjective language, the first person, and the active voice. A lab report is also informal, but because its purpose is to report the observations themselves—not the observer's reactions—it frequently relies on objective language and the passive voice ("The acid was poured" rather than "I poured the acid"). Perhaps the only thing that can be said with certainty about the level of diction of the various disciplines is that all of them use different degrees of formality to address different audiences and to fulfill different purposes.

Format   Each discipline has certain distinctive formats that govern the way in which written information is presented. A **format** is a way of arranging material that has become accepted practice in an organization or in a discipline. The most obvious format is the one that governs the arrangement of an entire piece of writing, such as a lab report, which has certain prescribed sections. Other formats determine how certain kinds of information are presented within a paper. For example, social scientists expect statistical data to be presented in tables or graphs. In some disciplines—particularly in the sciences and social sciences—writers often use internal headings in their papers, and in others—particularly in the humanities—they seldom do. Specific mechanical concerns, such as whether to spell out a number or use numerals, also differ from discipline to discipline.

Each professional society defines the guidelines that govern paper formats within the discipline (see 41c2). Typically, a professional society will issue or recommend a handbook or style sheet that defines the standards for spelling, mechanics, punctuation, and capitalization. This style sheet also gives explicit guidelines for the use and placement of information in charts, graphs, tables, and illustrations within a paper, and for typing conventions, such as the placement of page numbers on a paper and the arrangement of information on a title page. In addition, these style sheets discuss and illustrate the documentation format they recommend for research papers. Because significant differences exist from one discipline to another, always consult your instructor or the appropriate style sheet for the discipline before you write.

(2) Documentation

Different disciplines use different forms of documentation. Four of the most widely used formats are those recommended by the Modern Language Association (MLA), the American Psychological Association (APA), *The Chicago Manual of Style* (CMS), and the ▶ **See** Council of Biology Editors (CBE). Instructors in the humanities **Ch. 39** usually prefer MLA style, which uses parenthetical references within the text to refer to sources listed at the end of the paper, or CMS style, which uses footnotes or endnotes keyed to bibliographic citations at the end of the paper. Instructors in the social sciences and in education prefer the APA style, which uses parenthetical references that differ slightly from MLA style. Other disciplines—the physical and biological sciences and medicine, for example—prefer a number-reference format, similar to CBE style, which uses numbers in parentheses in the text that refer to a numbered list of works at the end of the paper.

Because of the lack of uniformity among the disciplines, it is especially important that you consult your instructor to see which documentation style he or she requires. Your instructor may expect you to use a certain style sheet which he or she will place on reserve in the library or ask you to purchase. But if this is not the case, it is your responsibility to determine which style to use. Regardless of which style you use, you should keep in mind the following general guidelines.

Guidelines for Documentation

- Make sure you understand what information must be documented **(see 39a).**
- Do not assume that the documentation style you use in one class is appropriate for another.
- Follow *exactly* the conventions of the format you decide to use.
- Use one system of documentation consistently throughout the paper.
- Make sure you have a copy of the appropriate style sheet so that you can consult it if problems arise.
- Leave yourself enough time to proofread the final draft of your paper. Make certain that you have documented all information that needs documentation and that you have punctuated all entries correctly.

WRITING IN THE DISCIPLINES

	Discipline	Research Sources	Assignment

Humanities	Languages
	Literature
	Philosophy
	History
	Linguistics
	Religion
	Art history
	Music
		Library sources
		Interviews
		Observations (museums,
		   concerts)
		Oral history
			Response statement
			Book review
			Art, music, dance, or
			   film review
			Bibliographic essay
			Annotated bibliog-
			   raphy
			Literary analysis
			Research paper

Social Sciences	Anthropology
	Psychology
	Economics
	Business
	Education
	Sociology
	Political science
	Social work
	Criminal justice
		Library sources
		Surveys
		Observation (behavior
		   of groups and indi-
		   viduals)
			Proposal
			Experience paper
			Case study
			Abstract
			Research paper

Natural and Applied Sciences	Natural science
	  biology
	  chemistry
	  physics
	  astronomy
	  geology
	  mathematics
	Applied science
	  engineering
	  computer science
	  nursing
	  pharmacy
		Library sources
		Empirical data (obser-
		   vations, experiments)
		Surveys
			Abstract
			Literature survey
			Laboratory report
			Research paper

Style and Format	Documentation Format
Style Specialized vocabulary Use of direct quotations *Format* Little use of internal headings, tables, etc.	English, languages, philosophy: MLA History, art: CMS
Style Specialized vocabulary, including statistical terminology *Format* Internal headings Use of charts and figures (graphs, maps, flow charts, photographs) Numerical data (in tabular form)	APA
Style Frequent use of passive voice Little use of direct quotation *Format* Internal headings Use of tables, graphs, and illustrations Exact formats vary from journal to journal	Biology: CBE Format varies from discipline to discipline and within disciplines as well

42

Writing in the Humanities

The humanities include a variety of disciplines, such as art, music, literature, languages, religion, and philosophy. In these fields research is often conducted in order to analyze or interpret a **primary source**—a literary work, a historical document, a musical composition, or a work of art—and perhaps to make connections between one work and another. Scholars in humanities disciplines may also examine **secondary sources**—commentaries on primary sources (**see 38a1**), in order to make critical judgments and sometimes to develop new theories.

42a *Research Sources*

Library research is an important part of study in many humanities disciplines. When you begin your research in any subject area, the *Humanities Index* is one general source you can turn to. Many specialized sources are available as you continue your research process.

(1) *Specialized library sources*

The following sources are used in various humanities disciplines.

Art

Art Index
Encyclopedia of World Art
Index to Art Reproductions in Books
New Dictionary of Modern Sculpture
Oxford Companion to Art
Praeger Encyclopedia of Art

Drama

The Crown Guide to the World's Great Plays from Ancient Greece to
Modern Times
A Guide to Critical Reviews
McGraw-Hill Encyclopedia of World Drama
Modern World Drama: An Encyclopedia
Oxford Companion to the Theatre

Film

The Film Encyclopedia
Guide to Critical Reviews
International Index to Film Periodicals
International Index to Multimedia Information
Lander's Film Reviews
Magill's Survey of Cinema
New York Times Film Reviews

History

America: History and Life (United States)
Cambridge Ancient History
Cambridge Medieval History
CRIS (Combined Retrospective Index to Journals in History,
1838–1974)
Dictionary of American History
Great Events in History
Guide to Historical Literature
Harvard Guide to American History
Historical Abstracts (Europe)
New Cambridge Modern History

Language and Literature

Annual Bibliography of English Language and Literature
Biography Index
Book Review Digest
Book Review Index
Cassell's Encyclopedia of World Literature
Children's Literature Abstracts
Contemporary Authors
Current Biography

Essay and General Literature Index
Language and Language Behavior Abstracts (LLBA)
Literary History of the United States (LHUS)
MLA International Bibliography
Oxford Companion to American Literature
Oxford Companion to Classical Literature
Oxford Companion to English Literature
PMLA General Index, v. 1–50
Princeton Encyclopedia of Poetry and Poetics
Salem Press Critical Surveys of Poetry, Fiction, Long Fiction, and Drama
Short Story Index
Twentieth Century Authors
Webster's Biographical Dictionary

Music

Harvard Dictionary of Music
Music Article Guide
Music Index
The New Grove Dictionary of Music and Musicians
The New Oxford Companion to Music

Philosophy

The Concise Encyclopedia of Western Philosophy and Philosophers
Dictionary of the History of Ideas
Encyclopedia of Philosophy
Philosopher's Index

Religion

Encyclopedia Judaica
Encyclopedia of Islam
The Hutchinson Encyclopedia of Living Faiths
New Catholic Encyclopedia
Oxford Dictionary of the Christian Church

(2) *Specialized databases for computer searches*

Many of the print indexes that appear on the above list of specialized library sources are also available online. Some of the most helpful databases for humanities disciplines include *Humanities Index,*

714

Art Index, MLA Bibliography, Religion Index, Philosopher's Index, Music Literature International (RRM), Essay and General Literature Index, Artbibliographies Modern, Historical Abstracts, the LLBA Index, Dissertation Abstracts, Arts and Humanities Search, and *OnLine.*

(3) Other sources of information

Research in the humanities is not always limited to the library. Historians may need to do interviews or archival work or consult records collected in town halls, churches, or courthouses. Art historians may visit museums and galleries, and music scholars may attend concerts.

Nonprint sources, such as the oral history interview excerpted below, can be important additions to a paper in any humanities discipline.

Excerpt from Interview with Arturo Tapia, a Registered Tigua Indian

My daddy never used to say he was Tigua Indian . . . we never talked about it . . . other Indians never liked us and the white people never allowed us in their bars or stores. I have gone up to people and told them I am Tigua and they say, "What a low class Indian," or "Them down there, the Mexicans," "They sold out."

The student who recorded this interview chose to use it in her paper's conclusion:

As many of the sources examined here have demonstrated, the history of the Tiguas is full of misconceptions. The New Mexico version of the Tiguas' migration is that they fled with a Spanish party to El Paso during the Indian uprising of August 10, 1680, but the Tigua version of their migration is quite different. The New Mexico Indians have portrayed the Tiguas of Isleta as a "Judas Tribe" who turned against their own people to ally with the Spanish. Even today the Tiguas face discrimination from other Indians as well as from whites and feel they are considered "low class" (Tapia).

42b *Assignments in the Humanities*

(1) *The response statement*

In some disciplines, particularly literature, you may be asked to write a *response statement,* in which you express (sometimes informally) your reactions to a work or performance—for example, a literary work, a painting, a film, a dance performance, or a concert. Such an assignment requires you to write a first-person account of your feelings and to explore the factors that influenced your response.

Sample Response Statement

```
     Rereading The Catcher in the Rye after two years, I
see a lot of weaknesses I didn't notice last time. The
style is too cute and too repetitive, and it calls
attention to itself. Salinger has Holden say things like
"I mean" and "if you know what I mean" too many times, and
he seems to use bad language for no particular reason.
Also, I don't like Holden as much as I did the first time
I read the book. Before I saw him as isolated and
misunderstood, a pathetic character who could have been
happy if only he'd stayed a child forever. Now he gets on
my nerves. I keep thinking he could do something to help
himself if he didn't have to blame everything on the
"phonies." All this probably says more about how I've
changed in two years than about how good or bad the book
is.
```

(2) *The book review*

A book review, which may be assigned in any humanities discipline (particularly in literature, history, and philosophy), asks you to respond critically to a book, judging it according to some external standard. In addition to your evaluation of the work, you also provide some context to enable readers to follow your discussion. Most book reviews, therefore, include a brief summary or overview of the work or an outline of the author's key points or arguments. (Reviews of performances or nonprint works are similar to book reviews in that they assess the worth of a work or an artist.) The book review that follows was written for a cross-disciplinary composition class.

Excerpt from a Book Review

In his thought-provoking book Chaos: Making a New Science, James Gleick chronicles the events of recent years that have shaped this new science and introduces the individuals responsible for those events. He begins with what is considered the starting point of the new science, Edward Lorenz's Butterfly Effect, and ends with a comprehensive discussion of the newest discoveries and the future of chaos. Most importantly, he explains in depth the equations, theories, and concepts that are the heart of chaos and traces the brainwork behind them. One example of how this new science is applied is Mitchell Feigenbaum's theory of universality. Using only a hand-held calculator, this physicist proved that simple equations from a simple system can be applied to a totally unrelated system to produce a complicated solution. Although Feigenbaum's theory was at first greeted with skepticism, it soon became the basis for finding order in otherwise unrelated irregularities. Gleick's clear analysis of this and other theories makes his explanation of chaos interesting to lay audiences as well as to scientists.

(3) The bibliographic essay

A bibliographic essay surveys research in a field and compares and contrasts the usefulness of various sources on a particular subject. Several publications in the humanities publish annual bibliographic essays to inform scholars of recent developments in the field. Students in advanced literature or history classes may also prepare this type of essay. The following excerpt, written by a student in an American literature class, comes from a bibliographic essay on Mark Twain's novel *Pudd'nhead Wilson*.

Excerpt from a Bibliographic Essay

Most early critics analyze the novel in terms of racial issues and the doctrine of environmental determinism. Langston Hughes, for instance, writes that "the basic theme [of Pudd'nhead Wilson] is slavery . . . and its main thread concerns the absurdity of man—made differentials, whether of caste or 'race'" (viii). James M. Cox also focuses on the racial issue, specifically on miscegenation, but in a more symbolic vein than does Hughes. Cox's analysis of the novel is very similar to Fiedler's. Like Fiedler, Cox believes the novel deals with American guilt; it is a "final unmasking of the heart of darkness beneath the American dream" (361). Tom serves as the white man's nemesis, spawned by the guilt of miscegenation, a violation of the black race. He is "the instrument of an avenging destiny which has overtaken Dawson's Landing" (353).

(4)   The annotated bibliography

Each entry in an annotated bibliography includes full source information and a *brief* summary of the source's main points or arguments. The example below is from a student's annotated bibliography of *Pudd'nhead Wilson*.

Excerpt from an Annotated Bibliography

Chellis, Barbara A. "Those Extraordinary Twins: Negroes
  and Whites." American Quarterly 21 (1969): 100—12.

  Chellis sees Pudd'nhead Wilson as an exposure of "the
fiction of law and custom" that has justified distinctions
between blacks and whites. Twain develops his theme
through his characterizations of Roxy, Tom, and Chambers.
According to Chellis, Roxy's ''crime''—condemning the
real Tom to slavery—stems not from the influence of her
race but from that of her white values. Tom is spoiled and
selfish—the kind of person produced by white society's
values. The invalidity of race distinctions is further
pointed out through the servility of Chambers, who is
white. Black servility is ultimately seen to be nothing
more than training.

(5)   The literary analysis

Students in literature classes are frequently called upon to analyze poems, plays, short stories, or novels. For an example of a literary analysis of a short story, **see 46d.**

► **See 46d**

42c   *Conventions of Style and Documentation*

(1)   *Style*

Although papers in the humanities may include abstracts and internal headings, they usually do not. Similarly, they do not generally present material in tables, charts, or graphs. Although each discipline has its own specialized vocabulary, clarity and restraint from the overuse of jargon are important considerations. Writing in the first person is acceptable when you are expressing your own reactions and convictions—for example, in a response statement. In other cases, however, you should use an objective tone and third-person point of view.

In writing papers about literature, certain conventions of literary analysis are followed. For example, direct quotations are frequently used, and present-tense verbs are generally used for plot summary. For a full discussion of writing about literature, see Chapter 46.

(2)   *Documentation*

Literature and modern and classical language scholars use MLA format (**see 39b**); history scholars use *The Chicago Manual of Style* (**see 39c**).

42d   *Sample Humanities Research Papers*

(1)   *Modern Language Association (MLA) Format*

For an example of a research paper that uses MLA format, see "The Italian Family: 'Stronghold in a Hostile Land'" (**40j**). For an example of MLA documentation style in a literary analysis, **see 46d.**

(2) *Chicago Manual of Style* (CMS) Format

The following excerpts from a history research paper, "Native Americans and the Reservation System," uses Chicago style. Note that because the instructor did not require a separate title page, the student included identifying information on the first page of her paper.

See ◄ 39c

1

Angela M. Womack

American History 301

December 3, 1992

Native Americans and the Reservation System

It is July 7th and 10,000 Navajo Indians make ready to leave land in Arizona that they have called home for generations. Their land has been assigned to the Hopi tribe by the United States government to settle a dispute between the two tribes over the land in question.[1] Ella Bedonie, a member of the Navajo tribe, says, "The Navajo and the Hopi people have no dispute. It's the government that's doing this to us. I think the Hopis may have the land for a while, but then the government . . . will step in."[2] The Hopis are receiving 250,000 acres to compensate them for the 900,000 acres they will lose in this land deal; however, the groundwater on this land is questionable due to possible contamination by a uranium mine upstream. To offset this unappealing aspect the government sweetened the deal with incentives of livestock.[3] This was the fate many Native Americans had to face as western expansion swept across the continent. Now consider that the incident mentioned occurred not on July 7, 1886, but on July 7, 1986. Indian relations with the

government are as alive and problematic today as ever
before, for the federal government's administration of the
reservation system both promotes and restricts the
development of the Native American culture.

A reservation is an area of land reserved for Indian
use. There are approximately 260 reservations in the
United States at present.[4] The term reservation can be
traced back to the time when land was "reserved" for
Indian use in treaties between whites and Native
Americans. Figures from 1978 by the Bureau of Indian
Affairs show that 51,789,249 acres of land are in trust
for Native Americans; 41,678,875 acres of this are for
tribes, and 10,110,374 acres are for individuals.[5] The
Native Americans are by no means restricted to these
areas, although this assumption is commonly made. They are
as free as any other citizen to leave these areas. The
reservation system provides benefits which promote the
development of the Indian culture, and many are not
offered to the general public. These benefits were
established to encourage Indian acceptance of living on
the reservation by guaranteeing that the Native American's
ways of life would be altered as little as possible. For
instance, each reservation has its own form of tribal
government and tribal laws.[6] Although a few federal laws
for crimes such as murder take precedence, most crimes
committed on the reservation are under the jurisdiction of
the tribal court.[7]

10

Notes

[1] Trebbe Johnson, "Indian Land, White Greed," <u>Nation</u>, 4 July 1987, 15.

[2] Johnson, 17.

[3] Johnson, 16.

[4] Ted Williams, "On the Reservation: America's Apartheid," <u>National Review</u>, 8 May 1987, 28.

[5] U.S. Bureau of Indian Affairs, "Information about . . . The Indian People," (Washington, D.C.: Government Printing Office, 1981), 6, mimeographed.

[6] Williams, 28.

[7] Bureau of Indian Affairs, 6.

11

Bibliography

"Adrift in Their Own Land." Time 6 July 1987: 89.

Arrandale, Tom. "American Indian Economic Development."
Editorial Research Reports 17 Feb. 1984: 127–142.

Battise, Carol. Personal interview, 25 Sept. 1987.

Cook, J. "Help Wanted––Work, Not Handouts." Forbes 4 May
1987: 68–71.

Horswell, Cindy. "Alabama–Coushattas See Hope In U.S.
Guardianship." Houston Chronicle 26 May 1987: 11.

Johnson, Trebbe. "Indian Land, White Greed." Nation 4 July
1987: 15–18.

Martin, Howard N. "Alabama–Coushatta Indians of Texas:
Alabama–Coushatta Historical Highlights." Brochure,
Alabama–Coushatta Indian Reservation: Livingston,
Texas [n.d.].

"A New Band of Tribal Tycoons," Time 16 March 1987: 56.

Philp, K. R. "Dillon S. Myer and the Advent of
Termination: 1950–1953." Western Historical Quarterly
Jan. 1988: 37–59.

[U.S. Bureau of Indian Affairs.] "Information About . . .
The Indian People." Washington, D.C.: Government
Printing Office, 1981. Mimeographed.

Williams, Ted. "On the Reservation: American's Apartheid."
National Review 8 May 1987: 28–30.

Young, J. Williams. T. American Realities: Historical
Realities From the First Settlements to the Civil
War. Boston: Little Brown, 1981.

Writing in the Social Sciences

The social sciences include anthropology, business, economics, education, political science, psychology, social work, and sociology. When you approach an assignment in the social sciences, your purpose is often to study individuals or groups in order to generalize about their behavior. You may be seeking to understand causes; predict results; define a policy, habit, or trend; draw an analogy between one group and another; or analyze a problem. Before you can approach a problem in the social sciences, you must develop a **hypothesis,** an educated guess about what you believe your research will suggest. Then you go on to gather data you hope will support that hypothesis. Data may be quantitative or qualitative. **Quantitative data** are essentially numerical—the "countable" results of surveys and polls. **Qualitative data** are less exact and more descriptive—the results of interviews or observations, for example.

43a *Research Sources*

Although library research is an important component of research in the social sciences, researchers are more likely to engage in field work. In the library, social scientists consult compilations of statistics, government documents, and newspaper articles in addition to scholarly books and articles. Outside the library, social scientists conduct interviews and surveys and observe individuals and groups. Because so much of their data are numerical, social scientists must know how to analyze statistics and how to read and interpret tables.

(1)   Specialized library sources

The following reference sources are useful in a variety of social science disciplines.

ASI Index (American Statistics Institute)
Bibliografia Chicana: A Guide to Information Sources
Dictionary of Mexican American History
Encyclopedia of Black America
Handbook of North American Indians
Harvard Encyclopedia of American Ethnic Groups
Human Resources Abstracts
International Bibliography of the Social Sciences
International Encyclopedia of the Social Sciences
The Negro Almanac: A Reference Work on the Afro-American
PAIS (Public Affairs Information Service)
Population Index
Social Sciences Citation Index
Social Sciences Index
Women's Studies: A Recommended Core Bibliography

The following reference sources are most often used for research in specific disciplines.

Anthropology

Abstracts in Anthropology
Anthropological Literature
Dictionary of Anthropology

Business and Economics

Business Periodicals Index
The Encyclopedia of Banking and Finance
The Encyclopedia of Management
Journal of Economic Literature
The McGraw-Hill Dictionary of Modern Economics
Personnel Management Abstracts

Criminal Justice

Criminology and Penology Abstracts
Criminal Justice Abstracts
Criminal Justice Periodicals Index
Encyclopedia of Crime and Justice
Police Science Abstracts

Education

Current Index to Journals in Education
Dictionary of Education
Education Index
Encyclopedia of Educational Research

Political Science

ABC Political Science
American Political Dictionary
CIS Index (Congressional Information Service)
Combined Retrospective Index to Journals in Political Science
Dictionary of Political Thought
Encyclopedia of Modern World Politics
Encyclopedia of the Third World
Encyclopedia of the United Nations and International Agreements
Europa Year Book
Foreign Affairs Bibliography
Information Services on Latin America
International Political Science Abstracts

Psychology

Biographical Dictionary of Psychology
Contemporary Psychology
Encyclopedia of Psychology
International Encyclopedia of Psychiatry, Psychology, Psychoanalysis
    and Neurology
Psychological Abstracts

Sociology and Social Work

Encyclopedia of Social Work
Encyclopedia of Sociology
Poverty and Human Resources Abstracts
Rural Sociology Abstracts
Sage Family Studies Abstracts
Sociological Abstracts

Government Documents   Government documents are important resources for social scientists because they contain the complete and up-to-date facts and figures on everything from technical, scientific, and medical information to information on home safety for children.

Government documents can be searched through the *Monthly Catalog*, which contains the list of documents published that month together with a subject index. Other useful indexes include *The Congressional Information Service Index*, *The American Statistics Index*, and *The Index to U.S. Government Periodicals*.

Newspaper Articles   Newspaper articles are particularly useful sources for researching subjects in political science, economics, and business. Students usually rely on the *New York Times*, whose indexes are available both in print and on microfilm. For information from newspapers from across the country, a useful source is *Newsbank*. Like the government's *Monthly Catalog*, *Newsbank* provides subject headings under the appropriate government agencies. For instance, articles on child abuse are likely to be listed under Health and Human Services. Once you find the subject area, *Newsbank* provides a microcard/microfiche number. On that microfiche you will find articles on your subject.

(2)   Specialized databases for computer searches

Many of the print sources cited above are listed in computer databases. Some of the more widely used databases for social science disciplines include *Cendata, Business Periodicals Index, Social Sciences Index, PsycINFO, ERIC, Social Scisearch, Sociological Abstracts, Information Science Abstracts, PAIS International, Population Bibliography, Economic Literature Index, ABI/INFORM, Legal Resource Index, Management Contents, Trade & Industry Index, PTSF + S Indexes* and *Facts on File*.

(3)   Other sources of information

Interviews, surveys, and observation of the behavior of various groups and individuals are important non-library sources for social science research. Assignments may ask you to use your classmates as subjects for surveys or interviews. For example, in a political science class, your teacher may ask you to interview a sample of college students and classify them as conservative, liberal, or radical. You may be asked to poll each group to find out college students' attitudes on issues such as nuclear energy, chemical waste disposal, or the problems of the homeless. If you were writing a paper on gifted programs in education, in addition to library research on the issue you might want to observe two classes—one of gifted students and one of students not eligible to participate in the gifted program. You might also want to interview students, teachers, or parents. Similarly, research in psychology and social work may rely on your observations of clients, patients, or their families. (For specific information on interviews, surveys, and observation, see 37c.)

43b *Assignments in the Social Sciences*

(1) *The experience paper*

Instructors in the social sciences often ask students to do "hands-on" research outside the library; one product of such research is the experience paper. This assignment asks students to record their observations and reactions to a field trip or site visit. For example, students in an education class might write up their observation of a class of hearing-impaired students, criminal justice students might record their reactions to a trial, business majors might write about their impressions of how a particular small business operates, and students in an abnormal psychology class could write an experience paper about a visit to a state-run psychiatric facility.

The following excerpt, written by a student in a Sociology of Religion class, describes visits to two different churches.

Excerpt from an Experience Paper

> The Pentecostal church service I observed was full of self-expression, motion, and emotion. People sang and praised the Lord in loud voices. In an atmosphere similar to that of a revival, people spontaneously expressed their joy and their reactions to the sermon. Each word the preacher spoke elicited responses like "Praise the Lord," "Hallelujah," "Thank the Lord," and "Amen." Rather than focusing on religious doctrine, the sermon concentrated on the problems of everyday life. The Presbyterian service I observed was very different. Compared to the Pentecostal service it seemed orderly, structured, and traditional. The sanctuary was quiet and still, with organ music the only sound. Worshippers did not shout or clap; the most

they did during the service was stand up. They conducted silent, almost whispering, prayers; even their hymns were quiet and solemn. Finally, the sermon was more analytical and less practical; it focused for the most part on the interpretation of theological doctrine and only tangentially addressed the doctrine's relevance to life.

(2) The case study

The case study is important for the presentation of information in psychology, sociology, anthropology, and political science, where it can examine an individual case, the dynamics of a group, or the functioning of a political organization. Case studies are usually informative, describing the problem at hand and presenting solutions or treatments. They generally follow a set format: the statement of the problem, the background of the problem, the observations of the behavior of the individual or group being studied, the conclusions arrived at, and suggestions for improvement or future recommendations.

Different disciplines make different use of case studies. In political science, case study methodology can be applied to deliberations in policy making and decision making. Foreign policy negotiations, for instance, may be described and written up as case studies, and issue analyses such as "Should government control the media?" can also be written as case studies. In psychology, social work, and educational psychology or counseling, the case study focuses on observation of an individual and his or her interaction with peers or with agency professionals. Such a case study usually involves describing the behavior of an individual or a group of individuals and outlining the steps to be taken in solving the problem that presents itself to the caseworker or researcher.

Excerpt from a Case Study (Social Work)

Mona Freeman, a 14-year-old girl, was brought to the Denver Children's Residential Treatment Center by her 70-year-old, devoutly religious adoptive mother. Both were personable, verbal, and neatly groomed. The presenting problem was seen differently by various members of the client system. Mrs. Freeman described Mona's "several years of behavior problems," including "lying, stealing,

729

and being boy crazy." Mona viewed herself as a
"disappointment" and wanted "time to think." She had been
expelled from the local Seventh Day Adventist School for
being truant and defiant several months earlier and had
been attending public school. The examining psychiatrist
diagnosed a conduct disorder but saw no intellectual,
physical, or emotional disabilities. He predicted that
Mona probably would not be able to continue to live in
"such an extreme disciplinary environment" as the home of
Mrs. Freeman because she had lived for the years from
seven until twelve with her natural father in Boston,
Massachusetts—a situation which was described as a
"kidnapping" by Mrs. Freeman. The psychiatrist mentioned
some "depression" and attributed it to Mona's inability to
fit in her current environment and the loss of her life
with her father in Boston.

(3)   The literature review

The literature review is similar in purpose and format to the
bibliographic essay assigned in the humanities (see 42b3). The literature review is often part of the background section of a social
science research paper (see 43d). By reading, summarizing, and
commenting on recent scholarship on a particular topic, students
gain a knowledge of the topic itself as well as an understanding of
the different approaches that may be applied to that topic. The
excerpt that follows, written for an introductory psychology class,
is from a literature review on the topic of depression among college
students.

Excerpt from a Literature Review

Negative events and outlook are not the only causes
of depression among college students (Cochran & Hammen,
1985; Brown & Silberschatz, 1988). In fact, some students
do not become depressed in the presence of one or more
negative events, while others are depressed even if no
negative event takes place (Billings et al., 1983).
Depression can be seen to arise from a range of social and

environmental factors, which can be seen as a combination
of stressful life events, poor coping style, and a lack of
social resources Vredenburg et al., 1985; Cochran &
Hammen, 1985).

(4) The proposal

A proposal, often the first stage of a research project, can help
to clarify and focus the research project's direction and goals.

In a proposal, you you have to make a convincing case for your
idea. To do so, you have to define your research project and defend
it. In the process you must adhere strictly to any specifications
outlined by your instructor or in the request for proposals issued
by the grant-giving agency.

Many proposals contain the following components.

Cover Sheet   The cover sheet contains your name, the title of
your project, and the person or agency to which your proposal is
submitted. It also provides a short title that expresses your subject
concisely. Thinking about who will read your proposal will help
you focus on your audience. Usually another line on this sheet states
the reason for the submission of the proposal—for example, to
satisfy a course requirement or to request funding or facilities.

> Advantages of the Maquiladora Project
>
> in El Paso
>
> Submitted to: Professor Lawrence Howley
>
> For: Fulfillment of Research Requirement
>
> for Sociology 412
>
> by Laura Talamantes

Sample of Cover Sheet Format

Abstract   Usually on a separate page, the abstract provides a
short summary of your proposal. **See 44b1** for information on
writing abstracts; for a sample, see the abstract accompanying the
social science research paper in **43d.**

Statement of Purpose   Essentially, your statement of purpose is
your thesis statement. It tells why you are conducting your research

and what you hope to accomplish—for example, "The Maquila-dora Project is an industrial development program that relies on international cooperation with Mexican industries to utilize Mexican labor while boosting the employment of U.S. white-collar workers."

Background of the Problem   This section explains why your perspective on your topic is important. It is usually a paragraph that summarizes previous research and indicates the need for your specific study.

Rationale   This section, which justifies further the need for your research project, should be persuasive. In it you explain why your research project is necessary and what makes it important at this time.

Statement of Qualification   This section demonstrates why you are uniquely qualified to carry out the research and the special qualities you bring to your work.

Literature Survey   This section usually contains a brief survey of each source you have consulted. Because it helps to establish your credibility as a researcher, this section should be thorough.

Research Methods   This section describes the exact methods you will use in carrying out your research and the materials you will need; its purpose is to demonstrate the soundness of your method.

Timetable   This section states the time necessary for carrying out the project.

Budget   Where applicable, this section estimates the costs for carrying out the research.

Conclusion   Here you restate the importance of your project.

Along with a proposal you usually send a cover letter, called a letter of transmittal, and a résumé, which lists your specific qualifications for the project. This résumé summarizes your relevant work experience and accomplishments and reinforces your qualifications as presented in the statement of qualification. For information on writing business letters and résumés, see Chapter 47.

43c   *Conventions of Style and Documentation*

(1)   Style

Social science writing tends to use a technical vocabulary. For instance, in the social work case study excerpted in 43b2, the student speaks of "the presenting problem"—that is, the reason the "subject," Mona, was brought to the Denver Children's Facility. Because you are addressing specialists when you write papers in these disciplines, you should use the vocabulary of the field. Also, in describing charts and tables, you should use familiar statistical terms, such as *means, percentages,* and *chi squares.* Keep in mind, however, that you should explain in plain English what percentages, means, and standard deviations mean in terms of your analysis.

A social science research paper typically uses internal headings (for example, Method, Results, Discussion or Statement of Problem, Background of Problem, Description of Problem, Solutions, and Conclusion). Unlike a humanities paper, each section of a social science paper is written as a complete entity with a beginning and an end so that it can be read separately, out of context, and still make sense. The body of the paper may present graphs, maps, photographs or flow charts as well as discussions of those figures. Finally, a social science paper frequently presents numerical data in tabular form.

(2) Documentation

The documentation style in the social sciences is more uniform than it is in the humanities or the sciences, with nearly all journals in the various disciplines using the documentation style of the American Psychological Association's *Publication Manual* (see **39d**).

43d Sample Social Science Research Paper

(1) American Psychological Association (APA) Format

The following psychology research paper, "Impression Formation in Customer-Clerk Interactions," uses APA documentation style.

Impression Formation
1

Impression Formation in Customer-Clerk Interactions

Jennifer Humble

Psychology 321

Dr. Barbara Bremer

December 11, 1992

Running head: IMPRESSION FORMATION

Sample Social Science Research Paper

Abstract

The present study examined the extent to which physical appearance and dress affect the quality of customer–clerk interactions. An observational study was conducted in which a well–dressed actor and a poorly–dressed actor posed as customers and engaged in customer–clerk interactions at nine different stores in a suburban shopping mall. The sociability of the clerk, time of initiation of interaction, duration of interaction, and prices of the first two watches shown were recorded. In support of the proposed hypothesis that dress and physical appearance will affect the quality of social interactions, the results indicated that the sociability of each clerk was significantly higher when interacting with the well–dressed actor than when interacting with the poorly dressed actor.

In an attempt to understand the factors that influence the quality of social interactions between customers and clerks, some theorists have proposed that the sociability of the customer is the critical factor in determining the sociability of the interaction (Hester, Koger, & McCauley, 1985). Hester et al. (1985) reported that the customer's sociability will determine the sociability of the salesperson, for the salesperson appears to adapt to and mimic the sociability of the customer. Furthermore, Segal and McCauley (1986) reported that sociability of customer-clerk interactions is only minimally affected by factors such as urbanism of location of interaction and business of the location. Thus they too indicated that customer sociability plays a crucial role in determining the quality of customer-clerk interactions.

Although customer sociability is believed to be a key factor in determining the quality of social interactions, one must also consider the effect of first impressions as a determinant of the quality of these interactions. Past research indicates that individuals tend to form impressions and make judgments of others on the basis of cues, including facial expression, gestures, and dress (Hamid, 1972). Hamid examined the effects of glasses and make-up on impression formation and judgments and discovered that female actors who wore no make-up and glasses were perceived as being conservative while actors who wore make—up and no glasses were perceived as intelligent, neat, and self—confident. These stereotypical responses occurred despite the fact that the subjects had neither seen nor communicated with the actors before. This indicates that individuals tend to make intrinsic judgments about a person based on external cues. Francis and Evans (1987) further demonstrated the significant affects of personal coloring and garment style on the assessment of personality trait factors such as emotional, sociable, adaptable, and scientific. Additional research has also confirmed that there is an overall general tendency to form impressions of strangers primarily on the basis of physical/biological traits (e.g., being well dressed and physically attractive) (Lennon & Davis, 1989).

The impressions that individuals form of others, while at times accurate judgments of intrinsic characteristics, nevertheless often prove to be inaccurate. In addition, once individuals integrate external information into their impression of a person it is very difficult to discount such information (Tetlock, 1983). One can see how impression formation can play a critical role in determining the quality of social interactions, for individuals tend to make intrinsic trait assumptions of others based on external cues. This tendency in turn alters their behavior toward the

Impression Formation
5

individual according to their preconceived perception of the individual. Furthermore, social interactions can be greatly hindered when the impressions one forms are inaccurate.

The purpose of the present study is to examine the effects of physical appearance and dress on impression formation and to determine how the formed impression of a customer will consequently affect the quality of customer-clerk interactions. Based on the previous research indicating the effect of dress cues on impression formation, it is proposed that the manipulation of dress and physical appearance will have a significant affect on the sociability of customer-clerk interactions.

Method

Subjects

The study included nine salespersons employed at various stores located in a large suburban shopping center. The subjects were unaware of the fact that an observational study was in progress.

Materials

A previously developed observational measure of sociability or friendliness of public interaction was used to determine the sociability of each clerk (Segal & McCauley, 1986). The clerk's sociability was scored based on the following six behaviors: (a) greeting; (b) conversation; (c) farewell (0=none; 1=routine, conversational; 2=friendly, personal recognition); (d) smiles; (e) facial regard (0=none; 1=one or two briefly; 2=three or more; 3=more or less continuous); and (f) overall tone (1=unfriendly; 2=functional, routine; 3=friendly; 4=personal recognition, willingness to go beyond business at hand). In addition, the time taken to initiate the interaction (minutes), the duration of the interaction (minutes), and the prices of the first two watches shown were recorded.

Procedure

The study was conducted by three experimenters (one male and two females) at a large suburban shopping center on a Sunday afternoon between 11AM and 4PM. The two female experimenters (Actor 1 and Actor 2) posed as customers in a customer-clerk interaction while the male experimenter served as the Stable Observer of the interaction. Additionally, Actor 1 and Actor 2 served as observers when not directly participating in the interaction.

To test the effects of dress and appearance cues on impression formation and the quality of customer-clerk interactions, Actor 1 was at first dressed in a beige tailored suit, wore high-heeled shoes, and carried a leather handbag. In addition, she wore gold jewelry and make-up and had her hair neatly arranged. Actor 2 wore an old blue hooded sweatshirt, blue sweat-pants, and old

Impression Formation

7

running sneakers. She additionally wore glasses, no make-
up, and no jewelry, and had her hair combed straight back.
In each interaction Actor 1 entered a store, approached a
jewelry counter, and began to look at watches. A jewelry
counter was chosen as a site for the interaction because
of the ease of observation of the interaction and the high
probability of obtaining the same clerk for both Actor 1
and Actor 2. Actor 2 and the Stable Observer also
approached the jewelry counter or surrounding areas
(within 10—20 feet of Actor 1) in order to record the
sociability of the clerk.

The basic scenario involved the salesperson
approaching Actor 1 and inquiring if she needed
assistance, to which Actor 1 was instructed to respond
that she was interested in purchasing a watch. If Actor 1
were asked if she had a price range in mind, she was to
respond that she had no price range. This measure was
taken to allow for the clerk to make a decision as to the
price of the watch that Actor 1 could afford based on
his/her impression of Actor 1. After being shown a minimum
of two watches, Actor 1 thanked the salesperson for
his/her help and departed.

After the interaction, Actor 2 and the Stable
observer scored the sociability of the clerk on small
notepads that had been concealed in their pockets during
the interaction. Actor 2 and the Stable Observer were on
opposite sides of Actor 1; thus, each was unaware of the

degree of sociability recorded by the other. After the
interaction involving Actor 1 was complete and the data
recorded, approximately five minutes elapsed before Actor
2 approached the same jewelry counter. Actor 2 then
engaged in an interaction with the clerk using the same
dialogue as Actor 1. The Stable Observer and Actor 1
scored the sociability of the clerk. The Stable Observer
also timed the initiation of each interaction and the
duration of each interaction. This procedure was repeated
in five large department stores and four smaller jewelry
stores. This measure was taken to determine whether the
clerk's sociability would vary according to store type.

Results

Analysis of the results of the sociability scale
indicated significant differences in each of the six
behavioral ratings of the clerk's sociability with respect
to Actor 1 and Actor 2. In Actor 1/Actor 2 evaluation of
the clerk's interaction with both Actor 1 and Actor 2,
significant differences were seen with respect to the
clerk's greeting ($t(16)=4.81$, $p<.000$), conversation ($t(16)$
$=2.98$, $p<.009$), farewell ($t(16)=3.58$, $p<.003$), smile
($t(16)=5.41$, $p<.000$), facial regard ($t(16)=8.50$, $p<.000$),
and overall tone ($t(16)=3.50$, $p<.008$) using two-tailed t-
tests for independent samples. Each clerk's sociability
rating tended to be higher when interacting with Actor 1
than when interacting with Actor 2. Means and standard

deviations of the six behavioral scores are presented in Table 1.

Insert Table 1 here

The results of the Stable Observer's evaluation of the clerk's behavior when interacting with Actor 1 and Actor 2 also indicated significant differences in the clerk's greeting ($t(16)=4.81$, $p<.001$), conversation ($t(16)=2.98$, $p<.009$), farewell ($t(16)=4.37$, $p<.000$), smiles ($t(16)=6.43$, $p<.000$), facial regard ($t(16)=8.50$, $p<.000$), and overall tone ($t(16)=4.38$, $p<.000$) using two-tailed t-tests for independent samples. The Stable Observer also rated the clerk as being more sociable when interacting with Actor 1 than when interacting with Actor 2. Means and standard deviations of the six behavioral scores are presented in Table 1.

Inter-rater reliability was shown to be significant in each of the six behaviors rated: greeting ($r=.94$), conversation ($r=1.00$), farewell ($r=.94$), smile ($r=.98$), facial regard ($r=1.00$), and overall tone ($r=.93$), $p<.001$, 1-tailed, for all correlations.

The overall evaluations by Actor 1/Actor 2 and the Stable Observer of clerk sociability in six behaviors over 18 interactions were shown to be strikingly similar. Means and standard deviations are presented in Table 2.

Insert Table 2 here

Significant differences were also noted in the prices of the first two watches shown to Actor 1 and Actor 2 (t(14)=5.73, and 2.95, respectively, p<.01, two-tailed t-test for independent samples). Actor 1 tended to be shown higher priced watches (watch #1, $\bar{x}$=$433.33; S.D.=98.68; watch #2, $\bar{x}$=$730.00; S.D.=457.24) than Actor 2 (watch #1, $\bar{x}$=$196.42; S.D.=51.94; watch #2, $\bar{x}$=$215.00; S.D.=38.30).

The amount of time until the initiation of the interaction (minutes) was also shown to be significantly shorter (t(16)=−3.91, p<.001) and the duration of the interaction significantly longer (t(16)=2.98, p<.009; two-tailed t-tests for independent samples) for interactions involving Actor 1 as opposed to Actor 2. Means and standard deviations are presented in Table 3.

Insert Table 3 here

Discussion

The results of the study clearly support the proposed hypothesis that physical appearance and dress influence impression formation which will consequently affect the quality of social interactions, namely customer–clerk interactions. It was demonstrated that each salesperson tended to be more sociable to the well–dressed Actor 1 than he/she was to the poorly dressed Actor 2 despite the lack of variation in behavior or dialogue between the two actors. Both the Stable Observer and Actor 1/Actor 2 rated each salesperson as generally exhibiting a more friendly greeting ($\bar{x}$=1.78; S.D.=.44) and conversation ($\bar{x}$=1.67; S.D. =.50) when interacting with Actor 1 as opposed to Actor 2. In addition, a higher degree of smiles ($\bar{x}$=2.67; S.D.=.50) and facial regard ($\bar{x}$=2.67; S.D.=.50) were recorded in each clerk's interaction with Actor 1. This suggests that each salesperson tended to form different impressions about Actor 1 and Actor 2 based on dress and physical appearance cues, for these two factors were the only intended differences between the interactions. The role of dress could be confirmed in future studies through the use of a single actor posing as both a poorly dressed customer and a well-dressed customer, thus eliminating the influence of differing personality factors of each actor on the clerk's sociability. Nevertheless, the differences in impressions formed led each clerk to behave in a more sociable manner to the well-dressed, physically attractive Actor 1.

The degree to which dress cues can influence impression formation and judgment is further demonstrated by the prices of the watches shown to Actor 1 (watch #1, $\bar{x}$=$433.33; watch #2, $\bar{x}$=$730.00) and Actor 2 (watch #1, $\bar{x}$=$196.43; watch #2, $\bar{x}$=$215.00). The salesperson in each case clearly made the assumption that a well-dressed customer would be interested in a more expensive watch, while a poorly dressed customer would be interested in a less expensive watch. The impression formation was so strong in one case that the clerk recommended Actor 2

Impression Formation
12

visit a store which sold less expensive watches. Thus,
each clerk made judgments about each Actor despite a lack
of information about the person's socioeconomic status.
The appearance of each Actor also influenced the amount of
time taken for service. In all cases the well-dressed
Actor was waited on sooner. In fact, in two stores the
poorly dressed Actor could not get waited on for 15
minutes and therefore, left the store. The duration of the
interaction was also shorter for Actor 2, and in most
cases the conversation was very routine, involving no
friendliness or personal recognition.

The results further indicated a high inter-rater
reliability in the subjective measurement of each clerk's
behavior. It must be noted that a potential weakness in
the results exists due to the fact that each observer was
previously aware of the hypothesis being tested. Thus, the
potential for biased observations does exist. However,
this factor appears not to have significantly influenced
the results, for the objective measurements (i.e., price
of watches shown, time of initiation of interaction, and
duration of interaction) also indicated the tendency of
each clerk to form different impressions of each Actor
based on appearance.

The results of the present study support previous
research indicating the effects of physical appearance and
dress on impression formation (Hamid, 1972; Francis &
Evans, 1987). This noted importance of dress cues on

Impression Formation
13

impression formation and resulting social interactions can have important implications in situations other than customer—clerk interactions, for dress is an integral part of one's appearance; thus, one must pay particular attention to mode of dress when trying to convey a given impression, particularly in situations such as job interviews.

Impression Formation
14

References

Francis, S. K., & Evans, P. K. (1987). Effects of hue,
value, and style of garment and personal coloring of
model on person perception. Perceptual and Motor
Skills, 64, 383–390.

Hamid, P. N. (1972). Some effects of dress cues on
observational accuracy, a perceptual estimate, and
impression formation. Journal of Social Psychology,
86, 279–289.

Hester, L., Koger, P., & McCauley, C. (1985). Individual
differences in customer sociability. European Journal
of Social Psychology, 15, 453–456.

Lennon, S. J., & Davis, L. L. (1989). Categorization in
first impressions. Journal of Psychology, 123(5),
439–446.

Segal, M. E., & McCauley, C. R. (1986). The sociability
of commercial exchange in rural, suburban, and urban
locations: A test of the urban overload hypothesis.
Basic and Applied Social Psychology, 7(2), 115–135.

Tetlock, P. E. (1983). Accountability and the
perserverance of first impressions. Social Psychology
Quarterly, 46(4), 285–292.

Table 1. Mean (S.D.) Scores, and Correlations of Inter-rater Reliability of Actor 1/Actor 2 and Stable Observer's Rating of Salesperson Sociability

| | Actor 1/Actor 2 Rating[c] | | | | Stable Observer's Rating[c] | | | | Inter-rater Reliability[d] |
| | Clerk 1[a] | | Clerk 2[b] | | Clerk 1[a] | | Clerk 2[b] | | Correlation Coefficient |
	$\bar{x}$	S.D.	$\bar{x}$	S.D.	$\bar{x}$	S.D.	$\bar{x}$	S.D.	
Greeting	1.78	0.44	0.78	0.44	1.78	0.44	0.78	0.44	0.87
Conversation	1.67	0.50	0.89	0.60	1.67	0.50	0.89	0.60	1.00
Farewell	1.78	0.44	0.89	0.60	1.89	0.33	0.89	0.60	0.94
Smile	2.56	0.53	0.78	0.83	2.56	0.53	0.67	0.71	0.98
Facial Regard	2.67	0.50	0.78	0.44	2.67	0.50	0.78	0.44	1.00
Overall tone	2.78	0.67	1.44	1.13	2.89	0.60	1.22	0.97	0.93

N = 9 for both Clerk 1 and Clerk 2.
[a]Clerk 1 is clerk interacting with Actor 1.
[b]Clerk 2 is clerk interacting with Actor 2.
[c]All means differ significantly, $p < .01$, by two-tailed t-test for independent samples.
[d]All correlations differ significantly, $p \leq .001$, by two-tailed t-test for paired samples.

Table 2. Mean (S.D.) Scores of Actor 1/Actor 2 and Stable
Observer's Overall Evaluation of Clerk Sociability

	Actor 1/Actor 2 Evaluation		Stable Observer's Evaluation	
	$\bar{x}$	S.D.	$\bar{x}$	S.D.
Greeting	1.28	0.67	1.28	0.67
Conversation	1.28	0.67	1.28	0.67
Farewell	1.33	0.67	1.39	0.70
Smile	1.67	1.14	1.61	1.14
Facial Regard	1.72	1.07	1.72	1.07
Overall Tone	2.11	1.13	2.06	1.16

$N = 18$
All means are significantly different, $p < .001$, by two-tailed
t-test for paired samples.

Table 3. Mean (S.D.) Scores of Prices of Watches, Time to Approach, and Time of Interaction

	Price of Watch #1		Price of Watch #2		Time to Approach (minutes)		Time of Interaction (minutes)	
	x̄	S.D.	x̄	S.D.	x̄	S.D.	x̄	S.D.
Actor 1	$433.33	98.68	$730.00	457.24	5.11	2.03	3.11	0.78
Actor 2	$196.43	51.94	$215.00	38.30	10.11	3.26	1.78	1.09

N=9 for all cases except for Actor 2 price of watch #1 and watch #2 (n=7).
All means differ significantly, $p < .01$, by two-tailed t-test for independent samples.

Writing in the Natural and Applied Sciences

Writing in the natural and applied sciences relies on **empirical data**—information derived from observations or experiments. Although science writing may be persuasive, it is often expository, concerned with accurately reporting observations and experimental data.

Basic to research in the natural and applied sciences is the **scientific method**—a way in which scientists gather and interpret information.

The Scientific Method

1. Define a problem you want to solve or an event you want to explain. Conduct a search of the literature to find out what previous work has been done on the problem.
2. Formulate a hypothesis that attempts to explain the problem.
3. Plan a method of investigation that will allow you to test your hypothesis.
4. Carry out your experiment. Make careful observations, and record your data.
5. Analyze the results of your experiment. Determine whether or not it supports your initial hypothesis. Revise your hypothesis, if you can, to account for any discrepancies. Plan further research that may help you account for the phenomena you have observed.

 **44a** *Research Sources*

The methods of data collection in the sciences frequently entail observation and experimental research. Most results are tabulated and presented graphically. In addition, however, scientists often carry out literature searches to determine what other work has been done in their areas of interest.

(1) Specialized library sources

The *Science Citation Index* is one of the most widely used indexes in the sciences. Because scientists are particularly interested in the number of times and the variety of sources in which an author is cited, they use citation indexes frequently. In addition to the *Science Citation Index,* the following specific sources are useful.

General Science

> *Applied Science and Technology Index*
> *CRC Handbook of Chemistry and Physics* (and other titles in the CRC series of handbooks)
> *Current Contents*
> *General Science Index*
> *McGraw-Hill Encyclopedia of Science and Technology*
> *Scientific and Technical Information Sources*

Chemistry

> *Analytical Abstracts*
> *Chemical Abstracts*
> *Chemical Technology*
> *Dictionary of Organic Compounds*
> *Kirk-Othmer Encyclopedia of Chemical Technology*
> *Van Nostrand Reinhold Encyclopedia of Chemistry*

Engineering

> *Engineering Index*
> *Environment Abstracts*
> *Government Reports Announcements* (NTIS)
> *HRIS Abstracts* (Highway Engineering)
> *Pollution Abstracts*
> *Selected Water Resources Abstracts*

Earth Sciences

> *Abstracts of North American Geology*
> *Annotated Bibliography of Economic Geology*
> *Bibliography and Index of Geology*

Bibliography of North American Geology
Climatology and Data (U.S. Environmental Data Service)
Encyclopedia of Earth Sciences
Geophysical Abstracts
Publications of the USGS

Life Sciences

G. F. Zimek's Animal Life Encyclopedia
Annotated Index to Nursing and Allied Health Literature
Biological Abstracts
Biological and Agricultural Index
A Dictionary of Genetics
Encyclopedia of Bioethics
Encyclopedia of the Biological Sciences
Environmental Abstracts Annual
Index Medicus
International Dictionary of Medicine and Biology

Mathematics

Current Index to Statistics
Encyclopedia of Statistical Sciences
Encyclopedic Dictionary of Mathematics
Mathematical Reviews
Universal Encyclopedia of Mathematics

Physics

Astronomy and Astrophysics Abstracts
Encyclopedia of Physics
Encyclopedic Dictionary of Physics
Physics Abstracts
Solid State Abstracts Journal

(2) *Specialized databases for computer searches*

As in other disciplines, many print indexes are available online. Helpful databases for research in the sciences include *BIOSIS Previews, CASearch, SCISEARCH, Agvicola, CAB Abstracts, Compendex, NTIS, Inspec, MEDLINE, MATHSCI, Life Sciences Collection, GEOREF, Zoological Record Online,* and *World Patents Index.*

(3)   Other sources of information

Specific sources outside the library vary greatly because of the many subjects that make up the sciences. In agronomy, for example, researchers collect soil samples; in toxicology, they test air or water quality. In marine biology, they might conduct research in a particular aquatic environment, while in chemistry they conduct experiments to identify an unknown substance. Scientists also conduct surveys: epidemiologists study the spread of communicable diseases, and cancer researchers question populations to determine how environmental or dietary factors influence the likelihood of contracting cancer.

44b   *Assignments in the Sciences*

Many writing assignments in a science class are similar to those assigned in other disciplines. Three additional assignments common in (but not limited to) scientific disciplines are the abstract, the literature survey, and the laboratory report.

(1)   The abstract

Most scientific articles begin with summaries called **abstracts,** which serve as road maps or guides for readers. Many scientific indexes also provide abstracts of articles so that researchers can determine whether an article is of use to them. An **indicative abstract** merely indicates what the content of an article is. It helps readers decide whether the article will be of use to them and whether they want to read it in full. An annotated bibliography is made up of short indicative abstracts that follow each complete citation in the bibliography. An **informative abstract** is detailed enough so that readers can obtain essential information without reading the article itself.

When writing an abstract, follow the format of the article. In 200 to 500 words, state the purpose, method of research, results, and conclusion in the order in which they occur in the paper, but include essential information only. Interpretation and criticism are not included in an abstract. Avoid quoting from the article or repeating the title. An abstract should provide clear information for a wide audience; therefore, use a minimum of technical vocabulary.

Abstract—Biology

"Purification to Near Homogeneity of Bovine Transforming
Epithelial Growth Factor," by Stephen McManus, Cooperative
Education Student, Smith, Kline & French.

The control of cellular proliferation is known to be
mediated at an extra-cellular level by polypeptide growth
factors; examples include epidermal growth factor (EGF),
platelet-derived growth factor (PDGF), and transforming
growth factors alpha and beta (TGF-a, TGF-β). The
transforming growth factors are so called because of their
ability to induce anchorage-independent growth of selected
target cell lines. Our studies have identified an
apparently novel growth factor activity associated with
epithelial cells and tissues. This activity, termed
epithelial transforming growth factor (TGFe), is
identified by the anchorage-independent growth of the SW13
epithelial cell line, derived from human adrenocortical
carcinoma. The purification of this factor was
accomplished by a multi-step chromatography and
electrophoretic process. The total purification was
estimated as 6×10^5-fold with 1% recovery, corresponding
to a yield of 0.1μg TGf-e/kg bovine kidney.

(2) The literature survey

Literature surveys are commonly used in the sciences, usually as
a section of a proposal or as part of a research paper. Unlike an
abstract, which summarizes a paper's points, a literature survey
summarizes the work of others and sometimes compares and contrasts it. By doing so, the literature survey provides a theoretical
context for the discussion.

Literature Survey—Parasitology

Ultrastructural studies of micro- and macrogametes
have included relatively few of the numerous Eimerian
species. Major early studies include the following (hosts
are listed in parentheses): micro- and macrogametes of E.

performans (rabbits), E. stiedae (rabbits), E. bovis
(cattle), and E. auburnensis (cattle) (Hammond et al.,
1967; Scholtyseck et al., 1966), macrogametogenesis in E.
Magna (rabbits) and E. intestinalis (rabbits) (Kheysin,
1965), macrogametogony of E. tenella (chickens) (McLaren,
1969), and the microgametocytes and macrogametes of E.
neischulzi (rats) (Colley, 1967). More recent
investigations have included macrogametogony of E.
acervulina (chickens) (Pitillo and Ball, 1984).

(3) The laboratory report

A laboratory report is perhaps the most common assignment for students taking courses in the sciences. It is divided into sections that reflect the stages of the scientific method and generally conform to the specifications for the laboratory report outlined below. Not every section will be necessary for every experiment, and some experiments may call for additional components, such as abstracts or references. In addition, a lab experiment will often include tables, charts, graphs, and illustrations. Much of the time the exact format of a student lab report is defined by the lab manual being used in a specific course.

In general, a lab report is an explanation of a process. For this reason, it is important for you to explain stages clearly and completely, to present steps in exact chronological order, and to illustrate the purpose of each step. In addition, you must provide clear descriptions of the equipment used in an experiment.

Laboratory Report—Chemistry

Purpose   In this section you describe the object of the experiment. In many cases you present the hypothesis that you are going to test or examine.

The purpose of this lab is to determine the iron
content of an unknown mixture containing an iron salt by
titration with potassium permanganate solution.

Equation to find % of Fe: $5Fe^{2+} + MnO_{4-} + 8H^+ = 5Fe^{3+} + Mn^{2+} + 4H_2O$

Equipment   In this section you present the equipment that you will use in the experiment. Often this section identifies and explains the methodology used.

Equipment includes two 60 ml beakers, a graduated
cylinder, a scale, 600 ml of distilled water, 2 grams of
H_2SO_4, 5 grams of $KMnO_4$, 100 ml of $H_2C_2O_4 \cdot 2H_2O$, and a Bunsen
burner.

Procedure   In this section you describe the steps of the experiment. You usually number the steps and present them in the order in which they occur.

1) Prepare a $KMnO_4$ solution by dissolving 1.5 grams of
$KMnO_4$ in 500 ml of distilled water.

2) Weigh two samples of $H_2C_2O_4 \cdot 2H_2O$ of about 0.2 grams
each.

3) Dissolve each sample in 60ml of H_2O and 30 ml of H_2SO_4
in a 250 ml beaker.

4) Heat the mixture to 80°C and titrate slowly with $KMnO_4$
until the mixture turns pink.

5) Repeat the procedure.

Results   In this section you present the results that you obtained from your experiments. These results can be observations, measurements, or equations.

Percentage of iron: 1st run = 12.51 ml

2nd run = 11.2 ml

Conclusion or Discussion of Results   In this section you explain your results or justify them in terms of the methodology you described in the *Purpose* section.

Calculation for % of iron

$$\frac{12.5 \text{ ml} \times .01894 \text{ M}}{1000 \text{ ml/1}} \times \frac{5 \text{ moles Fe}}{1 \text{ mole MnO}_4} \times \frac{55.85 \text{ g/mol}}{.5\text{g}} \times 100$$

$$= \frac{66.11}{500} = 13.22 \text{ % Fe}$$

44c *Conventions of Style and Documentation*

(1) Style

When writing a lab report or any scientific paper, you may want to use the passive voice to emphasize the tasks themselves rather than the person performing them. Avoid using the second person—that is, avoid giving instructions and directions. It is acceptable to use the first person when writing about your own experiment. Direct quotations are seldom used in scientific papers.

Think of the purpose of your writing as providing information for other scientists. You should attempt to write clearly so that scientists in your discipline can understand your meaning. Remember that overreliance on technical jargon can hamper the clarity of your paper. Many times a scientific paper will include a glossary that lists and defines terms that may be unfamiliar to readers (see **44d**).

Tables and illustrations are an important part of most scientific papers. Be careful to place tables as close to the discussion of them as possible and to number and label any type of illustration or diagram so that you can refer to it in your text.

In preparing any scientific paper, remember that different scientific journals follow different conventions of style and format. For example, although the *CBE Style Manual* governs the overall presentation of papers in biology, the *Journal of Immunology* might have a different format from the *Journal of Parasitology*. (The *CBE Style Manual* lists the different journals that use their own style formats.) Your instructor may ask you to prepare your paper according to the style sheet of the journal to which you might wish to submit your work. Although publication may seem a remote possibility to you, using a particular style helps to underscore the fact that writing in the sciences may involve writing for a variety of different audiences.

Each professional society also prescribes the formats of charts and the way they are to be referred to in the text. Therefore, you cannot use one format for all the sciences. You should also learn the various abbreviations with which journals are referred to in the reference sections of science papers. For example, *The American Journal of Physiology* is abbreviated Amer. J. Physiol., and *The Journal of Physiological Chemistry* is abbreviated J. of Physiol Chemistry. Note that in CBE style, the abbreviated forms of journal titles are *not* underlined in the reference list.

(2) Documentation

Documentation style varies from one scientific discipline to another; even within each discipline, style may vary from one discipline to another. For this reason, you should ask your instructor which documentation format is required. Most disciplines in the sciences

758

use the formats prescribed by their professional societies. For instance, electrical engineers use the format of the Institute for Electronics and Electrical Engineers, chemists use the format of the American Chemical Society, physicists use the format of the American Institute of Physics, mathematicians use the format of the American Mathematical Society, and biologists use the Council of Biology Editors (CBE) Style Sheet (**see 39c**).

44d *Sample Science Research Paper*

(1) Council of Biology Editors (CBE) Format

The following excerpts from a biology research paper, "Maternal Smoking: Deleterious Effects on the Fetus," uses one of the documentation styles recommended by the CBE Style Manual. Note that the full paper included an abstract like the one in 44b1.

Maternal Smoking

1

June M. Fahrman

Biology 306

April 17, 1992

Maternal Smoking: Deleterious

Effects on the Fetus

Introduction

The placenta, lifeline between fetus and mother, has
been the subject of various studies aimed at determining
the mechanisms by which substances in the mother's
bloodstream affect the fetus. For example, cigarette
smoking is clearly associated with an increased risk in
the incidence of low birthweight infants, due both to
prematurity and to intrauterine growth retardation. (1)

Introduction gives background and introduces problem.

Development of the Placenta

At the morula stage of development, less than one
week after fertilization, two types of cells can be
distinguished. . . .

This section presents an overview of how the placenta develops.

Maternal Smoking and Perinatal Events

Perinatal events associated with maternal smoking
during pregnancy have been the subject of numerous studies
over the past thirty years. One study, by M. Meyer et al.
(7), reported the following events. . . .

This section discusses the effect of smoking on the development of the fetus.

Proposed Mechanisms

Speculation abounds as to the mechanism involved by
which maternal smoking reduces fetal growth. Reduction in

This section discusses the various effects of smoking on fetal growth.

Maternal Smoking
2

maternal blood flow, inhalation of carbon monoxide,

nicotine, cadmium, and cyanide have been indicated. . .

Conclusion

Conclusion
summarizes
the study's
results.

    In summary, abundant evidence exists as to the

harmful effects maternal smoking may have on the fetus.

These include low birthweight, low IQ scores, minimal

brain dysfunction, shorter stature, perinatal mortality,

and premature birth. . .

Maternal Smoking
11

GLOSSARY

1. ABRUPTO PLACENTA--Partial or complete premature
   separation of a normally implanted placenta.

2. CATECHOLAMINES--Pyrocatechols with an alkylamine side
   chain; examples of biological interest are epinephrine,
   norepinephrine and dopa.

3. HYPOXIA--Decrease below normal levels of oxygen in air,
   blood, or tissue, short of anoxia.

4. MINIMAL BRAIN DYSFUNCTION--Also referred to as
   hyperactivity and/or attention deficit disorder.

5. NEONATAL PERIOD--Newborn; related to period immediately
   succeeding birth through the first 28 days.

6. PERINATAL PERIOD--Period before delivery from the
   twenty-eighth week of gestation to the first seven days
   after delivery.

Maternal Smoking

12

References

1. Rakel, Robert E. Conn's current therapy 1988.
   Philadelphia: W.B. Saunders; 1988.

2. Meberg, A.; Sande, H.; Foss, O. P.; Stenwig, J. T.
   Smoking during pregnancy—effects on the fetus and on
   thiocyanate levels in mother and baby. Acta Paediatr
   Scand 68:547–552; 1979.

3. Lehtovirta, P.; Forss, M. The acute effect of smoking
   on intervillous blood flow of the placenta. Brit Obs
   Gyn. 85:729–731; 1978.

4. Phelan, Jeffrey P. Diminished fetal reactivity with
   smoking. Amer Obs Gyn. 136:230–233; 1980.

5. VanDerVelde, W. J. Structural changes in the placenta
   of smoking mothers: a quantitative study. Placenta. 4:
   231–240; 1983.

6. Asmussen, I. Ultrastructure of the villi and fetal
   capillaries in placentas from smoking and nonsmoking
   mothers. Brit Obs Gyn. 87:239–245; 1980.

7. Meyer, M. Perinatal events associated with maternal
   smoking during pregnancy. Amer Epid. 103(5):464–476;
   1976.

Writing Essay Examinations

Taking examinations is a skill, one you have been practicing throughout your life as a student. Although both short-answer and essay examinations require you to study, to recall what you know, and to budget your time carefully as you write your answers, only essay questions ask you to synthesize information and to arrange ideas in a series of clear, logically connected sentences. To write an essay examination, you must do more than memorize facts; you must see the relationships among many facts and be able to infer from them a meaning that is greater than the sum of its parts. In other words, you must think critically about your subject.

45a *Planning an Essay Examination*

Because you are under pressure during an examination and tend to write quickly, you may be tempted to skip the planning and revision stages. But if you write in a frenzy and hand in your examination without a second glance, you are likely to produce a disorganized or even incoherent answer. With advance planning and sensible editing, you can write an answer that clearly demonstrates your understanding of the material.

Steps in Planning For An Essay Examination

1. Review your material.
2. Consider your audience and purpose.

---

continued

continued from previous page

> 3. Read through the entire examination.
> 4. Read each question very carefully.
> 5. Brainstorm to find ideas.

(1) Review your material

Be sure you know beforehand the scope and format of the examination. How much of your text and class notes will the examination cover—the entire semester's work or only the material covered since the last test? Will you have to answer every question, or will you be able to choose among alternatives? Will the examination be composed entirely of short-answer questions, or will it include one-sentence, one-paragraph, or essay-length answers? Will the examination emphasize your recall of specific facts or your ability to demonstrate your understanding of the course material by drawing conclusions?

Examinations challenge you to recall and express in writing what you already know—what you have read, what you have heard in class, what you have reviewed in your notes. Before you even begin any examination, then, you will have studied for it: reread your text and class notes, underlined key points, and perhaps outlined key sections of your notes. When you prepare for a short-answer examination, you may memorize facts—the definition of pointillism, the date of Queen Victoria's death, the formula for a quadratic equation, three reasons for the fall of Rome, two examples of conditioned reflexes, four features of a feudal economy, six steps in the process of synthesizing Vitamin C—without analyzing their relationship to one another or to a body of knowledge as a whole. When you prepare for an essay examination, however, you must do more than remember information; you must also make connections among ideas.

When you are certain you know what to expect, you should try to anticipate the essay questions your instructor might ask. As you study, note key concepts and the connections among them, and practice answering likely essay questions. Try out potential questions on classmates, and see whether you can brainstorm together on a few of them.

(2) Consider your audience and purpose

The *audience* for any examination is almost always the instructor who prepared it. He or she already knows the answers to the questions and a great deal more about the subject. As you read the questions, think about what your instructor has emphasized in class. Although you may certainly arrange material in a new way or use it to make your own point, keep in mind that your *purpose* is to demonstrate that you understand the material, not to make clever remarks or introduce irrelevant information.

You should also consider the wider academic audience your in-structor represents and make every effort to use the specific vocab-ulary of the field and to follow any discipline-specific conventions your instructor has discussed.

▶ **See 41c**

(3)   Read through the entire examination

Your time is usually limited when you take an examination, so you must plan carefully. How long should a "short-answer" or "one-paragraph" or "essay-length" answer be? How much time should you devote to answering each question? The question itself may specify the time allotted for each answer, so look for that information. More often the point value of each question or the number of questions on the examination will determine how much time to spend on each answer. If an essay question is worth 50 out of 100 points, for example, you will probably have to spend at least half and perhaps more of your time planning, writing, and proof-reading your answer.

Before you begin to write, read the entire examination carefully to determine your priorities and your strategy. First, be sure that your copy of the test is complete and that you understand the format each question requires. If you need clarification, ask your instructor or proctor for help. Then decide where to start. Responding first to short answers (or to questions whose answers you are sure of) is usually a good strategy. This tactic ensures that you will not be bogged down in a question that baffles you, leaving too little time to write a strong answer to a question you understand well. More-over, starting with the questions you are sure of can help build your confidence.

(4)   Read each question very carefully

To answer correctly, you need to know exactly what the question asks. As you read any essay question, you may find it helpful to underline key words and important terms.

SOCIOLOGY: Distinguish among Social Darwinism, instinct theory, and sociobiology, giving examples of each.

MUSIC: Explain how Milton Babbitt used the computer to
         expand Schoenberg's twelve-tone method.

PHILOSOPHY: Define existentialism and identify three influential exis-
              tentialist works, explaining why they are important.

Look carefully at the wording of the examination question. If the
question calls for a *comparison and contrast* of *two* styles of management, a *description* or *analysis* of *one* style, no matter how well
done, will not be acceptable. If the question asks for causes *and*
effects, a comprehensive discussion of causes alone will not do. The
wording of the question suggests what you should emphasize. For
instance, an American history instructor would expect very different
answers to the following two examination questions.

1. Give a detailed explanation of the major causes of the Great Depression, noting briefly some of the effects of the economic collapse on
   the United States. (1 hour)
2. Give a detailed summary of the effects of the Great Depression on
   the United States, briefly discussing the major causes of the economic
   collapse. (1 hour)

Although the questions above look somewhat alike, the first calls
for an essay that focuses on *causes,* whereas the second asks you
to stress the *effects.*

Key Words in Examination Questions

- Explain
- Compare
- Contrast
- Trace
- Evaluate
- Discuss
- Interpret

- Clarify
- Relate
- Justify
- Analyze
- Summarize
- Describe

- Classify
- Identify
- Illustrate
- Define
- Support
- Summarize

---

(5)   Brainstorm to find ideas

Once you understand the question, begin brainstorming. The
brainstorming process will help reveal the scope of your knowledge.
If you know your material well, you may be able to brainstorm
mentally. Generally speaking, though, you should quickly list all
the relevant points you can remember; then select key points and
delete less promising ones. You might even tentatively arrange the

key points you have arrived at. A quick review of your ideas should lead you toward a workable thesis for your essay answer. (Sometimes, particularly if you are very familiar with your material and have a thesis firmly in mind, you may find it more practical to brainstorm as you prepare your scratch outline.)

45b   *Shaping an Examination Answer*

(1)   *Finding a thesis*

Often you can rephrase the examination question as a thesis statement. For example, the second American history examination question above suggests this thesis:

EFFECTIVE THESIS

> The Great Depression, caused by the American government's economic policies, had major political, economic, and social effects on the United States.

An effective thesis addresses all aspects of the question but highlights only relevant concerns. The following thesis statements are not effective:

VAGUE: The Great Depression, caused largely by profligate spending patterns, had a number of very important results.

INCOMPLETE: The Great Depression caused major upheaval in the United States.

IRRELEVANT: The Great Depression, caused largely by America's poor response to the 1929 stock market crash, had more important consequences than World War II.

(2)   *Making a scratch outline*

Because time is limited, you should plan your answer before you write it. Therefore, once you have decided on a suitable thesis, you should make a scratch outline of your major points.

Write on the inside cover of your exam book or on its last sheet. Use the pattern of development suggested by the question—process, classification, or cause and effect, for instance—to shape your outline, and list your supporting points in the approximate order in which you plan to discuss them. Once you have an outline, check it against the question to make certain it covers everything the question requires—and only what the question requires.

A scratch outline for an answer to the American history question might look like this:

QUESTION: Give a detailed summary of the effects of the Great Depression on the United States, briefly discussing the major causes of the economic collapse.

THESIS: The Great Depression, caused by the American government's economic policies, had major political, economic, and social effects on the United States.

SUPPORTING POINTS: *Causes*
American economic policies: income poorly distributed, factories expanded too much, more goods produced than could be purchased.
Effects
1. Economic situation worsened—farmers, businesses, workers, and stock market all affected.
2. Roosevelt elected—closed banks, worked with Congress to enact emergency measures.
3. Reform—TVA, AAA, NIRA, etc.
4. Social Security Act, WPA, PWA

An answer based on this outline will correctly follow a *cause-and-effect* pattern (see **4f5**), with an emphasis on effects, not causes.

45c *Writing and Revising an Examination Answer*

Referring to your thesis and your outline, you can now draft your answer. A simple statement of your thesis that summarizes your answer is your best *introduction*, for it shows the reader that you are addressing the question directly. Do not bother crafting an elaborate or unusual introduction; your time is precious, and so is your reader's.

To develop the *body* of the essay, follow your outline point by point, using clear topic sentences and transitions to indicate your progression and to help the reader see that you are answering the question in full. Such signals, along with parallel sentence structure and repeated key words, make your answer easy to follow.

The most effective *conclusion* for an essay examination is a clear, simple restatement of the thesis or a summary of the essay's main points.

Essay answers should be complete and detailed, but they should not contain irrelevant material. Every unnecessary fact or opinion only increases your chance of error. Do not repeat yourself or volunteer unrequested information. Do not express your own feelings or opinions unless such information is specifically called for. Use objective evidence, and be sure to support all your general statements with specific facts or examples.

Finally, leave enough time to reread and revise what you have written. Try to view your answer from a fresh perspective. Have you left out words or written illegibly? Is your thesis clearly worded? Does your answer support your thesis and answer the question? Are your facts correct, and are your ideas presented in logical order? Review your topic sentences and transitions. Check sentence structure and word choice, spelling and punctuation. If a sentence—or even a whole paragraph—seems irrelevant, cross it out. If you suddenly remember something you want to add, you can insert a few additional words with a caret (∧). Neatly insert a longer addition at the end of your answer, box it, and label it so your instructor will know where it belongs.

The following one-hour essay answer, was written in response to the question in 45b2. Notice how the student restates the question in her thesis and keeps the question in focus by repeating key words like *cause, effect, result, response,* and *impact.*

Effective Essay Exam

Introduction—Thesis rephrases exam question	1 The Great Depression, caused by the American government's economic policies, had major political, economic, and social effects on the United States.
Summarizes policies leading to Depression (causes)	2 The Depression was precipitated by the stock market crash of October 1929. But its actual causes were more subtle; they lay in the U.S. government's economic policies. First, personal income was not well distributed. Although production rose during the 1920's, the farmers and other workers got too little of the profits; instead, a disproportionate amount of income went

769

to the richest 5 percent of the population. The
tax policies at this time made inequalities in
income even worse. A good deal of income also
went into development of new manufacturing
plants. This expansion stimulated the economy
but encouraged the production of more goods than
consumers could purchase. Finally, during the
economic boom of the 1920's the government did
not attempt to limit speculation or impose regulations on the securities market; it also did
little to help build up farmers' buying power.
Even after the crash began, the government made
mistakes: instead of trying to counter the country's deflationary economy, the government
focused on keeping the budget balanced and making
sure the United States adhered to the gold standard.

Transition
from causes
to effects

3   The Depression, devastating to millions of
individuals, had a tremendous impact on the
nation as a whole. Its political, economic, and
social consequences were great.

Early effects:
Paragraphs
4–8 summa-
rize impor-
tant results in
chronological
order

4   Between October 1929 and Roosevelt's inauguration on March 4, 1932, the economic situation
grew worse. Businesses were going bankrupt,
banks were failing, and stock prices were falling. Farm prices fell drastically, and hungry
farmers were forced to burn their corn to heat
their homes. There was massive unemployment,
with millions of workers jobless and humiliated,
losing skills and self-respect. President Hoover's Reconstruction Finance Corporation made
loans available to banks, railroads, and businesses, but he felt state and local funds (not
the federal government) should finance public
works programs and relief. Confidence in the

president declined as the country's economic situation worsened.

More effects:
Roosevelt's
emergency
measures

5   One result of the Depression, then, was the
election of Franklin Delano Roosevelt. By the
time of his inauguration, most American banks had
closed, 13 million workers were unemployed, and
millions of farmers were threatened by foreclo-
sure. Roosevelt's response was immediate: two
days after he took office, he closed all banks
and took steps to support the stronger ones with
loans and prevent weak ones from reopening.
During the first hundred days of his administration, he kept Congress in special session. Under
his leadership, Congress enacted emergency measures designed to provide "Relief, Recovery, and
Reform."

More effects:
Roosevelt's
reform mea-
sures

6   In response to the problems caused by the
Depression, Roosevelt set up agencies to reform
some of the conditions that had helped to cause
the Depression in the first place. The Tennessee
Valley Authority, created in May of 1933, was one
of these. Its purposes were to control floods by
building new dams and improving old ones and to
provide cheap, plentiful electricity. The TVA
improved the standard of living of area farmers
and drove down the price of power all over the
country. The Agricultural Adjustment Administration, created the same month as the TVA, provided for taxes on basic commodities, with the
tax revenues used to subsidize farmers to produce
less. This reform measure caused prices to rise.

More effects:
NIRA, etc.

7   Another response to the problems of the
Depression was the National Industrial Recovery
Act. This act established the National Recovery
Administration, an agency that set minimum wages

and maximum hours for workers and set limits on production and prices. Other laws passed by Congress between 1935 and 1940 strengthened federal regulation of power, interstate commerce, and air traffic. Roosevelt also changed the federal tax structure to redistribute American income.

More effects: Social Security, etc.

8   One of the most important results of the Depression was the Social Security Act of 1935, which established unemployment insurance and provided financial aid for the blind and disabled and for dependent children and their mothers. The Works Progress Administration (WPA) gave jobs to over 2 million workers, who built public buildings, roads, streets, bridges, and sewers. The WPA also employed artists, musicians, actors, and writers. The Public Works Administration (PWA) cleared slums and created public housing. In the National Labor Relations Act (1935), workers received a guarantee of government protection for their unions against unfair labor practices by management.

Conclusion

9   As a result of the economic collapse known as the Great Depression, Americans saw their government take responsibility for providing immediate relief, for helping the economy recover, and for taking steps to ensure that the situation would not be repeated. The economic, political, and social impact of the laws passed during the 1930's are still with us today, helping to keep our government and our economy stable.

Notice that the student does not digress by describing the conditions of people's lives in detail, blame anyone in particular, discuss the president's friends and enemies, or consider parallel events in other countries. She covers only what the question asks for. Notice, too, how topic sentences ("One result of the Depression. . . ."; "In response to the problems caused by the Depression. . . ."; "One of the most important results of the Depression. . . .") keep the primary purpose of the discussion in focus and guide the reader through the essay.

A well-planned essay like the one above is not easy to write. Consider the following ineffective answer to the same question.

INEFFECTIVE ESSAY EXAM

No clear thesis
Vague, subjective impressions of the Depression

1   The Great Depression is generally considered to have begun with the Stock Market Crash of October 1929 and to have lasted until the defense build-up for World War II. It was a terrible time for millions of Americans, who were not used to being hungry or out of work. Perhaps the worst economic disaster in our history, the Depression left its scars on millions of once-proud workers and farmers who found themselves reduced to poverty. We have all heard stories of businessmen committing suicide when their invest-ments failed, of people selling apples on the street, and of farmers and their families leaving the dust bowl in desperate search of work. My own grandfather, laid off from his job, had to support my grandmother and their four children on what he could make from odd carpentry jobs. This was the Depression at its worst.

2   What else did the Depression produce? One result of the Depression was the election of Franklin Delano Roosevelt. Roosevelt immediately closed all banks. Then Congress set up the Fed-eral Emergency Relief Administration, the Civil-ian Conservation Corps, the Farm Credit Administration, and the Home Owners' Loan Corpo-ration. The Reconstruction Finance Corporation and the Civil Works Administration were two other agencies designed to provide Relief, Recovery,

Gratuitous summary

and Reform. All these agencies helped Roosevelt

in his efforts to lead the nation to recovery
while providing relief and reform.

Along with these emergency measures, Roosevelt set out to reform some of the conditions he
felt were responsible for the economic collapse.
Accordingly, he created the Tennessee Valley
Authority (TVA) to control floods and provide
electricity in the Tennessee Valley. The Agricultural Adjustment Agency levied taxes and got
the farmers to grow less, causing prices to rise.

Unsupported generalization Thus these agencies, the TVA and the AAA, helped
to ease things for the farmers.

4   The National Industrial Recovery Act established the National Recovery Administration,
which was designed to help workers. It established minimum wages and maximum hours, both of
which made conditions better for workers. Other

Why were these agencies impor- tant? What did they do? important agencies included the Federal Power
Commission, the Interstate Commerce Commission,
the Maritime Commission, and the Civil Aeronau-
tics Authority. Changes in the tax structure at
about this time made the tax system fairer and
eliminated some inequities. Roosevelt, working
smoothly with his cabinet and with Congress, took
many important steps to ease the nation's economic burden.

Discussion of Roosevelt irrelevant to topic 5   Roosevelt, despite the fact that he was
handicapped by polio, was a dynamic president.
His fireside chats, which millions of Americans
heard on the radio every week, helped to reassure
Americans that things would be fine. This
increased his popularity. But he had problems,
too. Not everyone agreed with him. Private
electric companies opposed the TVA, big business
disagreed with his support of labor unions, the
rich did not like the way he restructured the tax

```
        system, and many people saw him as dangerously
        radical. Still, he was one of our most popular
        presidents ever, and he was elected to four
        terms.
```

Undeveloped
information

```
    6    Social Security Act--unemployment insurance,
        aid to blind and disabled and children
        WPA--built public projects
        PWA--public housing
        National Labor Relations Act--strengthened labor
        unions
```

This essay only indirectly answers the examination question. It devotes too much space to unnecessary elements—an emotional introduction, needlessly repeated words and phrases, gratuitous summaries, and unsupported generalizations. Without a thesis to guide her, the writer easily slips into a discussion that considers only the immediate impact of the Depression and never discusses its causes or long-term effects. Although the body paragraphs do provide the names of many agencies created by the Roosevelt administration, they do not explain the purpose of most of them. As a result, it appears that the student considers the formation of the agencies, not their contributions, to be the Depression's most significant result.

Because the student took a time-consuming detour, she had to list points at the end of the essay without discussing them fully. Although it is better to include undeveloped information than to skip it altogether, an undeveloped list has shortcomings. Essay answers are by definition made up of full paragraphs, and many instructors will not give credit if you do not write out your answer in full. More important, you cannot effectively show logical or causal relationships in a list. In addition, this student's digression left her no time to sum up her main points, even in a one-sentence conclusion.

45d *Writing Paragraph-length Examination Answers*

Some essay questions ask for a paragraph-length answer, not a full essay. A paragraph should be just that: not one or two sentences, not a list of points, not more than one paragraph.

▶ See Ch. 4

A paragraph-length answer should be *unified* by a clear topic sentence. Just as an essay answer begins with a thesis statement, a paragraph answer opens with a topic sentence that summarizes what the paragraph will cover. You should generally word this sentence to echo the examination question. The paragraph should also be *coherent*—that is, its statements should be linked by transitions that move the reader along. And the paragraph should be as *well developed* as possible, with enough relevant detail to convince your reader that you know what you are talking about.

A typical question on a business examination, reproduced below, calls for a paragraph-length response.

QUESTION: In one paragraph, define the term *management by objectives*, give an example of how it works, and briefly discuss an advantage of this approach.

EFFECTIVE PARAGRAPH-LENGTH ANSWER

Definition

As defined by Horngren, management by objectives is an approach in which a manager and his or her superior together formulate goals, and plans by which they can achieve these goals, for a forthcoming period. For example, a manager and

Example

a superior can formulate a responsibility accounting budget, and the manager's performance can then be measured according to how well he or she meets the objectives defined by the budget.

Advantage

The advantage of this approach is that the goals set are attainable because they are not formulated in a vacuum. Rather, the objectives are based on what the entire team, with knowledge of the constraints on its task, reasonably expects to accomplish. As a result, the burden of responsibility is shifted from the superior to the team: the goal itself defines all the steps needed for its completion.

In this answer, key phrases ("As *defined* by. . . ."; "For *example*. . . ."; "The *advantage* of this approach. . . .") clearly identify the various parts of the question being covered. The writer volunteers no more than the question asks for, and his use of the wording of the question helps make the paragraph orderly, coherent, and emphatic.

The student who wrote the response below may know what *management by objectives* is, but his paragraph sounds more like a casual explanation to a friend than an answer to an examination question.

INEFFECTIVE PARAGRAPH-LENGTH ANSWER

Sketchy, casual definition

No example given

Vague

> Management by objectives is when managers and their bosses get together to formulate their goals. This is a good system of management because it cuts down on hard feelings between managers and their superiors. Since they set the goals together, they can make sure they're attainable by considering all possible influ—ences, constraints, etc., that might occur. This way neither the manager nor the superior gets all the blame when things go wrong.

Just as with an essay-length answer, a paragraph answer will not be effective unless you take the time to read the question carefully, plan your response, and outline your answer before you begin to write. It is always a good idea to echo the wording of the question early in your answer and to reread your answer to make sure it explicitly addresses the question.

Writing About Literature

46a Approaching Literature

Literature is different from other kinds of writing. When writers create works of imaginative literature, they work within certain categories called **genres**: short stories, novels, plays, poems, and the like. Each of these types of literature has its own special characteristics. If you recognize these special forms and features, literary works will be more accessible to you because you will be able to approach literature with some basic assumptions about what it will and will not be.

To create a mood, imaginative literature may depend on experiments with language and form. The effect of a literary work is determined not just by its ideas but also by the artful arrangement of words and images and events. Literature has nearly limitless possibilities. In experimental modern fiction, a short story can consist entirely of an alumni magazine's class notes or a short series of diary-like entries moving backward in time to the narrator's birth; it can even consist of just a single paragraph. A poem may sound like prose, and may be just a few lines—or just a few words—long. It may be written entirely in lowercase letters, or its lines may be arranged in the shape of an animal. A play may have only a single character, or it may have a narrator who speaks directly to the audience. A novel may switch narrators with each section or chapter, and it can skip from one time period to another. In other words, literature has the power to surprise readers by doing what they do not expect it to do: by breaking the rules.

46b Reading Literature

When you read a literary work about which you plan to write, you use the same critical thinking skills and active reading strategies you apply to other works you read: you *preview* the work, *highlight* it to identify key ideas and cues to meaning, and *annotate* it carefully (see **38a**).

As you read and take notes, you focus on the special concerns of literary analysis, considering elements like a short story's plot, a poem's rhyme or meter, or a play's characters. You look for *patterns,* related groups of words, images, or ideas that run through a work. You look for *anomalies,* unusual forms, unique uses of language, unexpected actions by characters, or unusual treatments of topics. And you look for *connections,* links with other literary works, with historical events, or with biographical information.

Then, you *list* to organize into a useful order the material you have identified in your notes. As you arrange related material into lists, a structure for your paper may emerge.

These strategies, tailored to the special demands of writing about literature, help you to detect relationships among ideas, to uncover links to other works, and to find material to write about and a shape and central focus for your essay. When you read a work of literature, keep in mind that you do not read to magically discover the one correct meaning the writer had in mind. The "meaning" of a literary work is created by the interaction among a writer, a text, and its readers. This should not suggest that a work can mean whatever a reader wants it to mean; ultimately, your interpretation of a work must be consistent with the stylistic signals or thematic suggestions or patterns of imagery in the text. These elements may be subject to interpretation, but they cannot be ignored. Ideally, your writing about works of literature will represent a balance between what you know or can learn about the special qualities of literature and the unique reactions you bring to a work.

46c Writing About Literature

Just as literature is different from other kinds of writing, the writing you do *about* literature is different. When you write about literature, you respond to the possibilities created by a work's form, content, and style. As you write, you observe the conventions of literary criticism, which has its own discipline-specific vocabulary and forms. You also respond to certain typical assignments. For instance, you may be asked to **analyze** a work, taking it apart to consider one or more of its elements—perhaps the plot or characters in a story or the use of language in a poem. Or, you may be asked to **interpret** a work, trying to discover its possible meanings. Less often, you may be called upon to **evaluate** a work, to judge its merits and consider whether or not its author has been successful.

More specifically, you may be asked to trace the critical or popular reception to a work; to compare two works by a single writer (or by two different writers); to consider the relationship between a work of literature and a literary movement or historical context. You may be asked to consider the effect on a literary work of certain circumstances or events in a writer's life, or the relationship between a work and its author's writing process. You may be asked to analyze a character's motives or the relationship between two characters, or to comment on a story's setting or tone. In any case, understanding exactly what you are expected to do will make your writing task easier.

When you write about literature, you use all the skills you bring to any writing assignment. Your goal is to make a point and support it with appropriate references to the work under discussion or to related works or secondary sources.

Conventions of Writing About Literature

- Use present-tense verbs when discussing works of literature: "The character of Mrs. Mallard's husband *is* not developed. . . ."

- Use past-tense verbs only when discussing historical events ("Owen's poem conveys the destructiveness of World War I, which at the time the poem *was* written *was* considered to be. . . ."), presenting biographical data ("Her first novel, published in 1811 when Austen *was* 36, . . ."), or identifying events that occurred prior to the time of the story's main action ("Miss Emily is a recluse; since her father *died* she has lived alone except for a servant").

- Support all points with specific, concrete examples from the work you are discussing: briefly summarize key events, quote dialogue or description, describe characters or setting, or paraphrase ideas.

- Combine paraphrase, summary, and quotation with your own interpretations, weaving quotations smoothly into your paper.

- Be careful to acknowledge all sources, including the work or works under discussion. Introduce the words or ideas of others with a reference to the source and follow borrowed material with appropriate parenthetical documentation. Enclose the words of others in quotation marks.

- In accordance with MLA documentation style **(see 39b),** use parenthetical documentation and include a Works Cited list.

- Use correct reference form for fiction, poetry, and drama. When citing a part of a short story or novel, supply the page number (168); for a poem, give the line numbers (2–4); for a classic verse play, include act, scene, and line numbers (1.4.29–31 or I.iv.29–31). For other plays, supply act and/or scene numbers. When quoting more than four lines, follow the rules for setting off lines of prose or poetry **(see 30e).**

- Avoid subjective expressions like *I feel, I believe, it seems to me,* and *in my opinion.* These weaken your paper by suggesting that its ideas are "only" your opinion and have no inherent validity.

- Do not rely on excessive plot summary. Your goal is to draw a conclusion about one or more works and to support that conclusion with pertinent details. If a plot detail supports a point you wish to make, a *brief* summary alluding to a particular event or arrangement of events is acceptable. But plot summary is no substitute for analysis.

- Use literary terms accurately **(see 46e).** For example, be careful to avoid confusing *narrator* or *speaker* with *author*; feelings or opinions expressed by a narrator or character do not necessarily represent those of the author. You should not say, "In the poem's last stanza, Frost expresses his indecision" when you mean that the poem's *speaker* is indecisive.

- Identify works of literature correctly in your text: *underline* titles of novels and plays; set titles of short stories and poems within quotation marks.

46d *Writing About Fiction*

When you write about fiction, you follow the same process you use when you write any paper about literature. However, you concentrate on one or more of the elements the authors used in the work—for example, plot, character(s), setting, and point of view. Each of these elements contributes to the central idea or theme of the story.

STUDENT CASE STUDY

WRITING ABOUT FICTION

Carla Watts, a student in an introductory literature course, was asked to select a short story from a list supplied by her instructor and to write an essay exploring a central idea of the story. The following story, written in 1983 by Gary Gildner, is the one she decided to write about.

Sleepy Time Gal

In the small town in northern Michigan where my father lived as a young man, he had an Italian friend who worked in a restaurant. I will call his friend Phil. Phil's job in the restaurant was as ordinary as you can imagine—from making coffee in the morning to sweeping up at night. But what was not ordinary about Phil was his piano playing. On Saturday nights my father and Phil and their girlfriends would drive ten or fifteen miles to a roadhouse by a lake where they would drink beer from schooners and dance and Phil would play an old beat-up piano. He could play any song you named, my father said, but the song everyone waited for was the one he wrote, which he would always play at the end before they left to go back to the town. And everyone knew of course that he had written the song for his girl, who was as pretty as she was rich. Her father was the banker in their town, and he was a tough old German, and he didn't like Phil going around with his daughter.

My father, when he told the story, which was not often, would tell it in an offhand way and emphasize the Depression and not having much, instead of the important parts. I will try to tell it the way he did, if I can.

So they would go to the roadhouse by the lake, and finally Phil would play his song, and everyone would say, Phil, that's a great song, you could make a lot of money from it. But Phil would only shake his head and smile and look at his girl. I have to break in here and say that my father, a gentle but practical man, was not inclined to emphasize the part about Phil looking at his girl. It was my mother who said the girl would rest her head on Phil's shoulder while he played, and that he got the idea for the song from the pretty way she looked when she got sleepy. My mother was not part of the story, but she had heard it when she and my father were younger and therefore had that information. I would like to intrude further and add something about Phil writing the song, maybe show him whistling the tune and going over the words slowly and carefully to get the best ones, while peeling onions or potatoes in the restaurant; but my father is already driving them home from the roadhouse, and saying how patched up his tires were, and how his car's engine was a gingerbread of parts from different makes, and some parts were his own invention as well. And my mother is saying that the old German had made his daughter promise not to get involved with any man until after college, and they couldn't be late. Also my mother likes the sad parts and is eager to get to their last night before the girl goes away to college.

So they all went out to the roadhouse, and it was sad. The women got tears in their eyes when Phil played her song, my mother said. My father said that Phil spent his week's pay on a new shirt and tie, the first tie he ever owned, and people kidded him. Somebody piped up and said, Phil, you ought to take that song down to Bay City—which was like saying New York City to them, only more realistic—and sell it and take the money and go to college too. Which was not meant to be cruel, but that was the result because Phil had never even got to high school. But you can see people were trying to cheer him up, my mother said.

Well, she'd come home for Thanksgiving and Christmas and Easter and they'd all sneak out to the roadhouse and drink beer from schooners and dance and everything would be like always. And of course there were the summers. And everyone knew Phil and the girl would get married after she made good her promise to her father because you could see it in their eyes when he sat at the old beat-up piano and played her song.

That last part about their eyes was not, of course, in my father's telling, but I couldn't help putting it in there even though I know it is making some of you impatient. Remember that this happened many years ago in the woods by a lake in northern Michigan, before television. I wish I could put more in, especially about the song and how it felt to Phil to sing it and how the girl felt when hearing it and knowing it was hers, but I've already intruded too much in a simple story that isn't even mine.

Well, here's the kicker part. Probably by now many of you have guessed that one vacation near the end she doesn't come home to see Phil, because she meets some guy at college who is good-looking and as rich as she is and, because her father knew about Phil all along and was pressuring her into forgetting about him, she gives in to this new guy and goes to his hometown during the vacation and falls in love with him. That's how the people in town figured it, because after she graduates they turn up, already married, and right away he takes over the old German's bank—and buys a new Pontiac at the place where my father is the mechanic and pays cash for it. The paying cash always made my father pause and shake his head and mention again that times were tough, but here comes this guy in a spiffy white shirt (with French cuffs, my mother said) and pays the full price in cash.

And this made my father shake his head too: Phil took the song down to Bay City and sold it for twenty-five dollars, the only money he ever got for it. It was the same song we'd just heard on the radio and which reminded my father of the story I just told you. What happened to Phil? Well, he stayed in Bay City and got a job managing a movie theater. My father saw him there after the Depression when he was on his way to Detroit to work for Ford. He stopped and Phil gave him a box of popcorn. The song he wrote for the girl has sold many millions of records, and if I told you the name of it you could probably sing it, or at least whistle the tune. I wonder what the girl thinks when she hears it. Oh yes, my father met Phil's wife too. She worked in the movie theater with him, selling tickets and cleaning the carpet after the show with one of those sweepers you push. She was also big and loud and nothing like the other one, my mother said.

Carla began by reading the story through quickly. Then she reread it more carefully, highlighting and annotating as she read. A portion of the highlighted and annotated story appears below.

When do events take place?

In the small town in northern Michigan where my father lived as a young man, he had an Italian friend who worked in a restaurant. I will call his friend Phil. Phil's job in the restaurant was as (ordinary) as you can imagine—from making coffee in the morning to sweeping up at night. But what was (not ordinary) about Phil was his piano playing. On

Sat. nights = special— dancing, beer, etc. ?

(Saturday nights) my father and Phil and their (girlfriends) would drive ten or fifteen miles to a (roadhouse) by a lake where they would (drink beer) from (schooners) and (dance) and Phil would play an old beat-up (piano.) He could play any song you named, my father said, but the song everyone waited for was the one he wrote, which he would always play at the end before they left to go back to the town. And everyone knew of course that he had written the song for his girl, <u>who was as pretty as she was rich.</u> Her father was the banker in their town, and he was a tough old German, and he didn't like Phil going around with his daughter.

fairy tale style

My father, when he told the story, which was not often, would <u>tell it in an offhand way</u> and emphasize the (Depression) and not having much, instead of the important parts. <u>I will try to tell it the way he did, if I can.</u>

✳

Carla's next task was to make a brainstorming list to help her find ideas. Before she could decide on a topic for her paper, she had to decide on one area on which to focus. To do this, she found it helpful to brainstorm separately on plot, character, setting, point of view, and tone and style, to see which suggested the most promising possibilities. Then she brainstormed further to explore the story's theme and the way each of its elements contributed to that central idea. Carla's brainstorming list appears below.

Brainstorming List

Plot
Flashback — narrator remembers story father told.
Story: Phil loved rich banker's daughter, wrote song for her, girl married someone else, Phil sold song for $25.00, married another woman.
Ordinary, predictable story of star-crossed lovers from different backgrounds ("Probably by now many of you have guessed...."), but what actually happened isn't important.

785

Characters

Phil — Italian, never went to high
        school, ordinary job in restaurant,
        extraordinary piano player.
Girl — no name, pretty, rich, educated
Narrator — ?
Mother — romantic
Father — mechanic; gentle, practical

Setting

"Small town in northern Michigan"
Past — when narrator's father was a
        young man
In woods — near lake
Roadhouse — dancing, drinking, beat-up
        piano

Point of View

Narrator tells story to reader, but
        there's a story inside this story.
Father tells his story, mother qualifies
        his version (she's "not part of the
        story" but has heard it), narrator
        tells how they told it.
Point of view keeps shifting — characters
        compete to tell the story ("I would
        like to intrude further...").
Father's version: stresses Depression, hard
        times
Mother's version: stresses relationship,
        "sad parts"

Reader encouraged to find own point
of view; narrator of story
addresses readers.
Three characters invent and reinvent
and embellish story each time
they tell it.

<u>Tone and Style</u>

Conversational style—narrator talks
to reader ("Well, here's the kicker
part.")
Like fairy tale (girl = "as pretty as she
was rich"; father = a gentle but
practical man)
Casual speech: Contractions, "well," "some
guy," etc.

<u>Theme</u>

Which is "real" story?
Subject of Phil's story = missed chances,
failure.
Subject of narrator's story = the past?
Values of different characters? Conflict
between real events and memory?

When Carla looked over her brainstorming list, she saw at once that character and point of view suggested the most interesting possibilities for her paper. Still, she found herself unwilling to start drafting her essay until she could find out more about the story's title, which she felt sure could be an important source of material. She was so interested in the significance of the title that she asked around until she found someone who told her that it was the name of an actual song—and supplied the lyrics. She recorded her reactions to this information in a journal entry.

Journal Entry

"Sleepy Time Gal" = name of song
Mother says Phil got inspiration for
    song from the way his girl looked
    when she got sleepy. ** Does title of
    story refer to girl or to song? **
Song = fantasy about the perfect married life
    that should follow the evenings of
    dancing: in a "cottage for two" wife
    will be happy cooking and sewing for
    her husband and will end her
    evenings early. She'll be happy to
    forget about dancing and be a
    stay-at-home wife.
Maybe lyrics describe what Phil
    wants and never gets?

At this point Carla decided to identify patterns by **listing**. She arranged some of the most useful material from her brainstorming lists, journal entry, and annotations into the following groups of related ideas, reflecting the three versions of Phil's story presented in "Sleepy Time Gal."

Three Versions of Phil's Story

Mother's Version

"Likes the sad parts" and the details of
    the romance: the way the father
    made the daughter promise not to get
    involved with a man until she
    finished college, the way the women
    got tears in their eyes when Phil
    played his song.
Remembers girl's husband had French cuffs.
Remembers Phil's wife = "big and loud"

Notes people were trying to cheer Phil up
Remembers girl resting head on Phil's
    shoulder, and how he got idea for song.

Father's Version

Depression/money: mentions Phil's patched
    tires and engine, how he spent a week's
    pay on new clothes, how girl's husband
    pays cash for a new Pontiac
("Times were tough")

Narrator's Version

Facts of story — but wants to add more
    about Phil's process of writing song
    (because he, like Phil, = artist?), more
    about romance (" you could see it in
    their eyes"). Wants to embellish
    story. ("I wish I could put more
    in....")

Wonders about parts father doesn't
    tell — e.g. what girl thinks when she
    hears song.
Talks to reader about his creative
    process: "I couldn't help putting
    it in...."

Carla's notes and lists eventually suggested the following thesis for her paper: "'Sleepy Time Gal' is a story that is not about the 'gal' of the title or about the man the narrator calls Phil but about the different viewpoints of its three narrators." Guided by this tentative thesis, she went on to write and revise her paper, following the process detailed in Chapter 3. The final draft of Carla's paper begins below. Annotations have been added to identify the conventions that apply to writing essays about works of fiction.

Whose Story?

Midway through Gary Gildner's short story "Sleepy Time Gal" the narrator acknowledges, "I've already intruded too much in a simple story that isn't even mine" (215). But whose story is "Sleepy Time Gal"? It is presented as the tale of Phil, an ordinary young man of modest means who falls in love with a rich young woman, writes a song for her, and loses both the woman and the song, as well as the fame and fortune the song could have brought him, apparently because he is unwilling to fight for either. But actually, "Sleepy Time Gal" is not Phil's story, and it is not the story of the girl he loves; the story belongs to the three characters who compete to tell it.

> Title in quotation marks
> Quotation introduced

> Parenthetical documentation identifies number of page on which quotation appeared

> Thesis

The story they tell is a simple one; it is also familiar. Phil is a young man with an ordinary job. He has little education and no real prospects of doing anything beyond working in a restaurant doing menial jobs. He is in love with a girl whose father is a rich banker, a girl who goes to college. Phil has no more chance of marrying the girl than he has of becoming educated or becoming a millionaire. He has written a song for her, but he is doomed to sell the rights to it for twenty-five dollars. Phil may be a man with dreams and expectations beyond the small Michigan town and the roadhouse, but he does not seem to be willing to struggle to make

> Brief plot summary combined with interpretation

his dreams come true. Ironically, he never
achieves with his "gal" the happy married life
his song describes; his dreams remain just
dreams, and he settles for life in the dream
world of a movie theatre.

The character who seems to be the author of
Phil's story is the narrator's father: he is the
only one who knew Phil and witnessed the story's
events, and he has told it again and again to his
family. But the story he tells reveals more than
just what happened to Phil; it says a lot about
his own life, too. The father is a mechanic who
eventually leaves his small Michigan town for
Detroit. As the narrator observes, he is "a
gentle but practical man" (214). We can assume
he has seen some hard times; he sees Phil's story
only in the context of the times, and "times were
tough" (216). The narrator says, "My father,
when he told the story, . . . would tell it in an
offhand way and emphasize the Depression and not
having much, instead of the important parts"
(214). In the father's version, seemingly minor
details are important: Phil's often—mended car
engine, "a gingerbread of parts from different
makes" (215), and incidents like how Phil spent a
week's pay on a new shirt and tie, "the first tie
he ever owned" (215), and how the girl's husband
paid cash for a new Pontiac. These details are
important to the father because they have to do
with money. He sees Phil's story as more about a
particular time (the Depression era) than about
particular people. Whenever he hears Phil's song
on the radio, he remembers that time.

The narrator's mother, however, sees Phil's
story as a romantic, timeless story of hopelessly
doomed lovers. She did not witness the story's

Father's perspective

Past tense used to identify events that occurred before story's main action

Ellipses indicate words omitted from quotation

Mother's perspective

events, but she has heard the story often. According to the narrator, she "likes the sad parts and is eager to get to their last night before the girl goes away to college" (215). She remembers how the women in the roadhouse got tears in their eyes when Phil played the song he wrote. The mother's selective memory helps to characterize her as somewhat romantic and senti— mental, interested in people and their relation— ships (the way the girl's father made her promise to avoid romantic entanglements until after col— lege, the way Phil's friends tried to cheer him up) and in visual details (the way the girl rested her head on Phil's shoulder, the French cuffs on her husband's shirt). In the interac— tion between the characters she sees drama and even tragedy. The sentimental story of lost love appeals to her as the story of lost opportunity appeals to the father.

Point sup— ported by specific refer— ences to story

The narrator knows the story only through his father's telling and retelling of it, and he says, "I will try to tell it the way he did, if I can" (214). But this is impossible: he enhances the story, and he makes it his own. He is the one who communicates the story to readers, and he ultimately decides what to include and what to leave out. His story reflects both his parents' points of view: the focus on both characters and events, on romance and history. In telling Phil's story, he tells the story of a time, recreating a Depression—era struggle of a man who could have made it big but wound up a failure; however, he also recounts a story about people, a romantic, sentimentalized story of lost love. And, he tells a story about his own parents.

Narrator's perspective

The narrator, like Phil, is creative; he

needs to convey the facts of the story, but he must struggle to resist the temptation to add to them: to add more about how Phil went about writing the song, "maybe show him whistling the tune and going over the words slowly and carefully to get the best ones" (214—15), more about the romance itself. The narrator is clearly embellishing the story—for instance, when he says everyone knew Phil and the girl would get married because "you could see it in their eyes" (215), he admits that this detail is not in his father's version of the story—but he is careful to identify his own contributions, explaining, "I couldn't help putting it in there" (215). The narrator cannot help wondering about the parts his father does not tell, and he struggles to avoid rewriting the story to include them. Sometimes he cannot help himself, and he apologizes for his lapses with a phrase like "I have to break in here . . ." (214). But, for the most part, the narrator knows his place, knows it is not really his story to tell: "I wish I could put more in, especially about the song and how it felt to Phil to sing it and how the girl felt when hearing it and knowing it was hers, but I've already intruded too much in a simple story that isn't even mine" (215).

Narrator's perspective continues

Phil's story is, as the narrator acknowledges, a simple one, almost a cliché. But Gary Gildner's story, "Sleepy Time Gal," is much more complex. In it, three characters create and recreate a story of love and loss, ambition and failure, each contributing the details they feel should be stressed and, in the process, revealing something about themselves and about their own hopes and dreams.

Conclusion: reinforces thesis

Work Cited

Gildner, Gary. "Sleepy Time Gal." <u>Sudden Fiction: Ameri-</u>
<u>can Short-Short Stories</u>. Ed. Robert Shapard and
James Thomas. Salt Lake City: G. M. Smith, 1986.
214–16.

Carla's paper focuses on the story's shifting point of view and the contributions of the three central characters to Phil's story. She supports her thesis with specific references to "Sleepy Time Gal"—quotations, summary, and paraphrase—and interprets the story's events in light of the points she is making. Her paper does not include every item in her notes, nor should it: she selects only those details that support her thesis.

46e *Writing About Poetry*

When you write a paper about poetry, you follow the process you use when you write any paper about literature. However, you concentrate on the elements poets use to create and enrich their work—for example, voice, form, sound, meter, language, and tone. Each of these elements contributes to the poem's central idea, or theme.

Daniel Johanssen, a student in an introductory literature course, followed this process as he planned an essay about Delmore Schwartz's 1959 poem "The True-Blue American."

STUDENT CASE STUDY

WRITING ABOUT POETRY

Daniel's assignment was a general one; his instructor had asked only that each student choose a poem and react to it. After he chose his poem, Daniel read it several times. Then he read it aloud, paying special attention to the sound of the poem. As he read, he highlighted and annotated the poem, as illustrated below.

DELMORE SCHWARTZ (1913–1966)
The True-Blue American

Jeremiah Dickson was a (true-blue) — = *loyal;*
American, *faithful*
For he <u>was a little boy who un-</u> (*also* = "*red*
<u>derstood America</u>, for he felt *white & blue*"?)
that he must

Think about *everything;* because
    that's *all* there is to think
    about,
Knowing immediately the intimacy
    of truth and comedy,
Knowing intuitively how a sense ⎫ *intuitively* 5
why?   of humor was a necessity ⎬
·For one and for all who live in ⎭ *natively*
    America. Thus, natively, and *naturally*
Naturally when on an April Sun-
    day in an ice cream parlor
    Jeremiah
Was requested to choose between
    a chocolate sundae and a
    banana split
He answered unhesitatingly, hav-
    ing no need to think of it
Being a true-blue American, deter-
    mined to continue as he
    began: 10
Rejecting the either-or of Kierke- **?**
    gaard, and any another
    European;
Refusing to accept alternatives, re-
    fusing to believe the choice
    of between;
Rejecting selection; denying di-
    lemma; electing absolute
    affirmation: **?**
    knowing
        in his breast ⎫
            The infinite and the 15
                gold
            Of the endless fron- ⎬ *rhyme*
                tier, the death-
                less West ⎭
"Both: I will have them both!"
    declared this true-blue
    American.
In Cambridge, Massachusetts, on

*ambition, refusal
to settle for half.
Or just greed?*

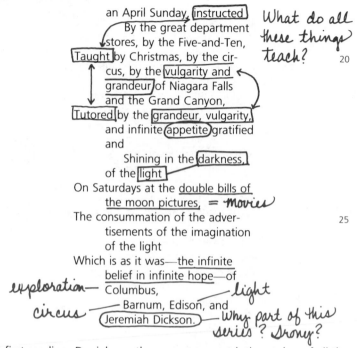

an April Sunday, instructed
    By the great department
    stores, by the Five-and-Ten,
Taught by Christmas, by the cir-
    cus, by the vulgarity and
    grandeur of Niagara Falls
    and the Grand Canyon,
Tutored by the grandeur, vulgarity,
    and infinite appetite gratified
    and
        Shining in the darkness,
    of the light
On Saturdays at the double bills of
    the moon pictures,   = Movies
The consummation of the adver-
    tisements of the imagination
    of the light
Which is as it was—the infinite
    belief in infinite hope—of
exploration— Columbus,   light
circus ——— Barnum, Edison, and
        Jeremiah Dickson. — Why part of this
                series? Irony?

What do all
these things
teach?   20

25

On first reading, Daniel saw the poem as a patriotic catalog of all the things that made America great; in fact, its seemingly patriotic theme was what made him select this poem to write about. The closer he looked, however, the more clearly he saw how deceptive his initial impression was. As he studied the poem, he saw how all its parts contributed to one impression: a critical look at American greed and materialism. Even though he did not like what he found, he could not ignore the clues to the poem's theme; the paper he finally wrote would have to interpret the poem in light of these clues.

As Daniel read and reread "The True-Blue American," he expanded his annotations in his journal, brainstorming and listing to find ideas for his paper. He began by brainstorming in a systematic fashion, considering voice, form, sound, meter, language, tone, and theme one by one. His brainstorming on the first four of these categories was not very productive: he concluded only that the poem's speaker was an anonymous voice, not identified as a particular person; that line length varied quite widely and did not seem to follow a particular pattern; and that the poem did not seem to have a regular rhyme scheme or meter. When he brainstormed about language, tone, and theme, however, he was able to discover some interesting ideas. The sections of Daniel's brainstorming list that pertain to language, tone, and theme follow.

Brainstorming List

Language

Repetition: true-blue American (3x + title),
Jeremiah Dickson (first and last
words of poem), vulgarity, grandeur,
infinite, light

Parallelism: "Knowing immediately...
knowing intuitively"; "Rejecting...
Refusing to accept... refusing to
believe... Rejecting... denying... elect-
ing... knowing";
"instructed by... taught by... tutored
by..."

Imagery: "moon pictures" — glowing in
the dark

Tone

Speaker's attitude seems angry, bitter,
disillusioned — why?
What does it mean to be "American"? to
understand America? Is being "true-blue"
a positive or negative goal?
Is title ironic?

Theme

Poem's stated subject = true-blue American, but what is true-blue American?
Is poem's real subject what it means
to be an American?
What is meaning of America? Is

America great, full of possibilities?
or corrupted by materialism and
greed?
What is significance of names of people
and places? How do they fit in
with the poem's theme?

After he had finished his brainstorming, Daniel made a more focused
list to organize some of the poem's key ideas and allusions.

Key Ideas and Illusions

Places

America: ice cream parlor, West (frontier),
    Cambridge Mass, department stores,
    Five-and-Ten, circus, Niagara Falls,
    Grand Canyon, movie theatre

People

Kierkegaard (?), Columbus, Barnum,
    Edison (+ Jeremiah Dickson, typical
    average American)

Miscellaneous

chocolate sundae, banana split,
    Christmas, advertisements

Contrasting ideas

Positive—
Promise of western frontier (infinite/
    endless/deathless)
grandeur
gold
imagination

light
hope
negative —
vulgarity
greed
appetite
darkness

Daniel's notes suggested many interesting paper topics. For example, he could contrast the poem's superficial patriotism with its actual pessimism or explore the relationship between language and theme. He could pursue the idea of making choices or the contrast between positive and negative images. He could do some research in order to consider the poem in the context of the United States in 1959, when it was written, or to consider how Delmore Schwartz's life or other works, or the works of his contemporaries, might be pertinent. He could examine the specific people and places mentioned in the poem and consider their possible significance. Finally, he could compare the poem to another poem with a similar—or contrasting—theme. Any of these possibilities would be perfectly appropriate. However, Daniel knew that it made sense to focus on a thesis his notes could support, and this eliminated some possible topics—for example, those focusing on the poem's sound or form.

As Daniel proceeded to find a thesis and an effective arrangement for his ideas, and, eventually, to write and revise his essay about "The True-Blue American" he followed the writing process outlined in Chapters 2 and 3 of this book.

EXERCISE

Review "The True-Blue American" and Daniel Johanssen's notes on pages 794–796. Brainstorm further if necessary, and arrange your material into lists of related ideas. Next, develop a thesis your notes can support, and write a paper about the poem. Finally, revise your paper according to the revision checklist below.

Revision Checklist: Writing about Literature

- Reconsider your topic. Is it specific enough? Do you focus on the concerns of your assignment?

continued

continued from previous page

- Does your introduction provide readers with the background or context they need to understand the discussion to follow? Would your introduction benefit from a quotation from the work? an overview of your research? a summary of your points?
- Do you clearly state your thesis? Does your thesis reflect your purpose? Does it clearly identify the aspects of the work you will discuss?
- Do you discuss the most pertinent points in your essay? Would other points about the work help you make a better case?
- How effective is the organization of your essay? Would your discussion be more effective if you arranged your points in a different order?
- Do you support your interpretations and judgments about the work? Would more support strengthen your case? Do you include too many points? Do you include a wide enough range of examples from the work and from your research? Do your examples actually support your points?
- Have you supplied the transitional words and phrases you need to reinforce the logical connections among your ideas?
- Have you included the plot details and definitions of literary terms that your readers need to understand your discussion?
- Does your conclusion reinforce your main points? Would a different strategy improve your ending?
- Have you documented all words and ideas that are not your own? Have you followed MLA documentation style?

46f *Using Literary Terms*

When you write about literature, you use a vocabulary appropriate to the discipline. The following glossary defines many of the terms you may use.

alliteration   repetition of initial sounds in a series of words, as in "dark, damp dungeon."

allusion   an unacknowledged reference to a historical event, work of literature, Biblical passage, or the like that the author expects readers to recognize.

antagonist   the character who is in conflict with or in opposition to the *protagonist*. Sometimes the antagonist is a force or situation, such as war or poverty.

assonance   repetition of vowel sounds in a series of words, as in "fine slide on the ice."

blank verse   lines of unrhymed iambic pentameter in no particular stanzaic form; approximates the rhythms of ordinary English speech.

character   the fictional representation of a person. Characters may be *round* (well-developed) or *flat* (undeveloped stereotypes), *dynamic* (changing and growing during the course of the story), or *static*) (remaining essentially unchanged by the story's events).

climax   the point of greatest tension or importance in a play or story; the point at which the story's decisive action takes place.

closed form   a poetic structure characterized by a consistent pattern of rhyme, meter, or stanzaic form.

conflict   the opposition between two or more characters, between a character and a natural force, or between contrasting tendencies or motives or ideas within one character.

consonance   repetition of consonant sounds in a series of words, as in "the gnarled fingers of his nervous hands."

denouement   the point in the plot of a work of fiction or drama at which the action comes to an end and loose ends are tied up.

end-stopped line   a line of poetry that ends with a full stop, usually at the end of a sentence.

enjambment   a line of poetry ending with no punctuation or natural pause so that it runs over into the next line.

exposition   the initial stage of the plot of a work of fiction or drama, where the author presents basic information readers need to understand the story's characters and events.

figurative language   language whose meaning is not literal. The most commonly used figures of speech are *hyperbole, metaphor, personification, simile,* and *understatement.*

free verse   poetry that does not follow a fixed meter or rhyme scheme.

hyperbole   a figure of speech that depends on intentional overstatement or exaggeration.

imagery   use of sensory description (description that relies on sight, sound, smell, taste, or touch) to make what is being described more vivid. A *pattern of imagery* collects a group of related images in order to create a single effect.

irony   the use of language to suggest a discrepancy or incongruity between what is said and what is meant *(verbal irony)*, between what actually happens and what we expected to happen *(situational irony;* also called *tragic irony)*, or between what a character knows and what the reader knows *(dramatic irony)*.

lyric poetry   poetry that expresses a speaker's mood or feelings. Lyric poems are usually short.

metaphor   a comparison that equates two things that are essentially unlike.

meter   the pattern of stressed and unstressed syllables in a line of poetry; each repeated unit of meter is called a *foot*. An *anapest* has three syllables, the first two unstressed and the third stressed; a *dactyl* has three syllables, the first stressed and subsequent ones unstressed; an *iamb* has two syllables, of which the second is stressed; a *spondee* has two syllables, both stressed; and a *trochee* has two syllables, the first stressed and the second unstressed. A poem's meter is described by the kind of foot (iamb, dactyl, and so on) and the number of feet in each line (one foot per line = monometer, two feet per line = dimeter, three feet = trimeter, four = tetrameter, five = pentameter, and so on). Thus a poetic line containing five feet, each of which contains an unstressed syllable followed by a stressed syllable, would be described as *iambic pentameter*.

monologue   an extended speech by one character.

narration   the recounting of events in a work of fiction. When an event that has already occurred is recounted in a later sequence of events, it is called a *flashback;* when something that will occur later in a narration is suggested earlier, the suggestion is called a *foreshadowing*.

open form   a poetic structure that is not characterized by any consistent pattern of rhyme, meter, or stanza form.

paradox   a seemingly contradictory statement.

persona   the narrator or speaker of a story or poem; the persona's attitudes and opinions are not necessarily those of the author.

personification   the assigning of human qualities to nonhuman things.

plot   the arrangement of events in a work of literature.

point of view   the perspective from which a story is told. A story may have a *first-person narrator,* who may be a major or minor character in the story. A story may have a *third-person narrator* who does not figure in the story's action. This narrator may be an *omniscient narrator,* who knows the thoughts and motives of all the story's characters, or a *limited omniscient narrator,* who sees into the minds of only some of the characters. A narrator who cannot be trusted—because he or she is evil, stupid, or self-serving—is called an *unreliable narrator.* The objective point of view that is limited to information you would get from watching the action unfold on stage is called the *dramatic* point of view.

protagonist   the principal character of a work of drama or fiction.

rhyme   the repetition of the last stressed vowel sound and all subsequent sounds. *End rhyme* occurs at the ends of poetic lines; *internal rhyme* is the rhyming of words within a line of poetry.

rhythm   the regular repetition of stresses and pauses.

setting   the background against which the action of a work of literature takes place: the historical period, locale, season, time of day, interior decoration.

simile   a comparison of two essentially unlike things using the word *like* or *as.*

soliloquy   a convention of drama in which a character speaks directly to the audience, revealing thoughts and feelings that the play's other characters, even if they are present on the stage, are assumed not to hear.

stanza   a group of lines in a poem, separated from others by a blank space on the page, that forms a unit of thought, mood, or meter. Common stanzaic forms include the *couplet* (two lines), *tercet* (three lines), *quatrain* (four lines), *sestet* (six lines), and *octave* (eight lines).

stock character   a stereotypical character who behaves consistently and predictably and who is instantly recognizable and familiar to the audience.

symbol   an image whose meaning transcends its literal or de-notative sense in a complex way. Its associations give it significance beyond what it could carry on its own.

theme   the main idea of a work of literature, made concrete by the work itself.

tone   the attitude of the speaker toward a work's subject, char-acters, or audience, conveyed by the work's word choice and arrangement of words.

understatement   intentional downplaying of a situation's signif-icance, often for ironic effect.

Practical Writing

47a *Composing Business Letters*

As a student you will probably have occasion to write letters—for example, to request information for a research paper, to appeal a decision or policy, to complain about a product or service, or to apply for employment.

(1) *Planning, writing, and revising your letter*

Before you sit down to write a business letter, you should think carefully about your purpose, audience, and tone. Many large organizations receive hundreds of letters each day, so your letter should be brief and to the point. Important information should appear early in the letter, and you should not digress. Be concise, and try to sound as natural as possible. Stilted or flowery language gets in the way of clear communication, and so do legalistic terminology *(in re: your letter)* and business jargon *(in regards to, herewith enclosed)*.

▶ See 1a

The first paragraph of your letter should introduce your subject and mention any relevant previous correspondence. The rest of your letter should present the facts readers will need to understand your points. If the matter is complicated, you may want to present information in a numbered list. Your conclusion should reinforce your message, and the whole letter should communicate your good will.

Type your business letter on good-quality 8½" × 11" paper. Leave wide margins, at least an inch all around, and center your letter on the page. Type your letter single-spaced and use a conventional format. One of the most common, the block format, is illustrated on page 807. (The semiblock format appears on page 810, and the indented format on page 812.)

After you proofread your letter, you may have to retype or reprint it. The appearance of your letter affects your reader's response to it. A neatly typed letter, free of smudges and errors, makes a favorable impression. A sloppy letter or one with misspellings or corrections made by hand presents you and your case badly. (See **47a2** for more information on the format of business letters.)

(2) Understanding the conventions of a business letter

The format of a business letter may seem arbitrary and prescriptive, but remember that this format has evolved in response to the special needs of the business audience. Using an inside address, for example, seems pointless until you consider that business letters often circulate to people other than the recipient, and to these readers knowing the original recipient is important. Dates are also necessary. Letters frequently become part of a permanent record, filed for some future use. These letters can have uses weeks, months, and even years later that no one could have originally predicted.

If you conform to the following conventions when writing business letters, your readers will know where to find each piece of information in your letter.

The Heading   The **heading** of a business letter consists of the sender's return address, but not his or her name, and the date the letter is written. If you use letterhead stationery, supply only the date, typing it two spaces below the letterhead. Each line of the heading falls under the one above it, flush to the left.

Spell out words like *Street, Avenue, Road, Place, East,* and *West* in full. You may, however, abbreviate the names of the states using postal abbreviations.

Revision Close-up

Be sure to punctuate the heading correctly. Commas separate the name of the city from that of the state and the day from the year, but no punctuation is used before the zip code, at the ends of lines, or in postal abbreviations for states.

The Inside Address   The **inside address** cites the *recipient's* name and address. It begins at the left margin four to six lines below the heading, depending on the need to use space for a balanced page. Include an appropriate title (Mr., Ms., Mrs., Miss, Dr.) with the

Sample Letter—Block Format

Heading	6732 Wyncote Avenue Houston, TX 77004 May 3, 1991
Inside address	Mr. William S. Price, Jr., Director Division of Archives and History Department of Cultural Resources 109 East Jones Street Raleigh, NC 27611
Salutation	Dear Mr. Price:
	Thank you for sending me the material I requested about pirates in colonial North Carolina.
Body	Both the pamphlets and the bibliography were extremely useful for my research. My instructor said that I had presented information in my paper that he had never seen before. Without your help, I am sure my paper would not have been so well received.
	I have enclosed a copy of my paper, and I would appreciate any comments you may have.
Complimentary close	Again, thank you for your time and trouble.
	Sincerely yours,
Written Signature	*Kevin Wolk*
Typed signature	Kevin Wolk
Additional data	Enclosure

recipient's name and the recipient's full address. Previous correspondence should be your guide to your recipient's correct name and title.

The Salutation   The **salutation** ("Dear _____") appears two spaces below the inside address, flush with the left margin. In business letters the salutation almost always ends with a colon, not a comma. It includes the person's title followed by the last name as it appears on the inside address.

If you are on a first-name basis with someone, you should still use his or her full name and title in the inside address. You may, however, use the first name, followed by a comma, in the salutation. If you are writing to someone you do not know—the Director of Personnel, for example—you can avoid the awkward phrase *To Whom It May Concern* by routing your letter to a specific department or by referring to a particular subject.

```
College Department
Harcourt Brace Jovanovich, Publishers
301 Commerce Street
Fort Worth, TX 76102
Attention: Director of Personnel
              or
Subject: Sales Position
```

Revision Close-up

If you are writing to a woman, refer to previous correspondence and use the title that she uses. If you do not know her preference, use *Ms.* If you know someone's initials but do not know whether the person is a man or a woman, you might call the company switchboard and ask. You can also use a neutral form of address—*Dear Editor* or *Dear Supervisor,* for example.

Keep in mind that salutations such as *Gentlemen* and *Dear Sirs* should be used only when you are certain that your audience is male. To use these salutations as general forms of address may offend some readers and should be avoided.

The Body   The **body** of your letter contains your message. Begin this section two spaces below the salutation, and single-space the text. In a short letter of two or three sentences, you may double-space throughout. In a block format letter you do not use paragraph indentations; in some other formats you indent paragraphs five spaces from the left-hand margin.

If your letter takes more than one page, place the addressee's name, the date, and the page number in the upper left-hand corner of the second page.

The Complimentary Close   The **complimentary close** appears two spaces below the body of the letter and flush left.

The most common complimentary closes are *Sincerely yours, Yours truly,* and *Yours very truly.* If you are on friendly terms with the recipient, *Best wishes* or *Cordially* is appropriate. Note that only the first word of the complimentary close is capitalized.

The Signature   Leave four spaces below the complimentary close, and type your name and title in full. Sign your name, without a title, above the typewritten line.

Additional Data   Indicate additional information below the signature, to the left.

Enclosures (Material enclosed along with letter)

cc: Eric Brody (Copy sent to the person mentioned)

SJL/lew (The initials of the writer/the initials of the typist)

47b *Writing Letters of Application*

The two most common letters of application you will write are letters requesting employment and letters requesting admission to graduate school.

(1) *Letter requesting employment*

When you apply for employment, your primary objective is to interest a prospective employer enough so that he or she will schedule an interview with you. Before you write, collect all the information you need for your letter—previous employment, employers, dates, and relevant courses, for example. Then consider why you want the job and what about you might interest a prospective employer. Next, make an informal outline, and then begin your rough draft.

Begin your letter by stating which job you are applying for and where you heard about it—in a newspaper, in a journal, from a professor, or from your school job placement service, for instance. Be sure to include the date of the advertisement and the exact title

Sample Letter Requesting Employment—Semiblock Format

```
                                    246 Hillside Drive
                                    Urbana, IL 61801
                                    October 20, 1991

Mr. Maurice Snyder, Personnel Director
Guilford, Fox, and Morris
Eckerd Building
22 Hamilton Street
Urbana, IL 61822


Dear Mr. Snyder:

My adviser, Dr. Raymond Walsh, has told me that you are
interested in hiring a part-time accounting assistant.
I feel that my academic background and my work
experience qualify me for this position.

I am presently a junior accounting major at the
University of Illinois. During the past year, I have
taken courses in taxation, trusts, and business law. I
have worked with a microcomputer and have developed my
own tax program. Last spring, I gained practical
accounting experience by working in the department tax
clinic.

After I graduate, I hope to get a Master's degree in
taxation and then return to the Urbana area. I feel
that my experience in taxation as well as my familiarity
with the local business community would enable me to
contribute to your firm.

I have enclosed a résumé for your examination. I will
be available for an interview any time after midterm
examinations, which end October 25. I look forward to
hearing from you.


                                    Sincerely yours,

                                    Sandra Kraft

                                    Sandra Kraft

                                    Enclosure
```

of the position. End your introduction with your thesis: a statement of your ability to do the job.

The body of your letter provides the information that will convince your reader of your qualifications. Mention any relevant courses you have taken and any pertinent job experience. Take care to address any specific concerns mentioned in the advertisement. Above all, emphasize your strengths.

Conclude by referring to your résumé. State that you are available for an interview, noting any dates on which you cannot be available.

EXERCISE 1

Look through the employment advertisements in your local paper or in the files of your college placement service. Choose one job, and write a letter of application in which you outline your qualifications and achievements and discuss why you want the position.

(2) Letters to Graduate or Professional Schools

Graduate and professional schools routinely ask applicants for autobiographies or statements explaining why they have applied. These personal statements reveal a great deal about you, including your goals, your level of maturity, and your ability to communicate. They are read carefully, and they help to determine whether or not you will be accepted.

As you plan, write, and revise, concentrate on what distinguishes you from others who are applying to the school. Be specific, offering examples from your experience to illustrate the points you make. Everything in your statement should underscore your thesis: that you are committed to the field and should be admitted to the program.

EXERCISE 2

Assume that you are applying to one of the following graduate programs.

Law school
Medical school
Business school
Journalism school
Social work school
A graduate program in an academic field

Sample Letter to Professional School—Indented Format

33513 Capstan Drive
Laguna Niguel, CA 92677
April 7, 1991

Donna Claxton-Deming, Assistant Dean of Admissions
Temple University School of Law
1719 N. Broad Street
Philadelphia, PA 19122

Dear Ms. Claxton-Deming:

During my sophomore and junior years in college, I worked part-time for a law firm in Cincinnati. I began as a file clerk and eventually was promoted to the research department of the firm. This experience was a turning point in my life. It helped me decide to become a lawyer and to take courses that would prepare me for this goal.

The firm in which I worked does general practice and also a good deal of community legal work. After being there for eight months, I was given the responsibility of screening legal-aid clients and assigning them to one of three lawyers. I consulted with attorneys and, at times, discussed specific cases with them. Eventually they allowed me to be present when depositions were taken.

My experiences with a law firm have given me a realistic picture of what the practice of law is and have enabled me to make a mature, informed decision to become a lawyer. I am certain that as a result, I will be an understanding and compassionate attorney, one who puts her clients' interests before her own.

To prepare for my legal career, I have majored in political science and minored in business. My grade point average has been good: 3.35 on a 4.0 scale. I have taken courses in political theory, government, accounting, and constitutional law. I have also taken a number of courses in sociology, psychology, and business writing. In addition, I am a member of my school's pre-law society, and I won honorable mention in a regional moot-court competition held last spring.

My background has made me realize my responsibility to the legal profession and to society. My involvement with the legal profession has provided me with the motivation to pursue a career in law. My academic record and my experience with legal work make me certain that a career in law is a realistic goal for me.

Sincerely,

Jacqueline Reyes

Jacqueline Reyes

Write a personal statement in which you tell the admissions officer what led you to choose your field. Be specific in describing your motivation, your experience, and your aspirations.

47c *Writing Résumés*

The letter of application summarizes your qualifications for a specific position; the résumé provides an overview of your accomplishments, focusing on your education and your work experience.

Before you compose your résumé, list all general information about your education, your job experience, your goals, and your personal interests. Then select the information that is most appropriate for the job you want, emphasizing the accomplishments that differentiate you from other candidates. If you have received academic honors or awards, or if you have financed your own education, include this information as well.

There is no single correct format for a résumé. Whatever its arrangement, however, it should be brief—one page is sufficient for an undergraduate—easy to read, and well organized. An employer should be able to see at a glance what your qualifications are.

Sections of a Résumé

- The **heading** includes your name, school address, home address, and phone number.
- The **education section**, includes the schools you have attended, starting with the most recent one and working back in time. After graduation from college, do not list your high schools unless you have a compelling reason to do so.
- The **summary of work experience** starts with your most recent job and works back.
- The **background section** lists special interests and community service. (Just a few examples will suffice.)
- The **references section** lists the full names and addresses of at least three references. If you already have a full-page résumé, a line saying that your references will be sent upon request is sufficient.
- If you can, include an **honors section** in which you list academic achievements and awards. In addition, you may include at the top of the page a statement of your *career objective.*

Sample Résumé

```
                    Michael D. Fuller
Address      Home                    Campus
             1203 Hampton Road       27 College Avenue
             Joppa, MD 21085         College Park, MD 20742
             Telephone:              Telephone:
             (301) 877-1437          (301) 357-0732

Education    University of Maryland, College Park, MD
1990-92      (sophomore). Biology major. Expected date
             of graduation: June 1994. Presently maintain
             a 3.3 average on a 4.0 scale.

1986-90      Forrest Park High School, Baltimore, MD.
             Basketball team, track team, debating
             society, class president, mathematics tutor.
             Graduated in the top fifth of the class.

Experience   University of Maryland Library, College
1991-92      Park, MD. Assistant to the reference
             librarian. Filed, sorted, typed, shelved,
             and catalogued. Earnings offset college
             expenses.

1990-91      University of Maryland Cafeteria, College
             Park, MD. Busboy. Cleaned tables, set up
             cafeteria, and prepared hot trays.

1990         McDonald's Restaurant, Pikesville, MD. Cook.
Summer       Prepared hamburgers. Acted as assistant
             manager for two weeks when manager was on
             vacation.

Background   Member of University Debating Society. Tutor
             in University Program for Disadvantaged
             Students.

References   Ms. Stephanie Young, Librarian
             Library
             University of Maryland
             College Park, MD 20742

             Mr. William Czernick, Manager
             Cafeteria
             University of Maryland
             College Park, MD 20742

             Mr. Arthur Sanducci, Manager
             McDonald's Restaurant
             5712 Avery Road
             Pikesville, MD 22513
```

Remember that federal law prohibits employers from discriminating on the basis of age, sex, or race, and you need not include such information in your résumé.

EXERCISE 3

Prepare a résumé to include with the letter of employment you wrote for Exercise 1.

47d *Writing Letters Requesting Information*

Students sometimes have to send letters requesting information from a person or a business. For instance, you might ask an instructor for a recommendation or write to an expert in a field to gather information for a research project.

Before you write such a letter, decide exactly what information you need. Make a list if necessary, and eliminate questions that you can answer yourself. Think about what you need the information for and how much time you have to get it. Usually you can limit your request to a few questions that can be answered quickly and easily.

Write a courteous and concise letter. Introduce yourself, and say clearly what information you want and why you want it. Be specific; your reader will be doing you a favor by responding, and you should not waste his or her time. If you have several requests, number them—and keep them simple.

EXERCISE 4

For a research paper on television situation comedies, write a letter requesting information from Dr. Alan Friedman (38 University Place, New York University, New York, NY 10003), a noted authority on the subject. Ask him four questions you would like him to answer. Remember that Dr. Friedman is very busy, but he will probably answer a short, businesslike letter.

Sample Letter Requesting Information—Semiblock Format

```
                              17 Maple Drive
                              Clinton, MS 39058
                              December 2, 1991

Dr. Norman Murphy
English Department
Louisiana State University
  at Shreveport
Shreveport, LA 75115

Dear Dr. Murphy:

I am a third-year English major at Clinton College, and
I am interested in pursuing a career in scientific and
technical writing. Dr. Stewart Lage, my adviser,
thought that you could give me advice about schools that
have graduate programs in this field.

Although I prefer to stay in the South, I am willing to
go to school in any part of the country. I am
particularly interested in schools that have internship
programs that would allow me to gain practical
experience in industry. I have already written to
Stanford University and am waiting for its catalog.

I am currently at home and will be back at school on
January 6th. I would appreciate any information you
could mail to me or to Dr. Lage.

I hope to hear from you soon.

                              Yours truly,

                              Daniel Howell, Jr.

                              Daniel Howell, Jr.
```

47e   *Writing Letters of Appeal*

Students often have occasion to write letters asking for a clarification of or change in college policy. For example, you may need to request permission to take a two-credit overload, to waive or change a particular requirement for graduation, to request a leave of absence, to appeal a faculty or administrative decision, or to request permission to live off campus. In such situations, the goal of your appeal is to convince the reader or readers of your letter that your point of view is worth considering. In many cases your audience will be inclined to hold a view different from yours, and you will have to convince them to change their minds.

As you write a letter of appeal, keep in mind the principles of writing an argumentative essay. Remember that the purpose of your letter is to convince your readers of the validity of your claims. To achieve this end, be sure that you maintain a rational tone. Support your points with facts and reasonable arguments, and avoid arguing against a policy simply because "it's not fair." Present yourself as a reasonable person who sees both sides of an issue, and remember that anger or sarcasm will only undercut your case. Revise your letter with your reader in mind. If your reader is unfamiliar with your case, begin with an overview, not an involved discussion of your problem. Arrange events in logical order, using transitions to make their sequence apparent. Be sure that your tone is firm but reasonable. Try to end on a positive note—at the very least asserting your belief in the fairness or goodwill of the reader.

▶ See Ch. 7

EXERCISE 5

Your college or university owes you a $250 refund from your tuition. Apparently they charged you twice for a student activities fee. After discovering the error you go to the registrar, who tells you that as a matter of policy all refunds are credited to the next semester's tuition. After a day and a half of hearing the same story at one office after another, you decide to write a letter to the president of the school. In this letter tell the president why you think the school should reimburse you now. Make a strong case, and present the facts clearly and logically.

Sample Letter of Appeal—Block Format

Room 405A
Building A
October 15, 1992

Ms. Andrea Perry, Director
Residential Life

Dear Ms. Perry:

I am writing this letter because I would like to keep my pet Burmese Python *(Python molurus bivittatus)* in my dorm room. This snake is nonpoisonous and is harmless to humans. Like all snakes, pythons make no noise, do not smell, and have no need of walks. I think that because of my background, I am uniquely qualified to attest to the desirability of having pythons as pets.

The first quality that makes Burmese pythons good pets is that they are safe. For two years, I worked at a large pet store in Philadelphia where I cared for more than two hundred snakes and other reptiles. During my employment, I was responsible for their care and feeding. I also kept many snakes as pets. Not one of the pets I kept ever caused any problems for either my parents or me. In addition, I was never harmed by any of the animals in the store nor by any of the snakes I kept at home.

In addition to being safe, Burmese pythons are inactive much of the day. The only time they become animated is when they are fed. After they eat their meal—one small mouse a week—they settle down to digest their food. As a result, they lie dormant for long periods of time, moving only to drink water or to change their position. This characteristic makes pythons ideally suited for the dorms.

My roommate, Derek Nelson (ext. 5647), is willing to have the snake in our room. My housemasters, Anthony Silverstein (ext. 8408) and Trish Mullen (ext. 8303), have also said that they would be willing to let me have a snake if you gave your permission. I realize that there is a rule against having pets in the dorm, but I feel that this pet is so easy to keep that an exception should be made. Finally, I believe that due to my years of experience working with snakes, I have the ability to care for my pet.

I would like to set up an appointment with you to discuss this matter. Thank you for your time and trouble.

Sincerely yours,

Christopher Mauro

Christopher Mauro

47f *Composing Memos*

The process of composing memos is much the same as the process of composing business letters. Unlike letters, however, memos communicate information *within* a business organization. They can communicate brief messages of a paragraph or two, or short reports or proposals. Their function is generally to convey information or to persuade. Regardless of their function, most memos have the following general structure.

The Opening Component   The **opening component**—*To, From, Subject,* and *Date*—replaces the heading and inside address of a letter (see sample, p. 820). This section establishes at a glance the audience and the subject of your communication. Because a memo often circulates beyond its original audience, all names and titles should be stated in full. The *subject line,* which exists to give your reader a clear idea what your memo is about, should include more than one word. "Housing" means very little to readers unfamiliar with your subject; "Changes in Student Housing Policy" states the subject more precisely.

The Body   The **body** of your memo should begin with a purpose statement containing key words that immediately convey your message. Some people like to present the purpose statement as a separate component with its own heading. In any case, the purpose statement should include a word that clearly defines your intention—for example, *evaluates, proposes, questions, reports, describes,* or *presents.*

The first paragraph of the body summarizes your conclusions; the rest of your memo tells readers how you arrived at your conclusions, backing them up with facts and figures. Often each paragraph of a memo has a heading that identifies its subject. These headings guide readers through the body of your memo.

The Conclusion   The **conclusion** of your memo should contain a detailed restatement of your points. If its purpose is to persuade your readers of something, you should include a list of recommendations. Because readers remember best what comes last, you should end your memo with a summary of the action that should be taken or the conclusions that should be drawn.

In the following memo from a student in a tutoring program, the writer uses headings to identify the major divisions of her discussion

TO: Ina Ellen, Senior Counselor
FROM: Kim Williams, Student Tutor Supervisor
SUBJECT: Construction of a Tutoring Center
DATE: November 10, 1991

The purpose of this memo is to propose the construction of a tutoring center in the Office of Student Affairs.

BACKGROUND
Under the present system, student tutors must work with students in a number of facilities scattered across the university campus. This situation has a number of drawbacks, including a lack of contact among tutors and the inability of tutors to get immediate help with problems if they need it. As a result, tutors waste a lot of time running from one facility to another—and often miss appointments. Most tutors agree that the present system is unwieldy and ineffective.

NEW FACILITY
I propose that we build a tutoring room adjacent to the Office of Student Affairs. The two empty classrooms adjacent to the office, presently used for storage of office furniture, would be ideal for this use. Incurring a minimum of expense and using its own maintenance workers, the university could convert these rooms into ten small offices. We could furnish these offices with the desks and file cabinets already stored in these rooms.

BENEFITS
The benefits of this facility would be the centralizing of the tutoring service and the proximity of the facility to the Office of Student Affairs. The tutoring facility could also use the secretarial services of the Office of Student Affairs, ensuring that student tutors get messages from the students with whom they work.

RECOMMENDATIONS
To implement this project we would need to do the following:

1. Clean up and paint rooms 331 and 333 and connect them to the Office of Student Affairs
2. Use folding partitions to divide each room into five single-desk offices
3. Use stored office equipment to furnish the center

I am certain that these changes would do much to improve the tutoring service that the Office of Student Affairs now offers, and I look forward to discussing this matter with you in more detail.

and emphasizes her recommendations by presenting them in list form. Her purpose is to persuade her audience; therefore, she addresses her reader's major concerns—cost, ease of construction, and projected benefits—and she ends with a list of recommendations.

EXERCISE 6

Your duties at your summer job with a public utility in your area include reading correspondence that goes from your division to the public. While reading a pamphlet that discusses energy conservation, you come across the following words and sentences: "Each consumer must do *his* part," "*repairman*," and "*Mothers* should teach their children about energy conservation." With the approval of your supervisor, you decide to write a memo to John Durand, Public Relations Manager, explaining to him that this inaccurate language could offend some readers. In your memo, explain to Mr. Durand why the language should be changed and some words and phrases he could use in their place. Mr. Durand is your superior, so maintain a reasonable tone.

A P P E N D I X

Preparing Your Papers

A clean, neatly typed or handwritten paper is a courtesy that you owe your readers. Sloppily typed or smudged papers not only make reading difficult but also detract from your ideas. Some of your instructors will give you specific guidelines for preparing a paper—and of course, you should follow them. But others will expect you to be familiar with the conventions for preparing a paper. The following instructions are standard and, in general, are consistent with those found in the MLA style sheet (3rd ed).

A1 *Typed or Printed Papers*

Submit typed papers whenever possible. Because typewritten papers are easier to read, they are worth the extra effort—even if you are a slow typist. Before you type, be sure that your keys are clean and that you have a fresh black ribbon or a new cartridge in your printer. Do not use "fancy" type, such as script, that could distract your readers. Be sure to make a copy for your files in case your instructor misplaces your paper.

Use white, twenty-pound weight 8½″ × 11″ bond paper. Avoid both erasable paper and "onionskin." Not only do they smudge, but they are also difficult to read. In addition, it is hard to make corrections in ink on coated paper. Remember, never use paper that is not white or that is smaller than 8½″ × 11″.

Double-space your paper throughout. Single-spacing is hard to read and does not leave enough room for instructors' comments or corrections.

A2 *Handwritten Papers*

If you have permission to submit a handwritten paper, use 8½″ × 11″ wide-lined paper. Do not use narrow-lined paper, unlined paper, or paper larger or smaller than 8½″ × 11″. Your best choice is paper that you can easily and neatly detach from a tablet. Do not use paper that leaves a ragged edge when torn from a spiral-bound notebook. Leave wide margins, write on every other line, and be sure to use only one side of each page. Use black or dark blue ink, never colored ink or pencil.

Make certain that you write clearly and that you form each letter carefully. If your handwriting is sloppy, try printing. Keep in mind that your instructor has many papers to mark and does not appreciate having to struggle with handwriting that is difficult to read.

A3 *Format*

Leave a one-inch margin at the top and bottom and on both sides of your paper. Indent five spaces for each new paragraph and ten spaces for a long quotation set off from the text.

Many instructors do not require a separate title page. If yours does not, type your name, the course number, your instructor's name, and the date (all double-spaced) one inch from the top of the first page of the paper, flush with the left-hand margin. Double-space again and center the title. If the title is longer than a single line, double-space and center the second line below the first. Capitalize all important words in the title, but not prepositions, conjunctions, articles, or the *to* in infinitives, unless they begin or end the title. Do not underline the title or enclose it in quotation marks. Underline words in the title if they are underlined in your paper (for example, book titles). Never put a period after a title, even if it is a sentence. Double-space between the last line of the title and the first line of text.

Number all pages of your paper consecutively—including the first—in the upper right-hand corner, one-half inch from the top, flush right. Do not put *p.* before the page numbers, and do not put periods or any other punctuation after them. To ensure that your instructor will be able to replace separated pages, put your name next to the page number of all pages.

Sample of First Page of Paper Without a Title Page

```
                                                    ½" ↕
                 ↕ 1"                                Williamson 1
     1"          ↓
     ↔→Mark Williamson
                          ←───── double-space
         Eng. 101

         Dr. Stevens
     double space ──→
         March 20, 1992


     center ──────────→Big Brother in George Orwell's 1984
     double space ──→
     indent 5 ──→Although the year 1984 has passed, Orwell's

         novel by the same name. . . .
```

Sample Page Format

```
                                                    ½" ↕
                 ↕ 1"                                Williamson 2
     1"          ↓                                  ½" ↕
     ↔→The language, manners, and mores of Orwell's world are
                                                                 1"
         determined by the state. When the characters in 1984 are faced ←─
         with a decision, they usually. . . .
```

(1) Subsequent pages of a paper with a title page

Some instructors prefer a separate title page and an outline like the ones appearing with the paper at the end of Chapter 40 (page 670). The title page carries the title; your name, course, and section number; your instructor's name; and the date you submitted your paper.

A2

When you use a title page, repeat your title on the first page of your manuscript. Subsequent pages follow the format for a paper without a title page. If your paper includes an outline more than one page long, number each page with a lowercase Roman numeral (i, ii, etc.). A single-page outline need not be numbered. All pages of the text include your last name and the page number.

Sample of First Page of a Paper with a Separate Title Page

```
                                                    ½"
                                                        Williamson 1
             1"
center              Big Brother in George Orwell's 1984
double space                                                         1"
indent 5    Although the year 1984 has passed, Orwell's novel by the
spaces
        same name. . . .
```

A4 *Typing Punctuation*

The conventions that determine the spacing of typed punctuation are illustrated below. Be sure to follow them consistently through-out the paper.

TYPED PUNCTUATION

Type of Punctuation	Typing Conventions	Examples
1. apostrophes	Leave no space before or after the apos-trophe unless the apostrophe ends a word.	Turner's landscapes The writer's local color novels

continued

continued from previous page

Type of Punctuation	Typing Conventions	Examples
2. commas and semicolons	Leave no spaces before commas or semi-colons; leave one space after commas and semicolons.	In fact, the story was untrue; the slave revolt failed.
3. colons, question marks, and exclamation points	Leave no spaces before these punctuation marks; leave one space after a colon and two spaces after a question mark or exclamation point.	Discuss the following: plot, character, and theme. Was he correct? Perhaps. Never! Tyranny can never triumph.
4. quotation marks	Leave no spaces between quotation marks and the words or punctuation marks they enclose.	The short story "The Gold Bug" is by Poe. "I come to bury Caesar," said Mark Antony, "not to praise him."
5. periods	Leave no space before a period at the end of a sentence. Leave two spaces after the period.	It has been an issue since 1938. The fight for intellectual freedom continues.
6. hyphens or dashes	A hyphen is one stroke; a dash is two unspaced hyphens.	quick-witted Ford was born poor-- not rich--on a farm.
7. ellipsis marks	Separate all periods of an ellipsis mark by one space. Do not leave a space before the period at the end of a sentence that is followed by an ellipsis mark.	It was . . . a bitter satire of the motion picture industry. The report examines many classes of people. . . .

Type of Punctuation	Typing Conventions	Examples
8. italics	Underline words to indicate italics. You can use an unbroken line or underline each word separately.	The Sun Also Rises The Sun Also Rises
9. parentheses, brackets	Leave one space before opening a parenthesis and one after closing a parenthesis. Do not space between the enclosed words and the parentheses. If the parentheses contain an entire sentence, leave two spaces before and after the parentheses. Brackets follow the same conventions as parentheses.	Charles Lindbergh attended the University of Wisconsin (1920–22) but left to learn how to fly. In 1907, Luther Burbank wrote *Training of the Human Plant.* (The pamphlet dealt with environment and human development.) In 1909. . . .
10. slashes	Leave no space before or after a slash except if the slash separates lines of poetry. In this case leave one space before and one after the slash.	The object travels at 800 m/sec in a parallel direction. "Nature's first green is gold. / Her hardest hue to hold." (Robert Frost)

A5 *Tables and Illustrations*

Tables and illustrations aid readers by summarizing material that is being presented. In order to carry out this function, tables and illustrations should be placed as close as possible to the part of the paper in which they are presented. Graphic aids should be integrated into the text, not just dropped into the middle of it. You can achieve this end by introducing tables and illustrations and by explaining their meaning to readers. For example, you might include a sentence such as "Table 3 shows the year-by-year increase in the national debt from 1980 to 1988."

Tables should be headed *Table* and given an Arabic numeral and a descriptive caption. Type the heading and the descriptive caption flush left on separate lines. Capitalize the heading and the caption as if they were titles. Give the full citation for the table (if it is borrowed from a source) and for any notes below the table beginning at the left-hand margin. Double-space the table text and the notes.

Table 2

Reading Miscues Based on the Reading Comprehension Test	
Reading Miscue Inventory	Percentile
Total miscues	53
Semantically inappropriate miscues	60
Miscues which alter meaning	51
Overall loss of comprehension	40
Retelling score	20

Source: Adapted from Alice S. Horning, "The Trouble with Writing Is the Trouble with Reading," Journal of Basic Writing 6(1987):46.

Illustrations—graphs, charts, line drawings, and photographs—should be labeled *Figure* (abbreviated *Fig.*) and given an Arabic number. The label, a descriptive caption, and the full citation are typed below the illustration beginning at the left-hand margin.

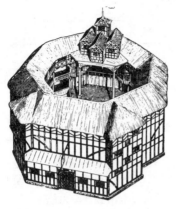

Fig. 1. Etching of the Globe Playhouse from Thomas Mark Parrott and Edward Hubler, Six Plays and the Sonnets (New York: Scribner's, 1956) 2.

A6 *Editing Your Final Draft*

After finishing the final draft of your paper, proofread it carefully and correct any errors. If a page is messy or if you have to make extensive corrections, retype or reprint the entire page. Make minor corrections with correction fluid. Never make corrections in the margin or below the line. If your instructor gives you permission, you may make some corrections in black ink. Use the proofreader's marks on the next page in moderation to indicate your changes.

A7 *Submitting Your Paper*

When you are ready to submit your paper, fasten the pages together with a paper clip in the upper left-hand corner. Do not staple the paper together like a book or use a binder that cannot easily be removed. Remember that your instructor cannot write comments on your paper if he or she cannot separate the pages.

Proofreader's Marks

Mark	Mark in text
∧	add; insert a ^word here
℘	delete; take a ℘ word out
⌣	close up; one w⌣ord
℘	delete; and close u↷p
# / ∧	add a#space
(stet)	disregard ~~change~~↻ (stet)
¶	¶ Begin new paragraph
/	lower-case /etter
≡	≡capital letter
∽	transpose lett⟋e⟍s
(ital)	italics (ital)
∽∽∽ (bf)	boldface (bf)
⟳	You can also indicate that you do not want to begin a paragraph.⟩ ⟨Draw a line to connect the two sentences.

Guide to Writing
with Computers

Why should you take valuable time from your other classes or your social life to learn how to use a computer? A long-range answer is that when you enter the working world, your employer will expect you to be computer literate.

A more immediate answer is that many of your classes will demand writing—sometimes a lot of it. A computer will make it easier for you to produce the kind of writing you will do in any course.

Since many different word-processing programs are on the market, it is difficult to give specific advice. In general, however, computers will not do the writing for you and word processing alone will not make you a better writer; classroom instruction in writing skills and hard work on your part are absolutely essential. Any word-processing program, however, will take much of the drudgery out of writing; in fact, many reluctant writers report that word processing makes writing more enjoyable.

General Advice for Writing with Computers

- Learn to type quickly and accurately.
- Know your software's capabilities.
- Do not allow yourself to mistake neatness for quality.
- Proofread carefully.
- Print your work frequently so you can see it in its entirety.
- Save your work frequently, perhaps every page or so—certainly after you have done anything that you would have a difficult time rewriting if lost.
- Take care of your files. Make a backup copy of every file on another disk.

---

1   *How Writing with Computers Can Help You*

Experienced writers recognize that writing is rewriting. A computer will allow you to rewrite papers with a minimum of time and effort. Because working on a computer makes revising and editing faster and easier, you may be more inclined to make revisions you might before have hesitated to make.

(1)   Note taking

Whether you are writing an essay or a research paper, you can type your preliminary notes or research ideas into a file you have created especially for that purpose. Or, you can take notes with pen and paper and enter them later into that special file. When you begin to write your paper, review these notes as you develop ideas and begin to organize them; you can even copy notes directly into your paper as you write.

(2)   Planning

You may find it advantageous to carry out planning and pre-writing strategies at the computer. Freewriting, for example, is much easier and more efficient with a computer. You can type faster; you can move the writing you produce directly into an essay without having to retype it; and you can easily group and organize your notes.

Word processing makes it easy to be spontaneous and create the kind of free-flowing writing that brainstorming and journals contain. If, however, you prefer doing your brainstorming, free writing, journal entries, and note taking by hand, you should do so. But you should try experimenting with the computer at all stages of the writing process. Writers who are comfortable planning and composing at the keyboard can save themselves a great deal of time.

(3)   Shaping

Your computer's ability to *move* parts of text—whether a single word or a number of paragraphs—from one location in a document to another is a powerful tool for organizing notes. For example, if you have created brainstorming or note-taking files, you can use the computer to organize your ideas. You can use the *delete* and *insert* commands to group similar notes together into "idea chunks." Experiment with putting the groups in different orders until you discover the best way to present your information.

You can use word processing in this way to arrange your notes into something approaching an informal outline or even a very rough draft. You can also make an outline by typing words or phrases representing main and supporting ideas, arranging and rearranging them until the order begins to make sense, and indenting them with the <Tab> key to indicate relative importance and subordination.

Following is an example of how Michael Schrader organized his first thoughts on what happened to the Italian family after immigration to the United States (note that the arrows indicate tabs):

▶ **See Ch. 40**

Immigrants who came from southern Italy
    → What were their customs in Italy?
    →   → Kept separate ones according to village of origin
    →   →   → Each village was really important
    →   →   → The family was important also
    → In America
    →   → They recreated the customs from Italy
    →   → They thought a lot about the old country
    →   → It was important to keep the Italian heritage

At a later stage in the writing process, Michael Schrader created a more formal outline by using the standard indicators of outline

---

Word-Processing Strategy: Planning

- Be sure you keep your planning and shaping material separate from your first draft. You can do this by creating different kinds of material. For example, if you are writing a paper on environmental issues in your community, you can call your planning and shaping file ENVIR-PS and your draft file ENVIR-D. In your ENVIR-PS file, you can store journal entries, brainstorming lists, notes on observations and readings, or informal outlines.

levels. (Note that he still needs to cast his thoughts in parallel constructions.)

→I. Immigrants from southern Italian villages
→ →A. In Italy
→ → →1. Separate customs maintained
→ → →2. Identification with family and village
→ →B. In America
→ → →1. Italian customs recreated
→ → →2. Identification with Italy

(4) Writing

As you write, keep in mind that writing is not a linear process; that is, a piece of writing usually does not proceed neatly and directly from a beginning right through to a conclusion. As writers write—sometimes while in the middle of developing a paragraph, or even writing a sentence—they go back to reread and think about what they have written and then, on the spot, edit or revise before going on. Experienced writers, in other words, are not trapped by what has been called the linear composing mode.

Because writing is not a neat, orderly process, the computer offers definite advantages. Text can easily be reshaped when you make changes and reformatted when you add new text or delete old text; thus, it is possible for you to begin in the middle or "end" at the beginning. As ideas come to you while writing, you can type them immediately and insert them wherever you think they ought to go—and, all the while, you can be certain that you can change their location (or even delete them) later on with little effort.

Although brainstorming is a good technique for inventing ideas, it is not something you can do only at the beginning of a writing assignment. Experienced writers often brainstorm whenever they need to generate ideas, no matter their current "stage" (*planning, shaping,* or *writing and revision*) in the writing process. Indeed, with a computer, the divisions between "stages" in the writing process tend to disappear.

Word-Processing Strategy: Writing

- As you write, enclose any comments or questions that occur to you in brackets or format them in bold or uppercase letters. Later, as you revise, you will easily be able to identify and react to these notes.

---

(5) *Revising*

Revising with a computer is much easier than revising with a typewriter or pen and paper. We have all been in the position of wanting to make changes in something we have written yet not wanting to retype the entire essay to add a sentence in the middle of a paragraph at the bottom of the first page.

A computer will not necessarily save you time; you will probably still spend just as many hours writing your essays. The difference will be that your time is spent more effectively. Instead of taking hours to type a neater version of an essay, you will be able to spend your time doing real revision—adding new paragraphs, deleting or rewording sentences, or moving a block of text.

The claim by some writing instructors that no writer ever did anything new with a computer contains a kernel of truth. But a word processor can help you do things faster and more accurately than you could do them by hand. A computer is especially efficient and helpful when it comes to finding potential problems in logic and organization in both paragraphs and complete essays.

Although some people revise exclusively the computer screen, this is not a good strategy. For one thing, you can only see a small portion of your text on the screen at any given time. For another, it is difficult for you to compare drafts. For these reasons, you should always print out a hard copy of each draft. This strategy enables you to see the entire paper and thus to make global revisions. You should make your handwritten changes on this hard copy and then enter them into your computer.

Word-Processing Strategies: Revising

- Use the *delete* and *insert* commands to move paragraphs around in your essay so that the order of the paragraphs is scrambled. Ask another student to try to discover the original order of the paragraphs. If he or she has trouble doing so, you may not have organized the material in a logical way or you may not have used transitions between paragraphs effectively.
- "Explode" a paragraph you have written by putting a <Return> after each sentence; this will format each sentence as a separate paragraph. Then, as you did with the paragraphs in your essay, use the *delete* and *insert* commands to scramble the text. (You can also use the search-and-replace function to replace spaces between sentences with paragraph returns.) Ask a classmate to try to put the sentences back in their original order. If he or she has difficulty

---

doing so, your paragraph may not be coherent—that is, the sentences may not be in a logical order or you may not have used transitions effectively.

- Take a typical paragraph you have written in which the topic sentence occurs at the beginning. Copy the paragraph twice so you have a total of three identical ones. Leave the topic sentence in the first paragraph in its original position at the beginning; move the topic sentence in the second paragraph to some suitable point near the middle; finally, move the topic sentence in the third paragraph to the end. In each case, ask yourself what advantages or disadvantages there are in having the topic sentence in that particular location. (Ask a classmate for his or her opinion.) When you place the topic sentence in a new location, do you have to make other changes in the rest of the paragraph? What changes? Why?

- As you revise, put material you might want to delete in **bold** characters, material you might want to rearrange in UPPER-CASE characters, and material you might want to add in underlined characters. After discussing possible changes with a peer editing partner, or in a small group of classmates, you can carry out the revisions you decide to make.

- Be careful about permanently discarding material that does not seem useful at the time. Get in the habit of moving unwanted material to the end of the file on which you are working, or to a special file until you are certain you really do not need it.

(6)   *Editing*

You may find it easier to spot surface-level problems—typing mistakes or grammar, punctuation, and spelling errors—if you can see what you have written in a different way or from a different perspective. Several strategies can help you accomplish this while you are editing your paper.

Word-Processing Strategies: Editing

- Try looking at only a small portion of text at a time. If your software allows you to split the screen and create another *window*, create one so short that you can see only one or two lines of text. Try this technique also while reading your essay backwards—last sentence to first—and you may find you can dramatically reduce the number of surface-level effors in your essays.
- Print a hard copy and work with a pen or pencil to mark final

continued

continued from previous page

> changes you want to make before entering the changes with the computer. Seeing your work on paper rather than a computer screen can help you find new ways to revise.
> - Use the *search* command to look for words or phrases about which your instructor has warned you, or for errors you commonly make—confusing *it's* with *its*, *lay* for *lie*, *effect* with *affect*, *their* with *there*, *its* with *it's*, or *too* with *to*. You can also search for examples of sexist language (*he*, *his*, *him*, *man*).

Finally, learn how to use the spell checker. Remember that it does not find "mistakes"; it simply identifies character strings that it does not recognize. Thus, a spell checker will not recognize *there* in "They forgot there books on the table" as incorrect, nor will it spot the typo in "Whatever he wanted to do, he dad." You still have the responsibility to proofread your papers carefully. In fact, your spell checker can lull you into thinking it will do all of the work for you. It will not.

(7) Formatting

When you write with a computer, you can easily tailor the format of your document for special audiences and occasions. With a little practice, you can make paragraphs look any way you wish for special kinds of documents.

> Here is a paragraph—the kind you will use most of the time for your essays—formatted in a conventional way, with the first line indented five spaces.

- Here is an indented paragraph preceded by a "bullet"—suitable, in some professional documents, for listing items or calling attention to something.

And here is a paragraph—the kind you might use in business letters—formatted with no indent.

With a computer you can quickly change the size of margins and the amount of space between lines. You might want to make such changes when you give a draft of an essay to a peer editor, printing it triple spaced, for example, or with extra-wide margins to leave room for written comments.

Finally, word processing can give your writing a neat, "finished" appearance. Keep in mind, however, that neatness does not equal correctness. Ironically, the ability of a computer to produce neat-looking text can disguise flaws that might otherwise be readily apparent. Because your writing has a professional look, you will have to take special care to ensure that spelling errors and typos do not slip by.

(8) Documenting

Word processing can eliminate much of the work, frustration, and confusion in documenting sources for research papers. Many programs will, with a few simple keystrokes, create notes, number the notes correctly, and automatically change the reference numbers of all subsequent notes if you add a new one or delete text that contains a reference number. Most software programs allow you either to place the notes at the bottom of the appropriate pages or to collect them at the end of the document (where they are called endnotes).

(9) Other kinds of software

Style checkers are special programs designed to perform operations such as identifying possible mistakes in grammar or punctuation, critiquing your writing style (for example, the length and complexity of your sentences), or commenting on proper word usage (slang terms or sexist language). Be careful how you use style checkers. Many are most helpful to experienced writers who know how to interpret a program's advice. The real danger is that you will depend too much on the style checker and not look critically at your own writing. Remember that style checkers are not "smart." Although they may point out weaknesses or problems in your writing, they can recognize only a limited number of writing patterns and are only as good as the programming behind them. You are— and should be—the final authority.

Tutorial programs are designed to provide practice in punctuation, mechanics, grammar, and usage. You can use them at your own pace for extra practice in specific areas.

Word-Processing Strategy

Be sure you have your instructor's permission before you use a style checker.

---

2 *Important Terms*

Software   A program, written in a computer language, that tells a computer what to do and how to do it.

File   A series of computer-generated characters—usually letters and numbers—stored on a *disk*. Each file is given a name so the computer can find it when commanded to do so. When you write an essay (or part of an essay) and *save* it, you create a *file* which remains on the floppy or hard disk and which you can access again later and change, display, or print.

Cursor   The blinking marker, usually a small bar or rectangle, on a computer screen. The *cursor* is the entry point for all text you create on a computer screen. As you type, text will appear immediately to the left of the *cursor*.

Hard copy   The printed version of material produced on a computer. A hard copy enables you to reconstruct your work if you lose or damage your floppy disk or accidentally erase or destroy your file.

Save   The command that makes a permanent copy of a document on either a *floppy* or *hard disk*. Until you *save* a document, it exists only as electronic impulses in the *memory* of your computer. If there should be an accidental power failure, all text produced since the last time you *saved* will be permanently lost. Learn the *save* command immediately and get in the habit of saving regularly.

Copy   A command which makes it possible for the user to reproduce either a whole file or part of a file in a different place.

Delete   A command which permanently removes a portion of text from a document or a complete *file* from a *disk*.

Insert   A command which adds a portion of text to a document. This command is frequently used along with the *delete* command to *move* text.

Move   A command which relocates text from one place to another in the same document or from one document to another document. The *move* command is actually composed of two other commands—*delete* and *insert*.

Search   A command that looks for a designated character string—

usually a word or a group of words chosen by the user—in a file. The command can help you find places in your writing where you might want to make changes or check for errors. For example, you can tell your word processor to *search* for the pronouns *he, him,* and *his* so that you can be sure you have avoided sexist language.

Replace   The command—usually used along with the *search* command—that substitutes one character string for another. The *replace* command allows you to make quick, systematic changes in your writing. For example, if you decided to change the name of a character in a short story, you could make the computer *replace* every instance of *Jim* with *Frederick.*

Glossary of Usage

This glossary of usage lists words and phrases that often give trouble to writers. As you use it, remember that this glossary is intended as a guide and that nothing in it is absolute. Language is constantly changing, so throughout this glossary an effort has been made to reflect current usage in college, business, and technical writing. When a usage is in dispute or in flux, the alternatives are discussed along with the advantages and disadvantages of each. In addition to the advice you receive from this glossary, your own sense of the language, as well as your assessment of your audience and purpose, should help you decide whether a particular usage is appropriate.

a, an   Use *a* before words that begin with consonants or words that have initial vowels that sound like consonants.

   a primitive artifact   *a* one-horse carriage

Use *an* before words that begin with vowels and words that begin with a silent *h*.

   an aqueous solution   *an* honest person

accept, except   *Accept* is a verb that means "to receive." *Except* is a preposition or conjunction that means "other than." As a verb *except* means "to leave out."

   The auditors will *accept* all your claims *except* the last two.

   Aliens who have lived in the United States for more than five years are *excepted* from the regulation.

advice, advise   *Advice* is a noun meaning "opinion or information offered." *Advise* is a verb that means "to offer advice to."

   The king sent a messenger to the oracle to ask for *advice*.

   The broker *advised* her client to stay away from speculative stocks.

affect, effect   *Affect* is a verb meaning "to influence." *Effect* can be a verb or a noun. As a verb it means "to bring about," and as a noun it means "result."

   A severe cutback in federal funds for student loans could *affect* his plans for graduate school.

   The arbitrator tried to *effect* a settlement that would satisfy both the teachers and the school board.

   The most notable *effect* of the German bombing of London was to strengthen the resolve of the British.

afraid, frightened   See **frightened, afraid.**

aggravate, irritate   *Aggravate* means "to worsen." *Irritate* means "to annoy." Avoid using *aggravate* as a colloquial term for *irritate*.

   The malfunction of the computer system *irritated* the project leaders, who worried that the breakdown would *aggravate* an already tense situation.

all ready, already   *All ready* means "wholly prepared." *Already* means "by or before this or that time."

> During the thirties President Roosevelt made the country feel that it was *all ready* for any challenge that might confront it.

> By the time Horatius decided to call for help, it was *already* too late.

all right, alright   Although there is a tendency in the direction of *alright*, current usage calls for *all right*.

allusion, illusion   An *allusion* is a reference or hint. In literature it is a brief reference to a person, place, historical event, or other literary work with which a reader is expected to be familiar. An *illusion* is something that is not what it seems.

> In *The Catcher in the Rye* the main character makes an *allusion* to *The Return of the Native*, a book by Thomas Hardy.

> The Viking landing proved that the canals of Mars are an *illusion* caused by atmospheric and topographical conditions.

a lot   *A lot* is always two words. It is used colloquially as a substitute for "many" or "a great deal" and should be avoided in college writing.

among, between   *Among* refers to groups of more than two things. *Between* refers to just two things. The distinction between these terms seems to be fading, and it is becoming increasingly acceptable when speaking to use *between* for three or more things when *among* would sound awkward. In formal writing situations, however, you should maintain the distinction.

> The three parties agreed *among* themselves to settle the question out of court.

> By the time of his death in 323 B.C., Alexander's empire encompassed all the territory *between* Macedon and India.

amount, number   *Amount* refers to a quantity that cannot be counted. *Number* refers to things that can be counted. Always use *number* when referring to people.

> Because he had missed several payments, the bank called in the full *amount* of the loan.

> Seeing their commander fall, a large *number* of troops ran to his aid.

an, a   See **a, an.**

and/or   In business or technical writing, use *and/or* when either or both of the items it connects can apply. In college writing, however, the use of *and/or* should generally be avoided.

> The data recorder can print *and/or* display the temperatures of the cooling vats.

> The painter uses a sponge, a brush, or both to create his masterpieces.

apt to   See **likely to, liable to, apt to**

as . . . as . . .   In such constructions, *as* signals a comparison; therefore, you must use the second *as*.

> **AWKWARD:** John Steinbeck's *East of Eden* is as long if not longer than *The Grapes of Wrath*.

> **CLEAR:** John Steinbeck's *East of Eden* is *as* long *as* if not longer than *The Grapes of Wrath*.

as, like   Current usage accepts *as* as a conjunction or a preposition. *Like*, however, should be used as a preposition only. If a full clause is introduced, *as* is preferred.

> In his novel *The Scarlet Letter* Hawthorne uses imagery *as* he does in his other works.

> In its use of imagery *The Scarlet Letter* is *like The House of the Seven Gables*.

When you use *as* as a preposition, it indicates equivalency or identity.

> After classes he works *as* a manager of a fast-food restaurant.

Like, however, indicates resemblance but never identity.

Writers *like* Carl Sandburg appear once in a generation.

as, than   When making comparisons, either objective or subjective case pronouns can follow *as* or *than.* To determine case, you must know whether the things being compared are subjects or objects of verbs. A simple way to test this is to add the missing verb.

Nassim was as tall *as* he (is tall).

I have walked farther *than* he (has walked).

I like Jim more *than* (I like) *him.* (*Him* is the object of the missing verb *like.*)

assure, ensure, insure   *Assure* means "to tell confidently or to promise." *Ensure* and *insure* can be used interchangeably to mean "to make certain." *Insure,* however, almost always means "the protection of people or property against loss."

Caesar wished to *assure* the people that if they surrendered, he would not plunder their city.

To *ensure* (or *insure*) the smooth operation of the mechanism, you should oil it every six months.

It is extremely expensive for physicians to *insure* themselves against malpractice suits.

at, to   Many people use the prepositions *at* and *to* after *where* in conversation. This usage is redundant and should not be used in college writing.

COLLOQUIAL: *Where* are you working *at?*
             Where are you going *to?*
STANDARD: Where are you working?
             Where are you going?

awhile, a while   *Awhile* is an adverb. *A while* consists of an article and a noun that you can use as an object of a preposition.

Before we continue we will rest *awhile.* (modifies the verb *rest*)

Before we continue we will rest for *a while.* (object of the preposition *for*)

bad, badly   *Bad* is an adjective and *badly* is an adverb.

The school board decided that *The Tin Drum* by Günter Grass was a *bad* book and deleted it from the high school reading list.

For the past five years American automobile makers have been doing *badly.*

After verbs that refer to any of the senses or any other linking verb, use the adjective form.

He looked *bad.* He felt *bad.* It tasted *bad.*

Bad meaning "very much" is colloquial and should be avoided in college writing.

COLLOQUIAL: Jake Barnes felt that he needed a vacation in Spain real *bad.*
STANDARD: Jake Barnes felt that he badly needed a vacation in Spain.

being as, being that   Colloquial for *because.* These awkward phrases add unnecessary words and weaken your sentences.

Because (not *being that*) the climate was getting colder, a great number of animals migrated southward.

beside, besides   *Beside* is a preposition meaning "next to" and occasionally "apart from." *Besides* can be either a preposition or an adverb. As a preposition, *besides* means "except" or "other than." As an adverb it means "in addition to."

Beside the tower was a wall that ran the length of the old section of the city.

The judge pointed out to the lawyer that his argument was *beside* the point.

Besides its industrial uses, laser technology has many other applications.

Edison not only invented the light bulb and the ticker tape, but the phonograph *besides.*

between, among   See **among, between.**

bring, take   *Bring* means to transport from a farther place to a nearer place. *Take* means to carry or convey from a nearer place to a farther one.

> In the late nineteenth century many Russian Jewish immigrants were able to *bring* to this country only the clothes they wore.

> *Take* this message to the general and wait for a reply.

but, however, yet   *But, however,* and *yet* should be used alone, not in combination.

> She thought her essay was adequate, *but* (not *but yet* or *but however*) she continued to revise.

can, may   *Can* denotes ability and *may* indicates permission.

> *Can* (are they *able* to?) freshmen participate in the work-study program if they have not completed composition?

> *May* (do they have permission?) registered aliens collect unemployment benefits?

censor, censure   To *censor* is to label as undesirable passages of books, plays, films, news, essays, etc. To *censure* is to condemn or criticize harshly.

> Many recording artists are concerned that their albums will be *censored.*

> In 1633 Galileo was *censured* by the Inquisition for holding that the sun was the center of the universe.

center around   This common colloquialism is acceptable in speech but not in writing.

> The report *centers on* (not *around*) the effects of cigarette smoking on the circulatory system.

compare to, compare with   Formal usage calls for *compare to* when you want to stress similarities, and *compare with* when you want to analyze similarities *and* differences.

> In one of Shakespeare's sonnets, the speaker *compares* his beloved *to* a summer's day.

> This study *compares* Nat Turner's revolt *with* other slave revolts that occurred in the eighteenth and nineteenth centuries.

complement, compliment   *Complement* means "to complete or add to." *Compliment* means "to give praise."

> A double-blind study would *complement* their preliminary work on this anticancer drug.

> Before accepting the 1949 Nobel Prize for literature, William Faulkner *complimented* the people of Sweden for their courtesy and kindness.

conscious, conscience   *Conscious* means "having one's mental faculties awake." *Conscience* is the moral sense of right and wrong.

> With a local anesthetic a patient remains *conscious* during this procedure.

> During the American Civil War, the Copperheads followed the dictates of *conscience* and refused to fight.

consensus   "Consensus of opinion" is redundant because *consensus* means an "agreement of the majority." Write "they reached a consensus," or use "they agreed" or "the majority view was."

continual, continuous   *Continual* means "recurring at intervals." *Continuous* refers to an action that occurs without interruption.

> A pulsar is a star that emits a *continual* stream of electromagnetic radiation. (It emits radiation at regular intervals.)

> A small battery allows the watch to run *continuously* for five years. (It runs without stopping.)

could of, would of   In speech, the contractions *could've* and *would've* sound like the nonstandard constructions *could of* and *would of*. Spell out *could have* and *would have* in college writing.

Macbeth *would have* (not *would of*) defied his wife if he *could have* (not *could of*).

couple of   *Couple* means "a pair," but *couple of* may mean loosely "several" or "a few." When you designate quantities, avoid ambiguity. Write "four points," "three reasons," or "two examples" rather than "a couple of."

criterion, criteria   Although many people use these singular and plural words interchangeably, *criteria*, from the Greek, is the plural of *criterion*, meaning "standard for judgment."

Of all the *criteria* for hiring graduating seniors, class rank is the most important *criterion*.

curriculum   *Curriculum*, from the Latin, is a noun meaning "a course of study." The correct plural form is *curricula*.

The premedical *curriculum* at this university is extremely demanding.

There are three *curricula* you can follow in the college of business.

data   *Data* is the plural of the Latin *datum*, meaning "fact." In everyday speech and writing *data* is used for both singular and plural. In college writing preserve the distinction.

The *data* discussed in this section *are* summarized in the graph in Appendix A.

different from, different than   *Different than* is used extensively in American speech. Stylists, who point out that *different than* indicates a comparison where none is intended, prefer *different from*. In college writing, use *different from*.

His test scores were not much *different from* (not *than*) mine.

discreet, discrete   *Discreet* means "careful or prudent." *Discrete* means "separate or individually distinct."

Because Madame Bovary was not *discreet* with her lover, her reputation suffered.

Current research has demonstrated that atoms can be broken into hundreds of *discrete* particles.

disinterested, uninterested   *Disinterested* means "objective" or "capable of making an impartial judgment." *Uninterested* means "indifferent or unconcerned."

The narrator of Ernest Hemingway's "A Clean, Well-Lighted Place" is a *disinterested* observer of the action.

Finding no treasure after leading an expedition from Florida to Oklahoma, Hernando de Soto was *uninterested* in going farther.

due to   *Due to* is always correct when used as an adjective following a form of the verb *be*. Many object to the use of *due to* as a preposition meaning "because of."

The cancellation of classes was *due to* a sudden snow storm.

Classes were cancelled *because of* (not *due to*) a sudden snow storm.

effect, affect   See **affect, effect**.

emigrate from, immigrate to   *To emigrate* is "to leave one's country and settle in another." *To immigrate* is "to come to another country and reside there." The noun forms of these words are *emigrant* and *immigrant*.

In 1887 my great-grandfather *emigrated from* the Russian city of Minsk and traveled by ship to Boston. During that year many other *emigrants* made the same trip.

The potato famine of 1846–1847 caused many Irish to *immigrate to* the United States. These *immigrants* became builders, politicians, and storekeepers.

ensure, assure, insure   See **assure, ensure, insure**.

enthused   *Enthused,* a colloquial form of *enthusiastic,* should never be used in college writing.

> President John F. Kennedy was *enthusiastic* (not *enthused*) about the United States space program.

especially, specially   *Especially* means "particularly" or "very." *Specially* means "for a particular reason or purpose."

> He was *especially* proud of his daughter's athletic abilities when he learned a scholarship had been created in her honor. The *specially* created college scholarship was earmarked for athletically gifted women.

etc.   *Etc.,* the abbreviation of *et cetera,* means "and the rest." Although *etc.* is common in popular writing and speech, do not use it in your college writing. Say "and so on" or, better, specify exactly what *etc.* stands for.

> UNCLEAR: Before beginning a research paper you should have paper and pencil, *etc.*
>
> REVISED: Before beginning a research paper you should have a pencil, bond paper, and a clean typewriter ribbon.

everyday, every day   *Everyday* is an adjective that means "ordinary" or "commonplace." *Every day* means "occurring daily."

> In the Gettysburg Address, Lincoln used *everyday* words to create a model of clarity and conciseness.

> In *The Canterbury Tales* Chaucer describes a group of pilgrims who tell stories *every day* as they ride from London to Canterbury.

except, accept   See **accept, except.**

explicit, implicit   *Explicit* means "expressed or stated directly." *Implicit* means "implied" or "expressed or stated indirectly."

> The director *explicitly* warned the actors to be on time to rehearsals. Her *implicit* message was that lateness would be grounds for dismissal from the play.

farther, further   The distinction between these words as adjectives has all but disappeared. In formal writing, however, *farther* is preferred to designate distance and *further* to designate degree.

> I have traveled *farther* from my home town than any of my relatives.

> Critics of the welfare system charge that government subsidies to the poor encourage *further* dependence.

Further has two additional uses. As a conjunctive adverb *further* means "besides." As a transitive verb, *to further* means "to promote" or "to advance."

> Napoleon I was one of the greatest generals in history; *further,* he promoted liberalism through widespread legal reforms.

> Tom Jones, the hero of Fielding's novel, is a poor boy who is able to *further* himself with luck and good looks.

fewer, less   Use *fewer* with nouns that can be counted: *fewer* books, *fewer* people, *fewer* dollars. Use *less* with quantities that cannot be counted: *less* pain, *less* power, *less* enthusiasm.

figuratively, literally   See **literally, figuratively.**

firstly (secondly, thirdly, . . .)   Archaic forms meaning "in the first . . . second . . . third place." Use *first, second, third.*

former   *Former* as an adjective means "preceding" or "previous." As a noun it means "the first of two things mentioned previously." It is often used in conjunction with *latter.*

> The *former* residents of this area, the Delaware Indians, were forced to cede their land in 1795.

A24

Two books mark the extremes of Herman Melville's career: *Typee* and *Moby-Dick*. The *former* was a best seller; the *latter* was generally ignored by the public.

freshman, freshmen   *Freshman* is singular and *freshmen* is plural. Even so, only *freshman* is used as the adjective form: *freshman* composition, *freshman* registration, *freshman* dormitories. To avoid sexist usage, use *first-year student.*

frightened, afraid   *Frightened* should be accompanied by the prepositions *at* or *by*; *afraid* by *of*.

Dolley Madison, wife of President James Madison, was *frightened at* the thought of the British burning Washington.

In Charles Dickens's *A Christmas Carol,* Scrooge is *frightened by* three ghosts.

Young children are often *afraid of* the dark.

further, farther   See **farther, further.**

good, well   *Good* is an adjective, never an adverb.

The townspeople thought the proposal for a new municipal water plant was a *good* one.

Well can function as an adverb or an adjective. As an adverb it means "in a good manner." Correct usage requires "He did *well* (not *good*) on the test" and "She swam *well* (not *good*) in the meet."

Well is used as an adjective with verbs that denote a state of being or feeling. Here *well* can mean "in good health": "I feel *well*."

good and   This colloquial phrase meaning "very" is not appropriate in college writing.

After escaping from the Iroquois, Natty Bumppo was *very* (not *good and*) tired.

got to   *Got to* is slang and not suitable in college writing. To indicate obligation use *have to, has to,* or *must.*

INAPPROPRIATE: Anyone who takes a literature course has *got to* get a copy of *A Glossary of Literary Terms* by M. H. Abrams.

REVISED: Anyone who takes a literature course *has* to get a copy of *A Glossary of Literary Terms* by M. H. Abrams.

hanged, hung   Both *hanged* and *hung* are past participles of *hang. Hanged* is used to refer to executions. *Hung* is used in all other senses meaning "suspended" or "held up."

Billy Budd was *hanged* from the mainyard of the ship for killing the master-at-arms.

The pictures in the National Gallery were *hung* to take advantage of the natural lighting in the various rooms.

he, she   Traditionally *he* has been used in the generic sense to refer to both males and females. To acknowledge the equality of the sexes, however, avoid the generic *he.* Constructions such as *he or she* or *he/she* are cumbersome, especially when used a number of times in a paragraph. To avoid problems, use the second person singular or first and third person plural pronouns when possible.

TRADITIONAL: Before registering, *each student* should be sure *he* has received *his* student number.

REVISION: Before registering, *you* should receive *your* student number.

REVISION: Before registering, *we* should receive *our* student numbers.

REVISION: Before registering, *students* should receive *their* student numbers.

hopefully   The adverb *hopefully* should modify a verb, an adjective, or another adverb.

During the 1930's many of the nation's jobless looked *hopefully* to the federal government for relief. (*Hopefully* modifies *looked*.)

Increasingly, however, *hopefully* is being used as a sentence modifier meaning "it is hoped." In college writing, use *hopefully* in its traditional sense to avoid ambiguity.

> AMBIGUOUS: *Hopefully*, scientists will discover a cure for the common cold within the next five years. (Who is hopeful? Scientists or the writer?)
>
> REVISED: Scientists *hope* they will discover a cure for the common cold within the next five years.

however   See **but, however, yet.**

if, whether   When asking indirect questions or expressing doubt, use *whether*.

> He asked *whether* (not *if*) the flight would be delayed because of the fog.
>
> The attendant was not sure *whether* (not *if*) the fog would delay the flight.

Use *whether or not* when expressing alternatives.

> He did not know *whether or not* to change his travel plans.

illusion, allusion   See **allusion, illusion.**

immigrate to, emigrate from   See **emigrate from, immigrate to.**

implicit, explicit   See **explicit, implicit.**

imply, infer   *Imply* means "to hint" or "to suggest." *Infer* means "to conclude from." When you *imply*, you *send out* a suggestion; when you *infer*, you *receive* or draw a conclusion.

> Mark Antony *implied* that Brutus and the other conspirators had wrongfully killed Julius Caesar. The crowd *inferred* his meaning and called for the punishment of the conspirators.

in, into   Use *in* when you want to indicate position. Use *into* when you want to indicate motion to a point within a thing.

> As he stood *in* the main burial vault of the tomb of Tutankhamen, Howard Carter saw a wealth of artifacts.
>
> Before he walked *into* the cave, Tom Sawyer grasped Becky Thatcher's hand.
>
> In 1828 Russia and Persia entered *into* the Treaty of Turkmanchai.

infer, imply   See **imply, infer.**

ingenious, ingenuous   *Ingenious* means "clever at inventing or organizing." *Ingenuous* means "open" or "artless."

> Ludwig van Beethoven is recognized as one of the most *ingenious* composers who ever lived.
>
> For a politician the mayor was surprisingly *ingenuous*.

inside of, outside of   *Of* is unnecessary when *inside* and *outside* are used as prepositions.

> He waited *inside* (not *inside of*) the coffee shop.

Inside of is nonstandard in references to time.

> He could run a mile in *under* (not *inside of*) eight minutes.

insure, ensure, assure   See **assure, ensure, insure.**

irregardless, regardless   See **regardless, irregardless.**

irritate, aggravate   See **aggravate, irritate.**

its, it's   *Its* is a possessive pronoun. *It's* is a contraction of *it is*.

> The most obvious characteristic of a modern corporation is the separation of *its* management from *its* ownership.
>
> *It's* not often that you see a collection of rare books such as the one housed in the Library of Congress.

-ize, -wise   The suffix *-ize* is used to change nouns and adjectives into verbs: *civilize, industrialize, immunize*. The suffix *-wise* is used to change a noun or adjective

into an adverb: *likewise, otherwise.* Unfortunately, some writers, particularly in advertising and gov- ernment, use these suffixes carelessly, making up words as they please: *finalize, prioritize, taste-wise, weather-wise,* and *policy-wise,* for example. Be sure to look up suspect *-ize* and *-wise* words in the dictionary to be sure that they are standard forms.

kind of, sort of   *Kind of* and *sort of* to mean "rather" or "somewhat" are colloquial and should not appear in college writing.

> COLLOQUIAL: The countess was surprised to see that Napoleon was *kind of* short.

> REVISED: The countess was surprised to see that Napoleon was *rather* short.

Reserve *kind of* and *sort of* for occasions when you categorize.

> Willie Stark, a character in Robert Penn Warren's *All the King's Men,* is the *kind of* man who begins by meaning well and ends by being corrupted by his success.

latter   See **former.**

lay, lie   See **lie, lay.**

leave, let   *Leave* means "to go away from" or "to let remain." *Let* means "to allow" or "to permit."

> Many missionaries were forced to *leave* China after the Communist revolution in 1948.

> As the liquid boils away, it will *leave* a dark brown precipitate at the bottom of the flask.

> In London it is illegal to *let* dogs foul the footpath.

less, fewer   See **fewer, less.**

let, leave   See **leave, let.**

liable to   See **likely to, liable to, apt to.**

lie, lay   *Lie* is an intransitive verb (one that does not take an object) that means "to recline." *Lay* is a transitive verb meaning "to put" or "to place."

Base Form	Past	Past Participle	Present Participle
lie	lay	lain	lying

> Each afternoon she would *lie* in the sun and listen to the surf.

> *As I Lay Dying* is a novel by William Faulkner.

> In 1871 Heinrich Schliemann unearthed the city of Troy, which had *lain* undisturbed for two thousand years.

> The painting *Odalisque* by Eugène Delacroix shows a nude *lying* on a couch.

Base Form	Past	Past Participle	Present Participle
lay	laid	laid	laying

> The Federalist Papers *lay* the foundation for the American conservative movement.

> In October of 1781 the British *laid* down their arms and surrendered to George Washington at Yorktown.

> After he had *laid* his money on the counter, he walked out of the restaurant.

> We watched the Amish stone masons *laying* a wall without using mortar.

like, as   See **as, like.**

likely to, liable to, apt to   *Likely to* implies a strong chance something might happen. *Liable to* implies that something undesirable is about to occur. *Apt to* implies a natural tendency.

> Medical researchers feel that in fifty years human beings are *likely to* have a life span of more than a hundred years.

> If we do not do something to correct the poor drainage in this area, we are *liable to* have a repeat of last year's flooding.

> Old books are *apt to* increase in value if you protect them from heat and moisture.

A27

literally, figuratively   *Literally* means "following the letter" or "in a strict sense." *Figuratively* means "metaphorically" or "not literally."

> *Literally*, the Declaration of Independence is a list of grievances that the English colonists had against their king. *Figuratively*, the Declaration of Independence is a document that elevates the rights of common people above the divine right of kings.

loose, lose   *Loose* is an adjective meaning "not rigidly fastened or securely attached." *Lose* is a verb meaning "to misplace."

> The marble facing of the building became *loose* and fell to the sidewalk.
>
> After only two drinks, most people *lose* their ability to judge distance.

lots, lots of, a lot of   These words are colloquial substitutes for "many," "much," or "a great deal of." Avoid their use in college writing.

> The students had several (not *lots of* or *a lot of*) options for essay topics.

When using these words informally, be careful to use correct subject-verb agreement.

> There are (not *is*) *lots of* possible topics.

majority, plurality   These words are often confused. *Majority* denotes more than half. *Plurality* means a larger number but not necessarily a majority. A candidate with a *majority* has over 50 percent of the votes cast. A candidate with a *plurality* has more votes than any of the other candidates, but not over 50 percent of the total. Use *most* rather than *majority* when you do not know the exact numbers.

> INCORRECT: The soprano got the *majority* of the applause.
>
> CORRECT: The soprano got *most* of the applause.

man   Like the generic pronoun *he, man* has been used in English to denote members of both sexes. This usage is being replaced by *human beings, people,* or similar terms that do not specify gender.

> The dinosaur was extinct long before *human beings* (not *man*) walked the earth.

may, can   See **can, may.**

may be, maybe   *May be* is a verb phrase. *Maybe* is an adverb meaning "perhaps."

> She *may be* older than the other students, but she is more enthusiastic than they are. *Maybe* her experience in the corporate world will give her an advantage in the management courses.

media, medium   *Medium*, meaning a "means of conveying or broadcasting something," is singular. *Media* is the plural form.

> Television has replaced print and film as the *medium* of communication that has the most profound effect on our lives.
>
> A good business presentation uses a number of *media* to make its point.

might have, might of   *Might of* is a nonstandard construction, not the written form for the contraction of *might have.*

> John F. Kennedy *might have* (not *might of*) been a great president had he not been assassinated.

number, amount   See **amount, number.**

OK, O.K., okay   While all three spellings are acceptable, this term should be avoided in college writing. Replace this term with a more specific word or words.

> The instructor's lecture was *adequate* (not *okay*), if uninspiring.

on account of   Use *because of.*

> The computer malfunctioned *because of* (not *on account of*) a faulty circuit board.

outside of, inside of   See **inside of, outside of.**

per   Acceptable for technical and business writing, *per* is not used in college writing.

His starting wage was only $5.25 *an* (not *per*) hour.

percent, percentage   *Percent* indicates a part of a hundred when a specific number is referred to: "10 *percent* of his weekly salary"; "5 *percent* of the monthly rent." *Percentage* is used when no specific number is referred to: "a *percentage* of the people"; "a *percentage* of next year's receipts." In technical and business writing it is permissible to use the % sign after percentages you are comparing. Write out *percent* in college writing.

phenomenon, phenomena   A *phenomenon* is a single observable fact or event. It can also refer to a rare or significant occurrence. *Phenomena* is the plural form.

Metamorphosis is a *phenomenon* that occurs in many insects, mollusks, amphibians, and fish.

John Stuart Mill was a *phenomenon*. He could read classical Greek at the age of five.

Comets are celestial *phenomena* that have been regarded with awe and terror and were once taken as omens of unfavorable events.

plenty   *Plenty,* when used as a noun followed by "of," means "abundance" or "a large amount." Avoid using *plenty* as a colloquial substitute for "very" or "quite."

There are *plenty of* benefits to recycling plastic.

Recycling can be *quite* (not *plenty*) time consuming but is well worth the trouble.

plus   As a preposition, *plus* means "in addition to." Avoid using *plus* as a substitute for "and."

Include the sum of the principal, *plus* the interest, in your calculations.

The amount you quoted was too high. Moreover (not *plus*), it was inaccurate.

precede, proceed   *Precede* means "to go or come before." *Proceed* means "to go forward in an orderly way."

Robert Frost's *North of Boston* was *preceded* by another volume of poetry, *A Boy's Will.*

In 1532 Francisco Pizarro landed at Tumbes and *proceeded* south until he encountered the Incas.

principal, principle   As a noun, *principal* means "a sum of money (minus interest) invested or lent" or "a person in the leading position." As an adjective it means "most important."

If you cash the bond before maturity, a penalty can be subtracted from the *principal* as well as the interest.

The *principal* of the high school is a talented administrator who has instituted a number of changes.

Women are the *principal* wage earners in many American households.

A *principle* is a rule of conduct or a basic truth.

The Constitution embodies the fundamental *principles* upon which the American republic is founded.

raise, rise   *Raise* is a transitive verb, and *rise* is an intransitive verb—that is, *raise* takes an object and *rise* does not.

A famous photograph taken during World War II shows American Marines *raising* the flag on Iwo Jima.

The planet Venus is called the morning star because when it *rises,* it is brighter than any light in the sky except the sun or moon.

real, really   *Real* means "genuine" or "authentic." *Really* means "actually."

With its ducklike bill, flat tail, and webbed feet, the platypus hardly looks *real.*

When news of the bombing of Pearl Harbor was first broadcast, many people did not believe that it had *really* happened.

In your college writing, do not use *real* as an adjective meaning "very."

> COLLOQUIAL: The planarian is a *real* flat worm that we studied in biology class.
>
> REVISED: The planarian is a *very* flat worm that we studied in biology class.

reason is that, reason is because   *Reason* should be used with *that* and not with *because*, which is redundant.

> The *reason* he moved out of the city *is that* (not *is because*) property taxes rose sharply.

regardless, irregardless   *Irregardless* is a nonstandard version of *regardless*. The suffix *-less* means "without" or "free from," so the negative prefix *ir-* is unnecessary.

> SLANG: *Irregardless* of what some people might think, drunk drivers kill more than twenty-five thousand people a year.
>
> REVISED: *Regardless* of what some people might think, drunk drivers kill more than twenty-five thousand people a year.

respectively, respectfully, respectably   *Respectively* means "in the order given." *Respectfully* means "giving honor or deference." *Respectably* means "worthy of respect."

> In this paper I will discuss "The Sisters" and "The Dead," which are, *respectively*, the first and the last stories in James Joyce's collection *Dubliners*.
>
> When being presented to Queen Elizabeth of England, foreigners are asked to bow *respectfully*.
>
> Even though Abraham Lincoln ran a *respectable* campaign for the United States Senate, he was defeated by Stephen Douglas in 1858.

rise, raise   See **raise, rise.**

set, sit   To *set* means "to put down" or "to lay." To *sit* means "to assume a sitting position."

Base Form	Past	Past Participle	Present Participle
set	set	set	setting
sit	sat	sat	sitting

After rocking the baby, he *set* her down carefully in her crib.

Research has shown that many children *sit* in front of the television five to six hours a day.

shall, will   *Will* is swiftly replacing *shall* to express all future action.

should of   See **could of, would of.**

sit, set   See **set, sit.**

so   Avoid using *so* alone as a vague intensifier meaning "very" or "extremely." Follow *so* with *that* and a clause that describes the result.

> She was *so* pleased with their work *that* she took them out to lunch (not *She was so pleased with their work.*)

sometime, sometimes, some time   *Sometime* means "at some time in the future." *Sometimes* means "now and then." *Some time* means "a period of time."

> In his essay "The Case Against Man," Isaac Asimov says that *sometime*, far in the future, human beings will not be able to produce enough food to sustain themselves.
>
> All automobiles, no matter how well constructed, *sometimes* need repairs.
>
> At the battle of Gettysburg, General Meade's failure to counterattack gave Lee *some time* to regroup his troops.

sort of, kind of   See **kind of, sort of.**

specially, especially   See **especially, specially.**

stationary, stationery   *Stationary* means "staying in one place." *Stationery* means "materials for writing" or "letter paper."

> When viewed from the earth, a communications satellite traveling at the same speed as the earth appears to be *stationary* in the sky.

> The secretaries are responsible for keeping departmental offices supplied with *stationery.*

supposed to, used to   Both *supposed to* and *used to* require the final *d* to indicate past tense.

> She was *supposed to* (not *suppose to*) turn in her paper yesterday.

> She always *used to* (not *use to*) turn in her papers on time.

take, bring   See **bring, take.**

than, then   *Than* is a conjunction used to indicate a comparison, and *then* is an adverb indicating time.

> The new shopping center is bigger *than* the old one.

> He did his research; *then* he wrote a report.

than, as   See **as, than.**

that, which, who   Use *that* or *which* when referring to a thing. Use *who* when referring to a person.

> In *How the Other Half Lives,* Jacob Riis described the conditions *that* existed in working-class slums in nineteenth-century America.

> *The Wonderful Wizard of Oz, which* was published in 1900, was originally entitled *From Kansas to Fairyland.*

> Anyone *who* (not *that*) visits Maine cannot help being impressed by the beauty of the scenery and the ruggedness of the landscape.

themselves, theirselves, theirself   *Theirselves* and *theirself* are nonstandard variants of *themselves* and are not acceptable in college writing.

> Pioneer families had to build their shelter and clear their land by *themselves* (not *theirself* or *theirselves*).

then, than   See **than, then.**

there, their, they're   Use *there* to indicate place and in the expressions *there is* and *there are.*

> I have always wanted to visit the Marine Biological Laboratory in Woods Hole, Massachusetts, but I have never gotten *there.*

> *There is* nothing we can do to resurrect a species once it becomes extinct.

Their is a possessive pronoun.

> James Watson and Francis Crick did *their* work on the molecular structure of DNA at the Cavendish Laboratory at Cambridge University.

They're is a contraction of *they are.*

> White sharks and Mako sharks are dangerous to human beings because *they're* good swimmers and especially sensitive to the scent of blood.

thus, therefore   *Thus* means "in this way," not "therefore" or "so."

> In Joseph Conrad's *Heart of Darkness,* Kurtz becomes a man-god to the natives. *Thus,* he is able to collect a fortune in ivory.

> INCORRECT: Throughout the past year, interest rates have dropped dramatically. Thus, businesses are able to buy the equipment they need to modernize their operations.

> REVISED: Throughout the past year, interest rates have dropped dramatically, so businesses are able to buy the equipment they need to modernize their operations.

till, until, 'til   Till and *until* have the same meaning, and both are acceptable. *Until* is preferred in college writing. *'Til,* a contraction of *until,* should be avoided.

to, at   See **at, to.**

to, too, two   *To* is a preposition that indicates direction.

> Last year we flew from New York *to* California.

Too is an adverb that means "also" or "more than is needed."

> "Tippecanoe and Tyler *too*" was William Henry Harrison's campaign slogan during the 1840 presidential election.

> The plot was *too* complicated.

Two expresses the number *2.*

> Just north of *Two* Rivers, Wisconsin, is a petrified forest.

try to, try and   *Try and* is the colloquial equivalent of the more formal *try to.*

> COLLOQUIAL: Throughout most of his career E. R. Rutherford was determined to *try and* discover the structure of the atom.
>
> REVISED: Throughout most of his career E. R. Rutherford *tried to* discover the structure of the atom.

-type   Deleting this empty suffix eliminates clutter and clarifies meaning.

> COLLOQUIAL: Found in the wreckage of the house was an *incendiary-type* device.
>
> REVISED: Found in the wreckage of the house was an *incendiary* device.

uninterested, disinterested   See **disinterested, uninterested.**

unique   *Unique* means "the only one," not "remarkable" or "unusual."

> COLLOQUIAL: Its undershot lower jaw makes the English bulldog *unique* among dogs.
>
> REVISED: Its undershot lower jaw makes the English bulldog unusual among dogs.
>
> CORRECT USAGE: In their scope and unity, Michelangelo's paintings are *unique.*

Because *unique* means "the only one," it can take no intensifiers. Never use constructions like "the most unique" or "very unique."

until   See **till, until, 'til.**

used to   See **supposed to, used to.**

wait for, wait on   *To wait for* means "to defer action until something occurs." *To wait on* means "to act as a waiter."

> COLLOQUIAL: I am *waiting on* dinner.
>
> REVISED: I am *waiting for* dinner.
>
> CORRECT: The captain *waited on* the head table himself.

well, good   See **good, well.**

were, we're   Some people pronounce these words alike, and so they confuse them when they write. *Were* is a verb; *we're* is the contraction of *we are.*

> The Trojans *were* asleep when the Greeks climbed out of the wooden horse and took the city.

> We Americans are affected by the advertising we see. *We're* motivated by the ads we see to buy billions of dollars worth of products each year.

whether, if   See **if, whether.**

which, who, that   See **that, which, who.**

who, whom   When a pronoun serves as the subject of its clause, use *who* or *whoever;* when it functions as an object in a clause, use *whom* or *whomever.*

Sarah, *who* is studying ancient civilizations, would like to visit Mycenae.

Sarah, *whom* I haven't seen in a year, wants me to travel to Greece with her.

To determine which to use at the beginning of a question, answer the question using a personal pronoun.

Who tried to call me? *He* called. (subject)

For *whom* is the package? It is for *her*. (object of a preposition)

Whom do you want for the job? I want *her*. (object)

who's, whose   Use *who's* when you mean *who is*.

Who's going to take calculus?

Use *whose* when you want to indicate possession.

The writer *whose* book was in the window was autographing copies in the store.

will, shall   See **shall, will.**

-wise, -ize   See **-ize, -wise.**

would of, could of   See **could of, would of.**

yet   See **but, however, yet.**

your, you're   Because these words are pronounced alike, they are often confused. *Your* indicates possession, and *you're* is the contraction of *you are*.

You can improve *your* stamina by jogging two miles a day.

You're certain to be impressed the first time you see the Golden Gate Bridge spanning San Francisco Bay.

Glossary of Grammatical and Rhetorical Terms

absolute phrase   See **phrase.**

abstract noun   See **noun.**

acronym   A word formed from the first letters or initial sounds of a group of words: NATO = North Atlantic Treaty Organization.

active voice   See **voice.**

adjectival   A word or word group used as an adjective to modify a noun: *dancing bear.* 25a; 25e

adjective   A word that describes, limits, qualifies, or in any other way modifies nouns or pronouns. A **descriptive adjective** names a quality of the noun or pronoun it modifies: *junior year.* A **proper adjective** is formed from a proper noun: *Hegelian philosophy.* Other kinds of words may be used to limit or qualify nouns, and they are then considered adjectives: **articles** *(a, an, the): the book; a peanut;* **possessive adjectives** *(my, your, his,* and so on): *their apartment, my house;* **demonstrative adjectives** *(this, these, that, those): that table, these chairs;* **interrogative adjectives** *(what, which, whose,* and so on): *Which car is yours?* **indefinite adjectives** *(another, each, both, many,* and so on): *any minute, some day;* **relative adjectives** *(what, whatever, which, whichever, whose, whoever): Bed rest was what the doctor ordered.;* **numerical adjectives** *(one, two, first, second,* and so on): *Claire saw two robins.* 21d; 25a

adjective clause   See **clause.**

adverb   A word that describes the action of verbs or modifies adjectives, other adverbs, or complete phrases, clauses, or sentences. Adverbs answer the questions "How?" "Why?" "Where?" "When?" "To what extent?" and "To what degree?". Adverbs are formed from adjectives, many by adding *-ly* to the adjective form *(dark/darkly, solemn/solemnly),* and may also be derived from prepositions *(Joe carried on.).* Other adverbs that indicate time, place, condition, cause, or degree do not derive from other parts of speech: *then, never, very,* and *often,* for example. The words *how, why, where,* and *when* are classified as **interrogative adverbs** when they ask questions *(How did we get into this mess?).* See also **conjunctive adverb.** 21e; 25c

adverb clause   See **clause.**

adverbial   A word or word group that is used as an adverb to modify a verb, an adjective, another adverb, or complete phrases, clauses, or sentences: *The sun rises in the east.; Our vacation begins Saturday.*

adverbial conjunction   See **conjunctive adverb.**

agreement   The correspondence between words in number, person, and gender. Subjects and verbs must agree in number (singular or plural) and person (first, second, or third): *Soccer is a popular European sport.; I play soccer too.* **24a** Pronouns and their antecedents must agree in number, person, and gender (masculine, feminine, neuter); *Lucy loaned Charlie her car.* **24b**

allusion   A form of **figurative language** in which the writer describes a subject by referring to a famous historical or literary person or event which the reader is expected to recognize. **18e5**

analogy   A form of **figurative language** in which the writer explains an unfamiliar idea or object by comparing it to a more familiar one: *Sensory pathways of the central nervous system are bundles of nerves rather like telephone cables that feed information about the outside world into the brain for processing.* **18e3**

antecedent   The word or group of words to which a pronoun refers: *Brian finally bought the stereo he had always wanted.* (*Brian* is the antecedent of the pronoun *he.*)

appositive   A noun or noun phrase that identifies, in different words, the noun or pronoun it follows: *Columbus, the capital of Ohio, is in the central part of the state.* Appositives may be used without special introductory phrases, as in the preceding example, or they may be introduced by *such as, or, that is, for example,* or *in other words: Japanese cars, such as Hondas, now have a large share of the U.S. automobile market.* In an inverted appositive, the appositive precedes the noun or pronoun it modifies: *The singing cowboy, Gene Autry, became the owner of the California Angels.* **8f4**

article   The word *a, an,* or *the.* Articles signal that a noun follows and are usually classified as adjectives. See also **adjective. 21d**

auxiliary verb   See **verb.**

balanced sentence   A sentence neatly divided between two parallel structures. Balanced sentences are typically **compound sentences** made up of two parallel clauses (*The telephone rang, and I answered.*), but the parallel clauses of a **complex sentence** can also be balanced. **10c**

cardinal number   A number that expresses quantity—*seven, thirty, one hundred.* (Contrast **ordinal.**)

case   The form a noun or pronoun takes to indicate how it functions in a sentence. English has three cases. A pronoun takes the **subjective** (or **nominative**) **case** when it acts as the subject of a sentence or a clause: *I am an American.* **22a1** A pronoun takes the **objective case** when it acts as the object of a verb or of a preposition: *Fran gave me her dog.* **22a2** Both nouns and pronouns take the **possessive** (or **genitive**) **case** when they indicate ownership: *My house is brick, Brandon's T-shirt is red.* This is the only case in which nouns change form. **22a3**

clause   A group of related words that includes a subject and a predicate. An **independent** (main) **clause** may stand alone as a sentence (*Yellowstone is a national park in the West.*), but a **dependent** (**subordinate**) clause must always be accompanied by an independent clause (*Yellowstone is a national park in the West that is known for its geysers.*). Dependent clauses are classified according to their function in a sentence. An **adjective clause** (sometimes called a **relative clause**) modifies nouns or pronouns: *The philodendron, which grew to be twelve feet tall, finally died* (the clause modifies *philodendron*). An **adverb clause** modifies single words (verbs, adjectives, or adverbs) or an entire phrase or clause: *The film was exposed when Bill opened the camera* (the clause modifies *exposed*). A **noun clause** acts as a noun (as subject, direct object, indirect object, or complement) in a sentence: *Whoever arrives first wins the prize* (the clause is the subject of the sentence). An **elliptical clause** is grammatically incomplete—that is, part or all of the subject or predicate is missing. If the missing part can be easily inferred from the context of the sentence, such a construction is acceptable: *When (they are) pressed, the committee will act.* **8d2**

climactic word order   The writing strategy of moving from the least important to the most important point in a sentence and ending with the key idea. **10a2**

collective noun   See **noun**.

comma splice   A sentence that occurs when two independent clauses are incorrectly joined by a comma. **14a–d**

> COMMA SPLICE: The Mississippi River flows south, the Nile River flows north.
> REVISED: The Mississippi River flows south. The Nile River flows north.
> REVISED: The Mississippi River flows south; the Nile River flows north.
> REVISED: The Mississippi River flows south, and the Nile River flows north.
> REVISED: Although the Mississippi River flows south, the Nile River flows north.

common noun   See **noun**.

comparative degree   See **comparison**.

comparison   The form taken by an adjective or an adverb to indicate degree. The **positive degree** describes a quality without indicating comparison (*Frank is tall.*). The **comparative degree** indicates comparison between two persons or things (*Frank is taller than John.*). The **superlative degree** indicates comparison between one person or thing and two or more others (*Frank is the tallest boy in his scout troop.*). **25d**

complement   A word or words that describes or renames a subject, an object, or a verb. A **subject complement** is a word or phrase that follows a linking verb and renames the subject. It can be an adjective (called a **predicate adjective**) or a noun (called a **predicate nominative**): *Clark Gable was a movie star.* An **object complement** is a word or phrase that describes or renames a direct object. Object complements can be either adjectives or nouns: *We called the treehouse the hideout.*

complete predicate   See **predicate**.

complete subject   See **subject**.

complex sentence   See **sentence**.

compound   Two or more words that function as a unit, such as **compound nouns:** *attorney at law; boardwalk;* **compound adjectives:** *hardhitting editorial;* **compound prepositions:** *by way of, in addition to;* **compound subjects:** *April and May are spring months.;* **compound predicates:** *Many have tried and failed to change his mind.*

compound adjective   See **compound**.

compound noun   See **compound**.

compound predicate   See **compound**.

compound preposition   See **compound**.

compound sentence   See **sentence**.

compound subject   See **compound**.

compound-complex sentence   See **sentence**.

conjunction   A word or words used to connect single words, phrases, clauses, and sentences. **Coordinating conjunctions** (*and, or, but, nor, for, so, yet*) connect words, phrases, or clauses of equal weight: *crime and punishment* (coordinating conjunction *and* connects two words). **Correlative conjunctions** (*both . . . and, either . . . or, neither . . . nor,* and so on), always used in pairs, also link items of equal weight: *Neither Texas nor Florida crosses the Tropic of Cancer.* (correlative conjunction *neither . . . nor* connects two words). **Subordinating conjunctions** (*since,* *because, although, if, after,* and so on) introduce adverb clauses: *You will have to pay for the tickets now because I will not be here later* (subordinating conjunction *because* introduces the adverb clause). **21g**

conjunctive adverb   An adverb that joins and relates independent clauses in a sentence (*also, anyway, besides, hence, however, nevertheless, still,* and so on): *Howard tried out for the Yankees; however, he didn't make the team.* **21e**

connotation   The emotional associations that surround a word. (Contrast **denotation**.) **18c1**

contraction   The combination of two words with an apostrophe replacing the missing letters: *we + will = we'll; was + not = wasn't.*

coordinate adjective   One of a series of adjectives that modify the same word or word group: *The glen was quiet, shady,* and *cool.*

coordinating conjunction   See **conjunction.**

coordination   The pairing of similar elements (words, phrases, or clauses) to give equal weight to each. Coordination is used in simple sentences to link similar elements into compound subjects, predicates, complements, or modifiers. It can also link two independent clauses to form a compound sentence: *The sky was cloudy, and it looked like rain.* (Contrast **subordination.**) **8a**

correlative conjunction   See **conjunction.**

cumulative sentence   A sentence that begins with a main clause followed by additional words, phrases, or clauses that expand or develop it: *On the hill stood a schoolhouse, paint peeling, windows boarded, playground overgrown with weeds.*

dangling modifier   A modifier for which no true headword appears in the sentence. To correct dangling modifiers, either change the subject of the sentence's main clause, creating a subject that can logically serve as the headword of the dangling modifier, or add words that transform the dangling modifier into a dependent clause. **15b**

  DANGLING: Pumping up the tire, the trip continued.

  REVISED: After pumping up the tire, they continued the trip.

dead metaphor   A metaphor so overused that it has become a meaningless cliché. **18f1**

declarative sentence   See **sentence.**

deductive argument   An argument that begins with a general statement or proposition and establishes a chain of reasoning that leads to a conclusion. **6b**

demonstrative adjective   See **adjective.**

demonstrative pronoun   See **pronoun.**

denotation   The dictionary meaning of a word. (Contrast **connotation.**) **18c1**

dependent clause   See **clause.**

descriptive adjective   See **adjective.**

direct object   See **object.**

direct quotation   See **quotation.**

documentation   The formal acknowledgment of the sources used in a piece of writing. **39a**

documentation style   A format for providing information about the sources used in a piece of writing. Documentation styles vary from discipline to discipline. **39b–e**

double negative   The illogical use of two negative words within a single sentence: *She didn't have no time.* Such constructions are nonstandard English. Revised: *She had no time* or *She did not have time.*

ellipsis mark   Three spaced periods used to indicate the omission of a word or words from a quotation: *"The time has come . . . and we must part."* **31f**

elliptical clause   See **clause.**

embedding   A strategy for varying sentence structure that involves changing some sentences into modifying phrases and working them into other sentences. **12b3**

enthymeme   A syllogism in which one of the premises—usually the major premise—is implied rather than stated. **6b3**

expletive   A construction in which *there* or *it* is used with a form of the verb *be: There is no one here by that name.*

faulty parallelism   See **parallelism.**

figurative language   Imaginative comparisons between different ideas or objects using common figures of speech—**simile, metaphor, analogy, personification, allusion, hyperbole,** and **understatement. 18e**

figure of speech   See **figurative language.**

finite verb   A verb that can stand as the main verb of a sentence. Unlike **participles, gerunds,** and **infinitives** (see **verbal**), finite verbs do not require an auxiliary in order to function as the main verb: *The rooster crowed.*

fragment   See **sentence fragment.**

function word   An article, preposition, conjunction, or auxiliary verb that indicates the function of and the grammatical relationship among the nouns, verbs, and modifiers in a sentence.

fused sentence   A **run-on sentence** that occurs when two independent clauses are joined either without suitable punctuation or without a coordinating conjunction. Fused sentences can be corrected by separating the independent clauses with a period, a semicolon, or a comma and a coordinating conjunction, or by using **subordination. 14a–d**

FUSED SENTENCE: Protein is needed for good nutrition lipids and carbohydrates are too.
REVISED: Protein is needed for good nutrition. Lipids and carbohydrates are too.
REVISED: Protein is needed for good nutrition; lipids and carbohydrates are too.
REVISED: Protein is needed for good nutrition, but lipids and carbohydrates are too.
REVISED: Although protein is needed for good nutrition, lipids and carbohydrates are too.

gender   The classification of nouns and pronouns as masculine (*father, boy, he*), feminine (*mother, girl, she*), or neuter (*radio, kitten, them*).
See **case.**

gerund   A special form of verb ending in *-ing* that is always used as a noun: *Fishing is relaxing* (gerund *fishing* serves as subject; gerund *relaxing* serves as subject complement). Note: When the *-ing* form of a verb is used as a modifier, it is considered a **present participle.** (See also **verbal.**)

gerund phrase   See **phrase.**

headword   The word or phrase in a sentence that is described, defined, or limited by a modifier.

helping verb   See **auxiliary verb.**

idiom   An expression that is characteristic of a particular language and whose meaning cannot be predicted from the meaning of its individual words: *lend a hand.*

imperative mood   See **mood.**

indefinite adjective   See **adjective.**

indefinite pronoun   See **pronoun.**

independent clause   See **clause.**

indicative mood   See **mood.**

indirect object   See **object.**

indirect question   A question that tells what has been asked but, because it does not use the speaker's exact words, does not take a question mark: *He asked whether he could use the family car.*

indirect quotation   See **quotation.**

inductive argument   An argument that begins with observations or experiences and moves toward a conclusion. **6a**

infinitive   The base form of the verb preceded by *to*, an infinitive can serve as an adjective (*He is the man to watch.*), an adverb (*Chris hoped to break the record.*), or a noun (*To err is human.*). See also **verbal.**

infinitive phrase   See **phrase.**

intensifier   A word that adds emphasis but not additional meaning to words it modifies. *Much, really, too, very,* and *so* are typical intensifiers.

intensive pronoun   See **pronoun.**

interjection   A grammatically independent word, which expresses emotion, that is used as an exclamation. Interjections can be set off by a comma, or, for greater emphasis, they can be punctuated as independent units, set off by an exclamation point: *Ouch! That hurt.* **21h**

interrogative adjective   See **adjective.**

interrogative adverb   See **adverb.**

interrogative pronoun   See **pronoun.**

intransitive verb   See **verb.**

inverted appositive   See **appositive.**

irregular verb   A verb that does not form both its past tense and past participle by the addition of *-d* or *-ed* to the base form of the verb. **23a**

isolate   Any word, including **interjections,** that can be used in isolation: *Yes. No. Hello. Good-bye. Please. Thank you.*

linking verb   A verb that connects a subject to its complement: *The crowd became quiet.* Words that can be used as linking verbs include *seem, appear, believe, become, grow, turn, remain, prove, look, sound, smell, taste, feel,* and forms of the verb *be.*

main clause   See **clause.**

main verb   See **verb.**

mass noun   See **noun.**

metaphor   A form of **figurative language** in which the writer makes an implied comparison between two unlike items, equating them in an unexpected way: *The subway coursed through the arteries of the city.* **18e2**

misplaced modifier   A modifier that has no clear relationship with its headword, usually because it is placed too far from it. **15a**

> MISPLACED: By changing his diapers, Dan learned much about the new baby son.
>
> REVISED: Dan learned much about the new baby son by changing his diapers.

mixed construction   A sentence made up of two or more parts that do not fit together grammatically, causing readers to have trouble determining meaning. **17f**

> MIXED: The Great Chicago Fire caused terrible destruction was what prompted changes in the fire code. (independent clause used as a subject)

REVISED: The terrible destruction of the Great Chicago Fire prompted changes in the fire code.

REVISED: Because of the terrible destruction of the Great Chicago Fire, the fire code was changed.

mixed metaphor   The combination of two or more incompatible images in a single figure of speech: *During the race John kept a stiff upper lip as he ran like the wind.* **18f2**

modal auxiliary   See **verb.**

modifier   A word that adds information to a sentence and shows connections between ideas.

mood   The verb form that indicates the writer's basic attitude. There are three moods in English. The **indicative mood** is used for statements and questions: *Nebraska became a state in 1867.* **23h** The **imperative mood** specifies commands or requests and is often used without a subject: *(You) Pay the rent.* **23i** The **subjunctive mood** expresses wishes or hypothetical conditions: *I wish the sun were shining.* **23j**

nominal   A word, phrase, or clause that functions as a noun.

nominative case   See **case.**

nonfinite verb   See **verbal.**

nonrestrictive modifier   A modifying phrase or clause that does not limit or particularize the words it modifies, but rather supplies additional information about them. Nonrestrictive modifiers are set off by commas: *Oregano, also known as marjoram and suganda, is a member of the mint family.* **27d1** (Contrast **restrictive modifier.**)

noun   A word that names people, places, things, ideas, actions, or qualities. A **common noun** names any of a class of people, places, or things: *Lawyer, town, bicycle.* A **proper noun,** always capitalized, refers to a particular person, place, or thing: *F. Lee Bailey, Chicago, Schwinn.* A **mass noun** names a quantity that is not countable: *sand, time, work.* An **abstract noun** refers to an intangible idea or quality: *bravery, equality, hunger.* A **collective noun** designates a group of people, places, or things thought of as a unit: *Congress, police, family.* **21a**

noun clause   See **clause.**

noun phrase   See **phrase.**

number   The form taken by a noun, pronoun, demonstrative adjective, or verb to indicate one (**singular**): *car, he, this book, boasts;* or many (**plural**): *cars, they, those books, boast.* **17d**

numerical adjective   See **adjective.**

object   A noun, pronoun, or other noun substitute that is influenced by a **transitive verb, verbal,** or **preposition.** A **direct object** indicates where the verb's action is directed and who or what is affected by it: *John caught a butterfly.* An **indirect object** tells to or for whom the verb's action was done: *John gave Nancy his butterfly.* An **object of a preposition** is a word or word group introduced by a preposition: *John gave Nancy his butterfly for an hour.*

object complement   See **complement.**

object of a preposition   See **object.**

objective case   See **case.**

ordinal number   A number that indicates position in a series: *seventh, thirtieth, one-hundredth.*

parallelism   The use of similar grammatical elements in sentences or parts of sentences: *We serve beer, wine, and soft drinks.* Words, phrases, clauses, or complete sentences may be parallel, and parallel items may be paired or presented in a series. When elements that have the same function in a sentence are not presented in the same terms, the sentence is flawed by **faulty parallelism. 10c; 16a–b**

participial phrase   See **phrase.**

participle   A verb form that functions in a sentence as an adjective. Virtually every verb has a **present participle,** which ends in *-ing* (*breaking, leaking, taking*), and a **past participle,** which usually ends in *-d* or *-ed* (*agreed, walked, taken*). Note: When the *-ing* form of a verb is used as a noun, it is considered a **gerund.** (See also **verbal.**) **Present participle:** *The heaving seas swamped the dinghy.* (present participle *heaving* modifies noun *seas*); **past participle:** *The aged deserve respect.* (past participle *aged* is the subject of the sentence)

parts of speech   The eight basic building blocks for all English sentences: *nouns, pronouns, verbs, adjectives, adverbs, prepositions, conjunctions,* and *interjections.*

passive voice   See **voice.**

past participle   See **participle.**

periodic sentence   A sentence that moves from a number of specific examples to a conclusion, gradually building in intensity until a climax is reached in the main clause: *Wan and pale and looking ready to crumble, the marathoner headed into the last mile of the race.*

person   The form a pronoun or verb takes to indicate the speaker (**first person**): *I am/we are;* those spoken to (**second person**): *you are;* and those spoken about (**third person**): *He, she, it is; they are.* **17d**

personal pronoun   See **pronoun.**

personification   A form of **figurative language** in which the writer describes an idea or inanimate object in terms that imply human attributes, feelings, or powers: *The big feather bed beckoned to my tired body.* **18e4**

phrase   A grammatically ordered group of related words that lacks a subject or a predicate or both and functions as a single part of speech. A **verb phrase** consists of an auxiliary (helping) verb and a main verb: *The wind was blowing hard.* A **noun phrase** includes a noun or pronoun plus all related modifiers: *She broke the track record.* A **prepositional phrase** consists of a preposition, its object, and any modifiers of that object: *The errant ball sailed over the fence.* A **verbal phrase** consists of a verbal and its related objects, modifiers, or complements. A verbal phrase may be a **participial phrase** (*Undaunted by the sheer cliff, the climber scaled the rock.*), a **gerund phrase** (*Swinging from trees is a monkey's favorite way to travel.*), or an **infinitive phrase** (*Wednesday is Bill's night to cook spaghetti.*). An **absolute phrase** usually consists of a noun or pronoun and a participle, accompanied by modifiers: *His heart racing, he dialed her number.* **8d1**

positive degree   See **comparison.**

possessive adjective   See **adjective.**

possessive case   See **case.**

predicate   A verb or verb phrase that tells or asks something about the subject of a sentence is called a **simple predicate:** *Well-tended lawns grow green and thick.* (*grow* is the simple predicate.) A **complete predicate** includes all the words associated with the predicate: *Well-tended lawns grow green and thick.* (*grow green and thick* is the complete predicate.) **8a**

predicate adjective   See **complement.**

prefix   A letter or group of letters put before a root or word that adds to, changes, or modifies it. **20b3**

preposition   A part of speech that introduces a word or word group consisting of one or more nouns or pronouns or of a phrase or clause functioning in the sentence as a noun: *Jeremy crawled under the bed.* **21f**

prepositional phrase   See **phrase.**

present participle   See **participle.**

principal parts   The forms of a verb from which all other forms can be derived. The principal parts are the **base form** (*give*), the **present participle** (*giving*), the **past tense** (*gave*), and the **past participle** (*given*).

pronoun   A word that may be used in place of a noun in a sentence. The noun for which a pronoun stands is called its **antecedent.** There are eight different types of pronouns. Some have the same form but are distinguished by their function in the sentence. A **personal pronoun** stands for a person or thing: *I, me, we, us, my,* and so on. (*They broke his window.*) A **reflexive pronoun** ends in -*self* or -*selves* and refers to the subject of the sentence or clause: *myself, yourself, himself,* and so on. (*They painted the house themselves.*) An **intensive pronoun** ends in -*self* or -*selves* and emphasizes a noun or pronoun. (*Custer himself died in the battle.*) A **relative pronoun** introduces an adjective or noun clause in a sentence: *which, who, whom,* and so on. (*Sitting Bull was the Sioux chief who defeated Custer.*) An **interrogative pronoun** introduces a question: *who, which, what, whom,* and so on. (*Who won the lottery?*) A **demonstrative pronoun** points to a particular thing or group of things: *this, that, these, those.* (*Who was that masked man?*) A **reciprocal pronoun** denotes a mutual relationship: *each other, one another.* (*We still have each other.*) An **indefinite pronoun** refers to persons or things in general, not to specific individuals. Most indefinite pronouns are singular—*anyone, everyone, one, each,*—but some are always plural—*both, many, several.* (*Many are called, but few are chosen.*) **21b**

proper adjective   See **adjective.**

proper noun   See **noun.**

quotation   The use of the written or spoken words of others. A **direct quotation** occurs when a passage is borrowed word for word from another source. Quotation marks (" ") establish the boundaries of a direct quotation: *"These tortillas taste like cardboard," complained Beth.* **30a** An **indirect quotation** reports someone else's written or spoken words without quoting that person directly. Quotation marks are not used: *Beth complained that the tortillas tasted like cardboard.*

reciprocal pronoun   See **pronoun.**

reflexive pronoun   See **pronoun.**

regular verb   A verb that forms both its past tense and past participle by the addition of -*d* or -*ed* to the base form of the verb. **23a–n**

relative adverb   See **adverb.**

relative clause   See **clause.**

relative pronoun   See **pronoun.**

restrictive modifier   A modifying phrase or clause that limits the meaning of the word or word group it modifies. Restrictive modifiers are not set off by commas: *The Ferrari that ran over the fireplug was red.* **27d1** (Contrast **nonrestrictive modifier.**)

root   A word from which other words are formed. An understanding of a root word increases understanding of other unfamiliar words that incorporate the root.

run-on sentence   An incorrect construction that results when the proper connective or punctuation does not appear between independent clauses. A run-on occurs either as a **comma splice** or as a **fused sentence.**

sentence   An independent grammatical unit that contains a subject and a predicate and expresses a complete thought: *Carolyn sold her car.* **8a** A **simple sentence** consists of one subject and one predicate: The season ended. **8e**; a **compound sentence** is formed when two or more simple sentences are connected with coordinating conjunctions, conjunctive adverbs, semicolons, or colons: *The rain stopped, and the sun began to shine.* **9a**; a **complex sentence** consists of one simple sentence, which functions as an independent clause in the complex sentence, and at least one dependent clause, which is introduced by a subordinating conjunction or a relative pronoun: *When he had sold three boxes* (dependent clause), *he was halfway to his goal.* (independent clause) **9b**; and a **compound-complex sentence** consists of two or more independent clauses and at least one dependent clause: *After he prepared a shopping list* (dependent clause), *he went to the store* (independent clause), *but it was closed.* (independent clause) **9c**

sentence fragment   An incomplete sentence, phrase, or clause that is punctuated as if it were a complete sentence. **13a–h**

shift   A change of *tense, voice, mood, person, number,* or *type of discourse* within or between sentences. Some shifts are necessary, but problems occur with unnecessary or illogical shifts. **17a–e**

simile   A form of **figurative language** in which the writer makes a comparison, introduced by *like* or *as,* between two unlike items on the basis of a shared quality: *Like sands through the hourglass, so are the days of our lives.; The wind was as biting as his neighbor's doberman.* **18e1**

simple predicate   See **predicate.**

simple sentence   See **sentence.**

simple subject   See **subject.**

split infinitive   An infinitive whose parts are separated by a modifier. **15a4**

> SPLIT: She expected *to* ultimately *swim* the channel.
>
> REVISED: She expected ultimately *to swim* the channel.

squinting modifier   A modifier that seems to modify either a word before it or one after it and that conveys a different meaning in each case. **15a**

> SQUINTING: The task completed simply delighted him.
>
> REVISED: He was delighted to have the task completed simply.
>
> REVISED: He was simply delighted to have the task completed.

subject   A noun or noun substitute that tells who or what a sentence is about is called a **simple subject:** *Healthy thoroughbred horses run like the wind.* (*horses* is the simple subject.) The **complete subject** of a sentence includes all the words associated with the subject: *Healthy thoroughbred horses run like the wind.* (*healthy thoroughbred horses* is the complete subject.) **8a**

subject complement   See **complement.**

subjective case   See **case.**

subjunctive mood   See **mood.**

subordinate clause   See **clause.**

subordinating conjunction   See **conjunction.**

subordination   Making one or more clauses of a sentence grammatically dependent upon another element in a sentence: *Preston was only eighteen when he joined the firm.* (Contrast **coordination.**) **9b**

suffix   A syllable added at the end of a word or root that changes its part of speech. **20b4**

superlative degree   See **comparison.**

suspended hyphen   A hyphen followed by a space or by the appropriate punctuation and a space: *The wagon was pulled by a two-, four-, or six-horse team.*

syllogism   A three-part set of statements or propositions, devised by Aristotle, that contains a major premise, a minor premise, and a conclusion. **6b**

tag question   A question, consisting of an auxiliary verb plus a pronoun, that is added to a statement and set off by a comma: *You know it's going to rain, don't you?*

tense   The form of a verb that indicates when an action has occurred or when a condition existed. **23b–f**

transitive verb   See **verb.**

verb   A word or phrase that expresses action (*He painted the fence.*) or a state of being (*Henry believes in equality.*). A **main verb** carries most of the meaning in the sentence or clause in which it appears: *Winston Churchill smoked long, thick cigars.* A main verb is a **linking verb** when it is followed by a **subject complement:** *Dogs are good pets.* An **auxiliary verb** (sometimes called a **helping verb**) combines with the main verb to form a **verb phrase:** *Graduation day has arrived.* The auxiliaries *be* and *have* are used to indicate the tense and voice of the main verb. The auxiliary *do* is used for asking questions and forming negative statements. Other auxiliary verbs, known as **modal auxiliaries** (*must, will, can, could, may, might, ought (to), should,* and *would*), indicate necessity, obligation, possibility, willingness, obligation, and ability: *It might rain next Tuesday.* A **transitive verb** requires an **object** to complete its meaning in the sentence: *Pete drank all the wine* (*wine* is the direct object). An **intransitive verb** has no direct object: *The candle glowed.* **21c1; 23a–n**

verb phrase   See **phrase.**

verbal   (nonfinite verb) Verb forms—**participles, infinitives,** and **gerunds**—that are used as nouns, adjectives, or adverbs. Verbals do not behave like verbs. Only when used with an auxiliary can such verb forms serve as the main verb of a sentence. *The wall painted* is not a sentence; *The wall was painted* is. **21c2**

verbal phrase   See **phrase.**

voice   The form that determines whether the subject of a verb is acting or is acted upon. When the subject of a verb performs the action, the verb is in the **active voice:** *Palmer sank a thirty-foot putt.* When the subject of a verb receives the action—that is, is acted upon—the verb is in the **passive voice:** *A thirty-foot putt was sunk by Palmer.* **10e; 17b; 23k–n**

Index

Literary Acknowledgments